D1599187

KANT

AND THE

CLAIMS OF TASTE

KANT

AND THE

CLAIMS OF TASTE

Paul Guyer

HARVARD UNIVERSITY PRESS

Cambridge, Massachusetts, and London, England
1979

Copyright © 1979 *by the President and Fellows of Harvard College*

All rights reserved

Printed in the United States of America

Publication of this book has been aided
by a grant from the Andrew W. Mellon Foundation

Library of Congress Cataloging in Publication Data

Guyer, Paul, 1948-
   Kant and the claims of taste.

   Includes bibliographical references and indexes.
   1. Kant, Immanuel, 1724-1804 — Aesthetics.
2. Aesthetics.   I. Title.
B2799.A4G85   111.8'5   78-19179
ISBN 0-674-50020-2

To my parents,
Betty and Irving Guyer

Acknowledgments

****

I cannot thank by name all of the many friends and colleagues who have helped me in my work on Kant's aesthetics, which has occupied me since 1971. Consequently, I will acknowledge the contributions of a very few. Stanley Cavell, teacher and friend, has long been a source of inspiration and assistance, and has constantly encouraged me in the completion of this book. John Cooper, teacher, friend, and former colleague, has often helped me clarify my arguments, and suggested a number of particularly useful revisions in the final draft of this book. Two other friends and former colleagues, Annette Baier and Alexander Nehamas, also read the final draft and made several helpful suggestions. Finally, the philosophical and linguistic sensibility of my wife, Pamela Foa, undoubtedly rescued me from many an obscurity.

Contents

****

Contents

Contents

KANT

AND THE

CLAIMS OF TASTE

Note: An asterisk attached to a note number indicates that the note contains substantive as well as bibliographic material. The notes begin on page 399.

Introduction

****

The Problem of Taste

Like his critiques of theoretical and practical reason, Kant's "critique of taste" is concerned with "part of the general problem of transcendental philosophy: How are synthetic *a priori* judgments possible?"[1] On Kant's view, the justification of a judgment of taste — for which he takes as a paradigm the judgment that a particular object, such as a rose or a painting, is beautiful — requires a deduction of a synthetic *a priori* judgment because in calling an object beautiful, we each express our own pleasure in it, yet go beyond the evidence furnished by that feeling to impute it to the rest of mankind, as the potential audience for that object. We presume that our feelings, just like our scientific theories and moral beliefs, can be the subject of publicly valid discourse, and that, although "there can be no rule by which anyone should be compelled to acknowledge that something is beautiful," we are nevertheless entitled to respond to a beautiful object with a "universal voice . . . and lay claim to the agreement of everyone."[2]* But the universal validity of our response to a beautiful object can neither be deduced from any concept of the object nor grounded on any information about the actual feelings of others, Kant believes, and so it can be based only on an *a priori* assumption of similarity between our own responses and those of others. Thus the presumption of aesthetic judgment can be defended only if we can answer this question: "How is a judgment possible which, merely from one's *own* feeling of pleasure in an object, independent of its concept, estimates *a priori,* that is, without having to wait upon the agreement of others, that this pleasure is connected with the representation of the object *in every other subject?*"[3]

I believe that when we use "beautiful" and many other aesthetic predicates, we do attempt to ground publicly valid assessments of objects on peculiarly private feelings and responses, and that Kant's critique of taste is

1

thus addressed to a question of perennial importance to aesthetics. The present book is a study of Kant's answer to this question. It is not a commentary on the whole of his *Critique of Judgment,*[4] nor is it a commentary on that work alone. It is, rather, devoted to a single theme: Kant's defense of the claims of taste, or his justification of the intersubjective validity of aesthetic judgment.

As did his theories of empirical knowledge and practical reason, Kant's view on aesthetic judgment grew out of long reflection on the work of his British and German predecessors, whose theories Kant himself named "empiricism" and "rationalism" in the "critique of taste."[5] Obviously, our understanding of the aims of Kant's aesthetic theory could be greatly enriched by a detailed study of the views of such thinkers as Hutcheson, Hume, Burke, Kames, Leibniz, Wolff, and the now little-known Alexander Gottlieb Baumgarten and Georg Friedrich Meier. But even a brief review of the theories of these thinkers, beginning with Kant's own remarks on them, can help make clear just what Kant had to accomplish in order to solve the problem of taste.[6]

Kant believed that empiricism in aesthetics, of which he took Edmund Burke as the foremost champion, "would obliterate the distinction that marks off the object of our delight" in beauty from the merely "agreeable,"[7] or reduce our pleasure in a beautiful object "wholly and entirely to the gratification which it affords through charm or emotion."[8] In other words, Kant thought that empiricism explained aesthetic response as a purely sensory response to the stimuli presented by particular external objects. And while such a theory might yield "empirical laws of the changes that go on within the mind" in actual cases of perception, Kant supposed,[9] these laws could be generalized only on the assumption that different "subjects are, contingently, similarly organized."[10] So such laws could yield only "a knowledge of how we do judge, but not command, how we should judge, and indeed in such a way that the command is *unconditioned.*"[11] But if empirical laws of taste could not justify such a command, then they could not justify a judgment of taste, for in making such a judgment one "declares that everyone *should* give [an] object his approval and, like himself, declare it beautiful."[12] In Kant's opinion, empiricism could establish only a "contingent congruence" among the pleasures of different persons, and any claim to agreement based on such a contingency would be resented and rejected in favor of the "natural right . . . to submit a judgment concerning the immediate feeling of one's own satisfaction to one's own sense and not to that of others."[13] By taking judgments of taste to be nothing but expressions of our strictly sensory gratifications in objects, Kant thought, empiricism precluded any explanation of the intersubjective validity of such judgments and any justification for actually making claims of taste.

In his criticism of rationalism, Kant did not argue that it undermined the intersubjective validity of taste, but focused exclusively on its failure to properly distinguish aesthetic response and judgment from a more purely intellectual satisfaction in the moral and ontological perfections of things. On rationalist theories, Kant held, "the judgment of taste is really a disguised judgment on the perfection to be discovered in a thing and in the relation of the manifold in it to an end, and is . . . called aesthetic only on account of the confusion that here besets our reflection."[14] This view, he supposed, denies any uniqueness to aesthetic judgment: "The distinction between the concepts of the beautiful and the good, which represents both as differing only in their logical form, the first being merely a confused, the second a distinct concept of perfection, but as otherwise alike in content and origin, is empty: for then there could be no *specific* difference between them, and the judgment of taste would be just as much a cognitive judgment as the judgment by which something is declared good."[15] Essentially, Kant's view was that in rationalism there is no real difference in either content or basis between aesthetic and cognitive judgment, but only a superficial difference in what he called logical (what we should probably call epistemological or even psychological) status—the difference, namely, between distinct and confused or indistinct conceptualization. And given this belief, Kant may well have assumed that the difficult question of the intersubjective validity of judgments of taste could not even arise within the framework of rationalist aesthetics.

Even these few remarks make clear one objective Kant's own theory has to accomplish to solve the problem of taste. When the *Critique of Judgment* distinguishes the pleasure we take in beautiful objects, and on which we found judgments of taste, from both the gratification which we take in a merely agreeable object and the esteem or approval which we feel toward an object which is good or of "objective worth,"[16] it suggests that the problem of taste cannot be solved if we confuse aesthetic response with sensory gratification or conceptual evaluation, or if we attempt to understand aesthetic response in terms of either one of these quite distinct states of mind. If, like the rationalists, we conflate aesthetic response with a conceptual judgment of practical value, the problem of the intersubjective validity of judgments of taste may not even arise; and if, like the empiricists, we reduce our pleasure in beauty to mere gratification of the senses, then this problem may be raised but can never be solved. If he is both to raise and to solve the problem of taste, Kant must first provide an analysis of the judgment of taste which shows its essential connection to feeling, but then discover an explanation of aesthetic response which, while treating it as a feeling — retaining its essential subjectivity — nevertheless allows its intersubjective validity.

And if we go beyond Kant's own comments on his predecessors, we can discover a further problem with their theories which Kant must confront. Though Kant does not make this clear, rationalism and empiricism actually did venture solutions to the problem of taste, and did not rest the intersubjective validity of either sensory gratifications or confused judgments of perfection on a merely contingent similarity of the constitutions of different persons. But the solutions which the rationalists and empiricists offered to the problem of taste could only be regarded, from the Kantian point of view, as flights into transcendent metaphysics.

Let us first consider the case of empiricism. There can be no doubt that the British philosophers, as Kant suggests, did attempt to understand the nature of aesthetic response by assimilating it to a mechanical model of sensory response to external stimuli. This assimilation was sometimes largely analogical, as in the cases of Hutcheson and Hume: thus Hutcheson invented a "Sense of Beauty" because of the similarities he saw between aesthetic response and ordinary sense perception, "Ideas of Beauty and Harmony, like other sensible Ideas, [being] *necessarily* pleasant to us, as well as immediately so";[17] while Hume maintained somewhat vaguely that "beauty is nothing but a form, which produces pleasure, as deformity is a structure of parts, which conveys pain; and . . . all the effects of these qualities must be deriv'd from the sensation."[18] Or the assimilation could go as far as Burke's completely physiological explanation of the "origin of our ideas of the sublime and the beautiful," according to which, for example, a beautiful object is pleasurable because it "acts by relaxing the solids of the whole system . . . and relaxation somewhat below the natural tone seems to me to be the cause of all positive pleasures."[19] But the proponents of such explanations of our response to beauty did not think that they reduced the universal validity of any judgment of taste to a mere contingency. Instead, they attempted to reconcile their explanations of aesthetic response with the universal claims of taste by appealing to a metaphysical conception of mankind as a single species, with certain essential, normal, or ideal properties, and by including a basic agreement in taste among these properties. Hutcheson claimed that we could "consult experience . . . as to the *universal agreement* of Mankind in their *Sense of Beauty*,"[20] but then revealed the metaphysical rather than empirical ground of this appeal by explaining away all "apparent Diversity of Fancys" as merely accidental.[21] Hume similarly supposed that nature had made "some internal sense or feeling . . . universal in the whole species,"[22] and postulated a clearly ideal "sound state of the organ," supposing that mere "defects" in the organ of taste could account for any observed differences in aesthetic judgment.[23] Burke too went beyond a "superficial view" to maintain that "the standard both of reason and taste is the same in all human creatures."[24] Finally, Kames made completely evident the naturalistic metaphysics underlying empiricism when he asserted that "we have a sense or conviction of a common nature, not only in our own species, but in every species . . . This common nature is conceived to be a model or standard for each individual that belongs to the kind."[25]* This common nature, Kames supposed, could serve as a standard by which to judge not only the different objects of taste, but also ourselves and our own responses, and so as a standard to determine "right" and "wrong" tastes. Thus he maintained that "the conviction of a common standard is universal and a branch of our nature,"[26] and that "the authority of that standard, even upon the most groveling souls, is so vigorous, as to prevail over self-particularity, and to make them despise their own taste compared with the more elevated taste of others."[27] In all of the empiricist theories, then, it was not merely supposed that there was a contingent convergence in the way that the senses of different persons operated; it was held that nature imposed an essential similarity on all members of the species, by means of an ideal "sound state" of or "common standard" for the sense of beauty, and allowed merely accidental or apparent divergences from that norm. But the postulation of such a norm, or the treatment of the sense of beauty as an essential property of a fixed species, was surely metaphysical — it had to transcend empirical observation, for, as Kant makes clear, that could reveal only the contingent fact of agreement, and could never demonstrate the existence of an ideal or standard of taste. Thus Kant's solution to the problem of taste could not lie in the empiricists' use of a metaphysical conception of a species and its essential properties.

The rationalist solution to the problem of taste, though not explicitly criticized by Kant, was actually even more blatantly metaphysical than that of the empiricists. As Kant suggested, the rationalists certainly did explain our response to the beautiful as a confused perception of the good. Building on Descartes's classification of knowledge by the senses as clear but confused rather than distinct knowledge, the rationalist thinkers from Leibniz on treated aesthetic response as either a special case of sensory knowledge or — in the case of Baumgarten, who treated the aesthetic as the "perfection of sensitive cognition"[28] — as the paradigmatic case of such knowledge, and thus analyzed it as a clear but confused knowledge of the same things that the intellect could, at least ideally, represent clearly and distinctly. Thus Leibniz maintained that "taste as distinguished from understanding consists of confused perceptions for which one cannot give an adequate reason."[29] Wolff explained "intuitive knowledge," knowledge through an image, as a kind of knowledge through the senses and thus as confused or indistinct,[30] and then defined pleasure, including that we take in beautiful objects, as an "intuitive knowledge of perfection."[31] Baumgarten defined "taste as the readiness to judge by the senses,"[32] and Meier summed up the tradition by asserting that the view "that beauty is in general a perfection, insofar as it is indistinctly or sensitively known, nowadays needs no proof."[33] These remarks may not appear to confirm Kant's claim that the rationalists treated aesthetic response as a confused perception of the *good,* since the concept of perfection was a clearly ontological one in the hands of Leibniz and Wolff, and Baumgarten also gave a completely abstract definition of perfection as the harmony which obtains "when many things taken together contain the sufficient reason of one."[34] But Meier made clear the practical nature of the concept of perfection by maintaining that in the case of aesthetic response the "focal point" of a perfection "must be a purpose";[35] and in his detailed discussion of the various perfections actually required of both sensitive knowledge itself and its objects, Baumgarten insisted that the kind of perfection required of the object of taste was "dignity" or "moral greatness."[36] So, in the end, the rationalists did treat the beautiful as the good, indistinctly known.

But the assimilation of aesthetic response to conceptual cognition did not, in fact, prevent the rationalists from seeing a problem about the universal validity of taste. It only meant that their solution to this problem had to proceed along the lines of their general solution to the problem of intersubjective agreement in knowledge. And this had two consequences which Kant could not have accepted. First, when the view that for every perfection of an object there is a rule which, if known distinctly, could settle all disputes about it was emphasized, as it was by Meier,[37] it became clear that unanimity in taste could be established only by removing the indistinctness which had been defined as essential to aesthetic response. This, of course, was the result of a lack of a truly specific differentiation of aesthetic response from ordinary cognition. Second, what supported all of the rationalist treatments of taste was the monadological metaphysics of the preestablished harmony. Though they did pose the problem of taste, the rationalists did not have to struggle with it. For while they supposed that the numerical difference of persons required a difference in their representations, which difference would manifest itself in their confused perceptions and thus in their aesthetic responses,[38] they also simply supposed that the divinely established harmony of the monads would establish a basic agreement among the views of different souls. Thus Leibniz held that God "is the cause of this correspondence among [different persons'] phenomena and . . . makes public to all that which is peculiar to one,"[39] and Baumgarten appealed to the strictly metaphysical claim that "in this and every world in which there are spirits, there is a general interconnection of spirits."[40] In fact, the rationalist definition of aesthetic response as confused or indistinct knowledge tended to make the intersubjective validity of claims of taste entirely insupportable in the empirical world, but their metaphysical refuge in the preestablished harmony functioned to guarantee this validity, completely though vacuously, at a higher level.

So neither rationalism nor empiricism actually failed to address the problem of the intersubjective validity of taste. But each attempted to solve it by means that the author of the *Critique of Pure Reason* could not have accepted — each attempted to solve it by transcendent rather than immanent metaphysics, by an appeal beyond the bounds of sense rather than to the principles of the possibility of experience itself. Even if Kant's criticisms do not address this point, it seems obvious to take it as a fundamental constraint on the *Critique of Judgment*'s theory of taste that it avoid any lapse into the kind of metaphysics once and for all destroyed by Kant's own critical philosophy. And, I shall argue, Kant did offer an argument for the intersubjective validity of taste which avoids both the simplifications of his predecessors' explanations of aesthetic response and the metaphysics of their guarantees of taste. We shall have to acknowledge, however, that in the end even Kant, as a theorist of taste rather than a critic of pure reason, did succumb to the lure of a "psuedo-rational" inference[41] and a "transcendental illusion,"[42] and ultimately attempted to found the universal validity of taste in a supersensible substratum underlying both man and nature.

With this background in mind, we can now see how Kant came to the problem of taste. From the time when he first recorded any thoughts on the matter, Kant took the claim to universal validity to be an essential component of aesthetic judgment. As early as 1769, Kant defined taste as "the faculty to choose in agreement with others that which sensitively pleases,"[43] and maintained that when one calls an object beautiful, "one declare[s] not merely [one's] own pleasure, but also that it should please others";[44] by 1776 Kant defined judgments of taste as "generally valid."[45] The *Critique of Judgment* defines the beautiful as "that which, apart from a concept, pleases universally,"[46] and taste itself as "the faculty of estimating what makes our feeling in a given representation *universally communicable* without the mediation of a concept."[47] So to justify any talk of taste at all, Kant had to demonstrate its universal validity; and to do this, he had to solve the two problems of explaining the pleasure of aesthetic response without assimilating it to any simple operation of sense or intellect, and of supporting the claims of taste without appealing to a meaningless metaphysics. How did Kant accomplish these objectives?

What Kant offered is a solution to the problem of taste which describes the judgment of taste — the assertion that a particular object is beautiful — as the outcome of a complex process of mental activity, consisting of two ideally distinct acts of reflection and depending upon both an empirically grounded assignment of a given pleasure to its internal source and an *a priori* assumption of the similarity of all judges of taste founded on an appeal to the general conditions of the possibility of experience. In barest outline, Kant's theory is this: a peculiar exercise of reflective judgment in the estimation of an object, in which no concepts are employed but in which the cognitive faculties of imagination and understanding are nevertheless involved, leads to a response to that object, a special state of mind, which may be thought of as a harmony or free play of these cognitive faculties. This subjective state manifests its existence by the occurrence of a feeling of pleasure — the pleasure in the beautiful, or aesthetic response itself. But the source of any given pleasure is not immediately apparent, so the decision that the pleasure felt in the presence of a particular object is in fact due to the harmony of imagination and understanding requires an empirical judgment about its origin. This judgment is reached by reflection on the context and history of one's own mental state, and thus by an exercise of the faculty of judgment which is at least theoretically distinct from that which first produced the felt pleasure in the object. And it is on the basis of this reflection on one's pleasure that a claim of taste can be erected, for it is precisely the attribution of a particular feeling of pleasure to the harmony of the faculties which licenses the attribution of the pleasure to other persons, or a claim of intersubjective validity for the pleasure

—the actual content of an aesthetic judgment. Further, such an extension of pleasure to others can be regarded as transforming the judgment of taste into a kind of *a priori* judgment, for it rests on an assumption of similarity between oneself and others which goes beyond any past experience of agreement. This assumption, however, plays no role in either the estimation of an object which actually produces pleasure or in the decision that a given pleasure is due to such estimation and the resultant harmony of the faculties; it is presupposed only in the universal imputation, by means of a judgment of taste, of a pleasure so produced.

The requirement of intersubjective validity set by Kant's analysis of aesthetic judgment, or by his definitions of the concepts of beauty and taste, imposes criteria for the evaluation of aesthetic response: any feeling of pleasure which is to serve as a ground for calling its object beautiful must be reasonably regarded as universally and necessarily valid for any audience of the object. But the explanation of aesthetic response as a harmony of the faculties of imagination and understanding, Kant supposes, in fact makes it rational to base a public claim to validity on something ordinarily so subjective as a feeling of pleasure. And that is not all that this explanation is taken to accomplish. Kant also uses it for the positive purpose of deriving the criteria of disinterestedness and finality of form, by means of which claims of universality and necessity for given pleasures may actually be justified; and at the same time he also suggests that this explanation sets limits on the certainty with which such claims may be made, and thus on the force which the justification of taste must attain. Kant's theory of aesthetic judgment thus comprises both an analysis of the demands made by judgments of taste and an explanation of the nature of aesthetic response which shows how such demands may be met. Underlying this theory is a model of mind more complex than any developed by Kant's predecessors, which enables Kant to avoid assimilating aesthetic response to either sensory gratification or the intellectual recognition of value, and yet to anchor the intersubjective validity of claims of taste on the intersubjectivity of knowledge in general.

That Kant's theory has the complicated structure I describe is far from obvious. Thus, instead of recognizing that the foundation of his view consists of two distinct but interlocking members, one recent commentator has claimed that the heart of Kant's theory is nothing but "a quite explicit conflation of talk about conceptual presuppositions or conditions of aesthetic appraisal with phenomenological descriptions of what goes on in the mind of the person making such appraisals," and that it is indeed difficult to find any aspect of Kant's exposition which "is not affected"—or afflicted—"by the same conflation of presuppositional and speculative-psychological arguments."[48] But although this is not the place for a general argument against the dogma that conceptual analyses can always be completely separated from commitments to phenomenological descriptions and psychological explanations, it does seem clear that Kant's theory of taste can never be understood if analysis and explanation are regarded as mutually exclusive alternatives. The interpretation which I have just sketched, and which I shall present in detail in what follows, tries to prove this point. I shall argue that Kant did indeed offer a speculatively psychological explanation of our pleasure in the beautiful—a phenomenon which Kant isolates, it should be noted, less by phenomenological description than by analysis of the concepts of subjectivity and of the aesthetic—but that he offers this explanation precisely in order to fulfill the demands imposed by his analysis of the presuppositions of aesthetic judgment as a form of public discourse. Paraphrasing a famous statement from the first *Critique,* I will contend that the analysis of aesthetic judgment without the explanatory theory of the harmony of the faculties would be empty, though the explanation without the analysis would surely be blind.[49] The full force of Kant's solution to the problem of taste can be appreciated only if we are willing to acknowledge that his analysis of the claims of taste and his explanation of aesthetic response in terms of a general model of mental activity are both equally fundamental constituents of his theory.

This is not to say that Kant was completely clear about the difference between the two parts of his theory or the exact character of their connection. In fact, there can be little doubt that he was not. There is every reason to believe that the *Critique of Judgment,* like Kant's other great works, was hastily written, and although its exposition shows a superficial concern with methodology, much is unclear about how its various arguments are really meant to cohere; Kant must have been somewhat confused about just what the structure of his theory really was. The real character of Kant's theory of taste is also obscured by the fact that the third *Critique* treats it as part of a larger theory of the reflective judgment of nature, although there are many ways in which the judgments of natural systematicity and purposiveness which are the concern of this larger theory are quite disanalogous to the judgments of beauty with which they are associated. And finally, we shall discover that Kant wrote the *Critique of Judgment* after a long period of indecision about the proper role of the concept of intersubjective validity in the analysis of taste, a period in which he entertained the radically distinct theories that the universal validity of our pleasure in the beautiful is a criterial condition of the judgment of taste, and that it is the universal validity of our response to a beautiful object which actually explains the pleasure we take in it. I will argue that it is the first of these views which is the key to Kant's mature theory of taste, but that he never entirely escaped from the grip of the second, and the fact that he did not caused some confusion in his own conception of the structure of his theory.[50]

It must thus be obvious that the interpretation offered in the following chapters will be, at least in part, a reconstruction of Kant's theory of taste. By this, I do not mean that I will attempt to argue for the conclusions of Kant's theory on the basis of any premises other than his own. Rather, what I mean is that I shall risk identifying certain concepts and arguments as those which are truly fundamental to Kant's theory and, where necessary, revise his own exposition to reflect the fundamentality of these premises. This will entail rejecting some of Kant's own statements about his procedure, and will also require me to argue that certain of the convictions which Kant presents as conclusions of his argument are not consequences of it at all. But I will argue that fallacies and paradox must result if one attempts to preserve every claim Kant makes, and thus that there can be no interpretation of Kant's theory of taste without some reconstruction of it. I do believe that the reconstruction I offer is persuasive, and that it employs no premises to which Kant himself was not deeply committed.

That Kant's theory of taste is interesting and illuminating, however, does not mean that his solution to the problem of taste is completely successful. I will attempt to show that Kant's theory of aesthetic judgment is far more plausible than has often been supposed. But I will also argue that Kant does not completely clarify his central explanatory concept of the harmony of imagination and understanding; that he does not fully succeed in his attempt to derive his highly restrictive constraints on particular judgments of taste, the requirements of disinterestedness and pure formalism, from this notion, nor in his attempt to show that it allows a completely secure justification of the universal claims of taste; and that he does not, in the end, completely avoid the kind of metaphysical guarantee of unanimity in taste to which his predecessors made such bald recourse. Nevertheless, I hope to demonstrate that Kant's aesthetics contains a sophisticated theory of aesthetic response and evaluation, and to suggest that it does contain profound insights into the character and complexity of the reflection that must underlie our discourse about the aesthetic merits of both natural beauties and artistic creations. If I show this much, I shall have shown that Kant's discovery of the reflective nature of aesthetic judgment was a permanent contribution to our understanding of matters of taste, and that the development and extension of his theory of taste must be part of the ongoing work of aesthetics rather than a mere exercise in its history.

I close this Introduction with a guide to the following chapters. In Chapter 1, I discuss some of Kant's early remarks on taste, and argue that they present a problem about the precise relationship between principles of intersubjective validity and our pleasure in the beautiful which must be solved by Kant's mature theory of taste. Chapters 2 and 3 consider the connections between this mature theory of taste and Kant's general theory of reflective judgment: Chapter 2 expounds this general theory, and points to a number of ways in which it can only distort the theory of taste; Chapter 3 argues that it nevertheless leads to the key to this theory, namely, the concept of the harmony of imagination and understanding as the explanation of aesthetic response, and offers an interpretation of this obscure and controversial idea. Chapter 4 begins my discussion of the Analytic of the Beautiful, where Kant expounds the four "moments" of the judgment of taste. In it, I first examine the superficial structure of this portion of Kant's text, and then present my arguments for revising Kant's own account of the order and relations among the four moments; I next give my interpretation of the analytical significance of the moments of universality and necessity, as the defining features of judgments of taste, and conclude the chapter by showing how Kant's explanation of aesthetic response can meet the demands of taste which this analysis imposes. In Chapters 5 and 6, I consider Kant's attempt to further his theory of aesthetic reflection by means of the substantive criteria of disinterestedness and finality of form; Chapter 5 is devoted to the first of these criteria, and Chapter 6 to the second. Chapters 7 through 9 are concerned with Kant's transcendental deduction of aesthetic judgment, his attempt to justify the intersubjective validity of taste. Chapter 7 offers an interpretation of the task of this deduction and of the constraints on any argument by which it might be accomplished; Chapters 8 and 9 interpret and assess the success of Kant's two main attempts to furnish such a deduction. Chapter 10 then considers Kant's final but unfortunate attempt to provide a metaphysical guarantee for the universality of taste. Finally, Chapter 11 turns to the view that Kant's deduction of aesthetic judgment can be completed only with the construction of a link between taste and morality. While there is much of interest in Kant's discussion of this link, I argue, his deduction of taste must be seen as depending on his account of the epistemology of our pleasure in the beautiful rather than on any analogy between aesthetic and moral judgment.

1

Kant's Early Views

****

The Norms of Taste

In December 1787, Kant wrote to his then disciple Karl Leonhard Reinhold that his long-standing interest in a "Critique of Taste" was suddenly
beginning to bear fruit. Finally, Kant claimed, he had discovered an *a
priori* principle for taste: "My inner conviction grows, as I discover in
working on different topics that not only does my system remain self-consis-
tent but also, when sometimes I cannot see the right way to investigate a
certain subject, I find that I need only look back at the general picture of
the elements of knowledge, and of the mental powers pertaining to them,
in order to discover elucidations I had not expected. I am now at work on
the critique of taste, and I have discovered a kind of *a priori* principle different from those heretofore observed."[1] It is clear that this letter represents a major revolution in Kant's thought. Though he had long hoped to
write the third critique which the letter announced — the famous letter
written to Marcus Herz in February 1772, announcing Kant's first conception of the *Critique of Pure Reason* as "The Limits of Sense and Reason,"
had even included the "universal principles of feeling, taste and sensuous
desire" among the topics of the proposed work[2] — Kant had still denied that
there could be *a priori* principles of taste in the early part of 1787.[3] But the
letter to Reinhold did not actually specify what the new *a priori* principle
of taste would maintain — it only hinted at some connection to the issue of
teleology — and the fact that the completion of the *Critique of Judgment*
itself, though promised for early 1788, was still more than two years away
may indicate that Kant had not yet discovered the particular principle by
which he was actually to prove the intersubjective validity of taste.

Indeed, before he could make good on his promise to Reinhold and
demonstrate that there is an *a priori* principle of taste, Kant had first to
determine exactly what role such a principle really plays in the pronounce-

ment of a judgment of taste, and this was an issue on which he had long been confused. Not until he finally understood the precise nature of the relationship between our pleasure in the beautiful and the claim to universal validity inherent in a judgment of taste could Kant see what the content of the *a priori* principle for taste would have to be, and not until the latter was determined could Kant know that such a principle was possible. Only with the discovery of the proper role of intersubjective validity in aesthetic judgment could Kant's bold announcement be defended.

The following review of the development of Kant's theory of taste up to the time of the *Critique of Judgment* will show that Kant's discovery of an *a priori* principle for taste did not follow a long period of uncertainty, for he had always firmly denied the possibility of such a principle. Rather, his discovery succeeded an extended period in which Kant maintained two different views on the role of intersubjective validity in matters of taste. On one of these views, a determination of intersubjective validity was a condition only of the judgment of taste, the assertion that a particular object of pleasure is beautiful, but on the other of these views the recognition of intersubjective validity was taken to be a constitutive factor in the occurrence of aesthetic response itself. Because Kant always held that the connection of pleasure to any particular object must be empirical, or wait upon the actual experience of the object (except in the special but irrelevant case of moral judgment), there could be no room for an *a priori* principle of intersubjective validity so long as any recognition of such validity was supposed to be involved in the actual occurrence of pleasure. But if a principle of intersubjective validity were not necessary for the feeling of aesthetic response itself, but only for an assessment of that response for the purpose of a judgment of taste, then it would be possible for such a principle to be *a priori* without belying the empirical conditions of aesthetic response. Thus we may conclude that it was Kant's resolution in favor of the first of his two theories which finally allowed the *Critique of Judgment* to fulfill his promise to Reinhold. We shall see, however, that the second of Kant's two early views never entirely lost its grip, and retained some influence even in the final composition of the third *Critique;* so we must conclude that Kant never became completely clear about the nature of his solution to the problem of taste. Consequently, an examination of his early remarks on this subject will not only prepare us to understand the accomplishment of Kant's mature theory of aesthetic judgment, but will also help explain some of its difficulties.

It was a constant in Kant's thinking before 1787 that there were no *a priori* principles appeal to which could confirm or justify judgments of taste. As early as 1764 Kant claimed that "one has no *a priori* grounds by which to justify a judgment of taste; rather only the general agreement in an age of reasonable estimation."[4] Kant's view was that there is no *a priori* principle on which the claim of intersubjective agreement represented by a judgment of taste might be based, so such a claim could only be grounded in the empirical observation of actual agreement in taste in a given community. Drawn from such observation, the principles by which judgments of taste might be justified could only be *a posteriori*. Kant also derived this conclusion from a connection of the thesis that aesthetic judgment depended on the senses with his original view that there were no *a priori* principles of sensibility; as he put it, "Taste offers no rules *a priori*, because it should be a sensuous judgment, which cannot be made according to such rules, but only in sensible intuition."[5] But it should be noted that this view of taste survived for many years after Kant's discovery, reported in the *Inaugural Dissertation* of 1770, that mathematics did contain *a priori* rules for sensibility; so that discovery must surely have been accompanied by a rejection of the Baumgartian view that aesthetic judgment represented the perfection or paradigm of sensitive cognition.[6]

Most of Kant's surviving fragments on aesthetics date from the 1770s, and they generally reflect this view on the possibility of *a priori* principles of taste. They also reflect a correspondingly negative evaluation of the philosophical status of the discipline of aesthetics itself. Thus one remark from 1769 or 1770 laconically reports that "fine arts allow only criticism [*Kritik*]. Home. Therefore no science of the beautiful."[7] Another fragment concludes that although "practical logic" is "demonstrable and therefore a theory . . . there is no theory of taste. There are aesthetic observations, but not *dogmata*. These rules are not established through reason, but through taste."[8] The appeal to taste may seem confusing, in light of Kant's eventual definition of this faculty, but what he means here by "taste" is not just the ability to choose objects in conformity with others, but such an ability as learned from observation of the choices of others, a "polishing" of judgment which can be acquired only through social intercourse and is thus thoroughly empirical.[9]

The empirical basis of taste is made manifest in several ways: the reference to Lord Kames is presumably meant to indicate our dependence upon experience for standards of taste; and a discipline which allows only "criticism" is also subjected to empirical limitation when Kant defines "criticism" by the possession of merely *a posteriori* rules. Thus he says that when rules may be known *a priori* and demonstrated, they are "dogmatic" and have the rank of logic; but when they are only *a posteriori,* they are "critical." In this case, one has not "doctrine" but "criticism." As an example of a discipline with the latter status, Kant mentions grammar.[10] Rules of criticism have a certain amount of force, but not the force of laws of logic. As Kant puts it, the *a posteriori* rules of taste "serve to elucidate and criticize taste, [but] not as precepts. The norm[s] of taste are examples, not of imitations [prescriptions], but of estimation."[11] *A posteriori* rules have a limited status: they may advise or direct, but not command. "Taste does not make a choice, but merely directs it."[12]

With only *a posteriori* grounds, any claims on the agreement of others contained in aesthetic judgments could have only the circumscribed force of induction from limited evidence. This conclusion led Kant to take sides with the empiricists in his early reflections on aesthetics. Thus in his lectures in logic — published in 1800, but actually based on the materials from the 1770s[13] — Kant says the following: "The philosopher Baumgarten in Frankfurt made the plan for an aesthetics as science. But Home more correctly called aesthetics criticism [*Kritik*], since it gives no rules *a priori,* which sufficiently determine the judgment, as logic [does], but derives its rules *a posteriori,* and only makes comparatively general the empirical laws, according to which we recognize the less perfect and more perfect (beautiful)".[14] This passage reiterates the claim that the principles of taste can be only *a posteriori,* or "empirical laws." However, the present characterization of these laws is misleading. Kant suggests that because the laws of taste are empirical, we can only make relative or comparative judgments that one thing is more or less beautiful than another, when the actual consequence of this fact is that we can only make judgments of taste with less than full certainty, regardless of what particular degrees of beauty they happen to claim for their objects. Nevertheless, Kant introduces an important new element into his contrast between the possession of *a priori* and *a posteriori* rules here: he says that because aesthetics has no *a priori* rules, it cannot sufficiently determine the judgment. That is to say, it provides no rules which by themselves can automatically decide whether or not an object is beautiful. That aesthetics could provide no rules of this sort was to remain a firm premise in all of Kant's thinking in aesthetics, and to stand in the way of the discovery of any *a priori* principle of taste as long as Kant supposed that if there were such a principle then it would automatically determine the judgment. Not until Kant realized that an *a priori* principle is needed to impute feelings of pleasure to other persons even if that principle alone cannot determine *which* occurrences of feeling to so impute could he acknowledge that judgments of taste might have an *a priori* principle yet still be made by an essentially empirical process of reflection.

But Kant did not see this possibility in the 1760s or 1770s, so the only way that he could argue against the rationalists' pretension that disputes in taste could be mechanically settled by rules—a pretense carried to the extreme when Meier offered no less than fifty rules of good taste[15]—was to take the strong position that any possible principles of taste are not merely limited in the determinacy of their application to specific objects but are strictly *a posteriori* in status as well. This view is expressed in many ways, frequently in the technical terms of eighteenth-century logic. Thus Kant says that while "aesthetics serves as critique, because the *principles* are derived *a posteriori*, [and] therefore are not *genetic;* logic [serves] as organon."[16] The precise significance of the contrast between "critique" and "organon" is not made clear here, but the difference seems to be one between a body of rules—also called "doctrine" or "discipline"—which not only govern the exercise of a faculty of mind, but may also be known in advance of such exercise,[17] and rules for guidance in the exercise of a faculty which can only be derived empirically. Rules of the latter sort can constitute, at best, a "logic of the healthy reason," or "common sense."[18] Such a logic can do nothing more than make one "attentive" to rules one already knows; it is only "negative (to avoid mistakes; aesthetic)."[19]

Kant also makes this point by using a distinction between "abstract" and "concrete." Abstract laws are those known prior to experience of their instances, and are truly universal; that which is concrete, however, can be known only on the basis of examples, and has a force limited to the range of examples on which it is based. Thus Kant differentiates logic from "the critique of taste, the principles of which are derived from the differentiations *in concreto* and are *a posteriori*." The force of the modifier "*in concreto*," in fact, is the same as that of "empirical" or "*a posteriori*": the limits of reason *in concreto*, Kant continues, "are determined by the field of experience."[20]

Even in his early period, then, Kant did understand judgments of taste as making claims to the agreement of all, but thought that such claims could be based only on past experience of actual agreements in taste, and had no real force beyond them. Thus such judgments could not have the force which Kant later assigned to them, when he argued that a judgment of taste claims that everyone *should* take pleasure in a beautiful object.[21] Kant's early view is well put in another passage from his *Logic:*

> In that logic is held to be a science *a priori,* or a doctrine for a canon of the use of the understanding and the reason, it is essentially distinguished from *aesthetics,* which as the mere *critique of taste,* has no canon, but only a *norm* (example or guideline merely for estimation) which consists in universal agreement. Aesthetics, namely, contains the rules of the agreement of knowledge with the laws of understanding and reason. The former has only empirical principles, and can never be a science or doctrine, insofar as one understands by "doctrine" a dogmatic teaching from principles *a priori* . . . [22]

In calling aesthetics a mere "critique" and any teaching from *a priori* principles "dogmatic," this passage reveals not only that Kant had not yet seen how to make room for any *a priori* principles of taste, but also that he had not yet arrived at his mature concept of a critique as the discovery of the *a priori* conditions of the possibility of experience.

Pleasure and Knowledge

In the 1760s and 1770s, Kant could not entirely commit himself to the aesthetic theory of either rationalism or empiricism, but had not yet developed his own alternative. His assumption that aesthetics concerned the agreement of knowledge with the laws of sensibility followed the tradition of Baumgarten's definition of aesthetics as "the science of sensitive cognition,"[23] and his assessment of the force of aesthetic principles followed what he took to be the views of such thinkers as Burke and Kames; but Kant had no idea yet that the existence of taste might depend on either a special faculty or a special use of judgment, nor did he yet suspect that he might adopt an *a priori* principle of taste without committing himself to the excessive view that individual judgments of taste could then be made *a priori.*

The idea of the agreement of knowledge with the laws of understanding, however, though not yet clearly distinguished from the idea of intersubjective agreement, does anticipate one element of Kant's mature theory of aesthetic judgment. This idea is an early expression of the view that the pleasure, the universal validity of which is claimed by the judgment of taste, is one occasioned by cooperation between our ordinary faculties of cognition, though perhaps under special circumstances. The possibility of such an explanation of our pleasure in the beautiful emerged by the mid-1770s, when Kant laid down the general law that "whatever agrees with the laws of a faculty of representation, pleases," and may please, in fact, either universally or privately.[24] Though it was not until the *Critique of Judgment* itself that Kant would hint at an explanation for such a thesis about pleasure, or see its full bearing on the problem of intersubjective validity, this claim did function as the basic premise of many of Kant's reflections on taste. In a large number of these reflections, a theory is sketched according to which our pleasure in a beautiful object is due to the unique facility with which such an object may be grasped by the senses, or to our ready comprehension of an object which is grasped with such facility.

This view was often expressed in terms drawn from Kant's rationalist predecessors. Thus one passage dating from the rich period of 1769-1770 maintains that "the form of logical perfection consists in truth (in concepts) and their means. The form of aesthetic perfection consists in comprehensibility [*Fasslichkeit*] in intuition."[25] But Kant modified the received model by transforming the idea of the sensitive perfection of cognition into a concept which could lead to a new theory of mental activity, the concept of the facilitation of knowledge. The connection of this concept to the problem of taste is made clear by one early passage: "In everything which is to be approved by taste there must be something which facilitates the differentiation of the manifold (delineation); which advances comprehensibility (relations, proportions); which makes the taking-together possible (unity); and finally, which makes possible differentiation from all [other] possibles (precision)."[26] Although he cannot yet say why, Kant is sure that a special facilitation of the attainment of such goals of cognition as differentiation, comprehension, and unification of ideas or objects must be the source of our pleasure in the beautiful.

Much about this theory is obscure. Though the phenomenon of "facilitation" is clearly supposed to differentiate aesthetic response from ordinary forms of cognition, Kant does not yet explain how it does so. Nor does he make it clear whether the pleasurability of beauty derives from its conformity to laws of sensibility alone, or whether it might derive from conformity to other laws of cognition, either instead of or in addition to the laws of sensibility. Some remarks suggest the first of these views, such as Kant's claims that "beauty has a subjective principle, namely, the conformity with the laws of intuitive cognition"—a Baumgartian phrase for sensibility.[27] But Kant also suggests alternative explanations when he says that "the essential form of the beautiful consists in the agreement of intuition with the rules of the understanding. [M]usic. [P]roportion,"²⁸ and when he continues the passage quoted in the previous paragraph by claiming that "the form of sensibility which facilitates the perfection of the understanding is the independently beautiful."²⁹ Thus Kant leaves open the possibilities that the conformity of an object which occasions pleasure may be with the understanding rather than with the sensibility, or—an early suggestion of his mature view—that aesthetic pleasure may have its source in a uniquely facilitated conformity of a given representation with both sensibility and understanding. The basic version of Kant's early view is that our pleasure in a beautiful object is due to its conformity with or facilitation of the workings of the laws of sensibility, but Kant's analysis of this notion of facilitation is too limited to exclude other cognitive faculties from entering into its explanation.

On one point of his early view, however, Kant was clear: the laws of sensibility to which a beautiful representation somehow conforms may be known only empirically. Thus the knowledge that a pleasure is occasioned by an accord with the laws of sensibility, and that the object occasioning this pleasure is beautiful, is dependent upon empirical knowledge of these laws. Any knowledge that a given pleasure stems from conformity to the laws of sensibility or a facilitation of their operation must be empirical, because the content and even existence of these laws can be known only on the basis of empirical observation of general agreement. Several passages from the mid-1770s make this particularly evident. In one, Kant defines the beautiful as "that which is in agreement with the subjective laws of mankind in general";³⁰ and a second remark adds that anything, such as "taste" or "feeling," where "the rule cannot be derived from objective, but from subjective, grounds . . . belongs to anthropology."³¹ By anthropology, Kant obviously means an empirical science of human response and behavior. A few remarks suggest that the empirical observations from which the subjective laws of mankind are derived may be confined to one's own case; thus one passage asserts that insight into these laws' generality "may be obtained from our self-inspection, without gathering external appearances."³² But this view, which would require some principle for extrapolating from one's own responses to those of others, is not developed, and Kant's basic theory seems to be that because aesthetic judgment concerns the workings of the subjective laws of sensibility, it can be founded only on empirical investigation into the agreement obtaining among different persons.

Some of Kant's early remarks on aesthetics, then, suggest a theory of the following sort. Our pleasure in beauty is founded in an object's conformity with the laws of sensibility, in the agreement an object allows between sensibility and understanding, or in the way that its effect on the sensibility facilitates the attainment of such objectives of the understanding as the comprehension and differentiation of objects. Such explanations seem to be intended by Kant's pregnant statement that what sets our mental faculties "into a harmonious play, is beautiful,"[33] and are more generally expressed by the thesis that when an object is in accord with the subjective laws of the mind, it is pleasing. And these laws, though they are subjective and can be known only by empirical observation, are valid for all mankind. Thus if one does have empirical knowledge of these laws, one may judge that a pleasure due to the harmony of an object with them will obtain for others as well; in other words, one may make an empirical judgment of taste.

Though this theory does not contain a clear distinction between aesthetic response, or our pleasure in beauty, and aesthetic judgment, or our claim that a given pleasure is generally valid, it seems to allow one, and to require an empirical knowledge of the similarity between oneself and others which subjective laws describe only for the actual judgment that an object is beautiful. On this theory, ignorance of the empirical laws of taste would not seem to preclude the occurrence of pleasure in the beautiful itself. But in some passages in his reflections Kant denies this inference. These remarks show that Kant entertained a second theory of our pleasure in the beautiful, according to which the intersubjective validity of our pleasure in the beautiful is not merely a criterion for the judgment of taste, but is a constitutive factor in the explanation of the occurrence of aesthetic response itself. Though Kant had to reject such a view before he could admit that a claim of intersubjective validity in taste might involve an *a priori* principle without allowing that our pleasure in beautiful objects could be linked to them by a rule, traces of this view will still surface in the *Critique of Judgment*.[34] It will thus be helpful if we now consider the antecedents of these passages in Kant's earlier reflections on aesthetics, and see that during the period of his development Kant simply entertained alternative theories of the relation between pleasure and intersubjective validity in the judgment of taste.

Pleasure and Communicability

On the view which anticipates Kant's mature theory of taste, I have maintained, the pleasure occasioned by a beautiful object can be felt without any consideration of intersubjective validity, although for such pleasure to license a possible judgment of taste it must in fact be determined to accord with the "subjective laws of mankind." Thus Kant says in 1771 that "in every case of beauty the object must please in itself through reflection, not through impression, for that is [merely] pleasant. It must please generally in accord with the laws of sensuous estimation, namely, in appearance."[35] Taste, as the ability to judge the intersubjective validity of pleasure, can obviously require an actual calculation of how an object will affect others, and if such a calculation can be made only by reference to empirically known laws about oneself and others, then judgments of taste can require an actual experience of society. On this view, then, it may be fairly concluded that "just because taste concerns how something pleases others, it occurs only in society."[36]

But Kant also asserts that in the case of taste pleasure arises "from agreement with a law, though empirical (of mankind),"[37] and this suggests the very different view that it is not merely the judgment of taste but the actual experience of pleasure in the beautiful itself which requires the existence and experience of society as its condition. One of the most striking expositions of this theory, though explicitly rejecting the facilitation theory of aesthetic response, dates from 1769 or 1770, and was thus maintained at the same time as the view it rejects: "That which pleases in taste is not really the facilitation of one's own intuitions, but predominantly the generally valid in the appearance, that in [taste], therefore, the merely private feeling is accommodated to the general intuition or the general rules of feeling . . . Therefore in isolation the proportions of sensibility can offer no delight."[38] According to this passage, universal validity is not merely a requirement for licensing a judgment of taste, but the ground of the feeling of pleasure itself. Neither an object of taste nor the mental state which it occasions, the facilitation of intuition, is the direct cause of our pleasure in the beautiful. It is only the generality of the mental state, the accord between oneself and others which the occurrence of the state represents, that is now claimed to be the ground of aesthetic response. In the terms of another passage, the beautiful is "what pleases because it can also please others."[39]

To say that the beautiful pleases because it also pleases others, though circular, clearly assumes that the intersubjective validity of a mental state has a constitutive role in the explanation of aesthetic response rather than a merely criterial role in the assessment of pleasure for the sake of aesthetic judgment. Kant makes both his attraction to such a view of intersubjectivity and its circularity evident in another reflection, which also emphasizes

the consequence which must attach to the absence of intersubjective validity on the present account of its role: "Beholding the beautiful is an estimation and no [mere] gratification [*Genuss*]. This appearance may offer some
enjoyment, but, by far, not in relation to the judgment of delight [*Wohlgefallen*] in the beauty; rather this consists solely in the judgment about the
generality of the delight in the object. From this it may be seen that, since
this general validity is useless in the absence of society, then also all charm
of beauty must be lost; just as little will even any inclination to beauty arise
in statu solitario."[40] This passage is certainly ambiguous, and its panoply of
different terms for pleasure almost seems designed to obscure its problems,
but it appears that the passage does maintain that it is not a mental state
per se but its general validity which causes pleasure; and it is from this
thesis that Kant derives the striking conclusion that in circumstances in
which no knowledge of intersubjective validity is possible there can be not
only no judgments of taste but also no pleasure in the beautiful — "in solitude there is indifference with respect to the beautiful."[41] On Kant's first
theory of taste, only the judgment of taste, and not aesthetic response itself,
would be affected by the ignorance of general validity which solitude must
impose.

Another early passage, in addition to showing Kant as holding his two
views of intersubjective validity at the same time, reveals a reason for his
adoption of the view that an empirical knowledge of intersubjective validity is not merely a criterion for but is constitutive of our pleasure in the
beautiful. This passage is found in the *Logik Blomberg,* a transcription of
some of Kant's lectures from about 1770:

> No one has yet been able to accurately connect, determine, and dis-
> cover the correct comparison of aesthetic perfection with logical per-
> fection. Much delicacy is required for this. That which favors our life,
> that is, which as it were sets our activity in play, pleases us. Something
> becomes easy for us, when it is in order. Order is, therefore, a means
> to the harmonization of our knowledge to the object to which it is ad-
> dressed. Further, what is novel pleases us especially, and not least the
> incredible, just because it is incredible, as long, only, as it is true . . .
> The surprising is always something pleasant for the sensibility, but
> also unpleasant for the understanding. Therefore one gladly hears the
> strangest stories. An aesthetic perfection is a perfection according to
> the laws of sensibility. One makes something sensible, when one ar-
> ranges it that the object awakes and touches a sensation, and when I
> [*sic*] make something capable of intuition. The greater art of taste
> [*Geschmacks-Kunst*] consists in my making sensible what at first I ex-

pounded only drily, in dressing it in objects of sensibility, but in such a way that the understanding loses nothing thereby. A perfection receives its value in that it allows of being communicated. In everything pertaining to taste, a sociability is the ground and therefore elevates taste much; he, who merely chooses what pleases himself but no one else, has indeed no taste. It is therefore impossible for taste to be isolated and private. Judgment about taste is therefore never a private judgment. From this we see, therefore,

1. Taste must relate itself to the judgment of everyone. Taste is a judgment of the most general agreement.
2. Taste has something sociable [*geselliges*], social [*gesellschaftlich*] about it.

   Sociability, however, gives life a certain taste, which it otherwise lacks, and this taste itself is sociable. If that, which is sensibly pleasing to me, must also actually please others, so it is said: I have taste. There are some persons who have nothing sociable about them, although they can otherwise be quite honest people.
   Solitary eccentrics never have taste. There is a certain principle in the human soul, which much deserves to be studied, namely, that our disposition [*Gemüth*] is communicable, and sympathetic, so that man as gladly communicates as he allows himself to be communicated [to]. Therefore men gladly communicate with one another, and a person seldom feels a proper enjoyment when he cannot communicate himself and his thoughts or inclinations to someone. Our knowledge is nothing, when others do not know that we know it. Thus it comes about, that one tests his judgment against the judgment of others, and that it pleases him, when his is in accord with theirs. It is therefore completely perverse to say: taste is a certain private judgment of a man about what he enjoys, what pleases him. Such a man has absolutely no taste. Taste also has generally valid laws, but may these laws be known *in abstracto* and *a priori?* No, but *in concreto;* for the laws of taste are not really laws of the understanding, but general laws of the sensibility.[42]

Some of the leaps and twists of this remarkable passage are undoubtedly due to the fact that it comes from a student notebook, but it is unlikely that one of Kant's students would have recorded two completely different views of taste unless the lecturer himself had suggested them. Thus this passage shows Kant entertaining two quite distinct theories of aesthetic pleasure even in the same hour, with no apparent recognition of their difference. Kant begins by linking an early form of the harmony theory of pleasure to the rationalist distinction between aesthetic and intellectual perfection, and by arguing that it is the play of mental activity in the perception of the beautiful—or the novel, or the marvelous—that pleases us. What pleases us in such a way, it is natural to conclude, is called a perfection just because it does so please us. But Kant then goes on to add an alternative explanation of our pleasure in a beautiful object. The value of an aesthetic perfection, he implies, lies *not* in the pleasure already described, nor indeed in anything intrinsic to the state induced by the object to which the perfection is attributed, but in the pleasure of communication. A beautiful object pleases us because it is an occasion for communication, and because we have a natural disposition to communication, the satisfaction of which brings us pleasure.

On this account, the absence of society precludes the judgment of taste, obviously enough: such a judgment makes a claim on the agreement of others, and can be made only on the basis of experience of others and their preferences. Their absence thus makes the judgment of taste logically incoherent and practically impossible. But the absence of others is also taken to deprive one of one's own pleasure in a beautiful object. Without anyone to share its experience with, Kant holds, one can have no "proper enjoyment" of the object itself, precisely because its pleasurableness lies in the fact that it is an occasion for communication. On the theory that it is the communicability of a mental state rather than the harmony of knowledge with its object which causes aesthetic pleasure, the conditions of both aesthetic response and aesthetic judgment are the same—namely, those which ground the possibility of communication. But as long as this identity was maintained, then Kant could not admit any *a priori* principle of the communicability of taste without making the occurrence of aesthetic response itself something that could be known *a priori*. And while neither this identity nor its consequence would follow from the theory of aesthetic perfection with which the passage from the *Logik Blomberg* opens, it seems clear that Kant did not yet distinguish his two views of intersubjective validity.

Kant's early confusion between the nature and conditions of aesthetic response and of aesthetic judgment is also revealed in another set of lecture notes, the *Logik Philippi*. Here, even more clearly than in the *Logik Blomberg*, Kant concludes that solitude must preclude aesthetic response as well as aesthetic judgment; thus he asserts that "in solitude man is very indifferent to the beautiful . . . Beautiful form seems to exist only for society . . . When we are alone, we never attend to the beautiful."[43] The pleasure of communication is not mentioned here, however, so Kant seems to be simply assuming that if the existence of society is a necessary condition for the possession of taste, it is also a necessary condition for the occurrence of the pleasures about which, under social conditions, judgments of taste might be made. Thus, in the paragraphs from which I have just quoted, Kant asks, "From whence does it come that in solitude taste disappears?" and answers that "in solitude we see to our private pleasures [*Privatgefallen*] only." This answer assumes that "beautiful form" is not intrinsically pleasing, but pleases us only when "we must direct ourselves according to the universal pleasure"; this may represent an implicit adoption of the explanation of pleasure in beauty by reference to its communicability, or a confusion of the question of whether in solitude one could be concerned with the publicity or privacy of a feeling of pleasure with the question of whether one could experience it at all in such a condition. Kant also states that "a person on a desert island would prefer the least feeling to all taste," as if "beautiful form" could not produce any feeling of pleasure on its own, but could please only when it provides an occasion for the exercise of taste in society. Similarly, on the next page of the *Logik Philippi,* Kant offers considerations concerning the development of *taste;* he maintains that "sociability is the cause and motivation of taste,"[44] or that only in society is it either of interest or possible to be discriminating about one's pleasures and their status. But if these facts are offered as reasons for the thesis that beauty brings no *pleasure* in solitude, Kant must again be either assuming the communicability theory of taste or else just confusing aesthetic response with aesthetic judgment.

The inclusion of two different theories of aesthetic response in a single lecture in 1770 shows that the pre-Critical Kant did not clearly distinguish the occurrence of pleasure in the beautiful from the reflection on this pleasure necessary to make a judgment of taste, and thus could not see that the availability of an *a priori* principle for use in such reflection would not mean that one's own pleasure in a beautiful object must occur, contrary to his firm conviction, in accordance with a rule. Eventually, Kant realized that the explanation of aesthetic response as due to any recognition of intersubjective validity was not the solution to the problem of taste, although his statement of this realization does not fully clarify the nature of the problem. The *Critique of Judgment* formally rejects any attempt to universalize a pleasure based on the "natural propensity of mankind to social life" because the existence of such a propensity can be demonstrated only "empirically and psychologically,"[45*] or can give rise only to *a posteriori* principles. But he does not make clear that identifying the condi-

27

tions of aesthetic response with those of aesthetic judgment, as this explanation attempts to do, means that there can be *a priori* principles for the
latter only if our pleasure in beauty is itself determinable *a priori,* and that
it was precisely because he wanted to deny this conclusion that he was earlier prepared to admit only "empirical and psychological" rules for the
judgment of taste. Nevertheless, it did become clear to the mature Kant
that the premise that intersubjective agreement is the basis of our pleasure
in the beautiful cannot be admitted in a theory which is to provide an *a
priori* principle of taste; the role of intersubjective validity in such a theory
must be other than explanatory.

Even before 1787 Kant was obviously concerned with the inconsistency
of his views on taste, for his early papers include evidence of several attempts to escape from his problems by distinguishing kinds of pleasure.
One such effort is recorded in a fragment from 1771: "What accords with
the universal subjective laws of knowledge (not of sensation) of mankind, is
beautiful [and] pleases [*gefällt*] in reflection, merely because it is in harmony with the conditions of reflection. The beautiful delights [*vergnügt*]
only in society, but it pleases [*gefällt*] also alone."[46] A distinction between
delight and mere pleasure might have solved Kant's problem if accompanied by a clear explanation of the difference between these two states,
but no such explanation was forthcoming. And, in fact, a solution to the
problem of taste was not to lie in a simple distinction between kinds of pleasure. Instead, the problem of these early texts could be solved only by a distinction between the conditions of the occurrence of a feeling of pleasure
and the conditions for judgment on such a feeling, together with a clear
recognition that the fact of its intersubjective validity plays a role not in the
actual production of pleasure in the beautiful, but only in that assessment
of pleasure which leads to a judgment of taste. It is this distinction which
underlies Kant's argument in the *Critique of Judgment.*

Kant's problem with two alternative theories of aesthetic pleasure, and
his tendency to think that intersubjective validity must have a constitutive
role in this response if it is to have any function at all, might be attributed,
at least in part, to the power of the tradition of regarding the whole of our
response to an object of taste as a single and basically simple mental act, a
tradition represented both in the rationalists' conception of "clear but confused cognition" and in the empiricists' "sense of beauty." Kant early recognized some of the complexity of aesthetic judgment — in a fragment from
1769 he wrote that "in every case of the beautiful, that the form of the object facilitates the operations of the understanding pertains to enjoyment

and is subjective; but that this form is generally valid, however, is objective"[47]—and from here it might have seemed but a short step to a distinction between the subjective process leading to this enjoyment and the further act of evaluating the general validity of such pleasure. But, still clinging to a simplistic conception of aesthetic response, Kant long wavered between linking our pleasure in the beautiful to the first or to the second of these factors, in either case treated as its cause, rather than distinguishing the pleasure we may take in the form of an object from the judgment of taste based on the intersubjective validity we ascribe to such pleasure. Kant did not yet have a model of mind which could provide a place for both the subjective and objective aspects here described in a complex act of judgment, or allow a clear distinction between aesthetic response and aesthetic judgment. In later chapters, I shall argue that Kant's mature theory of taste contains just such a distinction, although that it does so is obscured by the fact that Kant may never have become fully clear about the nature of his mature theory, and thus allowed a rejected explanation of aesthetic response to surface even in the text of the *Critique of Judgment* itself.

The Approach to an *A Priori* Principle

Another fact which tends to obscure the true structure of the solution to the problem of taste in the third *Critique* is the fact that both versions of its Introduction give more emphasis to the general discovery of *a priori* principles for reflective judgment than they do to Kant's advances in analyzing the structure of taste itself. This emphasis is in line with Kant's dominating concern with the possibility of *a priori* principles in general during the 1780s, leading to the conclusion that it was only because taste had an *a priori* principle that it could be included in the critical synthesis which this decade produced.[48] But this emphasis works to the disadvantage of Kant's exposition of the theory of taste itself: it allows the structure of aesthetic reflection to be described only after the existence of a principle for this reflection has been asserted and linked to another and not quite analogous *a priori* principle.

The problem of an *a priori* principle, as we saw, was raised early in Kant's thinking about taste. Initially, Kant thought aesthetics could have no such principle because its laws were laws of sensibility, or of the cooperation between sensibility and understanding, and these laws were only empirical. At the time of the *Inaugural Dissertation* of 1770, Kant decided that there were *a priori* laws for sensibility, those of mathematics. But this conclusion did not immediately lead him to revise his estimate of the possibility of *a priori* laws for taste; if anything, it may have inclined him to distinguish between the laws of sensibility and those of taste, as he began to do at about this time. In any case, Kant's insistence that the laws of taste are *a posteriori* long survived his discovery that there are some *a priori* laws of sensibility. Thus, at the time of the first edition of the *Critique of Pure Reason,* Kant still maintained that the rules of taste were entirely empirical, and for this reason even disparaged the philosophical respectability of the discipline of aesthetics itself. He argued this in a well-known footnote:

> The Germans are the only people who currently make use of the word "aesthetic" in order to signify what others call the critique of taste. This usage originated in the abortive attempt made by Baumgarten, that admirable analytical thinker, to bring the critical estimation of the beautiful under principles of reason, and so to raise its rules to the rank of a science. But such endeavors are fruitless. The said rules or criteria are, as regards their sources, merely empirical, and can therefore never serve as *a priori* laws, by which our judgments of taste must be directed; rather, the latter constitute the proper touchstone of the correctness of the former. For this reason it is advisable to give up using this name [for the critique of taste], and to reserve it for that theory [of sensibility] which is the true science (whereby one also approaches more closely the language and sense of the ancients, among whom the division of knowledge into *aistheta* and *noeta* was well known).[49]

This assessment of the status of the "critique of taste" does not differ from that found in Kant's earliest notes, for the possibility of an *a priori* principle for taste is still firmly denied.

In the second edition of the *Critique of Pure Reason,* published only several months before the letter to Reinhold was written, Kant's opinion on this question is still negative, but a slight modification may be observed. Kant changes the key sentence of the note just quoted to read: "the said rules or criteria are, as regards their *chief* sources, merely empirical, and can therefore never serve as *determinate a priori* laws, by which our judgments of taste must be directed"; and he alters the last sentence, now advising us *either* to reserve the name "aesthetics" for the subject treated in his Transcendental Aesthetic, the *a priori* laws of sensibility, "*or else to* share the denomination with speculative philosophy, taking 'aesthetics' partly in a transcendental sense, and partly in a psychological significa-

tion."⁵⁰ The latter concession, however, although at least allowing Baumgarten's subject its name, does not reveal a radical change in Kant's view of
the possibility of a critique of taste, for psychology was something that he
always regarded as a merely empirical study.⁵¹ But the first emendation
does indicate a new possibility, for it shows Kant as now committed only to
the denial that the critique of taste can produce *determinate a priori* principles by which aesthetic judgments might actually be decided. Thus it
leaves room for another sort of *a priori* principle, one which might not
provide concepts or rules for the objects of taste, as the categories of the
first *Critique* do for the objects of knowledge, but which might nevertheless
function in the justification of claims of taste. But although Kant's revisions may suggest that any *a priori* principle for taste will have to function
differently from the *a priori* rules of pure intuition and understanding,
they do not actually describe such a principle, nor do they really prepare us
for the discovery of one so confidently announced at the end of 1787.

The letter to Reinhold does indeed announce an *a priori* principle for
the solution of the problem of taste. But we cannot turn directly from this
letter to Kant's final analysis of the structure of taste and of its claims to
intersubjective validity. For while the announcement to Reinhold starts
with a reference to "the faculty of feeling pleasure and displeasure," the
third part of philosophy which this letter ultimately adds to theoretical and
practical philosophy, "each of which has its *a priori* principles," is not aesthetics at all but teleology.⁵² This is our only warning of what we actually
find when we turn to the Introductions to the *Critique of Judgment*. Although the history of Kant's thought might lead us to expect that this work
would begin directly with the question of intersubjective validity, and
make clear the existence of an *a priori* principle of such validity, it does
not; instead, it starts by submerging the problem of taste into a larger
problem of finding principles for a faculty of reflective judgment. In fact,
though all of Kant's earlier discussions of taste took works of art as the
paradigmatic objects of aesthetic judgment, the new context of reflective
judgment not only connects taste to the judgment of nature, but even leads
Kant to treat the judgment of taste as essentially a judgment on certain
aspects of nature *rather* than on art. Ultimately, we shall see, Kant's new
location of the theory of aesthetic judgment does not seriously deflect his
interest in the problem of taste or affect the character of his solution to it,
though it does distort some of his more particular conclusions. But the connection of aesthetic judgment to reflective judgment does initially obscure
Kant's theory of taste, and create some misleading expectations about its

character. Consequently, we shall have to pick our way rather carefully through the general theory of the Introductions before we can begin to discover Kant's mature views on the role and basis of intersubjective validity in taste, and before we can see that the letter to Reinhold really does announce a solution to the problem of taste after all.

2

The Theory of Reflective Judgment

****

Kant's Opening Analogies

In his early thought, Kant treated the problem of the universal validity of judgments of taste as a part of the problematic of "logic"—that is, what we would now call epistemology—and drew the materials for his attempts at its solution from his general views about knowledge. But in the texts which present his mature theory of taste—the two Introductions to the *Critique of Judgment*[1]* and its first half, the *Critique of Aesthetic Judgment*—Kant places the problem of aesthetic judgment in a new context. Prepared only by Kant's letter to Reinhold, we suddenly find the judgment of taste treated as a species of the more general class of what Kant calls "reflective" judgments. In this context, the problem of taste is not formulated as a problem about judgments on works of art, but is instead treated as part of a general problem about a class of judgments on nature which are not completely grounded by the principles of understanding established in the *Critique of Pure Reason.*

This new association between aesthetic and reflective judgment is crucial for the interpretation of Kant's theory of taste, but is also a source of several difficulties. On the one hand, the introduction of the concept of reflection into Kant's theory of mental activity is the key to the concept of the harmony of imagination and understanding, the basis for both Kant's explanation of our pleasure in beauty and the justification of aesthetic judgments which he builds on that explanation. On the other hand, however, the theory of reflective judgment not only adds a layer of often internally obscure doctrine to Kant's theory of taste;[2]* in some ways, it actually masks the real character of that theory. The general problem of reflective judgment is presented as the problem of grounding the systematicity of judgments in natural science, and its *a priori* principle as one which attributes the property of systematicity to nature itself. Correspondingly, Kant's Introductions sometimes suggest, the problem of taste must be a problem about the basis for beauty as a special property of natural objects, and its principle one which attributes such a property to those objects. But on Kant's deepest analysis, judgments of taste do not predicate a special property of nature alone, and can predicate beauty of either nature or art; and what must really be shown to prove the possibility of judgments of taste is not that they have a basis in the properties of objects distinct from ourselves, but that there is a foundation for their claims to intersubjective validity in the shared features of the human capacities for knowledge and feeling. Though Kant's Introductions would suggest otherwise, the only *a priori* principle of taste which he actually defends is concerned with our own characters as judges, and not with any necessary properties of the objects of our judgment.

Kant's discussion of reflective judgment cannot keep the true structure of his theory of taste from emerging, even within the two Introductions to the *Critique of Judgment.* But in some respects its final context in Kant's system does distort his treatment of taste; notably, the implication that aesthetic judgments, like other reflective judgments, are paradigmatically or even uniquely concerned with the beauties of nature founds a bias against aesthetic judgments of art which is characteristic of the whole third *Critique,* though not required by Kant's fundamental account of taste itself.[3*] Clearly, then, the two Introductions, with their emphasis on the general theory of reflective judgment — and with their further argument for the metaphysical significance of judgment as a link between the realms of nature and of freedom, a topic which I shall largely suppress[4*] — provide an approach to Kant's theory of taste which is both illuminating and confusing, and which requires careful examination. To provide this examination, the present chapter will expound the general theory of reflective judgment, and then explain the problems it creates for the interpretation of Kant's actual solution to the problem of taste. Chapter 3 will then show that, in spite of its problems, the theory of reflective judgment does contain the foundation for Kant's theory of taste, insofar as it does lead to the idea of the harmony of imagination and understanding and provide an important clue to its interpretation.

Each of Kant's Introductions begins with a set of appeals to architectonic considerations — claims within Kant's faculty psychology — that are meant to establish both a connection between our faculty of judgment and our ability to feel pleasure and displeasure and the existence of an *a priori* principle for judgment to use in this connection. These analogies may appear highly artificial, and their artificiality has been held to undermine Kant's whole argument in the *Critique of Judgment*.[5] I will argue that these analogies are unpersuasive, but that they do not really damage Kant's argument. For we do not have to treat them as actual premises for Kant's subsequent argumentation, and may instead regard them as mere anticipations of points to be more deeply grounded in the sequel. Kant's opening claims may not seem convincing, but we will ultimately see that there are grounds for the connections they assert.

Kant starts by dividing the higher or cognitive faculty of the mind — all those capacities that contribute to knowledge except sensibility — into three parts: "first, the capacity for knowledge of the *universal* (of rules) — *understanding;* second, the capacity for *subsumption of the particular under the universal — judgment;* and third, the capacity for the *determination* of the particular through the universal (deduction from principles) — *reason.*"[6] Understanding and reason, Kant says, have already been shown to furnish *a priori* principles, the laws of nature and freedom,[7*] and these might appear to be the only *a priori* principles possible in philosophy.[8] But that conclusion cannot be drawn. There is still the question of *a priori* laws for the faculty of subsumption, or judgment. This question is raised in the Preface to the third *Critique,* when Kant asks if judgment has *a priori* principles, and, if so, whether they are constitutive or regulative, and whether they "give a rule *a priori* to the feeling of pleasure and displeasure."[9] An answer to this question is intimated by the opening move of the first Introduction, which suggests that if understanding and reason both furnish *a priori* laws, "we may expect by analogy that judgment, which mediates between the other two faculties, will likewise afford its special *a priori* principles."[10]

Neither of these passages actually makes an argument by analogy for the existence of *a priori* principles for judgment; they might be regarded as merely posing the question to be answered by further argument. But as Kant continues he does in fact commit himself to an argument by analogy. Thus the Preface argues that judgment *must* contain in itself an *a priori* principle, "for otherwise it would not be a cognitive faculty the distinctive character of which is obvious to the most commonplace criticism";[11] and in Section II of the published Introduction, after again associating the *a priori* laws of nature and freedom with understanding and reason, Kant goes on to assert that "we may reasonably presume by analogy that [judgment] may likewise contain, if not a special authority to prescribe laws, still a principle peculiar to itself upon which laws are sought, although one merely subjective *a priori.*"[12] It appears as if the third *Critique* assumes at the outset precisely what should be most difficult to prove, and what Kant had previously flatly denied.

But even if he does suppose that the analogy between judgment on the one hand and understanding and reason on the other can establish the existence of some *a priori* principle for judgment, Kant immediately places a strong qualification on his argument. So far, Kant has defined judgment only as the faculty of subsuming particulars under universals, or of applying concepts to intuitions. This might lead us to ask why judgment should need any principles at all other than those furnished by the concepts it applies. Kant does not yet offer an answer to this question, but he does warn us of the possible difficulty of an infinite regress of principles. He maintains that whatever the principle of judgment is, it cannot be objective, that is, offer determinate concepts of objects. The understanding furnishes concepts of objects, and if judgment needed further concepts in order to apply those already supplied by the understanding, there would be no reason to preclude even further concepts being needed to apply those of the faculty of judgment, or that "another faculty of judgment would again be required to enable us to decide whether the case was one for the application of the rule or not."[13] But such a multiplication of faculties would be absurd, so Kant concludes that the principle or principles of judgment cannot be determinate and objective, or furnish "cognition of a thing." They will not specify qualities the presence or absence of which in a particular object may entail the predication of a determinate concept of it, and will have to be some other sort of rule altogether. In the terms of contrast suggested by the Preface, it appears, such principles may be regulative rather than constitutive, for Kant argues that only understanding is constitutive or capable of providing determinate concepts of objects. Only understanding has a "realm" of objects, a set of objects over which it exercises "legislative authority."[14] The principles of judgment may have at best a "territory," a field of objects to which they apply without being legislative.[15]

Kant's argument for this conclusion may be sound, but its content is obscure: the distinction between "realm" and "territory," the first of numerous political analogies which Kant uses in the third *Critique,* is not clear, and no description has yet been given of what even a regulative principle of judgment would actually maintain. And, in any case, the supposition that judgment has any *a priori* principles still rests on nothing but analogy, and seems entirely gratuitous. Kant needs stronger arguments for this claim, based on more than mere architectonic isomorphism. But before we can pursue these arguments, we must consider the second of Kant's opening analogies, for this first prepares the way for a theory of taste by linking judgment to the feeling of pleasure and displeasure.

In the Preface Kant simply asserts that "those estimates which are called aesthetic, and which relate to the beautiful and the sublime," demonstrate a connection between judgment and the capacity for pleasure and "evidence an immediate bearing of" the faculty of cognition "upon the feeling of pleasure or displeasure according to some *a priori* principle."[16] This is obviously intended only as a statement of what is to be proved in the body of the work, and not as an actual argument. Both versions of the Introduction, however, early introduce another argument by analogy to associate the faculty of judgment with the feeling of pleasure. First, considering now "all the powers of the human mind," and not just the higher cognitive faculty, Kant maintains that these too may be divided into three: the faculty of knowledge, the feeling of pleasure and displeasure, and the faculty of desire."[17*] Next Kant asserts that for each of the faculties already shown to have *a priori* principles, these principles have derived from a part of the higher cognitive faculty: the legislative principles for the faculty of knowledge in general from the understanding, and the principle which is legislative for desire (the moral law) from reason. Since both these parts of the cognitive faculty contain *a priori* principles, Kant then states, "we may, provisionally at least, assume that judgment likewise contains an *a priori* principle of its own."[18] And since both of the elements of the higher cognitive faculty already considered furnish principles for one of the three more basic faculties of mind, Kant continues, nothing is "more natural" than to conclude that judgment, the remaining one of the parts of the higher cognitive faculty, is linked to the feeling of pleasure and displeasure, the remaining one of the more basic faculties. Pursuing the analogy, Kant concludes that the link between pleasure and judgment, just as in the other cases, is "that the latter will contain principles *a priori* for the former."[19]

In the published Introduction, Kant explicitly characterizes this as an argument by analogy,[20] and it certainly is. It builds upon his first analogy, according to which judgment has *a priori* principles, and adds to that a new analogy, between the feeling of pleasure and displeasure and other basic faculties of the mind. Kant thus infers that this faculty of feeling has *a priori* principles; then, relying on the completeness of his divisions, he concludes that the faculty of judgment is the only remaining source for such principles.

But in the first Introduction, Kant goes beyond this second analogy. He maintains that "analysis of the mental powers in general incontestably shows a feeling of pleasure which is independent of determination by the faculty of desire," and argues that "the connection of this in a single system with the other two faculties requires that this feeling of pleasure, like the other two faculties, rest not on merely empirical grounds but on an *a priori* principle."[21] In other words, he adds to the analogy of the published Introduction the premise that there are cases of pleasure which are fundamental states of mind, in that they cannot be explained by reference to understanding or desire, and suggests that it is these cases of pleasure which require an *a priori* principle. Some pleasures, Kant tells us, are connected to the existence of an object in an "empirically knowable" way, and thus involve no *a priori* principle.[22] Others are connected to the representation of objects *a priori,* but only because their objects are seen "under the rational concept of freedom." In this case, the pleasure either follows immediately from the determination of the will, or "is perhaps nothing but the sensation of the capability of the will for determination by reason itself"; but in either case, such pleasure "is not a special feeling and unique receptivity which demands a special place among the properties of the mind."[23] However, a feeling of pleasure which is both connected to the representation of an object *a priori* and does not depend upon any practical law recommending the willing of such an object can be neither explained nor justified by reference to understanding or desire alone. It thus demands its own principle.

As long as the supposition that there is such a pleasure is unproven, this argument cannot show that judgment must supply an *a priori* principle bearing on our general ability to feel pleasure or pain. Though it does suggest that *if* we go beyond experience to make some as yet undescribed *a priori* claim about pleasure, we will have to find a principle for this claim distinct from any supplied by theoretical or practical reason, Kant's analogical argument cannot convince us that pleasure in fact has any *a priori* principle. Nor can his trichotomies persuade us to assign such a principle to the faculty of judgment.

In the first Introduction, however, Kant amplifies these merely architectonic considerations, and first begins to expound a new theory of mental activity. Building on the claim that whatever principles judgment does furnish, as a merely subsumptive faculty it cannot furnish new concepts of objects, Kant adds that "judgment is always relative to the subject and produces no concepts of objects for itself alone." Alternatively, he says that "the feeling of pleasure or displeasure is only sensitivity to the state of the subject." Taking this as a premise, Kant next infers that "if the judgment is always to determine something for itself alone, that probably could be only the feeling of pleasure; and conversely if the latter is always to have a principle *a priori,* it could only be found in the judgment."[24] Again, this argument by itself does not seem to reveal an adequate ground for Kant's withdrawal of his earlier rejection of *a priori* principles for taste. Its second clause depends on the prior assumption that pleasure does have an *a priori* principle, and its first clause does not follow from the premise, for Kant has not shown that pleasure or displeasure is the *only* form of sensitivity to the state of the subject, and thus that, if judgment bears on that state, it must bear on pleasure and displeasure. Formally speaking, this argument does not advance Kant's case beyond the point already reached by his opening analogies, and this is not surprising. What Kant has been attempting in these initial arguments is a deduction of the existence of an *a priori* principle for pleasure from the bare outlines of a model of mind, without a demonstration that we make any *judgments* — claims — *about* our pleasures which might actually require an *a priori* principle. We would hardly expect such an enterprise to get very far. Nevertheless, this last argument is significant. By introducing the idea of a judgment *about the state of the subject,* it does point the way to the deeper theory of an *a priori* judgment of taste which Kant ultimately offers. But instead of proceeding immediately to this theory, Kant now submerges the present suggestion in his general theory of reflective judgment. We must follow him in this twist.

Reflective Judgment and the Systematicity of Nature

The Introductions' initial characterizations of the faculty of judgment limit it to the role already allowed it in the first *Critique,* that of subsuming particulars under concepts given to it by the understanding. As his argument develops, however, Kant expands on this definition, giving judgment a more general concern with matching particulars and universals. In fact, he now describes two different ways in which judgment can operate: depending upon whether it is first furnished with a universal or a particular, judgment may be "determinant" or "reflective."

"If the universal (the rule, principle, or law) is given, then the judgment which subsumes the particular under it is *determinant,*" Kant writes in the published Introduction.[25] In the earlier version, he defines determinant judgment as the "capacity for *making determinate* a basic concept by means of a given empirical representation,"[26] suggesting that judgment in this form of its exercise supplies schemata for concepts furnished by the understanding.[27] On either definition, the faculty of determinant judgment is obviously merely the capacity to apply concepts already given, particularly pure concepts, to appropriate particulars. (Kant does not define the particular judgments which result from the exercise of this faculty, but presumably they would be called determinant judgments.) As such a capacity, determinant judgment does not require its own *a priori* principles. "The law is marked out for it *a priori,* and it has no need to devise a law for its own guidance to enable it to subordinate the particular in nature to the universal."[28] If it did, the problem of an infinite regress of principles would arise.

There is, however, a second possible relation between particulars and universals: that obtaining when the particular is given, but a universal has to be found for it. The capacity to respond to the situation defined by this relation is reflective judgment[29] (and the products of such response, presumably, are reflective judgments). This, at least, is how Kant defines reflective judgment in the published Introduction. The first Introduction offers what will turn out to be a more illuminating account. Here, Kant defines reflective judgment as "a capacity for reflecting on a given representation according to a certain principle, to produce a possible concept."[30] This seems to assign reflective judgment the same task given to it in the published Introduction, that of finding an appropriate universal for a given particular, but Kant goes on to intimate a broader interpretation. To reflect, he says, "is to compare and combine a given representation either with other representations or with one's cognitive faculties, with respect to a concept thereby made possible." Reflective judgment still seems to be concerned with the search for a concept, but Kant now suggests two alternatives to the direct application of an already given concept rather than one. Reflective judgment may be concerned with certain relations among objects which are not immediately evident in the pure or empirical concepts individually applicable to them, but which obtain only among groups of such concepts; or it may be concerned with aspects of the relation between an individual object and a subject of cognition which are not represented by any given concepts at all. The latter possibility, it will turn out, is Kant's ground for treating aesthetic judgment as a species of reflective judgment, for Kant will ultimately use the notion of a "possible concept" to connote not merely possible concepts themselves but also the general condition for the application of concepts, the harmony between imagination and understanding.[31] What it is for reflective judgment to compare and combine a given representation with one's own cognitive faculties, however, is not immediately apparent, nor does Kant quickly explain his suggestion. Instead, he next turns to a lengthy explanation of the first form of reflective judgment, which he interprets as our capacity for detecting systematic connections among the diversity of our empirical concepts of nature. And while it is in his consideration of systematicity that Kant's deeper motivations for postulating an independent faculty of reflective judgment with its own *a priori* principles first emerge, this discussion also contains much to obscure the true nature of Kant's theory of taste. While looking to the theory of reflective judgment for a key to Kant's critique of aesthetic judgment, we must also be aware that aspects of this theory can confuse our interpretation of his treatment of taste, and may even have distorted Kant's own development of the latter.

The first task which Kant assigns to the faculty of reflective judgment is the discovery or establishment of systematic order among the concepts and laws which constitute our empirical knowledge of nature. By the time Kant came to write the *Critique of Judgment,* he had apparently concluded that systematicity, though a fundamental objective of scientific knowledge, was a property not only of science but also of nature itself which could not be accounted for by the *Critique of Pure Reason's* foundation of science in the principles of determinant judgment, and thus required an independent foundation in a faculty of reflective judgment. And it may well have been Kant's recognition that there was a gap in the system of the first *Critique* with regard to judgments of systematicity that led him to conclude that it contained a gap for the phenomenon of judgments of taste as well, and thus to place aesthetic and reflective judgment in their new connection. But whether this is the case or not, we must begin our examination of the faculty of reflective judgment by determining just what gap it is supposed to fill.

In the *Critique of Pure Reason,* Kant sometimes assumed that the principles derived from the pure concepts of the understanding are sufficient for the actual foundation of a body of scientific laws describing the "order and regularity in the appearances, which we entitle nature."[32] For the construction of an actual body of scientific knowledge, only experience need be added to these principles. This view was particularly evident in the Transcendental Deduction of the first edition, where Kant held that the "affinity" of appearances, or the complete subsumption of appearances under "universal rules of thoroughgoing interconnection,"[33] rests on the *a priori* rules of synthesis alone: "The objective unity of all empirical consciousness, that of original apperception, is thus the necessary condition of all possible perception; and the affinity of all appearances, near or remote, is a necessary consequence of a synthesis in imagination which is grounded *a priori* on rules."[34] In the second edition, Kant was somewhat more cautious. He suggested a distinction between empirical laws establishing necessary connection among empirical intuitions and the necessary unity of apperception itself, and intimated that the necessary truth of particular laws cannot follow from the necessary unity of apperception alone.[35] He then concluded that while "nature (considered merely as nature in general) is dependent upon these categories as the original ground of its necessary conformity to law . . . Pure understanding is not . . . in a position, through mere categories, to prescribe to appearance any *a priori* laws other than those which are involved in a *nature in general,* that is, conformity to law of all appearances in space and time."[36] Thus the categories alone do not fully determine the individual laws of nature discovered by natural science. However, the discovery of such laws does not appear to require any *principles* other than the categories. Rather, Kant's argument suggests that the categories need to be supplemented only by the strictly empirical method of induction. Thus Kant concluded the paragraph just quoted simply by adding that "to obtain any knowledge whatsoever" of the actual empirical laws of nature "we must resort to experience."

Now, both editions of the first *Critique* do contain an appendix entitled "Regulative Employment of the Ideas of Pure Reason"[37] in which the "systematic unity of the knowledge of the understanding," as distinct from the affinity established by the Transcendental Deduction, is described as the legitimate and necessary aim of the faculty of reason.[38] And one passage in this appendix does assert that the "law of reason which requires us to seek for . . . unity, is a necessary law, since without it we should have no reason at all, and without reason, no coherent employment of the understanding, and in the absence of this no criterion of empirical truth."[39] But this suggestion that some search for systematicity may actually be necessary for the pursuit of empirical knowledge itself is isolated. On the whole, Kant seemed to believe that reason's idea of systematicity is necessary only to motivate the understanding and to assist it in reaching coherent results in occasional cases of its failure,[40] and not that systematicity is one of the necessary conditions of empirical knowledge. The Transcendental Deduction and the

Analytic of Principles are taken to have stated all of the latter, and the idea of systematicity seems to be an afterthought, something to occupy reason once it has been deprived of transcendent metaphysics.[41*]

In the *Critique of Judgment,* however, Kant takes the problem of the gap between the categories and a systematically organized or interconnected body of empirical laws or concepts very seriously. He now seems to believe both that such a system of knowledge is necessary and that empirical methods alone cannot guarantee that such a system can be built on the foundations provided by the categories. So the latter must be supplemented by some further *a priori* principle. And because the gap which this principle must bridge can be seen as one between universal and particular — between the universal laws of the categories and the particular laws or concepts of an actual empirical science of nature — Kant assigns the responsibility for bridging it to the faculty of reflective judgment. So there is a reason deeper than mere architectonic analogy for the assignment of an *a priori* principle to the faculty of judgment. It is not yet clear, however, exactly *what* aspect of systematic scientific knowledge it is that neither experience nor the pure understanding can ground, and so both the nature of and the need for an *a priori* principle for reflective judgment remain obscure. As we continue, we shall see that Kant sheds some light on these issues, but that some aspects of his theory of reflective judgment are never fully clarified; this, of course, cannot bode well for the development of a theory of taste from this foundation.

In the first Introduction, Kant argues that the mechanism of the first *Critique* cannot guarantee the existence of a "systematic connection of empirical laws . . . whereby it becomes possible for judgment to subsume the particular under the universal . . . proceeding to the highest empirical laws and their appropriate natural forms."[42] The categories alone can insure that any appearances of which we are conscious at all will be subject to concepts, but not that nature will not present "such an infinite multiplicity of empirical laws and so great a heterogeneity of natural forms" as to preclude an experience of nature "as a system according to empirical laws."[43] But the details of Kant's concept of systematicity are obscure, and it is thus not obvious what must actually be supplied to guarantee that such systematicity will obtain. In general, the concept of systematicity seems to imply an Aristotelian ordering of class-concepts, with more particular concepts of species being subsumed under more and more abstract concepts of genera until some upper limit of universality is reached, or at least approached. Thus Kant describes the work of reflective judgment as a "comparison of empirical representations, so as to perceive in natural things empirical laws and the corresponding *specific* forms, and yet through comparison of these with others to detect *generically* harmonious forms," or as the examination of nature "as adapted to a *logical system* of its manifold under empirical laws."[44] The essence of systematicity, then, seems to be logical systematicity, or the existence of highly defined relations of inclusion among the concepts we apply to nature.

But there are several problems with this. First, while Kant clearly conceives of systematicity as a relation obtaining among empirical laws when some number of them may be subsumed under either some single "common principle"[45] or under some smaller group of "higher although still empirical principles,"[46] he does not make it clear whether the relationship among laws which he intends can really be that of species-genus subsumption. Kant does not actually give an example of the kinds of empirical laws he has in mind, so it cannot be determined whether the higher-order laws which unify more particular laws of nature are just supposed to be abstract *descriptions* of similarities among the lower-order laws, which might conform to the species-genus model, or rather first principles from which the lower-order laws might actually be *deduced,* which would not follow from this model. And even when, in the published Introduction, Kant does hint at what kinds of laws he has in mind, he does not settle the issue of the precise logical nature of their relationship to higher principles. He says that "while it seems . . . unavoidable for our understanding to assume for the specific variety of natural operations a like number of various kinds of causality, yet these may all be reduced to a small number of principles,"[47] thus suggesting that what he has in mind is a unification of laws describing such processes as crystallization, combustion, generation, and the like; but he still does not make clear whether these laws will be unified descriptively or deductively.

The assumption that the systematicity of empirical laws and of empirical concepts share the same logical form is not the only problem with Kant's exposition of the goal of reflective judgment. Kant also seems to commit himself to the view that one and the same ordering of ideas will be at the same time a systematic connection of empirical laws, such as those describing causal connections, and empirical concepts, those figuring in a taxonomic classification of the forms of the objects of nature. Thus Kant does not just describe all systematicity in terms of stipulations on classifications in natural science, such as that they show that nature is "rich in varieties but poor in species";[48] he also describes as a single task that of finding unity in "the variety and dissimilarity of [empirical] laws and also of the corresponding natural forms."[49] But Kant does not actually argue that systematicity among the laws governing the behavior of natural objects requires or implies taxonomic systematicity in our classification of those objects, nor is it apparent that explanatory and classificatory systematicity are really the same thing. Kant may well have assumed so, just because he thought of concepts as rules, and thus as laws; but his actual argument seems simply to slide between the consideration of concepts and that of laws. Thus he characteristically maintains that "the condition of the possible application of logic to nature" is that we assume that "nature in its unlimited plurality has hit upon a division into genera and species which enables our judgment to find harmony when comparing natural forms, and to reach empirical *concepts* and their interconnection by ascending to more universal, yet empirical *concepts,* i.e., the judgment posits *a priori,* and hence by a transcendental principle, a system of nature under empirical *laws* as well."[50]

But of course the biggest problem about Kant's argument is just why such systematicity, whether of concepts or laws or both, should be necessary at all. The first Introduction to the *Critique* does not contain a clear answer to this question. While its Section IV might suggest that a connection of all appearances under an integrated system of empirical laws is a condition of the unity of apperception itself, or that "the unity of nature under a principle of the thoroughgoing connection of everything contained in this sum of all appearances . . . requires a system of potential empirical knowledge according to universal as well as particular laws,"[51] Kant does not actually defend such a strong view. Rather, he attributes the need for systematicity not to the conditions of apperception (the unity of consciousness itself), but only to a need on the part of the faculty of judgment to exercise its "capacity of subsuming the particular given laws under more general ones, which are not given."[52] The faculty of judgment itself, Kant implies, simply requires an ascent from more particular laws to more universal ones.

A different view of the problem of empirical laws is hinted at in the published Introduction, where Kant suggests that empirical laws need a basis beyond the principles of understanding in order to secure their very status *as* empirical laws. They need a ground for their necessity, and the requirement of systematicity follows because a ground of necessity can be supplied by the relational property of position in a unified system of laws: "These laws, being empirical, may be contingent as far as the light of our understanding goes, but still, if they are to be called laws (as the concept of a nature requires), they must be regarded as necessary on a principle, unknown though it be to us, of the unity of the manifold. The reflective judgment which is compelled to ascend from the particular in nature to the universal, therefore, stands in need of a principle."[53] Initially, this passage might appear to postulate the same simple need for systematicity that the first Introduction does, or just to make it judgment's special assignment to find a "unity of all empirical principles under higher, though likewise empirical, principles."[54] Kant does, however, suggest that it is actually the necessity rather than the mere systematicity of empirical laws which is judgment's ultimate concern, and that systematicity is required as a ground for necessity. Thus he adds to the bare need for unity a requirement for the *necessity of* the unity of empirical laws, and speaks of judgment's need for a principle to establish that "what is contingent in the particular (empirical) laws of nature nevertheless contains unity of law in the synthesis of its manifold in an intrinsically possible experience."[55] That is, individual empirical laws cannot be contingent, as they were left in the *Critique of Pure Reason,* but must be regarded as necessary; and, Kant seems to suggest, they can derive at least an approximation to this necessity only by being included in a hierarchical system of laws, with lower-order laws represented as deducible from higher-order ones. While the necessity of such a system of laws as a whole would remain opaque to us, its unity would lend an appearance of necessity to individual laws within it just in virtue of the way they are connected to other laws within the system. The categories cannot establish the existence of such a system, so an additional principle must be adopted.

But Kant does not make his commitment to a view such as this unequivocal. If the underlying ground for the objective of systematicity were that individual laws of nature must be established to be necessarily true in order to ground necessary connections in apperception, and if their integration in a system were the only condition under which they could appear to be necessarily true, it would seem to follow that systematicity is a condition of the possibility of experience itself. In this case, it would seem that systematicity should be on a par with the constitutive principles of the understanding itself. Kant, however, refrains from drawing this conclusion. Instead, he maintains that the goal of systematic unity "only represents the unique mode in which we must proceed in our reflection upon the objects of nature . . . and so is a subjective principle, i.e., a maxim of judgment."[56] The *Critique of Judgment,* like the *Critique of Pure Reason,* treats the goal of systematicity as a regulative idea rather than a constitutive principle, in spite of its increased emphasis on this goal. Before we can fully understand the peculiarity of this conclusion, however, or its implications for the yet to be considered question of the status of any principle of aesthetic judgment, we must consider a question that is too pressing to be put off any longer — namely, what is the actual content of the *a priori* principle of reflective judgment? What assertion is it which must support judgment's search for systematicity?

According to Section II of the first Introduction, the *a priori* principle of judgment is actually just the *a priori* representation of the possibility of success in the work of judgment, rather than any specific concept, transcendental or empirical, of individual natural objects. And what acts as such a condition is in fact nothing but the principle that *nature itself is systematic*. This is clear from Kant's first statement of the principle: "should there be a concept or rule which has sprung originally from the faculty of judgment, it would have to be a concept of things *in nature so far as nature conforms to our faculty of judgment*" and its need to subsume particular laws under more general ones.[57] In Section IV, a similar view is presented. Here, Kant asserts that the understanding alone does not provide the "principle of the affinity of the special laws of nature,"[58] but that judgment does furnish such a principle in the form of "a subjectively necessary, transcendental *presupposition* that this dismaying, unlimited diversity of empirical laws and this heterogeneity of natural forms do not belong to nature, that, instead, nature is fitted for experience as an empirical system."[59]

We thus see that the *a priori* principle of reflective judgment is nothing but the postulation that the object of this faculty, nature itself, possesses a special property in virtue of which it conforms with the objective of this faculty, that is, the property of systematicity. The "principle of reflection on any given natural object" is nothing but the postulation that reflective judgment may be successful, or "that for all things in nature empirical concepts can be found . . . that one can always presuppose in the creations of nature a form which is possible under universal laws accessible to our knowledge."[60] But there are two obvious problems with such a principle. First, it might seem that the principle of systematicity adds no actual criteria to the rules for empirical knowledge already developed in the first *Critique;* second, it must seem that this principle does nothing but transform our own need for systematicity into a self-serving delusion that nature is systematic.

The more serious of these questions is the second, concerning the justifiability of postulating that nature is systematic. Kant himself calls attention to this problem with his insistent qualification of the epistemic status of the principle of reflective judgment. Thus he calls it a principle for nature as "art," or for a "technic of nature," which is apparently meant to express a contrast with a principle for an actual *science* of nature; a principle for a technic furnishes no "knowledge of objects and their nature" but only "a principle for progression in accordance with empirical laws through which the investigation of nature is possible."[61] Kant also describes the "technical" or "artistic" principle of reflective judgment as a "universal but at the same time undefined principle of purposive, systematic ordering of nature,"[62] but claims that this "is neither a concept of nature nor of freedom, since it attributes nothing at all to the object," but only concerns our mode of reflection on it.[63] We shall see in a moment, however, that these terms of qualification cannot mean that the principle of judgment is not, at least grammatically, predicated of nature, and even believed true of nature, for the principle must have a motivational force, which is possible only if it is understood to actually attribute the property of systematicity to nature. So what do these qualifications mean?

Apparently, they mean simply that this principle is not, after all, a necessary condition of the possibility of any experience at all. Kant states his qualification by describing the principle of reflective judgment as a "necessary *presupposition*" rather than a law,[64] or as prescribing a law merely to judgment itself rather than to nature.[65] He does not define the nature of a "presupposition" or the precise force of a contrast between a presupposition and an actual transcendental law of nature. But it appears that in the end he does not recognize the concept of systematicity as a criterion of empirical truth, or a condition without which "there might exist a multitude of perceptions, and indeed an entire sensibility, in which much empirical consciousness would arise in my mind, but in a state of separation, and without belonging to a consciousness of myself."[66] The idea of systematicity is not an idea which we must use to link individual perceptions into a single experience; it is only the idea of a further layer of organization which we hope to find among the empirical concepts which we do use to secure such a connected consciousness. Consequently, the principle of systematicity cannot be regarded as a constitutive principle, without which any experience would be impossible, but can only be regarded as a principle which motivates the search for system among the concepts of experience. In this sense, the principle may be regarded as merely regulative in its epistemological force.

Kant thus presents the principle that nature is systematic as an answer to judgment's "own subjective laws, its need,"[67] but not as an "objective basis for the determination of the universal concepts of nature."[68] Nevertheless, in spite of the hedges we may place on its assertion, this principle must be taken to be about nature and not just about our own subjective cognitive needs with respect to nature. For Kant presents it as the representation of a condition under which success in the fulfillment of our cognitive requirements can be rationally expected, and such a condition is certainly different from the mere concept of the requirement itself. Thus, at least in form, the principle of reflective judgment is about a property which nature itself possesses, and we must still ask what justifies us in assuming any such principle. Kant's answer appears to be that representing nature as a whole as systematic makes the search for system a well-motivated activity.

Thus the language of the first Introduction suggests that judgment needs a principle because the activity of investigation would be irrational without a promise of success. Kant states that without a principle of judgment, reflection on possible laws of nature beyond the categories themselves would be mere "groping about among natural forms," and that success in reflective judgment would be "entirely fortuitous."[69] Similarly, if we did not presuppose the conformity of nature to our demand for systematicity, the investigation of its empirical laws "would be carried on at random and blindly, and as a result with no sound expectation of its agreement with nature."[70] Or, to the question "how one could hope to arrive at empirical concepts" conforming to the ideal of systematicity,[71] Kant answers that one could not so hope without supposing that nature itself is systematic. For the activity of reflection to be rationally motivated, one must believe that nature itself is systematic — that "our judgment is favored, as it were, by nature,"[72] or that nature itself "specifies its universal laws to empirical ones, according to the form of an empirical system, for the purpose of the judgment."[73]

It is doubtful, however, that any need for motivation in scientific activity can actually justify this *a priori* principle of reflective judgment. First, one may question whether a guarantee of success in an activity, rather than a rule for proceeding in it, is appropriately called a "principle." But even if one does not wish to quibble over usage, one may also wonder whether Kant is not employing an overly strong model of rationality here. Kant's idea appears to be that our faculty of judgment imposes the requirement that our science be fully systematic, and that activity aimed at developing such a science will be made rational only if we postulate that nature is fully systematic, for only such a postulation can guarantee that we will, sooner or later, achieve such an articulated body of scientific knowledge. But a reason to believe that a venture *must* be successful may be more motivation than we generally need to make undertaking it rational, especially if the value of success in the enterprise would compensate for a risk of failure. To rationally undertake some pursuit, success in which would clearly be valuable, it may be enough to lack any reason to believe it must fail;[74] and to rationally persevere in an enterprise, it may be enough that *some* headway be made toward its objective, either because partial success may confirm the initial supposition that success is not impossible, or because even partial success may have its own value. Without a more informative account than he gives of why our body of knowledge must be systematic, Kant cannot convince us that the efforts of reflective judgment will be rational only if we have a guarantee that nature itself is fully systematic. And finally, of course, one must wonder whether merely postulating or presupposing that an object will meet one's needs, rather than obtaining evidence that it does which is completely independent of one's own wishes, can make it rational to behave as if that object really will meet those needs. A delusion, after all, is no rational basis for action, yet the difference between the present presupposition and a mere delusion is not at all obvious.

The principle of systematicity, as presented in the Introductions to the third *Critique,* has something to do with our motivation in scientific research, but Kant's argument in its favor is not convincing. But this does not damage his case for his theory of taste, we will see, for the principle of systematicity is actually irrelevant to that theory. For one thing, its problematic ascription of the property of systematicity to nature itself is not, in the end, mirrored in the case of aesthetic judgment, for the principle of taste makes no claim about either natural or artificial *objects* of taste, but concerns only ourselves as the makers of such judgments. Second, Kant does not attempt to justify the *a priori* principle of taste by any reference to the present argument for the existence of a principle of reflective judgment. Rather, he gives an entirely independent deduction of the principle of taste, turning on the intersubjective rather than objective condition for cognitive success in general. This argument, to be sure, has its own problems, but they are quite different from those connected with what appears to be a rather gratuitous postulation of the systematicity of nature. And, most crucial, we shall see that what Kant's theory of asethetic judgment can adopt from his general theory of reflective judgment is the idea of a cognitive goal, analogous to that of systematicity, the satisfaction of which is a constant objective on our part, but *not* the idea that the fulfillment of such a goal must or even *can* be postulated in advance of the experience of particular objects. In fact, what we shall discover is that Kant's ultimate connection between the faculty of reflective judgment and our pleasure in objects of taste depends on the fact that fulfillment of the aesthetic analogue of systematicity *cannot,* if it is to be pleasurable, be anticipated on the basis of any conceptualization of the object of taste.[75]* Thus a principle which allows us to postulate *a priori* that nature possesses a property in virtue of which it conforms to our own faculty of reflective judgment is not merely irrelevant to Kant's theory of taste; it is actually precluded by the explanation of aesthetic response which lies at the basis of that theory. Therefore, the justifiability of the transcendental presupposition that nature is systematic need not concern us here.

Instead, we may return to the first of the two earlier questions about this principle of reflective judgment, that of its criterial content. Kant does have more to say about the content of this principle than I have so far considered. Systematicity does require more than a mere conglomeration of empirical concepts. Rather, a group of well-known and even "fashionable" formulae — that "nature takes the shortest path," "does nothing in vain," "makes no leaps in the manifold of forms," and that "she is rich in varieties but poor in species" — actually constitutes the content of the concept of systematicity, or expresses the "transcendental utterance of the judgment laying down for itself a principle for experience as a system" which "neither understanding nor reason can establish."[76] These principles do not place any specific constraints on the content of individual empirical concepts, such as the categorial constraints that they be substantival or causal concepts; and they are certainly not themselves particular empirical concepts, like, say, the concepts of *aqua regia* or gravitational attraction. But they do place constraints on *groups* of empirical concepts; they require that such groups display the greatest possible variety, continuity, and unity among themselves.[77] In stating such constraints, these maxims do give content to the idea of systematicity by stating directions — other than mere conformity with the data and with the categories — which are to be followed in the search for specific empirical concepts. These directions can guide judgment in reflection on the relation of possible empirical concepts to other, perhaps already adopted empirical concepts, and thus act as rules for the first form of reflective judgment, the comparison of given representations with one another.

Kant's connection of these maxims, as he also calls them, to the general idea of systematicity shows that this concept, though not a specific concept of individual objects, does give rise to certain more specific, though still not completely determinate rules, which may be used as conditions for its application. The maxims are criteria for conformity with the general requirement of systematicity, stating guidelines for its fulfillment, though providing neither a guarantee nor a decision procedure for full compliance with it.

The indeterminacy of the function of these maxims in the application of the general principle of reflective judgment is a second reason for concluding that this principle may be understood on the model of a regulative rather than a constitutive principle — that is, a principle which has an "excellent, and indeed indispensably necessary regulative function, namely, that of directing the understanding toward a certain goal upon which the routes marked out by all its rules converge."[78] The concept of systematicity, even when analyzed into the concepts of manifoldness, affinity, and unity which underlie the popular maxims of nature's parsimony and continuity,[79] does not supply specific concepts which can be directly predicated of individual objects, nor does it supply the general forms of particular empirical concepts. Rather, this concept applies to the relations of the concept of one object to the concepts of other objects — the kinds of relations that we find, for instance, in the subsumption of species under genera or of one level of explanation, such as chemical explanation, under another, such as physical. And this means that there can be no automatic procedures for determining sufficient compliance with the requirement of systematicity. Its criteria, the maxims of natural science, are only indefinite imperatives. They command continued investigation in the face of any apparent setback in the pursuit of systematicity, but they cannot prescribe any specific point at which, say, a large enough number of varieties and a small enough number of species may have been included in our system of empirical concepts; that nature takes the shortest path cannot tell us how short the shortest path is. That must be determined by empirical research, and is always open to revision. We can always conceive of laws both more specific and more general than any we are considering, or classifications more fine-grained than any we have; the principle of systematicity may prescribe a search for such laws or classifications, but cannot tell us when, if ever, to suspend it.

Thus the principle of reflective judgment is regulative rather than constitutive in function as well as in force: it does not furnish actual concepts of objects, but only certain goals for our systems of concepts; and it prescribes these goals without any definite specification of what constitutes their fulfillment. This feature of the function of regulative principles is described in the *Critique of Pure Reason,* where Kant writes: "The remarkable feature of these principles . . . is that they seem to be transcendental, and that although they contain mere ideas for the guidance of the empirical employment of reason—ideas which reason follows only as it were asymptotically, i.e., ever more closely without ever reaching them— they yet possess, as synthetic *a priori* propositions, objective but indeterminate validity, and serve as rules for possible experience."[80] It is not clear that the *Critique of Judgment* grants regulative principles objective validity, but it is more than clear that it agrees that the principles of reflective judgment are applicable to specific cases only with a certain indeterminacy.

The principle of reflective judgment is thus a peculiar kind of presupposition which can be applied to specific cases only with a certain degree of indeterminacy. It is natural to assume that these qualifications on the status of the principle of systematicity are meant to exemplify properties of principles of reflective judgment in general, thus including the principle of aesthetic judgment. This assumption must, however, be made with caution. We shall see that the principle of taste for which Kant eventually argues is indeed indeterminate in its application to particular aesthetic judgments, and it too might be best regarded as a regulative rather than constitutive principle of knowledge. However, we shall also see that the epistemological grounds for uncertainty in particular applications of this principle are quite distinct from those obtaining in the case of the principle of systematicity, and that, in spite of his insistence on the merely regulative status of the general principle of reflective judgment, Kant is actually quite hesitant to admit that the principle of aesthetic judgment is less than fully constitutive. The epistemological restrictions which Kant places on the principles of systematicity are thus suggestive of his eventual restrictions on the principle of taste, but are by no means identical to them. But before we can understand the differences between these principles, of course, we must first see how Kant actually develops his theory of taste from his general theory of reflective judgment. And before we can see that, we must conclude the examination of the theory of reflective judgment by considering two aspects of it which are intimately connected with Kant's transition to the theory of taste but inimical to its development. These aspects are Kant's concept of the finality of nature and his introduction of the individual forms of natural objects as special objects of reflective judgment.

The Finality of Natural Forms

Kant presents the concept of "purposiveness" or "finality" (*Zweckmässigkeit*) as the "characteristic concept of the reflective judgment";[81]* it, unlike the concept of systematicity itself, is clearly intended as a concept which can be directly predicated *of objects,* either individually or collectively, rather than of their concepts, in order to indicate their conformity to the demands of reflective judgment. Thus the concept of finality is at least grammatically analogous to substantival and causal concepts, which can be predicated of empirical objects in order to express their conformity to the principles of the understanding. But this analogy may be misleading, for it can create the expectation that there must be some independently specifiable criteria or descriptive rules for an object's possession of purposiveness — analogous to the specific spatiotemporal schemata of permanence and successiveness by means of which such abstract concepts as "substance" and "cause" are applied to empirical objects — which are not just equivalent to the requirements of reflective judgment, but rather first allow it to be determined that given objects actually conform to these requirements. That is, we might suppose that the concept of finality is supposed to supply an empirically applicable rule by which the purely logical notion of systematicity can be applied to appearances, just as the schemata of substance and causation give empirical sense to the purely logical concepts of a subject and a ground-and-consequence relation. Kant warns against this expectation, and in the general case of systematicity his warning may be sufficient. But we shall later see that in the case of aesthetic judgment Kant may succumb to it himself, and try to derive from the finality of the objects of taste more specific constraints on their aesthetic properties than are really implied. Indeed, one may wonder why Kant bothers to introduce the concept of finality at all, if not in the hope that it will somehow assist the work of reflective judgment by providing at least an analogue to the schemata which enable determinant judgment to function.[82]*

Though I have so far avoided mentioning it, the concept of finality is actually employed from the beginning of Kant's argument, at least in the published version of the Introduction, to characterize the special property which reflective judgment must attribute to nature as the ground of a systematic unity of empirical laws. Thus the systematicity of nature itself is more properly called its finality,[83] and this eventually leads to the characterization of beauty as a variety of finality as well. But the concept is problematic from the start. Kant defines finality as if it were a property which could *explain* nature's conformity to our own cognitive needs, and yet denies finality any explanatory function in its connection with reflective judgment.

Kant defines an "end" or "purpose" (*Zweck*) as a concept of an object which "contains the ground of the actuality of this object" — that is, which is causally responsible for the existence of the object — and "finality" as "the agreement of a thing with that constitution of things which is only possible according to ends."[84] So, Kant implies, an object of a kind which possesses finality could come into existence only through action involving the representation of a concept, or through the agency of a being capable of being guided by concepts. Then Kant introduces the special concept of the "finality of nature"; explicitly, it refers only to the fact that even in its multiplicity nature is subsumable under a system of empirical laws, but it seems to be introduced because of the explanatory significance of the concept of finality. For Kant's claim is that through the concept of the finality of nature "nature is represented as if an understanding contained the ground of the unity of the manifold of its empirical laws."[85] To say that nature is final, and not just systematic, is apparently to refer to the ground of its systematicity.

Before going any further, we may ask why Kant should have connected nature's conformity to a system of empirical laws to any notion of intentionality. The answer to this must lie in his unstated assumption that only creation in accordance with rules can explain necessity, and that these rules must be rules apparent to an understanding which acts on them. Thus just as the necessity of the universal laws of the understanding is due to the fact that we prescribe them to nature ourselves, our further goal of grounding the necessity of particular laws of nature can be accomplished only if we think of them too as if prescribed by an understanding. The unity of empirical law may be regarded as necessary only if we think that "an understanding ([even] though it be not ours) had supplied [these laws] for the benefit of our cognitive faculties, so as to render possible a system of experience."[86] To suppose this is to think of nature as final, for it assumes that conformity to our requirement of a ground for necessity can be ascribed to nature only as a product of design in accordance with a concept.

It is hardly obvious that purposiveness in general can only be understood by reference to any form of intentionality; descriptions of varieties of purposive action free of conceptual guidance have been common since Aristotle.[87] But the more pressing problem for Kant is just what the content of his concept of finality of nature really is. For Kant actually deprives it of its explanatory significance, and insists that it must not imply the actual existence of a designer, moved by an actual purpose. Such an understanding must not be "actually assumed," Kant maintains, for finality is, after all, only a concept of reflective rather than determinant judgment.[88] Thus the "adaptation of nature to our cognitive faculties" is merely "presupposed *a priori* by judgment" on its own behalf, and recognized as contingent by the stricter standards of the understanding; we ascribe to nature a merely "transcendental purposiveness in respect of the subject's faculty of cognition,"[89] without finding any actual reference to ends in the "products of nature."[90] But how could such a presupposition explain the necessary unity of empirical laws? Kant's argument supposes that systematicity can be understood only if explained by reference to an agent, and yet denies that we are really entitled to believe that any such agent exists. Nor is the relevance of a belief in such an agent obvious. For while Kant's argument is motivated by the assumption that necessary truth is possible only if self-imposed by the mind that acknowledges it, it also ignores this assumption. Even if an understanding other than our own could be legitimately postulated as the source of the necessary unity of empirical law, the transparency of necessary truth that is crucial to its recognition would be lost when this understanding is assigned to another agent, no matter how like ourselves it might be.

The first Introduction's discussion of finality is equally confusing. This text does not make express reference to a possible designer distinct from nature which may have had the systematicity of nature as its purpose. But it does describe the principle of judgment not as the mere assumption that nature *is* systematic, but as the presupposition "that nature itself *specifies* its transcendental laws by some principle."[91] Thus it too seems to imply that nature's conformity to our own requirement of systematicity can be understood only if regarded as the product of some agency on the part of nature itself, or if "through its principle judgment conceives of a finality of nature in the specification of its forms through empirical laws."[92] But here too Kant is insistent in denying this presupposition of purpose any objective or constitutive validity. Just as the published Introduction maintains that calling the products of nature purposive does not really imply a "practical finality ([as] in human art or even in morals), though it is doubtless thought after this analogy,"[93] so the first Introduction asserts that in judgment's presupposition of finality "the end is posited not in the object but always in the subject, and in fact in the latter's mere capacity for reflection."[94] But this must mean, in fact, that the *only* purpose actually involved in calling nature final is *our own objective of systematicity,* and the only basis for calling nature final is *its conformity to this purpose.*

So the first Introduction too deprives the finality of nature of the explanatory force associated with Kant's original definition of finality, and in so doing reveals the fundamental problem with this concept. For if "finality is conformity to law on the part of that which is in itself contingent,"[95] the possession of finality not only remains unexplained, but also turns out to amount to *nothing but* an object's contingent conformity to the requirements of the reflective judgment. Once the explanation of that conformity dissolves into a mere "presupposition," nothing is left but the bare fact that a given object does conform to the needs of judgment, whether specified by the maxims of systematicity or in some other way. No further and more specific form, appearance, quality, or history of an object is invoked by calling it final, no criterion of systematicity established other than the indeterminate maxims of natural science already stated. *Any* property on the basis of which an object may be subsumed under a system of empirical laws, or in virtue of which it fulfills another objective of reflective judgment, entitles it to an ascription of finality. Thus no new property of objects which might be directly manifested in their individual or collective appearances is provided; the concept of finality cannot found a schematism for reflective judgment.

The concept of finality is thus a purely grammatical addition to Kant's theory of reflective judgment. Kant claims that natural laws can be called purposive because they "resemble the case in which the possibility of a thing presupposes the representation of it as a ground,"[96] but denies that nature is actually intentional; eventually, he makes it clear that "experience does exhibit ends [*Zwecke*], but nothing can prove that these are also intents [*Absichten*]."[97] But the grace of this concession cannot hide the fact that Kant's concept of finality picks out no property in virtue of which conformity to our cognitive requirements can be independently specified. This is actually of little consequence in the case of systematicity, for Kant does specify criteria for this notion without using the concept of finality, namely, the maxims of natural science. But we shall see that in the case of aesthetic judgment, where these maxims cannot serve as criteria for reflection, the concept of finality will offer a false promise of specificity. But we are far from ready to see why this is the case. Rather, we are just now at the point where we can begin to consider how the topic of aesthetic judgment is introduced into the general theory of reflective judgment, and see both the foundation which Kant's theory of taste acquires and the bias it suffers from its connection to this theory.

Kant's two Introductions opened with a direct approach to the topic of aesthetic judgment, the attempt to link pleasure and judgment by means of their analogous positions in the trichotomies of the higher cognitive faculty on the one hand and the faculties of mind as a whole on the other. This topic was then dropped while Kant pursued the questions of why there should be a faculty of reflective judgment at all and why its principle should be that of the systematicity of nature. But we may now recall that Kant began his consideration of reflective judgment by maintaining that it might take either of two forms — to reflect, Kant said, "is to compare and combine given representations either with other representations or with one's cognitive powers"[98] — and that the principle of systematicity, in spite of its relation to our own cognitive powers, is intended as the principle of the first form only of reflective judgment. It is the second kind of reflective judgment, however, that is connected with aesthetic judgment; and both its explanation and its principle remain to be given.

Kant reveals that the argument so far considered bears on only one of the two applications of the faculty of reflective judgment in a number of places, beginning with Section VI of the first Introduction. Here, he says that in thinking of nature as purposive in the way already described, it is not the forms of particular objects of nature themselves "that are thought of as purposive, but only their relation to one another, and their adaptability . . . to a logical system of empirical concepts."[99] When judgment considers how the species of objects are to be subsumed under their genera, and how the laws that govern their behavior are to be systematized, it is considering the forms of those objects, to be sure. But it is not considering how any one of those forms relates to our own cognitive faculties; rather, it is comparing and combining them with one another to determine how they stand under a system of concepts and laws. The principle of systematicity, Kant now emphasizes, "does not extend so far as to decide about the production of natural forms which are *final in themselves*," or, in other words, it does not bear on "the *absolute* finality of natural forms," the external forms or internal structures of individual objects of nature.[100] So, Kant continues in Section VII, "since this principle of finality is only a subjective principle of the division and specification of nature, it determines nothing in regard to the forms of nature's products. Thus far, the finality would remain purely conceptual, and supply a maxim of the unity of the empirical laws of nature for the logical use of the judgment in experience . . . but there would be no natural objects as products whose form corresponds with this special sort of systematic unity."[101] However, Kant now adds that reflective judgment does in fact concern the particular "forms of nature's products" too, or that "the concept of reflective judgment which makes possible the inner perception of a finality of representations can also be applied to the representation of the [individual] object."[102] It is the second form of reflective judgment, that in which it compares and combines a given representation with one's own cognitive faculties, which makes this possible, or which leads to a perception of finality in the representation of individual objects.

This is how Kant introduces aesthetic judgment into his theory: the basis of aesthetic response, the harmony of imagination and understanding, is the result of the exercise of the second variety of reflective judgment, and beauty is the finality of an object in virtue of which it can occasion this response. Kant contrasts reflection on the systematicity of a collection of empirical concepts with "simple [*blossen*] reflection on a perception," where "it is not a matter of reflecting on a determinate concept but in general only [a matter of reflecting] on the rule of a perception in behalf of the understanding, as a faculty of concepts"; in this form of reflective judgment, one considers the comparison of the relationship in which imagination and understanding "must stand to each other in the faculty of judgment with that in which they actually stand in the case of a given representation."[103] And such a comparison may lead to an aesthetic judgment, or a reflective judgment on the finality of an individual form:

> If, then, the form of a given object is so produced in empirical intuition that the *apprehension* of its manifold in the imagination agrees with the *presentation* of a concept of the understanding (regardless of which concept), then in simple reflection understanding and imagination mutually harmonize for the furtherance of their business and the object is perceived as final for the judgment. Hence the finality as such is thought [of] as merely subjective, since a definite concept of the object is neither needed nor produced by it, and the judgment made is not cognitive. Such a judgment is called an *aesthetic judgment of reflection*.[104]

We shall see in Chapter 3 that this idea of reflective judgment as furthering the work of imagination and understanding — a clear descendant of Kant's original explanation of aesthetic pleasure as consisting in the facilitation of knowledge—is the key to his mature theory of aesthetic response, for it is his thesis that it is this mutual harmony of the cognitive faculties which is the basis of our pleasure in the beautiful. How this key works, however, will take all of that chapter to explain; and what I will emphasize now is only Kant's unargued assumption that this variety of reflective judgment is uniquely linked to the particular *forms* of objects *of nature.*

Kant introduces his theory of the aesthetic judgment of reflection as the ground for a "technic of nature," or a method for judging "natural objects as products whose form corresponds with *this special sort* of systematic unity, namely, that according to the representation of a purpose."[105] He thus arrives at the topic of aesthetic judgment by isolating a form of reflective judgment on "indeterminately purposive natural forms" rather than one on either the systematicity of sets of concepts for natural objects or— an entirely different contrast which Kant adds in concluding Section VII of the first Introduction—actual "natural ends."[106] But this restriction of aesthetic judgments to objects of nature, we will see, is not implied by Kant's actual explanation of how the comparison of an object with our own faculties in reflective judgment can produce pleasure in its beauty. It is based only on the context in which this explanation is first introduced and on an unexamined concept of form. Thus the kind of apprehension involved in the aesthetic judgment of reflection is taken to be directed toward natural objects just because it is reflection on nature in general which has been under consideration; but nothing in the explanation of the connection between that apprehension and pleasure implies that nonnatural objects— works of art—might not also be objects of this special form of reflective judgment. And the thesis that it is the *forms* of individual natural objects which are the objects of apprehension in reflective judgment is derived only by a simple exclusion of their concepts, as constituting the concern of the first variety of reflective judgment in its search for systematicity. If this is so, however, we must note that we can only infer about the form of an object which occasions the aesthetic judgment of reflection that it must comprehend *any* feature of the object which could figure in the "apprehension of its manifold in the imagination" without a comparison of the determinate empirical concepts which classify and explain that object to concepts of other objects. Nothing Kant says in introducing aesthetic judgment into his general theory of reflective judgment can actually link taste to a more specific concept of form.

Section VII of the first Introduction takes the crucial step of adding to the theory of reflective judgment the concept of a variety of judgment which reflects on the condition of one's own cognitive faculties. But it is also a fateful section for Kant's development of his theory of taste. For this section must be seen as at least partially responsible for Kant's opinion that it is objects of nature rather than of art which are primary for aesthetic judgment, and for his belief that aesthetic response must be derived from the form of objects alone. Even worse, however, the thesis that the aesthetic judgment of reflection is based on the form of natural objects gives rise to the most misleading impression created by Kant's subsumption of taste under reflective judgment: the idea that the *principle* of aesthetic judgment itself, like the principle of systematicity, is a principle concerning the properties possessed by objects in nature distinct from ourselves.

This view of the principle of taste is, fortunately, not suggested by either Section VIII of the first Introduction or Section VII of the second, which constitute Kant's real introduction to his theory of taste; these sections, which will be considered in the next chapter, make it clear that the need for an *a priori* principle arises in connection with taste's claim to universal validity, and direct our attention to the source of intersubjectivity within the human faculties of cognition. But Section IX of the first Introduction and the parallel Section VIII of the published text do suggest that the principle of taste must be a principle attributing a special property of finality to nature itself.

This impression arises from a discussion which introduces a new distinction between aesthetic and teleological judgment, but in so doing also tends to obliterate Kant's previous distinction between the aesthetic judgment of individual forms and the more general reflective judgment of the systematicity of nature. Kant's original distinction between the two basic forms of reflective judgment, that in which it reflects on the relation of concepts of objects to one another and that in which it reflects on the relation of particular objects to the subjective condition of our cognitive faculties, leads to a distinction between judgments on finality in the "division and speciation of nature"—systematicity—and those on the finality of individual forms in nature,[107] or aesthetic judgments. After his initial discussion of aesthetic judgment, however, Kant inserts a new distinction into his argument: that between the "*formal* technic of nature," or its finality in intuition, and its "*real* technic," or finality according to concepts.[108] The exact character of this distinction, or its difference from the earlier one, is not immediately apparent; but the published Introduction, by asserting that "there are two ways in which finality may be represented in an object given in experience,"[109] suggests that the new distinction is one between two ways in which *individual* objects may be regarded as final, both of which must be distinguished from the finality exhibited by *groups* of objects in nature insofar as they are systematic. One of these two forms of finality is the "finality of the form of the object," or the purely subjective finality discovered in the apprehension of an object.[110] The other is the conceptual, though not objectively valid, finality attributed to objects insofar as they are represented as "natural ends"—that is, things the structure "of which presupposes a purpose and hence a concept which is the underlying condition of the causality of their production"[111] or in which we discover a "harmony of the form of the object with the possibility of the thing itself according to an antecedent concept of it containing the ground of this form."[112] Judgments of the first kind are aesthetic judgments of form; judgments of the second kind of finality, which are judgments of purposive connections within the structure of particular objects, are teleological judgments—an illustration is the judgment that "the crystalline lens in the eye has the *purpose* of accomplishing by a . . . refraction of the light rays the focusing of those emanating from a point into a point on the retina."[113] Teleological judgments, which are the topic of the second half of the *Critique of Judgment,* are supposed to serve as principles for conducting research into natural objects without actually determining the latter through concepts of purposes, that is, attributing "to nature a causality by the representation of ends—i.e., *intentional* action."[114]

I mention teleological judgment here only so that we may consider the implications of the way in which Kant distinguishes this new form of judgment from aesthetic judgment for his theory of taste. What we must notice is that in making his final contrast between aesthetic and teleological judgment, Kant writes as if aesthetic judgment were the *only* other form of reflective judgment, and thus suggests that everything he had previously argued about reflective judgment in general *applies to aesthetic judgment.* But this suggests that the principle of aesthetic judgment is in fact the same as, or similar to, the principle of systematicity—which is, though a mere "presupposition," a principle about the systematicity *of nature.* Kant creates the impression, in other words, that while the principle of teleological judgment is not a principle about the actual properties of nature, *the principle of aesthetic judgment is.*

The assimilation from which this suggestion arises may be found in the third paragraph of the first Introduction's Section IX. This section, with its opening distinction between the formal and the real technic of nature, begins without any reference to judgments of systematicity. But systematicity is then introduced as if the judgment of the systematicity of nature's laws were identical with the aesthetic judgment of the finality of its individual forms:

> Although *a priori* aesthetic judgments are not possible, *a priori* principles nonetheless exist in the necessary idea of the systematic unity of experience, and they include the concept of a formal finality of nature for our judgment; from these principles the possibility of aesthetic judgments of reflection founded on *a priori* principles becomes apparent. Nature is necessarily harmonious, not merely in regard to the agreement of its transcendental laws with our *understanding,* but also in respect of the agreement of its empirical laws with the *judgment,* and the power of the latter to exhibit an empirical apprehension of nature's forms by means of the imagination.[115]

This passage seems to contrast to the necessary affinity of nature under the categories a *single* further harmony of nature with our cognitive faculties, namely, the systematicity of its empirical laws *and* the exhibition of this systematicity in the individual forms apprehended in the free play of the imagination. And this can only lead to the suggestion, which Kant here makes explicit, that the *a priori* principle of aesthetic judgment is in fact identical with that of systematicity, and must thus postulate the harmony of nature with our own cognitive faculties, as the latter principle does.

The intimation that the principle of aesthetic judgment must be a principle about the natural objects of taste rather than about the faculties of those who make judgments of taste might appear to be in order, for it does recur in the very first of the later sections of the third *Critique* which Kant devotes to the deduction of the principle of judgments of taste.[116] Nevertheless, we must note that Kant's actual analysis of the claims of taste, as expounded in the sections of the Introductions explicitly devoted to the problem of aesthetic judgment and in the later Analytic of the Beautiful and Deduction of Pure Aesthetic Judgments, neither restricts judgments of taste to natural objects (though the opinion that they are so restricted is reiterated) nor shows them, even when directed to natural objects, to make any assumption which requires an *a priori* principle *about nature.* What we shall see is that the only component of an aesthetic judgment which is in any sense *a priori* is its claim to the agreement of everyone, and thus that the only *a priori* principle on which it depends is an assumption of the similarity of cognitive faculties among human beings. Aesthetic judgments make no *a priori* claims about the natural existence of beautiful objects or postulations that such objects exist; they do make *a priori* claims about the intersubjective validity of the pleasures occasioned by beautiful objects.

Thus what is needed to support such claims is an *a priori* principle about the cognitive faculties of persons making such judgments and those of the others from whom agreement is claimed, but not a principle applicable to the *objects* of such judgments — the things, natural or artificial, which are called beautiful.

That a later paragraph of Section IX may retract its initial assimilation of aesthetic judgments to judgments of systematicity, by distinguishing "logically reflective" judgments from aesthetic reflective judgments,[117] does not undo the damage of its opening, for the suggestion that the principle of taste must be an *a priori* principle about nature is not affected. And this suggestion is made even more strongly by the published Introduction, which asserts that "in a Critique of Judgment the part which deals with the faculty of aesthetic judgment belongs to it essentially, for this part alone contains a principle which the faculty of judgment makes, fully *a priori,* the ground of its reflection on nature, namely, that of a formal finality of nature according to its particular (empirical) laws for our faculty of cognition."[118] This clearly implies that aesthetic judgment concerns the forms of natural objects in virtue of which they can be described by a systematic science. But we shall see that the only principle of taste which Kant ever actually *states* or *defends* has *no* essential connection to the problem or principle of systematicity, and that it is only in his final lapse into metaphysics that Kant makes another attempt to connect the underlying similarity of those who make judgments of taste, which is the actual topic of the principle of aesthetic judgment, with any aspect of nature itself.[119] The principle of aesthetic judgment may concern ourselves as judges *of* nature, but it does not concern either nature itself or even any of our properties as creatures *in* nature. Insofar as we are the latter, Kant believes, we are subjects "for explanation by empirical psychology"; but aesthetic judgments "claim to be necessary, and assert, not that everyone does judge thus" — all that empirical psychology could ever explain — "but that one *should* so judge."[120] It is to ground this "should" that aesthetic judgment needs an *a priori* principle, and the only kind of principle which can ground this claim is one concerning our own faculties of mind.

Aesthetic and Reflective Judgment: Final Comments

Thus we must conclude that Kant's association of the problem of taste with that of the systematicity of nature leads to a deeply misleading suggestion about the actual content of the *a priori* principle of taste. We may use the theory of reflective judgment to interpret Kant's model of aesthetic response, but not to identify the *a priori* principle of aesthetic judgment.

In the next chapter, I shall suggest that Kant's connection of aesthetic with reflective judgment is far from a total disaster, for this association does lead to the idea of a judgment which explicitly concerns the relation of particular objects to our own faculties of cognition; and a thesis about the satisfaction of cognitive objectives which Kant attaches to the general theory of reflective judgment does provide the basis for his eventual explanation of the pleasurability of aesthetic response by means of the harmony of the faculties. But the theoretical location of Kant's discussion of taste is damaging. We have already seen that the theory of reflective judgment includes a highly questionable concept of finality, a concept which easily creates a false impression of criterial specificity; and I shall argue in Chapter 6 that Kant's theory of taste does suffer from its use of the concept of finality. And we have just seen that Kant's introductory exposition also creates the false impression that there is a special connection between taste and nature, or that his analysis is essentially restricted to the case of natural beauty.[121] This connection is not required by the actual structure of his explanation of aesthetic response or by his analysis of aesthetic judgment. My next concern will be to show just what this explanation and this analysis really do imply. Before doing so, however, I will record three further warnings about the expectations which Kant's initial statement of the theory of reflective judgment may create.

First, as we have seen, the concept of systematicity is associated with four "maxims" of natural science — that "nature takes the shortest path," that "she does nothing in vain," that "she makes no leaps in the manifold of forms," and that "she is rich in varieties but poor in species."[122] These maxims might be regarded merely as rules of thumb for applying the idea of systematicity, or, perhaps more accurately, they might be thought of as actually specifying, in somewhat anthropomorphic terms, what constitutes the systematicity of a set of concepts of nature. In either case, however, all four rules function in the same way: each rule specifies a property of nature either grounding its systematicity or partially constituting it. Without giving a clear division of their functions or making apparent any relations of subordination among them, Kant also lists four "moments" of aesthetic judgment — the requirements of disinterestedness, universality, finality without purpose, and necessity — which are to serve as rules for aesthetic judgment, or "definitions" of beauty.[123] It might thus be expected that these moments, like the four maxims of science, will all have the same kind of function in the making of judgments of taste. Such a conclusion, however, would be another misleading result of the connection of aesthetic to reflective judgment. In fact, it is absolutely crucial to Kant's theory of taste that the four moments of aesthetic judgment be divided into two groups, reflecting two radically different functions in the making of aesthetic judgments. The moments of universality and necessity state the goal of intersubjective agreement in taste, and those of disinterestedness and the finality of form rather than purpose provide criteria for determining that particular aesthetic responses can license claims to such agreement. No such division of function is suggested by Kant's general theory of reflective judgment, but my next four chapters will be devoted to showing that the true import of Kant's solution to the problem of taste can be understood only if this distinction is introduced into the argument of the Analytic of the Beautiful.

Second, it has been observed that the concept of systematicity which is the heart of Kant's theory of reflective judgment of nature is an indeterminate concept, that is, a concept the application of which cannot be governed by any automatic decision procedure. So are the particular concepts —richness in species, parsimony in genera, and the like—by means of which this general concept is applied. This suggests that indeterminacy may also be a feature of the criteria of aesthetic judgment. We will see that this is indeed the case, but that caution must nevertheless be used in associating the indeterminacy of aesthetic judgment with that of reflective judgment in general. In fact, both the nature and the source of the indeterminacy of judgments of taste are different from those of the indeterminacy of judgments of systematicity. The uncertainty of the latter form of judgments arises from the indefinite extent to which systems of species and genera concepts may be developed; the indeterminacy of judgments of taste has nothing to do with that, but derives instead from the uncertainty of the judgments about ourselves on which claims to intersubjective validity must be based.

Finally, we have seen that the most appropriate model for the status of the idea of systematicity and the maxims subordinated to it is that of the regulative employment of a transcendental idea. This might lead us to expect that the goal of intersubjective validity in taste will be treated as a regulative ideal, and its principles as regulative principles. But it is by no means clear that this is Kant's intention. Although Kant does hint once that the principle of taste may be merely regulative in force,[124] he will actually argue for it as if it were a constitutive principle of the possibility of experience itself. We shall see, however, that this is one point at which Kant's theory of taste might have been benefited rather than distorted by the theory of reflective judgment, for there are serious problems with his attempt to produce a constitutive principle of taste.

The connections between Kant's theories of reflective judgment and of taste are far more tenuous than the programatic argument of his two Introductions would have us believe. There is a deep connection between Kant's theory of reflective judgment and his explanation of the harmony of the faculties as the basis of aesthetic response; at the same time, however, Kant's explanation of aesthetic response is at odds with his characterization of the principle of reflective judgment, and the principle of taste has nothing to do with the latter. In some ways, Kant goes too far in attempting to assimilate the theory of taste to the general theory of reflective judgment; yet he does not go far enough in pursuing the possible similarity in the epistemological status of their distinct *a priori* principles. At this point, however, we may set aside these difficulties and turn to the real significance of the theory of reflective judgment: its suggestion of the idea of the harmony of the faculties.

3

The Harmony of the Faculties

****

Pleasure and Subjectivity

We can now begin to consider the true nature of Kant's theory of taste. This theory has two fundamental components: an analysis of the judgment of taste — the judgment that a given object is beautiful — as a claim of subjective universal validity for the feeling of pleasure occasioned by that object; and an explanation of such feelings of pleasure as due to the harmony between imagination and understanding occasioned by beautiful objects. Precisely because a pleasure due to this source is universally valid, the attribution of a given feeling of pleasure to the harmony of the faculties can license the claim that the object which occasions it is beautiful; and thus the criteria which can be employed to assign a feeling of pleasure to this state of harmony — namely, disinterestedness and formal finality — can also be used as criteria to justify the claim to universal and necessary validity for that pleasure.

That we can distinguish between the analytical and explanatory components in Kant's aesthetic theory might lead us to think that only one of them can be truly fundamental, or even legitimate, and to ask which that is. Given both contemporary philosophical prejudices and the order of Kant's own exposition in the Analytic of the Beautiful, we might think that it is Kant's analysis of the requirements of the judgment of taste, as a form of public discourse, which is either his true starting point or even the only legitimate part of his enterprise.[1*] However, the nature of Kant's argument in the two Introductions to the *Critique of Judgment* could suggest that it is his explanation of aesthetic response — our pleasure in the beautiful — which is the true foundation of his view.[2*] But to reduce Kant's theory of taste to either its analytic or its explanatory aspects would be a mistake. Rather, the key to this theory is Kant's perception of the intimate relation between analysis and explanation — the analysis of aesthetic judgment poses questions that can be answered only by an explanation of aesthetic response.

But while Kant's analysis of the claims of taste and his explanation of our pleasure in the beautiful are inseparably connected, an exposition of his theory of taste must begin with one of these components. It might seem best to begin with the demands of taste, and then see how they are to be answered. But Kant's own presentation, having begun with the general problem of reflective judgment, first introduces the concept of the harmony of the faculties, the result of one form of reflective judgment, and thus begins with the explanatory aspect of his theory. I will follow him, and in this chapter will show how, by expanding on the claim that judgment may reflect on the relation of a representation to our own cognitive faculties as well as to other representations, Kant develops a model of the judgment that an object is beautiful as the outcome of a complex process involving both the production of pleasure by the faculty of reflective judgment and the estimation of the intersubjective validity of such pleasure by that same faculty. In subsequent chapters I will show how this theory is used to answer the claims of taste, and how it is to prove the possibility of intersubjective validity in aesthetic judgment.

In each version of the introductory section designed to connect the problem of taste with the general theory of reflective judgment, Kant constructs an argument which is supposed both to establish that judgments of taste do in fact concern the pleasure produced by beautiful objects and to explain how the exercise of reflective judgment can produce such a pleasure. Kant's argument for the first of these points may seem somewhat perfunctory, but that is not too much of a problem: first, because Kant's readers would have accepted this claim without any argument at all; second, because he does support it at greater length in the first and second moments of the Analytic of the Beautiful; and third, because he could in any case just have stipulated that by an aesthetic judgment he *means* a judgment which ascribes intersubjective validity to the pleasure occasioned by a given object, whether or not this is how others understand such judgments, and concerned himself solely with a defense of their possibility. But Kant's arguments on the second issue — the actual explanation of aesthetic response — are more crucial, both because they are more controversial and because the success of his introductory exposition is in fact assumed throughout much of the main body of the *Critique of Judgment.* Since Kant's initial explanations of aesthetic response are obscure, clarifying their significance will be my major concern in this chapter.

Section VII of the published Introduction — which, biased by the theory of reflective judgment, is entitled "The Aesthetic Representation of the Finality of *Nature*"[3] — approaches the topic of aesthetic judgment through the concept of subjectivity. Kant begins by revealing the complexity of this concept. In any of its senses, obviously, it involves some reference to the subject or possessor of knowledge — to call something subjective is to say that it depends upon the constitution of some subject for its existence or for the way it appears. But the force of describing something as subjective can vary with the nature of the dependence, and representations which are ontologically subjective, or depend upon the constitution of a subject for their existence, can nevertheless have a cognitive import that requires describing them as epistemologically objective. Thus the forms of space and time are ontologically subjective — "in the sense-representation of external things the quality of space in which we intuit them is the merely subjective side of my representations"[4] — or are explained by reference to the subject. Nevertheless, these forms are necessary conditions of our representations of objects, and are thus objectively valid — valid of all the objects of our experience. "Despite its purely subjective quality, space is still a constituent of the knowledge of things as phenomena."[5] In the *Critique of Pure Reason,* only the pure forms of intuition and the pure concepts of the understanding are allowed objective validity; in the third *Critique,* however, Kant allows that impure representations such as color sensations, which are subjective in being dependent upon the physiological constitution of the perceiver, may be included in our empirical concepts of objects. Thus what is ontologically subjective may in this case too be epistemologically objective, or form part of *"objective* sensation."[6*] By making objective employment of such data as color sensations, to be sure, one might limit the claims of empirical knowledge. Spatial and temporal structure can be validly ascribed to an object for any human perceiver, but a concept which includes reference to color might provide knowledge of an object only for a particular group of physiologically similar perceivers. Nevertheless, the subjective origin of a representation does not necessarily preclude its objective validity, for it might still be connected by a rule to the concept of an object.[7*]

Objective validity is the availability of a representation for "the determination of the object (for the purpose of knowledge)"; Kant also calls this status "logical validity."[8*] In the first *Critique,* Kant paid little attention to the question of *intersubjective* validity, or the rational expectation of agreement among different subjects on the representation of given objects. The few remarks he did devote to this question suggest that he believed intersubjective validity to be a consequence of objective validity, and to be expected only on the basis of the latter. Thus sensations such as colors and tastes, "since they cannot rightly be regarded as properties of things, but only as changes in the subject," cannot be the topic of intersubjectively valid judgments—they are properties, rather, "which may be different in different persons."[9] Conversely, the existence of intersubjective validity can be used as an empirical criterion or "touchstone" for objective validity; for there is "at least the presumption that the ground of the agreement of all judgments with one another, notwithstanding the differing characters of individuals, rests upon the common ground, namely, upon the object."[10] And in the *Prolegomena to Any Future Metaphysics,* Kant even asserts that "objective validity and necessary universality (for everybody) are equivalent terms."[11] But in the third *Critique,* Kant separates the question of inter-subjective acceptability from that of objective validity, and thus implies a complex division of the status of representations. All representations may, of course, be regarded as ontologically subjective. But epistemologically, they may be objectively valid, or furnish knowledge of phenomenal objects; they may enjoy no form of validity, and be entirely different from one person to the next; or finally, they may be intersubjectively valid, the topics of intersubjectively acceptable judgments, without being objectively valid.

If aesthetic judgment is to be possible, then the third *Critique must* argue that there are representations which are intersubjectively valid without being objectively valid. For Kant begins his analysis of aesthetic judgment by maintaining that there is an element of the subjective side of representation which is not objectively valid, or is *"incapable of becoming an element for cognition."*[12] This element is the feeling of pleasure or displeasure connected with cognition; and this feeling is the subject of aesthetic judgment. Thus Kant calls "that which is purely subjective in the representation of an object, i.e., what constitutes only its reference to the subject,"[13] its "aesthetic quality," and then holds that the feeling of pleasure and pain is the only such quality. Aesthetic judgment must concern the pleasure or pain occasioned by objects.

In Section VIII of the first Introduction, Kant opens by considering the term "aesthetic" rather than the concept of subjectivity, but arrives at the same result. He notes first that in a phrase such as "an aesthetic mode of representation," the word "aesthetic" connotes the subjective contribution of a form of sensibility to a representation, and is thus compatible with the objective validity of the representation. This usage — Kant's own in the first *Critique* — follows the Baumgartian tradition in which the aesthetic is the sensible component of knowledge.[14] As Kant suggested in the second edition of the *Critique of Pure Reason,* however, we may grant a second sense to "aesthetic."[15] Calling a mode of representation aesthetic may also express our "intention of relating a representation not to the cognitive faculty but to the feeling of pleasure or displeasure."[16] In this sense, Kant points out, the aesthetic makes no contribution to the knowledge of objects, but concerns only a sensitivity on the part of the subject; what is aesthetic in this sense is purely subjective in ontological significance. Again, Kant connects the aesthetic with the subjective, and thus prepares to link aesthetic judgment with the noncognitive feeling of pleasure and pain.

Because there are two senses of "aesthetic," Kant next notes, the phrase "an aesthetic mode of representation" (*eine ästhetische Vorstellungsart*) is ambiguous. It can refer either to the pleasure or pain aroused by a representation, or to the contribution of sensible intuition to the content of a given representation. This ambiguity does not, however, attach to the phrase "aesthetic judgment." If we think of a judgment as a knowledge claim, we realize that the senses alone can make no judgment. "Intuitions can indeed be sensuous," but an actual knowledge claim always involves the understanding. So an aesthetic judgment cannot be a knowledge claim based on sensible intuition alone, as its name implies if taken in one sense.[17] Consequently, it must be the other sense, the reference to pleasure or displeasure, which is intended in the phrase "aesthetic judgment." Kant thus concludes that "an aesthetic judgment of an object" refers, grammatically, to a relation of a representation to an object, but is actually "a judgment conveying the determination of the subject and his feeling rather than of the object."[18] An aesthetic judgment is, then, one which concerns a feeling, presumably caused by a given object; instead of making a knowledge claim about the object, however, it makes a claim about the feeling it occasions. In fact, we shall see, this feeling is the feeling of pleasure, and what is claimed for it is not objective but intersubjective validity: that the pleasure which the object occasions in the person judging it should be felt by every other member of its eventual audience as well.

But Kant is not actually ready to introduce intersubjectivity into the argument. So far, he has only claimed that aesthetic judgment concerns the subject's feeling of pleasure or displeasure, a result arrived at by consideration of the term "subjective" in one version of his argument and of "aesthetic" in the other. He next links these considerations to the theory of reflective judgment, and argues that in making one kind of judgment about the pleasure occasioned by an object we are making a judgment about the relation of the representation of that object to our cognitive faculties. It is here that Kant's explanation of aesthetic response begins to emerge; though this explanation will ultimately ground judgments of taste, it is introduced before any analysis of the actual content of such judgments.

In any act of judgment, the faculties of imagination—which Kant treats as "the faculty of intuitions or presentations" in the third *Critique,*[19] and which must thus perform the functions assigned to both sensibility and imagination in the first *Critique*—and understanding "are regarded as mutually related." Ordinarily, this relation is "objective and cognitive"; it results in the understanding's assignment of some definite concept to an intuition presented by the imagination. In such a case, what we are generally concerned with is not the relationship between the two faculties, but the knowledge claim which is the product of judgment; we are interested in a proposition rather than in the mental event of judgment itself. However, Kant argues, we can also consider the mental state from which a cognition issues. "This same relationship of two cognitive faculties can also be regarded purely subjectively, with respect to how one helps or hinders the other in a given representation and thereby affects one's mental state, hence as a relation which is sensible."[20] We may be conscious of the mental state which is the effect of an object on our cognitive faculties, and this consciousness is given by a sensation which is not itself predicated of the object. This sensation is not a "sensuous representation of an object," but is "subjectively connected with the embodiment of the concepts of the understanding in sensation by means of the judgment, being the sensuous representation of how the condition of the subject is affected by an act of that faculty."

So to the distinction between the conjunction of representations and concepts—the knowledge claim—which is the product of judgment, and the mental state or relation between the mental faculties which is the source of that product, Kant has now added the claim that there is a *sensation* which rather than representing any property of the object judged represents or manifests the existence of the mental state of judgment itself. Kant's next major step is to forge a new link between the faculty of judgment and the feeling of pleasure and displeasure by urging that the lack of objective reference on the part of this feeling makes it the appropriate sensory expression of the subjective side of judgment, or the existence of the act of judgment itself. Before he makes this connection, however, Kant must expand on the present distinction. So far, he has only distinguished between the content of a judgmental state and the occurrence of that state *with regard to ordinary cognition.* If aesthetic pleasure were linked to even the merely subjective side of this distinction, its occurrence would be dependent upon the occurrence of cognition. This would limit aesthetic judgment to cases in which cognitive judgments may be made, making such judgment derivative from a more basic mode of mental activity. And this would hardly allow Kant to advance beyond rationalism, or to prove that aesthetic judgment is a fundamental power of mind, requiring its own critique and its own *a priori* principle.

To establish the possible independence of the feeling connected with the subjective side of judgment, Kant maintains that the subjective condition of judgment, or the mental state which ordinarily underlies knowledge, may obtain even when its ordinary product, an actual cognition, does not result. Thus Kant writes that

> a merely *reflective* judgment about a particular object *can be aesthetic,* however, if, even before it contemplates comparing the object with others, the judgment, with no concept antecedent to the given intuition, unites the imagination (which merely apprehends the object) with the understanding (which produces a general concept) and perceives a relation between the two cognitive faculties which forms the subjective and merely sensible [*empfindbar*] condition of the objective employment of the faculty of judgment — namely, the harmony of the two faculties with each other.[21]

Thus there is a subjective state in which the conditions of judgment are met; the existence of this state may be perceived by means of a sensation; and, further, this state may obtain independently of the making of an actual knowledge claim about an object. This subjective state is the harmony of the cognitive faculties; the feeling by which it is perceived is that of pleasure; and the claim that it is the existence of this state which is manifest in aesthetic response is the foundation of the explanatory side of Kant's aesthetics.

But what is the subjective and merely sensible condition of the objective employment of judgment? And how can it obtain without an actual cognitive judgment? These are basic questions for the interpretation of the harmony of the faculties. They are best approached, however, by further consideration of the thesis that pleasure is the sensation linked to this state, for

Kant's deepest reason for making this claim is also our best clue to the nature of the harmony of the faculties itself. To see this, though, we must advance beyond the rather abstract considerations by which Kant actually connects pleasure and the subjective condition of judgment in the two sections of the Introductions explicitly devoted to aesthetic judgment. These considerations may be sufficient to link aesthetic judgments with feeling, but are not enough to explain *why* the harmony of the faculties should produce pleasure in the beautiful.

In both Introductions, Kant's official connection of the harmony of the faculties to the feeling of pleasure and displeasure seems to depend on an inadequate argument by elimination. In the first version, the argument proceeds as follows. An aesthetic judgment is one "whose predicate can never be cognitive, although it may contain the general subjective condition for a cognition." Thus its "ground of determination," or the evidence on the basis of which such a judgment is made, must be sensation; otherwise it will not be an aesthetic judgment at all. And if the judgment is to be directed to the state of the subject rather than the nature of the object, the sensation on which it is based must be one which cannot form part of the concept of an object. "However, there is only one unique, so-called sensation which can never become part of the concept of an object, and this is the feeling of pleasure or displeasure . . . Thus an aesthetic judgment is one whose ground of determination lies in a sensation immediately connected with the feeling of pleasure and pain."[22] Such a sensation may be brought about in two ways. It could be caused directly by the empirical intuition of an object, without the involvement of any higher cognitive faculties at all. A report of such a sensation would be an "aesthetic judgment of sense." Or it might be "effected by the harmonious interplay of the judgment's two cognitive faculties, imagination and understanding, when the former's power of apprehension and the latter's power of presentation are mutually assisting each other in a given representation." The expression of such a state would be an "aesthetic judgment of reflection."[23] And assuming that a judgment of taste—an aesthetic judgment in our own sense—claims validity beyond what can be justified by empirical intuition alone, Kant then implies that such a judgment must be based on a sensation of pleasure produced in this second way.[24]

When we can see what "mutual assistance" is and why it should produce feeling, we will understand Kant's explanation of aesthetic response. But let us consider the opening claims of Kant's argument first. Two facts, require comment. First, this argument assumes that the feeling of pleasure

and pain is the *only* feeling incapable of objective employment. That pleasure and pain are so incapable is an old assumption—witness Locke's assimilation of the sweetness and whiteness of manna to the sickness and pain
it produces in order to make the former appear as subjective as the latter,[25]
and Berkeley's generalization of Locke's argument to deny the reality of
material substance altogether.[26] But that pleasure and pain are in fact of
purely subjective significance, and the only sensations so purely subjective,
could use proof. Second, insofar as Kant's argument turns only on the subjectivity of sensation, it treats of a single feeling, and does not discriminate
between pleasure and pain. It may seem quite natural that pleasure and
pain should be connected with the subjective state of our cognitive faculties, but Kant's indirect argument does not in fact show why only pleasure
—and not merely pleasure *or* pain—should express a harmonious state of
these faculties.

The published Introduction offers another indirect argument, associating the subjectivity of the feeling of pleasure with the subjectivity of finality
rather than with that of the mental state of judgment. As we have seen,
Kant opens Section VII of this text with the claim that what is purely subjective in a representation of an object is its "aesthetic quality" and thus,
presumably, the subject matter of aesthetic judgment.[27] He then asserts
that it is the feeling of pleasure or displeasure which is this "subjective side
of a representation," and thus the aesthetic quality. Then, Kant makes an
unfortunate attempt to employ the confused concept of finality, which he
has deployed in his general theory of reflective judgment. He asserts that
"the finality of a thing, so far as represented in our perception of it, is in
no way a quality of the object itself." (In fact, he thinks, this is so even
when finality "may be inferred from a cognition of things," apparently
because even in this case it is not a quality of the kind "that can be perceived"; but only his present view that finality is subjective when it is independent of or precedes (*vorhergeht*) any actual knowledge of an object is at
issue here.) And then he infers that "the finality, therefore, which precedes
the cognition of an object, which even, without any will to use the representation of the object for cognition, is yet immediately connected to it, is
the subjective aspect of it [the representation], which cannot become a
constituent of knowledge." But this makes the feeling of pleasure and displeasure and the property of finality both subjective sides of representation, and Kant thus connects the two. The feeling of pleasure or displeasure becomes the representation of that finality of an object which precedes
any cognition of it: "Hence the object is called final, only because its repre-

sentation is immediately connected with the feeling of pleasure; and this representation itself is an aesthetic representation of the finality."[28]

This argument is intended to link the feeling of pleasure directly to the peculiarly nonobjective property of finality, our understanding of which is presupposed, and to make finality the "aesthetic quality" of objects. As it stands, however, it is unsatisfactory. We have seen that in the case of reflective judgment an ascription of finality means only that an object fulfills some subjective requirement, but the present argument's assertion that objects may be called final in virtue of producing pleasure apart from cognition does not provide an independent characterization of the goal which a finality preceding knowledge can fulfill, or an explanation of why a feeling of pleasure should be the sensory representation of such finality. That is, instead of explaining either finality by pleasure or pleasure by finality, Kant has merely linked these two phenomena by their common status of subjectivity. But then a question like that raised about the argument of the first Introduction remains open: if it is merely the fact of subjectivity which associates feeling with finality, why should it be just pleasure and not pleasure *or* pain which represents finality? The connection of pleasure to purposiveness may be even more intuitive than is its connection to the functioning of our cognitive capacities—it might even seem to contradict the laws of nature to suppose that the fulfillment of any purpose could produce anything other than pleasure[29]—but Kant's argument is still indirect, and falls short of an actual explanation of the link between the sensation of pleasure and the harmony of the faculties.

Perhaps, however, the paragraph I have been considering is merely meant to introduce the claim that our pleasure in the beautiful is linked to an aesthetic quality of finality, rather than to argue for it; Kant does, after all, conclude the paragraph by stating that "the only question is whether such a representation of finality exists at all."[30] This suggests that a deeper consideration of what the subjective sensation of pleasure represents is required, and from this further examination a reason *why* pleasure should express the harmony of the faculties could emerge. And, in fact, the present connection of pleasure and finality, though itself indirect and unpersuasive, does lead to the heart of Kant's theory.

That his argument may depend upon an actual explanation of the production of pleasure by a certain kind of mental activity, rather than on a mere association of pleasure with some other phenomenon because of the common epistemological status of subjectivity, is intimated by Kant's next paragraph:

If pleasure is connected with the mere apprehension (*apprehensio*) of the form of an object of intuition, apart from any relation to a concept for a determinate cognition, then the representation is not thereby related to the object, but merely to the subject; and the pleasure can express nothing but the conformity of the object to the cognitive faculties which are in play in the reflective judgment, so far as they are in play, and hence [it expresses] a merely subjective formal finality of the object. For this apprehension of forms in the imagination can never occur unless the reflective judgment, even if unintentionally [*auch unabsichtlich*], at least compares them with its faculty of relating intuitions to concepts. If now in this comparison the imagination (as the faculty of intuitions *a priori*) is through a given representation unintentionally [*unabsichtlich*] set into harmony with the understanding (as the faculty of concepts), and a feeling of pleasure is thereby aroused [*erweckt*], then the object must be regarded as final for the faculty of reflective judgment.[31]

We now see how the reflective judgment's capacity to "compare and combine" a given representation with the subject's own cognitive capabilities rather than with other representations can be the basis of a theory of aesthetic response. For Kant is maintaining that the faculty of reflective judgment can inaugurate a comparison of apprehended form with our general ability to connect intuitions and concepts — a comparison in some sense "unintentional" — and so produce a harmony between imagination and understanding which causes a feeling of pleasure, and the existence of which that pleasure expresses. Such pleasure is, of course, subjective; but now, instead of merely linking it to the finality of an object by virtue of the latter's similar subjectivity, Kant suggests that the object's "subjective formal finality" *consists in* its conformity to our cognitive faculties, "so far as they are in play," or *in its disposition to produce* this state of play without judgment having to contemplate the object's relation to a concept for the purpose of acquiring knowledge. That is, an object is subjectively or formally purposive *because* by producing free play between the imagination and the understanding it produces pleasure; the free play of the cognitive faculties must somehow be the requirement of the reflective judgment, conformity to which *constitutes* an object's finality.

This argument, unlike the earlier ones, does not turn on the mere fact of subjectivity, and does specifically relate pleasure rather than just pleasure *or* pain to the exercise of a form of reflective judgment. It raises many questions. It is still not clear just what the play or harmony of imagination and understanding is, or why this state should be an end, so that an object which produces it is final. Nor is it clear what the meaning of Kant's statement that reflective judgment acts unintentionally in bringing about the harmony of the faculties is. Answers to these questions, however, will emerge from a consideration of an even deeper question: why should the harmony of the faculties arouse, or cause, a feeling of pleasure?

There can be no answer to this question without a connection of the explanation of aesthetic response to a general theory of pleasure, and the section of the published Introduction I have been considering does not contain such a theory. The corresponding Section VIII of the first Introduction does contain what Kant describes as a "definition" (*Erklärung*) of this feeling, a definition which Kant claims to be general because it ignores *"the distinction of whether it accompanies sense perception, or reflection, or the determination of the will."* This defines pleasure as "a *state* of the mind in which a representation is in harmony with itself, as the ground, either simply for preserving itself (for the condition of mutual assistance among faculties of the mind in a representation does preserve itself), or for bringing forth its object."³²* But this definition, although it explains the *effects* of the feeling of pleasure — the determination of the mind either to remain in a state which does bring it pleasure or to act toward the production of an object which will allow it to so remain — does not illuminate what is important to us, namely, the conditions under which this feeling is *first produced*. There is, however, one place in his mature texts on aesthetics where Kant does imply a general theory of the production of pleasure. This is Section VI of the published version of the Introduction, which connects the phenomenon of pleasure to the general theory of systematicity. It is in light of this section, then, that we must interpret Kant's theory of the pleasure of aesthetic response and its production by the harmony of the faculties.

Pleasure and the Goal of Cognition

Essentially, Kant finally connects pleasure to the faculty of reflective judgment by the theory that all pleasure results from the fulfillment of some aim of the subject. As he puts it, "the attainment of every aim [*Absicht*] is coupled with a feeling of pleasure."³³ The same thesis is reiterated with what will turn out to be a key amplification in the "General Remark" which concludes the Analytic of the Beautiful: here Kant says that "the accomplishment of any, even problematical, objective [*Absicht*]" — including the specific case of an "end [*Zweck*] in respect of knowledge" — "is invariably connected with delight."[34]* Now, these remarks state that the fulfillment of an objective always produces pleasure, and not that pleasure is produced only by the fulfillment of some aim; so, it might be objected, Kant is not in fact committed to the view that all pleasure is linked to the satisfaction of an aim. Given Kant's repeated use of the term "unintentional" (*unabsichtlich*) to characterize the activity of reflective judgment, and his frequent insistence that aesthetic pleasure is not connected to desire,[35] it might further be objected that the explanation of pleasure as due to the satisfaction of an aim cannot possibly be involved in the case of aesthetic response.[36] But the remarks I have quoted are Kant's only general statements on the conditions under which pleasure occurs; and we shall see that these statements do in fact illuminate Kant's connection of pleasure to the harmony of the faculties without conflicting with any key characterization of aesthetic judgment.

To see this, however, we must differentiate between a broad notion of objectives and the ordinary concept of desires, and allow Kant the view that the faculty of desire is not involved in every one of our objectives. For Kant's theory of pleasure depends on the view that each of the faculties of mind has the objective of producing the state which it is capable of producing, and that the satisfaction of this objective — under certain conditions, at least — produces pleasure. Kant states the fundamental presupposition of the *Critique of Judgment's* explanation of aesthetic response when he writes, in the *Critique of Practical Reason,* that "to every faculty of mind an interest can be ascribed, i.e., a principle which contains the condition under which alone its exercise is advanced."[37] His terminology changes between the two *Critique*s, for, to mark the distinction between pleasure produced by reflective judgment and that connected with desire, Kant gives up the use of the term "interest" in connection with the former.[38] But the idea that each faculty has its own objective is crucial to the third *Critique*. Thus the attainment of knowledge is the fulfillment of the objective of the faculty of cognition and, at least ideally, the occasion of a pleasure which does not fulfill an objective set by desire. Correspondingly, the satisfaction of an objective set by the faculty of desire itself may be regarded as the cause of pleasure that does not involve the objectives of the faculty of cognition. And, finally, the successful employment of the faculty of reflective judgment must also be seen as the occasion of a pleasure which is independent of the practical aims of the faculty of desire.

Kant explicitly applies his general theory of pleasure to reflective judgment only in the case of the judgment of the systematicity of nature, and not in the case of the aesthetic judgment of reflection on individual forms in nature; thus it might be natural to approach the latter case by a study of Kant's argument in the former. Before doing so, however, I will raise a difficult question. What is the status of Kant's thesis that pleasure is always produced by the satisfaction of an objective? Kant introduces the claim without argument, and immediately proceeds to use it for a sketch of an argument for the validity of intersubjective claims about pleasure ("now where such attainment," he says, "has for its condition a representation *a priori*—as here a principle for the reflective judgment in general—the feeling of pleasure also is determined by a ground which is *a priori* and valid for all men.")[39] Kant thus employs his statement as a lawlike and fundamental premise. But why is it entitled to such status?

Kant says nothing on this point. It is clear that the thesis cannot be analytic, for it does not assert merely that whatever state persons are in on the attainment of their objectives shall be called "pleasure." Rather, it connects the attainment of objectives with a feeling of pleasure, a feeling which Kant's entire argument makes clear is a single pyschological state, in some respects at least phenomenologically identical in all of its occurrences.[40] Thus this thesis is a matter of fact, not of definition; it must be synthetic rather than analytic. But is it synthetic *a priori* or synthetic *a posteriori?* Kant's use of his thesis to found *a priori* claims and his remark in the first Introduction that a definition of the feeling of pleasure "must be transcendental"[41] (a remark followed by the "definition," earlier quoted, concerning the consequences rather than causes of pleasure) might suggest that his theory of pleasure is meant to be synthetic *a priori*. But Kant offers no sketch of a transcendental deduction of his proposition, and it is not clear how adoption of the principle that the attainment of every objective produces pleasure could be a condition of the possibility of human knowledge.[42*] The possibility remains, then, that this basic thesis of Kant's theory of pleasure might be synthetic *a posteriori:* not *a priori* at all, but a law, even a fundamental law, of human psychology—a law perhaps never disconfirmed, but at least conceivably disconfirmable. That a law which links a specific feeling to a specific mental state should be empirical may well be the most natural conclusion.

It is obvious that such an interpretation would not be congenial to Kant's purposes, for it would introduce an empirical law into the foundation of his explanation of aesthetic response, and this could later threaten his argument for an *a priori* principle of taste. Instead of considering this problem now, however, I will submerge it in my later consideration of

Kant's transcendental deduction of aesthetic judgment, where I will argue that Kant's attempt to defend an *a priori* principle for aesthetic judgment does have an ultimate limit in empirical psychology. For the moment, I will examine only Kant's application of his general thesis to the reflective judgment of nature. This cannot resolve the question of whether the thesis is *a priori* or not, but does cast light on the meaning of the harmony of the faculties in Kant's theory of aesthetic judgment.

Kant explains our pleasure in the systematicity of nature as follows. We do not find that the subsumability of perceptions under the general laws of nature stated by the categories produces any "effect on the feeling of pleasure." This is so because in the case of such subsumption understanding necessarily proceeds — and succeeds — according to rules set by its own nature. But the discovery that nature displays the higher-order organization demanded by our ideal that its laws be systematic does produce a feeling of pleasure, because it is the satisfaction of an objective which the nature of the understanding itself cannot guarantee will be fulfilled. Thus Kant says, "that two or more empirical heterogeneous laws of nature are allied under one principle that embraces them both, is the ground of a very appreciable pleasure, often even of admiration."[43] Kant concedes that we may not detect any noticeable pleasure in such comprehensibility of the division of nature into species and genera as is necessary to make empirical concepts possible, but asserts that it must have been there in its time, and that when something makes us attentive to the finality of nature for our understanding, we do notice pleasure. In particular, when the conformity of nature to the requirements of judgment is seen by us as contingent, or not necessitated by the mere nature of our own cognitive faculties, it produces a conscious pleasure. Thus, given our endeavor to bring the heterogeneous laws of nature together under other, higher empirical laws, the contingent fact of success in this endeavor produces pleasure: "on meeting with success, pleasure may be felt in this accord [of the laws] with our cognitive faculty, which is regarded by us as purely contingent."[44] Success in reflective judgment's objective of systematizing the understanding's knowledge of nature produces a feeling of pleasure.

There are a number of problems with this brief argument. First, it suffers from several obscurities. Thus it is not in fact clear whether the lack of pleasure in the coincidence of nature with the categories is really due to the fact that the fulfillment of this objective is always guaranteed, or whether Kant supposes that this coincidence is not a cognitive objective at all; the opening sentence of the third paragraph of Section VI might suggest the latter, although everything else in this section points to the former. It is also not entirely clear whether a guarantee of success really precludes the occurrence of pleasure, or only prevents us from noticing it; again, Kant's opening claim implies the former, but his later statements the latter. And it is not clear whether the thesis that the attainment of an objective produces a feeling of pleasure is being treated as an *a priori* law, in which case it can be asserted that even in ordinary cognition pleasure must have occurred, whether it was noticed or not, or as an empirical law, describing a psychological process subject to alteration by our expectations or past experience.

These obscurities do not mask the central contention of the theory: that when pleasure is felt in the systematicity of nature, it is felt because the perception of systematicity represents the fulfillment of a general cognitive objective in a case in which such success is not guaranteed and cannot be predicted on the basis of the necessary conformity of nature to the mere conditions of the possibility of our experience itself. Whether or not we always notice pleasure in the fulfillment of our objectives, Kant may be taken to say, we certainly do notice it where that success is contingent; psychologically speaking, success which cannot be predicted, and is thus a surprise, produces a noticeable feeling of pleasure. Furthermore, because the finality of nature amounts to nothing but its conformity to the needs or objectives of our cognitive faculties — reflective judgment's demand for systematicity included — we may also say that the discovery of finality in nature is the occasion for a feeling of pleasure.

The clarity of Kant's central contention, however, does lead to a deeper problem with the present argument: namely, the problem of its very compatibility with Kant's conception of the *principle* of reflective judgment. The present argument connects pleasure to the perception of systematicity in virtue of the contingency of such perception, or the fact that systematicity is not guaranteed by the laws of the understanding; but the principle of reflective judgment, that nature itself is systematic, was apparently designed precisely to guarantee that such a perception would occur, or would at least not seem to be contingent. Thus the principle of reflective judgment seems to be incompatible with the only way in which that faculty can be linked to the feeling of pleasure.

But this difficulty need not deter us from using this general theory of pleasure to interpret Kant's explanation of aesthetic response. I have already suggested that an analysis of what *a priori* claim a judgment of taste actually makes will show that its *a priori* principle must be quite distinct from the *a priori* postulation of nature's systematicity. The fact that the latter principle turns out to be incompatible with Kant's fundamental explanation of pleasure as a product of judgment is just one more reason for concluding that this principle is irrelevant to the case of judgments of taste. What Kant's theory of taste draws from the general theory of reflective judgment is in fact only the latter's theory of pleasure, and not its model of an *a priori* principle.

Let us now see how this general theory of pleasure bears on the case of aesthetic response. The theory just considered is, in fact, radically different from the attempts to link pleasure and judgment previously considered. It does not link the two by the analogical positions of judgment and the feeling of pleasure in Kant's two tables of faculties. Nor does it associate feeling with either the subjective conditions of knowledge or the subjective finality of objects on the basis of the mere fact of shared subjectivity, a connection which could not actually explain why pleasure rather than pain should be so associated. This argument offers a positive explanation of why the discovery of systematicity should produce a feeling of pleasure: it does so just because this discovery falls into a larger class of events, the attainment of objectives, which are invariably coupled with pleasure—at least when contingent. And it is through this explanation that the argument suggests why pleasure should be connected with the occurrence of the harmony of the faculties, or with reflective judgment's comparison of the form of an object with our own cognitive capacities. If we are to regard this connection as explained by the general theory of pleasure Kant offers, then we must infer that the harmony of the faculties produces pleasure because it too represents a state in which a general cognitive objective, analogous to our requirement of systematicity, is fulfilled without the guarantee ordinarily provided by the subsumability of intuitions under the categories. And this, finally, not only explains why the harmony of imagination and understanding produces pleasure; it also provides the basis for saying what this state is.

The mental state of the harmony of the faculties produces a feeling of pleasure because it represents success in the attainment of a general cognitive objective—an "end in respect of knowledge"[45]—in conditions where such success is contingent. But what is the cognitive objective which is fulfilled in this state? Recalling the first Introduction's phrase "the subjective and merely sensible condition of the objective employment of the faculty of judgment" may now help us answer this question, although previously Kant's equation of this condition with the harmony of the faculties could only pose our problem.⁴⁶ For what this passage suggests is that we may look at knowledge from two points of view, the objective and the subjective. Suppose that we take the acquisition and possession of knowledge as our most general cognitive aim. This supposition is unexceptionable, for it does nothing but describe knowledge as a state of affairs which can serve as a goal for our activity. However, the goal of knowledge may actually be characterized in two ways, corresponding to our two points of view on knowledge itself. Our aim in regard to knowledge might be strictly objective, in which case our goal would be the discovery or acquisition of true beliefs or objectively valid judgments. But we may also describe the goal of knowledge from the subjective point of view, as simply consisting in the synthesis or unification of our manifolds of intuition, however achieved. To be sure, the doctrine of Kant's first *Critique* seems to be that there can be no synthesis of manifolds without objectively valid judgments. Leaving that aside for the moment, however, we can say that from a psychological point of view the synthesis or unification of a manifold is what produces an objectively valid judgment. As the mental event which has knowledge as its outcome, this synthesis may be thought of as the subjective condition of cognition, and as itself a goal in cognition. Supposing, then, that the harmony of the faculties is a state in which the subjective condition of knowledge exists without the use of a concept, and thus without any objective judgment actually being made, we can think of this state as one in which a manifold of intuition, presented by the imagination, is unified or, at least, appears to be unified, without the use of a concept. Since it is the use of a concept which ordinarily guarantees the unification of a manifold, unification without a concept could obviously be regarded as the contingent and unexpected fulfillment of our aim in knowledge, described from the subjective point of view. It would thus be the occasion of a "noticeable pleasure."

This conclusion may be confirmed by reconsidering Kant's statement that the harmony of the faculties is the "sensible" as well as the "subjective" condition of knowledge. As I remarked earlier, the third *Critique* characterizes the imagination as the faculty of intuitions, thereby assigning it the roles of both sensibility and imagination in the first *Critique*.⁴⁷* The "sensible condition" of knowledge might thus be taken to be the contributions of both sensibility and imagination, as contrasted with understanding, to the production of cognition. If we turn to the *Critique of Pure Reason*'s model of the actual production of knowledge, namely, the first edition's theory of threefold synthesis, we will see that this includes all the aspects of synthesis except the actual application of a concept of the understanding to the manifold of intuitions. Specifically, the "sensible condition" of knowledge, or of the objective employment of judgment, must include the "synthesis of apprehension in intuition"[48] and the "synthesis of reproduction in imagination."[49] The harmony of the faculties is a state in which a manifold of some duration, or one in which "the mind distinguishes the time in the sequence of one impression upon another," is first "run through, and held together."[50] It is also a state in which "the various manifold representations that are involved" not only "must be apprehended by me in thought one after another," but also are "set in a relation whereby . . . one of these representations can . . . bring about a transition of the mind to the other," or a state in which I can reproduce representations "while advancing to those that follow."[51] Because Kant maintains that the synthesis of apprehension is "inseparably bound up with the synthesis of reproduction," and that the two together constitute the "transcendental ground of the possibility of all modes of knowledge whatsoever," prior to the "synthesis of recognition in a concept" — the actual application of a concept to the apprehended manifold — we may think of the "sensible condition" of knowledge as being constituted by these two syntheses. The harmony of the faculties is then a state in which, somehow, a manifold of intuition is run through and held together as a unity by the imagination without the use of a concept. This state represents the attainment of the objective of knowledge, subjectively described as the unification of a manifold of intuition, apart from its ordinary guarantee, and thus, again, occasions pleasure. Finally, it may be noted, while this account of the harmony of the faculties does not assign an active role to the understanding, it does describe a state in which the imagination is in harmony with the understanding, in the sense of accomplishing everything that is ordinarily requisite for the successful relation of the understanding to a manifold of intuition.

The "subjective condition" of knowledge represented by the harmony of imagination is not just that a given manifold be *unifiable*. This is a necessary condition of any form of consciousness at all, aesthetic or cognitive, and represents not a subjective contribution to knowledge but a condition on the given manifold which must be met for any mental activity at all to be possible. Rather, the "subjective condition" of knowledge obtains when a given manifold is in some sense actually perceived as unified. How this can occur without the use of a concept, or how there can be a synthesis of reproduction in imagination in which one representation brings about a transition of the mind to another but *not* "in accordance with a fixed rule,"[52]* is obviously a question that must eventually be answered. Before considering this substantive problem, however, I will tackle the interpretative problem of reconciling the present account of the harmony of the faculties with Kant's actual characterizations of this state—for my interpretation, although suggested by Kant's general theory of pleasure, is far from self-evident.

Although it is the first Introduction's reference to the "subjective and merely sensible condition" of judgment which gives us our clue to the application of Kant's general theory of pleasure to the case of the harmony of the faculties, its descriptions of this concept are less than lucid. Several of them employ the metaphor of a relationship of "mutual assistance" between the two faculties of imagination and understanding. Thus Section VII of this Introduction states that "in simple reflection on perception"— the exercise of the reflective judgment that leads to the harmony of the faculties and the arousal of the feeling of pleasure—"it is not a matter of reflecting on a determinate concept but [of reflecting] in general only on a rule of perception in behalf of the understanding as a faculty of concepts."[53] But what it is for a perception to be presented by the imagination "in behalf of" (*zum Behuf*) the understanding is far from clear, and at first we may notice only Kant's repetition of the metaphor of assistance. Thus the next paragraph of Section VII states that if "the form of a given object is so produced in empirical intuition that the *apprehension* of its manifold in the imagination agrees with the *presentation* of a concept of the understanding (regardless of which concept), then in simple reflection understanding and imagination mutually harmonize for the furtherance of their business [*zur Beförderung ihres Geschäfts*]."[54] In Section VIII, Kant states that when we consider the subjective aspect of the relationship of the two faculties involved in cognition, what we actually consider "is how one helps or hinders the other in a given representation and thereby affects one's mental state."[55] Finally, a page later, Kant says that the feeling of pleasure which is the "ground of determination" for an aesthetic judgment of reflection is "effected [*bewirkt*] in the subject" by the "harmonious play of judgment's two faculties of cognition, imagination and understanding," and this state is defined as that in which "in a given representation the former's power of apprehension and the latter's power of presentation are mutually assisting each other [*einander wechselseitig beförderlich sind*]."[56]

Even though they are metaphorical, these remarks are not entirely unilluminating. For they describe imagination and understanding as working together for a common "business"—or purpose—and what can this be but the preparation of a manifold for cognition? If the explanation of its plea-surableness precludes actual cognition in the case of aesthetic response, or if no determinate concept is actually applied to the manifold, then this "mutual assistance" can only consist in the imagination's performance of the syntheses of apprehension and reproduction, or in its unification of a manifold without a concept. This is a task ordinarily performed "on behalf of" the understanding, and thus the imagination in aesthetic response is in harmony with the usual requirements of the understanding, even though the latter does not apply any determinate concept in the state of free play. And, though this is a separate matter, these passages also make the impor-tant point that the imagination accomplishes its synthesis of apprehension on the manifold *provided* "in a given representation" or *by* "the form of a given object . . . in empirical intuition." That is, the mind is ordinarily *dis-posed* to the harmony of the faculties *by* an object, which we may provi-sionally suppose is beautiful in virtue of this disposition. This would ex-plain why Kant does attribute finality to the object of aesthetic response, although that finality is nothing more than its disposition to produce the harmony of the faculties.

This interpretation is also compatible with remarks from the first Intro-duction which do not employ the metaphor of assistance. In a sentence quoted in the last chapter, Kant said that "in a merely reflective judgment, imagination and understanding are regarded in the relationship in which they stand to each other in the judgment in general, contrasted with the actual relationship between them in a given perception."[57] This suggests that the harmony of the faculties consists in the unification of a manifold without the use of a determinate concept, which is what would be involved in ordinary cases of perception. So does the claim quoted above that imagi-nation's apprehension of a manifold agrees with the understanding's "pre-sentation of a concept . . . (regardless of which concept)." This somewhat inept wording might suggest the idea of a concept which is no concept in particular, much like the idea of a triangle that is "neither oblique, nor rectangle, equilateral, equicrural, nor scalenon" to which Berkeley so vig-orously objected.[58] But it is surely more charitably interpreted as describ-ing a state in which the ordinary condition for the application of a concept — the imagination's unification of a manifold — obtains without the appli-cation of any concept at all. This is even more clearly suggested by Kant's statement that "an aesthetic judgment can thus be defined as that sort of judgment whose predicate can never be cognitive (a concept of an object) (although it may contain the subjective conditions for cognition in general)."⁵⁹ Reflective judgment, it turns out, leads to aesthetic response not by finding a *possible concept* for a given particular, but by discovering that a given object fulfills the *general condition for the possibility of the application of concepts* without having any concept at all applied to it.⁶⁰*

Many of the published *Critique of Judgment*'s characterizations of the harmony of imagination and understanding share the metaphorical tone of the first Introduction's remarks, and depend upon the language of faculties. We have already seen Kant's major description of the play of the faculties in Section VII of the Introduction, where he explained the pleasure connected with the apprehension of the mere form of an object as expressing "nothing but the conformity of the object to the cognitive faculties which are in play in the reflective judgment," and as resulting from the reflective judgment's "unintentional" comparison of forms "with its faculty of relating intuitions to concepts."⁶¹ Other key passages in the text are similar. Thus looking ahead to §9 of the Analytic of the Beautiful—the crucial but problematic section in which Kant links his explanatory model of aesthetic response with his analysis of aesthetic judgment—we see that Kant describes the feeling of pleasure which is the determining ground of the judgment of taste as the "mental state which presents itself in the mutual relation of the powers of representation so far as they refer a given representation *to cognition in general.*" This relationship is one of "mutual accord" between imagination and understanding, "as is requisite for *cognition in general,*" and is also called a relation of "free play," "because no definite concept restricts" these two faculties "to a particular rule of cognition."⁶² More obscurely, the concluding paragraph of §9 calls the sensation produced by the harmony of the faculties one of the "quickening [*Belebung*] of both faculties (imagination and understanding) to an indefinite, but yet, by means of the occasion of the given representation, harmonious activity, which belongs to cognition in general."⁶³ But even from all this figurative language, the point emerges that the harmony of the faculties is a state in which the ordinary general condition of knowledge obtains without the use of any concept. This can only be a state in which the imagination conforms to the understanding's demand for the unification of our manifolds of intuition, without the understanding performing its customary role of applying a concept to a manifold as the rule for its unification.

Kant's explanation of the harmony of imagination and understanding in §35, which recapitulates his theory of aesthetic response in preparation for his deduction of aesthetic judgment, is in some ways even more elusive than the versions just considered. This section begins by maintaining that since "the judgment of taste is not determinable by means of concepts . . . it can only have its ground in the subjective formal condition of a judgment in general," but defines this condition obscurely as "the judging faculty itself." And while Kant does say that this condition requires the "harmonious accordance" of "the imagination (for the intuition and the combination [*Zusammensetzung*] of the manifold of intuition) and the understanding (for the concept of the representation of the unity of this combination)," he does not completely clarify his point by saying that, in the case where no concept of an object is employed, this condition consists "only in the subsumption of the imagination itself . . . under the condition that the understanding in general pass from intuition to concepts." Nor does he clarify the point by adding that "taste as a subjective faculty of judgment contains a principle of subsumption, not of intuitions under *concepts,* but rather of the *faculty* of intuitions (that is, the imagination) under the *faculty* of concepts (that is, the understanding), insofar as the former *in its freedom* accords with the latter in its *lawfulness* [*Gesetzmässigkeit*]."[64] What is involved in the "subsumption" of one faculty under another is unclear, since Kant elsewhere uses the term to characterize only relations among representations: intuitions are subsumed under concepts, or less general concepts are subsumed under more general concepts.[65] Still, Kant does suggest that, ordinarily, the accord between faculties consists of imagination's combination of a manifold and the understanding's representation of this combination by a concept. This seems to imply that the present, peculiar "subsumption" of faculties, differing from their ordinary relationship by the absence of a concept, must consist in the "combination" of a manifold by the imagination, which thus harmonizes with the understanding's requirement of unity by its own action. In this case, Kant intimates, the unity of the manifold is represented by a feeling rather than a concept.

These conclusions are also suggested by two other features of the present passage. First, there is Kant's remark that the harmony of the faculties consists in the general condition of the *transition* from intuition to concepts: this condition can only be the completion of the syntheses of the manifold *presupposed* by the synthesis of recognition in a concept. Second, there is Kant's further remark that "the freedom of the imagination" — what is intended by the idea of "free play," that is — consists precisely in the fact that it "schematizes without a concept."[66] In the typical case of cognition, "schematism" is the imagination's provision of a rule for the application of a pure concept of the understanding to the data of intuition; in the present case, since schematism is to occur without a concept, we can only understand it as a "synthesis of the imagination" which "aims at no special intuition" *or concept,* "but only at unity in the determination of sensibility."[67]

All of these passages, then, confirm the interpretation of the harmony of the faculties as a state in which a manifold of intuition is in some sense apprehended as unified without being subsumed under any determinate concept, or in which the imagination meets the understanding's general requirement of "lawfulness" without the use of a concept, and in which the unexpectedness of such an imaginative grasp of unity produces pleasure. Further, these passages suggest at least one meaning for Kant's introductory remark that in the aesthetic case of reflective judgment imagination is "unintentionally [*unabsichtich*] brought into accord with understanding."[68] This need not mean that the exercise of reflective judgment which produces aesthetic response *has* no general objective, but only that this objective is attained without the direction ordinarily furnished by a concept as a rule. At this point, then, it would be natural to ask how the idea of imagination synthesizing a manifold without a concept can conceivably be reconciled with the first *Critique*'s theory of knowledge. Before I turn to that topic, however, I will consider two more passages which shed light on the nature of the harmony of the faculties. In view of both the importance and the difficulty of getting beyond metaphor in the interpretation of Kant's central explanatory concept, no clue can be disregarded.

The first of these further passages is the "General Remark" which is appended to the conclusion of the Analytic of the Beautiful.[69] Kant begins this remark by stating that his analysis leads to the concept of taste as a "faculty for estimating an object in relation to the *free lawfulness* of the imagination."[70] This state of the imagination Kant explains in the following way. If the imagination is free, then it cannot be purely reproductive, entirely subject to laws of association, but must be in some sense productive. Nevertheless, it is still bound to the apprehension of a given object of sense; so for the imagination to be free, two other conditions are required. First, the object must be thought of as supplying to the imagination "just such a form . . . as the imagination, if it were left free, would itself project in accord with the understanding's *lawfulness* in general"; and second, the understanding must not actually supply any law — or concept — for the arrangement of the manifold.[71] Thus the state of aesthetic response must be a state of "lawfulness without a law," or a "subjective harmony of the imagination without an objective one," one in which "the representation would be related to a determinate concept of an object."[72] This "subjective harmony" can only be a sense of the unity of a manifold which is not determined by any concept of a rule determining the form of an object, particularly any concept referring to a possible purpose.

Kant illustrates this thesis with a discussion of "geometrically regular figures." These are often thought of as beautiful, but, Kant says, they are much too easily looked at "as mere presentation of a determinate concept by which a figure has its rule," and too easily related to definite purposes. What is required, instead, is an object which produces a manifold unifiable by the imagination, but does not provoke immediate reference to a determinate concept. If the latter condition is met, then the following analysis applies: "The regularity that conduces to the concept of an object is, in fact, the indispensable condition (*conditio sine qua non*) of grasping the object as a single representation and determining the manifold in the form of such. This determination is an end [*Zweck*] in respect of knowledge; and in this connection it is invariably coupled with delight (such as attends the effecting of any, even problematic, purpose [*Absicht*])."[73] In short, for aesthetic response to occur, the ordinary condition for cognition must be met without the imagination feeling constrained by consciousness of a rule—or, as it turns out, by a sense of repetition that is just as constraining as a rule. This last point emerges in Kant's discussion of an explorer tiring of the regularity of a garden in comparison with the freedom of nature, and may introduce a certain empirical element into Kant's characterization of the freedom of the imagination.[74]

.The second passage I want to consider comes from a section toward the end of the *Critique of Judgment,* one of a number in which Kant is dealing not with taste in general but with our taste for art in particular. Some of these sections constitute Kant's discussion of "aesthetic ideas," which can illuminate the interpretation of his model of aesthetic response, but which also introduces complexities that cannot be considered here.[75*] Kant's discussion of our enjoyment of music, however, bears directly on the present issue, and provides one of his few illustrations of his key concept. Kant considers the role of concepts in our response to music in the specific form of mathematical rules which might describe the relationships between the tones or individual representations constituting the manifold in an actual experience of music. Consciousness of such rules is not required for or involved in music's production of pleasure, he declares: "mathematics, certainly, does not play the least part in the charm and movement of the mind produced by music. Rather, it is only the indispensable condition (*conditio sine qua non*) of that proportion of the combining as well as changing impressions which makes it possible to grasp them all in one and prevents them from destroying one another, and to let them, rather, harmonize toward a continuous movement and quickening of the mind by affections that are consonant with it and thus [lead] to a comfortable self-enjoyment."[76] If we assume that the enjoyment of music, as of any other object of taste, depends on the occurrence of the harmony of the faculties, then what we have here is a lucid description of a pleasure produced by a unification of a manifold achieved without any consciousness of conceptually formulated rules. Though an explanation *of the object's disposition* to produce that harmony might involve reference to such rules—perhaps this is what Kant's "indispensable condition" means—the explanation *of the enjoyment* of the harmony turns on just the fact that the general cognitive objective of grasping a manifold and holding it together in the mind has been achieved without consciousness of constraint from any concept.

I have now presented sufficient evidence for the interpretation of the harmony of the faculties as a state in which the subjective condition of cognition, the unification of the manifold of intuition, occurs without the use of a concept, and for the explanation of aesthetic response as the feeling of pleasure produced by this state of harmony between the activity of the imagination and the goal of the understanding. A number of serious questions about both the possibility of such a mental state and the precise nature of its relation to the feeling of pleasure must be raised and answered before we can consider how this notion of the harmony of the faculties is incorporated into Kant's larger theory of taste. Before I turn to these issues, however, I would like to make one further point about the nature of the harmony of the faculties.

As I have interpreted it, the harmony between imagination and understanding is the attainment or fulfillment of an objective. As so described, it may be natural to think of this state as a kind of event—a state the preparation for which may extend through some amount of time, but the occurrence of which occupies only a brief and specific moment of time. Kant's general claim that this state produces and, as we shall soon see, is only manifest in a feeling of pleasure tends to confirm this impression, insofar as such a feeling itself seems to be a temporally discrete and confined event. And both Kant's introduction of the general model of reflective judgment's accomplishment of a cognitive objective and his initial interpretation of aesthetic response in terms of this model also suggest this view. Kant's first example of such an accomplishment is that of "the discovery . . . that two or more empirical heterogeneous laws of nature are allied under one principle that embraces them both," serving as "the ground of a very appreciable pleasure";[77] and a discovery would seem to be an event which, no matter how long it is in preparation, is actually made in a single moment. The same conclusion seems to be implied by Kant's application of the general theory of pleasure to the case of aesthetic response, when he holds that if, in reflective judgment's comparison of forms in the imagination with its general capacity for relating intuitions to concepts, "imagination . . . is unintentionally brought into accord with understanding," then "a feeling of pleasure is thereby aroused"[78] — the use of the preterite tense suggests that both the occurrence of the harmony and the arousal of pleasure are events of a given moment.

However, though it may be natural to think that in any case of the accomplishment of a goal, there is a specific moment at which the accomplishment takes place, after which it is true to say that the goal *has been* accomplished, it would seem peculiar to think of aesthetic response — our enjoyment of a painting or, even more to the point, of a musical or dramatic performance — of being anything like instantaneous. And not only does it seem natural to think of aesthetic response as temporally extended in a way that an event of accomplishment or moment of fulfillment is not, but it also seems that Kant sometimes describes the harmony of the faculties as a temporally extended state. In calling the harmony of the faculties a "play" of the mental powers "as quickened by their mutual accord," or in characterizing "the sensation the communicability of which is postulated by the judgment of taste" as the "quickening of both faculties (imagination and understanding) to an indefinite but . . . harmonious activity,"[79] Kant definitely suggests that both the feeling of aesthetic response and its ground, the fulfillment of the general objective of cognition without the employment of a concept, are extended through time — are like an activity rather than an act or event. Such a conclusion is even more obviously suggested by Kant's reference, in the discussion of music recently quoted, to the production of "a continuous movement and quickening of the mind by affections that are consonant with it and thus [lead] to a comfortable self-enjoyment."[80] In such passages, Kant describes what is clearly a unified but also a temporally extended psychological state. Is there any contradiction between such characterizations of the harmony of the faculties and the purely epistemological interpretation of it as the fulfillment of an objective?

I think that there is not, but that, in fact, the interpretation of the harmony of the faculties as the fulfillment of an objective naturally leads to the present characterizations of a form of continuous mental activity, and explains the pleasurability of such extended activity. First, we may note that while the concept of attainment or accomplishment might be taken as that of a kind of event, the concept of fulfillment can be thought of as that of a state of affairs, obtaining throughout a period in which certain conditions are fulfilled. Thus, while there might be a particular moment at which a given manifold of intuition first comes to be unified, it may also be the case that the presentation or reproduction of a manifold occupies a period of time, and that the *state* of its unification can likewise be regarded as occupying that extended period of time. Such an explanation would be natural in the case of an object of aesthetic response like a musical performance, which occupies an extended period of time and our enjoyment of which extends throughout that whole period—in part, at least, because the continuation of the unity through the period is contingent, and will thus produce a continued pleasure. But in fact, because all manifolds of intuition are temporally successive,[81] whether they are presented by objects which, like paintings, themselves exist complete at the first moment of intuition or by objects which, like musical performances, are actually developing while being successively intuited, it may always be appropriate to think of their unification as a temporally extended activity, even when it is also natural to specify a moment at which unification can be said to have been achieved. Just because the pleasure of aesthetic response depends upon an unexpected unification of a manifold, it can obtain as long as the manifold continues to be presented *and* its unity retains its appearance of contingency. (This second condition must be met, of course, because the fact that aesthetic response may permit of temporal extension does not entail that any particular pleasure in beauty permits of indefinite extension. For when the unity of a given manifold comes to be expected, even if it is not traced to a determinate concept, the pleasure of aesthetic response must fade. As in Kant's example, the Sumatran explorer need only pass a day in his charming pepper garden "to discover that if, through [the garden's] regularity, the understanding sets itself in the disposition to order, which it always needs, then the object no longer entertains him, but rather imposes a tedious constraint on the imagination.")[82*]

Second, even when the fulfillment of a goal may be regarded as having been completely accomplished at or in a particular moment, it would still be natural to think of the enjoyment engendered by that accomplishment as occupying a longer period of time. One savors an accomplishment, continues to enjoy it in reflection upon its occurrence, and so on—even if the ground of pleasure is the occurrence of an act or event, the pleasure it produces may be a continuous psychological state more akin to an activity. Thus the epistemological interpretation of the harmony of the faculties as the fulfillment of an objective would lead to its psychological characterization as an extended state of play or quickening. If the manifold presented by an object of taste is itself temporally continuous, then the response to it will be an extended and developing sense of its unity; and even if the manifold itself is fully unified at any given time, the pleasure it engenders may still be temporally extended.

So there is no contradiction in interpreting the harmony of the faculties as an event or accomplishment, like a discovery, and yet also describing it in terms of a temporally extended mental activity. The idea of the fulfillment of the subjective conditions of cognition allows us to think of the harmony of the faculties as a state which may be brought about at a particular moment, but also as one which may obtain through a period of time, and, in either case, as a state which may produce an extended feeling of pleasure. Kant's two ways of describing his basic notion of aesthetic response, as a state of the unification of a manifold and as the play or activity of the imagination and understanding through a period in which the requirement of unity is unexpectedly fulfilled, pose no threat to our interpretation of this concept; instead, they recommend it, for both sorts of description characterize aspects of psychological states which fulfill the general aim of cognition in the absence of a determinate concept, and which are pleasurable for that reason.

At this point, the basic content of the idea of the harmony of the faculties should be clear, though more needs to be said about the precise nature of the consciousness of this state and about the relationship between this consciousness and the feeling of pleasure which this state grounds. Before we can turn to these questions, however, a question of a different sort must finally be answered: that of the very possibility of the existence of such a mental state. Though it may seem intrinsically plausible to suppose that we can have a feeling of unity even when we are not conscious of the subsumption of an object under a concept, it is quite another matter whether the author of the *Critique of Pure Reason* could have reasonably affirmed the existence of such a state, or can reasonably have such an affirmation ascribed to him.

This question must be asked because aesthetic response has been held to involve a kind of synthesis without a concept, while the triumphant conclusion of the first *Critique*'s Transcendental Deduction is just that: "All synthesis . . . even that which renders perception possible, is subject to the categories; and since experience is knowledge by means of connected perceptions, the categories are conditions of the possibility of experience, and are therefore valid *a priori* for all objects of experience."[83] In the face of this thesis, how could Kant even consider the possibility of any apprehension of a manifold without a concept, let alone actually affirm the existence of such a state of mind?

Obvious as this question might seem to his reader, Kant never raises it in the *Critique of Judgment,* and gives no hint at a solution. So the commentator can only speculate on its answer. We may quickly reject one possible reconciliation of the two *Critiques.* The theory of reflective judgment, as I pointed out in Chapter 2, responds to Kant's view that there is a gap between the categories, as the merely necessary conditions of experience, and the actual form of our empirical knowledge. So, just as the reflective judgment on the systematicity of nature is one way of filling the gap, aesthetic judgment on the forms of objects might be another. Why this will not do can be stated in several ways. First, even though reflective judgment adds something to the rules for experience beyond the categories, it seems that the latter must retain a role in all synthesis precisely because they are necessary conditions of experience, even if merely necessary conditions. More subtly, one might argue that the status of the categories as necessary conditions for any synthesis of perceptual manifolds actually entails that all synthesis must employ determinate empirical concepts, and can be applied to intuitions only through specific concepts. No substance merely causes a change in another, one could say; one substance mechanically changes another, or chemically changes it, and so on. If the application of the categories to intuitions is a necessary condition of any synthesis of perception at all, then, in fact, so is the application of empirical concepts, whether or not these must be systematic. The gap filled by reflective judgment in general is one between concepts or laws and systems of concepts or laws, but not one between concepts and the manifolds of intuition themselves.

A deeper solution to the problem of reconciliation is required, and could be provided only on the basis of a full analysis of the argument of the *Critique of Pure Reason.* That cannot be offered here, but I will sketch a possible way of reconciling the two *Critiques.* The first step would be to distinguish between psychological and epistemological elements in Kant's analysis of knowledge: a theory of syntheses as mental processes by which mental states of cognition are *produced,* and a theory of the categories as rules by which the *verification* of claims to cognition may proceed. Then, one could argue that the employment of the categories is a necessary condition for the synthesis of any manifold, as "the manner in which given modes of cognition are brought to the objective unity of apperception,"[84] only where that synthesis is counted as *knowledge* that different "representations given in intuition one and all belong to me,"[85] and not as mere *belief* or *feeling* that they belong together. The employment of the categories, and of the empirical concepts which apply to actual empirical intuitions, would then be not a necessary condition for the occurrence of the psychological *process* of synthesis, but only a condition for the verification of claims to actual knowledge of the members of one's manifold and their position in one's mental history, or in the objective unity of apperception.[86]

Such an interpretation of the Transcendental Deduction is hardly uncontroversial.[87]* But it has considerable power in the present context, for the imagination's unification of a manifold without a concept might be thought of as a state in which the psychological concomitants of knowledge obtain in the absence of an actual claim to knowledge; and this interpretation would drive a wedge between the occurrence of the psychological states ordinarily associated with the unification of manifolds and the absolute subjection of the latter to the categories. Such a wedge is required if the psychological concomitants of knowledge which are involved in the harmony of the faculties — the appearance of memory, the feeling that different representations belong together and constitute a continuous whole, and the other sorts of feelings which Kant's discussion of music suggests actually exemplify the harmony of the faculties — are to occur without the use of concepts. With such an interpretation, the Transcendental Deduction would entail not the impossibility of the harmony of the faculties, but only the absence of any means for verifying claims to knowledge ventured on the basis of such a mental state. The harmony of the faculties could thus be thought of as something like the occurrence of the psychological basis for knowledge without the actual employment of concepts, whether pure or empirical.

Exactly how this view should be developed is far from clear, and it might be suggested that what Kant's account of asethetic response describes is actually a sense of coherence in an object which goes *beyond* the unities imposed by whatever concepts apply to it, rather than one which occurs without the application of any concepts at all. But this proposal too would represent a break with the first *Critique*'s strict association of unity of consciousness with the application of concepts to objects. Thus it does seem clear that however its details are worked out, the interpretation of the harmony of the faculties does require a separation of the psychological and epistemological components of Kant's theory of synthesis to explain the possibility of that harmony as a mental state which affects our capacity for feeling pleasure as if it were the attainment of our general cognitive objective, the unification of the manifold of intuition, without providing a counter-example to the conclusion of the first *Critique*'s Transcendental Deduction.[88*] This interpretation of Kant's explanation of aesthetic response would also have profound implications for his theory of aesthetic judgment. One result, quite congenial to Kant's argument, is that there will be an element of uncertainty in consciousness of the occurrence of the harmony of the faculties itself, just because this state requires the absence of the ordinary conditions for the verification of judgments about the mental states within one's own transcendental unity of apperception. We will see later that the ultimate uncertainty of aesthetic judgments is indeed a constant theme in Kant's theory of taste,[89*] and this problem about aesthetic response might be its deepest explanation. Less welcome to Kant, however, would be the fact that an interpretation of the harmony of the faculties in psychological rather than purely epistemological terms must allow an element of empiricism into the foundations of aesthetic judgment. I will argue later, however, that close analysis of Kant's deduction of aesthetic judgment points to the same problem; such an implication, then, would constitute not an objection to my interpretation of it, but an indication of the limits of Kant's theory of taste itself.[90*]

Pleasure and the Consciousness of Harmony

The question of the very possibility of the harmony of the faculties undoubtedly requires a fuller answer than I have given, but I cannot provide this here. Instead, I must now turn to the question of the precise nature of the relationship between this basis of aesthetic response and its manifestation in the feeling of pleasure. Two questions are crucial here. First, is our pleasure in a beautiful object *caused* by our independent consciousness that it has produced a state of the harmony of the faculties, or *is* the feeling of pleasure itself our sole consciousness of the existence of that state? And, second, is it in any case permissible to speak of the harmony of faculties as *causing* a feeling of pleasure?

A number of passages suggest that we may be directly conscious of the occurrence of the harmony of faculties by having a sense or even a thought of the unity of a given manifold, and these passages could thus incline us to the view that our consciousness of pleasure is consequent on a prior consciousness of the harmony of the faculties. One such passage is that on the experience of music, already quoted from §53.[91] This might be taken to say that listening to music produces feelings of unity and wholeness in a manifold of "combining as well as changing impressions," and as stating that the feeling of "comfortable self-enjoyment," which is produced by the mind's grasping all these impressions as unified without a rule, is a consequence of the awareness of such feelings. Another remark suggestive of such a view appears in the first Introduction's Section VIII, where, in distinguishing the judgment of taste from a mere expression of sensory gratification, Kant writes that "if reflection on a given representation precedes the feeling of pleasure (as the determining ground of the judgment [of taste]), then the subjective finality is *thought* before it is *felt* in its effect, and in that case the aesthetic judgment, according to its principles, belongs to the higher faculty of cognition, and indeed to the judgment, under whose subjective and yet thereby general principles the representation of the object is subsumed."[92] This passage appears to be one of Kant's fundamental explanations of the conditions under which an expression of a feeling of pleasure can in fact be judgment of taste at all. Thus what it asserts — that in the case of aesthetic judgment some kind of thought of an object as subjectively final, or producing the harmony of the faculties, *precedes* the feeling of pleasure — would seem to be basic to Kant's theory.

However, the first of these passages need not be read as stating that a *consciousness* or "thought" of the unity of a piece of music produces our pleasure of it, but only read as saying that some kind of mental grasping of unity — conscious or not — causes this pleasure. And the last sentence quoted cannot be regarded as definitive of Kant's view, for there are passages both elsewhere in the first Introduction and in the published text of the third *Critique* which point to a different position. The text just considered appears to imply that a consciousness of the subjective finality of an object is the ground for our feeling of pleasure in it. But later in Section VIII, Kant writes that "the aesthetic faculty of reflection thus only judges the subjective finality of an object, not its perfection, and the question arises whether this judgment is *by means of* the experienced pleasure or pain, or rather *concerning* it, so that a judgment may concurrently determine that pleasure or pain is *necessarily* connected with the representation of the object;"[93] and then answers this question by saying that the judgment of taste is *both* made by means of *and* concerns the experienced feeling of pleasure (or pain). The implications of the latter part of this claim need not concern us yet; but the statement that aesthetic judgment is made *by means of* the experienced pleasure suggests that it is the feeling of pleasure itself which is the ground for thinking that the object produces the harmony of the faculties, rather than the reverse. And, as we have already seen, the property of finality is just the fact of an object's conformity to our own needs; if the existence of such conformity is manifested by the feeling of pleasure, then any determination of finality must rest on the feeling of pleasure, rather than *vice versa*.

The text of the third *Critique* itself also allows this conclusion. In its key §9, Kant states that before we can consider "whether, and how, aesthetic judgments are possible *a priori*," we must "occupy ourselves with the lesser question: in what way do we become conscious of a reciprocal subjective accord of the cognitive faculties in a judgment of taste—aesthetically by mere internal sense and sensation, or intellectually through the consciousness of our intentional activity in bringing these powers into play [?]"[94] Kant's answer to this question suggests that it is indeed the feeling of pleasure which is the basis for consciousness of the harmony of the faculties. Thus he begins by arguing that the consciousness of the union of imagination and understanding in a given representation cannot be intellectual, for that would require the use of a concept; so it must instead be accomplished by means of a sensation. As Kant puts it, "the subjective unity of that relation can therefore make itself known only through sensation. The quickening of both faculties" to a "harmonious activity, such as belongs to cognition in general," is the sensation "which is the subject of the judgment of taste."[95] But since, as we will see, the sensation which is this subject—or "the sensation, the universal communicability of which the judgment of taste postulates"—is nothing but the feeling of pleasure itself, this answer seems to imply that it is in feeling pleasure that we first become conscious of the harmony of imagination and understanding. This might not be entirely apparent from §9, which continues by asserting that "no other consciousness" of the harmony of the faculties is possible "except through sensation of its effect, which consists in the facilitated [*erleichterten*] play of the two faculties enlivened through their mutual accord"; this could be taken to mean that the consciousness of the harmony of the faculties is indeed indirect, but also that the sensation which provides such consciousness can be characterized as something like a feeling of the unity of the faculties rather than just as a feeling of pleasure. But Kant's position is made unequivocal only three sections later, when he maintains that "the consciousness of mere formal finality in the play of the cognitive faculties attending a representation whereby an object is given, is the feeling of pleasure itself."[96] It is not merely the case that the harmony of the faculties, being independent of the employment of a concept, must make its presence known to consciousness through *some* sensation; it must manifest or express[97] itself in a feeling of pleasure.

This thesis may seem both implausible and inconsistent with Kant's own explanation of aesthetic response. It seems absurd to suppose that we can take pleasure in a state of affairs—in this case, a state of mind—without first knowing that state to obtain, and yet this is just what Kant's claim that the occurrence of the harmony of the faculties is first made manifest to consciousness by the feeling of pleasure itself implies. Further, it seems particularly bizarre to suppose that we might take pleasure in the fulfillment of some objective without the awareness both that we have the objective and that it is fulfilled being conceptually independent of and prior to our pleasure in it; this would certainly be the case insofar as we think of an object's conformity to our fulfillment of some objective of ours as a ground or reason for taking pleasure in it. For example, in Kant's own first case of reflective judgment's production of pleasure—the pleasure produced by the discovery that several empirical laws may be subsumed under some higher principle—it was certainly clear that we could be directly conscious of such a discovery, and that it was precisely through such consciousness that the discovery served as the ground of our "very appreciable pleasure."[98] So why is Kant's theory of aesthetic response not that we have a direct consciousness of the harmony of the faculties, in some sort of feeling of unity, and that our awareness that such a feeling constitutes a fulfillment of our general though subjective aim in cognition is in turn the ground of a feeling of pleasure?

It might be attractive to suppose that Kant is making the phenomenological point that in responding to beautiful objects we do not have two distinct kinds of feelings, feelings of unity or harmony and feelings of pleasure, and that, in fact, there is no distinct feeling of pleasure at all, but rather that feelings of unity just *are* pleasurable. Such a supposition would reduce the difficulty of Kant's claim that the harmony of the faculties produces pleasure in virtue of fulfilling an objective and yet that we know of this fulfillment only through the feeling of pleasure. But such a supposition would have little to do with the actual basis of Kant's thesis. For Kant's claim does not involve the thesis that different kinds of feelings may be pleasurable in their own ways, but instead depends on the diametrically opposed view that all feelings of pleasure are qualitatively identical, coupled with the further belief that the feeling of pleasure (or pain) is the *only* kind of sensation entirely devoid of objective significance. The feeling of pleasure is the only feeling which cannot generally be included in our empirical concepts. We saw this in Section VIII of the first Introduction, where Kant derived the result that aesthetic judgment concerns the pleasure produced by objects by defining such judgment as one in which "sensation is the ground of determination" and then asserting that "there is only a single so-called sensation, which can never become a concept of an object, and this is the feeling of pleasure and pain."[99] And we may now note, what we previously overlooked, that in concluding the main portion of this same section, Kant also argues that reflective judgment, not being based on concepts, must relate itself *merely* to such a sensation, because the "rule" of such reflection "is itself only subjective, and agreement with it can only be recognized in something else which in the same way merely expresses a relation to the subject, namely, sensation." This sensation can only be that of pleasure or pain[100] — or, now that we have the theory of cognitive fulfillment behind the idea of the harmony of the faculties, the feeling of pleasure alone. In other words, because the harmony of the faculties is a cognitive state of a subject which obtains apart from actual knowledge of an object, and because the feeling of pleasure is the only kind of sensation that manifests a state of a subject without being connectable to any determinate property of an object, only the feeling of pleasure can actually make the harmony of faculties manifest to consciousness.

Kant's argument is fallacious, for it infers from the (purported) fact that the feeling of pleasure is the only feeling which can *never* furnish knowledge of an object the conclusion that it is the only feeling which can *ever* be used to express the psychological state of a subject without also being used for knowledge of an object. This does not follow, for even if it were true that pleasure is the only feeling which never supplies knowledge of objects, there might be others, such as feelings of unity, harmony, or continuity, which are sometimes subsumed under concepts of objects and sometimes not; in the latter case, they too could figure in aesthetic response, even figure as our reasons for taking pleasure in the objects that produce them. But Kant does make the argument that only the feeling of pleasure itself can manifest the harmony of the faculties, and my reconstruction of his argument must employ this fundamental premise.

One might still wonder how Kant's claim can be reconciled with his explanation of the origination of aesthetic response itself. For even if it were true that pleasure were the only feeling which may express a psychological state of purely subjective significance, one might suppose that its production by the fulfillment of an objective must still require *some* antecedent awareness of that fulfillment. To this objection, I can only say that while Kant's theory of aesthetic judgment is clearly a theory of the relations between judgments and their grounds, his theory of aesthetic response is a theory of mental processes, or of the relation between mental states and their internal causes, for which a requirement of consciousness is not so obviously necessary as it is for the relation between reasons and the judgments they ground. If Kant were treating the harmony of the faculties an object produces as a *reason* for taking pleasure in that object, some awareness of the harmony would be a presupposition of the feeling of pleasure. But he does not treat the connection between the harmony and the pleasure in this way; instead, they are seen as related by a psychological process or mechanism, in virtue of which the harmony of the faculties *causes* a feeling of pleasure; and, as with Kant's theory of psychological processes in general—that is, his theory of synthesis—there is no absolute requirement that such processes be manifest to consciousness except by their results. This view is particularly evident in Kant's exposition of the theory of threefold synthesis, according to which it is only with the application of a concept to the manifold of intuition that a synthesis of recognition takes place.[101] This implies that it is only with the application of a concept that success in synthesis ordinarily becomes fully manifest to consciousness, an implication allowing the conclusion that the prior syntheses of apprehension and reproduction at least may be conducted unconsciously. But if it is just these syntheses which take place in aesthetic response, with the feeling of pleasure substituting for the application of a concept, then it seems that it would be by that feeling that the success in synthesis which constitutes the harmony of the faculties is actually recognized. Thus the mental activity which leads to that pleasure, though ascribed to a faculty of reflective judgment and thus naturally thought of as taking place consciously, may in fact be treated by Kant as the operation of a psychological mechanism to which consciousness is not necessary. Intrinsic as the requirement of awareness might seem to be to the production of pleasure by the fulfillment of an objective, Kant may have associated his general theory of pleasure with a model of mental activity in which this requirement does not figure.

Kant's general theory of pleasure is without doubt deeply problematic, but my project here is only to show how it forms the basis for his theory of taste. Thus I must be more concerned with its consequences than with its ultimate acceptability. One consequence that we may now note is that Kant's thesis that it is only in the feeling of pleasure itself that the state of the harmony of the faculties is manifest to consciousness can further explain his remark that reflective judgment's comparison of the representation of an object to our cognitive faculties is "unintentional" (*unabsichtlich*). The one thing that cannot be meant by the use of this term in the published Introduction's first explanation of aesthetic response is that reflective judgment's activity in producing the harmony of the faculties is not connected to any purpose (*Absicht*) or objective at all, for the explanation of the pleasurableness of this state requires its being the fulfillment of some sort of objective. One thing which Kant can mean, as we have already seen, is that reflective judgment is not guided by a concept, although such guidance is a condition of ordinary intentional activity. And we have now seen one more idea which Kant may have had in mind. If the harmony of the faculties is not manifest to consciousness directly, but is only manifested in the feeling of pleasure, then the activity which *leads* to that state may also be an object of only indirect consciousness. While the mental activity of comparing a representation to our cognitive faculties is undertaken in the service of the general goal of cognition, it is not guided by any specific concept, and may not even be consciously conducted. Imagination's search for unity in its manifolds, strange as this sounds, might be an unconscious activity, fully revealed only in its success—on some occasions, in the application of a concept to a manifold, and on others, in a feeling of pleasure. Insofar as the activity of reflective judgment which leads to this pleasure is not consciously undertaken, it may be called "unintentional," though it is still in the service of an ultimate cognitive objective.

Kant's argument that the harmony of the faculties is manifest only in the feeling of pleasure which it produces is hardly unproblematic. It assumes that concepts and sensations are the only forms of representation, and that because any sensations except those of pleasure and pain may be used as constituents of empirical concepts, pleasure and pain are the only forms of consciousness which are genuine alternatives to conceptualization. These assumptions can surely be questioned. Further, Kant's argument may seem implausible insofar as our acceptance of his explanation of aesthetic response might depend on our own assumption that feelings of unity could be recognized as fulfilling our aim in cognition, and thus be taken as reasons for pleasure. In fact, the difficulty of accepting the account of the relationship between the consciousness of the harmony of the faculties and the feeling of pleasure which Kant suggests, as well as some of Kant's own remarks about the nature of this relationship, has led some writers to deny that this relation can be understood as a causal mechanism at all. Thus before we can turn to the chief question which Kant's theory of pleasure as the consciousness of harmony raises — namely, how reflective judgment can assign a particular pleasure to the harmony of the faculties, if the occurrence of the pleasure is our only direct evidence for the existence of that state — we must first consider whether Kant's text can actually be interpreted in the causal language I have been employing.

As with so much at the fundamental level of his theory, the evidence of Kant's intentions on this issue is ambiguous. On the one hand, a number of his most basic statements of the theory of aesthetic response employ clearly causal terminology. Thus the first Introduction's earliest statement that we may be conscious of the subjective condition of our cognitive faculties by means of a sensation rather than a concept describes such a sensation as "the sensuous representation of the condition of the subject that is affected [*afficirt*] by an act of that faculty [of judgment]."[102] In the differentiation of judgments of taste from other reports of pleasure which follows, Kant describes the feeling of pleasure in "aesthetic sensory judgment" as "immediately brought forth [*hervorgebracht*] by the empirical intuition of the object," and that in the aesthetic judgment of reflection as "effected [*bewirkt*] in the subject" by the "harmonious play of the two cognitive faculties of the judgment." Kant ascribes the feelings of pleasure connected with the two judgments to different states of affairs, but in both cases his terminology suggests a causal connection between the feeling and its basis. And the conclusion of the paragraph which distinguishes the two forms of aesthetic judgment repeats the causal term *bewirkt:* Kant says that in the case of "mutual assistance" between imagination and understanding, "this relation . . . effects a sensation which is the determining ground of a judgment, and which is therefore termed aesthetic."[103] Another causal term is used in the published Introduction. Here, as we have seen, Kant begins his basic explanation of his theory by asserting that pleasure is connected with the apprehension of the form of objects in the case of aesthetic judgment, and goes on to explain this by saying that the feeling of pleasure is "aroused" (*erweckt*) by the occurrence of harmony between imagination and understanding.[104] All of these remarks suggest a causal relationship between the harmony of the faculties and the feeling of pleasure. The general law that success, especially unexpected, in the attainment of an objective produces pleasure appears to function as a causal law relating kinds of states of affairs, and to explain the case of aesthetic response by means of a causal relationship between two psychological states that is an instance of this more general law.

As we have seen, however, it might seem more intuitive to think of the attainment of an objective as a reason for pleasure rather than as a cause of pleasure, and there are passages in Kant's text which appear to conflict with the relation between harmony and pleasure as a causal one. The remark of the first Introduction that subjective finality must be thought before pleasure is felt could be taken in this way.[105] Even more problematic is §12 of the Analytic of the Beautiful. Kant begins this section by maintaining that "to determine *a priori* the connection of the feeling of pleasure or displeasure as an effect, with some representation or other (sensation or concept) as its cause, is utterly impossible; for that would be a causal relation [*Causalverhältniss*], which (among objects of experience) in every case can be known only *a posteriori* and by means of experience."[106] This seems to preclude the possibility of a causal relation between pleasure and its ground. For it states that such a relation must be known *a posteriori,* yet the thesis of the section is that "the judgment of taste rests on *a priori* grounds";[107] therefore, it apparently follows, it cannot concern a causal relationship. Further, Kant states that in the connection of pleasure and moral judgments, "the mental state present in the determination of the will by any means is at once in itself a feeling of pleasure and identical with it, and so does not issue from it as an effect [*folgt also nicht als Wirkung daraus*]"; and then makes the vague remark that the pleasure in aesthetic judgment is "disposed" in a "similar way" — so, it may seem, it cannot issue from some other mental state as its effect. These remarks appear to require a noncausal rather than a causal interpretation of the relation between the harmony of the faculties and the feeling of pleasure.[108]

But this evidence is not conclusive. First, insofar as Kant denies that the relation between a "representation" and the feeling of pleasure is causal, because it would then be *a posteriori,* he could be interpreted as denying that the relation between pleasure and its *object* — the thing which is beautiful — is causal, leaving the relation between pleasure and the other *state of mind* which produces it, the harmony of the faculties, untouched. But this possibility is not actually helpful, for it seems perfectly plausible to say that the object which disposes the imagination to harmony with the understanding is at least a partial cause of that harmony, and it might in fact only be an object's causal link to pleasure which allows it to be called the object *of* that pleasure.[109] What is more important is that §12's reason for apparently denying that the link between pleasure and its ground is causal is no reason at all. The argument suggested in §12 is that the connection of pleasure to the representation which occasions it cannot be causal, because in that case it could not be known *a priori*. But in §37, Kant asserts that "with no representation can I connect *a priori* a determinate feeling (of pleasure or displeasure)," except in the case of moral judgment. He then points out that what is represented as *a priori* in a judgment of taste is *not* the connection of pleasure to a given object, but the *universal validity* of a pleasure which is connected *a posteriori* to an object; the bare "judgment to the effect that it is with pleasure that I perceive and estimate some object is an empirical judgment."[110] This version leaves open the possibility that the connection of pleasure both to its object and to the state of mind through which the object produces the pleasure may be essentially causal, because it is the subject of a judgment which is in part (though only in part) empirical.[111]

In addition, the evidence furnished by Kant's claim that the connection between the state of mind in the determination of the will and the feeling of pleasure is not that the latter is the effect of the former, and by his suggestion that something similar is the case with aesthetic response, is in fact ambiguous. Kant could be taken to mean that the determination of the will by reason does not causally produce a feeling of pleasure as its effect, but he could also be taken to mean something quite different from this. By the "state of mind" (*Gemütszustand*) of a determined will Kant may well mean not the psychological *fact* of the will's being determined, but rather the *consciousness* of the determination of the will;[112*] interpreted thus, he would be saying not that the determination of the will, like the harmony of the faculties, does not causally effect a feeling of pleasure, but only that in the case of the determination of the will, *just* as in the case of the harmony of the faculties, there is no awareness that this psychological state obtains except for the feeling of pleasure. There is thus no other feeling or conscious representation from which the feeling of pleasure issues forth as an effect; but this does not mean that this feeling is not related by causal connection to the state of mind — the activity of the mental faculties — which underlies and produces it, and of which it is the conscious expression.

Finally, there are the following considerations. First, the fact that the harmony of the faculties is manifest only in the feeling of pleasure means that these two states of mind do not fit Kant's standard schema for causation, in which we are presented with two distinct representations and a search for a link between them (a schema, of course, adopted from Hume).[113] This fact could certainly have made Kant hesitate to *acknowledge* that this relationship is a causal one, although he does not actually hesitate to *treat* it as one. Second, the fact that Kant tends to equate the possibility of causal connection with the formulability of a determinate empirical law linking states of objects, combined with the impossibility of linking the harmony of the faculties to the objects which produce it by any such law, may have led him to be suspicious of the idea that the harmony of the faculties and the pleasure it *produces* are causally connected. But this does not follow. Although the peculiarities of the relation between the feeling of pleasure and its ground in the harmony of the faculties make it an anomolous causal connection, they do not undermine the basically causal nature of Kant's account of this connection; and Kant himself has stated the causal law which relates the two states in his general theory of pleasure.

Kant uses causal terms to describe how pleasure emerges from the harmony of the faculties. His only explanation of the pleasurability of aesthetic response suggests that this response is an instance of a general causal connection in human psychology between pleasure and accomplishment. Finally, Kant's view that a judgment of taste can emerge from aesthetic response only by a process of reflective judgment also suggests a causal theory of pleasure, for the reflection on a feeling of pleasure which precedes the judgment of taste is best understood as a search for the cause of a given effect. This may not fit Kant's standard case, in which we are given two events and consider whether there is a connection between them; what Kant describes is a situation in which, given an effect and a limited number of ways in which it could have been caused, we search for its actual cause. Nevertheless, the employment of such a model is dependent on the belief that the relation between pleasure and what "effects" or "arouses" it is a fundamentally causal connection: only such a connection could in fact create both the need for reflection and the possibilities for error in judgment which are, as we shall see, essential parts of Kant's theory of taste.

Although there may be difficulties in reconciling all of Kant's statements about aesthetic response with a causal theory of our pleasure in the beautiful, such a theory is more consistent than any other with his theory of aesthetic judgment as the outcome of a complex process of reflective judgment, in which a particular feeling of pleasure is assigned to its proper source in "simple reflection" and on that basis claimed to possess intersubjective validity. In spite of the argument of §12, that is, Kant's treatment of the judgment of taste's *a priori* claim to the agreement of others presupposes the reflection that a given pleasure has been caused by the harmony of the imagination rather than by something else. Thus our consideration of Kant's explanation of aesthetic response may be best concluded if we now turn to his introductory exposition of the structure of aesthetic judgment, that is, the judgment that a given object is beautiful.

Two Kinds of Reflective Judgment

The key to Kant's theory of the judgment of taste is the recognition that the declaration that an object is beautiful rests on two conceptually distinct acts of the faculty of reflective judgment: one, the "unintentional" reflection which produces the pleasure of aesthetic response; the other, that further and quite possibly intentional exercise of reflective judgment which leads to an actual judgment of taste, or determines that the feeling of pleasure occasioned by a given object *is* such a pleasure, and thus is validly attributed to anyone perceiving that object. The judgment that a feeling of pleasure has a certain source and status is a mental act with a particular propositional content — the assertion of the intersubjective validity *of* a given pleasure — which is clearly distinguishable from both the feeling of pleasure that is its subject and the production of that pleasure. This is so even if the two acts of reflective judgment, which lead to the pleasure on the one hand and the determination of its status on the other, are not always phenomenologically distinct or temporally successive, for while making a judgment about a pleasure certainly presupposes the occurrence of that pleasure, the latter does not entail the former. However, although there is overwhelming evidence for attributing this distinction to Kant, he does not manifest his commitment to it by adopting a consistent terminology for its expression.

On particular occasions, Kant does use pairs of terms in ways that in fact distinguish between judgment's production of pleasure and judgment's reflection on the production of pleasure. In Section VIII of the first Introduction, for instance, Kant speaks of the activity of reflection which produces the harmony of the faculties and the feeling of pleasure as "simple reflection." This is opposed to the "aesthetic judgment," which is always a "reflective judgment" and meets the criterion of "the claim of a judgment to universal validity and necessity."[114] Thus one might use "simple reflection" to mean the pleasure-producing exercise of the faculty of judgment, and "aesthetic judgment" to mean the act as well as the product of reflection on this exercise (as I have done and will continue to do). But Kant himself does not suggest that he is introducing a distinction in technical terminology here, nor does he use this terminology every place he might.

Another place where Kant provides possible technical terms is §9 of the third *Critique*. Here, Kant uses the phrases "the estimation of the object" and "the judgment of taste" (*Beurteilung des Gegenstandes* and *Geschmacksurteil*).[115] The former refers to the activity of reflection which precedes the feeling of pleasure, and the latter refers to the actual claim of "the universal communicability of this pleasure." We might thus distinguish between "estimating" an object and "judging" a pleasure as the two stages of reflection leading to a judgment of taste. But Kant does not employ these terms consistently, either; though §9 talks of pleasure resulting from "estimation," Section VII of the published Introduction uses the form "estimated" (*beurteilt*) in connection with the judgment that a "pleasure is . . . combined necessarily with the representation" of an object[116]—the judgment which is the product of reflection upon the fact that the felt pleasure was produced by what §9 calls "the estimation of the object." So §9, too, fails to introduce terminology which consistently reflects the distinction which Kant's theory requires.[117]*

But though Kant does not consistently distinguish between the "estimating" of an object and the "judging" of a pleasure, we must, for his theory is intelligible only if we distinguish two conditions for making the judgment of taste. The issuing of such a judgment depends both upon the occurrence of the mental activity which actually produces an intersubjectively valid feeling of pleasure, and on the logically independent recognition of the intersubjectivity of that feeling. In spite of the fluidity of his terminology, close attention to the arguments of Kant's two Introductions establishes that an aesthetic judgment must be the outcome of such a complex process of reflection.

The need for distinguishing two aspects of reflection emerges in the first Introduction's basic explanation of aesthetic response itself. In Section VIII of this text, already noted, Kant asserts that in aesthetic judgment in general sensation, in particular the sensation of pleasure and pain, is "the ground of determination"; specifically, in the judgment of taste the "harmonious play of the judgment's two cognitive faculties . . . effects a sensation, which is the determining ground of a judgment."[118] In this sentence, I suggest, Kant refers to three phenomena: the "unintentional" and non-rule-governed exercise of reflective judgment in the act of "simple reflection on a perception,"[119] which produces the feeling of pleasure; the feeling of pleasure itself, which as the "ground of determination" is both the evidence for and the subject of the further act of the faculty of judgment which leads to the judgment of taste; and that judgment itself, which is the claim of universal validity made about the given pleasure on the basis of the belief that it has in fact been produced by the harmony of the faculties in the perception of its object.

The necessity of distinguishing two acts of judgment might be most simply demonstrated by pointing to the fact that Kant describes the feeling of pleasure as both the product of judgment and the ground of determination for judgment; yet if aesthetic judgment resulted from a single act, this would be to say that the same feeling of pleasure both succeeded, as its product, and yet preceded, as its evidence or ground, a single judgment. This is clearly absurd.[120]* But this circularity can be avoided only if we take Kant to be referring to two distinguishable acts of the faculty of judgment when he describes this faculty as both producing a feeling of pleasure and taking such a feeling as the ground of determination for an aesthetic judgment on the beauty of an object.[121]*

The argument I have just stated is sufficient to compel adoption of the distinction between two kinds of reflection. Further textual evidence shows that such a distinction is in accord with Kant's actual intentions, even if not implied by his terminology. We have already seen that Kant concludes Section VIII of the first Introduction by asking whether aesthetic judgment is *by means of* the felt pleasure or *concerning* it — either alternative implying that the felt pleasure precedes this judgment — and by suggesting that if the judgment does concern this pleasure, what it does is to "determine that pleasure or pain is necessarily connected with the representation of the object." Clearly, establishing this fact about a given pleasure is different from actually producing the pleasure. The presupposition of the existence of the pleasure at the stage of reflection at which a judgment like this can be made is also manifest when Kant continues that if, as he assumes, his entire analysis of aesthetic judgment can be defended by "a deduction from an *a priori* ground of determination," aesthetic judgment "would indeed determine something *a priori* through the cognitive faculty (namely, the judgment) by means of the sensation of pleasure or pain, but at the same time [something] concerning the universality of the rule connecting the feeling with a given representation."[122] Again, *judging* that the connection between a given representation and a feeling of pleasure is universal must differ from *producing* such a feeling, and must presuppose its existence.

Why the mental act which compares a given representation to the subject's cognitive powers and in so doing produces a harmony between imagination and understanding should be called reflective judgment has already been seen; why the further judgment which decides that a given pleasure is due to this activity should also be so called is yet to be seen. Before considering this question, however, I will present further evidence, from the published Introduction, for Kant's commitment to the distinction between two kinds of reflective judgment. This text makes the structure of aesthetic judgment quite explicit through a serial exposition of its stages. If aesthetic judgment is the claim that the pleasure occasioned in oneself by a given object is also valid for everyone else, then it can only result from the assignment of a felt pleasure to the harmony of the faculties, as its cause. Thus, following his now familiar statement that the unintended accord of imagination and understanding which results from the conformity of an object to the cognitive faculties at play in reflective judgment arouses the feeling of pleasure, Kant continues:

> When the form of an object (not the material of its representation, as sensation), in simple reflection on it, without the intention of deriving any concept from it, is estimated [*beurteilt*] as the ground of a pleasure in the representation of such an object, then this pleasure is also judged [*geurteilt*] to be necessarily connected with such a representation, that is, as [so connected] not merely for the subject which apprehends this form, but for every judging [subject] in general. The object is then called beautiful; and the faculty of judging by means of such a pleasure (and thus with universal validity) is called taste.[123]

The concluding line of this passage suggests what only the Analytic of the Beautiful will actually argue, that calling an object beautiful depends upon the judgment that the pleasure it occasions is universally valid. But the first part of the quotation makes it clear that such a judgment can only follow from the "estimation" or judgment that the pleasure has resulted from the act of simple reflection — the reflective judgment's production of pleasure through the harmony of the faculties described in the preceding lines. And if this is how a judgment of taste is made, then it is clear that reflective judgment's production of pleasure and its conclusion that a given pleasure has been produced in a given manner must be distinguished.

The same result may be derived from this passage, which occurs later in the second Introduction's Section VII:

> one who feels pleasure in simple reflection on the form of an object without regard to a concept rightly makes claim to everyone's agree-

ment, even though that judgment is an empirical and singular judgment: for the ground of this pleasure is to be met with in the universal
though subjective conditions of the reflective judgment, namely, the
final harmony of an object (whether it be of nature or art) with the
mutual relation of the cognitive faculties (imagination and understanding) which is required for every empirical cognition. In the case
of a judgment of taste, the pleasure is, to be sure, dependent on an
empirical representation and cannot be connected *a priori* with any
concept (one cannot determine *a priori* which object will accord with
taste, or not: one must test it); but it is yet made the determining
ground of this judgment only insofar as one is conscious that it rests
merely on reflection and on the universal, although merely subjective,
conditions of the harmony of reflection with the knowledge of objects
in general, for which the form of the object is final.[124]

This passage is worth presenting in full, because it lays bare the foundations of Kant's aesthetics. As clearly as anything in the Introduction, it
foreshadows the analysis of the judgment of taste as the claim to everyone's
agreement in a given pleasure, or as the *"universal voice* in respect of a delight that is not mediated by concepts."[125] Equally clearly, it suggests that
such a judgment must be justified by the explanation of the given pleasure
as due to the harmony of the faculties produced by reflection on its object,
and it hints at the strategy of Kant's deduction of aesthetic judgment — the
argument that attribution of pleasure to the harmony of the faculties
makes it universally valid just because this state is the subjective condition
of knowledge in general. Finally, this passage indicates that it is the feeling
of pleasure which is the determining ground of the judgment of taste, or
the evidence for the existence of the harmony of the faculties; but it also
reveals that the feeling of pleasure can play this role only if one is in fact
conscious that it does indeed stem from simple reflection rather than from
something else. Thus the production and the awareness of pleasure must
logically precede the conscious conclusion that an object is beautiful, and
an act of reflection upon the nature of one's pleasure must be required in
order to reach the latter conclusion — or, certainly, to justify it.

This last requirement calls for reflection upon the sources of one's feelings of pleasure, which is why the judgment of taste as well as the production of pleasure can reasonably be attributed to a faculty of reflective judgment. Kant makes this point only obscurely in the published Introduction,
when he says that since the pleasure which grounds the judgment of taste is
not connected with the representation of its object by a concept, it "must

always be recognized as connected with this only through reflected perception [*reflectirte Wahrnehmung*]."[126] The argument of the first Introduction makes somewhat clearer why it is appropriate to call the "estimation"
of the source of one's pleasure a form of reflection. Here, it will be remembered, Kant began by defining an aesthetic judgment as one based on the
feeling of pleasure. He pointed out, however, that two different kinds of
aesthetic judgment are possible: an aesthetic judgment of sense and an aesthetic judgment of reflection. The former is the mere expression or report
of a feeling of pleasure produced "directly by the empirical intuition" of an
object, or by purely physiological response to it. The aesthetic judgment of
reflection is the judgment of taste, which "belongs to the higher faculty of
cognition" and makes the universal claim we have just encountered.[127]
Now, even in the case of the latter, since there can be "no definite concept
of its determining ground, this ground can only be given by the feeling of
pleasure, so that aesthetic judgment is always a reflective judgment." That
is, since two different kinds of judgment may be licensed by feelings of
pleasure produced in different ways, reflection is needed to decide, in the
case of a given feeling of pleasure, which form of judgment is actually in
order. For such reflection, a criterion for ascribing different pleasures to
their sources is required.

Kant seems to suggest this as he continues the first Introduction. He
writes: "It is in the [main body of this] treatise that the criterion [*Merkmal*]
for distinguishing the two can best be brought out. It consists in the claim
of a judgment to universal validity and necessity; for if an aesthetic judgment carries these in itself, it also claims that the basis of its determination
must lie *not merely in the feeling* of pleasure, but *equally in a rule* of the
higher cognitive faculties."[128] But this first use of the term "criterion" in
Kant's aesthetic theory does not reveal the full problem for reflection.
These lines explain the *force* of using a feeling of pleasure to ground a genuine judgment of taste rather than a mere judgment of sense, or, in the
language of the Analytic of the Beautiful, of calling an object beautiful
rather than merely personally agreeable.[129] The former judgment, but not
the latter, claims universal validity and necessity for the feeling of pleasure.
Insofar as these define the claim of the judgment of taste, they may be
called its "criterion." But this is not a "criterion" in the sense of *evidence*
for a judgment, or what justifies it. A criterion in the latter sense would be
what allows the attribution of a feeling of pleasure to the harmony of the
faculties, and thus *licenses* the claim to universality. But here a problem
arises. Kant has argued that the feeling of pleasure is the sole conscious

manifestation of the harmony of the faculties, that not all feelings of pleasure manifest this state, and that a judgment of taste can be licensed only if
reflection decides that a given feeling of pleasure is due to this state. Yet
Kant nowhere argues that there are qualitative or phenomenological differences between pleasures, which would make differences in their sources
self-evident, and in many places he suggests the opposite. Reflection, then,
would seem to require criteria for its decision that are provided neither by
the ideas of universality and necessity nor by the mere relation of pleasure
to the harmony of the faculties — for it is precisely this relation which requires some kind of evidence. What could such criteria be?

Kant answers this question only in the text of the Analytic of the Beautiful; and it would thus now be appropriate to turn to that section of the *Critique of Judgment*. Before doing so, however, I will consider the claim that
Kant does not postulate qualitative differences between kinds of pleasure a
bit further, for this is both controversial and important to my picture of
Kant's model of the complex process of reflective judgment in taste.

Kant's distinction between the sensation of pleasure brought forth by
empirical intuition and that produced by the harmony of imagination and
understanding,[130] or the expanded distinction, offered in §5 of the Analytic, between the kinds of pleasure taken in the agreeable, the beautiful,
and the good,[131] can easily be taken as a distinction of qualitatively different kinds of pleasures. On this view, Kant believes that feelings of pleasure
can be sorted into kinds on the basis of some internal features, and that it is
this fact which allows one to make a judgment of taste on some occasions
but not on others. One simply notices which kind of pleasure one has in the
presence of a given object, and then either just reports the pleasure of
agreeableness or else makes a claim to intersubjective validity.[132]*

But Kant, in fact, never says anything which commits him to this view.
What he does say is that "the agreeable, the beautiful, and the good . . .
denote three different relations of representations to the feeling of pleasure
and displeasure, as a feeling in respect of which we distinguish different
objects or modes or representations."[133] As Lewis White Beck has put it,
"There are only two elementary feelings — pleasure and pain. All other
feelings, such as the feeling of the sublime, the beautiful, and respect are
defined by the accompaniments, contexts, causes, or 'objects' of the pleasure or pain we feel. Whether the origin of the pleasure lies in some physical stimulation, the physical fulfillment of a desire, or some idea held in
contemplation, the feeling is always an effect upon our sensibility . . . there

is no place for qualitative differences."[134] Kant always refers to the feeling of pleasure in the singular, implying that, however various instances of pleasure may differ in origin or intersubjective validity, the nature of the feeling itself is always the same. And much of the force of calling aesthetic judgment a "reflective judgment" depends on the very fact that it cannot be made on the basis of introspection of a single sensation taken in isolation, but requires reflection on the context and cause of the feeling, or on its particular "relation to representation." It is for this reason that the judgment of taste calls for criteria concerning the state of mind from which a pleasure issues and the aspects of the object which occasion it — the criteria ultimately provided by the "moments" of disinterestedness and the form of finality.

Kant's actual definitions of pleasure are few. In fact, in one place he maintains that "pleasure and displeasure, not being modes of cognition, cannot at all be defined in themselves, and will be felt, but not understood"[135] — a statement which suggests that there are no internal differences by which kinds of pleasure can be distinguished. But all of Kant's descriptions of pleasure do conform to the view that feelings of pleasure are qualitatively identical, differing only in the sorts of relations which Beck mentions. This passage from the *Critique of Practical Reason* is one of Kant's clearest statements: "However dissimilar the conceptions of the object, be they proper to the understanding or even to the reason instead of the senses, the feeling of pleasure, by virtue of which they constitute the determining ground of the will . . . is always the same. This sameness lies not merely in the fact that all feelings of pleasure can be known only empirically, but even more in the fact that the feeling of pleasure always affects one and the same life-force which is manifested in the faculty of desire, and in that respect one determining ground can differ from any other only in degree."[136] This passage was written before Kant finally adopted the view that the feeling of pleasure could be occasioned by the faculty of judgment as well as by sensuous or rational desire, and thus might be held to express the very view that is overturned in the *Critique of Judgment*. But there is nothing to indicate that Kant revised his view on the qualitative uniformity of the feeling of pleasure itself, even after this discovery that some instances of this feeling could be grounded in the higher cognitive faculties and thus possess universal subjective validity. In his letter to Reinhold which announces this revolution in his theory of taste, Kant claims to have found a new and *a priori* principle for pleasure, but not a new kind of pleasure.[137]

The few definitions of pleasure which Kant does offer demonstrate a continuity in his view of this feeling which survives other changes in his aesthetic theory. In the second *Critique,* Kant defines pleasure "as the idea of the agreement of an object or action with the *subjective* conditions of life."[138] In the first Introduction to the third *Critique,* the same idea of a feeling of harmony with the subject's requirements emerges: "*Pleasure* is a *state* of the mind in which a representation is in harmony with itself, as the basis either simply for conserving itself . . . or else for creating its object."[139] Whether the feeling of pleasure is one of contemplation or desire, this suggests, its content as a conscious state of the mind is the same. The definition of pleasure as a feeling of agreement is also expressed in §10 of the *Critique of Judgment:* "the consciousness of the causality of a representation in respect of the state of the subject as one tending to *preserve a continuance* of that state, may here be said to denote in a general way what is called pleasure."[140] Finally, the *Anthropology from a Pragmatic Point of View* (published in 1797) defines "*sensuous* pleasure" — which includes both pleasure "through the *senses* (enjoyment) or . . . through *imagination* (taste)" — as "what directly prompts me to maintain [my] state (to remain in it)."[141] Even after the *Critique of Judgment,* Kant still implies that there is a single feeling of pleasure, regardless of how it is produced, and regardless of whether or not a given occurrence of it allows me "to choose, not merely for myself according to sensation, but also according to a certain rule that I represent as valid for everyone."[142] And this feeling continues to be defined in the same way as before — a definition which not only implies the phenomenological uniformity of different feelings of pleasure, but also, by explaining pleasure as due to the conformity of an object to the subjective conditions of life, or our own objectives, confirms the interpretation of the harmony of the faculties for which I have argued.

The feeling of pleasure itself, then, is always the same. It can be the ground of determination for different kinds of judgment only if it can be assigned to one source or another — even when that source is itself an act of reflection. This is the kind of process which Kant describes in the Analytic of the Beautiful; and it is the need for such a process of finding the right cause for an observed effect which makes the model of causal connection the most informative interpretation of the relation between the harmony of the faculties and the feeling of pleasure in aesthetic judgment, despite Kant's occasional reservations about the applicability of the standard analysis of causation to this case.

In the next three chapters, I will examine Kant's development of his introductory idea of a complex form of reflection into a detailed analysis of aesthetic judgment and its criteria. Before I do so, however, a final remark on Kant's theory of aesthetic response is in order. The view that all feelings of pleasure are a qualitatively uniform kind of sensation may strike us now as wildly archaic. To us, pleasures seem as much like attitudes as they seem like sensations, and appear to be, at least often, intrinsically intentional — bearing a relation to their object in their content and not solely in their causal history. We might thus be inclined to dismiss Kant's theory of aesthetic response as an outmoded form of sensationalism. But we must note one profound fact about it. By treating pleasures as much alike, and thus as internally opaque with regard to their diverse causal histories or relations to their objects, Kant undermines the traditional view that the nature of our mental states must always be immediately transparent to us. He thus makes room for both reflection and uncertainty in our own assessment of our pleasures. Even if he arrives at the insight that aesthetic judgment is the product of a complex and uncertain reflection on our own feelings by a simplistic account of what those feelings are actually like, the insight itself remains valid. Our own belief that pleasures are diverse should certainly make us aware of how complexly they may be intertwined in the case of aesthetic response — where it is often so hard to sort out our pleasures and displeasures with respect to the different perceptual, conceptual, emotional, and ideological routes by which they arise — and this can only make us welcome Kant's discovery of the opacity of pleasure, in spite of the anachronistic form it might seem to take.

4

A Universal Voice

****

The Organization of the Analytic

The *Critique of Judgment*'s two Introductions have presented a complex picture of the relations between pleasure and reflection in the judgment of taste. Kant's argument began with an attempt to establish a connection between our ability to feel pleasure or pain and our faculty of judgment, on the basis of their analogous positions in two divisions of our mental capacities. This argument claimed a general connection between pleasure and judgment, but left obscure the exact nature of the relationship intended. It was only after Kant introduced the notion of reflective judgment as an ability to compare given representations not only with each other, but also with our own cognitive faculties, that his aesthetic theory began to take on more definite shape. For the theory of reflective judgment led to Kant's thesis that the pleasure we take in beautiful objects is a product of the contingent harmony between imagination and understanding which results from "simple reflection" on such objects. But it became apparent that the production of pleasure could not be reflective judgment's only role in aesthetic judgment, for Kant's explanation of aesthetic response is not the whole of his theory. When the Introductions employed Kant's analysis of the claims of aesthetic judgment, the structure of his theory began to show more fully; the judgment of taste makes a claim about the status of the pleasure occasioned by a given object which can be sustained only if that pleasure is explained as due to the harmony of the faculties.

Kant's view is that in making an aesthetic judgment — not just responding to an object with pleasure, but calling that object beautiful — one is not merely reporting an experience of pleasure; one is claiming that the pleasure one has felt is intersubjectively valid, or reasonably imputed to other persons. Calling an object beautiful does not involve predicating an objectively valid concept of it, or attributing to it properties connected by determinate rules. No determinate relation holds between being beautiful and any specific properties of empirical objects analogous to that which holds between being gold and such properties as being yellow, ductile, malleable, and soluble in *aqua regia*. Nevertheless, Kant maintains, the judgment of taste does "claim, like every other empirical judgment, to be valid for everyone."[1] Such a claim, the Introductions suggest, is to be justified by invoking Kant's explanation of aesthetic response. Explaining a given pleasure as in fact due to the harmony of the faculties is the basis for reasonably claiming it to be universally and necessarily valid.

The Introductions offered an argument for the explanatory role of the harmony of the faculties. The analytical aspect of Kant's theory, however, was introduced without argument. Thus, as Kant himself suggested,[2] the analysis of the judgment of taste's claim to intersubjective validity remains to be defended in the Analytic of the Beautiful, the first major division of the text of the *Critique of Aesthetic Judgment* itself. Also still requiring defense, obviously, is the thesis that attributing a feeling of pleasure to the harmony of the faculties *does* justify a claim of universal and necessary validity. This defense, however, although sketched in the penultimate section of the Analytic, is basically reserved for Kant's subsequent Deduction of Pure Aesthetic Judgments. But these two arguments will hardly complete Kant's theory of taste. As we saw in the last chapter, actually making a judgment of taste requires an exercise of reflection in addition to that which produces pleasure, by means of which it may be decided that a given feeling of pleasure is due to the harmony of the faculties rather than to anything else; and the nature of such further reflection is still unclear. Its task, to be sure, is clear enough. In the terms of the published Introduction, it is to "estimate" that it is "the form of an object . . . in the mere act of reflecting on it" which is "the ground of a pleasure in the representation of such an object."[3] But Kant has argued that it is the feeling of pleasure itself which manifests the existence of the harmony of the faculties — the result of that mere act of reflecting — and this seems to imply that the feeling of pleasure, the source of which is the problem for the further reflection required for the judgment of taste, is also the only evidence available for such reflection.

The criteria of universal and necessary validity which Kant mentioned in the first Introduction cannot solve this problem. They state the content of aesthetic judgment's claim, or are criteria by which this form of judgment may be distinguished from a mere report of one's response to any object. So they are not criteria by means of which this claim may be justified. Rather, it is the factors of disinterestedness and the form of finality which play this second role. That a given feeling of pleasure is disinterested, and that it has been occasioned by the perception of the purposiveness of a given object's form,[4*] are facts about it which, in Kant's view, may be manifest to consciousness, may be used to assign it to the harmony of the faculties rather than to some other source, and which, consequently, may be used to justify the claim of intersubjective validity for that pleasure.

The Analytic of the Beautiful thus imposes a complex set of constraints on our reflection on aesthetic response. Universality and necessity are constraints on the status of a given pleasure, required if its occurrence is to be the basis for calling an object beautiful. Disinterestedness and connection to the form of finality are constraints on the actual production of a pleasure, or on the state of mind from which it issues, that are required if a claim to intersubjective validity is to be justified. Universality and necessity, we might say, are defining criteria for the judgment of taste, and disinterestedness and the form of finality are justificatory criteria.

The Analytic of the Beautiful, then, has a twofold task: it must present the analytical argument by which Kant's interpretation of the claims of taste is to be defended, and it must argue for the justificatory employment of the concepts of disinterestedness and the form of finality. In this and the next two chapters, I will examine Kant's attempt to accomplish these objectives. In this chapter, I will first consider Kant's analysis of the judgment of taste, an analysis which is independent of his explanation of aesthetic response, though it calls for such a theory. I will then show how Kant does connect his analytical and explanatory theories. In the subsequent chapters, I shall look at Kant's arguments for the justificatory criteria of taste. These arguments are not independent of the theory of the harmony of the faculties; rather, they represent Kant's attempt to derive substantive criteria for taste from his more general theory of aesthetic pleasure. It is at this state of his argument that Kant attempts to bridge the gap between abstract theories of taste and substantive rules for critical judgments.

I have just sketched an interpretation of the Analytic of the Beautiful according to which it contains two strands of argument, analytical and explanatory, and on which its four "moments" are divided into two groups of criteria, differing in function and status. Universality and necessity, Kant's second and fourth moments of the judgment of taste, define the status necessary for a feeling to ground this judgment, and are derived from an analysis of its form as a judgment. Disinterestedness and the form of finality, Kant's first and third moments, are criteria by which particular feelings of pleasure may be decided to have the requisite status for justifying a judgment of taste, and are derived primarily from the explanation of aesthetic response. Further, we will see, the nature of these criteria can explain how claims of taste may both be necessarily less than completely certain and represent a rational form of thought.

This interpretation, I believe, can show that the Analytic of the Beautiful offers an articulated theory of the conditions of the judgment of taste. It also provides the basis for an assessment of the internal coherence of Kant's argument, and is thus a prerequisite for any serious criticism of Kant's views. Nevertheless, there are obstacles to the acceptance of my description of the structure of the Analytic. First, Kant's own arrangement of the Analytic of the Beautiful into four moments of the judgment of taste does not suggest their division into two functionally distinct groups of criteria. Second, Kant's own "key to the critique of taste,"[5] §9 of the second moment of the Analytic, is contradictory. It does suggest that the relation between aesthetic judgment and aesthetic response for which I am arguing is the correct one. But it also suggests a quite different analysis, on which aesthetic judgment is the condition of aesthetic response, rather than *vice versa*. Before I can argue for my interpretation of the Analytic of the Beautiful, then, I must explain why certain aspects of what is apparently Kant's own view about the structure of his theory should be disregarded.

Although the Introductions to the third *Critique* contain some remarks that may be thought of as methodological, there is little in the text of the work itself which is explicitly addressed to questions of method and structure. The surface structure of the Analytic does not itself reveal a division of its four moments into two groups of differently functioning criteria. Instead, Kant simply offers a sequential discussion of four moments of the judgment of taste, each resulting in a "definition" or "explanation" (*Erklärung*)[6] of the beautiful. This discussion is organized on the basis of an analogy to the fourfold division of judgments employed in the *Critique of Pure Reason*.[7] No suggestion is made that these "definitions" make claims about the judgment of taste or its object different from the claims the headings of the table of judgments make about ordinary cognitive judgment. Nor does Kant's division of his analysis into four moments, resulting in four "definitions" of the beautiful, suggest that any of these definitions makes a claim about aesthetic judgment different from those made by any of the others. To the extent that the whole Analytic constitutes a single argument, further, it seems that the first moment — the discussion of disinterestedness — is where this argument begins, and that the remaining three moments must simply represent subsequent stages of the argument.

The first section of the text — included as part of the first moment's discussion of disinterestedness, but actually introducing all of the Analytic — presents both the substantive and methodological bases for the argument which follows. In it, Kant recapitulates the Introductions' argument that the judgment of taste is "subjective" and "aesthetic," that is, not a claim to knowledge of an object, but a judgment in which "we relate the representation to the subject and its feeling of pleasure and displeasure" or, "what is more, to its feeling of life — under the name of the feeling of pleasure or displeasure." Kant insists that this feeling "denotes nothing in the object," and makes clear his opposition to the rationalist model of aesthetic response. Thus, he holds, "to apprehend a regular and appropriate building with one's cognitive faculties, be the mode of apprehension clear or confused, is quite a different thing from being conscious of this representation with an accompanying sensation of delight."[8] The noncognitive nature of our pleasure in the beautiful appears to be the premise for the rest of Kant's analysis of the judgment of taste, and this analysis thus seems based on his introductory explanation of aesthetic response.

The only methodological statement in this section appears in a footnote appended to its title; this note thus actually opens the Analytic of the Beautiful. What Kant says to account for the structure of his text is this:

> The definition of taste, which is here the foundation, is that it is the faculty of estimating the beautiful. But what is required in order to call an object beautiful must be discovered by the analysis of judgments of taste. I have searched for the moments to which this faculty of judgment in its reflection pays attention according to the guidance of the logical functions of judgment (for in a judgment of taste there is always a relationship to the understanding). I have first brought the moment of quality into consideration, because the aesthetic judgment on the beautiful takes regard of this first.[9]

The "logical functions" of judgment are the forms of judgment, or the headings used to divide the table of categories — quantity, quality, relation, and modality. On the basis of the claim that aesthetic judgment, although not cognitive, does have a "relationship" to the faculty of understanding, Kant assumes that these four functions will be appropriate for the analysis of judgments of taste as well as of knowledge. The only alteration that he thinks is needed for these concepts to serve their new analytic purpose is that of reversing the position of "quantity" and "quality." Kant begins the argument of the Analytic with the moment of quality—or disinterestedness of pleasure—for the reason that this is what aesthetic judgment first regards.

But the force of this reason is obscure. It is taken to mean that a theoretical analysis of aesthetic judgment must begin from the concept of disinterestedness, but this does not follow from what actually seems to be asserted, that in actually making a particular aesthetic judgment, one must begin by looking for evidence of disinterestedness. In fact, I will argue, it is only in the *practice* of aesthetic judgment that the moment of quality comes first. The starting point of Kant's foundational *analysis* of aesthetic judgment itself lies not in his discussion of disinterestedness, but in his discussions of the moments of quantity and modality, or universality and necessity. Nevertheless, Kant uses this unclarified remark as justification for beginning his exposition with the moment of disinterestedness, and proceeds to offer an analysis of the judgment of taste—or its object, the beautiful— which, at least on the surface, has the following form.

The quality of the beautiful consists in the disinterestedness of the delight it occasions. Kant bases this assertion on direct consideration of what is required "in order to say that [an] object *is beautiful*,"[10] and also on the differentiation of the pleasure of aesthetic response both from any pleasure arising merely from sensation,[11] and from any pleasure dependent for its existence on the faculty of desire, whether the desire in question be provoked by sensation or reason.[12] This differentiation of aesthetic pleasure from pleasure in the agreeableness of sensation and in the goodness of that which is esteemed as of objective worth leads to the "definition" of taste as "the faculty of estimating an object or mode of representation by means of a delight or aversion apart from any interest," and a definition of the beautiful as the object of such a delight.[13] Furthermore, from the disinterestedness of the delight in the beautiful and his definition of an interest as a delight in the existence of an object,[14] Kant also concludes that a disinterested pleasure is not connected to any concern for the existence of an object. This inference has led many to suppose that for Kant the object of aesthetic response is not an ordinary empirical object, or an ordinary representation of such, but instead a nonempirical object of some sort.[15]*

Kant's exposition then turns from the moment of quality to that of quantity. Kant claims that from the fact that the delight that we take in the beautiful is disinterested, it may be "deduced" (*gefolgert*) that the beautiful is the object of a universal delight.[16] Universality is superficially introduced into the argument of the Analytic as a consequence of the disinterestedness of a given pleasure. This introduction is then buttressed by an appeal to a difference between the ways in which the words "beautiful" and "agreeable" themselves are correctly used. We may properly say, Kant maintains, that some canary-wine is "agreeable *to me,*" but, it would be "ridiculous" to say that a building or a poem is "beautiful *to me.*"[17] In other words, it follows from common usage as well as from the fact of disinterestedness that calling something beautiful is making a judgment which claims to be valid for all. This "quantity" of aesthetic judgment, however, must be carefully distinguished from the "logical quantity" of universality, the property that characterizes a proposition such as "All roses have thorns." The logical quantity of an aesthetic judgment is always singular. It has the form "This rose is beautiful," and a logically general statement such as "All roses are beautiful" could never be more than an empirical generalization from genuine singular aesthetic judgments. The quantity of an aesthetic judgment is not "objective universal validity," or validity for all objects falling under a given concept (such as "rose"). It is "subjective universal validity," or validity for all subjects encountering a particular object, quite apart from any general concept under which it might fall.[18]

At this stage of the Analytic, where he is ostensibly still making deductions from the moment of disinterestedness, Kant reintroduces the claim that aesthetic judgment does not involve the employment of any concept and, thus, of any "rule according to which anyone is to be compelled to recognize anything as beautiful."[19] Only if this is the case will the universal validity of the delight be subjective. On the basis of this exclusion of concepts from aesthetic judgment, Kant then introduces the concept of the harmony of the faculties into his exposition, maintaining that the "cognitive powers brought into play" by a representation which occasions a disinterested but universal delight "are here engaged in a free play, since no definite concept restricts them to a particular rule of cognition."[20] He also argues as if the relation of the feeling of delight to the harmony of the faculties added another ground for the claim to universality intrinsic to the concept of the beautiful to that derived from disinterestedness, since "we are conscious that this subjective relation suitable for cognition in general must be just as valid for everyone, and consequently as universally communicable, as is any determinate cognition, which always rests upon that relation as its subjective condition."[21] On its surface, then, Kant's analysis does not introduce disinterestedness as a criterion for the occurrence of the harmony of the faculties, but instead proceeds from the starting point of disinterestedness to both the status of the judgment of taste and the ground for this status. Kant's second "definition," that "the *beautiful* is that which, apart from a concept, pleases universally,"[22] is presented as if it were a consequence of his previous conclusion that it is the object of a disinterested delight, and Kant does not suggest that there is any difference in function between these two moments.

From quality and quantity, Kant turns to relation, considering "judgments of taste according to the *relation* of ends which are drawn into consideration in them."[23] This moment does not concern a relational form present in the structure of aesthetic judgment, which is logically categorical, but a relation between judgment and its object. Kant argues that the correct object of the judgment of taste, or what is genuinely beautiful in an object of universal delight, is purposiveness or finality of form perceived apart from any consciousness of an actual end. From the fact that the delight in a beautiful object is both disinterested and perceived without any concept, Kant concludes that we can perceive in it only the "bare form" of finality.[24] From the fact that our pleasure in such an object is occasioned by the harmony of the faculties, he argues, it also follows that our pleasure is in its purposiveness for our cognitive faculties. Thus the object of our pleasure is a "formal finality" in the object. Kant then equates the "form of finality" in an object with the finality of its form, and argues that the object of our pleasure cannot be any matter for sensation. Thus delights stemming from mere "charm" and "emotion" are excluded from the judgment of taste,[25] as are such things as the color in a painting, as opposed to its design, or tones in music, as opposed to composition.[26] From the fact that the delight in a beautiful object is felt without the application of any particular concept to it, Kant further infers that aesthetic pleasure is not a delight in any perfection of the object, for such a pleasure would presuppose "a concept of *what sort of a thing it is to be.*"[27] Here Kant introduces his famous distinction between "free beauty" and "dependent beauty." The perception of the former presupposes no concept of the object of delight, but that of the latter presupposes such a concept and the perception of "an answering perfection of the object."[28] From this distinction, Kant attempts to derive the conclusion that such abstract and nonrepresentational objects as "designs *à la greque,* foliage for frameworks or on wallpaper," which "have no intrinsic meaning," and "represent nothing—no object under a determinate concept"—are the only proper objects of a

purely aesthetic judgment.[29] Objects which involve empirical or moral concepts—for instance, the ideal of human beauty—can at best permit of
mixed aesthetic and intellectual judgment.[30]

Finally, Kant comes to "the modality of the delight" in a judgment of
taste. A beautiful object has a necessary relationship to delight. This necessity is neither "theoretical objective necessity," derivable *a priori* from the
concepts applied to an object, nor "practical necessity," due to thinking of
something as an object of rational will according to an objective law.[31]
Rather, the necessity of aesthetic judgment is "exemplary." A judgment of
taste exemplifies necessity because calling an object beautiful entails claiming that "everyone *ought* to give the object in question his approval and follow suit in describing it as beautiful"; and this amounts to treating an object as an "example of a universal rule" even though no such rule can be
given.[32] Such necessity, Kant argues, follows from the universal validity of
the beautiful, and depends on the presupposition that there is a "common
sense," or shared subjective condition of cognition, at the basis of formal
finality.[33] Thus the moment of modality is derived from the quantity of
taste as well as its relation. The discussion of the fourth moment also reveals that the attribution of pleasure to the harmony of the faculties, here
in the guise of a "common sense," is the condition of aesthetic judgment's
claim to universality and necessity. At this point, Kant essays one attempt
to defend this justificatory use of his explanatory theory, but defers its full
consideration until later.[34]

There is considerable difference between the outward form of this exposition and the analysis of the four moments which I sketched at the beginning of this chapter. But Kant's organization of his theory involves grave
difficulties, which can be resolved only by discarding its surface appearance in favor of a deeper view of the interrelation of his four moments. I
now turn to these problems.

First, the mere organization of Kant's analysis by means of headings bor-
rowed from the first *Critique*'s division of the logical functions of judgment
is problematic. Kant himself points to a disanalogy between the analyses of
cognitive judgments and of aesthetic judgments only in the ordering of the
headings of quality and quantity, but there is a profound difference between the actual content of the two analyses. This may be obscured by
Kant's use of the term "moment"—a term not used in the first *Critique,*
and thus of no clear architectonic or methodological significance—but the
fact is that the logical functions of cognitive judgment and the moments of

aesthetic judgment do not describe analogous properties of judgments. With the exception of the categories of modality, the logical functions of judgment characterize differences in the content of judgments, or differences that may obtain between various judgments considered as formal objects, without regard to their truth or warrant. The moments of aesthetic judgment, by contrast, do not describe differences in the possible contents of particular aesthetic judgments or, indeed, any way in which one judgment of taste may differ from another. Rather, these moments describe features of epistemological status common to all aesthetic judgments—the acceptability they claim to enjoy, the kinds of evidence on which they may be based, the positions from which they must be made.[35*]

This disanalogy may be easily demonstrated. Employing the particular categories of quantity, quality, relation, and modality as logical functions of judgment, we can formulate a large number of formally different judgment types. There are apodeictic universal affirmative categorical judgments, and problematic singular negative hypothetical judgments, and assertorical particular negative disjunctions, and many more.[36] According to Kant's own analysis, only the modal categories have anything to do with the epistemological status of judgments, for possibility and impossibility, existence and nonexistence, and necessity and contingency[37*] "do not in the least enlarge the concept to which they are attached as predicates [but] only express the relation of the concept to the faculty of knowledge."[38] All of the other functions concern only differences in the content of various judgments—in Kant's terms, enlargements or restrictions of the concepts to which they are attached as predicates. The situation is quite different in the case of aesthetic judgment, however, for Kant actually insists that all aesthetic judgments have the same logical form. "In their logical quantity all judgments of taste are singular judgments."[39] Similarly, they all have the same quality, relation, and modality: every aesthetic judgment of taste is a judgment of the form "This . . . is beautiful".[40*] Every aesthetic judgment makes the same assertion about its object—in terms of the logical functions of judgment, every aesthetic judgment is an assertoric singular affirmative categorical judgment. The four moments of aesthetic judgment thus do not characterize differences in the way in which the predicate "beautiful" may be attached to its subject. Instead, they characterize the epistemological status of such judgments: that they are, though subjective, universally and necessarily valid, that they must be made from a position of disinterestedness, and be based on a delight occasioned by the mere form of finality.

Since the logical functions of judgment describe differences in the contents of judgments, and the moments of aesthetic judgment describe quite different features of the status and ground of judgments, there is no reason why the order or even the number of the former should provide an appropriate framework for the analysis of the latter. In fact, Kant's sequential arrangement of the four moments as four "definitions" of the judgment of taste obscures the difference in function between those describing the requirement of intersubjective acceptability and those describing criteria by which such a requirement may be judged to be fulfilled. With the exception of modality, all of the logical functions make the same contribution to a form of judgment — they determine its content. But, as we shall see, only the moments of quantity and modality can be considered to determine the content or meaning of aesthetic judgment's claim; quality and relation concern the evidence for making such a claim, a contribution to judgment not covered at all by the first *Critique*'s division.

The difference between the logical functions of judgment and the criteria actually described by the four moments of aesthetic judgment is a sufficient reason for suspending our natural presumption in favor of Kant's own structuring of his argument. Why Kant should have adopted a method of exposition so ill-suited to the real content of his theory is a question that merits some attention. The answer cannot be a mere obsession with the architectonic, for this itself could not dictate the particular architectonic elements to be employed — in the *Critique of Practical Reason,* for instance, while Kant did retain the general divisions into an analytic and a dialectic, and into a doctrine of elements and a doctrine of method, he did not rely on the table of categories for the basic outline of his exposition.[41*] That he did so in the case of the third *Critique* must mean that Kant thought, at least at some point, that this table was particularly appropriate to aesthetics.

In fact, the analogy between the moments of aesthetic judgment and the logical functions of judgment is a remnant of the rationalist view of aesthetic perfection with which Kant grew up, and which retained its grip on him even when his thinking on aesthetics was also influenced by empiricism. The rationalist theory of aesthetic response as a kind of cognition, with the different perfections of cognition, was rejected by the mature Kant, but left its trace in the organization of the Analytic of the Beautiful. One note, written sometime between 1776 and 1779, clearly shows Kant trying to work out "subjective" and "aesthetic" equivalents for the perfections of ordinary cognition, in a manner reminiscent of Baumgarten. This note presents the following table:

Quality: Distinctness (subjective) (lively, particular) (aesthetic: clarity of intuition.)

Relation: Truth (2. subjective truth in appearance.) (2. The aesthetic relation is to the subject. Charm and emotion.)

Quantity: Universality (subjective) (3. The universal in the particular.) (subjective for all.)

Modality: Certainty. Necessity (of cognition in general. The usual, custom . . .) (4. empirical necessity. Approval. Universal. The customary. Taste).[42]

This note represents Kant's thinking on taste at an early and confused stage. But the very fact that Kant could use the headings for the logical functions of judgment even in this early phase suggests that there is no intimate connection between the division of the four moments and the real content of Kant's mature theory. Kant's division of the four moments really preceded his final conviction that aesthetic judgment was not a form of cognitive judgment, but this division was such a long-standing habit of thought that he continued to employ it even after the disanalogies between aesthetic and cognitive judgment had become greater than the analogies. Kant's employment of this framework in the third *Critique* is thus anachronistic as well as misleading.

A second problem with Kant's exposition in the Analytic of the Beautiful concerns not its outward form, but its actual substance if taken literally. This problem arises in the transition from the first to the second moment. As we saw, Kant begins what is meant to be an analysis of aesthetic judgment with the feature of disinterestedness. Such a beginning may be acceptable, to the extent that it presupposes nothing but our pretheoretical intuitions — intuitions to which Kant appeals when he says that "everyone must admit that a judgment on beauty which is mingled with the least interest is very partial and not a pure judgment of taste."[43] But beginning with disinterestedness may be misleading, when the requirement so stated is derived from the exclusion of any role for the faculty of desire, whether sensuous or rational, from aesthetic response[44] — for this presupposes Kant's explanatory use of the harmony of imagination and understanding, which is not introduced until the second moment. The most serious problem in starting with disinterestedness, however, emerges when Kant claims that it may be "deduced" [*gefolgert*] from this moment that the beautiful is the object of a universal delight, on the ground that "where anyone is conscious that the delight [in an object] is in his own case free of all interest, then he cannot but estimate it as containing a ground of delight for everyone"[45] — for this "deduction" is invalid. From the fact that a delight is not caused by any interest or desire, it does not follow that it is valid for everyone. It might be entirely accidental, or based on some other kind of merely private condition. Universality cannot be deduced from disinterestedness alone, nor does it follow that in requiring disinterestedness of a pleasure one is requiring that it be universal; one may simply be requiring a source other than interest, quite apart from any consideration of intersubjective validity at all. Indeed, one might maintain that unless the requirement of disinterestedness is already a normative[46]* requirement for intersubjective acceptability, trying to deduce such a requirement from disinterestedness confuses a factual matter with a normative requirement.[47]*

The remarks with which Kant himself amplifies his opening claim that universality may be deduced from disinterestedness suggest that the latter is not really prior to the former in the philosophical analysis of aesthetic judgment, and does not entail the requirement of universality; rather, disinterestedness provides evidence for a claim to universality in the actual practice of aesthetic judgment. Kant's text describes a person trying to evaluate the intersubjective validity of his response and using disinterestedness to comply with the presupposed demand for universality. Thus Kant writes that when a subject does not think his delight is based on any inclination or "other deliberate interest," but instead "feels himself completely *free* with respect to the delight he accords to the object," he will not be able to find "any private conditions as the grounds for his delight." On this basis, and the — yet to be defended — assumption that a disinterested delight rests on a ground which is common to all, he will then "believe that he has reason for demanding a similar delight from everyone."[48] In other words, Kant characterizes a situation in which the request for universality, or a reason to demand the same delight from everyone, is already given, and the disinterestedness of one's own delight is invoked as a reason for claiming such universality. Disinterestedness is evidence which justifies one in claiming that an object is universally pleasing, but not a ground for the analytical thesis that universal validity of response is what is required if an object is to be called beautiful. Kant's invalid deduction of the second moment from the first is not the real lesson of the transition between the two. Instead, his exposition suggests that the requirement of disinterestedness is a justificatory criterion of taste, and that of universality a defining criterion. If this is the case, of course, then an argument for the requirement of universality will constitute the true foundation of Kant's analysis of aesthetic judgment.

The priority of the moment of universality is revealed at another point in the discussion of the second moment. In §8, where Kant clarifies his distinction between objective and subjective universal validity, he maintains that "the claim to universality is so essential to a judgment in which we declare something to be beautiful, that were this not to be thought, it would never enter into anyone's head to use this expression."[49] The term "essential" (*wesentlich*) is not used of any of the other moments of taste, not even of the quality of disinterestedness, which we "first regard" in making an aesthetic judgment.[50] This fact again suggests that it is the second moment in Kant's analysis which makes the basic claim about the epistemological condition for calling an object beautiful, and not the first moment. Disinterestedness is our "first regard" or "what we want to know" in *answering* the demand for universality.[51] It is not a condition directly imposed by the *meaning* of "beautiful," but is instead a ground by which we may justify the claim to universality dictated by the logically prior argumentation of the second moment.

The difficulties in Kant's use of the headings from the first *Critique*'s table of judgmental functions and in his transition from the first to the second moment are enough to undermine our confidence in his presentation of his theory, and to make clear the need for some reconstruction of his argument. Further argument will show that the fourth moment's requirement of necessity belongs with the call for universality as a defining condition, and that the third moment's concept of the form of finality, like disinterestedness, is an attempt to state a condition under which the demand for universality and necessity in response may be fulfilled. These conclusions will emerge in due course, however; at this point, I turn to Kant's actual foundation for his analysis of aesthetic judgment in the second moment.

A Universal Voice

The second moment of the Analytic of the Beautiful starts with the claim that "the beautiful is that which, without concepts, must be represented as the object of a universal delight,"[52] and offers Kant's most direct argument for universality as a defining condition of aesthetic judgment. It even goes so far as to assert that to speak of taste without assuming the possibility of universal agreement "would be to say as much as that there is no such thing as taste."[53] The second moment also introduces Kant's explanatory concept of the harmony of the faculties into the body of the Analytic. It thus not only founds his analysis of aesthetic judgment, but also shows how this can be complemented by his explanation of aesthetic response to produce a solution to the problem of taste.

As we have just seen, the second moment begins in some confusion. Its opening §6 commences with the ill-fated claim that the definition of the beautiful as the object of a universal delight is deducible from the definition of it as the object of a delight free of any interest. This inference is fallacious, for it leaves open the possibility that a delight might stem from some source of privacy other than an interest, and thus be disinterested but still not valid for others. But §6 does suggest that a subject making an aesthetic appraisal will be examining himself for "personal conditions to which his own subjective self alone might be party" because the question of intersubjective validity is what is crucial in reflection upon aesthetic or pleasurable responses. Should the subject find no evidence that his pleasure is due to "personal conditions" — should he find, for instance, that it stems from a disinterested frame of mind — he may call the object occasioning his pleasure beautiful. We use the grammar of objectivity, in other words, though the actual topic of our reflection is our own feeling of pleasure. We "speak of the beautiful as if beauty were a quality of the object," Kant argues, "and the judgment logical (forming a cognition of the object by concepts of it), although it is only aesthetic . . . because it still bears this resemblance to the logical judgment, that it may be presupposed valid for all persons."[54]

From an ontological point of view, Kant is suggesting, the object of aesthetic judgment is something subjective rather than objective — a feeling rather than any specific property of the object. But ontology is not the only factor determining the grammar of our judgment; we adopt a grammatically objective mode of expression in this case because we are in fact willing to claim the same status of intersubjective validity for some of our feelings about objects that we do for our perceptions of their ordinary properties. When I call something red I am not just describing how it appears to me — I do that by saying "It seems red" — but rather describing how I expect it will appear to anyone in certain circumstances, in virtue of certain specific properties it has. When I call something beautiful, I am likewise not saying merely that it pleases me, but rather that it ought to please everyone perceiving it. I do not make this claim on the basis of any specific properties of the object, as I might call an object red because it reflects light of a certain wave length. But if my use of the predicate "beautiful" is not to be irrational, I must have "some reason for demanding a similar delight from everyone." The objective form of aesthetic judgment involves a claim to intersubjective validity, and such a claim requires a ground.

Kant may seem to be taking the use of the predicate "beautiful" for granted, and then arguing that, because there is a claim to intersubjective validity implicit in the predicate form itself, there must be a justifiable claim to intersubjectivity at the basis of judgments of taste, in spite of the fact that beauty "is only aesthetic, and contains merely a relation of the representation of the object to the subject." But Kant's argument is not meant to move so fast. First, it is obvious that at this point Kant is only analyzing the claim of aesthetic judgment, and not begging the question of a transcendental deduction of this form of judgment by assuming that its claim is in fact justified. Second, the next section (§7) makes it clear that Kant is not supporting his analysis just on his own view of predication. Rather, Kant supports the criterial role of the claim to universality on a broader appeal to linguistic usage. Invoking in §§7 and 8 his introductory distinction between aesthetic judgments of sense and of reflection,[55] Kant argues that there is a difference in our linguistic expectations about the objects of such judgments, the agreeable and the beautiful.

First, he analyzes our use of "agreeable":

> As regards the *agreeable* every one concedes that his judgment, which he grounds on a private feeling, and through which he says of an object that it pleases him, is also limited merely to his own person. Thus he is quite satisfied if, when he says that canary-wine is agreeable, another corrects the expression and reminds him that he ought to say: It is agreeable *to me* . . . A violet color is to one soft and lovely; to another dead and faded . . . To quarrel over such matters with the intention of reproaching another's judgment as incorrect when it differs from our own, as if two judgments were logically opposed, would be folly.[56]

The correct expression or what we "ought to say" with regard to the term "agreeable" allows indexing the term to particular users, or allows for expecting purely private validity.[57*] This term functions merely to report the occurrence of a feeling of pleasure in a specific person, perhaps even on a specific occasion. Correct usage of "agreeable" involves no claim on the agreement of others, for it permits the explicit denial of any such claim by the addition of the words "to me."

With the term "beautiful," however, our linguistic expectations are quite different:

> It would be . . . ridiculous, if someone who prided himself on his taste were to think of justifying himself by saying: this object (the building we see, the dress someone is wearing, the concert that we hear, the poem submitted to our estimation) is beautiful *for me*. For if it merely pleases *him*, he must not call it *beautiful*. Many things may have charm and agreeableness for him — no one cares about that; but when he proclaims something beautiful, he imputes the same delight to others: he judges not merely for himself but for everyone, and then speaks of beauty as if it were a property of things.[58]

In §8 Kant also links the use of the term "beautiful" to the "particular determination of the universality of an aesthetic judgment" — which he notes is a "curiosity" not for the "logician" but for the "transcendental philosopher," thus revealing that the universality of an aesthetic judgment has indeed nothing to do with the logical function of universal extension, but is concerned with the epistemological fact of universal acceptability. He establishes this link in a passage already quoted in part: "One must first of all become fully convinced that by the judgment of taste (upon the beautiful) the delight in an object is imputed to *everyone*, yet without being founded upon a concept (for then it would be the good), and that this claim to universality is so essential to a judgment by which we declare something to be *beautiful*, that were it not for its being thought it would never enter into anyone's head to use this expression."[59] Clarifying the first Introduction's suggestion that universality (to be joined by necessity) is the criterion for distinguishing between aesthetic judgments of sense and of reflection, Kant now states that it is the claim to universality which is meant or intended in calling something "beautiful" rather than merely "agreeable."

The claim to intersubjective validity is a condition on the meaningful use of "beautiful." That "beautiful" implies such a claim is what distinguishes the use of this term from a mere report of the occurrence of a feeling of pleasure in oneself. In calling an object agreeable, one merely reports the occurrence of such a feeling; in calling it beautiful, one goes beyond that to "impute" the pleasure to others as well, although on the basis of its occurrence in oneself. This criterial significance of universality is implicit in the correct use of the expression "beautiful." Just as the essential privacy of agreeableness is revealed by the permissibility of adding the index "to me" to "agreeable," so the publicity inherent in the meaning of "beautiful" is revealed by the fact that it would be "ridiculous" to place such a restriction to oneself on the scope of its validity. Without the intention of universality, the distinction between "beautiful" and "agreeable" would collapse. Denying that the aesthetic judgment makes no such claim by saying that "everyone has his own taste . . . would be equivalent to saying that there is no such thing as taste at all, that is, no aesthetic judgment which can make a rightful claim upon the assent of everyone."[60]

This excursion into common usage, unparalleled in Kant's other *Critiques*, is obviously meant to be the extrasystematic foundation for Kant's analysis of aesthetic judgment. But his view of the methodological significance of such an appeal is unclear. Yet some features of Kant's procedure in these sections are clear enough. Thus it is obvious that Kant is not simply taking the fact that the claim to universality constitutes the essential difference in meaning between "agreeable" and "beautiful" to mean that we are necessarily justified in claiming universal validity. This must be shown by independent argument; and Kant's analysis of correct expression is meant only to show what must be argued—what we must be able to justify if we are to meaningfully employ two terms of appraisal rather than one. This appeal to what we ought to say is meant to show what we must justify to defend our use of the term "beautiful" from a skeptic's reproach, because of the very criterion by which the meaning of that term is defined; but it does not itself offer that defense. It is thus also clear that Kant is denying that the defense of intersubjectively valid judgments of taste can be taken up as a mere afterthought to other concerns with aesthetic experience.[61*] Such a defense must constitute the heart of a critique of taste, for it is a condition of the possibility of any intelligible discourse about taste at all. The distinction between mere private validity and intersubjective validity of response is analogous to that between subjective and objective sequences of representations in the first *Critique:* as the latter is what judging of objects is all about, so the former is what taste is all about, and it is what must be defended to show judgments of taste possible.

It is clear, then, that in §§7 and 8 Kant means to transcend his own interest in *a priori* judgments and to suggest that his concern with justifying a claim to universality in aesthetic response is imposed on him by the nature of our basic term of aesthetic appraisal itself. It is also clear that by so doing he means only to pose the question of a transcendental deduction of taste, and not to beg it. But it is not clear what force he thinks actually attaches to an appeal to what we ought to say, for Kant certainly has no general theory of the philosophical significance of ordinary language. Kant could be treating the claim to universality as part of the definition of "beautiful" in common usage, and thus attributing the status of analytic truth to the second moment's "definition" of the beautiful. But this seems unlikely: first, because Kant thought philosophy could not start from definitions, but only argue to them;[62] and second, because no one as familiar with the controversies of eighteenth-century aesthetics as was Kant could have reasonably assumed that there was any common agreement on a definition of beauty. Yet neither does Kant suggest that anything like common usage could function as the third thing or "unknown $= x$"[63] by which a synthesis between the concepts of beauty and universality could be effected; it seems improbable that Kant would have regarded the proposition that the beautiful is the object of a universally valid delight as a *synthetic a priori* truth founded on a shared but merely linguistic practice. In other words, neither of the two interpretations of the status of a fundamental proposition that are possible within Kantian methodology—that it is analytic *a priori* or synthetic *a priori*—seems to fit the case of his basic claim about the significance of aesthetic judgment very well.

In fact, Kant's silence on the status of the implications of ordinary language in the case of the second moment is only one instance of the methodological reticence of the third *Critique*. Although Kant does carefully explain that particular aesthetic judgments have both empirical and *a priori* components, he never comments on the status of his four "definitions" of taste themselves. He does not say whether they are analytic or synthetic, *a priori* or *a posteriori,* and no position can be inferred from his imprecise term *Erklärung*. One can only speculate on what Kant thought he was doing in his unusual appeal to correct expression.

Perhaps Kant did anticipate the modern view that language is essentially a shared enterprise, and that the use of the linguistic form of predication presumes an intersubjectively valid basis for what is asserted. Sometimes, of course, this presumption might be surrendered—and our language itself may acknowledge this, as when it accepts the addition of "to me" to "agreeable." But unless ordinary usage does admit such a disclaimer, the argument might run, grammar's presumption of intersubjective validity must be sustained. Thus Kant may have had in mind a linguistic version of the first *Critique*'s claim that the "copula *is*"—and the predicative form of judgment which uses it—"is employed to distinguish the objective unity of given representations from the subjective."[64] This claim, coupled with the *Prolegomena*'s assertion that "objective validity and necessary universality (for everybody) are equivalent terms,"[65]* could lead to the view that our language itself dictates that the schema "*a* is F" be used only when *a* is believed to be F for everyone, unless that same language defeats this demand by allowing or requiring the addition of "to me" to the predicate F. From this it would follow that the acceptability of adding "to me" to "agreeable" defeats the claim to universal validity inherent in the act of predication itself, but that the unacceptability of this addition in the case of "beautiful" means that this claim stands, even though this predicate concerns subjective feelings.

Or perhaps Kant had no such theory of language at all, but appealed to ordinary usage for a strategic reason. He may have thought that the "definition" of the beautiful as the universally pleasing was no discovery of his own, but a commonly held belief. Thus it need not be pressed upon the reader by an elaborate metaphysical deduction, as in the case of the definition of the concept of an object through the categories. Instead, Kant may have viewed his own contribution as consisting merely in the defense of the claim to universality. If so, then the appeal to what we ought to say may have been meant not to provide an argument for the claims of aesthetic judgment, but to draw the reader into Kant's deduction — to remind him that, unlike a skeptic, he does not concede that "there is no disputing of tastes" although he cannot say why, and therefore has a stake in Kant's subsequent argument. Kant may have thought that the place for a sophisticated argument, a true defense of a synthetic *a priori* proposition, was not in the analysis of aesthetic judgment, but in its deduction. If the latter could be accomplished, then any objections to his analysis would fall under the combined weight of our presumption in its favor and Kant's proof that the task it imposes can in fact be accomplished.

As with the foundation of his explanation of aesthetic response in a general theory of pleasure, Kant hardly more than suggests a basis for his analysis of aesthetic judgment. In his appeal to correct expression, we have seen what Kant has to say in support of his analysis of the term "beautiful" and the judgment using it as imposing the condition of universal or intersubjective acceptability. We must now consider just how Kant formulates this requirement of taste.

The terms with which Kant expresses the criterion of universal validity are somewhat surprising — they all suggest not so much *expecting* the occurrence of a mental state in another person, or *attributing* a state to another, but rather *demanding* or *requiring* something from someone, even *imposing* some kind of obligation on another.

The word which Kant uses most often is *Anspruch,* which is generally translated as "demand." Thus aesthetic judgment is described as involving "a demand for validity from everyone," "a demand for subjective universality,"[66] a "rightful demand for everyone's agreement,"[67] "A demand for universal validity,"[68] and "a demand for the accession of everyone"[69] — what one has when one "believes oneself to have a universal voice" in matters of taste. A more literal translation of *Anspruch* would be "title." Kant would thus be saying that one has a title to the agreement of others, suggesting not only that, when one makes a judgment of taste, one has the right to demand agreement from others, but that they have some sort of obligation to furnish it. Kant also uses a number of verbs, all of which mean expecting, demanding, or requiring something — typically, a performance of some kind — from someone. Thus, in §7, Kant says that in calling something beautiful "one does not as it were reckon on the agreement of others in one's judgment of delight . . . rather one *requires* [*fordert*] it of them"; he also states that one "demands" (*verlangt*) that others have taste.[70]

A large number of passages employ the verb *zumuten,* which is translated as "demanding" or "exacting," as well as "imputing." The published Introduction has already said that the "strange thing" about the judgment of taste is that it "exacts" the feeling of pleasure from everyone, or "imputes" it to them (*dass es . . . ein Gefühl der Lust . . . jedermann zumutet*),[71] and this term recurs in each of §§6, 7, and 8. In the first of these sections, as we saw, a belief in the disinterestedness of one's own pleasure is supposed to provide a ground "to demand a similar delight from everyone."[72] In §7, a person who proclaims something beautiful "imputes the same delight to others";[73] and the verb *zumuten* occurs several times in §8, when Kant speaks of demanding or imputing "agreement in one's judgment of taste."[74]

In this last passage, Kant also uses the verb *ansinnen,* another word meaning to expect or require; thus, through a judgment of taste one "require[s] the pleasure in an object from everyone." And Kant distinguishes the judgment of taste from a mere aesthetic judgment of sense by saying that in the latter case one may actually find others in agreement with one's own pleasure, but one does not "require" it of them.[75] *Ansinnen* and *zumuten* do not mean precisely the same thing, for the latter conveys the sense that one's demand is impertinent (at least in contemporary usage), but both do generally refer to a demand or request. This sense may be somewhat attenuated if one translates *zumuten* by "impute," as in an imputation of responsibility—but even this sense may involve reference to a demand, perhaps for payment of a penalty.

There are also several passages outside of the second moment where Kant uses apparently moral language to state the claim of taste. Concluding §40, Kant raises the suggestive question of "how the feeling in the judgment of taste is attributed to everyone as a sort of duty," or "as [if] it were a duty."[76] And, according to both English translations, §19 says that in declaring an object beautiful one intends that "everyone *ought* [*solle*] to give the object concerned his approval"[77]—although there is in fact no reason why Kant should not be translated as making the more neutral assertion that "everyone *should* give the object concerned his approval."

There are shades of difference between Kant's terms, but all of them suggest the imposition of a demand or request of some sort on another person, an imposition which would ordinarily require some legal or moral basis. The imputation of responsibility may be a slightly different matter, but that too is surely a moral or legal concept. This fact has led some commentators to argue that aesthetic judgment's demand for agreement is a moral claim, and requires a foundation in a moral justification.[78]* But though Kant does eventually attempt to establish that there is a moral interest in at least judgments on the beauty of nature—with limited success, I will argue in Chapter 11—it is hasty to conclude that these terms are meant to introduce a moral element into the analysis of the second moment. Kant may be using these words to convey the importance of finding a reason for making claims about the responses of others, but at this stage in his argument it is reasonable to assume that he is describing an epistemological rather than a moral responsibility—describing a requirement of rationality rather than of morality.

Several considerations support this interpretation. First, Kant himself attempts to derive the second moment from the first, and it is quite unlikely that he could have meant to support a moral demand for any kind of performance on a requirement of disinterestedness: so far, the disinterestedness of aesthetic judgment appears to separate it entirely from any connection to morality. Second, Kant's arguments in §§8 and 9 concern epistemological grounds for a title to universality, to the exclusion of any moral grounds. Finally, Kant does use some terms with cognitive rather than practical connotations in describing the claim of taste. Two sentences from §6 are especially revealing. First, there is Kant's description of the condition under which one may have ground to "demand" a pleasure from another: "it must be seen as grounded in that [condition] which can be pre-supposed in everyone else." A few sentences later, Kant again uses the cognitive term "presuppose" instead of any such practical term as "demand": he says that aesthetic judgment is similar to logical judgment in "that one can presuppose its validity for everyone."[79] The judgment is presupposed valid for others, and this entails that its ground of determination may be presupposed to obtain for others as well. But this just means that aesthetic judgment "presupposes" the feeling of pleasure in others, or attributes it to them.

Since Kant's argument in §9 — the key to the critique of taste, after all — is addressed solely to the question of under what circumstances a feeling of pleasure can be attributed to others, or assumed to be communicable, and since what Kant explicitly entitles the "Deduction of Judgments of Taste"[80] is similarly limited in scope, it seems correct to take such an attribution to be what is meant by demanding pleasure from others or imputing it to them. In any case, demanding pleasure of others in particular circumstances may be held to presuppose both that one is justified in supposing them capable of it and that one could know one's demand to be fulfilled, or could attribute pleasure to them; so whether or not there is a moral claim in taste, its epistemological claim must be considered first. The epistemological presumption involved in that claim — that of assuming that one can know how others will respond to an object on the basis of one's own pleasure — may be enough of an impertinence to explain Kant's terminology.

In spite of the terms in which it is described, the judgment of taste's imputation of pleasure or agreement about pleasure to others cannot yet be any sort of moral or legal claim on them. What sort of claim is it? Our clues for an answer to this question lie primarily in the contrasts Kant draws between the claim of aesthetic judgment and more ordinary forms of empirical prediction and *a priori* inference.

In §§7 and 8, Kant contrasts the judgment of taste with a prediction made by induction from empirical evidence. This is asserted directly in §7, when Kant says that a person making a judgment of taste "does not reckon on the agreement of others in his judgment of delight because he has often found them in accord with his own [judgment], but he *requires* it of them."[81] In §8, Kant makes the point indirectly, by adding to the assertion that an aesthetic judgment is not made by induction the statement that it cannot be defeated by empirical evidence of a counter-example. This is "strange," Kant concedes: in the case of a mere report on agreeableness, or a judgment of "sensory-taste" (*Sinnen-Geschmack*), one does not impute agreement to others, "although a quite extensive unanimity is often found even in these judgments"; however, "the taste of reflection" (*Reflexions-Geschmack*) requests such general agreement, even though, "as experience teaches, it often enough finds its claim to the universal validity of its judgment (on the beautiful) for everyone dismissed."[82] An imputation cannot be an inductive prediction, then, for it is neither "reckoned" on the basis of a body of confirming evidence, nor defeated by what apparently may be even a large body of conflicting evidence.

Taste's imputation of agreement also fails to conform to philosophy's other model of rational prediction, that based on *a priori* inference from concepts. Kant makes this clear in the concluding paragraph of §8: "The judgment of taste itself does not *postulate* everyone's agreement (for only a logically universal [judgment] can do that, since it can adduce grounds)," and such a postulation is different from a judgment of taste precisely because the latter cannot make a predictive inference from concepts. Rather, "it merely imputes this agreement to everyone, as a case of a rule, in respect of which it expects confirmation not from concepts but from the accession of others."[83]

The judgment of taste, then, is a claim about the responses of others, but not a prediction based on induction or deduction; it expects its confirmation from the accession of others, but is not defeated by evidence that others do not in fact agree. What kind of claim is this? Kant's introduction of the metaphor of a "universal voice" only deepens the problem. This figure is deployed in the two final paragraphs of §8. The first of these sharpens our conception of the epistemological impertinence of the claim of taste by describing how one's own use of the universal voice is coupled with an insistence on oneself's feeling pleasure as a condition of concurrence in another's judgment of taste. Kant asserts that no evaluation of an object based on concepts is a judgment of its beauty, and that no judgment of beauty can be based on concepts, or compelled by the application of a rule to the object. Thus, instead of allowing oneself to be talked into a recognition of something (a dress, a house, a flower) as beautiful by any sort of reason or principle, "one wants to submit the object to one's own eyes, just as if its delight depended on sensation; and nevertheless, if one then calls the object beautiful, one believes oneself to have a universal voice and claim title to the accession of everyone, while on the contrary any private sensation would be decisive only for the observer alone and his own delight."[84] So, one takes a feeling of pleasure in oneself to be a ground for

speaking with a universal voice, or attributing agreement about that pleasure to others; but since one's own agreement with another's judgment will
not be forthcoming with one's own experience of the claimed pleasure, one
must not be asking for mere verbal agreement from others; one asks that
they too actually experience the pleasure. Speaking with a universal voice is
imputing feelings of pleasure to others on the basis of one's own feeling.

This tells us more about the circumstances of taste's imputation, but still
does not clarify the epistemological status of such a claim itself. The final
paragraph of §8 is our last hope, but its opening sentences only offer further difficulty. Kant begins by saying that "nothing is postulated in the
judgment of taste but such a *universal voice* in respect of delight without
mediation by concepts; thus the *possibility* of an aesthetic judgment, which
can at the same time be considered valid for everyone."[85] This sentence
introduces the concept of "postulation" into the argument, and suggests
that this may be our clue to the nature of the claim to intersubjective validity. But there is less of a clue here than may at first appear.[86*]

First, there is a problem about what Kant describes as being postulated.
Kant says here that the judgment of taste postulates only the possibility of a
judgment which is both aesthetic — that is, made on the basis of a felt pleasure — and yet valid for everyone. But that is too weak a characterization of
the content of aesthetic judgment, for such a judgment asserts not merely
that others *may* feel the pleasure I feel — that is always possible — but that,
at least under certain conditions, they *do* or *will* feel such a pleasure.

Perhaps this problem is only verbal, and a minor rewording could save
Kant's exposition. But even then, the deeper problem of the obscurity of
the concept of postulation itself would still remain. Kant's use of the concept here is, in fact, both contradictory and vague. It is contradictory because the sentence just quoted suggests that aesthetic judgment may have
the status of a postulation; but the very next sentence is the one, already
quoted,[87] in which Kant contrasts postulation with imputation, stating
that the former sort of claim can be made only by logical judgment from
grounds. In addition, Kant's use of the concept of postulation here is vague
because it functions as a technical term with no clear sense: in fact, Kant's
other works describe three different kinds of postulation (or postulates),
and none of them fits the case of aesthetic judgment.

One usage of "postulate" is to describe the principles of modality, or
Kant's definition of the possible, the actual, and the necessary.[88] This
seems an unlikely candidate for the usage in the sentence under consideration because it is supposedly dealing with the quantity rather than the

modality of aesthetic judgment. And Kant's explanation of why he calls these principles postulates does not seem to help: the principles of modality are so called because "they do not increase our concepts of things, but only show the manner in which [things are] connected with the faculty of knowledge."[89] Aesthetic judgment, like reflective judgment, is concerned with the connection of objects to our general faculty of cognition, but on this definition of a postulate one can say that an aesthetic judgment has such status because it asserts that an object of taste is connected to our cognitive faculty with universal validity—and that much we already know.

A second sense of "postulate" is that drawn from mathematics, to which Kant contrasts the sense just considered.[90] A postulate in this sense is clearly defined in Kant's *Logic* as "a practical, immediately certain proposition or a fundamental proposition which determines a possible action of which it is presupposed that the manner of executing it is immediately certain," as in mathematical construction.[91] But this cannot illuminate the nature of the claim of taste, for, as we shall shortly see, this claim is not immediately certain.

Finally, there is the sense of "postulate" employed in the *Critique of Practical Reason* and Kant's other discussions of the idea of God, freedom, and immortality. In this sense, a postulate is "a theoretical proposition which is not as such demonstrable, but which is an inseparable corollary of an unconditionally valid practical law,"[92] or, in Beck's paraphrase, "an assertion of the possibility or actuality of an object as a corollary to the acknowledgment of a necessary law."[93] But because it is Kant's thesis in §8 itself that taste's claim to universal validity cannot be derived from any law, theoretical or practical, and his thesis in the first moment that taste is not connected to any practical interest, the claim of taste cannot be a corollary of any practical law. Thus the judgment of taste is not a postulate in this sense either.

Kant's description of what the universal voice postulates, then, is not quite right, nor does his characterization of its claim as a postulation cast much light on its status.[94*] The concluding sentences of §8, however, are more helpful. Having distinguished aesthetic judgment's *imputation* of agreement from an actual *postulation* of agreement, Kant continues:

> The universal voice is therefore only an idea [*Idee*] (on what it rests, will not be examined here). That he who believes himself to be making a judgment of taste actually judges in accord with this idea, may be uncertain; but that he relates his judgment to such an idea, insofar as it is a judgment of taste, is proclaimed by his expression of "beauty."

> For himself he can be certain through his mere consciousness of the abstraction of everything pertaining to the agreeable and the good from the delight remaining to him; and this is all for which he promises himself the agreement of everyone: a claim, which under these conditions he would also be justified in making, were it not that he often sinned against them and therefore made an erroneous judgment of taste.[95]

An imputation of pleasure or agreement in pleasure is not an induction, deduction, or postulation in any of their usual senses, but it is an "idea," a concept of objective but indeterminate validity.[96] Its validity is indeterminate because it rests on two conditions the fulfillment of which is uncertain Aesthetic judgment's imputation of pleasure to others is an attribution of pleasure to them, subject to the dual conditions that one's own feeling of pleasure, the basis for this attribution to them, in fact be "abstracted" from any sensually or conceptually determined pleasure, and that others be in a like condition of abstraction. Such "abstraction," of course, requires attributing the feeling of pleasure to the harmony of the faculties— the ground which Kant is not yet ready to pursue—and in any given case, the occurrence of this state both in oneself and in others is uncertain; Kant's momentary suggestion that one can be certain of the abstraction of one's pleasure from improper sources is retracted as soon as he makes his crucial claim that one often sins against the conditions of taste. The imputation of taste, then, is an attribution of pleasure to others which is indeterminate or ideal[97]* because of the uncertainty of its evidence, and it is not necessarily defeated by disagreement either because one may in fact have been wrong about the source of one's own pleasure or because another, who disagrees, may himself not have performed the requisite abstraction. But though the aesthetic judgment's claim is thus not an empirical induction, or an inference from any determinate concepts, it is not irrational, but founded on a ground: the concept—or idea—of the harmony of the faculties. This remains to be argued in §9, but Kant is now clearly pointing to such an argument.

An imputation of pleasure is, then, an attribution of pleasure to others, subject to conditions on the certainty of one's knowledge of both oneself and others, and founded on the indeterminate concept of the harmony of the faculties as the ground of aesthetic response. It is, after all, a prediction, but an ideal prediction—a prediction which presupposes ideal knowledge of one's own responses and ideal circumstances of response for others. To formalize this conclusion somewhat, we might say that the judgment that a particular object *x* is beautiful amounts to the claim that everyone who perceives *x* should, apart from any predication of a concept of it, take pleasure in it, or that, under ideal conditions — of noninterference from purely sensory pleasures and abstraction from any concepts that might effect an interested response — everyone who perceives *x* will take pleasure in it. We might then distinguish this analysis of the truth conditions of an assertion that some *x* is beautiful from a description of the evidence on the basis of which a person may reasonably make such an assertion. A person may reasonably assert that an object *x* is beautiful only if he takes pleasure in *x* and believes that his pleasure in *x* is due to the harmony to which the perception of *x* disposes his imagination and understanding. What the last lines of §8 then imply, and what shall be further shown in the sequel, is that though one can have evidence for a belief that one's pleasure in a given object is due to such a harmony, one can never be completely certain that one's pleasure has been so caused; so it is possible that one may assert that an object is beautiful on the basis of the evidence just described, and yet be wrong. In such a case, one will have made an erroneous judgment of taste, a judgment in which the conditions on the evidence for a judgment of taste have been met but its truth conditions have not. One might then want to say that only true rather than erroneous judgments of taste are justified, but I would suggest that Kant's argument calls for a weaker interpretation of justification in the case of judgments of taste. Since one can never be certain of judgments of taste, but yet can reasonably make them, a judgment of taste will be justified if the person asserting it reasonably believes himself — on the basis of due and careful reflection — to have the requisite evidence for such a judgment, even if he in fact turns out to be wrong in his assessment of the source of his own pleasure.

In §9, Kant makes it clear how the ascription of one's own pleasure to the harmony of the faculties can ground an imputation of it to others, or function as evidence for the assertion of a judgment of taste, and first suggests what sort of deduction will be necessary to show why such an ascription should in fact count as such evidence. Before we can consider the argument of §9, however, we must examine some further aspects of Kant's characterization of the claims of taste in §8.

The Singularity of Aesthetic Judgment

Both Kant's description of the imputation of taste and the defense of his theory turn on the thesis that aesthetic judgment is not determined by the subsumption of an object under a concept, which would be required for either empirical induction or *a priori* inference. The opening of §8 makes it appear as if this thesis is derived from the characterization of the judgment of taste as disinterested, and from the differentiation of judgments of beauty from judgments of goodness which emerged from that discussion. Thus the first statement in §8 that a judgment of taste imputes delight in an object to everyone says that it does so "without being founded on a concept (for then it would be the good)."[98] If, however, the demonstration that taste is disinterested is not analytically prior to the thesis of universality, and if—as I shall argue in the next chapter—the differentiation of the beautiful from the good presupposes the thesis of beauty's independence of concepts rather than grounding it, then this distinction cannot be the basis of the latter thesis. But that thesis can be regarded as a consequence of the definition of aesthetic judgment which was introduced in §1 as a premise for the whole of the Analytic, and of Kant's explanation of aesthetic response. Kant began the Analytic with the definition of aesthetic judgment as "one whose determining ground *cannot be other than subjective*," or one which is made on the basis of the experience of pleasure itself.[99] Further, pleasure, according to both §1 and the Introductions, "denotes nothing in the object, but is a feeling which the subject has of itself, as it is affected by the object."[100] If this is so, then none of the ordinary concepts predicated of an object can express the fact of its pleasurableness; and so "from concepts there can be no transition to the feeling of pleasure or pain."[101*] But then aesthetic judgment cannot be based on the subsumption of an object under a determinate concept; *a fortiori,* its claim to universal validity cannot depend on such a subsumption.

The same conclusion would result if we viewed Kant as arguing from his explanation of aesthetic response as arising from subjective rather than objective conditions of knowledge, and we could interpret §8 as relying upon this explanation rather than on the moment of disinterestedness. But because Kant's explanatory model is not explicitly introduced into the argument until §9, perhaps we should let the present account of the derivation of taste's independence from concepts suffice, and turn to §8's contrast between the universality of aesthetic judgment and ordinary logical universality. This distinction is made on the basis of aesthetic judgment's independence of concepts: "a universality which does not rest on concepts of objects (even if only empirical) is not logical, but aesthetic, that is, it contains no objective quantity of the judgment, but only a subjective [quantity], for which I also use the expression *universal validity* [*Allgemein-*

gültigkeit], which designates not the validity of the relation of a representation to the cognitive faculty, but [the validity of the relation of the representation] to the feeling of pleasure and pain for every subject."[102] Logical universality, or what Kant also calls "objective universal validity," is simply the formal property of universal quantification, or the validity of a particular predicate for any object falling under a certain subject-concept. Objective universal validity is the quantity manifested in the propositional form "All Fs are G," and characterizes the content of a given proposition quite apart from its truth or acceptability. The universality of an aesthetic judgment, by contrast, is not an internal or formal feature of its content, but is its epistemological status — its imputability to or acceptability for all judges or subjects. This is why Kant calls it "subjective universal validity."[103] A logically universal judgment connects a predicate-concept to a subject-concept in such a way that the former is valid of any object falling in the extension of the latter; the extension of a subjectively universal judgment, by contrast, is not a class of objects, but the class of possible human judges. "Aesthetic universality" thus does not connect a predicate with the concept of an object, "considered in its whole logical sphere," but rather "extends [the predicate of beauty] over the whole sphere of the *judging* [subjects]."[104]

That aesthetic universality cannot be identical with logical universality is a consequence of the fact that the judgment of an object's pleasurability is made independently of its subsumption under any concept, and cannot be implied by its subsumption under a concept. If the judgment that a given rose is beautiful cannot be inferred from the object's being a rose, then it is obviously not derived from a proposition of the form "All roses are beautiful," nor need it be taken to offer support for such a proposition. Kant expresses this by saying that "with respect to logical quantity all judgments of taste are *singular* judgments"; they are always of the form "This rose is beautiful." In such a judgment, the use of the referring expression "this rose" may serve to pick out the object of attention, but does not provide the basis for calling it beautiful.

Kant's exposition of this point is somewhat confused. First, if universal subjective validity is simply the status of universal acceptability or imputability, it should not be called "aesthetic universality"; obviously all kinds of judgment may enjoy this status, whether they are logically singular or universal, cognitive or aesthetic. Aesthetic universality is just a special case of subjective universal validity, namely, such status when not entailed by an object's subsumption under any concept. Second, Kant's statement that a judgment which "has *objective universal validity* is always subjectively [universally valid]" is not quite right, and conflates the question of truth or acceptability with that of logical form. No judgment is valid for all subjects just in virtue of being logically universal. What can be said, however, is that any objectively universal statement which is *true* is also subjectively universally valid; that is, if it is true that all Fs are G then it is valid or acceptable for any person to judge either that this F is G or that all Fs are G. But Kant's point is, nevertheless, clear enough. The universality claimed by aesthetic judgment is the imputability of delight, and thus the validity of the judgment, for all subjects. Because of the independence of aesthetic response from the synthesis of manifolds under concepts, this validity cannot be inferred from the classification of an object under a concept, and does not imply that any object falling under a classification which happens to be used to refer to a given object in asserting beauty of it will be beautiful.

An aesthetic judgment is thus logically singular but subjectively universally valid: it asserts of a given object, and that object only, that it may be expected to occasion pleasure in every subject responding to it; or rather, it "imputes" all of this, because it is subject to the dual conditions which make the universal voice an "idea" rather than any more ordinary "postulate." This thesis about the judgment of taste cannot be too carefully described, for it shows us in precisely what way aesthetic judgment is independent of concepts. Feelings of pleasure are not produced by the subsumption of objects under concepts (except in the special case of moral feeling), and thus aesthetic judgment cannot proceed by subsuming objects under ordinary concepts of objects. This is not to say that the *content* of aesthetic judgment does not involve *any* concepts — such as the concept of other persons — or that its expression does not employ concepts — such as the concept of beauty itself, or the particular concepts of objects which must be used to designate the reference of particular aesthetic judgments. Nor does Kant's thesis entail that under certain circumstances concepts, or at least representations of concepts, cannot themselves be part of the *object* of aesthetic judgment. All that Kant is actually arguing is that the subsumption of an object under a classificatory concept is not a basis for responding to it pleasurably *or* for validly imputing that response to another person; in this sense, aesthetic judgment, as the complex activity of reflective judgment and its outcome, is independent of the subsumption of its object under concepts.[105]*

How can aesthetic judgment claim any form of universal validity without employing a concept of an object, when it is apparently only such a concept "which prevents our modes of cognition from being haphazard or arbitrary"?[106] Kant's answer to this question is given by §9's "key to the critique of taste," which explicitly links his explanation of aesthetic response to his analysis of the requirements of aesthetic judgment to show that an intersubjectively valid claim about pleasure can indeed be made. But while §9 does contain clear confirmation of the complex model of aesthetic reflection I am attributing to Kant, it also makes several unsettling claims about the basis of our pleasure in aesthetic judgment. This section must be approached carefully, and it will be helpful if we first review the picture of Kant's theory so far developed.

The Key to the Critique of Taste

Everything so far considered has led to an interpretation of the judgment of taste as the outcome of a double process of reflection both producing pleasure and evaluating it. In the presence of a particular object, a person experiences pleasure. Given the way we use the predicate "beautiful," he may then ask whether it is universally valid. To answer this question, he seeks to determine the source of his delight. By excluding as the source of his pleasure "personal conditions" to which he alone might be party,[107] or achieving a "consciousness of the separation of anything belonging to the agreeable and the good from the delight remaining to him,"[108] he may attribute his feeling to a ground which "he may presuppose in every other person"—the harmony of the faculties, as §9 will argue—and thereby justify its imputation to others. Such an imputation will be uncertain, because a person must base it on an empirical judgment about his own state of mind, or on a hypothesis about a stretch of his own mental history, where there is always room for error and hidden motivation. But if the person is right about the source of his pleasure, his reflection on it will lead him to the conclusion that it has been produced by "simple reflection" on the object rather than by anything else; and he will take this fact about it to license his claim to speak with a universal voice, or call the object beautiful.

It is a fundamental assumption of this analysis that the occurrence of the feeling of pleasure is logically independent of and prior to that reflection on its intersubjective validity which results in an actual judgment of taste. Simply put, unless the feeling of pleasure precedes reflection on intersubjective validity, there is nothing to reflect about; in Kant's terms, the feeling of pleasure is the ground of determination for the reflective judgment of taste, and must logically precede the latter.[109]* This emerges quite clearly in those passages where Kant explicitly describes a subject making an aesthetic judgment as one reflecting on the sources of a *given* pleasure, seeking to determine whether or not it is grounded in personal or private conditions. Now, if the pleasure in a beautiful object is independent of any consideration of its intersubjective validity, and is instead the precondition of such consideration, it would seem impossible that the fact of intersubjective validity, though a condition of the *judgment of taste,* could itself be the ground or occasion of the *feeling of pleasure.*[110]*

Most of Kant's argument in §9 conforms to this view of aesthetic reflection, and fills in its details by putting the explanatory concept of the harmony of the faculties into its justificatory role. But several apparently key statements in §9 conflict with this view, and threaten to undermine our entire understanding of Kant's theory. I will first show how §9 confirms my interpretation, and then consider the threats to this interpretation.

The purpose of §9 is to investigate the question "whether in the judgment of taste the feeling of pleasure precedes the estimation of the object, or whether the latter precedes the former."[111] Kant is asking whether in the case of aesthetic judgment pleasure must result from some sort of reflection on an object, and his answer — "the key to the critique of taste and so worthy of all attention" — begins just as we would expect:

> If the pleasure in the given object were to precede [the estimation of it], and should only the universal communicability of this pleasure be attributed to the representation of the object in a judgment of taste, then such a procedure would be self-contradictory. For such a pleasure would be none other than mere agreeableness in sensation, and, in accord with its nature, could have merely private validity, because it would depend immediately on the representation through which the object *is given.*[112]*

This first paragraph of §9 is somewhat confusing, for it may suggest that there is a contradiction in merely raising the question of intersubjective validity[113]* in the case of a sensory pleasure, or even worse, that there is a contradiction in the concept of a judgment whose content is simply a claim of intersubjective validity for a felt pleasure. But it seems clear that Kant does not mean to undermine the analysis of aesthetic judgment or the description of aesthetic reflection in this way; obviously, all he means is that universal validity cannot be rationally attributed to a pleasure whose origination precedes all reflection or estimation, and is instead due entirely to sensation. If universal communicability is to be attributed to a given pleasure, then that feeling must be regarded as having been preceded by a use of the higher cognitive faculties in estimation of the object. Only such an origin, and not sensation, could support a claim of intersubjective validity.

After an initial sentence to which we shall shortly return, Kant's next paragraph continues predictably enough:

> But nothing can be universally communicated except knowledge and representation, so far as it belongs to knowledge. For only thus is [representation] objective, and only then does it have a universal point of relation, with which everyone's faculty of representation is obliged to accord. If, now, the ground of determination of the judgment on this universal communicability of representation is to be thought [of] as merely subjective, that is, without a concept, it can be nothing but that mental state which is encountered in the relation of the faculties of representation to each other, so far as they relate a given representation to *knowledge in general.*

This mental state, clearly, is the harmony of imagination and understanding. Thus the third paragraph of §9 goes on: "The cognitive faculties, which are set into play by this representation, are thus in a free play, because no determinate concept limits them to a particular rule of knowledge. Therefore the mental state in this representation must be one of a feeling of the free play of the faculties of representation in a given representation for knowledge in general." Such a free play, we know, is that relation between imagination and understanding which is the subjective condition of knowledge, or the harmony of the faculties. And if it is this state rather than a mere state of sensation which is the source of a pleasure, or which is felt in a given pleasure, then universal communicability or validity can indeed be claimed for that feeling, and the requirement of aesthetic judgment met. For, as the present paragraph concludes, "this condition of a *free play* of the cognitive faculties in a representation, through which an object is given, must allow of universal communication [*muss sich allgemein mitteilen lassen*]: because cognition, as a determination of the object, through which given representations (in whatever subject it may be) must accord, is the only mode of representation which is valid for everyone."[114] Kant must mean, of course, that either knowledge or its subjective condition, and not just actual knowledge itself, is universally valid, or else his whole argument collapses; and, equally obviously, the proof of this thesis remains to be given. But his intention is clear; if a given pleasure can be attributed to the harmony of the faculties rather than to any mere sensation, interest, or other private condition, then it can be attributed to a condition which may indeed be presupposed in every person, as a mental state which may be expected to occur in others, at least under ideal conditions. Thus although aesthetic response can be neither produced nor inferred from the subsumption of an object under any determinate concept, it is linked to a universally valid state of our shared cognitive faculties, and hence is subject to a valid imputation to others.

Thus the fifth paragraph of §9 answers the section's opening question: "Now, this merely subjective (aesthetic) estimation of the object, or of the representation through which it is given, precedes the pleasure in it and is the ground of this pleasure in the harmony of the cognitive faculties; [and] on this universality of the subjective condition of estimation alone is grounded this universal subjective validity of delight, which we connect with the representation of an object when we call it beautiful."[115*] So §9 confirms my interpretation. Simple reflection or estimation of an object produces the harmony of imagination and understanding, thereby producing pleasure; and given the theory of the Introduction, it will do so whether the question of beauty and intersubjective validity is considered or not. But if, once pleasure has been felt, the latter question should be raised, then the universality of this particular source of pleasure can be invoked, or the pleasure itself granted universal subjective validity — supposing, of course, that the question Kant next considers, namely, how we can become conscious of the harmony of the faculties, can be answered.

The "key to the critique of taste," then, consists in Kant's explanation of our pleasure as due to the harmony of the faculties, which is both the fulfillment of the subjective aim of cognition and a source which can justify the imputation of one's own pleasure, subjective feeling though it be, to other persons. Or does it? Two passages from §9 must give us pause. The first of these is the initial sentence of its second paragraph, which I omitted from my earlier quotation. Here, after denying that the judgment of taste can be based on a pleasure which precedes all reflection, Kant says: "therefore it is the universal communicability [*Mitteilungsfähigkeit*] of the mental state in a given representation which, as the subjective condition of the judgment of taste, must serve as its ground [*demselben zum Grunde liegen*], and must have the pleasure in the object as its consequence."[116*] This sentence makes two assertions: that the universal communicability of a state of mind occasioned by an object is the ground or condition for a judgment of taste on that object; and that such communicability is also what produces our pleasure in the object. The first of these assertions is unexceptionable. But the second is remarkable, for it appears to make the fact of communicability the explanation of the pleasure in aesthetic response, or to give intersubjective validity a role in the actual constitution of pleasure, rather than in the mere evaluation of it, which has not figured at all in Kant's explanatory theory.[117] This is problematic, for while the harmony of the faculties could produce pleasure under any circumstances, whether communication is possible or not, the present explanation suggests that in a solipsistic situation, where there is no possibility of communication, one could take no pleasure in a beautiful object. Kant's peculiar early view, that in solitude there is no pleasure in beauty, suddenly seems a serious danger. Further, this assertion is also incoherent, for both the opening paragraph of §9 and its concluding paragraphs make pleasure itself "the mental state in a given representation," and Kant's present statement is thus equivalent to the assertion that the universal communicability of a mental state of pleasure is the cause of that pleasure. This is obviously absurd.

A related difficulty emerges in the fourth paragraph of §9, which I have also omitted from my exposition so far. Here, Kant writes that "the subjective universal communicability of the mode of representation in a judgment of taste, since it is to obtain without presupposing a determinate concept, can be nothing other than the mental state in the free play of imagination and understanding (so far as they harmonize with each other, as is requisite for a *cognition in general*)."[118] This paragraph concludes by asserting, predictably, that this state of harmony is valid for everyone and thus universally communicable, just as is an ordinary determinate cognition. But its opening clauses make the strange claim that the communicability of a representation is itself the mental state of free play. If the fact of communicability were equivalent to the state of the harmony of the faculties, this might explain how the former, instead of the latter, could be said to cause the feeling of pleasure. But, clearly, Kant's statement identifies a property of a mental state with that state itself; and this is not a way out of the circularity implied two paragraphs earlier, but a category mistake just as absurd as that earlier incoherence.

If we did not consider implications from elsewhere in Kant's text, these lines from §9 could be either interpreted or revised without great difficulty. If we did not assume that "the mental state in a given representation" had already been established to be a state or feeling of pleasure, then the first offender could in fact be coherently read as claiming that it is the communicability of a mental state which causes us to take pleasure in it. And the problematic line from the fourth paragraph, even though its identification of a property of a state with that state itself is internally incoherent, could just be revised to bring it into line with such an explanation of pleasure. This sentence could be taken to say, not that the property of communicability *is* the state of free play, but rather that it is the property of that state which *makes* it pleasurable. But such an interpretation of these lines must be rejected. First, it must be noted that Kant himself explicitly abjures an explanation of aesthetic response as due to the fact of communicability, on the ground that this would preclude an analysis of the judgment of taste as in any sense *a priori*.[119*] Kant argues this point in the sixth paragraph of §9:

> That being able to communicate one's mental state (even only in respect to the cognitive faculties), is accompanied by pleasure, could easily be demonstrated (empirically and psychologically) from mankind's natural inclination to sociability. But this is not adequate to our intention. In a judgment of taste, we impute the pleasure we feel to others as necessary, just as if it were regarded as a property of the object, determined to [belong to] it according to concepts.[120]

Though Kant has not yet argued that taste's imputation of pleasure to others is necessarily as well as universally valid, his point is clear enough. To license a judgment of taste, one's pleasure must be attributed to an internal source which may rationally be supposed to exist in others as well.[121] But a psychological inclination to communication, the satisfaction of which might produce pleasure, can be known to exist only by empirical investigation. On the basis of past experience, it may be regarded as an ordinary feature of human psychology, but cannot be presupposed to exist in every human subject, or be attributed to others *a priori*. Thus a pleasure produced by this implication cannot reasonably be imputed to everyone. An object's production of pleasure by such a mechanism could be reported only by the weak assertion "this is agreeable *to me*," or "to me and such others as actually have this inclination."

   That it could ground only an empirical rather than an *a priori* generalization of pleasure is not the only reason why the suggested explanation of aesthetic response by communicability must be rejected, however. A deeper reason lies in the fact that its possible intersubjective validity simply plays

no role in Kant's explanation of how reflective judgment can produce pleasure, or why aesthetic response is in fact pleasurable. Kant's theory is that
the harmony of the faculties causes pleasure because it represents an unusual fulfillment of our most general objective in cognition, the unification
of the manifold of imagination, and neither the Introductions to the *Critique of Judgment* nor the *Critique of Pure Reason* ever argues that universal validity is equivalent to cognition in this sense, or is itself a fundamental
objective in cognition. Kant's characterization of knowledge as the synthesis of a manifold in accordance with rules does not presuppose that such
knowledge must be shared, or even shareable. He explains knowledge in
such a way that even a solipsist could possess it, though his account does
entail that if there are many subjects with similar sensibilities and under-
standings, they will share at least the same framework for knowledge.
There is no reason to suppose that the situation is different when the aim of
cognition is satisfied by the mere subjective condition of harmony rather
than by the subsumption of the manifold under concepts. The implication
of Kant's basic theory of our pleasure in the beautiful is that the occurrence
of the harmony of the faculties occasions pleasure, whether that state is
communicable or not. Of course, the universal validity of the judgment of
taste depends upon the communicability of that state, and the fact of that
communicability might itself be a further ground for pleasure, as Kant
himself has suggested. But the fact of communicability is irrelevant to the
mechanism by which the harmony of the faculties actually produces pleasure in the beautiful; it is crucial to the *judgment of taste,* but not to *aesthetic response* itself.

Thus the thesis which these lines of §9 imply, even when they are freed of
internal incoherence, must be rejected, for they imply a theory of aesthetic
response which is different from that to which everything else in the third
Critique points. How could Kant have suggested an alternative theory of
pleasure in the very section which introduces his real theory of pleasure
into his analysis of taste, and which even explicitly rejects the pretender?
One might just suppose Kant to have been careless; but the errors of these
lines are so great that they call for deeper explanation.

One possible explanation is historical. As noted in Chapter 1, Kant
entertained two alternative theories of aesthetic response for the better part
of the three decades preceding the publication of the *Critique of Judgment.* One of these theories linked our pleasure in the beautiful to the
"facilitation" of knowledge, and eventually became Kant's mature theory
of the harmony of imagination and understanding. The other theory took

the fact of the communicability of a "perfection" to be the cause of pleasure. Either of these theories could be used as long as Kant believed—as he
did as late as 1787—that aesthetic judgments were empirical; but the communicability theory had to be rejected once Kant decided that taste had an
a priori element, as the sixth paragraph of §9 itself reveals. Nevertheless, it
is possible that a theory so long entertained retained a powerful influence,
and exercised it in Kant's exposition in the opening paragraphs of §9.[122]* It
is certainly true that Kant's view that pleasure in the beautiful is not compatible with solitude, originally a consequence of the communicability
theory, retained its grasp on him even in the third *Critique;*[123] and this suggests that Kant may never have become completely clear about the difference between the theory on which communicability is a necessary condition
of aesthetic judgment, and that on which it is a necessary condition not
only for aesthetic judgment but for the occurrence of aesthetic response—
pleasure in the beautiful—itself.

   A less speculative explanation is also possible. In Chapter 3, I noted that
Kant did not introduce a clear terminological distinction between reflection as the source of pleasure and reflection as the condition of the judgment of taste. The first Introduction suggested a distinction between "simple reflection" and "reflective judgment," and §9 itself suggests a distinction between the "estimation of an object" and the "judgment of taste";
but Kant does not use these distinctions consistently.[124] Perhaps this fact
reflects an inadequate understanding of the difference between the two
aspects of reflection which his theory entails. If this is so, then the confu-
sions of §9 might be explained as due to Kant's failure to differentiate
clearly between reflection as leading to pleasure, to which the fact of communicability is irrelevant, and reflection on pleasure as leading to the judgment of taste, to which the communicability of the first form of reflection
is relevant indeed.

   The difficulty with our first problem passage may certainly be diagnosed
in this manner. Kant opened §9 by asking whether, in the case of aesthetic
judgment, the estimation of the object precedes the feeling of pleasure. His
answer began by denying that the pleasure could precede the estimation,
for the reason that such a pleasure could only be one of sensation and could
not license an intersubjectively valid judgment. But confusion arose when
Kant then inferred that therefore the universal communicability of a mental state not only must be the ground of the judgment of taste but also must
have pleasure as its consequence, suggesting that the judgment of taste itself precedes the feeling of pleasure.[125]* Obviously, what has happened is

that Kant has conflated the three phenomena considered in his initial question — estimation, pleasure, and the judgment of taste — into two phenomena, a feeling of pleasure and an undifferentiated exercise of reflection identified with the judgment of taste, or judgment of communicability. Considering only these two factors, Kant then concludes that if pleasure cannot precede judgment, then judgment must precede pleasure; so he ends up with the paradoxical suggestion that pleasure is the consequence of the judgment of communicability even though that judgment must in fact presuppose the feeling of pleasure in order to have any subject at all. This inference, of course, depends upon an equivocation between two concepts of reflection, and the appearance of paradox can be removed as soon as we distinguish the simple reflection or estimation which leads to the feeling of pleasure from reflection on the communicability of that pleasure. We can then say that simple reflection has pleasure as its consequence, and precedes it, and that reflection on that pleasure can result in the judgment that it is universally communicable or valid. It is this complex model of reflection which is the "key to the critique of taste."[126]*

The incoherence of the fourth paragraph of §9 may be resolved by dissecting another conflation, in this case not of two stages of reflection, but rather of the facts of the existence of a mental state and its epistemological status. When Kant identifies the universal communicability of a representation with the mental state of the free play of the faculties, what he is doing is identifying a mental state (characterized in terms which explain its pleasurableness) with that aspect of its status which allows it to serve as the ground of an intersubjectively valid judgment. This conflation, too, can be seen as a failure to distinguish adequately between the estimation of the object and the judgment of taste. In this case, it is as if Kant confused the cause of pleasure, the harmony of the faculties, with the condition of aesthetic judgment, universal validity. Once these concepts are separated, the true form of Kant's theory is again apparent. Properly stated, what Kant is arguing is that the harmony of the faculties, as a "free" occurrence of the subjective conditions of knowledge, produces a feeling of pleasure; and this state, as a universally communicable mental state, allows the pleasure it produces to be imputed to others. It is the occurrence of this state which explains aesthetic response, and the fact of its intersubjective communicability which grounds aesthetic judgment.

Properly interpreted, then, §9 does not imply the theory that intersubjective validity is the basis of our pleasure in the beautiful, but instead shows how the criterial requirement of such validity can be fulfilled with an explanation of our pleasure in the beautiful as due to the harmony of the faculties. This section concludes by raising the question of how we actually "become conscious of a mutual subjective accord of the cognitive faculties" — aesthetically, by mere inner sense and sensation, or intellectually, through awareness of an intentional (and concept-directed) activity?[127] I have already discussed Kant's answer to this question in Chapter 3. He asserts that "the subjective unity of the relation can make itself known only through sensation." He then characterizes this sensation as "the enlivening of both faculties," but this is again a conflation of an effect with its cause; the actual "sensation of the effect, which consists in the facilitated play of the two mental faculties . . . enlivened by mutual accord,"[128] must be the feeling of pleasure itself. Thus we return to the problem first raised for the Analytic, that of explaining how reflection can actually attribute a given feeling of pleasure to the harmony of the faculties. The second moment has shown why such an attribution will solve the problem of taste; the moments of disinterestedness and the form of finality will attempt to show how the required reflection may proceed. However, before we can consider those moments, the "quality" and "relation" of the judgment of taste, we must examine Kant's discussion of necessity, or the "modality" of taste.

The Necessity of Aesthetic Judgment

I have argued that Kant's discussion of the subjective universal validity of aesthetic judgment in the second moment of the Analytic both states the fundamental requirement of epistemological status imposed by the judgment of taste, and explains how this condition may be fulfilled. But in his own initial consideration of how the judgment of taste may be distinguished from a mere judgment of sensory pleasure, Kant stated that "the criterion for deciding this difference . . . consists in the claim of a judgment to universal validity and necessity."[129] And in my own rearrangement of the four moments of Kant's analysis, I argued that the moments of quantity and modality, universality and necessity, together define the status of aesthetic judgment, particular claims to which are to be justified by reference to the moments of quality and relation. We must then ask whether the requirement of necessity in fact differs from the requirement of universality.

Ordinarily, universality and necessity are neither identical nor inseparable. True universal statements need not be necessarily true; witness the difference between "All ravens are black" and "All bachelors are unmarried."

And it has at least been supposed that necessarily true statements need not be universal statements; consider the difference between "God exists" and "Socrates exists." Yet in the first *Critique* Kant argued that the transcendental requirements of universality and necessity are always coextensive; he asserted that "necessity and strict universality are thus sure characteristics of *a priori* knowledge, and are inseparable from each other."[130] The fulfillment of either criterion, Kant held, entails the fulfillment of the other, and it is only advisable to use the two criteria separately because it may sometimes be easier to demonstrate "empirical limitation" than contingency, or to show necessity rather than "unlimited universality." How are these two moments related in the case of aesthetic judgment? Are the universality and necessity of a judgment separate requirements, or do they both impose the same condition on our reflection on feelings of pleasure?

Kant's exposition in the opening sections of the fourth moment suggests the latter interpretation, for his description of the requirement of necessity is almost indistinguishable from his exposition of the demand for universality. His argument in §18, which is to say "what the modality of a judgment of taste is," starts differently than §8, but reaches the same conclusions. Kant begins by associating different forms of aesthetic judgment with the three varieties of modality. A synthesis of pleasure with any representation is at least possible; in calling an object "*agreeable* I assert that it *actually* causes pleasure in me"; but in the case of the beautiful, we are concerned with "a necessary connection to delight."[131] These categories were not mentioned in §8, which instead employed a contrast between universal and singular judgments to characterize the claim of taste. But Kant's explanation of the "peculiar kind" of necessity involved in aesthetic judgment does not seem new. It is not a "theoretical objective necessity," which would allow us to make the ideal prediction or know *a priori* "that everyone *will feel* this delight in the object called beautiful by me." Nor is it a "practical" necessity, derivable from "concepts of a pure rational will." And, obviously enough, it cannot be "inferred from the universality of experience (a thoroughgoing unanimity of judgments on the beauty of a particular object)," because no amount of empirical evidence can itself sustain a claim of necessity. Rather, Kant asserts, the necessity involved in aesthetic judgment can "only be called *exemplary*": it is "the necessity of the assent of *all* to a judgment which is regarded as an example of a universal rule which cannot be furnished."[132] Kant's descriptions of what the necessity of aesthetic judgment is not are reminiscent of §8's statements that the general or public validity of taste is derived neither from concepts nor from the "actually quite extensive unanimity" which often prevails in sensory prefer-ences.[133] His explanation of what this necessity is was anticipated by §9's assertion that "in a judgment of taste, the pleasure which we feel is im-puted to others as necessary, just as if it were a property of the object, determined to [belong to] it according to concepts."[134] The idea that the necessity of everyone's assent allows us to regard the judgment as an exam-ple of a universal rule which cannot actually be stated seems to be an addi-tion; but it is similar to the notion of agreement with a concept "regard-less" of any particular concept which is employed in the first Introduc-tion.[135] Both are merely clumsy ways of stating that in aesthetic judgment certain of the ordinary consequences of knowledge obtain without the actual application of a concept, because certain of cognition's usual condi-tions are fulfilled. Thus the characterization of aesthetic judgment's neces-sity as "exemplary" is not a new element in Kant's analysis.

In §19, Kant also simply reiterates his earlier thesis: "the judgment of taste imputes agreement to everyone, and whoever declares something beautiful intends that everyone *should* give the object concerned his ap-proval and likewise declare it beautiful." The term "should" may connote a sense of necessity, but *what* is necessitated is precisely what has been at-tached to the judgment of taste by the second moment, namely, the agree-ment of all. This section is important, for it amplifies §8's concluding char-acterization of the claim of taste as conditional, making it clear that aes-thetic judgment always retains an element of uncertainty. As Kants puts it, "The *should* in aesthetic judgments . . . is yet pronounced only condition-ally. One courts everyone else's agreement, since one has a ground that is ·common to all; and one could also count on this agreement, if one were only always certain that the case had been correctly subsumed under that ground as a rule of approval."[136] As he did before, Kant suggests that one cannot in fact be certain that a given pleasure has been correctly attributed to a common ground — that is, the harmony of the faculties. Kant separates the question of the rationality of aesthetic judgment from the question of its certainty, and thus frees the eventual deduction of aesthetic judgment from the impossible task of showing that there can be no errors in taste.[137*] But, in spite of this significance, §19 does not show that the moment of necessity actually adds a new feature to Kant's analysis of taste.

This is not to say that the fourth moment is of no interest.[138*] In fact, the similarities between the formulations of the claim of taste offered in the second and fourth moments suggest that both universality and necessity must be mentioned in the statement of this demand. What taste actually calls for is necessary agreement in response, though this agreement will occur only under ideal conditions, and the assertion that it obtains is never completely certain. Kant himself makes it clear that agreement alone is not a sufficient condition for aesthetic judgment when he argues that even quite considerable unanimity in mere sensory pleasure cannot license a judgment of taste, because it is contingent. Similarly, his insistence that actual disagreement does not mean that a judgment of taste is false shows that it is not simply intersubjective validity which aesthetic judgment requires, but rather an agreement which is necessary, though only under ideal conditions.[139] What the judgment of taste requires as a condition of calling an object beautiful is that it occasion a pleasure which could be felt — and which under ideal conditions would be felt — by any human observer of that object, because it is produced by the object's effect on a ground common to all. And in attributing a pleasure to such a source, one is claiming that it is a pleasure which is in a sense necessary rather than contingent. A pleasure due to the harmony of imagination and understanding is a pleasure which one has just in virtue of possessing the faculties necessary for cognition, rather than because of some contingent fact about one's own physiology or interests. It is by assigning a pleasure such status that one makes rational its imputation to other persons.

Both the moments of universality and necessity ultimately place the same demand on the judgment of taste. Both require that a person calling an object beautiful rationally expect that others will take pleasure in it, unless he has in fact erred in assigning his own pleasure to its proper source. This demand can be met only if the pleasure is attributed to a ground which is neither private nor contingent, but is instead a necessary constituent of human nature; in other words, the demand of taste can be met only by an object which disposes one's imagination and understanding to the harmonious state of free play. In the words with which Kant concludes §9, "A representation which is singular and not compared to others, yet nevertheless is harmonious with the conditions of generality, which constitute the business of the understanding in general, brings the cognitive faculty to the proportionate disposition which we require for knowledge in general and which we therefore also hold valid for everyone who must judge through understanding and sense together (for every human)."[140] The attribution of pleasure to the harmony of the faculties to answer the demand for subjective universal validity thus furnishes precisely what Kant takes the moment of necessity to require — namely, a "subjective principle . . . which determines what pleases or displeases, through feeling and not through concepts, but yet with universal validity."[141]

From one point of view, my argument may suggest that it is actually the requirement of necessity which is fundamental to the judgment of taste. For the demand for universal validity can be satisfied only by a pleasure which is connected with a necessary rather than a contingent feature of the subject; and one can rationally believe that the requirement of intersubjectivity is satisfied only if one believes that a given pleasure is in this sense necessary rather than contingent. In the justification of an aesthetic judgment, in other words, it is the necessity rather than the universality of a feeling of pleasure which is the decisive criterion. But there are also both analytical and strategic reasons for considering the requirement of universality first, as Kant does. First, it is by means of this demand that Kant connects his analysis with the pretheoretical intuitions about taste that constitute the extrasystematic anchor of his argument. Ordinary language supports taste's claim to universal agreement, and it is only to *answer* this claim that we must discover a necessary source of pleasure. Second, the debate about taste from which Kant's aesthetics emerged focused on the possibility of agreement in taste, rather than on the idea of necessity in aesthetic response. In view of this, it is only natural that Kant's strategy is first to stake out his position with his thesis that the possibility of agreement is a condition of taste, and then to defend it with a proof that taste possesses an "exemplary" necessity.

The proof that our pleasure in the beautiful in fact enjoys such status has yet to come; and before we come to that, we must consider Kant's justificatory criteria of taste. However, one final point about Kant's concept of necessity in his analysis of taste should be made. In the fourth moment, Kant has argued that the judgment of taste requires that one's delight in a beautiful object be regarded as having a "necessary relation" to that object. Yet he also suggests that it cannot be necessarily true of a beautiful object that it is beautiful, for it cannot be known *a priori* that a given object is beautiful. Rather, Kant insists, one's connection of pleasure to an object — a connection presupposed in judging it to be beautiful — can be made only on the basis of actual experience of the object, or empirically. This was implied earlier in §8, when Kant said that even when one intends to speak with taste's universal voice, one must also have "the object submitted to one's own eyes."[142] The point is made more explicitly when Kant prepares to present the deduction of aesthetic judgment. Thus in §37 Kant writes:

That the representation of an object is immediately connected with pleasure can only be internally perceived and would, if one wished to indicate nothing more than this, yield only a merely empirical judgment. For I cannot connect a determinate feeling (of pleasure or displeasure) with a representation *a priori,* except where an *a priori* principle of reason serves as a ground determining the will; [but] the pleasure (in moral feeling) . . . cannot even be compared with the pleasure in taste, for it requires a determinate concept of a law; whereas the latter should be immediately connected with simple estimation prior to any concept.[143]

On the one hand, the delight which grounds an aesthetic judgment must be a necessary delight; but on the other, except in the irrelevant case of moral feeling, no pleasure can be connected *a priori* with the representation of an object. How, "although the predicate (the personal pleasure connected with the representation) is empirical,"[144] can its connection to the object possess any necessity?

The answer to this question lies in interpreting Kant's present denial of apriority as founded on his thesis that the reflection leading to aesthetic judgment links the feeling of pleasure to the subjective state of the harmony of the faculties rather than to any subsumption of the object of pleasure under concepts. That is, Kant is arguing that the predication of delight of a beautiful object is not *a priori,* in the sense that it is not entailed by the predication of any determinate concept of that object. Thus the paragraph just quoted from §37 concludes by reminding us of the thesis of §8: pleasure cannot be connected to an object *a priori,* for "all judgments of taste are singular judgments, since they do not connect their predicate of delight with a concept, but with a given singular empirical representation."[145] One's judgment that an object is beautiful cannot proceed from any conceptual characterization of the object, but must await one's own experience of it.

But to deny that the feeling of pleasure can be produced *a priori* is not to deny that one's reflection on one's pleasure can produce an *a priori* judgment, or that the *judgment of taste* has an *a priori* element. For reflection on one's pleasure in an object can reveal that the feeling is due to a necessary rather than a contingent source, or a public rather than a private condition, even though it could not have been predicted in advance that the object would in fact please. Once having felt the pleasure, one can attribute it to the harmony of the faculties. On the basis of this attribution, the *a priori* judgment that the object is beautiful—that the pleasure it produces may be imputed to others — can be made. As Kants puts it: "Thus it is not the pleasure which is represented *a priori* in a judgment of taste as a universal rule for judgment, valid for everyone, but the *universal validity of this pleasure.* That I perceive and estimate an object with pleasure, is an empirical judgment. But that I find it beautiful, that is, that I may impute that delight to everyone as necessary, is an *a priori* judgment."[146] My pleasure in a given object must wait upon my experience of it, and a judgment which merely reports that I feel such pleasure is thus a purely empirical judgment. This is so whether my pleasure is produced by simple reflection or by a merely sensory process. But if I take the further step of reflecting on the sources of my pleasure, then I may judge — though still empirically — that my pleasure is necessary rather than contingent, and this licenses its *a priori* imputation to others.

The judgment that a given object is beautiful thus has both empirical and *a priori* elements. Insofar as it reports my own pleasure, it is empirical, for it depends on my experience of the object. And insofar as it attributes my pleasure to the harmony of the faculties, it is also empirical, for it is a judgment about a particular causal link in my own mental history. But insofar as it takes the last attribution as a basis for imputing my pleasure to others, the judgment of taste is *a priori*. For it depends not upon actual experience of shared responses, but on the *a priori* assumption that what occasions the harmony of the faculties is the same for all. And since the imputation of pleasure to others is part of the actual content of a judgment of taste, this judgment not merely rests on an *a priori* assumption, but also makes an *a priori* claim.[147]*

That a single judgment — the judgment of beauty in a given object — can be made both empirically and *a priori* is possible only if it involves two distinguishable acts of reflection. The present analysis thus confirms my interpretation of Kant's model of the mental activity leading to a judgment of taste, as well as the analysis of the apriority of aesthetic judgment suggested at the end of the last chapter. It also shows both where the source of uncertainty in taste lies — in the fact that taste requires hypotheses about one's own mental history — and where the judgment of taste requires further support — namely, in its *a priori* assumption that the harmony of the faculties is indeed similarly produced "in everyone who must judge through understanding and sense together." Before Kant's defense of this assumption can be considered, however, we must consider the criteria by which a given feeling of pleasure can actually be ascribed to the harmony of the faculties. I will begin with Kant's discussion of disinterestedness.

5

The Disinterestedness of Aesthetic Judgment

****

Problems in the Official Exposition

The first moment of the Analytic of the Beautiful defines the "quality" of the judgment of taste by means of a constraint on the states of mind on which it may properly be grounded and to which it may lead. This constraint is not expressed in the opening section of the text, for its claim that "the judgment of taste is aesthetic" states what is merely a presupposition of Kant's entire analysis.[1] Rather, what the moment of quality requires is first stated by the title of §2, which asserts that "the delight which determines the judgment of taste is without any interest."[2] This broad claim is made only slightly more specific in Kant's final statement of the thesis of the first moment at the end of §5. Here, Kant writes that "taste is the faculty of estimating an object or a mode of representation by means of a delight or aversion *without any interest*. The object of such a delight is called *beautiful*."[3] None of these statements directly defines the judgment of taste itself; they instead describe a property of its ground, object, or originating faculty. But it is easy to draw such a definition from Kant's statements: a judgment of taste is a judgment of an object grounded on a delight in it which is without any interest. The fact that a particular pleasure is felt apart from any interest, further, may be referred to as the disinterestedness of that pleasure. Thus the first moment requires that the judgment of taste be made by means of, or on the basis of, a disinterested pleasure.

Two points must be noted immediately. First, Kant's definitions do not mention disinterestedness; what they require is an absence of any interest. So the persuasiveness of Kant's arguments will largely depend on the clarity of his conception of interest. Second, Kant's statements apparently deny *any* connection between interest and the pleasure of aesthetic response. The first moment does not merely assert that our pleasure in the beautiful cannot *originate* from any interest, or, as Kant puts it in §5, that in the case of the beautiful "no interest, whether of the senses or of reason, extorts approval."[4] Kant's bald denials of *any* connection between interest and aesthetic response also imply that the pleasure in the beautiful does not *create* any interest in its object. This implication is made explicit in a footnote to §2, where Kant asserts that "in themselves judgments of taste found no interest at all."[5]

To secure the argument of the first moment, then, we have to explain both why pleasure in the beautiful must originate apart from any interest and why it cannot lead to any interest in the existence of its object; to establish that it contributes a criterion for the justification of aesthetic judgment, we must discover how the absence of an interest may be recognized. But none of this may easily be achieved with the simple definition of interest (*Interesse*) as any "pleasure which we connect with the representation of the existence of an object"[6] that opens the argument. Consequently, the argument of the present chapter will be complex. First, I will have to demonstrate the difficulties that arise in attempting to interpret Kant's analysis of disinterestedness by means of the third *Critique*'s official definition of interest. Next, I will introduce another concept of interest, drawn from Kant's writings on moral philosophy, and argue that Kant's arguments may be better understood on the basis of this concept; but I will also show that the apparent force of some of Kant's stronger claims must be reduced if they are to be founded on this concept of interest. In particular, both his thesis that the pleasure of aesthetic response is not connected to the existence of its object and his thesis that aesthetic judgment grounds no interest in its objects will be shown to have more restricted significance than is often supposed. Only after Kant's definition of interest has been revised and the structure of his arguments untangled will I be able to explain the criterial significance of the moment of disinterestedness.

As we saw, the second moment makes it clear that the requirement of disinterestedness is meant to serve for the justification of judgments of taste. As Kant puts it, if a person is aware that his own pleasure in an object is without any interest, "then he cannot but judge that it must contain a ground of delight for everyone." But this inference assumes that the exclusion of interest from the basis of one's own delight is equivalent to the exclusion of *any* merely private ground for it. This is revealed as Kant continues: "For since [the delight] is not grounded on any inclination of the subject (nor on any other considered interest), but the judging subject feels himself completely *free* in respect of the delight which he accords the object, he can discover no private conditions as grounds for his delight, to which his subject alone is party, and must therefore see it as grounded in that which he may presuppose in everyone else."[7] This argument, however, involves a concept of interest which is either too strong or trivial. If an interest is taken in its normal sense, as something seen as being to one's advantage, then it is surely too strong to assume that every subjective or private ground for delight is an interest; and if an interest is simply any such private ground for pleasure, then Kant's argument is trivial. In any case, this argument cannot itself establish that there *is* any truly public ground for delight. It seems intuitively obvious that the exclusion of delights based on interest will exclude a large number of merely private delights from invalid imputation to others, and thus that the disinterestedness of one's pleasure may be employed in the attribution of pleasure to an intersubjectively valid source in the harmony of the faculties. But this general promise of justificatory significance for disinterestedness cannot be redeemed until we are given a more determinate concept of interest.

How such a concept should be derived is not made clear by the structure of Kant's exposition. As noted at the beginning of the last chapter, Kant writes as if his analysis of aesthetic judgment actually begins with disinterestedness, and as if both the requirement of universal validity and the explanation of aesthetic response expounded in the second moment could be derived from this starting point. But this assignment of analytical priority to the first moment is untenable. Unless interest is simply identified with any private cause of pleasure, the inference that any disinterested pleasure is universally valid is false; and if the identification is made, Kant's argument is circular. Further, as we shall shortly see, Kant's argument for disinterestedness cannot really derive the same sort of support from pretheoretical intuitions as does his analysis of the beautiful as the universally valid. The justificatory role of disinterestedness may make it what is "first regarded" in actually making an aesthetic judgment,[8] but putting the requirement of freedom from interest first in the analysis of aesthetic judgment only draws attention away from what must be our real basis for interpreting Kant's concept of disinterestedness — the fact that the disinterestedness of aesthetic response is a consequence of its explanation as due to the harmony of imagination and understanding, rather than *vice versa*.

In the actual practice of aesthetic reflection, the absence of an interest may be what we look to in attempting to assign a feeling of pleasure to the harmony of the faculties. But at the level of aesthetic theory, the necessity of this procedure must be derived from the antecedent analysis of the requirements of aesthetic judgment and from the explanation of aesthetic response. Kant himself suggests as much in his concluding survey of the Analytic, when he writes that "that is beautiful which pleases in simple estimation (thus not by means of [mere] sensory feeling [nor] according to a concept of the understanding). From this it follows at once that it must please without any interest."[9] Kant's own presentation of the first moment is distorted by a misleading conception of what the argument for its requirement of disinterestedness really is, and by what will turn out to be an inadequate definition of the central concept of interest itself. To arrive at a proper understanding of what Kant's theory really entails, we must follow the lead given in the last quotation, and interpret Kant's analysis of disinterestedness on the basis of his explanation of aesthetic response. But first we must examine Kant's own exposition of his argument.

Kant's analysis of aesthetic judgment calls for a discrimination of the pleasures occasioned by different objects into those which themselves lead to judgments about their objects and those which do not, and, among the former, those which may be imputed to others and those which may not. The first of these distinctions calls for a discrimination of aesthetic response from the pleasure that may accompany moral judgment or action, because the latter is not the basis of any moral judgment. The second distinction requires separating aesthetic response from mere sensory pleasure; both of these pleasures found some form of judgment, but only the pleasure of aesthetic response may be rationally imputed to others.

Such a set of distinctions is the obvious consequence of the definition of the judgment of taste as a universally valid judgment founded on a feeling of pleasure, and in §5 Kant dignifies it with a special vocabulary. An object which merely arouses sensual pleasure, such as some drink or food, is said to "gratify" (*vergnügen*) a person, and is called "agreeable" (*angenehm*). An object which pleases because of its "objective worth" or subsumability under a moral law is called "good," and is "esteemed" or "approved" (*geschätzt, gebilligt*). Finally, an object which "merely pleases" (*gefällt*)[10] is called "beautiful." Alternatively, Kant distinguishes three kinds of delight — not three different feelings, of course, but "three different relations of representations to the feeling of pleasure and displeasure, in relation to which we differentiate objects."[11] There is delight based on inclination, or delight in the agreeable; delight based on respect, or delight in the good; and delight based on favor, or delight in the beautiful.[12]

This division supplies names for the different mental states from which pleasure might result—inclination, respect, and favor—and for the objects which occasion such states—the agreeable, the good, and the beautiful. It is also the classification of pleasures to which Kant connects the criterion of disinterestedness. Kant maintains that "favor" (*Gunst*), or the "taste in the beautiful," is the "one and only disinterested and *free* delight; for with it, no interest, whether of sense or reason, extorts approval." The criterion of disinterestedness is thus claimed to make the same division of pleasures as the classification of pleasures into the agreeable, the good, or the beautiful. Pleasures in the first two sorts of object are always connected to an interest, and only pleasure in the beautiful is free of such connection. In Kant's words, "neither an object of inclination, nor one which is imposed on us as a desire by a law of freedom, leaves us freedom, to make of anything an object of pleasure." Both inclination and rational desire are connected with interest, and "all interest either presupposes a want, or calls one forth; and as the determining ground of approval does not allow the judgment on the object to be free."[13]

In defining the "quality" of aesthetic judgment Kant is not making a phenomenological distinction between different kinds of feelings of pleasure, but a distinction between the ways in which different instances of pleasure may be occasioned. Just because feelings of pleasure are all more or less the same, any classification of a given pleasure must be made by reflection on its context, cause, or object.[14] What Kant is now suggesting, then, is that the presence or absence of a connection to interest may serve as a criterion for the reflective classification of given pleasures. Understood this way, §5's division of pleasures is unexceptionable, and leads us directly to the question of what an interest actually is. An argument in §3, however, threatens to undermine our whole understanding of reflection on pleasure, and thus the present interpretation of the role of disinterestedness. Before we can turn to Kant's characterization of interest, then, we must consider this argument.

The ostensible point of §3 is to show that "delight in *the agreeable* is connected with interest," and that this differentiates it from pleasure in the beautiful. But only the last of the section's four paragraphs actually addresses these concerns. The first three paragraphs, surprisingly, appear to constitute an argument against the thesis that "all delight [*Wohlgefallen*] is (people say or think) itself sensation (of pleasure [*Lust*])." If this is supposed, Kant maintains, then anything that pleases would please because of the agreeableness of the sensation it engenders, and different pleasures would differ only in their intensity or relation to other feelings. "But if that were conceded, then impressions of sense, which determine inclination, or principles of reason, which determine the will, or mere reflected forms of intuition, which determine the faculty of judgment, would all be the same in their effect on the feeling of pleasure";[15] they would all produce mere agreeableness in the sensation of one's state. In that case, none of the labor of these faculties would produce "any evaluation of things and their worth, except that consisting in the enjoyment they promise"; and, Kant implies, nothing but a purely hedonistic comparison between pleasures, concerning their intensity and the ease with which they may be attained, would have any point.[16] Apparently, this conclusion would preclude aesthetic judgment.

This argument is supposed to reveal a danger in supposing that all delight is equivalent to a sensation of pleasure, and Kant responds to it by distinguishing two senses of "sensation." In one sense, this term denotes an "objective representation of sense," or a representation available for knowledge of objects. The sensation of green, for instance, is such an "*objective sensation*," because it can become a component in empirical concepts, such as that of grass. But when "sensation" is used in connection with pleasure or pain, it "is related merely to the subject and does not serve for any knowledge, not even for that by which the subject *knows* itself." This kind of sensation "must always remain purely subjective." It is the form of sensation properly called "feeling." Through it no objects are represented, though on its account objects are regarded as objects of delight.[17]

This distinction is presumably meant to avert the problems consequent to the identification of all forms of delight with sensation. Kant does not say how it does this, however, and in fact this distinction does not avoid the purported difficulty. What he has called for is a distinction between kinds of pleasure, but what Kant supplies is instead a distinction between feelings of pleasure and all other kinds of sensation. If there is in fact a problem in assuming that all pleasures consist in a sensation of gratification, then Kant's distinction only aggravates it; it simply confirms the view that pleasure consists in a special kind of sensation. Further, Kant's exposition of his solution creates another problem. Aesthetic judgment has been argued to depend upon an assignment of one's own feelings of pleasure to their proper source, and that suggests that aesthetic judgment requires a form of self-knowledge. But here Kant seems to deny that the feeling of pleasure can be the basis for any form of knowledge, even self-knowledge.

Fortunately, the failure of Kant's distinction of kinds of sensation to separate kinds of pleasure is not damaging, for in fact he has no need to disprove the view that delight always consists of the same sensation of pleasure — the view, of course, which he himself generally maintains. First, the questionable thesis hardly entails hedonism, as Kant suggests, for the basic identity of all pleasures does not imply that pleasure is the only ground for action. Second, Kant's argument in both the Introductions and §5 is perfectly compatible with the thesis that §3 attacks. Section 5 makes it clear that to distinguish between the agreeable, the good, and the beautiful, we need to differentiate not kinds of pleasure, but rather relationships in which objects stand to the feeling of pleasure, or ways in which they may occasion occurrences of this feeling. While different objects, or different uses of our own faculties (sense, reason, judgment), may all produce the same effect on our faculty of pleasure — namely, a feeling of pleasure — there is still room for discrimination. Even if they involve the same sensation, different occurrences of pleasure can be judged to differ in precisely the way taste requires — in their grounds and in their intersubjective validity.

Further, there is actually nothing in the argument of §3 to undermine the interpretation of Kant's view of aesthetic reflection which I have presented. The distinction between objective and subjective sensation does not in fact entail that pleasure cannot serve for self-knowledge, at least in any sense in which I have claimed it can. This distinction simply asserts that some sensations are referred to the object, and others (pleasures) to the subject; by itself, this implies only that sensations of pleasure cannot provide knowledge *of objects*. This does not affect their potential service for self-knowledge. To be sure, the qualitative identity of all pleasures prevents the mere occurrence of a pleasure from providing knowledge of the path by which one has come to feel it. But the interpretation of Kant's theory of aesthetic response for which I am arguing does not, of course, imply that feelings of pleasure can serve for knowledge in this way; it denies this, and holds only that aesthetic judgments must be based on a kind of knowledge about one's own mental history that arises from reflection on the grounds of one's pleasures.

This is not to say that there is no difficulty at all in thinking of reflection on one's pleasures as producing true *knowledge* of the self, or of the judgment of taste as resting on an acquaintance with the states of the self which fully qualifies as knowledge. We have already seen[18] that Kant's explanation of aesthetic response excludes the use of the ordinary condition of apperception, or of concepts by means of which beliefs about one's own mental states may be verified. Knowledge about the kind of person one is — that

173

one responds in one way to one kind of object, and in another to a second might also seem precluded in the case of a pleasure which cannot be linked to any determinate concept of objects. But the distinction of two kinds of sensation does not itself raise these problems, nor does it create any new difficulty for thinking of reflection on the source of given feelings of knowledge as producing knowledge about one's mental history (or, at least, knowledge *claims* — the condition of uncertainty expressed in §§8 and 19 remains). In any case, using the presence or absence of an interest in connection with a pleasure as a basis for determining the proper classification of that feeling does seem like a cognitive exercise, though one producing knowledge of one's pleasure rather than of an object; and the argument of the first moment as a whole thus suggests that we should ignore §3's apparent denial of this interpretation.

Why Kant should have raised a false problem for his theory, and then offered an irrelevant solution to it, is not easily answered. Perhaps, as in the case of §9's confusion of the origin of aesthetic response with the condition of aesthetic judgment, Kant simply became confused over the distinctions to which his theory commits him, and which he even sometimes states clearly. Kant's theory of taste is based on a distinction between ontological subjectivity and epistemological subjectivity, and §3 appears to confuse these two forms of subjectivity; it is also based on the assumption that the sources of feeling may differ even when the feeling itself is the same, and this too is overlooked. I can give no explanation for such failures, and will simply rely on §3's obvious conflict with §5 and internal incoherence to prevent this section from standing in the way of my discussion.

I will now turn to Kant's own exposition of the argument for the disinterestedness of aesthetic response. This begins in §2 with a definition of interest and an argument for the claim that our pleasure in the beautiful is not connected with an interest so defined; this argument appears intended to appeal not to Kant's own system but to our pretheoretic intuitions, like that of §7. In §§3 and 4, Kant argues that our pleasures in the agreeable and the good do betray the presence of interest.

Kant defines interest as a "delight which we connect with the representation of the existence [*Existenz*] of an object."[19] This is an inauspicious beginning. First, it defines interest as a *kind* of pleasure, rather than a *ground* of pleasure; but if the aim of reflection in aesthetic judgment is to isolate pleasures due to the harmony of the faculties by excluding those *due to* interest, it would seem that interest must be a *source* rather than a kind of pleasure. Second, the significance of the phrase "representation of the existence of an object" is not clear. Other versions of Kant's definition do not include the term "representation." In §4, interest is more simply defined as "delight in the existence [*Dasein*] of an object or action,"[20] and in §41, interest is said to consist in "pleasure in the existence" (*Lust an der Existenz*) of an object.[21] Since representation and actual existence might naturally be taken as opposites, Kant's opening definition can cause confusion.[22*] Finally, just what connection between delight and the existence of its object is intended is obscure; as it stands, the definition would call an interest any delight connected with existence, whether it precede, accompany, or succeed it. This will cause difficulty. To supplement his definition, however, Kant adds only the opaque remark that "such a [delight]²³* is therefore always related to the faculty of desire, either as a determining ground thereof or else as necessarily connected" with such a ground.[24]

The immediate context of Kant's first definition of interest makes it clear that some clarification of his concept of interest is needed. His subsequent definitions make this need even clearer. For they suggest that the difference between interested and disinterested pleasures may be understood by reference to a difference in their intentional objects—namely, that the latter are pleasures in the representations of objects, and the former in their existence. But Kant is the philosopher who introduced the idea that "*being* is obviously not a real predicate,"[25] or that existence is not a genuine property of things. And this means that to link a pleasure solely to the existence of a thing is entirely uninformative. For on a causal account of the objects of pleasure such as Kant's, to link a pleasure to an object is to say that there is some property or disposition of the object in virtue of which it produces pleasure, but the mere fact that a thing exists does not itself characterize it or provide any ground for pleasure. Some further fact about the properties of things, or features *of* their existence, must be linked to the notion of interest before any contrast with aesthetic response can emerge. So if the concept of interest is to be illuminated, it must be by the arguments with which Kant follows his opening definition.

Kant begins these with a series of examples, our intuitions about which are to support the claim that "when the question is whether something is beautiful, one does not want to know whether we or anyone else is at all concerned with the existence of the thing, or even could be, but rather, how we estimate it in mere contemplation (intuition or reflection)."[26] On Kant's definition of interest, proving this would amount to proving the disinterestedness of our response to the beautiful. The examples offered in support of the claim are characteristic responses to the question of whether a given object is beautiful; we are supposed to see that they are all irrelevant, because they reveal an inappropriate concern for existence, and thus an interest. Thus: when asked whether a given palace is beautiful,[27*] I may answer that I do not care for objects made merely to be gaped at; or, like a visiting Iroquois, that I would prefer a good Parisian bistro; or I may reply by decrying the "vanity of the great who waste the sweat of the people on such superfluous things."[28] I may even contend that, could I do so merely by wishing, I would not replace my modest hut with such a palace.[29] All of these answers may have their place, Kant argues, but none of them will be accepted as a reply to the question asked. In this case, "One only wants to know whether the mere representation of the object is accompanied in me with delight, no matter how indifferent I may be to the existence of the object of this representation. One readily sees that in saying an object is *beautiful,* and proving that I have taste, what I can make of this representation in myself is at issue, and not any way in which I might depend on the existence of the object." Our readiness to dismiss all these answers to a request for aesthetic judgment, in other words, is supposed to show that we all acknowledge the difference between contemplation of a representation and approval of actual existence, and that the identity of aesthetic response with the first of these may serve as a starting point for aesthetic theory. The disinterestedness of aesthetic pleasure, it seems, is no special claim, but a matter of common consent: "Everyone must concede that a judgment on beauty, in which the least interest mingles, is very partial [*parteiisch*] and no pure judgment of taste. One must not be in the least prejudiced in favor of the existence of the thing, but be quite indifferent in this respect, in order to play the judge in matters of taste."[30]

That the replies Kant lists will be rejected by anyone who understands the request for a judgment of taste seems clear enough; but it may be questioned whether Kant has here offered an argument as basic as that provided in §7. For one thing, the source of Kant's claims in §2 is not clear. In §7, the thesis that a judgment of beauty requires intersubjective validity was drawn directly from common usage, or argued to be understood by anyone familiar with the correct use of the expression " . . . is beautiful." Kant does not make such a claim in the case of disinterestedness, so it is not clear whether he means to draw on a common usage of *terms* of aesthetic judgment or, what would be less fundamental, a putatively common *theory* of aesthetic response. Moreover, even if it is granted that we would all indeed dismiss Kant's sample answers as inappropriate to the request for a judgment of taste, it is not obvious that we could only do so on the basis of a distinction between mere representation and existence. Without mentioning such a distinction at all, one might contend that these objections arise from applying the wrong kind of standard to an object. They are irrelevant, one might say, because they employ some standard of utility or morality rather than of mere beauty—even, one might add, because they are connected to personal interests rather than free of such concern. This much, anyone at all might indeed concede. But that anyone at all will express this by saying that these replies concern the existence of an object rather than the mere contemplation of its representation is unlikely. Kant must prove that our intuitions about relevant and irrelevant grounds for taste involve this distinction, for it cannot be drawn directly from common usage.

Kant himself suggests that §2's appeal to intuition may not be sufficient to prove the disinterestedness of aesthetic response, let alone his own interpretation of this requirement. He closes the section by saying that there is no better way of demonstrating his thesis than by "contrasting the pure, disinterested delight in the beautiful with that connected with interest: especially if we can also be certain that there are no more forms of interest than those presently to be named."[31] The next two sections, then, do not merely draw conclusions from the argument of §2, but are themselves essential parts of Kant's defense of disinterestedness. How do they fare?

As we have already seen, the discussion in all but the last paragraph of §3 is concerned with the distinction between pleasure and other sensation, and thus irrelevant to a distinction of "quality" among pleasures. Only the last paragraph actually bears on the question of interest. Here, Kant argues that affirming that an object is agreeable expresses an interest in it, "because through sensation it [my judgment, apparently] excites a desire for other objects of the same sort; thus the delight presupposes not the mere judgment in the object, but the relation of its existence to my condition, insofar as it is effected by such an object." Thus we say of the agreeable not that it pleases (*gefällt*), but that it gratifies (*vergnügt*); in the case of the agreeable, there is no "mere approval, but rather inclination is aroused."[32]

This is a peculiar argument. First, it treats interest not as a simple delight in the existence of a given object, but rather as a *desire* for pleasure from objects of a certain type. Agreeableness is interested, it seems, not because of how this pleasure is produced by its object (the chocolate, say, which actually produces one's pleasure), but because it creates a desire for

177

more such objects. On the surface, the existence which is involved in agree-ableness is not that of the given agreeable object, but that of other objects similar to it. Kant may mean to suggest that agreeableness is a delight con-nected with existence, because only the actual existence of an object can have this effect on the faculty of desire, but he hardly states this very clearly. Second, this argument presupposes that delight in the beautiful is disinter-ested, rather than proving it. Kant apparently takes the fact that delight in an agreeable object provokes a desire for more such objects as a ground for distinguishing it from delight in the beautiful,[33*] but this fact entails a dis-tinction only if it is already assumed that in the case of the beautiful there is no interest in the existence of either the given object or others of its type. This was in fact asserted in the footnote to §2,[34] but we are still looking for its proof.

If only an effect of existence on sensation can stimulate desire, then agreeableness would seem to be a delight in the existence of an object, and an interest on Kant's definition, because it does stimulate desire. But the argument of §3 seems to introduce a new conception of interest, as a desire for pleasure from objects of a certain type; and it also assumes what at this point must still be proven about pleasure in the beautiful — that it depends on contemplation rather than sensation, and that it creates no interest. Only by making these assumptions does §3 imply a contrast between the agreeable and the beautiful. This suggests that §3 cannot be taken as a starting point for Kant's theory of aesthetic response, but actually derives consequences from the latter. This, of course, is what is entailed by my reconstruction of the Analytic of the Beautiful.

On the most straightforward reading of §3, the agreeable and the beau-tiful differ, not because any interest precedes delight in the agreeable, but because interest — a form of desire rather than delight — succeeds this kind of pleasure. We might suspect that the good will differ from the beautiful because in its case interest does precede delight. The first two paragraphs of §4[35*] do suggest this. But they also reveal the inadequacy of §2's defini-tion of interest, and further confirm the impression that Kant's discussion of disinterestedness presupposes the argument of the second moment in-stead of introducing it.

Kant defines the good as that "which by means of reason pleases through its mere concept." The good is divided into "the *good for something* (the useful), which pleases only as a means," and the *"good in itself,"* which pleases on its own account. The good for something pleases because it is conceived as a means to something else which pleases, and an object good in itself pleases without reference to any other object at all. But even the latter does please in connection with a concept, for "in both cases there is a concept of an end." Presumably, the good for something pleases because it is a means to something else which fulfills an end, and the good in itself pleases because it itself fulfills an end. Further, because in either of its forms the good involves an end, it also involves "the relation of reason to (at least possible) willing, and thus delight in the *existence* of an object or action, i.e., some interest or other."[36]

Kant thus establishes a connection between the good and interest that, we are apparently to understand, does not obtain in the case of the beautiful. But there are two problems in his continuation of the argument. First, his explicit contrast between the beautiful and the good does not mention interest, but turns on the question of connection to a concept. Second, the move which Kant makes from connection to a concept to connection to interest does not in fact make it clear that our pleasure in the beautiful does not involve "delight in the existence of an object."

In the second paragraph of §4, Kant maintains that to find something good, one must know "what sort of object the thing should be," and thus have a concept of it.[37] That which is good, then, not only can please through its concept, but also cannot be seen as pleasing unless classified under some concept. An object which is judged to be good is judged to be so because it is an instance of a certain concept or class of things, and it pleases as such an instance. This is not the case in the judgment of the beautiful. A beautiful object can please, and be judged to be beautiful, without having any determinate concept applied to it.[38*] Kant illustrates this fact with several examples of objects which can please without consideration of any concept, and lays the ground for a strong restriction on the proper objects of aesthetic judgment. "Flowers, free drawings, lines aimlessly intertwining," or foliage, he says, "signify nothing, depend on no determinate concepts, and yet please." He then asserts that "the delight in the beautiful must depend upon the reflection on an object, which leads to some concept (not definitely determined)." Thus delight in the beautiful differs from that in the good because it requires no reference to a determinate concept; and it also differs from that in the agreeable because it does require some form of reflection.[39]

The idea of reflection leading to an undetermined concept is clumsy, but obviously meant to suggest the notion of reflection producing the harmony of the faculties without using any concept. This concept of reflection is introduced into the present context as if it followed from the preceding contrast between the beautiful and the good; but, in fact, the beautiful has not been contrasted with the good in any way which implies this thesis about it. The first paragraph of §4 does not propose a contrast with the beautiful from which the theory of aesthetic response as a special kind of reflection can be derived. The intention of this section appears to be to argue that because the good is connected to a concept and the beautiful not, the former is connected to an interest and the latter not; but this implied contrast can only be derived if Kant's explanation of aesthetic response as free of any determinate concepts is presupposed. This does not preclude the use of disinterestedness as a criterion for particular aesthetic judgments, but does undermine Kant's pretense of beginning the argument of the Analytic from the fact of disinterestedness.

By assuming that the judgment of beauty does not require applying a determinate concept to an object, or classifying an object as an instance of a given kind, §4 does reveal one difference between the judgment of beauty and the judgment of goodness. Judging an object to be good does seem to require subsuming it under some concept; for instance, to decide whether the splashing about at the end of the dock is good, one must know whether it is an attempt at water ballet or an attempt to save a drowning child. One does not need to know anything like this to decide whether it is beautiful. But this difference does not entail that the pleasure in the beautiful is disinterested, so long as interest is defined merely as delight connected with real existence. What the opening paragraph of §4 argues is that conceiving of something as good implies a delight in its existence, because such a conception of an object is a reason for willing its existence. But this does not entail that we can have an interest in an object only if it is judged to be good, or that seeing an object as good under some concept is necessary for taking a delight in its existence. Unless we know more about Kant's notion of existence, it cannot be obvious that a delight felt in an object without any subsumption of it under a concept is not a delight connected with existence.

The last paragraph of §4 might be thought to argue the disinterestedness of pleasure in the beautiful more successfully. Here, after having discussed various differences between the agreeable and the good, Kant argues that the agreeable, the useful, and the morally good are all alike "in being invariably coupled with an interest in their object." This is because each of these may be an object of the will; and "to will something and to take a delight in its existence, i.e., to take an interest in it, are identical."[40] If this is so, then that which is not an object of the will is not an object of interest, and if the beautiful is not an object of the will, then our pleasure in it is not connected with an interest.

But an argument of this form — the final steps of which Kant does not actually assert — would also fail to prove that our delight in the beautiful is not connected to any interest. For Kant has shown neither that the beautiful cannot be an object of the will, nor that willing something and taking a delight in its existence are identical.

Obviously, anything seen as a good may also serve as an end or an object of will. The good is that which pleases through its concept, or, we might say, an object the concept of which promises pleasure in advance of its actual existence.[41]* In the third moment, Kant defines an end as "the object of a concept so far as this concept is regarded as the cause of the object (the real ground of its possibility)."[42] An object the mere concept of which promises pleasure is obviously fit to be an end. Since the concept promises pleasure, it will be an incentive for its own instantiation — for the actualization of the object which will fulfill the promise of pleasure. Thus a thing seen as good can become an end, or an object of the will; in Kant's terms, its concept can be the cause of its own existence, or the real ground of its possibility. And once we connect the concept of a good to the concept of an end, we can establish a further connection with the concept of real existence. For while it is not obvious that willing something is identical with taking a delight in its existence, it does seem that willing presupposes such a delight, for willing something is identical with willing its existence. When we will something we act in ways designed to bring it into existence; we might even say that willing is meant to add existence to something we already have the concept of. Presumably, we act in such a way because we expect to take pleasure in the existence of the object of our will. Thus we will what we take to be a good, because the delight promised by conceiving of something as a good is, in fact, a delight in its existence.

But although this analysis may establish that we have or expect a delight in the existence of anything we will, it establishes neither that willing always requires a concept which promises pleasure nor that willing something and taking pleasure in its existence are identical. A concept of a thing as good, or good for something, may be a ground for willing its existence, but is not obviously the only such ground. And though willing something may presuppose that we expect a delight in its existence, it does not follow either that willing *is* taking a delight in the existence of an object, or that we can take pleasure in the existence only of objects that may be willed.

If we assume Kant's theory of aesthetic response, then we may suppose that the beautiful cannot be an end or object of the will in a certain sense. For that theory holds that there is no determinate concept under which a beautiful object may be subsumed which entails that we take pleasure in it, and if a concept's promise of pleasure is what acts as an incentive for the will, then we cannot have such a promise in the case of the beautiful. At the same time, however, the very fact that we do take pleasure in the beautiful would seem to suggest that beauty may affect the will. In the *Anthropology*, it will be recalled, Kant defines pleasure—whether it be due to the senses or to the imagination—as "what directly prompts me to maintain [my] state,"[43] and within the text of the Analytic of the Beautiful itself this is asserted to be true of pleasure in the beautiful. "Even this [pleasure] has an inner causality, namely, to preserve the condition of representation itself and the occupation of the cognitive faculties without a further objective [*Absicht*]."[44] If the pleasure of aesthetic response is like any other pleasure, then on Kant's own account it must create an inclination toward its own continuation. And if that pleasure is produced by the effect of an object on the imagination and understanding, so that the object is a condition of the occurrence of the pleasure, the continued existence of the object will presumably also be an object of the inclination which Kant links with pleasure, almost by definition. It would seem, then, that the beautiful may in fact be an object of the will—or, at least, of inclination—and thus may be connected to an interest.[45*]

Kant's argument in the first moment is seriously flawed. First, there is the fact that it actually presupposes the theses expounded in the second moment, rather than leading to them. But there are difficulties in its content as well as in its structure. In §3, Kant differentiates pleasure in a beautiful object from that in an agreeable one by claiming that the latter produces an interest in further experiences of the same sort, and implying that the former does not. However, it appears to be a defining characteristic of any kind of pleasure that it produce an interest in its own continuation, and this makes the difference between the beautiful and the agreeable obscure indeed. In §4, Kant distinguishes pleasure in the beautiful from that in the good by reference to the fact that the latter, but not the former, presupposes the application of a concept to its object. But it is not apparent why this should mean that only the delight in a good object is connected with its existence, or is an interest as defined by §2. Nor is it obvious why its independence from determinate concepts should prevent the beautiful from being an object of the will—especially given Kant's own theory of pleasure — and thus the object of an interest in an ordinary sense. Even if it seems plausible that aesthetic judgment cannot be determined by any prior interest, the thesis that the judgment of beauty creates no interest in its object is certainly implausible.[46*] The beauty of irreplaceable masterpieces like the Parthenon or *The Last Supper* seems to provide very good reason indeed for even strenuous and expensive efforts for the continued existence of these objects; and nothing in Kant's argument appears adequate to undermine our temptation to think of such efforts as stemming from an interest produced by aesthetic judgment.

Interests and Concepts

Without a more informative concept of interest, Kant's theory of disinterestedness threatens to collapse. Both the precise nature of the connection between delight and existence in the case of an interest and the meaning of the concept of existence itself need clarification. In fact, a basic problem with the argument I have been considering is that it employs an overly simple definition of interest, equating an interest with any state of delight connected in any way with the existence of an object, when a more complicated definition is required. Such a definition is suggested by the *Critique of Practical Reason.* In this work — published only two years before the *Critique of Judgment,* and undoubtedly fresh in the memories of both author and readers of the later work — Kant defines an interest as "an incentive of the will so far as it is presented by reason."[47] This definition reveals that an interest is too complex to be simply equated with a kind of pleasure. Rather, it involves two components: it is a mental state which is an incentive, or furnishes a motive for action; and it does this by means of the application of a particular concept to an object or action. That is, through reason it represents something as a reasonable end or object of the will; and reason surely works through concepts. On this definition, an interest may *presuppose* a delight in the existence of an object if a particular conceptualization of an object acts as an incentive for the will by promising a delight in its existence. But the interest is more intelligibly equated with the conceptualization of the object as promising delight than with the feeling of pleasure itself.

One passage in the *Foundations of the Metaphysics of Morals* might be read as supporting the third *Critique*'s definition of interest rather than that taken from the second. In a footnote in the third section of this work, Kant defines interest as "that by which reason becomes practical, i.e., a cause determining the will."[48] If a feeling of pleasure itself can determine the will to a particular action, then this definition may be thought to equate interest with such a feeling. But even in the *Foundations,* the concept of interest always involves a role for reason and thus, one may suggest, a role for a concept of the object of the will. An earlier footnote in this work defines interest as "the dependence of a contingently determinable will on principles"; and even in the case of a "pathological interest in the object of the action," or an interest founded in mere feeling or inclination, the will is dependent on "principles of reason for the purpose of inclination, since reason . . . gives the practical rule by which the needs of inclination are to be aided."[49] This suggests that even if an interest is *founded* on pleasure or the expectation of pleasure, it cannot be *equated* with such a feeling of delight. In a rational creature — even when it acts pathologically, and reasons only instrumentally — the will is determined by rules of reason; at the least, an interest must thus be a practical rule by which the satisfaction of inclination may be aided. Such a rule would be a concept of an object as promising delight, and not a feeling of delight itself.

Such an interpretation may also be derived from another passage in the *Critique of Practical Reason,* where Kant defines an "object" or "material" of the faculty of desire as a "determining ground of the will." This, in turn, is defined as "the conception of an object and its relation to the subject, whereby the faculty of desire is determined to seek its realization."[50] A determining ground of the will is a conception of an object which offers a reason for efforts toward its realization, or toward its existence. Such a conception would seem to be equivalent to an incentive for the will; and if "from the concept of an incentive there comes that of an interest,"[51] then an interest must also either be or depend on a conception of an object which offers a reason for its realization.

We must be careful about the way in which pleasure and the existence of objects are linked in this interpretation of interest. In his discussion of the material of the will in Theorem I of the second *Critique,* Kant specifies the relation to the subject which determines the will as "pleasure in the reality of the object" — a phrase obviously synonymous with the third *Critique*'s phrase "delight in the existence of an object." This suggests that the reason for action toward the realization of an object is always a pleasure promised or predicted by the classification of the object under a determinate concept, as a consequence of its existence; and this seems to be confirmed by Kant's declaration that this relation "must be presupposed as the condition of the possibility of the determination of the choice."[52] Such a promise could be founded on past experience of a given sort of object as always accompanied by a feeling of pleasure, with that feeling then being taken up into the empirical concept of that sort of object; that being done, thinking of a given object as of that sort would then promise pleasure.

This explanation of interest would not equate it with pleasure in the existence of the object, but would link it closely to the latter, for a promise of such pleasure would always be the basis of interest. Such a conception would allow us to see how an interest may be formed in the case of the agreeable, and in the case of the mediately good, which is a means to the pleasure of agreeableness. But it would also seem to limit the application of the concept of interest to these cases of pleasure. This would undermine Kant's connection of interest to the good in itself, and thus his differentiation of the beautiful from the good by reference to interest. It is obvious, however, that Kant's conception of interest is not so limited, and thus that a promise of pleasure in its existence is not the only conception of an object which serves as an incentive for the will, or as an interest. In the case of a moral determination of the will, the expectation of pleasure in the existence of the object of action is not the reason for acting. Instead, the subsumption of an object or action under the formal law of reason, the categorical imperative, itself creates a reason for its realization, and thus an interest in the action itself, or a moral interest.

That the central contention of Kant's ethics is that the will both may and must be determined by reason alone, or that "the sole principle of morality consists in independence from all material of the law (i.e., a desired object) and in the accompanying determination of choice by the mere form of giving universal law,"[53] hardly needs proof here. Nor does it have to be argued that it is Kant's view that "respect for the moral law is therefore the sole and undoubted moral incentive."[54] What does need emphasis, however, is the fact that this means that interest may be founded on moral law as well as on pleasure, and that for this reason too the concept of interest cannot be explained as simply delight in the existence of an object. Kant makes it clear that moral law as well as pleasure gives rise to interest in several places. In the *Foundations,* he contrasts "pathological interest in the object of the action" with "practical interest in the action" itself; the former is based on inclination, on the expectation of pleasure from the object of the action, and the latter involves "only the dependence of the will on principles of reason in themselves."[55] The same work also distinguishes two kinds of interest, the moral and the pathological, as "direct" and "indirect" interest. "A direct interest in [any] action is taken by reason only if the uni-

versal validity of its maxim is a sufficient determining ground of the will";
such an interest is "pure." If, however, the will is determined "by means of
another object of desire or under the presupposition of a particular feeling
of the subject" — for instance, pleasure in the existence of an object — then
reason takes an interest in action which is indirect, empirical, and "not a
pure interest of reason."[56]

It is beyond doubt that Kant's ethics postulates an interest in action
which is founded on purely formal considerations, as well as an interest
founded on pleasure in the reality of objects.[57*] The only question is
whether there is any way in which a connection between the idea of interest
as a formal incentive for action and the idea of interest as a conception of
an object which promises pleasure in its existence may be preserved.

The answer to this lies in an analysis of the concept of willing and in
Kant's theory of moral feeling as a subjective delight in moral action. First,
as we have seen, willing something is always willing the existence of some
object or state of affairs. Whatever else it may be, "the will is the faculty
which makes a rule of reason the efficient cause of an action which can
make an object real."[58] This is so whether the rule of reason involved is a
merely material rule, predicting pleasure in connection with the object, or
is a formal law. Thus any incentive to will or realize an object is an incentive to will its existence, even when that incentive is merely the formal conformity of the proposed willing to the moral law. But second, at least in
human beings, even moral willing is often connected with a feeling of pleasure. Although willing something on the ground of its moral correctness is
not willing it *because* of an expected pleasure, such willing does bring
about a "subjective feeling of satisfaction," which seems to be a feeling of
pleasure.[59*] But this feeling of pleasure does not depend on the actual existence of an object; for it is a consequence of the correctness of one's act of
willing, and this does not depend on success in realizing the object of the
will. The pleasure that arises from morally correct willing is thus also independent of whether or not a morally motivated action succeeds in its effect,
and hence independent of the actual existence of the willed object. Nevertheless, because willing is always willing existence, even the pleasure of
satisfaction in moral willing is linked with the representation of the existence of an object, in that it is connected with willing this existence, though
not causally dependent on it.

Kant suggests something of the actual complexity of the relations between pleasure, desire, and existence subsumed under the general concept
of interest in the *Metaphysics of Morals,* a later work than the *Critique of*

Judgment. Here, Kant makes it clear that pleasure may be related to the faculty of desire (and thus to action) in two different ways, and that the concept of interest comprehends both relations. "The pleasure which is necessarily connected with desire," Kant states, "may be called practical pleasure, whether it is the cause or the effect of the desire"; and as long as such a connection may be perceived by reason, it may be called an interest: "the connection of pleasure with the faculty of desire, insofar as this connection is judged to be valid according to a general rule . . . is called interest."[60]* Thus an interest is present whether a feeling of pleasure, expected or actual, is the cause or effect of a given desire or determination of the will. In the case of "the determination of the faculty of desire which is caused by" and, accordingly, preceded by this pleasure, "we have appetite or inclination, [and an] interest or inclination. On the other hand, if the pleasure can follow only upon an antecedent determination of the faculty of desire, then it is an intellectual pleasure, and the interest in the object must be called an interest of reason."[61]

A view of this sort is basic to Kant's moral philosophy, and makes it clear that the simple definition of interest as delight in the real existence of an object which Kant employs in the third *Critique* is misleading. The connections between interest, pleasure, and existence are, in fact, complicated. If an interest is defined as a conception of an object which furnishes an incentive for the will, or as a conception of an object and its relation to the subject whereby the faculty of desire is determined to seek its realization, we can see what these connections are. First, an interest is always a concept of an object or action which has a relation to the faculty of desire: it is a cognitive representation which is an incentive for that faculty. Second, an interest is always connected to the existence of an object, for an incentive of the will is always an incentive to will the existence of something. Third, interest is always connected to delight, for an incentive to will something is either a promise of pleasure in its existence or the conformity of the object of the will to the moral law, the consciousness of which produces a feeling of or like pleasure. Delight either is promised in the real existence of something, and thus a reason for willing, or is a consequence of the willing.

On this more complex definition of interest, aesthetic response is certainly disinterested in origin, and differs from the pleasures in the agreeable and the good in being so. Since an interest, whatever else it is, is always a concept of an object, and since the beautiful is the object of a judgment made apart from any concept of an object, the beautiful must be the object of a judgment made apart from any interest. This provides an easy contrast between judgments of beauty and judgments of goodness. Since a judgment on the goodness of an object depends on a particular conception of the object, and can create an interest in it only through that conception, judgments of goodness and of beauty are not identical. This is true if the goodness is mediate, and we are interested in a given object only because of some inclination that it may fulfill, or if the goodness is absolute, and we are interested in the object because of the moral law. It must be noted, however, that this differentiation of judgments of the beautiful and the good turns not on interest's connection to *existence,* but on its connection to *concepts*—a fact reflected by Kant's actual argument in §4.

The difference between the beautiful and the *agreeable* with respect to interest, however, is less obvious. The delight in an object or action judged to be morally good is interested because it presupposes a concept. The delight follows from the subsumption of the object under a moral conception, or practical law, and the resolution to act under the law. The delight in something agreeable, however—ultimately, any delight which is not moral or aesthetic, since the ends of action are either the formal end of conformity to the moral law or the material end of pleasure—does not presuppose an interest. An agreeable object pleases by means of a purely physiological effect on the senses, and no particular conception of the object is required for its production of this pleasure. However, if the experience of pleasure in an agreeable object does depend on the senses alone, and is due to a causal relation between properties of the object and one's own physiology, then one may come to believe in a lawlike connection between objects of that sort and the experience of pleasure—at least for oneself. [62]* Past experiences of pleasure from objects of a given sort might lead to the inclusion of a promise of pleasure in one's own empirical concept of that sort of object. This concept could then form the basis of an interest. Given one's past experiences of agreeableness, thinking of a given object under a certain concept—say, chocolate—would provide a promise of pleasure, and thus an incentive for action toward the realization or possession of the object. Agreeableness may presuppose no interest, but in this way it can produce one.

This conclusion does show how connection to an interest distinguishes pleasure in the agreeable from that in the beautiful, though it does depend on Kant's special concept of interest. For pleasure in the beautiful cannot produce an interest of the type just described. The pleasure derived from a particular beautiful object, according to Kant's theory, is not associated with any general concept under which the object may be subsumed, and cannot be linked with the predicates defining such a concept. Thus this pleasure cannot be predicted of an object in virtue of its having the features picked out by any empirical concept, and the representation of an object as having such features could not serve as an incentive by promising the pleasure of aesthetic response. Although the associability of sensual pleasure with the characteristic properties of chocolate might make the representation of anything as chocolate an incentive—at least for me—there is no such representation connected with the pleasure in beauty. Since no classification of an object under a determinate empirical concept is involved in its production of the harmony of the faculties, no inference to beauty may be drawn from any particular conceptualization of it. While what makes something a sonata or statue may be determinable by concepts, what makes it beautiful is not; and if we take pleasure in something not because it is a sonata or statue, but because it is a beautiful one, then whatever concepts we can predicate of an object of aesthetic response will not serve to found an interest. In this way, then, beauty does not produce interest.

This argument, however, has limited force, for it turns on the thesis that an interest always requires a general concept. Apart from its freedom from determinate concepts, there is nothing in Kant's explanation of our pleasure in a beautiful object which would entail an absence of the ordinary concomitant of pleasure, namely, a desire to continue in that state; nor, if the existence of the object is itself a condition of that state, does it follow that we would not desire its continuation—in the ordinary sense, be interested in it. Thus while merely conceiving of a possible object as a sonata might not be an incentive for its actualization, there is nothing in Kant's argument to suggest that we cannot have a very definite desire for the continued existence and experience of a sonata already judged to be beautiful. In such a case, our pleasure may have to be connected with the proper name we use to identify an object of taste rather than a general concept—with "Les Adieux" rather than with "sonata"—but nothing except Kant's own definition of interest prevents us from taking particulars rather than types as objects of interest. Such an interest would presuppose an experience of beauty, but interest in an agreeable object also presupposes an actual experience of pleasure from at least one instance of its type.

Once it is understood that Kant's explanation of aesthetic pleasure precludes an interest in the beautiful only in the narrow sense of "interest," other ways of restricting Kant's broad claim that judgments of taste found no interest also became obvious. First, there are pleasures other than that in beauty which might be called aesthetic. Someone might be interested in a certain form or genre, such as the sonata or picaresque novel, and the classification of an object as falling into this form might be enough to promise him a certain pleasure in the object, even if he neither expects nor finds it to be beautiful. Such a person's pleasure and interest in, say, a particular sonata may not be intersubjectively valid, but that is another matter. Second, it might be argued that either merely thinking of objects as beautiful or knowing that they belong to classes of objects which in the past often have turned out to be beautiful is itself ground for a clearly aesthetic, though indeterminate, interest in them. The belief that there are beautiful objects in a museum, or that it has a large collection of Rembrandts, is, after all, surely an incentive for going to visit it. To be sure, not every museum lives up to its reputation, and not every Rembrandt is beautiful; so the interest founded on the mere idea of beauty or on a classification like "by Rembrandt" may not have the determinacy required by Kant's concept of interest, and the promise of pleasure which such an incentive offers cannot have the degree of certainty that Kant attributes to interests. Perhaps no concept applicable to paintings can promise me pleasure in the particularly secure way that the concept of chocolate does, or that thinking of an action as in accord with morality does for any moral agent (though Kant hardly proves that this is so). Nevertheless, only Kant's own definition of interest prevents one from calling *whatever* incentives we do have to experience beautiful objects interests. But nothing in this definition requires us to deprive aesthetic response of pleasure's typical effect on desire.

Once the third *Critique*'s definition of interest is replaced by the more complex notion found in Kant's ethical writings, it becomes apparent how pleasure in the beautiful differs from pleasures connected with interests. Unlike pleasure in both the instrumentally and the morally good, pleasure in the beautiful is not produced by recognizing that a given object falls under any particular empirical concept. Unlike pleasure in the agreeable, pleasure in the beautiful cannot produce an interest in a determinate class of objects. These theses follow from Kant's explanation of aesthetic response, rather than leading to it, and follow only as long as we adhere to Kant's restriction of interest to the objects of determinate concepts, rather than allowing interest in particulars or in the objects of indeterminate concepts, such as the concept of beauty itself. Thus Kant's claim that beauty produces no interest cannot be accepted without qualification.[63*]

This is not to say, however, that there is no criterial significance to a more limited interpretation of the difference in interest between pleasure in the beautiful and other forms of pleasure. Certainly, the presence or absence of a concept in the origination of one's pleasure may be reflected upon in making aesthetic judgment. Further, Kant could well have argued that the presence of an inexhaustible desire for experience of a certain kind of object is a sign that the pleasure in it is sensual rather than reflective; for since the latter form of pleasure depends on the freedom of the imagination from constraint by rules, it may well not able to bear repetition in the same way as a pleasure can which involves only the senses and not the imagination.[64*] Still, the criterion of disinterestedness cannot be employed in the broad way that Kant may have intended, for his argument simply provides no reason to believe that our response to the beautiful not only is independent of antecedent determination by concepts of desire but also has no effect on the faculty of desire.

Interests and Existence

An interest in Kant's sense is a conception of an object which serves as an incentive for its realization, either because its existence promises pleasure or because willing its existence is in accord with moral laws, in which case the act of willing itself has a feeling of pleasure as its consequence. So far, both my defense and my criticism of Kant's thesis of disinterestedness have turned on the role of concepts in interest; and if the disinterestedness of an aesthetic response is derived from its explanation by the harmony of the faculties, this is appropriate. But what Kant actually emphasizes in §2's example of the criterial use of disinterestedness is our concern with the existence of objects in the case of interested pleasure, and our purported indifference to such existence in the case of beauty; indeed, as we saw, only the connection to existence is mentioned in the third *Critique*'s official definition of interest. This suggests that the presence or absence of a concern for actual existence may be used in evaluating one's feelings of pleasure, and in deciding whether or not they may ground judgments of taste. But what is a concern for the actual existence of an object? How can the judgment of taste have an ordinary empirical object or event — a rose, a statue, a musical performance — as its object, and yet be indifferent to its existence?

Kant's argument in §2 contrasts the "mere representation" of an object with its "existence," maintaining that the judgment of beauty concerns only the effect of the former but that agreeableness and goodness involve dependence on the latter.[65] In opening §5, Kant expands on this contrast. Here, he claims that both the agreeable and the good involve a relation to the faculty of desire, and because of this relation are attended with a feeling of delight — either "pathologically" (physiologically) conditioned delight, or "pure practical delight." The occurrence of such delights, he then adds, is determined not "merely by the representation of the object," but rather "by the represented connection between the subject and the existence of this [object]." In such a case "it is not merely the object, but also its existence that pleases." Judgments on these objects are then opposed to the judgment of taste, which Kant now calls "contemplative." Revealing the dependence of his argument on the thesis that aesthetic judgment is not cognitive, and is "neither *grounded* in concepts nor *aimed at them*," Kant argues that the contemplation which produces a judgment of taste is "indifferent with respect to the existence of an object," and "only compares its character [*Beschaffenheit*] with the feeling of pleasure and displeasure."[66] But what is meant by dependence on existence, or a "represented connection" to such existence, is not made clear.

Indeed, this characterization is puzzling, for Kant's original explanation of the subjectivity of aesthetic response turned on the fact that it is a "determination of the subject and its feeling" in an object, or a relation between subject and object, rather than a representation of a property of the object alone.[67] This would seem to link such pleasure with a "represented connection" between a subject and the existence of an object. But Kant's own earlier investigation of the categories of modality had led to the conclusion that existence itself is not a mere property or predicate of objects,[68] and that in thinking of a concept as actualized in an object, we consider only the relation of that concept to ourself and our experience.[69] How, then, does our relation to an object in aesthetic response differ from a relation to its actual existence, or not involve such a relation?

While the first *Critique*'s slogan that being is not a genuine predicate poses the problem, the first *Critique*'s examination of the ontological argument suggests an answer to it. Kant argues that existence is not a genuine predicate because it adds no new property to the concept of an object of which it is asserted. "The real contains no more than the possible," Kant insists, for if existence were a genuine predicate, asserting existence of an object would ascribe a new predicate to it, and change its identity. However, there is certainly a difference between an actually existing object and a merely possible object, though not a difference in concept. As Kant puts it, "my financial position is . . . affected very differently by a hundred real dollars than it is by the mere concept of them (that is, of their possibility.)"[70] The difference between a possible and a real object lies not in any intrinsic feature of the object itself, but in the network of causal connections and dependencies, of which a real object is part, but a possible object is not. If we could argue that our delight in an agreeable or good object depends on the causes and effects of its existence in a way that our delight in the beautiful does not, we might then give sense to the contrast between mere representation and actual existence. Perhaps this would reveal the difference between aesthetic response as a relation between an object and the subject's feeling of pleasure, and other forms of delight as depending on connection to an object's existence.

A mere representation can, however, hardly be equated with a concept of a possible object, because a representation is not a concept at all. Nor can Kant's criterion for actuality be used without modification to explicate the third *Critique*'s concept of existence. In the first *Critique*'s "Postulate of Empirical Thought," Kant defines the actual as "that which is bound up with the material conditions of experience, that is, with sensation."[71] We can know that something exists only if "it is bound up with certain perceptions, in accordance with the principles of their empirical connection (the analogies)"—that is, with causal laws governing the behavior of objects and our perceptions of them.[72] Now, although Kant's concern to distinguish the agreeable and the beautiful sometimes leads him to write as if aesthetic response were free of any sensation of objects,[73] his customary examples of aesthetic objects—flowers, foliage, and the like[74]—are clearly empirical, perceptual objects.[75]* Beautiful objects exist and are perceived in the same way as any other objects, although the empirical laws that explain their perception cannot explain why they dispose the imagination and understanding to the harmonious state of free play. We cannot explain the peculiarity of aesthetic response by denying that its objects cause perceptions in us, for the very reason that the experience of beauty depends on the perception rather than mere conception of objects.

But an analogue of Kant's criterion for the difference between the possible and the actual might serve to explicate the use of existence as a criterion of interest. If we think of the delight of contemplation as dependent on the presence of an object *just* for its perception, but of other delights as dependent on more than mere perception of the presence of their objects, we may be able to state a criterion for distinguishing disinterested from at least some interested pleasures. If our pleasure in an object is dependent not just on perception of it, but on either consumption, use, possession, or any other such "represented connection" with it, or even on judgment about such connections of the object, then we may regard it as a pleasure dependent on the existence of an object. If our pleasure requires no relation to its object other than that of perception, whether in judgment or in practical activity, it may be a contemplative pleasure in the mere representation of the object.

A number of Kant's early reflections on aesthetics point to this conclusion; but while supporting the interpretation, they also reveal a problem in Kant's theory. One note contrasts delight in an object itself with delight in its consequences for our condition: "The delight [is] either in the object or in the existence of the object. The latter [is] in the consequences of the existence of the object for our condition, the other in the object itself. Delight in the enlivening of the sensibility, or the understanding and reason, or both in agreement. That, the existence of which pleases, [is what] interests."[76]* Delight in the enlivening of the sensibility—a typical early characterization of aesthetic response—is connected with the object alone, but the kinds of delight perceived by the understanding and reason stem from the consequences of the object's existence on our condition; so, it seems, the force of relating pleasure to the existence of an object, and to interest, is to relate it to such consequences or judgment of them. This note does not indicate what these consequences for our condition are, but other reflections do. Several written between 1769 and 1771 are particularly illuminating. This reflection from 1770 draws a clear contrast: "There are three kinds of pleasure in an object [*Sache*] through feeling: immediate pleasure through sensation. 2. The pleasure in our condition, concerning the possession of this object. 3. The pleasure in our own person. When the first pleasure obtains without the second, it serves for estimation [*Beurtheilung*]."[77] This passage suggests no distinction between pleasures of sense and of reflection, but does suggest a distinction between an immediate pleasure in an object itself (whether through sensation or reflection), and pleasure in the further practical relations in which it might stand to us, ways in which it might affect our practical circumstances or moral condition. The former but not the latter pleasure is linked with "estimation," thus suggesting that pleasure in the beauty of an object is meant to be contrasted with pleasure in the practical and moral consequences of its existence. The latter kind of pleasure, then, would be pleasure dependent on the actual existence of an object, or on judgment about such existence.

This interpretation of the criterion of connection to existence is suggested by another note from this period. Here, Kant writes that "agreeableness and beauty are noticed immediately through sensibility, without judgment by means of the understanding, which attends to the connection of cause and effect. Only the reason can recognize usefulness. This usefulness consists in the relation of something, as a means, to something which pleases."[78] Again, Kant does not yet separate the sensory pleasure of agreeableness and the reflective pleasure of beauty, but he clearly opposes these "immediate" forms of pleasure to two other kinds. Aesthetic responses are contrasted with pleasures which can be felt only on the basis of judgments of cause and effect about an object — judgments about its history, intention, purposes, effects, capabilities, and the like — or on the basis of practical judgments about the uses to which it may be put, or the pleasures which it might ultimately provide, not in itself, but as a means to some further experience. Here, Kant suggests two ways in which pleasure in beauty may be taken in mere representation rather than actual existence. Pleasure may be felt apart from knowledge of actuality by causal laws — though this does not mean that its object is in any way nonactual — and it may be felt without reference to the effects an object may have beyond mere perception or contemplation.

A delight which is "indifferent to existence" is not directed toward any special kind of object, nor is it necessarily unsuited for creating an interest in the continued existence of its object. It is simply a delight that can be felt upon mere perception or contemplation of an object, without requiring further penetration into the causal nexus of the object — either cognitively, by judgment about its causal history or causal potential, or practically, either by consumption, use, or possession, or by judgment about such relations. It is in this sense that aesthetic response is directed to the representation of an object, as opposed to the connection between the subject and the existence of the object. At the same time, as pleasure, this response does express a relation between the representation of the object (or simply, the object) and the cognitive faculties of the subject. Delight in the beautiful is a pleasure which must be available merely from contemplation of an object, as opposed to requiring a further relation to the object — consumption of it, possession of it, the ability to dispose of it, and the like. This contrast may well be expressed as one between "what I can make of the representation" of an object and ways in which I "depend on the existence of the object."[79] For aesthetic response, a representation of an object — either in the Kantian sense of its presentation to consciousness or, in fact, in the ordinary sense of a (perhaps perfect) reproduction — is all that is required, but in an interested response to an object, the full ramifications of its actual existence may be involved. Pleasure from cognition goes beyond an object's appearance to its causal connections; practical pleasure may require not just the representation, but control over an object and access to it.

One note from the mid-1770s gives examples of the sorts of interest in existence that must be excluded from the basis of aesthetic response. Kant writes that "the beautiful must betray no alien interest, but please apart from any self-interest [*uneigennützig*]. It is not to betray any affection for art, any pride in wealth, any charm in the acquisition of goods, any need for economy. It must please in itself, like virtue."[80] This clearly contrasts pleasure in the mere contemplation of an object with kinds of pleasure that can come only with its possession, one form of delight in existence.

One last passage from this period makes the same contrast, but then takes it too far:

> Taste shows itself if one does not choose merely *on account of usefulness*. Therefore, a porcelain button is more beautiful than a silver one. The beauty of lace consists in the fact that it does not last long. Clothes are therefore chosen of delicate colors, because they are perishable. Flowers have their beauty in their perishability. (Nature has given the least beauty to that which is enjoyable because it nourishes: cows, bees, swine, sheep; to that which refreshes in enjoyment, somewhat more: fruit; that which smells nice, more: and that which can merely please the eyes, the most.)[81]

Like the third *Critique* in its insistence that pleasure in beauty not only presupposes but also creates no interest in its object, this passage misinterprets the requirements of disinterestedness. Instead of merely separating taste from practical dependence, it proposes an actual conflict between beauty and practicality. But the inverse relationship between beauty and usefulness which Kant describes is no consequence of disinterestedness. This criterion demands only that the delight we take in a beautiful object be purely contemplative, and not based on any of those cognitive or practical facts which may be involved in its actual existence, or implicated in judgments about this existence.

Kant's insistence that aesthetic judgment must be founded in pleasure produced by the mere perception or contemplation of the representation of an object, rather than by its actual existence, does not mean that aesthetic response is caused by anything other than an ordinary object of experience. It means only that it cannot be determined by either the use, possession, and so on, of an object, or by judgments about such matters—for pleasure in either of these must depend on conceiving of the object as of a certain sort, or possessing a certain kind of existence, and aesthetic judgment cannot depend on such a conceptualization of its object. This must certainly be the case whenever the conceptualization of an object or its possible use would provide rules for the determination of our response to it, and when our assessment of the object would thus not have to wait upon our actual experience of it. This must be kept in mind, for it could be objected to Kant's argument that while the usefulness of such things as ships or buttons is certainly not identical to their possible beauty, the use of a painting or sculpture is just to engender aesthetic response, so our actual response to such objects can hardly be unconnected to their use, a fact about their actual existence. But while it may be plausible to assign such a use to objects of taste, it remains true that no consideration of their use can determine our pleasure in them, or decide the issue of their beauty. Whereas the use of other sorts of objects might provide rules by which their value can be determined, the decision that a particular painting could serve a purely aesthetic use can only *follow* from the decision that it is in fact beautiful, and would provide no rules for the former decision. What is crucial is that the nature of the existence of an object of taste provides no rules for its evaluation, although this is just what considerations about the actual existence of objects often do.

On this interpretation of indifference to actual existence, it is obvious that §2's examples of unacceptable answers to a question of beauty do indeed manifest inappropriate interests in the existence of the object of discussion. Disapproving of a palace because it was made for mere spectacle depends on judging its causal history rather than the character of its representation alone. Preferring a restaurant to the palace expresses a judgment not on the representations of the two places, but on the sensual pleasures to be derived from interactions going beyond mere perception—namely, the pleasures to be had in actually eating in one place or the other. Again, condemning the vanity of those who spent the sweat of the people on the palace expresses not a judgment on the representation or appearance of the building, but a moral judgment on the injustice of its having been built. Each of Kant's examples contrasts pleasure in the mere contemplation of an object with approval of its existence, depending upon judgments about the causal connections comprising its actuality. But none entails that the object of aesthetic judgment is anything but an ordinary object or event.[82*]

We may also note that Kant's contrast between mere representation and the judgment of actual existence, like his true concept of disinterestedness itself, concerns only the bases on which objects may please, or the grounds for judgments of approval. It implies only that aesthetic response cannot be based on an interest in an object or its use, a concept of which could create an incentive for willing its existence in advance of actual experience of it. Kant's contrast cannot preclude that once having found the contemplation of a particular object pleasurable, we should desire the continued availability of its representation and thus, ordinarily, the continued existence of the object itself. The true force of disinterestedness does not conflict with the "intrinsic causality" of all pleasure as creating a disposition for its own preservation.[83] The disinterestedness of aesthetic response does not entail that beauty produces no interest in its object, or even in its existence, except on Kant's own restrictive conception of interest.

Before considering how the criterion of disinterestedness may be applied in the actual justification of a judgment of taste, however, we must briefly examine two problems concerning Kant's differentiation of pleasure in the beautiful from *both* gratification *and* esteem by means of the concept of indifference to actual existence. First, there is a problem with any suggestion that simple reflection on an object is independent of its actual existence and that it differs from pleasure in the agreeable in this regard. Second, Kant's view that aesthetic response depends on neither cognitive nor practical concern with the actual existence of its object seems to conflict with many of our beliefs about attitudes toward beautiful objects of both art and nature.

Kant's early notes all contrast immediate pleasure in perception with pleasures dependent on more than merely perceptual relations to objects — characteristically, with the effects of objects on one's practical or moral condition. This contrast is certainly plausible — in spite of both Hume and the Bauhaus, we do think of such utilitarian features as usefulness and such aesthetic merits as beauty as distinct values of objects. Thus differentiating the beautiful from the good by the criterion of indifference to real existence seems admissible. But it is not so clear that this criterion can be used to distinguish the beautiful from the agreeable. When he first developed this criterion, Kant did not distinguish between these two objects of pleasure, and thus did not employ the distinction between the representation of an object and its existence[84] for this purpose. Aesthetic judgments of sense and aesthetic judgments of reflection were not separated until Kant wrote the *Critique of Judgment* itself; earlier, he identified aesthetic response with "immediate pleasure through sensation."[85] There was no contrast between beauty and agreeableness in the view that "the perfection of objects of experience is harmony with the law of the senses, and this, as appearance, is called beauty; it is, so to speak, the outer side of perfection, and the object pleases merely in being contemplated."[86] The contrast between a merely contemplative attitude toward an object and interested relations to it is easily applied when we oppose both sensual and aesthetic pleasures to judgments of relative and absolute goodness. But can it really be used to make Kant's mature distinction between sensual gratification and aesthetic response?

The notion of indifference to actual existence can, in fact, make this distinction only with some difficulty. Part of the meaning of the disinterestedness of aesthetic response, as we saw, may be interpreted without any special concept of existence. This is Kant's thesis that the experience of sensory gratification can generate an interest in a class of objects, subsumable under an empirical concept, in a way that the experience of beauty cannot. This claim does not have as much force as Kant may have thought, but need not be questioned here. However, Kant may also have meant that the experience of sensory gratification is dependent on the existence of its object in a way that pleasure in the beautiful is not. He not only says that the agreeable creates interest; he also claims that in the "pathologically conditioned" delight in the agreeable "it is not merely the object, but also its existence, that pleases."[87] This is indeed problematic, for the experience of beauty seems to depend on the perception of an actual empirical object just as much as does the experience of sensory gratification, which differs from the latter only in involving the harmonious play of the higher cognitive faculties and not just the physiological reaction of the senses.

Kant does sometimes argue as if the play of the higher faculties of knowledge excluded rather than depended on ordinary sense perception. For instance, he asserts that it is the design rather than the color of a painting which is "the proper object of a pure judgment of taste,"[88] even though the view that a design of colors is an object of taste might be an equally plausible interpretation of the theory of the harmony of the faculties. In the next chapter, however, I will argue that Kant's tendency to oppose sense perception and aesthetic response is not a necessary consequence of his theory; and we may note now that there is a much more acceptable interpretation of the differentiation of agreeableness and beauty by reference to real existence. Kant's basic idea is that of the contrast between the mere representation of an object and the full nexus of its causal relations; and while both the beautiful and the agreeable are causally related to us, only in the case of the latter can we have empirical knowledge of its causal basis. A physiological response can be the subject of empirical investigation and empirical causal laws; thus the agreeableness of an object, at least for given persons, may be included among the network of causal connections which constitute the real existence of an object. No knowledge of causal connections is required to feel sensory pleasure, but judgments about the agreeableness of an object may take the form of ordinary empirical judgment. Beauty, however, cannot be linked with any determinate empirical concepts of an object; thus judgments of beauty are not empirical judgments about the causal connections or existence of their objects. This might be a second meaning of differentiating pleasure in the beautiful from that in the agreeable as a delight independent of the existence of its object.

This argument does not, however, imply that the experience of beauty is any less dependent on the actual perception of an object than is the sensory response of gratification. Indeed, if aesthetic judgment cannot be made on the basis of concepts alone, intuitions provided by such perception *must* be necessary for aesthetic response. The free play of the cognitive faculties which differentiates beauty from agreeableness may make beauty incapable of connection with determinate causal concepts, but it does not make the experience of beauty independent of an existent object. The different grounds of sensory and aesthetic pleasure may imply a difference in potential for forming interests in their objects — or a difference in the kind of interests that may be formed — but not a difference in dependence on the actual existence of the objects of judgment.

We must conclude, then, that simple reference to existence does not lead to a very neat distinction between the agreeable and the beautiful. I now turn to a different kind of problem for Kant's theory. If what is excluded from aesthetic judgment, as connected to actual existence, is the network of an object's causal connections, and thus its entire causal history, many features of an object that we would ordinarily consider proper objects of aesthetic attention will in fact be excluded from the judgment of taste — for instance, the very fact that an object is a work of art rather than of nature, and has thus come to be in a certain sort of way;[89] the particular intentions with which a work has been made;[90] or the significance that it may have in virtue of the artistic or semantic intentions behind it. The limitations imposed by the requirement of indifference to real existence apparently preclude attention to many of the ordinary concerns of criticism.

This objection raises the problem of Kant's "formalism," and will be more fully treated in the next chapter. Here, I will only point out that in-difference to real existence is not a condition for *any* judgment we might make about works of art, but is a condition for the *judgment of beauty*. For purposes of this judgment, whether an object is natural or artificial and intentional is indeed irrelevant. It must be kept in mind that in Kant's usage "aesthetic" is not synonymous with "artistic,"[91] but connotes only the subjective pleasure we take in objects. Thus limitations on aesthetic judg-ment are not necessarily limitations on our judgments about art. Kant's thesis that judgments of beauty concern the mere representation of an ob-ject rather than any aspect of its causal history is a thesis not about all judg-ments of art, but only about the specifically aesthetic merit of beauty.

Indeed, Kant's exclusion from aesthetic judgment of many of the factors ordinarily influencing our evaluation of art may count in favor of his theory. Kant's thesis that the judgment of taste is not about an object as a member of any determinate class, but is instead a logically singular judg-ment, has sometimes been taken to mean that aesthetic judgment has a special concern with the uniqueness of aesthetic objects, or even that it may actually be made in virtue of the uniqueness of aesthetic objects.[92] Taking pleasure in the uniqueness of an object, however, would really express a concern with the conditions of its actual existence rather than with the character of its representation. For instance, if we value an original in ways in which we do not value even a perfect copy, or if we value a novelty more than an object in a well-defined tradition, we may be responding to the his-tory of the physical object before us rather than to the representation it occasions. If we value a work of art just because it is the only one of its kind, we are taking pleasure in the uniqueness of its existence. Some of the ways in which we take pleasure in the uniqueness of an object depend on facts which Kant would connect with its existence, and an appreciation of uniqueness would thus be precluded by Kant's theory of aesthetic judg-ment. But this is a perfectly acceptable conclusion. If our appreciation of an object suffers because there are others like it, we must not be appreciat-ing it for its beauty at all, but for some such factor as its rarity or its mone-tary value. If, however, we could derive the same pleasure from a perfect reproduction of an object (which may, of course, be impossible in some media) as we could from the object itself, this suggests that our pleasure is in fact founded on the harmonious effect of the representation of the ob-ject on our cognitive faculties, and not on anything like rarity or price. The compatibility of our pleasure in an object with indifference to its unique-ness indicates that our pleasure in it is due to the intersubjectively valid state of the harmony of the faculties, and not to some interest in its existence. Indifference to the uniqueness of an object's real existence would thus be a valid criterion for the judgment of taste. Indeed, it may be a salutory criterion when concern with such matters as the novelty, rarity, or value of works of art all too often overshadows genuinely aesthetic appreciation of objects.

Let me make clear what I am not saying here. First, I am not denying that the uniqueness of a work of art is a good reason for taking an interest in its existence. If only one object can occasion a particular beautiful representation — if only the *Mona Lisa* originally painted by Leonardo can give us an adequate representation of the *Mona Lisa* — then it is completely natural that the pleasure we derive from the representation of that object should lead us to desire its continued existence. Second, I am not arguing that a genuine delight in the beautiful need be able to survive any amount of repetition or imitation. As we have seen, the effect of repetition on aesthetic response may be the same as that of rule-governedness, namely, destruction of the at least apparent contingency of synthesis on which pleasure in the beautiful rests. Too much familiarity with a given manifold, or kind of manifold, may make its unification entirely as expected as would its subsumption under a concept. But if the nature of aesthetic response requires uniqueness, what is needed is uniqueness of representations relative to the subject, and not uniqueness of the objects of taste themselves. Truly aesthetic appreciation of an object concerns the character of its representation rather than the uniqueness of its existence. For this reason, considering whether one could obtain the same pleasure from a perfect representation of an object as from the object itself might indeed be a useful criterion for the judgment of taste.

The Evidence of Disinterestedness

We have now seen what an interest is, and to what extent it is true that our pleasures in the agreeable and the good are interested, but our pleasure in the beautiful disinterested. The question that now remains is, how is the criterion of disinterestedness applied in the justification of a judgment of taste? How does one become conscious that a given pleasure is disinterested?

Kant makes it clear enough that consciousness of disinterestedness does play a criterial role in claiming intersubjective validity for aesthetic response. We are familiar with §6's assertion that when "one is conscious that one's delight in [an object] is without any interest, [it] cannot be estimated except as containing a ground of delight for everyone"; and on this inference from disinterestedness to intersubjectivity is based the grammatically objective attribution of beauty to an object. Indeed, Kant writes as if consciousness of disinterestedness were a necessary and sufficient condition for aesthetic judgment. But he is less explicit about the form of this consciousness than he is about its role. Is the disinterestedness of a feeling of pleasure something which is *felt?*

Supposing that it is would be consistent with the requirement that any aesthetic judgment, whether sensory or reflective, be founded on feeling; and §6 might be read as suggesting that there is a special feeling of disinterestedness. Kant writes that a subject may conclude that there are no merely private reasons for his delight, and attribute it to others, because "since it is not founded on any inclination of the subject (or on any other considered interest), the judging [subject] rather feels himself fully *free* in respect of the delight which he directs to the object."[93]

But disinterestedness cannot be manifested by a special and characteristic feeling. First, Kant has claimed that pleasure itself is the only sensation which cannot become part of the concept of an object, or is a true feeling,[94] and this implies that the feeling of freedom in the synthesis of a manifold could only be the feeling of pleasure itself. Second, Kant also suggests that, just as the freedom of imagination is nothing but the absence of any conceptual constraint on it,[95] so the freedom of pleasure is nothing but its independence of any interest. In §5, as we have seen, Kant says that pleasure in the beautiful is the "one and only uninterested [*sic*] and *free* delight," and "*favor* the only free delight," because in the case of this pleasure "no interest, whether of sense or of reason, extorts approval."[96] Freedom and disinterestedness, in other words, are merely different names for one fact, the absence of a proscribed connection between pleasure and interest. The freedom of pleasure is not a unique feeling which can be used as evidence for its disinterestedness.

Consciousness of disinterestedness is not awareness of any phenomenologically unique feeling. The conclusion that a given feeling of pleasure is disinterested, then, must depend on consciousness of the presence or absence of other facts or states of mind associated with it. In fact, if an interest in an object is a concept of it which offers an incentive for willing its existence, then consciousness of the interestedness of a pleasure must consist in the consciousness of a pleasure in an object, consciousness of a concept of it which represents the existence of an object of its type as desirable, and an accompanying judgment that this conceptualization of the object is either the cause or effect of one's pleasure in it. Conversely, consciousness of the disinterestedness of a pleasure must consist in an awareness of it without an accompanying awareness of any such concept, or without ground for any such judgment as to the cause or effect of the pleasure.

A judgment of disinterestedness, then, is not made on the basis of a simple introspection of feeling; it is, rather, an indirect judgment linking a felt pleasure to the harmony of the faculties in virtue of the absence of evidence for certain other judgments about the cause or effect of that pleasure. A judgment of disinterestedness cannot be the direct consequence of a judgment that a feeling of pleasure is due to the harmony of the faculties, because of Kant's thesis that in this case there is no consciousness of the harmony except for the pleasure itself, or no consciousness of the cause except through its effect. But this problem does not affect judgment on other pleasures. Where pleasure is caused by the subsumption of an object under a concept, we may be conscious of the concept as well as of the pleasure, and thus have the necessary evidence for venturing a causal connection between them. Similarly, where interest is supposed to be the effect rather than the cause of pleasure, we may be conscious of the interest — as a certain concept of a type of object — as well as of the pleasure itself, and then link the two by a causal judgment. The lack of a separate consciousness of the ground of aesthetic response is why aesthetic judgment must be the product of reflection. The criterion of disinterestedness does not reveal any new form of evidence which can be a direct object of consciousness in such reflection, but it does establish an indirect method by which reflection can proceed.

Because it can be applied only indirectly, the criterion of disinterestedness cannot be stated simply, except, of course, as requiring the absence of an interest. But my exploration of the concept of interest should make it obvious what sorts of circumstances may suggest the presence or absence of interest. Now that I have given an interpretation to the contrast between the representation and the existence of an object, this distinction gains criterial potential. Thus, if one is taking pleasure in a reproduction of a work rather than in the physical presence of the work itself, one has evidence for believing one's pleasure to be disinterested — though not conclusive evidence, for even a reproduction can be the object of an interested pleasure (that in proving a point, for instance). Circumstances may also suggest that one's pleasure in an object is interested. If one finds oneself thinking of the money to be derived from its sale while looking at a painting, or gleefully contemplating the cries of envy that will result when friends see the new acquisition, that would be evidence for believing one's pleasure to be interested — though, again, not conclusive evidence, for one might be having such thoughts and yet still be pleased by the mere beauty of the painting itself.

These examples — which could easily be multiplied — turn on the connection between interest and existence. The connection between interests and general concepts can also provide a tool for aesthetic reflection. Certain concepts will be obvious signs of interest. If one finds oneself looking at a painting and thinking how useful it would be for teaching children the virtue of honesty and thrift, the suspicion that one's pleasure in it is interested is clearly in order. The mere thought of such moral or practical concepts may be enough to suggest their responsibility for one's pleasure. However, the criterion of connection to a concept cannot always be so easily applied. For any object of which one is conscious, one is sure to be aware of some *a priori* concept under which it falls (for example, substance), and almost as sure to be aware of various empirical concepts which also apply to it (for example, statue, rose, composition by Mozart). So aesthetic judgment is never likely to be grounded on a simple absence of concepts from the context of one's pleasure. But we can still imagine tests by which one might decide whether or not one's pleasure is *due to* the subsumption of the object under such concepts. One could consider whether one would still take pleasure in it even if one did not know what it was, or whether one is pleased by any object falling under the concept. If one thinks one would still be pleased by the object without knowing it to be a rose, or knows that one does not take pleasure in everything written by Mozart, that would be reason to believe that such classifications were not the ground of pleasure. Attributing the pleasure to the harmony of the faculties would then be a reasonable alternative.

The tests for the presence or absence of interest which I have described do not provide conclusive evidence, and this is a fundamental fact about them. Establishing that a pleasure is disinterested is a matter not of incorrigible introspection, but of hypothesis and conjecture about causal connections in one's mental history. Linking a pleasure to an interest requires a particular causal judgment, and causal judgments are empirical judgments subject to error. But the intrinsic corrigibility of causal judgment is not the only source of the uncertainty of aesthetic judgments founded on the criterion of disinterestedness. While the efficacy of an interest with respect to a given pleasure may never be conclusively established, at least the presence of the interest may be certain. A claim of disinterestedness, however, requires the absence of any interest, and no failure to turn up evidence of an interest after a search of any particular length can prove that no interest caused one's pleasure. If the search for an interest is a search in the network of one's own thoughts and associations, it is always possible that one has not looked long enough or in the right direction. Any pleasure may be caused by an interest which one has failed to notice. As Kant put it in the *Foundations of the Metaphysics of Morals,* "Who can prove by experience the nonexistence of a cause when experience shows us only that we do not perceive the cause?"[97]

Further, reference to Kant's moral theory can remind us that the very fact that the cause of pleasure which aesthetic reflection seeks to exclude is an *interest* is another ground of uncertainty. The fact that a finite search may conclusively establish the presence of a possible cause, but not its absence, is a problem for causal judgment in general. Interests, however, are incentives, or motives, and it is a basic tenet of Kant's moral epistemology that one can never be fully certain of what motives stand behind one's actions—that in a search for motives, "even the strictest examination can never lead us entirely behind the secret incentives."[98] Although Kant does not mention this thesis in the *Critique of Judgment,* there is no reason to suppose that it does not apply to incentives for approval as well as to those for action, and if it does, it provides yet another explanation for the uncertainty of aesthetic judgment.

This interpretation of the criterial role of disinterestedness in the justification of aesthetic judgment makes it clear why its conditions are so frequently sinned against,[99] why one can never really be sure that a given feeling of pleasure has been "correctly subsumed" under the harmony of the faculties as its "rule of approval."[100] Yet this analysis also shows that the uncertainty of judgments of taste is due at least in part to the general uncertainty of empirical self-knowledge, and not to any problem unique to aesthetic judgment. This is surely the reason why Kant can claim that in matters of taste the possibility of "an incorrect application to a particular case of the right which a law gives us [does] not suspend the right in general."[101] Further pursuit of the question of certainty, however, would lead directly to the deduction of aesthetic judgment, and before that can be considered, Kant's attempt to find another criterion for aesthetic judgment in the "form of finality" must be examined. I thus now turn to the third moment of the judgment of taste.

6

The Form of Finality

* *

Objective Rules for Taste

In specifying the "quality" of the delight in judgments of taste, the requirement of disinterestedness does not pick out a qualititatively distinct kind of
pleasurable feeling as the ground for aesthetic judgment, but does function
as a constraint on the subjective grounds for ascriptions of beauty to objects. It requires that only pleasures thought to have originated independently of any interest in the existence of their objects be imputed to everyone else. This is not because any pleasure unconnected to interest must
automatically be intersubjectively valid, but because the absence of interest is the best evidence one can have for the hypothesis that a given pleasure
is indeed due to the harmony of imagination and understanding; and this
state, though he has yet to argue it, Kant does believe to be intersubjectively valid.

The first moment of aesthetic judgment thus functions as a criterion for
judgments of taste by restricting the relation between subject and object to
one of several that might cause pleasure, or by limiting the subjective
grounds for pleasure in such judgments. According to its title, the third
moment considers "the *relation* of ends which are brought into consideration" in judgments of taste;[1] and if the exclusion of interest is thought to
exclude relation to any ends except the general objective of cognition itself,
this might suggest that the third moment must cover much the same
ground as the first. But this conclusion cannot be drawn so quickly. In the
end, I will argue, the third moment largely does just continue the argument of the first, placing restrictions on our subjective grounds for the approval of the "proper object for the pure judgment of taste,"[2] though ex-
tending the earlier argument in some particulars. But Kant's intentions in
the third moment are clearly greater than this. The third moment represents Kant's attempt to accomplish the traditional objective of aesthetics:

that of directly specifying certain properties or even kinds of objects which license judgments of taste, without a need for further reflection on our response to these aspects or kinds of objects.

By arguing that "beauty is the form of *finality* in an object, so far as it is perceived in it *without representation of an end,*"[3] Kant attempts to introduce not only a criterion applicable to our own response to objects, but also a general criterion directly applicable to the objects of taste themselves — namely, that of the "form of finality."[4*] This, in turn, is further specified in a number of ways. Kant argues that aesthetic judgment must be based on pleasure occasioned by the perceptual form of objects, as opposed to pleasures connected with any sensations of them or any concepts applicable to them; he further suggests that aesthetic response must be occasioned by a specific range of perceptual forms, those which have the appearance of design. He also apparently argues that genuine aesthetic response must be limited not only to this particular aspect of objects, but to a particular kind of objects as well — objects of nature rather than of human art.[5*] Thus, by means of the concept of finality, the third moment attempts to introduce some rules for judgments of taste directly applicable to the objects of such judgment.

Naturally, Kant does not try to provide *determinate* rules by which it could be mechanically and definitively decided that any particular object is beautiful. The possibility of such rules is excluded by his basic explanation of our pleasure in the beautiful, and Kant never forgets this. Thus the final section of the third moment asserts that "no objective rules of taste can be given which would determine what is beautiful through concepts," and says that it would be a "fruitless endeavor" to "seek a principle of taste which would provide a universal criterion of the beautiful through determinate concepts."[6] A famous passage in §34 reiterates this conclusion: "Thus although critics, as Hume says, may reason more plausibly than cooks, they must still have the same fate. The determining ground of their judgments cannot be expected from the force of demonstrations, but only from the reflection of the subject on his own condition (of pleasure and displeasure), to the exclusion of precepts and rules."[7] But objective rules as precepts based on determinate concepts are not the only kinds of constraints we might place on objects. There might be more general — or indeterminate — rules which could link the possibility of proper aesthetic response to either certain aspects or certain kinds of objects, without thereby creating any procedure by which it could be mechanically decided that a given object is beautiful. In particular, there might be rules which exclude certain aspects or kinds of objects from among the proper objects of taste without implying that any instance of an aspect or kind of object which survives this exclusion is necessarily beautiful. The discovery of such rules might not fulfill every hope of traditional aesthetics, but would certainly offer some valuable criteria for aesthetic judgment. It is for such general rules that Kant searches in the third moment.[8]*

But Kant's objective criteria for judgments of taste, even if indeterminate, are still problematic. What we find in the third moment is Kant's attempt to bring his abstract analysis of aesthetic response and judgment closer to the level of actual rules for criticism characteristic of his century by means of several formalist constraints on the objects of taste. These are his theses that pure judgments of taste must be based on response to the perceptual form of objects, their design and composition rather than color and tone;[9] that they must be based on the form of objects rather than on what might be represented by them;[10] and perhaps even that aesthetic judgment requires natural objects, which embody no purposes, rather than works of art, which do.[11] But such constraints on beautiful objects cannot be directly derived from the basic premises of Kant's theory of taste. This theory comprises the analysis of aesthetic judgment as requiring the intersubjective validity of pleasure, and the explanation of aesthetic response as due to the harmony of the faculties and thus the ground of such validity. If substantive constraints on the objects of taste could be deduced from the explanation of aesthetic response, Kant would certainly have a powerful argument for such criteria. But Kant's derivations of such constraints actually depend either on fallacious arguments, or on a questionably direct application of the requirement of intersubjective validity to empirically observed facts of agreement and disagreement, or on the employment of aspects of the *Critique of Pure Reason*'s theory of perception that are not implied by the idea of the harmony of the faculties itself. For these reasons, although Kant's argument that the objects of pure judgments of taste must be regarded as having the mere "form of finality" is not devoid of criterial significance, and does amplify some of the suggestions of his earlier arguments, his attempt to move beyond the analysis of disinterestedness to a delimitation of special aspects or types of aesthetic objects, falling under a concept or concepts of aesthetic form, is seriously flawed, and illustrates only the false promise of his concept of finality.

But this may not be an entirely unwelcome conclusion. For if my argument shows that Kant's general theory of taste and his formalist aesthetic opinions are not so intimately connected as has traditionally been supposed, and that the latter involve assumptions which are only historically connected to the former, then it will also show that the general theory is not necessarily damaged by the criticisms which may be directed against some of Kant's particular opinions about the proper objects of taste or by our own departures from both the psychology and the sensibilities of the eighteenth century.

To see just what problems there are in Kant's attempt to derive his formalist opinions from his general theory of taste, we will have to examine the argument of the third moment in some detail. This argument may be regarded as composed of four main layers. Its first and most general claim is that the judgment of taste must in fact be a response to the "form of finality" in an object. This is argued in the first paragraph of §10 and in §§11 and 12. There are then three further arguments by means of which Kant lends some specificity to this general claim. The first is found in the second paragraph of §10, and in some examples scattered elsewhere in the *Critique of Judgment;* in this argument, Kant intimates a connection between the form of finality and an appearance of design. With the considerations advanced in §§13 and 14, Kant then tries to connect the notion of the form of finality to a distinction between the form and matter of appearance, thus establishing perceptual form as the proper object of the judgment of beauty. Finally, in §§15 and 16, Kant attempts to link the beauty of an object to its form rather than to any perfection or conceptual significance it may have,[12*] and suggests that this connection restricts taste to natural objects. So with three different arguments, Kant attempts to associate the general concept of the form of finality with a more specific kind of form.

As we examine Kant's various arguments, however, we should keep in mind that the thesis that aesthetic response is directed to the form of natural objects has already been inserted into the arguments of the two Introductions. In the published Introduction, Kant simply asserted that it is the form of objects which disposes the imagination and understanding to their harmonious cooperation.[13] In the first Introduction, Kant divided the general sphere of reflective judgment into judgments on the purposiveness of relations between natural objects and judgments on the finality of the forms of individual natural objects, and treated aesthetic judgment as the latter.[14] In so doing, he anticipated the third moment in both its limitation of aesthetic response to the forms of objects and its intimation that natural objects are the paradigmatic objects of taste. Indeed, Kant may have regarded these introductory claims as having laid the groundwork for his for-

malism, and have intended the third moment merely to apply rather than
to defend his view. But Kant's introductory assertion that taste concerns
the forms of natural beauties was derived solely from the context of the
general theory of reflective judgment, and was not otherwise supported. In
what follows, I will thus assume that the Analytic of the Beautiful has so far
made no real case for the restriction of aesthetic judgment to any particular forms or kinds of objects, and consider whether its third moment now
makes such a case.

The Form of Finality

In the first stage of his argument, Kant employs the results of the first two
moments of the Analytic to argue for a concept of subjective or formal finality as that in virtue of which objects are beautiful, and that in them to
which aesthetic judgment is properly limited. Kant's notion of subjective
finality, however, fails to escape the difficulty of his original concept of finality as nature's conformity to the needs of reflective judgment: that is,
while the concept of finality grammatically connotes a property of objects
rather than of our own responses, it in fact attributes to objects only the
disposition to produce a certain response in us, and does not place any definite restrictions on the properties through which objects may exercise this
disposition.

As in the first moment, Kant begins with a definition; but just as his
definition of interest was misleading, so is his definition of "end," which
actually applies to only one of the two sorts of ends relation to which must
be excluded in the case of aesthetic judgment. Kant defines an "end" or
"purpose" (*Zweck*) as "the object of a concept so far as this concept is regarded as the cause of the object (the real ground of its possibility)."[15] He
claims that this is a definition of the concept of an end "according to its
transcendental determinations," presupposing reference to nothing empirical, including the feeling of pleasure.[16] This suggests that in calling something an end, we are not saying anything about its particular relation to
motivation or desire, but are instead saying something else. In fact, we are
saying that a thing which is an end is the product of causality through a
concept, or of action undertaken by an agent capable of conceptual representation. An end is the product of an action, but by calling something an
end we do not refer it to the desire which presumably motivates the action.
Instead, we assert that it is an object whose nature is such that it could
come into being only by a process which involves a representation of its na-

ture prior to, and as a condition of, its existence. Thus Kant maintains that one thinks of an object as an end not merely where one supposes that cognition of it requires a concept, but "where the object itself (its form or its existence) as an effect is thought to be possible only through a concept of the latter." In calling something an end, we make a claim about the nature of the causality that produced it, namely, that "the representation of the effect is here the determining ground of its cause and precedes the latter."[17]

The basic sense of "finality" (*Zweckmässigkeit*) is then derived from this definition of "end." Kant first explains finality as a property of the kind of *concept* which can lead to the production of an end, or as "the causality of a *concept* in respect of its object." In the second paragraph of §10, however, Kant uses the term "finality" not to refer to the causal efficacy of a concept which produces an end, but rather in reference to an "object, a state of mind, or even an action."[18] Kant does not pause to make explicit the revision in his initial definition of finality. But it should be obvious that if the finality of a concept is its efficacy in producing an object, then the most natural meaning of "finality" when applied to an *object* will be that it has been produced by a final concept, or a prior representation of itself in an agent capable of action according to concepts. Thus to attribute finality to an object is to attribute to it a certain kind of causal history. An object which is final is an object of a kind which can be produced only by a prior representation of itself, or one which has actually been so produced.

It is immediately apparent that no judgment about the finality of an object can ground a judgment of taste. For if a judgment of finality is a judgment about the causal history of an object, then it must be a judgment, employing determinate concepts, about those relations of the object to other objects constituting its actuality and existence; and just such judgments have been excluded from the basis of aesthetic response by means of the doctrine of disinterestedness developed from Kant's fundamental notion of the harmony of the faculties. For Kant to deny that the judgment of taste is a judgment of finality as so far defined, or to deny that it can consider any relation to ends, is no great revelation. Nor will it be any surprise if he argues that any finality which the objects of taste do enjoy must be different from that so far considered. However, the content of the third moment is not limited to the claim that aesthetic judgment does not concern the causal history of its objects. Kant's attempt to introduce substantive constraints on the objects of pure aesthetic judgment requires a broader thesis than this.

That Kant intends the third moment to do more than just reiterate the independence of aesthetic judgment from judgments of causality is quickly revealed by §11, which implicitly widens §10's concept of an end and in so doing undermines its definition of finality. Kant opens this section thus:

> Any end, if it is regarded as a ground of delight, implies an interest as the determining ground of the judgment on the object of pleasure. Therefore, no subjective end can serve as the ground of a judgment of taste. But neither can any representation of an objective end, that is, of the possibility of the object itself according to principles of connection to an end, determine the judgment of taste, and consequently neither can any concept of the good: because it is an aesthetic and not a cognitive judgment, which therefore concerns no *concept* of the constitution [*Beschaffenheit*] and internal or external possibility of an object through this or that cause, but merely the mutual relation of the faculties of representation, so far as they are determined by a representation.[19]

This paragraph refers to two sorts of ends, only one of which falls under the definition offered in §10. An objective end in the present paragraph corresponds to an end as first defined, and refers to an object represented as possible only on the basis of a certain kind of causal history. Obviously enough, since aesthetic judgment is not determined by causal considerations, the representation of an object as an objective end cannot determine the issue of its beauty. But the concept of subjective end with which this paragraph opens has nothing to do with this sense of "end." This is apparent from the fact that Kant's first claim about such an end is that it implies a connection to interest, even though §10's definition of an end proceeded without any relation to pleasure, and thus, presumably, without any relation to interest. In fact, a subjective end is not an object with a certain kind of history, but rather, in its primary sense, a certain aim, purpose, or interest that a person may have. This is the force of calling it "subjective." When Kant denies that the judgment of taste rests on a subjective end, he is thus denying that it depends on seeing an object as fulfilling an interest of the person taking pleasure in it; hence regarding an object as a subjective end is regarding it as an object which fulfills a subjective end in this first sense.

To call an object an end in this new sense is not necessarily to say anything about its causal history, but rather to say something about its causal efficacy, or, we might say, its causal future. It is to call it an end because it can satisfy an interest, and not because of the way in which it was produced. This must be the case, simply because natural objects can fulfill interests even though they are not produced through concepts. If we assumed that rational creatures create objects only when they see them as fulfilling some interest, it might follow that all objective ends are also subjective ends; but this does not imply that all subjective ends are objective ends, or that all objective ends are subjective ends — fulfillments of interests — for those who may respond to them, rather than those who created them.

In denying that objects are judged to be beautiful because of their status as either subjective or objective ends, then, Kant is making a broader claim than that which would be made by denying that objects are beautiful because of their possession of finality as defined by §10. So far, however, he is still not making any *new* claims. The first paragraph of §11 only repeats what we already know, that we do not judge objects to be beautiful either because they are judged to satisfy some interest or because they are judged to have some particular causal history. From a grammatical point of view, this initial stage of the third moment may appear to place constraints on the objects of taste rather than on the states of mind in aesthetic response, just as Kant's original introduction of the concept of the finality of nature appeared, at least grammatically, to define an independent criterion for systematicity. The argument of §11 denies that an object's possession of certain kinds of finality can be a basis for calling it beautiful. But, as in the earlier argument, the appearance of a new criterion is in fact merely grammatical. If an object may be regarded as a (subjective) end just in virtue of fulfilling an interest, then to say that the object of taste cannot be an end is simply to reiterate that it cannot be regarded as beautiful just because it pleases by fulfilling that interest. And if representing an object as an (objective) end is to regard it as having a certain kind of history, then to deny that the representation of it as such an end can determine the judgment of taste is only to repeat that determinate causal judgment plays no part in taste. So far, no new constraints have actually been placed on the objects of taste, and no objects have been excluded from the class of possible beauties. As in the first moment, only certain grounds of approval have been excluded.

This is not to say that no gains at all can result from Kant's statement of his position in §§10 and 11. While Kant's denial that an object of taste can be regarded as a subjective end adds nothing to his previous claim that the beautiful does not please by satisfying an interest, the thesis that objects are not judged beautiful because of their status as objective ends does make more explicit a claim that was less clear in the first moment. This is the view that aesthetic judgment must disregard not only the effect of the actual existence of an object on its perceiver or audience,[20] but its causal history in general, including its causal connections to its creator. One's pleasure in a beautiful object cannot be dependent on the perception of it as having been created in the intentional fulfillment of a concept, because the role of a concept in its creation cannot be considered in aesthetic judgment of an object. *A fortiori,* an object of taste does not please as an object which successfully fulfills a certain intention.[21*] Thus, Kant's discussion of finality leads to the criticism of one form of intentionalist fallacy, namely, the assumption that a work's success in fulfilling its maker's intentions for it is itself a ground for aesthetic appreciation.[22*] This conclusion is stated in §15, where Kant denies that aesthetic judgment is a judgment on the perfection of an object in relation to some concept of what it should be, although, as we shall see, Kant is actually less than willing to apply this conclusion to the case of art.[23*] But even if this thesis was not completely clear before, it was in fact entailed by Kant's distinction between representation and actual existence and by his denial that aesthetic judgment depends upon determinate empirical judgment. And it still places constraints only on what we may consider in making a judgment of taste, rather than on the objects of taste themselves. How can Kant's consideration of finality or the relation of objects to ends lead to any such constraints?

Kant's attempt to provide substantive constraints on the properties of objects which may be considered in aesthetic judgment begins with the establishment of a sense of "finality" implying no connection with the two kinds of ends proscribed in the first paragraph of §11. Kant asserts that if a judgment of beauty can be determined neither by the agreeableness of an object as a subjective end nor by its perfection as an objective end, then "the delight, which we estimate as universally communicable without a concept, and which constitutes the determining ground of the judgment of taste, can be constituted by nothing other than the subjective finality in the representation of an object without any end (whether objective or subjective), consequently the mere form of finality in the representation through which an object is given to us."[24] This maintains that an object or its representation may possess the "form" of finality without, we might say, possessing the usual "matter" of finality—that is, actual relation to some subjective end or recognized status as an objective end. But what is the "form" of finality? Kant's alternative expression "subjective finality" suggests that an object has the form of finality when it stands in a certain relation to a subject who perceives and enjoys it. This suggestion may be confirmed not only by turning ahead to §12, but also by turning back to the two Introductions, where, in fact, Kant first deployed the concept of subjective or formal finality.

Section VII of the unpublished Introduction first established the notion of subjective finality in explaining how reflective judgment can perceive finality in the representation of a single object rather than in the representation of relations among objects.[25] Here, it will be remembered, Kant argued thus: "If, then, the form of a given object in empirical intuition is so constituted that the *apprehension* of its manifold in the imagination harmonizes with the *presentation* of a concept of the understanding (regardless of which concept), then in simple reflection understanding and imagination mutually harmonize for the furtherance of their business, and the object is perceived as final merely for the judgment; thus the finality itself is considered merely subjective."[26] The published Introduction similarly explained "subjective formal finality" in connection with an object's production of the harmony of the faculties. Here, Kant argued that when pleasure is felt in the apprehension of an object but without any relation of the object to "a concept for a determinate cognition," "the pleasure can express nothing but the suitability [*Angemessenheit*] of the object itself to the cognitive faculties, which are in play in the reflective judgment, so far as they are in play, and therefore merely a subjective formal finality of the object."[27] According to these two passages, the subjective or formal finality of an object does indeed consist in its standing in a certain relation to a subject — namely, that of being able to dispose the imagination and understanding of the subject to their state of free play. The form of finality in an object consists precisely in its tendency to produce the harmony of the faculties, or its suitability for allowing this state to result from the contemplation of it. Such a tendency, it might be noted, may be called final or purposive because the harmony of the faculties itself pleases as an unusual accomplishment of our general cognitive aim or purpose. This implies that though a beautiful object does not please as a "subjective end" in reference to some specific desire or interest in the subject perceiving it, it does in fact please in reference to a more general aim on the part of subjects — the aim of cognition itself, on which Kant's entire theory of aesthetic response depends.

The same conclusion is implied by the argument of §12, although perhaps more obscurely. Basically, §12 reiterates the explanation of aesthetic response already presented in the Introductions and the second moment of the Analytic in a way which justifies calling that response "final" and attributing finality to the objects which occasion it. Kant accomplishes this by arguing that although the feeling of pleasure does not stand in an ordinary causal connection to its object, it is nevertheless linked to an "internal" and an "intrinsic causality" (*innere Causalitat* or *Causalitat in sich*).[28]

Kant begins §12 by maintaining that the feeling of pleasure cannot be linked to any representation ("sensation or concept") by an *a priori* law describing the latter as cause and the former as effect, for the simple reason that connections of cause and effect can be known only "*a posteriori* and by means of experience."[29] Instead of suggesting that there may be such an *a posteriori* causal connection between aesthetic response and the representation which is its object, however, Kant proceeds to emphasize the disanalogy between aesthetic judgment and ordinary empirical investigation which, I have argued, inspires the enterprise of the Analytic. This is the fact that our consciousness of pleasure in the beautiful is our sole direct consciousness of the ground of this pleasure. Kant argues that in the case of moral judgment the mental state (by which he apparently means consciousness) of the determination of the will and the feeling of pleasure are identical, and then asserts that the situation is similar in the case of aesthetic judgment: the consciousness of the free play of the faculties just is the consciousness of pleasure. Specifically, what Kant is suggesting is that in the case of aesthetic judgment, the recognition of the finality of an object does not require a causal judgment about the relation between pleasure and an end, but is given by the feeling of pleasure itself. Thus he maintains: "The consciousness of the merely formal finality in the play of a subject's cognitive faculty in the case of a representation by which an object is given is the pleasure itself, because an aesthetic judgment involves a determining ground of the activity of the subject with respect to the enlivening of its cognitive faculties, and thus an internal causality (which is final) in respect to cognition in general, but without being limited to a determinate cognition, and consequently a mere form of the subjective finality of a representation."[30] This passage cannot be taken to maintain that there is no causal judgment involved in any stage of aesthetic judgment. As we have seen, the occurrence of a feeling of pleasure is only a necessary and not a sufficient condition of such judgment. Deciding that an object is beautiful, as this very passage could be taken to imply, does require the judgment that it occasions the felt pleasure through the causality of the harmony of the faculties rather than through anything else. Rather, the point of this passage is that the finality of an object of taste does not consist in its relation to any specific end, but just in the causality of the object in respect of the general condition of cognition.

In other words, the merely formal or subjective finality of the representation of an object consists in the fact that it can dispose the faculties of imagination and understanding to the state of free play, itself internally causal in producing feeling of pleasure. A representation which causes aesthetic response may be called final because it is in fact related to a general objective — not a specific interest, but the general aim of knowledge itself. Insofar as this objective can be satisfied without any judgment about the relation of an object to any determinate interest or intention, an object which produces the harmony of the faculties possesses a finality distinct from that defined in §10. And insofar as the unification of our manifolds, as the general subjective aim in cognition, might be thought of as a "formal" end (the form of knowledge without its usual matter or content, specific empirical judgments), the finality which an object possesses in virtue of producing the harmony of the faculties may be thought of as a formal finality. Formal finality is simply the power of an object — or its representation — to satisfy a formal end or purpose.

As Kant first defined finality in §10, it was a kind of causality — the causal power of a concept to produce an object. The formal finality of an object also turns out to be a kind of causality: the power of an object to satisfy the general aim of cognition apart from any determinate judgment, or to occasion a free play between imagination and understanding. This is not the only kind of causality which Kant connects with aesthetic response. He continues §12 by arguing that although our pleasure in the beautiful is not due to a practical ground of agreeableness or goodness, still it resembles pleasure in the agreeable or good in involving "an intrinsic causality, namely, that of *preserving* the condition of representation itself and the occupation of the cognitive faculties without ulterior aim," a causality which explains why "we *dwell* on the contemplation of the beautiful."[31] This *intrinsic* causality is not identical with the causality of a representation in respect to the general aim of cognition which has just been discussed. The *internal* causality first mentioned in §12 is the power of a representation to produce a feeling of pleasure by producing the harmony of the faculties; the *intrinsic* causality next mentioned is the efficacy of the feeling of pleasure itself to produce a tendency toward its own continuation and the preservation of anything on which it depends. The second kind of causality is simply a general effect of any feeling of pleasure;[32] it is only the first kind of causality which is unique to aesthetic response. A pleasure's tendency to produce an inclination toward its own continuation may, of course, be connected to the fact that pleasures result from the satisfaction of objectives — on the supposition that objectives not only have to be satisfied, but have to remain satisfied — but this is not what constitutes the finality of an aesthetic object. That consists in its tendency to produce pleasure in the first place.

By the argument of §12, then, Kant succeeds in defining a sense of "finality" in which it denotes a property in objects of taste in virtue of which they may be said to produce aesthetic response. However, the question must again be raised whether Kant has introduced a constraint on objects of taste which is new in anything besides its grammar. Does the assertion that a beautiful object must please because of its formal or subjective finality restrict aesthetic response to any particular aspects or kinds of objects? Does it lead to any criteria directly applicable to objects by means of which some of the pleasures they occasion may be recognized to be pleasures in their beauty, and others not? In particular, does formal finality, or "the bare form of finality in the representation whereby an object is given to us," necessarily pertain to the form of objects? Is the form of finality finality of form?[33]

At this stage of Kant's argument, the answer to this question must surely be no. Kant has attributed the form of finality to the object of taste by emphasizing the role of the representation of an object in the production of that harmony of the faculties which satisfies our subjective but purely formal cognitive objective. But he has not shown that any particular properties or kinds of objects are uniquely suitable for producing the state of free play. To attribute formal finality to an object is to claim that it is suitable for occasioning this state, but not to claim that it does so in virtue of any specific properties. Naturally, given the way the formal end to which beautiful objects are related has been defined, certain of what are at least grammatically an object's properties may be excluded from the basis of aesthetic response. Those properties which an object has in virtue of standing in relation to certain of our own desires or requirements may be excluded. An object's utility is not a property which makes it beautiful, because it is a property it has in virtue of its connection to some specific interest we have. An object's subsumability under some concept does not make it beautiful, because that is a property it has in relation to the determinate concepts we possess. But excluding such properties from the appropriate bases of taste does not disqualify any of the more ordinary sorts of an object's properties from a potential role in producing the harmony of the faculties, or from contributing to its formal finality. So far, it is not obvious that only design but not color can contribute to formal finality, or that only composition but not tone can occasion the harmony of the faculties. Nor does anything in Kant's notion of the form of finality entail that free beauties of nature but not representational works of art should be proper objects of pure judgments of taste.

The concept of the mere form of finality, in other words, is not identical with any particular notion of aesthetic form, and does not itself imply a restriction of taste to the kinds of properties Kant offers as examples of aesthetic form. The notion of form which Kant develops in §§11 and 12 of the third moment does not add any criterion for aesthetic judgment to those developed in the first two moments. How can Kant suppose that it does? As I pointed out, Kant has already used his classification of aesthetic and teleological judgment as the two species of reflective judgment to associate the former with the judgment of individual natural forms, as opposed to the relations between natural objects;[34] and his Introductions have already asserted that it is in the apprehension of the form of an object that imagination and understanding may be brought into their unintended accord.[35] Nevertheless, these earlier passages do not offer any actual analysis of the concept of form. It is only in the third moment that Kant attempts to move from the epistemological notion of formal finality to more restrictive notions of aesthetic form. This move has not occurred in §§11 or 12; if it is to be found at all, it must be found in the three specific arguments which I distinguished at the beginning of this chapter. I now turn to the first of these.

The Appearance of Design

The first paragraph of §10 defined finality in terms of causal history, suggesting that any judgment about finality must be a judgment about causality. In a way, §12 has confirmed this suggestion, even for the case of aesthetic judgment. In the second paragraph of §10, however, Kant writes:

> An object, or a state of mind, or even an action may be called final, although its possibility does not necessarily presuppose the representation of an end, just because its possibility can only be explained and comprehended by us if we assume a causality according to ends as its ground, that is, a will that would have arranged it according to the representation of a particular rule. Finality can therefore obtain apart from an end, insofar as we do not posit the causes of this form in a will, but can yet make the explanation of its possibility comprehensible to ourselves if we derive it from a will. Now we do not always have to

examine what we observe through reason (with respect to its possibility). Therefore, without basing it on a purpose (as the matter of the *nexus finalis*) we can at least observe a finality with respect to form [*eine Zweckmässigkeit der Form nach*] in objects, although we can notice it only by reflection.[36]

To understand this argument fully, we must attribute to Kant the view that knowledge requires not only the synthesis of representations of objects according to rules, but also the production of objects themselves according to rules, and that where we cannot see a comprehensible object as due to our own action according to rules, we must postulate—though we cannot actually know—some other rule-governed agent as its cause. I cannot examine this doctrine here. What I do wish to consider, however, is Kant's reason for invoking this view at all in the present context. This appears to be the assumption that certain objects have an appearance of design, an appearance which forces us to postulate a designer for them. Such an appearance might be considered a mere form of finality—this would be suggested if we read Kant's phrase *eine Zweckmässigkeit der Form nach* as contrasting with the "actual matter of the *nexus finalis,*" that is, a finality in real causal history. But Kant also intimates that this appearance is a finality *of form.* What we have to explain by this peculiar postulation of a designer is the form of an object. Thus Kant seems to believe that there are certain phenomenal forms which are characteristic of designed objects, and to imply that such forms are the appropriate objects of taste.

This is, at least, the traditional interpretation of §10. Donald Crawford, for instance, interprets Kant as claiming that "we can call an object . . . *purposive* on the basis of its formal organization (structure) even when we do not or cannot actually place the cause of this form in a will . . . An object's 'purposiveness' is what we perceive in it—its form or organization—which leads us to say that it resulted from a concept."[37] But we must ask whether there are in fact any forms characteristic of designed objects, or whether a suggestion that pleasure in the beautiful is a response to apparent design actually limits the form of finality to any specific notion of aesthetic form.

Again, our answer must be that this argument cannot imply any constraint on objects of taste other than the already established conclusion that they must please without being subsumed under determinate concepts of cause or interest. First, we might argue that the only purpose which beautiful arguments can appear designed to fulfill without actually being judged to be designed is the general purpose of cognition itself. But unless we have already placed some constraints on the features by which objects can produce the harmony of the faculties, their appearing designed for this purpose can imply no such constraints. Second, we may undermine Kant's suggestion by considering more specific sorts of purposes, which might be expected to make the notion of an appearance of design more specific. If we do this, we shall surely recognize that human purposes — let alone those of other possible wills — are too various to imply any restriction on the appearance of objects that may satisfy them. For *any* perceptual property an object might have, we may readily imagine a purpose which that property could satisfy; we can easily construct purposes objects might satisfy by their color or tone, as well as by their geometrical design or temporally extended organization. And *within* any range of properties objects have, there are none that cannot be imagined to fulfill some conceivable purpose. Within the realm of shapes, for example, any, from the simplest and most regular to the most complex and irregular, may satisfy some human objective. Neither the concept of the formal end of cognition itself, then, nor reflection of specific human purposes can place any constraints on the features on account of which objects may appear designed for some purpose. The appearance of design is a vacuous criterion for aesthetic judgment, for any appearance might satisfy some design. Alternatively, if we tried to interpret the mere form of finality as consisting of perceptual features which *cannot* be taken to satisfy any subjective or objective ends, we would be left with no candidates for finality of form at all. Obviously, if any perceptual properties of an object might satisfy some imaginable end, then there are none which cannot satisfy such an end.

The argument of §10 may be meant to make a transition from the concept of the form of finality to a concept of the finality of form, but it cannot succeed in so doing. Consideration of Kant's own examples of objects which appear to be designed without being known to be so only confirms this conclusion. Kant gives two examples of objects which occasion "a certain finality in the representative state of the subject" and which thus tempt the subject to the thought of purpose, without providing any knowledge of purpose. The first of these is in §15. Here Kant writes that "if in a forest I come upon a lawn, around which the trees make a circle, and I do not thereby represent any purpose, such as that it should serve for country-dances, then not the least concept of a perfection will be given by the mere form."[38] In the *Critique of Teleological Judgment,* Kant offers a second example of an appearance which can occasion the thought of an end and, in this instance, a postulation of finality through a teleological rather than an aesthetic judgment: "If someone in an apparently unoccupied country perceived a geometrical figure traced in the sand, say, a regular hexagon, his reflection, while it worked on a concept of it, would become aware through reason, although obscurely, of unity of principle in its production."[39] These examples involve arguments beyond the scope of §10, but are certainly supposed to suggest to us the kinds of forms associated with ends. Of the second example, for instance, Crawford writes that "the object in this case is conceived as having a purpose . . . owing to our apprehension of certain formal relationships exemplifying a rule."[40] But there is nothing about the pure *form* of the objects involved in these examples which requires the thought of finality. If we encounter the geometrical form of circularity not in a forest clearing, but when a raindrop hits a still pond, we need not be tempted to thoughts of purpose; and if we find a hexagon in the cell of a beehive,[41]* or in a crystal, rather than apparently drawn in the sand, we will not be inclined to think of a will as its cause. That is, it is not the nature of any form itself which suggests design, but, at best, its context. To think of any object as even merely apparently designed, we must not only perceive its form but also consider the causal nexus of its actual existence. The mere thought of design cannot pick out either any particular forms or any range of perceptual properties as formal ones, to serve as the proper objects of taste.

The belief that intelligible form or proportion requires the action of an intelligent creator goes back to the roots of Western philosophy,[42] and Kant may well have been in its grasp when he supposed that regular forms were obviously appearances of design. But he does not attempt to delimit any set of forms which can be taken as such appearances, or to show that an object's disposition to satisfy our general objective in cognition — its formal finality — must actually lie in any specific features of its apparent organization, or in finality of form. Thus Kant's first attempt to replace the concept of the form of finality with a more concrete notion of form is a failure. We must now consider his two remaining attempts in the final five sections of the third moment. We must keep in mind that in the actual composition of these sections Kant may have simply assumed that the concepts of the *form of finality* and the *finality of form* are identical, which they are not. Nevertheless, I will now consider how these sections fare if regarded as independent arguments for the thesis that it is in fact only the form of objects which is responsible for their formal or subjective finality.

Form and Matter

If Kant's aesthetic theory consists of two fundamental doctrines, the requirement of universality and the explanatory model of the harmony of the faculties, he might attempt to derive specific criteria for the justification of aesthetic judgments from either of these two bases. Kant's argument in §§13 and 14 contains elements of both strategies, but basically rests on a parallel between his analysis of aesthetic judgment and the theory of perception employed in the *Critique of Pure Reason*. In what follows, I will examine the actual structure of Kant's argument in these sections, and consider to what extent his conclusions can really be seen as entailed by the fundamental doctrines of his aesthetic theory alone.

The key to these sections is the classification of judgments concerning felt pleasures with terms drawn from the first *Critique*. I have already used the adjective "pure" of judgments of taste, connoting by the expression "pure judgment of taste" simply a genuinely valid aesthetic judgment of reflection. In §§13 and 14, Kant canonizes this terminology and exploits it in defense of his formalism. The first paragraph of §14 displays the basis of his new scheme: "Aesthetic judgments, just like theoretical (logical) ones, can be divided into empirical and pure. The former are those which predicate agreeableness or disagreeableness of an object or its mode of representation, the latter, those which predicate beauty of it; the former are judgments of sense (material aesthetic judgments), the latter (as formal) alone [are] genuine judgments of taste."[43] This classification does not itself imply any new constraints on the objects of taste, for, like the scheme of the first moment,[44] it divides judgments of taste solely by reference to the history of the pleasures occasioning them. Empirical or material judgments of taste are simply those which assert that objects are agreeable, and are grounded on feelings of pleasure ascribed to the physiological effects of objects on the senses. Pure or formal judgments of taste are those which ascribe beauty to an object, and must be founded on the attribution of the felt pleasure to the harmony of the faculties, and on the *a priori* imputation of pleasure so felt to other persons. Nothing not already known about *how* objects can dispose us to the state of free play is thereby entailed.

This is also evident in §13, where Kant basically just supplies some new names for interested and sensory pleasures. Thus this section begins by repeating the thesis that "every interest corrupts the judgment of taste and deprives it of its impartiality," and asserts that the extent of the influence of interest on a given judgment of taste is equivalent to the degree to which the judgment is affected by the sensations through which something merely gratifies or occasions pain. Such sensory and interested feelings of pleasure are now called "charms" and "emotions" (*Reize* and *Ruhrungen*), and so Kant's separation of judgments on objects determined by feelings of interest and agreeableness from those based on disinterested pleasure is reformulated as a distinction between judgments influenced by charm and emotion and those truly concerned with beauty. Thus "a judgment of taste on which charm and emotion have no influence (although they may allow of association with the delight in the beautiful), and which therefore has merely the finality of form as its determining ground, is a pure *judgment of taste.*"⁴⁵ This sentence suggests that a judgment of taste must be a response to finality of form, rather than to the mere form of finality. But merely renaming interested feelings of pleasure "charms" and "emotions" and contrasting "empirical" judgments of pleasure with "pure" ones provides no new justification for the assumption that true pleasure in beauty is a response only to the form of objects. Nor does the introduction of the terms "matter" and "form" into §13 provide such justification. Kant says that when charms are counted as genuine beauty, "the matter of delight is passed off for the form." But this cannot mean that feelings of charm are occasioned by "matter" *in objects* and true feelings of beauty by their "form." At best, it can be only another way of saying that interested pleasure is occasioned by the merely empirical or "material" nature of sensory gratification—our *response to* objects—and pleasure in the beautiful by the "formal" state of the harmony of the faculties.

Yet §14 proceeds directly from these considerations to the assertion that judgments of taste must always be associated with the formal rather than material elements *of the objects of perception themselves*. It is here that Kant lays down his famous restrictions:

> In painting, sculpture, indeed in all formative arts, in architecture and horticulture, insofar as they are beautiful arts, the *design [Zeichnung]* is what is essential; in these, it is not what gratifies in sensation which constitutes the basis of any disposition for taste, but solely what pleases through its form. The colors which illuminate the outline [*Abriss*] belong to charm; they can indeed in themselves enliven the object for [the faculty of] sensation, but they cannot make it worthy of intuition and beautiful . . .
>
> All form of objects of senses (of the outer senses and also, mediately, of the inner sense) is either *figure [Gestalt]* or *play [Spiel]*, in the latter case, either the play of figures (in space, mime, or dance) or the mere

play of sensations (in time). The charm of colors or the agreeable tones of the instruments may be added, but the *design* in the former and the *composition* in the latter constitute the proper object of the pure judgment of taste.[46]

In these passages, Kant finally asserts a genuinely restrictive doctrine of formalism. Strictly sensory and physiological aspects of perception such as colors or tones are maintained to contribute to nothing but charm or gratification in their objects, and only such purely formal features of spatial and temporal organization as "design" or "drawing," "outline," "figure," "play," and "composition" are allowed to contribute to actual beauty. Only these features of objects, in other words, are supposed able to dispose the imagination and understanding to their harmonious fulfillment of the subjective conditions of knowledge. The form of finality is finally linked to the finality of form, by being assigned to these purely formal features of spatially and temporally extended objects of perception.

Kant's thesis is not just that such individual contents of sensations as *particular* colors or tones, being purely physiological, cannot produce any aesthetic response themselves, and must be experienced in a complex manifold if they are to present any occasion for a harmony between imagination and understanding. One might place this interpretation on Kant's first mention of color and tone in §14, when he says that "a mere color, such as the green of a lawn, or a mere tone (as distinguished from sound and noise), such as that of a violin, is declared to be beautiful in itself by most people, although both seem to have only the matter of representation, that is, mere sensation, for their ground, and thus deserve to be called only agreeable."[47] This remark could lead one to suppose that Kant's view is that colors or tones by themselves are merely agreeable, but that *complexes* of colors or tones might be beautiful—stimulate a harmony of the faculties—in virtue of the coloristic or tonal relations obtaining among their members. However, Kant's use of such terms as "drawing" and "outline" suggests that nothing but the lineal, geometrical, or spatial properties of even complexly colored objects are responsible for their beauty. Colors, whether singly or in groups, can never do more than add charm to beauty. Similarly, Kant's treatment of composition as a purely temporal play of sensations suggests that in music it is only the temporal organization of notes which is beautiful, and that even such complex features of tones as instrumentation, registration, and coloration can never contribute anything but charm to our response.

How could Kant move from his division of judgments on pleasure to such a thesis about the proper objects of pleasure? In what follows, we will see several reasons which inclined Kant to this view. Perhaps the most fundamental, however, is that Kant in fact adopted more than just the words "form" and "matter" from the *Critique of Pure Reason.* Having classified judgments of agreeableness and beauty as material and formal judgments, Kant then imported the full perceptual theory of the first *Critique* into his aesthetic theory, and supposed that a material judgment of taste must be occasioned by the matter of appearance, and that a formal judgment of taste can be occasioned only by the form of sensation. To understand Kant's inferences in §14, we must begin by looking at his earlier theory of perception.

The views on which Kant's aesthetic formalism depend are all stated in the opening paragraphs of the first *Critique*'s Transcendental Aesthetic, where Kant prepares the way for his theory of pure and empirical judgment by breaking appearance up into formal and material constituents. First, sensation is defined as "the effect of an object upon the faculty of representation, so far as we are affected by it."[48]* Empirical and pure representations are then defined in terms of their connection to sensation. "That intuition which is in relation to the object through sensation is entitled *empirical*'; by contrast, Kant terms "all representations *pure* (in the transcendental sense) in which there is nothing that belongs to sensation." By extension, empirical and pure judgments are those which depend, respectively, on empirical and pure representations or intuitions. But Kant's claim that pure representations contain nothing belonging to sensation needs interpretation, for it does not mean that such representations have no connection to sensory representation or appearance at all; rather, what it means is that they relate to perception through the form of appearance.

Thus the distinction between pure and empirical judgments in Kant's epistemology depends on the distinction between the form and matter of appearance. This is stated thus: "That in the appearance which corresponds to sensation I term its *matter;* but that which so determines the manifold of appearance that it allows of being ordered in certain relations, I term the *form* of appearance." This remark is profoundly important, for it suggests that form is *whatever* is responsible for the unity of a manifold of perceptions. This could make it true by definition that it is the form of an aesthetic object which is responsible for its production of the harmony of the faculties; and this definition undoubtedly does much to explain Kant's ready assumption that finality of form is indeed the proper object of taste. But to understand how this definition can lead to the specific opinions of the third *Critique*'s §14, we must consider several further theses of the Transcendental Aesthetic. First, by assuming the empiricist doctrine that perception can present us with discrete particulars but not the relations between them, Kant asserts that "that in which alone the sensations can be posited in a certain form, cannot itself be sensation"; consequently, while the matter of appearance is actually given by sensation, "its form must lie ready for the sensations *a priori* in the mind, and so must allow of being considered apart from all sensation." The object of pure *a priori* judgment thus must be the "pure form of sensible intuitions in general, in which all the manifold of intuition is intuited in certain relations, [and] which must be found in the mind *a priori*." Second, Kant argues that this pure *a priori* form of appearance is space and time. Thus if we "separate from [sensibility] everything which belongs to sensation . . . it will be found that there are two pure forms of sensible intuition, serving as principles of *a priori* knowledge, namely, space and time."

Space and time are the *a priori* forms of intuition, and spatial and temporal structure the *a priori* and formal aspects of objects of experience. This leads to a doctrine of abstraction according to which the formal aspects of the representation of objects can be separated from both the matter of sensation and, it turns out, conceptual addition: "Thus if I take away from the representation of a body that which the understanding thinks in regard to it, substance, force, divisibility, etc., and likewise what belongs to sensation, impenetrability, hardness, color, etc., something still remains over from this empirical intuition, namely, extension and figure. They belong to pure intuition."[49] The doctrine of the first *Critique* is, then, that the form of appearance is what allows intuitions to be ordered in cognitive relations, and that what actually fills that role is spatial and temporal form. Further, the spatial and temporal aspects of objects are subject to abstraction and can be judged *a priori*. Thus the secondary qualities of objects—Kant's list of what belongs to mere sensation is not identical with Locke's list of secondary qualities, but his contrast certainly suggests Locke's classification[50*]—are subject to merely empirical judgment, but such primary qualities as "extension and figure," as well as the temporal analogue "play," are subject to pure *a priori* judgment, based on abstraction of the form of appearance from its matter.

The formalism exemplified in §14 of the *Critique of Judgment* depends on the importation of this theory of perception into the context of aesthetic response and judgment. The notion of purity furnishes the linchpin in Kant's transition from the character of aesthetic response to that of its proper object. A passage from §16 reveals Kant's strategy in its neat parallel of my last quotation from the Transcendental Aesthetic: "Now just as the connection of agreeableness (of sensation) with beauty, which properly concerns only form, hinders the purity of the judgment of taste; so the connection of the good (on which, that is, the manifold of a thing is good according to its purpose) with the beautiful does the same sort of damage to the purity of this judgment."[51] A pure judgment must be based on a pure aspect of objects, and on the theory of the first *Critique* that means it can be determined neither by the sensory qualities of objects themselves nor by the concepts which apply to them, but only by their spatial and temporal forms, their figure and play. And for this to be possible, it would seem, the mind must have a power of abstraction in aesthetic response quite analogous to that which it exercises in arriving at *a priori* knowledge of pure intuition itself, or geometry and arithmetic.

I shall return to the issue of abstraction at the end of this chapter; at this point, I will consider the more general question of Kant's justification for using this theory of appearance in his theory of taste. There are several ways in which Kant's distinction between the form and matter of appearance might be thought of as being introduced into the argument of §14. First, there is the most obvious reading of the section. On this, Kant would be seen as simply assuming that formal and material judgments of pleasure must take the form and matter of appearance as their objects. This corresponds most closely to the actual structure of the text. Unfortunately, it does not support a very convincing argument. One may contend that the classification of judgments of beauty and agreeableness as formal and material is based on a mere analogy with the first *Critique*'s division of theoretical judgments, and argue that such an analogy simply cannot license the conclusions which Kant draws from it. Second, one might view Kant as revolving the argument on the notion of the harmony of the faculties. Treating this harmony as a relation among items in a manifold of appearance, Kant would then be using the definition of form as what grounds such a relation, and assuming that, as with cognition in general, so in the case of the merely subjective harmony of the faculties it is spatial and temporal form which fills this role. An argument such as this would be less arbitrary than a mere argument from analogy. Still, it could be contended that it must be an independent question whether spatial and temporal form are the only features of a manifold of imagination which can cause what is, after all, a mere feeling of unity, or whether, say, nonspatial and nontemporal relations among colors or tones might not also allow the free play of the faculties. Finally, one can see Kant as making this argument: since the sensory matter of appearance can ground only empirical judgments, and only the pure form of appearance can ground *a priori* judgments, and since the requirement that aesthetic judgment possess subjective universal validity precludes its dependence on strictly empirical judgment, the judgment of taste must be a pure judgment in the sense of the first *Critique*—that is, a judgment on spatial and temporal form.

Insofar as the second and third of these arguments rest on more than mere analogy, they require careful consideration. As far as the view that the explanation of aesthetic response as due to the harmony of the imagination and understanding implies the restriction of its proper objects to spatial and temporal form is concerned, it may be safely objected that nothing in the concept of the free play of the faculties itself requires its association with the first *Critique*'s separation of the form and matter of appearance. Kant's explanation of our pleasure in the beautiful does entail that this must be more than a merely physiological gratification in the sensory qualities of objects, and must instead involve reflection upon a complex manifold of imagination. But this does not imply that the features of such a manifold in virtue of which the imagination can present it as unified may not themselves be such sensory qualities as color or tone. Certain colors or tones, while nothing but sensations themselves, might be felt to belong together in just such a way as to satisfy the understanding's requirement of unity in the manifolds imagination presents to it; indeed, one might even suggest that the very fact that such features of objects are not pure *a priori* elements of their appearance and thus not susceptible to the schematism of the *a priori* concepts of the understanding makes it all the more likely that they could serve for the felt synthesis without concepts which founds aesthetic response.

Examples for this objection are easily constructed. Criticizing Kant's theory of aesthetic form several decades ago, Barrows Dunham wrote that "violet, as a single color, may be liked or disliked as you please, even though no experience will yield you a sensation of violet alone. In a painting, however, where the violet serves a definite artistic purpose, it cannot avoid being a necessary part of the total effect. The solitary notes of a trombone may be pleasant perhaps only to the player, but in the performance of a symphony they may be so necessary that the music would be

Form and Matter

crippled by the loss of them."[52] Dunham's talk of "artistic purpose" and what is "necessary" in a work or performance may cloud the issue, but his point is well taken. Consider, for example, a set of paintings from Josef Albers' "Homage to the Square" series,[53*] a large group of paintings each of which has the same geometrical form—they look like sets of nested squares—but is done in a different selection of colors. Suppose that we find some of these paintings beautiful and others not; to what could we then ascribe the difference in our responses to them? Since the geometrical form is exactly the same in each painting, differences in regard to their beauty can be due only to the fact that in some of them the colors are felt to belong together and to please us in a way not true in others. In the words of Hilton Kramer, "the singularity of an Albers painting does not reside at all in its formal invention, but exclusively in the particular confluence of colors which are brought together within their assigned forms." Yet it can hardly be supposed that the fact that it is only the colors of these paintings which really occupy our imagination means, as Kant's thesis implies, that our response to them is nothing but charm or emotion.[54] In fact, we respond to them with a purely formal unity of imagination and understanding; as Kramer points out, these paintings involve "nothing less than the elimination of all those notations of feeling which traditionally invest a painting with its pictorial meaning and make of it something more than a design."[55] In other words, these paintings conform fully to the Kantian constraints on aesthetic response, but do so because their color rather than their form produces a harmony between imagination and understanding. Indeed, Kant's general theory of aesthetic response is perfectly suited to explain our pleasure in some of these paintings, and can do so as long as we recognize that Kant's assumption that only "figure" or "play" can ground a response to beauty is entailed by his commitment to the first *Critique*'s theory of perception rather than by the concept of the harmony of the faculties itself.

Kant's restriction could be attacked with many more examples. Thus to impugn Kant's exclusion of tone from the proper objects of taste in the case of music, Dunham simply asks us to "imagine the performance of a symphony in which the violin parts are played by the horns and the horn parts by the violins"; imagining this will surely lead us to agree "that the finest music in the world will not survive ill-treatment of its tonal qualities."[56] The point I wish to emphasize, however, is not that Kant is, as it were, just wrong about the facts of beauty. Rather, the point is that his own general theory of the harmony of the faculties need not exclude harmonies among colors and tones from the objects of taste; only if this theory is supplemented by the quite independent assumption that it is only spatial and temporal forms which can order manifolds in relations, even purely subjective ones, can it actually have the restrictive consequences he assigns to it. The notion of the harmony of the faculties is certainly linked with Kant's general theory of cognition as synthesis, and must be interpreted in the light of that connection. But Kant's general theory of knowledge and its conditions is far from identical with the specifics of his views on sensation and perception. Kant's theory of cognitive judgment can be understood apart from the Transcendental Aesthetic's distinction between the form and matter of appearance; and so, I would contend, can his theory of taste.[57*]

Several further points may be made about the connection between Kant's abstract explanation of aesthetic response and his commitment to specific formalist opinions. The first is that Kant's own discussion of a condition under which such material qualities of sensation as color or tone might in fact be objects of genuine pleasure in beauty by no means accommodates the kind of criticism which I have brought against him. Kant does allow one circumstance in which such sensations as color or tone might be entitled to be called beautiful—the circumstance where they are themselves pure.[58] The reason for Kant's exception of pure sensations from his general proscription of the matter of appearance rests in his adoption of Euler's theory of color and tones.[59*] Kant assumes that colors are "isochronous vibrations of the ether," and tones similar vibrations of the air, and that in being conscious of pure colors or tones, one is in fact conscious of "formal determinations of the unity of a manifold of sensations." In this case, one's pleasure in them would be not the effect of "mere sensations, but rather the effect of an estimation of form in the play of a manifold of sensations."[60] There are problems with this, however. One problem is that for this theory to work, Kant has to suppose that in perceiving color and tone "the mind not only perceives by sense their effect in stimulating the organ [of sense], but also perceives through reflection the regular play of impressions (thus the form in the connection of different representations)."[61] This not only seems unlikely; it also conflicts with what Kant says much later on about the aesthetic effect of music, namely, that it depends not on any consciousness of the mathematical basis of the relations among impressions, but simply on the mind's sense of the unity or continuity of a manifold of notes.[62] Another problem is that an aesthetic appreciation of pure colors or tones is hardly what we need to explain by the theory of the harmony of the faculties. It is not "simple colors" in isolation which are beautiful, but cominations of colors, as in the case of the Albers paintings. Kant does not try to reconcile the beauty of *manifolds* of colors or tones to his theory, but instead adopts the strained view that single colors or tones are themselves really manifolds allowing the play of the imagination. This forces him to suggest that we really are conscious of a manifold in being conscious of a single or pure color or tone, when it would in fact be much more plausible to allow that manifolds of colors or tones can occasion the harmony of imagination and understanding and produce the pleasure of aesthetic response. It is not plausible to suppose that the simple constituents of manifolds — whether they be pure colors or simple determinations of space, such as points or lines — are themselves beautiful; it is only plausible to assume that manifolds of such items can be appreciated as beautiful or felt to belong together without being subordinated to any rule.[63]* Kant's concession of beauty to *pure* colors or tones is no acknowledgment of the independence of the theory of aesthetic response from the first *Critique*'s theory of perception.

The second point I want to make, however, is that the theory of aesthetic ideas which Kant expounds later in the third *Critique* must derive from Kant's own exploitation of the gap between the general idea of the harmony of the faculties and the particular formalist opinions of the third moment. An aesthetic idea "is a representation of the imagination, annexed to a given concept, with which, in the free employment of imagination, such a multiplicity of partial representations are bound up that no expression indicating a definite concept can be found for it,"[64] or which induces "on its own accord such a wealth of thought as would never admit of comprehension in a definite concept."[65] An aesthetic idea involves a manifold of the imagination the constituents of which are felt to belong together, and to illustrate a given concept, although, as with aesthetic response in general, this coherence does not derive from a rule imposed by the concept being illustrated or by any other concept. As with other objects of taste, so in the case of aesthetic ideas "the imagination is represented . . . in its freedom from all guidance by rules, but still as final for the presentation of the given concept."[66] Thus the explanation of our pleasure in the contemplation of a work which presents an aesthetic idea is the same as that of our pleasure in beauty, namely, the harmony of the faculties. Indeed, in §51, Kant goes so far as to assert that "beauty in general (it may be beauty of nature or of art) may be called the *expression* of aesthetic ideas."[67] But it is clear that the constituents of an aesthetic idea are *not* limited to pure spatial or temporal forms. Kant calls the members of the

233

manifold of an aesthetic idea "secondary representations of the imagination," and gives as an example — illustrating the idea of the king of heaven — "Jupiter's eagle with the lightning in its claws." Such an attribute does not "represent what lies in our concepts of the sublimity and majesty of creation"; instead, it is something else, "something that gives the imagination occasion to spread itself over a host of related representations."[68] The constituents of the manifold in the case of an aesthetic idea thus function as more than mere spatial or temporal forms. Kant's example suggests that they work by presenting conceptual contents in addition to such forms; but if we were to supplement his example from poetry with analyses of the effects of, say, monumental painting and opera, colors and tones might also be brought into the explanation of the effect of a given work on the imagination.

Again, the point is simply that the explanation of pleasure as due to the harmony of the faculties does not itself place a constraint on the possible *contents* of the manifold of the imagination, or determine which of its features may allow it to be grasped in a unified but free play of the higher cognitive faculties. Kant's explanation of aesthetic response places constraints on what kinds of approval can found judgments of taste, but not, it seems, on what sorts of properties of objects may contribute to their beauty.

The strategy of linking formal aesthetic judgments to the form rather than the matter of appearance through the concept of the harmony of the faculties does not appear promising. What about the third argument which may be read into §14, that on which Kant eliminates the matter of appearance from the proper objects of taste by direct appeal to the analytical requirement of universal subjective validity?

That Kant subscribes to such an argument is beyond question. In the *Critique of Pure Reason,* he commits himself to the view that representations which "belong merely to the subjective constitution of our manner of sensibility . . . as in the case of sensations of color, sounds, and heat . . . since they are mere sensations and not intuitions, do not of themselves yield knowledge of any object."[69] And because "these cannot rightly be regarded as properties of things, but [can] only [be regarded] as changes in the subject," they are "changes which may, indeed, be different for different persons." A rose, for instance, "in respect of its color, can appear differently to every observer."[70] The *Critique of Judgment,* at least in its third moment,[71]* retains this conclusion, and argues that if the matter of sensation cannot be expected to be the same from one observer to the next, *a fortiori* neither can its disposition for causing pleasure or pain. This emerges in Kant's discussion of pure colors and tones, which are not favored solely because they can supposedly explain the harmony of the faculties, it turns out. They are also favored because they are supposed to be exceptions to the lack of intersubjective validity which generally obtains for the matter of appearance: "one must also notice that sensations of color as well as of tone are only correctly held to be beautiful in themselves insofar as they are *pure,* which is a determination that already concerns their form, and is also the only one which can be universally communicated of these representations with certainty: since the quality of sensations itself cannot be assumed to agree in all subjects, and it can hardly be assumed that the agreeableness of one color as opposed to another, or of the tone of one musical instrument rather than another, will be estimated by everyone in the same way."[72] There is no doubt, then, that Kant uses the generally conceded variability of the quality of sensations from one person to the next as itself a ground for excluding such sensory qualities as color and tone from the proper objects of taste. But what are we to make of such an argument?

The first point to be made is that the thesis of the variability of sensation must be regarded as quite independent of Kant's explanation of aesthetic response. Even supposing that, say, both the appearance and the agreeableness of colored objects varies from person to person, there is no reason to suppose that certain combinations of colors could not produce the harmony of the faculties in any given person. Only an *a priori* assumption that what can produce the harmony of the faculties must be the same in all could lead to such a conclusion, and Kant has hardly argued for such an assumption at this point in his text. Second, it might be noted that the thesis of the variability of sensation can be regarded as an empirical rather than an *a priori* proposition. If it is so regarded, one can wonder whether it can be employed for the derivation of any restrictive criteria for the judgment of taste without removing Kant's theory of taste from the realm of *a priori* judgment to that of the merely empirical and psychological, which he consistently attempts to avoid.[73*] But perhaps most important, the use of a direct appeal to the requirement of universal subjective validity to exclude any objects from the proper sphere of taste raises a deep problem about the relative status of the two keystones of Kant's aesthetic theory. What is the real force of Kant's thesis that aesthetic response must be intersubjectively valid? We saw earlier that the ultimate foundation of such a constraint on taste is an appeal to common usage, but what is the strength of such an appeal? Can it really found an absolute constraint on what we should count as an aesthetic response, or should it, rather, be taken to base a regulative principle, motivated by our desire to communicate about our feelings and pleasures, but also to be weighed against other considerations? In particular, where the history of a given pleasure seems to conform to the *explanation* of our response to beauty, but *not* to the analytical requirement of intersubjective validity, should we take the concept of the harmony of the faculties to be the true base of the theory of beauty, and allow that such a pleasure is a response to beauty? Or should we take the criterion of universal agreement as fundamental to the concept of an object of taste, and discount such a response from the realm of taste? Should we consider the possibility that the concepts of beauty and taste might not be completely coextensive?

These are hard questions, and they are not readily answered. Basically, I believe, Kant did not really consider the possibility that the range of objects which can produce the harmony of imagination and understanding and the range of those about which there must be universal agreement might not be identical, although, as my study of his deduction of aesthetic judgment will reveal, he should have. Nevertheless, we may guess how he would have answered my questions. I think he would have given primacy to the requirement of universal subjective validity as *defining* both taste and beauty, and banished from the realm of genuine taste qualities of objects which can occasion irresolvable disagreement, even if they should also produce the harmony of the faculties. But it is not obvious that we should follow Kant in this assessment. We might find his explanation of aesthetic response most attractive, and thus be willing to weaken the requirement of intersubjective agreement, treating it as a regulative rather than a constitutive principle. We might suppose that intersubjective agreement is indeed a genuine desideratum in aesthetic judgment, but not be willing to conclude that some of our pleasures in objects are not genuine aesthetic responses for the *sole* reason that they do not conform to this requirement.

In subsequent chapters, I will argue that Kant's attempt to justify the assumption of intersubjective validity for pleasures founded on the harmony of the faculties can in fact ground only a regulative principle of taste. I will also argue that Kant's attempts to justify the demand for agreement in taste by the exploitation of various analogies between aesthetic and moral judgment cannot support an interpretation of the requirement of intersubjective validity as a true imperative. These conclusions may support my present question as to whether the fact of intersubjective variability can itself imply that a given pleasure is not in fact due to the harmony of the faculties. Perhaps the issue should be left thus for now.

Form and Concepts

We have now seen that there are serious difficulties with the first two of Kant's attempts to develop a specific doctrine of aesthetic formalism from his more general explanation of pleasure in the beautiful as a response to the form of finality. At this point, I will turn to Kant's final arguments, in which he employs not a contrast between the form and matter of appearance, but rather one between the form of appearance and the concepts applicable to appearances. One would not think that Kant's consideration of this contrast, which occupies §§15 through 17, could reveal a fundamentally new constraint on the objects of taste. Unlike the contrast between the form and matter of appearance, which had been occasionally invoked but not really discussed until §§13 and 14, the contrast between aesthetic response to objects and conceptual judgment of them seems to have been fully explored in the first and second moments. It would be surprising if Kant could now do more than rephrase what he had previously argued about the character of aesthetic response in terms applicable to the objects of that response.

However, these sections are not entirely repetitive. In §§16 and 17, several theses emerge which, if valid, would place constraints on the kinds of objects which can properly exemplify taste. Kant appears to argue both that objects of nature rather than art are proper objects of aesthetic judgment, and that to the extent that works of art can be proper objects of taste, they must be abstract rather than representational works of art. Further, Kant makes the even more startling suggestion that insofar as anything can be a true "model" or "ideal" of beauty, it can only be human beauty. These conclusions would certainly constitute new substantive criteria for aesthetic judgment, and offer rules concerning objects which could be appealed to in the discussion and justification of particular aesthetic judgments.

Unfortunately, these theses are not valid consequences of Kant's basic aesthetic theory. As in the case of §14, Kant fails to effect a convincing transition from the analysis of constraints on aesthetic response to any particular restrictions on the objects which might occasion such response by disposing the imagination and understanding to their mutual accord.

No new doctrines are obvious in §15, although some new terms are introduced. Kant begins by making it clear that an object of taste is independent of determinate ends because the judgment of taste is independent of determinate concepts. "*Objective* finality," he asserts, can be only "recognized through the relation of the manifold to a determinate end, and thus through a concept"; but since the judgment of beauty is a response to "a merely formal finality, a finality without an end" — here Kant actually uses the famous words *Zweckmassigkeit ohne Zweck* — that judgment cannot be determined by any concept. From this, Kant concludes that the beautiful is "independent of any representation of the good."[74] Apparently, he assumes that any concept of an end is a concept of a (or the) good; a reason for this will emerge shortly.

This conclusion is no surprise, and represents no advance over, say, §11. In the second paragraph of §15, however, Kant does employ new terminology. Objective finality, he maintains, can take either of two forms. It may be "external" finality, or "utility"; or it may be "internal" finality, or "perfection." That a judgment of beauty is not a judgment of utility, Kant says, is "sufficiently" evident from the arguments of the first two moments.[75*] He does not say the same of the claim that a judgment of beauty is not a judgment of perfection, although, since such a judgment involves the subsumption of an object under a concept, this is also evident. Instead, Kant takes the occasion to criticize his rationalist predecessors. Perfection or internal finality, he notes, has been taken to be beauty, "when it is thought confusedly."[76] However, he will argue, the judgment of beauty cannot be founded in a confused perception of perfection, for it is not a judgment of perfection at all.

The claim that the judgment of beauty is not a judgment of utility or perfection rephrases Kant's earlier claim that this judgment does not rest on either an interest, or subjective end — a conception of an object external to its actual existence — or on a conception of the object itself as an objective end dependent on "connection to an end" or purposive action[77] — a conception internal to the history of the object's existence. This becomes clear as Kant characterizes the particular kind of perfection which is internal finality, and from which he means to dissociate the judgment of beauty. If the exclusion of perfection from aesthetic judgment is to depend on the exclusion of consideration of ends, then such perfection must be connected to an end, that is, to something "the *concept* of which may be regarded as the ground of the possibility of the object itself." But only one of two forms of perfection depends on such an end. Perfection may be either "qualita-

mate of such free beauties, Kant maintains, "the judgment of taste is pure. No concept of any purpose for which the manifold should serve the given object and which the latter should thus represent is presupposed."[86] By contrast, the beauty of certain other things "presupposes a concept of what the thing should be, thus a concept of its perfection," and is thus "adherent" or dependent beauty. As examples Kant then gives "the beauty of a person . . . the beauty of a horse, of a building (as church, palace, arsenal, or garden-house)."[87]

The intent of Kant's examples seems obvious enough. If we judge that an object is beautiful without considering any purpose it might have or fulfill, we make a pure judgment of taste; if we approve of a thing on the basis of consideration of its relation to the concept of some end — if we approve of a horse because its speed will mean prizes at the races, or of an arsenal because its solidity implies security in time of siege — we do not make a pure judgment of taste. In fact, however, Kant's distinction is not so simple, for his examples actually imply that objects may be classed as dependent beauties for two different reasons. Some of the dependent beauties are objects which may be either natural or manmade, but which in either case can serve a purpose and be judged according to a concept of what a thing should be in order to serve that purpose. Horses serve purposes of work and pleasure, as do, perhaps, human beings. Such artifacts as buildings also serve purposes — they can be used for worship, recreation, defense, and the like. All of these might please because they are judged to have perfections answering to the concepts of such purposes.[88] But there is another class of dependent beauties, the members of which are all manmade objects, and the criterial feature of which is not so much that the objects have *purpose* as that they have *content*. When Kant contrasts dependent beauties to designs *à la grecque* and music without words, or to "mere aesthetical painting, which has no determinate theme,"[89] he does so because these free beauties do not *mean* or *represent* anything (*etwas bedeuten* or *vorstellen*). They do not stand in semantic or symbolic relationships to things outside of themselves — they do not depict or portray any content. Dependent beauties do, however. But it is hardly obvious that to depict or mean something is the same as to serve a purpose, or that if objects which serve purposes must be excluded from the proper objects of pure judgments of taste, then so must representational objects or works of art with content.[90]*

This is an important point, for any claim that Kant succeeds in adding the exclusion of content to the exclusion of matter in his development of formalist constraints on the objects of taste depends upon the argument of

§16, and it is not clear that Kant's classification of representational works of art as dependent beauties can be derived from the connection of such beauties to purposes. The use of concepts to *interpret* the content or meaning of a work is not identical with the use of concepts for the *evaluation* of objects subsumed under them; yet it is only the latter use of concepts which Kant's explanation of aesthetic response must clearly exclude from aesthetic judgment. Why should Kant assume that representational art must be the object of less than pure aesthetic judgment?

Several explanations of Kant's ambiguous illustrations of dependent beauty may be offered. First, it is possible that Kant may just be confusing two different concepts of representation. He speaks both of things representing purposes and of things representing other objects, and may suppose that there is a single concept of representation here, when there are actually two. On the one hand, to represent an end is simply to serve that end, or instantiate the concept of it; such representation would be not a semantical relation, but a matter of classification or practical significance. On the other hand, to represent "an object under a determinate concept" may have nothing to do with purposes, but rather mean to depict, portray, or refer to something, as might be done by music with words, for instance, or a historical painting as opposed to a mere painted arabesque. It is possible that what is depicted by such an object can be an end — a use or intention — in itself, and that an object might both serve and illustrate a particular purpose.[91] A devotional painting, for instance, might both illustrate and serve the purpose of worship. But that such an object should represent an end in both function and content is surely contingent; the two kinds of representation are themselves distinct. Thus judging that something illustrates, by its content, some end, would be quite different from judging it as an object which serves that end, and which has its merit because of *this* relation to an end. The latter judgment must clearly be excluded from our response to beauty, but it is far from clear that the former must.

If Kant's theory of dependent beauty turns on such a confusion, then it is obviously fallacious, and there is no reason to suppose that a restriction of pure aesthetic judgment to nonrepresentational art can follow from Kant's basic theory of aesthetic judgment. It is possible, however, that Kant may have had something more than mere confusion in mind. He often writes as if the purpose of art were to depict or portray, and may have supposed that our pleasure in representational art is based on our approval of its success in accomplishing its purpose of representation — and hence is pleasure in dependent beauty. Thus in §48 Kant claims that "a natural beauty is a *beautiful thing;* an artistic beauty is a *beautiful representation* of a thing,"[92] and goes on to attribute a special excellence to fine art which depends on its representational function. This virtue is its capacity to describe—or depict—beautifully objects which would be ugly or offensive if actually encountered in nature.[93*] In the theory of aesthetic ideas, Kant also proceeds as if art were essentially representational. An aesthetic idea is the instrument by which an artist "seeks to approximate to a representation of rational concepts (of intellectual ideas)," or by means of which "a poet dares to make sensible rational ideas of invisible beings, the kingdom of the blessed," and the like.[94] That is, an aesthetic idea is a representation of the imagination which depicts or illustrates some (usually rational) object, although its character cannot be fully determined by its reference to the latter.[95] Indeed, Kant supposes, "beauty . . . in general may be termed the *expression* of aesthetic ideas," linking beauty and representation very closely indeed.[96*] He even adds that the arts may be classified on the basis of their analogies with various aspects of linguistic expression. In all of these remarks, Kant reveals an assumption that the representation of concepts or themes is the characteristic *purpose* of art, in spite of the examples of abstract art which he provides in §16 itself. He might then have concluded that art pleases us by succeeding in this purpose, and that our pleasure in it is linked to our consideration of this purpose.

If Kant did subscribe to such an explanation of our response to art, then his inclusion of representational art among dependent beauties would not be a mere mistake. Representing—as depicting—something would be an instance of representing—as serving—an end, namely, the end of depiction or mimesis. Nevertheless, it might still be argued that the exclusion of such art from the objects of pure judgments of taste is not a necessary consequence of Kant's aesthetic theory. First, Kant does not actually argue that art must serve the purpose of depiction; *a fortiori,* he does not argue for this thesis on the basis of any premises central to his theory of aesthetic response and judgment. Second, even if art not only is representational but has the purpose of representing, it still does not follow that our pleasure in its beauty is dependent upon consideration of this purpose. To find something beautiful is quite different from finding it accurate, illustrative, or informative; and the frequency with which illustrative or heuristic artworks are aesthetically indifferent makes it clear that successful representation is hardly a sufficient condition of any kind of beauty. Beauty and representation may be compatible but distinct features of a work of art.

Kant's distinction between free and dependent beauty, then, does not lead to one criterion for pure aesthetic judgment to which he apparently supposed it did lead. It does not entail the classification of representational art as merely dependent beauty. But this is not the only problem with Kant's distinction. Two other questions must be asked about the argument of §16. First, given the basis of his distinction, why does Kant describe it as a distinction between two kinds of beauty, rather than between beauty and some other form of value? Second, why does Kant formulate his distinction as one between two species of beauty, rather than as one between two kinds of judgments of beauty?

The first question stems from the fact that judgments of dependent beauty are described as judgments of the perfection of objects which fall under the concepts of particular ends. According to everything that Kant has argued before §16, such judgments are not aesthetic judgments at all. Why, then, should he classify them as any kind of judgment of beauty in §16? Kant offers no reason for his sudden enlargement of the concept of beauty, and his commentators have not had much to say on the subject either.[97]* But it is certainly not plausible to suppose that the concept of dependent beauty is just a mistake, as I have supposed in the case of several other peculiarities in Kant's exposition; that concept departs too radically from a position about which Kant was too clear for a mistake to be possible. Two speculations, however, may be worth considering.

The first turns on the fact that Kant does sometimes use a rhetorical strategy of stating an argument with terms more in accord with the accepted opinion on a matter than with his own conclusion, in order to gain a hearing for what he is about to argue. Such a strategy explains why, for instance, he begins the first *Critique*'s Transcendental Deduction by supposing that "appearances can certainly be given in intuition independently of functions of the understanding," when this is, of course, just what his argument ultimately denies.[98] Thus if we were to suppose that Kant took the ordinary understanding of beauty to be perfection according to a concept of some end, we might conclude that he decided to classify this as a species of beauty distinct from that which was his main concern rather than as no kind of beauty at all, in order to make his own view seem less radical.[99]* If such a concession to the common view of beauty is the intent of Kant's concept of dependent beauty, however, then it is peculiar that it is made after Kant has already expounded the better part of his own view rather than before.

A second explanation is even more speculative than this, but perhaps more interesting as well. This is the suggestion that judgments of dependent beauty in fact are aesthetic judgments, though not pure ones, because though they do involve concepts of purpose, these concepts do not fully determine our approval of their objects. Ordinarily, we could argue, when the merit of an object is determined by its subsumption under some concept, our approval is fully governed by rules derivable from that concept. If something is to be declared good for some purpose or a good instance of some concept, and approved solely on that account, then that concept dictates what properties the object must have, and makes the judgment of its goodness a matter of cognition. But this is not the case with some of Kant's examples of dependent beauty. Although our pleasure in a church or arsenal is connected with its purpose, the concept of the purpose does not provide any rules by which the beauty of the building can be mechanically determined. The concept of its purpose imposes *some* constraint on the freedom of the imagination with respect to the appearance of a church, but still leaves that faculty such latitude within this constraint that pleasure may yet be produced by its free harmony with the understanding's demand for unity. Thus while the general purpose of worship and such more specific requirements as that of a cruciform floor plan may place limits on what can please us in a church, these hardly provide rules which are sufficient for producing a beautiful church or judging one. The concept of its purpose leaves room for a genuine aesthetic response to the beauty of a church, although it places some limits on the forms which might constitute that beauty.

This example, and Kant's own suggestion that the "flourishes and light but regular lines" of Maori tattooing are *incompatible* with the dignity of the humans they decorate, imply that the relation between purpose and dependent beauty is a negative one: the purpose functions to constrain the forms which may produce the harmony of the faculties but *not* to fully determine them. This might be an inadequate interpretation of Kant's claim that judgments of dependent beauty *presuppose* concepts of what objects should be and the recognition of perfections answering to those concepts, for on the present proposal the concepts of purpose would merely function to exclude certain forms as imperfections in objects to which they apply. They would constrain the imagination rather than actually guide it in its reflection. But such an interpretation of the role of concepts in the case of dependent beauty may be the only one which can leave room for both reference to purpose and the freedom of the imagination. It is also consistent with some of Kant's other remarks about concepts in dependent beauty, for two passages within §16 characterize such concepts as means by which the freedom of the imagination is "restricted" (*eingeschränkt*).[100] If we suppose that our approval of dependent beauties is meant not to be fully determined by a concept, but merely constrained or limited by it, or set within boundaries, then we can see how judgments on them might be impure but still aesthetic judgments.

A solution to the first problem with Kant's distinction is thus possible. I will now turn to the second problem that I raised above, namely, why Kant distinguishes free and dependent *beauties,* rather than two forms of *judgments on* beauty. This question, in fact, leads to a fundamental problem about Kant's explanation of aesthetic response which has not been considered so far, but which becomes pressing in the present context. This is the question of the real conditions of the freedom of the imagination.

Abstraction and the Freedom of the Imagination

Given his general view that beauty is not a property of objects but rather a relation between objects and human pleasure, mediated by human judgment, as well as his specific claim that the difference between free and dependent beauty lies in whether or not a purpose or perfection is involved in our judgment of an object, it would seem natural for Kant to distinguish free and dependent judgments of beauty rather than free and dependent beauties. This is in fact what Kant is generally taken to mean by his distinction.[101]* And some of Kant's own formulations apply the adjectives "free" and "dependent" to judgments rather than to their objects. Thus in one of the passages alluded to a moment ago, Kant states, "Now if the judgment of taste in respect of [the delight in the beautiful] is made dependent on a purpose . . . and thereby restricted, it is no longer a free and pure judgment of taste."[102] A sentence like this suggests that Kant's distinction is properly one between two ways of judging objects, and that its expression as one between two kinds of beauties, or two kinds of objects themselves, is at best elliptical.

If this were so, then particular objects would not be intrinsically free or dependent beauties, but would be either free or dependent beauties, depending on whether they had been made objects of free or dependent judgments of beauty. Some of Kant's remarks suggest this conclusion. The final paragraph of §16 implies that it is a matter of choice whether we regard a given object as a free or dependent beauty, and holds that this fact may be crucial for the resolution of disputes in taste:

A judgment of taste in respect of an object with a determinate internal end would only be pure if the person judging it either had no concept of this end, or abstracted from it in his judgment. But then such a person, although he made a correct judgment of taste insofar as he estimated the object as a free beauty, would be blamed and accused of a false judgment by someone else (who looked to the purpose of the object), although both judged correctly in their own way: the one according to what he had present to his senses, the other according to what was present to his thought. Through this distinction one can settle many a quarrel about beauty between judges of taste, insofar as one shows them that the one is dealing with free and the other with dependent beauty, and the former making a pure, the latter an applied [*angewandtes*] judgment of taste.[103]

Either this passage implies that objects themselves are not intrinsically free or dependent beauties, but either, depending on how they are regarded; or it implies at least that objects are not intrinsically one or the other kind of beauty, but may be both if they allow of being regarded both with and without reference to purpose.

But there are also passages in which Kant denies that there is such liberty in the judgment of objects as free or dependent beauties. I have already quoted one passage, from §48, in which Kant apparently claims that *any* judgment on the beauty of a work of art must consider its perfection with respect to a concept of what it ought to be. In §16 itself, Kant's treatment of the examples of dependent beauty suggests that such things as churches and horses *must* be regarded from the point of view of their purposes. He speaks of "the beauty" of a human being, horse, or building as presupposing a concept of purpose and perfection[104] as if these things could be beautiful only in connection with such a concept, or as if the nature of these objects themselves required that they be judged as dependent beauties. And in §17, Kant implies a similar position. Appended to this section's closing statement that *"beauty* is the form of *finality* in an object so far as perceived *without the representation of an end"* is a footnote in which Kant considers the special case of objects which are supposed to have ends, although we are ignorant of what they actually are. He has in mind objects found in ancient tombs and the like, "the forms of which certainly had some purposes, though we do not know them." Of these he says: "that one regards them as works of art is sufficient to establish that one refers their figure to some aim and some determinate purpose. Therefore, there is indeed no immediate delight in their intuition."[105] This is peculiar. The first sentence is compatible with the standard view of Kant's position on free and dependent beauty, for it holds only that a consideration of its purpose is a necessary condition of classifying something as a work of art. But the second sentence makes a stronger claim, for it asserts that an object's status as art actually makes a judgment of free beauty impossible. That is to say, it is not arbitrary or up to us whether something is regarded as a free or dependent beauty. If a thing has a purpose, it seems, it can *only* be judged according to that purpose, or as a dependent beauty. On this view, Kant's distinction between free and dependent beauties would not be merely elliptical, for things are not either free or dependent beauties if we so regard them; rather, certain things are intrinsically dependent beauties.

If we assume that judgments of free beauty and pure judgments of taste are equivalent, this conclusion would certainly provide a substantive constraint on the proper objects of taste not encountered earlier in Kant's argument. On Kant's own theory of art, every work of art has some purpose. Even nonrepresentational works such as abstract paintings or wallpapers and music without themes have purposes—to cover walls, to earn livings for their composers, and so on. If simply having *any* purpose with respect to which a judgment of perfection may be made insures that something cannot be the object of a judgment of free beauty, then no work of art could be the proper object of a pure judgment of taste. Only natural beauties could be genuine objects of taste.

To state this conclusion is sufficient to object to Kant's position, for his own examples make it clear that at least some works of art can be regarded as free beauties. The problem is not what is wrong with a theory according to which art is never the object of pure aesthetic judgment, but to explain how Kant could have come to suggest it.[106*] This explanation, I believe, must lie in a problem basic to Kant's entire aesthetic theory, the indeterminacy of his conception of the freedom of the imagination, linked to his uncertainty about the scope of the power of abstraction. The problem of free and dependent beauty and of Kant's attitude toward art, it turns out, is connected to some obscurity in the most fundamental concepts of his aesthetic theory.

Throughout his exposition Kant consistently maintains that the freedom of the imagination is the necessary condition of aesthetic response. This freedom is not total freedom from constraint, for pleasure in the beautiful is meant to be a response to the manifold presented by an object or its form, and thus to something which is independent of the imagination.

This represents some constraint, for "in the apprehension of a given object of sense [the imagination] is bound to a determinate form of this object," even though, if the object is to be found beautiful, its form must be felt to be one the imagination could have designed itself.[107] Where the freedom of the imagination does lie is in its freedom of constraint by concepts. The harmony of the faculties must be produced by a manifold which is given to the imagination, but it cannot be produced by any concept which is forced on the understanding in connection with the manifold.

However, what now turns out to be less than obvious is the precise nature of the circumstances under which the freedom of the imagination from constraint by concepts can actually obtain. It is clear that any actual occurrence of the harmony of the faculties requires the presentation of a manifold which is unifiable without concepts. But it is not clear whether the mere *presence* of any concepts—the mere knowledge of their applicability to a given manifold, or even the mere fact of such applicability—is sufficient to constrain the imagination, or whether the imagination can always abstract from concepts known to apply to objects. In other words, it is not clear whether the freedom of the imagination is a negative condition, which obtains only if a given object presents or forces no concepts on the mind, or a positive condition, a power of the imagination by which it can actually free itself of the constraints of whatever concepts actually—and perhaps even obviously—apply to the given object.

Kant's remarks that aesthetic judgment involves abstraction from an object's unity as end[108] and that an aesthetic judgment may be pure if the person making it is *either* ignorant of concepts of ends applicable to the object of his judgment *or* abstracts from such suggest the latter interpretation.[109] So does Kant's apparent assumption that pure aesthetic judgment requires abstraction from the matter of appearance as well as from concepts, or from the charms and emotions of colors and tones. Abstraction appears to be a power of the mind by which it can free itself from the constraints of both sensation and concepts, and thus at least set the stage for a free play between imagination and understanding. But Kant's examples of dependent beauties and his remarks on the necessity of judgments of perfection in the case of art suggest that the mind is not always free to abstract, at least from the concepts which apply to objects. Under some circumstances, it seems, the freedom of the imagination can obtain only if no knowledge of even undetermined or indeterminate purposes imposes itself upon our attention. The knowledge that an object is a human being or a church, or a work of art produced according to some intention, appears to be such that it simply cannot be abstracted from for the sake of a pure judgment of taste.[110*]

The discussion of §§15 and 16 has revealed two open questions: whether the judgment of art must always be a judgment of perfection, and whether it must always be a judgment of dependent beauty. A decision on these questions is impossible without a decision on the scope of our power of abstraction, and thus of the freedom of the imagination to create the conditions in which its harmony might occur. However, basic though the concept of abstraction must be to Kant's explanation of aesthetic response, his references to it are actually too few to provide an adequate basis for such a decision. Nor do even his more extensive explanations of the nature of the harmony of the faculties provide such a basis, for they all emphasize the peculiarities of the state that results from aesthetic reflection rather than the scope of the powers which enable it to occur. It is easy to see what position Kant should have taken, though. Since it is not just concepts of purposes which can constrain the imagination, but, in fact, any empirical concepts which furnish rules for the synthesis of the manifold, and since a multitude of empirical concepts can apply to almost any empirical object, anything less than a very broad power of abstraction will make aesthetic response a rare occurrence. So will the fact that we are rarely given anything approximating pure design or composition, but are generally presented with forms embodied in such material qualities as colors and tones. The nature of sensation and empirical knowledge, were the imagination constrained by everything these present, would preclude our finding many objects beautiful. Clearly, Kant did not mean to imply such a conclusion. But there is little evidence that he realized how extensive the power of abstraction must be to avoid this difficulty, or just what the implications of such a power of abstraction for his theory of art must be. In particular, he may have failed to notice that a power of abstraction broad enough for his general theory of aesthetic response would also be broad enough to allow free judgments on the beauty of objects which are, as a matter of fact, works of art and even of representational art.

It may seem strange that Kant had so little to say on such a fundamental issue as the relation between the harmony of the faculties and our power of abstraction. I believe that the explanation of this oddity must lie in Kant's attempt to construct a transcendental rather than empirical aesthetic theory, or a "transcendental exposition of aesthetic judgments" as opposed to a merely "physiological" one.[111] He attempted to characterize aesthetic response entirely in terms of the conditions of the possibility of knowledge in general and the most abstract explanation of the grounds of pleasure. He may well have felt, however, that the question of whether it is always in our power to abstract from certain sorts of concepts — the question, say, of whether concepts of purpose may be as easily ignored as more ordinary empirical concepts of classification — is not a transcendental question, but an empirical question, and refrained from pursuing it for this reason.[112]* As interesting as the work of "Burke and many acute men among us" may have been, the laws that their empirical exposition of taste might discover could "only make known how things are judged, but not command how they should be judged."[113] But what the role of abstraction in Kant's discussion of free and dependent beauty suggests is that the transcendental theory of taste itself may not be sufficient to produce substantive constraints on the proper objects of aesthetic judgment. Just as the basic conception of the form of finality has to be supplemented with a theory of perception to produce Kant's restriction of taste to the form of appearance, so must it be supplemented with an additional theory about abstraction from concepts to provide any criterial distinction between objects which *must* be regarded as free beauties and those which *must* be seen as dependent beauties.

We have now seen that each of Kant's three basic attempts to add to his criteria governing the subjective sources of pleasure criteria which might aid in the justification of aesthetic judgment by providing constraints on the possible objects of taste themselves fails. Kant never supposed that determinate rules could be provided which would govern the application of the predicate "beautiful" to particular objects. But in arguing that beauty lies in the form rather than the matter of appearance, that judgments of free beauty require nonrepresentational rather than representational objects, and perhaps even that such judgments can be made only of nature rather than art, Kant tried to formulate certain loose constraints which may be applied directly to objects of pleasure rather than to the subject's state of mind or mental history. He did not attempt to formulate determinate rules of taste, but he certainly tried to argue for indeterminate or regulative criteria, perhaps analogous to the maxims of scientific judgment. However, each of Kant's arguments goes beyond what may be inferred from the concept of the harmony of the faculties alone. Either his arguments involve a direct appeal to the criterion of universality coupled with an empirical hypothesis about the scope of human disagreement, or else they involve specific theories about the nature of perception, the purpose of art, or our power to abstract from purposes. In no case do Kant's substantive formalistic opinions express views which we must accept simply on the basis of his explanation of aesthetic response alone.

In §17, Kant offers an argument the point of which is obscure, but which may be regarded as one last attempt to provide some constraints on the proper objects of taste in spite of the absence of any determinate rules of beauty. Kant begins this section, as we have seen, by reiterating the view that there are no such rules, or that it is a waste of effort to look for a "universal criterion" of beauty in determinate concepts.[114] Thus, he concludes, only the "universal communicability of the sensation (of delight or displeasure)" can provide any criterion for taste; and only objects which have actually been found—empirically—to provide or at least approximate to such a shared pleasure can be regarded as proper objects of taste. These objects are called "exemplary" or "models of taste" (*Muster des Geschmacks*).[115] Kant then introduces the notion of the "highest model" of taste, or its "archetype" (*Urbild*), and launches a search for this—presumably as a search for a proper object of taste. Briefly, what he argues is that this highest model or archetype must not be a mere *idea*, but an *ideal*— "the representation of an individual being as adequate to an idea."[116] He then considers various ways of arriving at norms—as average or composite figures[117]—but concludes that none of these can actually fix any individual form of beauty as its highest model or archetype. Only the example of the human figure, he concludes, can serve as such, because it is in fact an ideal "expression of the *moral,* apart from which the object would not please at once universally and positively."[118] Because it can please universally, the human figure becomes the ideal of taste; although Kant hastens to add that "estimation according to such a standard can never be purely aesthetic, and that the estimation according to such an ideal of beauty is no pure judgment of taste."[119]

What the significance of this argument is meant to be is far from clear. It could be supposed that it is designed to introduce the view, which I will later consider, that the universal validity of aesthetic judgment requires a moral as well as an epistemological foundation.[120] It is conceivable that this is Kant's purpose, although his consideration of such a moral foundation for taste seems out of place at this point in his argument, and the human figure does not play a central role in Kant's other attempts to link aesthetic and moral judgment. I think that Kant's intention was something else. Perhaps he recognized that his basic account of aesthetic response could not, in the end, provide any very specific constraints on the objects of taste, or be of much help in criticism's traditional search for models of beauty. He may then have decided that only some supplementation of this account with an external constraint on taste could point toward a specific model of beauty. If this was his intent, however, his argument is quite unsatisfactory. For in inferring from the existence of exemplary products of taste the possibility of an ideal of taste, the argument suggests that a theory of taste requires not just that objects which are properly judged beautiful be pleasing to all, but that there be some *one* object or type of object which best fulfills the canons of taste. But nothing in Kant's prior analysis of taste implies such a thesis, and his own conclusion that the choice of the human figure as the ideal of beauty rests on a dependent rather than a free judgment of taste essentially acknowledges as much. Kant might have turned to the model of the human figure in one final attempt to place even some indeterminate constraint on the objects of taste, but the argument of §17 must be regarded as an aberration.

I have now argued that Kant's search for justificatory criteria oriented toward the objects rather than subjects of taste is a failure. This is not to say that Kant has failed totally in his attempt to derive concrete criteria for aesthetic judgment from his general theory of taste, for that theory has led to genuine results in the discussion of disinterestedness, and some of these results have been clarified in the third moment of the Analytic of the Beautiful. But — a conclusion that might be welcome rather than disappointing — Kant's aesthetics cannot lead to the introduction of any specific restrictions on the kinds of objects that might turn out to be beautiful, or place *a priori* limitations on our search for natural or artistic beauty. Only if his transcendental theory is supplemented with particular theories of art and perceptual and cognitive psychology — theories, it may be noted, characteristic not only of Kant but of many in his century — can it possibly lead to such constraints.

I shall now turn to Kant's attempt to guarantee the universal validity of taste by a transcendental deduction of aesthetic judgment. Here too we must consider how well Kant succeeds in confining his argument to the transcendental plane and keeping it free of assumptions from other spheres, especially empirical psychology.

7

The Task of the Deduction

****

The Universal Validity of Pleasure

Making a judgment of taste requires a complex process of reflection. Faced with the question of beauty, namely, whether the pleasure occasioned by a given object can rationally be imputed to others, one considers whether this pleasure has been felt apart from any reflection on an interest its object might serve or an end it might represent. If one does conclude that one's feeling is disinterested and linked to the mere form of finality in the object, one may also conclude that it has been occasioned by an estimation of the object which has led to a harmonious accord between imagination and understanding. On the basis of this conclusion, one may then impute the pleasure to other disinterested observers of the object. The requirement that these observers be disinterested, of course, means that one cannot say that everyone *does* or *will* like the object, but one can rationally claim that "everyone *should* give the object in question his approval and likewise declare it to be beautiful."[1]

But attributing a feeling of pleasure to a source in the harmony of the higher cognitive faculties can ground a rational claim to intersubjective validity only if this harmony is itself subject to a valid imputation of intersubjectivity, or if the occurrence of this harmony in the presence of a given object may rationally be expected in anyone who does abstract from interest in its existence and confine his attention to its mere form of finality. Thus Kant must provide an argument that the harmony of the faculties occurs in different persons under the same conditions, or that in attributing a pleasure to this state one is indeed linking it to a public source which "he may also presuppose in everyone else" rather than to some "private condition" to which he alone might be party.[2] This argument will be the deduction of pure aesthetic judgment.

The Universal Validity of Pleasure

That the deduction must establish the intersubjective validity of the ground of aesthetic judgment is not made clear in §30, the first of the sections by which Kant prepares for the formal "Deduction of judgments of taste" presented in §38 of the third *Critique*. But it does emerge quite clearly in the intervening §§31 to 37.

Section 31 makes it plain that the need for a deduction of the judgment of taste derives solely from this judgment's presumption that the pleasure a particular person takes in a given object can have a "thoroughgoing validity for everyone."[3] Kant arrives at this view in the following way. First, he asserts that in general "the obligation to furnish a deduction, that is, a guarantee of the legitimacy of judgments of a particular kind, only arises where the judgment lays claim to necessity." Then he implies that this is the case even where the necessity in question is not the necessity that anything exist, or the objective necessity that any determinate concept be predicated of a particular object, but only the subjective necessity of agreement among the responses of different persons. In Kant's own words, his statement of the reason why a deduction is necessary holds even for a judgment which requires only "subjective universality, that is, the agreement of everyone: while it is not a cognitive judgment, but only one of pleasure or displeasure in a given object, [it is yet] a presumption of a subjective finality that has a thoroughgoing validity for everyone, which should not be grounded on any concept, since it is a judgment of taste." Some deduction is needed for any assumption of universal validity, but particularly for one made in the absence of its ordinary ground, the predication of a determinate concept of an object; and such a deduction can be given only by showing that the extraordinary ground of aesthetic judgment, the subjective finality of an object, also has universal validity. And if the subjective finality of an object is in fact nothing but its disposition to produce the harmony of the faculties, such a deduction can proceed only by showing that a pleasure explained as due to this source is valid for all.

This becomes even clearer as Kant continues §31 by maintaining that all we need to demonstrate in order to justify aesthetic judgment is the possibility of "the *universal validity* of a *singular judgment,* which expresses the subjective finality of an empirical representation of the form of an object," and by claiming in turn that we can accomplish this just by explaining, first, "how it is possible that something can please in mere estimation" and, then, "how just as the estimation of an object for the sake of *a cognition* in general has universal rules, the delight of any one person may also be pronounced as a rule for every other."⁴ That is, the deduction of aesthetic judgment is a justification for moving from the explanation of aesthetic pleasure as a response produced by mere estimation to a universal imputation of that pleasure, and can be given only by demonstrating the universal validity of any pleasure due to the mere estimation of an object. That it must establish the intersubjective validity of pleasure is also implied when Kant describes the deduction of aesthetic judgment as "the solution of the logical peculiarities" that arise in the case of a claim to universal validity which is not "based on a collection of votes and an investigation of the sensations of others," but which must instead rest, "as it were, on an autonomy of the subject judging the feeling of pleasure (in the given representation)."⁵

The same conclusion may be drawn from the further consideration of the "task of a deduction of judgments of taste" that Kant offers in §§36 and 37.⁶ The first of these sections describes this task as arising from the fact that a judgment of taste "is not merely a judgment of sensation, but a formal judgment of reflection, which imputes . . . delight to everyone as necessary." Given this, a deduction is needed to supply an *a priori* principle which can "make it intelligible how an aesthetic judgment can lay claim to necessity."⁷ And that the deduction of aesthetic judgment must demonstrate the intersubjective validity of the pleasure which is its ground becomes even more clear when Kant argues, in §§36 and 37, that aesthetic judgment is in fact a variety of synthetic *a priori* judgment, so that the problem of a deduction of aesthetic judgment may therefore be considered "part of the general problem of transcendental philosophy: How are synthetic *a priori* judgments possible?"⁸ For surely what requires a deduction in the case of a synthetic judgment is just whatever *a priori* claim it contains or implies, and what is *a priori* in the judgment of taste is precisely its attribution of intersubjective validity to particular feelings of pleasure.

According to §36, judgments of taste are synthetic because they go beyond the concept of an object, and even beyond its intuition, "to join to the latter as [its] predicate something which is not even a cognition at all, namely, the feeling of pleasure (or displeasure)." But they are *a priori*, "or will be held as such," precisely because they concern "an agreement required of everyone."⁹ In §37, Kant expands on these claims. Alluding to earlier arguments, he maintains that "it can only be internally perceived that the representation of an object is immediately connected with a pleasure" because there are no concepts applicable to any representation (except in the special case of the moral law) which can allow one to make an *a priori* connection of pleasure to that representation. But if this is so, then insofar as one simply reports the occurrence of pleasure in the presence of a given object, one makes a merely empirical judgment. It is only if one adds to one's observation of pleasure a claim of universal validity for that pleasure, or for the perceived connection between pleasure and the object, that an *a priori* judgment is made. "Hence it is not the pleasure which is represented *a priori* as a universal rule for the judgment, valid for everyone, in a judgment of taste, but the *universal validity* of this pleasure, which is perceived as connected in the mind with the mere estimation of the object. It is an empirical judgment that I perceive and estimate an object with pleasure. But it is an *a priori* judgment that I find it beautiful, that is, that I may impute that delight to everyone as necessary."[10] This paragraph is clumsy, for claiming universal validity for a pleasure attributed to mere estimation is indeed representing it as a valid rule for everyone, that is, supposing that any subject ought to feel pleasure in a given object. But Kant's point is clear enough. The mere report that a given object produces pleasure in oneself does not transcend the limits of empirical knowledge, and so makes no claim requiring a transcendental deduction. It is only in attributing this pleasure to others that one goes beyond the limits of one's own experience and makes an *a priori* claim calling for such a deduction. Thus what requires a deduction in aesthetic judgment is the transition from the empirically ascertainable occurrence of pleasure in oneself to the imputation of that pleasure to others, a claim for which empirical evidence cannot suffice but which is nevertheless made in calling an object beautiful rather than merely agreeable.

In §36, Kant describes the task of the deduction of an *a priori* judgment as the provision of an "*a priori* principle" to act as its ground. A deduction must explain the possibility of a synthetic *a priori* judgment. In the case of the judgment of taste, its deduction must answer this question: "How is a judgment possible which, merely upon one's *own* feeling of pleasure in an object, independent of its concept, estimates this pleasure *a priori* as attached to the representation of the same object in *every other* subject, that is, without having to wait upon the [actual] agreement of others?"[11] Answering this question, and no other, will provide a transcendental deduction of aesthetic judgment; and whatever is the key to this answer will turn out to be the true *a priori* principle of taste, whether or not it bears any resemblance to the *a priori* principles of theoretical or practical reason or even to reflective judgment's own principle of systematicity.

Sources of Confusion

The conclusion of the previous section should come as no surprise, although it may be surprising to realize that it is only as late as §§36 and 37 that Kant formulates the problem of taste with his standard model for the presentation of philosophical problems — that is, as a problem about the possibility of a form of synthetic *a priori* judgment.[12] Nevertheless, the present delimitation of the task of the deduction must be made explicit, for several aspects of Kant's exposition — some of his characterizations of the claims of taste, his location of the deduction of aesthetic judgment with respect to the general divisions of his text, and his statements in §30 about just what sorts of aesthetic judgments need a deduction — can create misleading impressions about what the deduction of aesthetic judgment must actually accomplish. Needless to say, it is only if we are clear about what the deduction must prove that we can decide whether it proves it.

In this section, I will briefly consider three problems which might appear to arise for the interpretation of the task of the deduction. Two of these problems will be dealt with quickly, at least for the moment; the third will require a separate section for its solution. Following that section, I will return to the main themes of the deduction, and discuss the constraints which, according to Kant, the very nature of aesthetic judgment imposes on its own deduction.

First, the present analysis of the aims of the deduction has characterized it in purely epistemological terms. The judgment of taste has been treated as a claim about, or on, the cognitive conditions of other persons, the imputation of a particular mental state to them even though this state is not connected with the subsumption of an object under any determinate concepts; and the deduction of aesthetic judgment has been introduced as if it must justify only the epistemological presumption of claiming to know about the subjective states of others. But, as noted earlier,[13] it is possible to read aesthetic judgment's insistence "that everyone *should* give the object in question his approval"[14] as expressing more than a purely epistemological demand. When Kant asks "how the feeling in the judgment of taste comes to be exacted from everyone as a sort of duty"[15] and then suggests that "everyone expects and requires consideration of universal communicability from everyone else, just as if it were part of an original compact, dictated by humanity itself,"[16] he appears to imply that the presumption of taste is not limited to an epistemological imputation of pleasure to others, but also assigns them some sort of duty or obligation to take pleasure in beautiful objects. Clearly, such a claim could not be defended solely by a demonstration that the harmony of the faculties is a public source of knowledge; it would also require a proof that there is some moral significance to the existence of taste. Thus, for instance, Donald Crawford has supposed that Kant's deduction of aesthetic judgment must be a multistaged argument culminating in the claim that "the beautiful is a symbol of the morally good, and consequently . . . gives pleasure with a justifiable claim for the agreement of everyone."[17]

If the deduction of a form of judgment comprised all the arguments necessary to support its every transcendence of a merely empirical connection of subject and predicate — in the present case, every way in which aesthetic judgment goes beyond the mere expression of agreeableness — we might indeed think that Kant's deduction could be completed only with a demonstration of the moral significance of taste. But while appeal to both epistemological and moral considerations may be necessary to fully explicate taste's demand for agreement, the justifications of the epistemological and moral aspects of this demand are as distinct as are the rationality of *expecting* agreement in matters of taste and the morality of *exacting* it from anyone. Kant's defenses of the two aspects of the demand for agreement in aesthetic response are logically independent, and stand or fall apart from each other.

For this reason alone, the epistemological deduction of the judgment of taste may be considered apart from the analogies between beauty and morality by which Kant attempts to add the extra element of obligation to this judgment, even if one does regard these analogies as constituting a part of the complete deduction of aesthetic judgment. But it may also be noted that the only section which Kant himself actually entitled "Deduction of judgments of taste" presents only epistemological grounds for the justification of the universal imputation of agreement.[18] Thus it appears that Kant's intentions will be more accurately interpreted if the deduction of pure aesthetic judgment is equated only with his proof of the intersubjectivity of the harmony of the faculties, and if the support for taste's exaction of agreement is excluded from its deduction. Indeed, such a restriction of the scope of the deduction not only is justified, but, I believe, will also be beneficial. For the current insistence upon the moral aspect of Kant's deduction has actually deflected attention from the important and logically prior question of the strength of his epistemological argument.[19*] Consequently, I will confine my discussion of the deduction of aesthetic judgments to Kant's argument for the intersubjective validity of aesthetic response, and examine his analogies between aesthetics and morality only when this discussion has been completed.

A second problem in the interpretation of the deduction concerns the explanation of its location in Kant's text. Actually, there are two problems about the location of the deduction. The first is that of actually *locating* it, for there are three different and widely separated places in his text where Kant attempts to support the intersubjective validity of aesthetic judgment, and none of these passages makes any reference to either of the others. This problem I shall deal with at the end of the chapter. What concerns me now is the problem of the placement of the explicitly titled "Deduction of judgments of taste"—§38 and the surrounding sections—in Kant's text.

I have already noted one occasion where Kant's organization of the third *Critique* serves him badly in the exposition of his aesthetic theory: his employment of the first *Critique*'s logical functions of judgment to expound his theory of the four moments of the judgment of taste.[20] In the case of the "Deduction of judgments of taste," Kant's organization does not so much misserve him as break down altogether. Like the *Critique of Pure Reason,* the *Critique of Aesthetic Judgment* has a Doctrine of Elements broken down into two major sections, an Analytic of Aesthetic Judgment and a Dialectic of Aesthetic Judgment.[21]* Unlike that of the first *Critique,* however, the Analytic of the third is further divided into two "books," the Analytic of the Beautiful and the Analytic of the Sublime, and this occasions confusion. For instead of presenting the deduction of pure aesthetic judgment either as a part of the Analytic of the Beautiful or else as a separate section serving both Analytics, Kant includes it in the Analytic of the Sublime. But he also explicitly denies that judgments of the sublime require any deduction beyond their mere exposition, maintaining instead that the search for a deduction of judgments of taste may be confined to judgments on the beauty of things in nature. This, to say the least, makes the location of the deduction in the Analytic of the Sublime peculiar. Furthermore, the large set of sections which Kant calls the "Deduction of Aesthetic Judgment" seems not only to be subsumed under the wrong heading, but also itself to subsume inappropriate material. Kant titles all of §§30 through 54 the "Deduction," but only §§30 through 40 concern the synthetic *a priori* status of judgments of taste and the principle on which this status depends. The sections beginning with §41, or in any case with §43, do not bear on the justification of taste's claim to intersubjective validity at all. Instead, these sections expound Kant's theory of art and of the purportedly different grounds for interests in natural and artistic beauty.

Whether §§41 and 42, which consider "empirical" and "intellectual" interests in the beautiful, are meant to contribute to the justification of aesthetic judgments or not is a moot point,[22*] but the sections following §42 certainly constitute only applications of Kant's aesthetic theory to some specific problems about our relation to nature and the character of artistic creation, rather than any further investigation of the foundations of the aesthetic theory itself. So it seems clear that the location of the deduction in the Analytic of the Sublime, and the inclusion in it of Kant's theory of art, is a mistake, and should be ignored. Failing to do so could only lead to wild speculations — that although judgments of taste involve only the harmony of imagination and understanding, their deduction must include reference to the faculty of reason involved in the experience of the sublime; or that even though judgments of taste must be judgments of free beauty, their deduction must involve reference to the content and intentionality characteristic of art. Fortunately, Kant's own account of what a justification of the apriority of judgments of taste must demonstrate makes it clear that such hypotheses could have nothing to do with his deduction of aesthetic judgment. Carelessness can be the only explanation of the location of the deduction in the architectonic of the third *Critique*.

There is a third problem about Kant's treatment of the relation between his theory of sublimity and his deduction of aesthetic judgment. In §30, which officially opens that deduction, Kant asserts that "the deduction of aesthetic judgments upon objects of nature must be directed not to what we call sublime in nature, but only to the beautiful."[23] As I have just observed, this makes the location of the deduction in the Analytic of the Sublime unintelligible. But what is worse, it also suggests that a deduction is needed only for aesthetic judgments on objects of nature, and thus not for judgments of taste on works of art. That Kant should intimate this may not be inexplicable, given his earlier hints that judgments on art may never in fact be pure judgments of taste; and insofar as these intimations are rejected (as I have argued they should be), we might see no need to worry over the present restriction. However, Kant's exclusion of both judgments of the sublime and of art from the scope of the deduction is not, at least explicitly, based on his distinction between free and dependent beauty. Instead, it appears to arise from a misconception on his part of what the deduction must accomplish — a misconception which, though it surfaces only in §30, may be deeply connected to Kant's earlier subsumption of aesthetic judgment under the reflective judgment of nature in general. For Kant's putative restriction of the deduction to judgments of natural beauty seems to stem from the idea that the deduction must explain the *existence* of naturally beautiful forms, an explanation which could not be required in the case of either natural sublimity or artistic beauty.

If the deduction of aesthetic judgment is to justify the imputation of subjective responses to others, then it will apply to any judgment which involves such an imputation, whether that judgment concerns natural beauty or any other source of aesthetic response. This may be clear enough, but to put it beyond doubt, we must now pause to unravel the peculiar argument which leads to the problematic assertion of §30.

Sublimity, Natural Beauty, and Artistic Beauty

Why should Kant have held that only judgments on natural beauty, and not those on either sublimity or artistic beauty, stand in need of a deduction? A brief consideration of Kant's theory of the sublime will show why he distinguished between judgments of sublimity and natural beauty in this regard; and such a consideration will prove a worthwhile digression, for it will also reveal an argument, though an unpersuasive one, for the separation of natural from artistic beauty in Kant's opening description of the task of the deduction.

In the Analytic of the Beautiful, Kant maintained that our pleasure in the beautiful is a response to the form of an object, and thus that the judgment of beauty relates a feeling of pleasure to the form of an object. In the Analytic of the Sublime,[24] by contrast, Kant describes a satisfaction in the formlessness rather than in the form of objects. Our pleasure in the sublime, he argues, is evoked by the very fact of formlessness, or the incapacity of imagination and understanding by themselves to grasp any unity of form in certain objects. In such cases, the unity that we nevertheless do feel can be attributed only to the faculty of reason, and the superiority of this faculty over our other higher faculties of cognition is the actual ground of our pleasure in sublimity, for which the sublime object is merely an external occasion. This doctrine is apparent throughout the discussion of the sublime, and a few quotations will suffice to illustrate it. In §23, Kant defines the fundamental difference between beauty and sublimity thus: "The beautiful in nature concerns the form of the object, which consists in limitation; the sublime is to be found, on the contrary, even in a formless object, insofar as *limitlessness* is represented in it through its instigation, and yet totality is also attributed to it: so that the beautiful seems to be taken as the presentation of an indeterminate concept of the understanding, but the sublime as the presentation of an indeterminate concept of reason."[25] The sublime, in its formlessness, may actually be regarded as "abusive" (*gewalttätig*) of the imagination, and yet is satisfactory for just that reason: the inadequacy of sensuous presentation in the case of an object which is formless or limitless incites "the mind to abandon sensibility, and occupy itself instead with ideas involving a higher finality."[26] It is in the revelation of this higher power of the mind which it occasions that a sublime object pleases.[27]

It is not obvious that the fact that it is the formlessness of an object which reveals this "higher finality," or, as it were, makes us conscious of a pleasing disharmony between reason and imagination rather than of a pleasing harmony between understanding and imagination, obviates any need for a deduction of judgments of the sublime. These judgments, like other aesthetic judgments, do claim universality; even in their case, "everything which should please the reflective judgment apart from any interest must import subjective and as such universally valid finality in its representation, although here no finality of the *form* of an object grounds our estimation of it."[28] The judgment of the sublime makes the same claim on the agreement of others as the judgment of beauty does, and like it must rest on the assumption that one's own faculties—now imagination and reason rather than understanding—are affected by given objects in the same way as those of everyone else. Nevertheless, in §30, Kant maintains that "the exposition of judgments on the sublime in nature was at the same time their deduction."[29]

This exposition, however, claims intersubjective validity for only one of the faculties involved in the response of sublimity, namely, reason, the source of all ideas transcending the finite capacities of imagination. Tacitly equating reason in general with practical reason, Kant holds that since the judgment of the sublime relates the imagination to reason, we attribute necessity to this judgment "only under a subjective presupposition (which, however, we believe we are justified in having to impute to everyone), namely, that of the moral feeling in mankind"; with this, we attribute necessity to aesthetic judgments on the sublime.[30] But even if we are justified in presupposing the existence of the faculty of reason in everyone else—and in equating reason as the source of the moral feeling with reason as the source of limitless ideas in general — we must also assume that everyone has a similar faculty of imagination. The universal imputation of the judgment of sublimity presupposes that all persons have the same limits on their imagination, and that this faculty will interact with reason in the same way in the case of any given object. If a transcendental deduction is needed to justify such an assumption about the imagination and its harmony with another faculty of cognition in the case of beauty, then it is also needed for the judgment of sublimity, which likewise assumes the fundamental similarity of faculties among human subjects. That the feeling of sublimity is a response to formlessness rather than to form does not affect this requirement.

Kant does not acknowledge this in §30 because of an inappropriate concern with the existence of the forms of nature as objects of aesthetic judgment. Kant begins this section by stating that "the claim of an aesthetic judgment to universal validity for every subject, as a judgment which must stand on some *a priori* principle, requires a deduction (that is, a legitimization of its presumption)."[31] This is no surprise, and one simply assumes that what needs deduction is the presupposition of intersubjective similarity by means of which an attribution of any pleasure to a free play of the faculties licenses the imputation of that feeling to others. But Kant does not focus upon intersubjectivity. Instead, he proceeds as if it were some peculiarity of the object of aesthetic judgment which creates the need for a deduction: the latter "must be something more than the exposition [of the judgment] if it concerns a delight or dissatisfaction in the *form of the object.*" It is apparently when "the finality has its ground in the object and its outward form" that a deduction is required, suggesting that what must be deduced is some assumption about the existence of beautiful objects, rather than about the nature of judging subjects.

Kant's final remarks in the opening paragraph of §30 also intimate that the deduction must furnish an explanation of the existence of beautiful forms in nature: "With respect to the beautiful in nature, therefore, one may raise a number of questions which concern the cause of this finality of their forms: e.g., how one would explain why nature has spread beauty about prodigally, even in the depth of the ocean where the human eye (for which alone it is final) but seldom penetrates." This looks like a query that must be answered by an explanation of the unexpected existence of beautifully formed objects.

If this were what the deduction of aesthetic judgment actually had to explain, it would justify §30's implied restriction of the deduction to cases of natural rather than artistic beauty, as well as its express exclusion of judgments of the sublime. The latter restriction is stated in the remaining paragraphs of §30. Kant begins by reiterating his view that "the sublime in nature . . . may be regarded as quite without form or figure, and nonetheless be looked upon as an object of pure delight, and reveal a subjective finality of the given representation."³² But, he continues, it is actually inappropriate to refer to objects in nature as being themselves sublime. Rather, sublimity "must properly be attributed only to the attitude of thought, or even more to the foundation of this [attitude] in human nature"—that is, it seems, human reason. This is why the mere exposition of the sublime is supposed to explain all that one needs to know for any claim about sublimity, the claim to universal validity included. Apparently, since sublimity is not a property of objects of nature in even the attenuated sense in which beauty is, no question of an explanation of its existence need even arise.

Were this conclusion correct, the inclusion of the deduction in the Analytic of the Sublime would be misleading, but the restrictions of §30 would themselves make sense. No deduction of aesthetic judgments on art would be necessary, because the existence of beautiful forms in that sphere could be easily explained as the result of our own action. And no deduction of judgments of the sublime would be needed, because they would make no claims about objects at all. But Kant's argument in §30 cannot be accepted. First, if an explanation of their existence were really needed in the case of beautiful objects, it would be just as appropriate in the case of the sublime, in spite of the "form" of the former and the "formlessness" of the latter. The need for an explanation of the existence of natural beauty could only arise from the fact that it is not the forms of all natural objects which lead to a harmony of the human cognitive faculties. Only some forms do, and this raises the teleological question why *those* forms should exist, especially where no human being may ever see them. However, the very same question may be raised with regard to the sublime, even if Kant is more insistent on the subjectivity of sublimity than of beauty. After all, not *every* formless object in nature disposes the mind to the satisfying recognition of the superiority of reason over the inadequate imagination which constitutes the experience of sublimity; the formlessness of a weed-grown lot does not occasion the same response as that of a wild mountain range. If the existence of beauty as an exceptional case of form calls for an explanation, so does the existence of sublimity as an exceptional case of formlessness.

Further, the question of §30 also conflicts with Kant's argument in all of the remaining sections devoted to the deduction of aesthetic judgment. First, Kant's concluding remark in §38, where he attempts to evaluate the true force of his deduction, specifically excludes any *a priori* explanation of the existence of beautiful objects in nature—a deduction of their existence—from the realm of aesthetics. Thus Kant writes: "But if the question were, how is it possible to assume *a priori* that nature is a complex of objects of taste? the problem would then be related to teleology, because it would have to be regarded as an end of nature, essentially connected to its concept, that it exhibit forms final for our faculty of judgment. But the correctness of this assumption is much to be doubted, even while the reality of natural beauties lies open to experience."[33] The question for which §30 suggests the deduction of aesthetic judgment must supply an answer is not a question for aesthetic theory at all. Second, both Kant's statement of the question of the deduction in sections subsequent to §30 and his actual answer to this question show that what is at issue is not the existence of beautiful objects at all, but rather the similarity among human objects that grounds the possibility of universal subjective agreement. But in this case, a deduction must be just as necessary for judgments of artistic beauty as for those of natural beauty, and for cases of sublimity as well as of beauty, just as long as judgments on any of these claim intersubjective validity for subjective responses.[34]*

Constraints on the Deduction

So the transcendental deduction of judgments of taste must accomplish just what we would expect on the basis of my earlier analysis of aesthetic judgment, in spite of the misleading impressions which may be caused by its location in the text and by Kant's argument in §30. Before examining Kant's actual attempts at such a deduction, however, we must consider the constraints which the explanation of aesthetic response imposes on any possible deduction of aesthetic judgment. These constraints are developed in §§32 to 34, which also contain most of what Kant has to say about the force of criticism as a practical means for working toward the intersubjective agreement intended by aesthetic judgment. My concern, though, will not be the general question of how much of a theory of criticism might be drawn from these sections,[35]* but only how Kant's characterization of the force of critical discourse reveals key limits on the deduction of taste. In this regard, we shall see that even though these sections constitute no real departure from the Analytic of the Beautiful, they do put some of its results in a particularly illuminating perspective.

According to §31, the judgment of taste "has a double and indeed logical peculiarity." First, Kant maintains, the judgment of taste "has universal validity *a priori,* yet not a logical universality according to concepts, but the universality of a singular judgment." Second, it has "a necessity (which must always rest upon *a priori* grounds) but one which depends upon no *a priori* grounds of proof, by the representation of which the assent which the judgment of taste imputes to everyone could be enforced."[36] If the requirements of universality and necessity impose essentially the same constraint on aesthetic reflection, these two "peculiarities" do not impose different constraints on aesthetic judgment or its deduction.[37] Both make the same point: to call an object beautiful is to make a "singular judgment," and does not depend on the predication of any determinate concepts of that object; yet calling an object beautiful is to claim a universal assent ordinarily justifiable only when it can be enforced by the subsumption of an object under determinate theoretical or practical concepts. Thus the peculiarity of the necessity of aesthetic judgment is actually explicated in terms of universality; in Kant's words, it consists in the fact that, although aesthetic judgment "has merely subjective validity, it yet makes a claim on *all* subjects, as could otherwise be made only if it were an objective judgment, which rested on cognitive grounds and could be enforced by a proof."[38] But although the peculiarities of aesthetic judgment's universality and necessity do not imply two different constraints either on this judgment or on its deduction, two crucial constraints on that deduction do emerge in the two sections which Kant devotes to these peculiarities. These constraints are not as closely linked to the requirements of universality and necessity as they are to Kant's basic explanation of aesthetic response.

In §32, Kant maintains that taste makes claim to "autonomy," and that "to make the judgments of others the determining ground of one's own [judgment of taste] would be heteronomy."[39] That is, a judgment of taste cannot be made on the basis of any induction from other persons' expressions of approval, but must be "pronounced *a priori.*" This, it seems, is no accident, but part of the concept of taste itself: an aesthetic judgment must be made on the basis of one's own feeling to qualify as a judgment of taste at all. In Kant's terms, "for every judgment, which should reveal the taste of a subject, it is required that the subject judge for himself, without having to grope about among the judgments of others and inform himself of their delight or dissatisfaction in advance [of his own judgment]; thus, his judgment should be pronounced *a priori,* not as an imitation because a thing actually happens to generally please." That is, a judgment of taste not only has an *a priori* claim as part of its content, but must be made in a manner which is in some sense *a priori.* It can only be made on the basis of one's own feeling of pleasure and reflection on it. In other words, while one's own feeling of pleasure may not be sufficient evidence for a judgment of taste, it is a necessary piece of evidence.

Kant illustrates this claim by the example of a "youthful poet" who "allows himself to be dissuaded from his conviction that his poem is beautiful neither by the judgment of the public nor by his friends." In so doing, he is not being particularly egocentric or demonstrating any adolescent stubbornness. He is merely complying with the requirement of taste that he base his judgment on his own feelings of pleasure or displeasure. Only if his own feelings actually change can he "freely depart from his former judgment." In this, he acts as reasonably as he would in any other kind of judgment — a judgment of reason in Kant's example — for what he is doing is just refusing to change his judgment until he can detect a change in the appropriate evidence. In an aesthetic judgment, one's own feeling is the crucial evidence.

Kant does not make explicit why judgments of taste must be autonomous in the way he describes. One could suppose that he just takes this to be a consequence of the fact that a judgment which makes an *a priori* claim cannot be supported by the merely empirical evidence which could be obtained from inquiry into the responses of others. One might then object that the fact that such a judgment cannot have an empirical foundation, and instead requires one that is *a priori,* does not actually imply that one can only make it if one has a feeling of pleasure oneself. Since the content of an aesthetic judgment could be expressed in the subjunctive — as in "Any disinterested observer would take pleasure in this object" — it is at least conceivable that one could judge an object beautiful without taking pleasure in it, if one knew that one's own response was in fact interested and therefore irrelevant. However, Kant's point may be that this is not a real possibility: since aesthetic pleasure cannot be linked to an object by a concept, nothing but the actual occurrence of pleasure can reasonably suggest that a given object is beautiful. If this is so, then one's own feeling of pleasure must be a necessary condition for reasonably thinking an object beautiful. The autonomy of aesthetic judgment might even be thought to be a consequence of the fact that such a feeling is *only* a necessary condition of aesthetic judgment, and that this judgment also requires reflection on the source of one's pleasure for its assignment to the harmony of the faculties. The requirement of autonomy might then express the fact that one cannot conduct such reflection on the reported pleasures of others, but can only so reflect on one's own feelings.

But whatever Kant's exact reasons for the doctrine of autonomy are, it clearly has an important consequence for the deduction of aesthetic judgment, and clarifies Kant's notion of the imputation of pleasure. If an aesthetic judgment requires that others assent to it, but if anyone can reasonably assent to a judgment of beauty only if he actually feels pleasure in the object concerned, then any argument which can justify this form of judgment must do more than just allow us to attribute certain beliefs or cognitive contents to other persons. It must justify us in attributing certain feelings or specific kinds of experiences to others. It must permit us to attribute to other persons neither just certain conclusions nor the dispositions to make certain utterances, but rather particular states of mind. This is as strong a requirement as we make in any case of shared knowledge, and stronger than what we require in many cases.

Ordinarily, we think of intersubjective agreement as requiring that other persons hold the same beliefs as we do and possess adequate evidence for those beliefs. But we do not require that the states of mind which embody their beliefs have any particular affective value, or be pleasurable or painful. And in many cases, we do not specify that the adequate evidence for their beliefs be constituted by any specific experiences—let alone sensations—though we may assume that their beliefs must be linked to certain situations or occasions for certain observations. Even in cases where another's justified possession of a particular belief may appear to require that he have a particular sensation, alternative forms of evidence might be possible. For example, we might think someone justified in believing an object to be red only if he is capable of having the sensation of red, but we would have to allow an alternative justification if he can discriminate the wave lengths of light reflected from objects even without sensing red. But Kant's requirement of autonomy means that the deduction of aesthetic judgment must demonstrate that we are justified in imputing the specific capacity for aesthetic pleasure to other persons, and even that we are justified in attributing that feeling to them in very particular contexts.

Kant's deduction, then, must prove more than that we are justified in attributing a general capacity for aesthetic response to other persons. For his exposition of the logical peculiarities of the judgment of taste emphasizes that a judgment of taste is a logically singular judgment. It is a claim

The Task of the Deduction

about a particular, and imputes pleasure in this particular to other persons. As Kant says, "To say this flower is beautiful, is only to repeat its own individual claim to the delight of everyone."[40] The feeling attributed to others in a judgment of taste is a feeling occasioned by a specific object. If one's own justified assent to a judgment of beauty requires that one actually be pleased by that object, then a justified demand of assent from others requires a justified belief that they too will take pleasure in that particular. The deduction of aesthetic judgment must then be an argument sufficient to justify the imputation of specific feelings to others on specific occasions, and this is a very strong constraint. As Hume insisted, the problem of a "standard of taste" really becomes pressing "when critics come to particulars,"[41] and Kant's own analysis of aesthetic judgment requires that his deduction come to particulars.

Thus the first constraint on the deduction of aesthetic judgment is that it show we may make an assumption about other persons which is as strong as any we ever make in claiming intersubjective validity for a belief. The second constraint, which emerges in §33, is that this deduction show we can assume intersubjective validity for aesthetic judgment even though the very nature of this judgment deprives us of the *means* by which intersubjective acceptance of beliefs is ordinarily obtained. What Kant emphasizes in his discussion of the "second peculiarity" of taste is that "the judgment of taste is not determinable by grounds of proof [*Beweisgründe*], just as if it were merely *subjective*."[42]

As before, Kant illustrates his claim with what appears to be an acceptance of youthful individualism or a nascent romanticism. "In the first place," he says, "if someone does not find a building, view, or poem beautiful, then he does not let his approval be pressed out of him by a hundred voices, all praising it highly." And, second, a judgment of beauty cannot be determined by "a proof *a priori* according to rules." "Someone may adduce Batteux or Lessing, or even older and more famous critics of taste, and all the rules they proposed for proof that his poem is beautiful . . . [but] I stop my ears, will hear no grounds and no arguing, and would rather assume that the rules of the critics are false . . . than let my own judgment be determined *a priori* by proofs, for it must be a judgment of taste and not of understanding or reason."[43] But, again, Kant is not celebrating obstinacy; he is only reminding us that the deduction of aesthetic judgment must be compatible with the fact that particular judgments of taste cannot gain assent by induction or deduction—by the acclaim of a hundred voices or by a proof *a priori*.

Kant denies the possibility of supporting judgments of taste by either ordinary induction or deduction when he claims that such judgments are not determinable by proofs or "grounds of proof." A proof of a judgment of taste would be possible only if there were a "principle of taste, by which one would understand a premise [*Grundsatz*], under the condition of which one could subsume the concept of an object, and then, by a syllogism [*Schluss*], draw the inference that it is beautiful."[44] That is, the judgment that an object is beautiful cannot be concluded from the fact that any other concept or conjunction of concepts applies to it. This follows from Kant's explanation of aesthetic response as a synthesis of a manifold achieved without the use of any concept, though Kant does not refer to this explanation in the present context, only invoking its consequence that "as a matter of fact the judgment of taste is invariably made as a singular judgment on an object."[45] A singular judgment is one which may use a general concept ("tulip," in Kant's example), to identify the object of which it makes a predication, but which does not base its predication on any inference from that general concept.

That all of this is true of aesthetic judgment was clear from §8 of the Analytic of the Beautiful. It may be asked, however, why Kant excludes both the "empirical *ground of proof*" constituted by the praise of a hundred voices, and the "proof *a priori* according to definite rules" as furnished by a Batteux or Lessing, as cases of *syllogistic* proof. The latter kind of proof surely fits Kant's general definition, but trying to support an aesthetic judgment by inductive appeal to the approval of others does not seem to involve appealing to a general concept under which the object falls. If a hundred voices could all identify the object of their approval by mere ostension, then one could base one's own judgment on theirs without subsuming the object under any general concept at all. Perhaps what Kant believes, though, is that such an appeal to the experience of others is ordinarily involved in one's own employment of empirical concepts for cognition, since one ordinarily draws many inferences from the application of an empirical concept which are neither purely *a priori*[46*] nor based on one's *own* experience. If that is so, then proof by subsumption under empirical concepts at least sometimes depends on an induction from the experience of others. Thus Kant suggests that for one to appeal to the beliefs of others may be permissible in cognition but not in taste: "that others may possibly see and observe for him, and that many have seen in one way what he believes to have seen in another way, may serve as a sufficient proof for him in the case of theoretical and thus logical judgement, but what has pleased others can never serve as the ground of an aesthetic judgment."[47] Kant cannot be arguing that induction is impermissible in the case of aesthetic judgment just because that judgment cannot employ any empirical concepts, since though these concepts may really represent inductions from the experiences of others, such inductions could also be made apart from the use of empirical concepts. But Kant's whole argument could be interpreted thus: no subsumption of an object under a general concept can determine aesthetic judgment, both because concepts in general—whether they are well-founded empirical concepts or the *a priori* rule of critics—are not involved in aesthetic response, and because the use of empirical concepts represents an implicit use of induction incompatible with the *a priori* claim made by aesthetic judgment.

But however these claims of §33 are interpreted, they do not yet go beyond points already made in the Analytic of the Beautiful. Where this section does break new ground is in its intimations about the limited force of ordinary modes of argument in the case of aesthetic judgment. If neither induction nor deduction can determine the judgment of taste, then the usual means of producing assent to a belief are inapplicable to aesthetic disputes. Kant expresses this by considering the case in which others find an object beautiful but one does not find it so oneself. If one disagrees with the consensus of others, "he may even begin to doubt whether he has formed his taste through acquaintance with a sufficient number of objects of a particular kind (as one who believes to recognize as a wood something in the distance which everyone else regards as a town may doubt the judgment of his own eyesight) . . . [But though] the unfavorable judgment of others may rightly make us dubious in respect to our own, [it] can never convince us of its incorrectness."[48] The same argument could be made with respect to disagreement with the rule-governed pronouncements of a critic. Further, the argument can also be made with regard to others rather than oneself. If one's own assent cannot be enforced by appeal either to consensus or to concepts, then one cannot reasonably expect that such appeals will bring others around to one's own judgment of taste. But this means that an aesthetic judgment makes a claim on the agreement of others which is at least as strong as any other claim to intersubjective validity, and perhaps stronger than most, but which cannot be enforced by any of the normal means for producing cognitive agreement. It cannot appeal to the evidence of induction, to the results of such induction incorporated into empirical concepts, or to any *a priori* concepts.

The deduction of aesthetic judgment, then, faces the task of justifying the rationality of a claim to intersubjectivity to which the ordinary means for securing agreement are inapplicable. This may not seem to imply a constraint on the possible form of this deduction,[49*] although the absence of the usual instruments of intersubjectivity does mean that we may not be predisposed to assume its possibility, and that the deduction of aesthetic judgment will have to be a very persuasive argument indeed. But Kant's discussion of the "second peculiarity" of the judgment of taste does at least hint at one possible constraint on the form of the deduction itself. Kant has argued that judgments of taste do not employ any concepts except, incidentally, to secure their reference; but, on at least one interpretation, Kant's transcendental deductions are arguments which justify a particular form of judgment precisely by showing that we are justified in using, or even compelled to use, some *concept* which has an essential role in that form of judgment.[50*] On this model, the judgment that every event must have some cause, for instance, is justified by the fact that the *concepts* of cause and effect are required for the absolutely unimpeachable purpose of making any distinction between subject and object, or subjective and objective sequences of apprehension. Indeed, Kant suggests in the *Critique of Pure Reason* that a transcendental deduction must turn on such a necessary use of certain determinate concepts: "The transcendental deduction of all *a priori* concepts has . . . a principle according to which the whole inquiry must be directed, namely, that they be recognized as *a priori* conditions of the possibility of experience, whether of the intuition which is to be met with in it or of the thought. Concepts which yield the objective ground of the possibility of experience are for this very reason necessary."[51] This suggests that a transcendental deduction can be constructed only if certain concepts can be shown to be necessary conditions of the possibility of experience. But if a form of judgment employs no determinate concepts, it is difficult to see how it can thus be deduced; and aesthetic judgments, as we have once again seen, employ no determinate concepts, whether empirical or *a priori*.

The absence of determining concepts from judgments of taste certainly constitutes a constraint on their possible deduction. But it may not make this justification impossible, for the kind of argument that has just been sketched is not the only model for a transcendental deduction. It is also possible to suppose that transcendental arguments proceed by demonstrating that certain *judgments* are necessary conditions of the possibility of experience, or of certain other, unimpeachable judgments, and that they show particular *concepts* to be necessary only indirectly, by justifying the judgments in which those concepts are employed.[52]* On this interpretation, the transcendental deduction of the first *Critique* would work by showing that judgments about objects are conditions of the unquestionable possibility of judgments which merely assign different experiences to the same manifold of intuition, and by then showing that such concepts as those of cause and effect are required to formulate judgments about objects. And if this is how transcendental deductions proceed, then it is at least conceivable that a deduction of aesthetic judgments can be given. Even though such judgments do not employ determinate concepts, they might still be shown to be judgments which we must be capable of making if we can make some other, less questionable kind of judgment.

Kant himself suggests that this must be his strategy when he claims that what makes the deduction of aesthetic judgment so easy is that "it has no need to justify the objective reality of a concept," but instead "only asserts that we are justified in universally presupposing in every person the same subjective conditions of the faculty of judgment which we find in ourselves."[53] In the next two chapters, I will show that Kant tries to carry out this strategy by proving that possession of the capacity to enjoy aesthetic response, even in particular circumstances, is entailed by the capacity to make any cognitive judgments at all.

But if this is his strategy, two questions must be asked. First, does Kant's deduction of aesthetic judgment proceed from some assumption which is really as unimpeachable as the first *Critique*'s assumption that we are capable of judgments which merely assign different items to the same manifold, or are capable of affixing the representation "I think" to any of our other representations?[54] Or does it at least depend on a presupposition which he shows to be a genuine consequence of such an unquestionable judgmental ability? Second, even supposing that his deduction of aesthetic judgment does proceed from such a starting point, does it really succeed in showing that such a capacity entails the ability to make aesthetic judgments? In what follows, I shall argue that these questions must be answered in the negative. Although it is of considerable force, and perhaps even as strong as it really need be, Kant's deduction of pure aesthetic judgment cannot conform to the parameters for success in transcendental deduction which the model of his own *Critique of Pure Reason* implies.

One problem, earlier mentioned but not discussed,[55] must still be considered before turning to Kant's actual deduction. This is the fact that Kant addresses the issue of the intersubjectively valid ground for pleasure not once, but three times, in three separate passages none of which so much as hints at the existence of either of the others.

The problem of the intersubjective validity of our pleasure in the beautiful is first tackled in the fourth moment of the Analytic of the Beautiful. Here Kant claims that the judgment of taste can be made "only on the presupposition that there is a common sense"[56] and then offers a problematic account of the justifiability of this presupposition: first, he maintains that the supposition of a common sense is the "necessary condition of the universal communicability of our knowledge,"[57] suggesting that it may be as readily deduced as any principle in the first *Critique;* but he then undermines his position by asking whether the existence of a common sense is to be regarded as a constitutive or a regulative principle, and by stating that this question cannot yet be resolved, in spite of the just announced claim that a common sense is a necessary condition of knowledge.[58] Then, in §§30 to 40, which are expressly concerned with the deduction of pure aesthetic judgment, Kant offers an argument which appears quite similar to that expounded in the fourth moment; but, strangely, he neither mentions that he has already made one attempt at a deduction nor addresses the one point which might most obviously explain a second attempt: namely, the open question of whether aesthetic judgment rests on a constitutive or a regulative principle. Finally, the question of the universal validity of the judgment of taste is brought up again in the Dialectic of Aesthetic Judgment. The argument we find here, however, does not even consider the conditions of the communication of knowledge, but rather concerns the existence of a supersensible ground underlying both the objects and subjects of judgments of taste.[59] All of this naturally raises the question why should Kant make three attempts to prove the justifiability of judgments of taste, and how do these three attempts stand in relation to one another?

Nothing that Kant actually says in his text casts any light on this issue.[60] Given what Kant says in §30, one might suppose that these arguments stand in the following relation: that of §21 demonstrates the intersubjective validity of aesthetic response, on purely epistemological grounds; that of §§38 and 39, answering the question of §30, explains the natural existence of objects engendering such response; and that of the Dialectic supplies a crucial metaphysical premise missing from the earlier two arguments. However, such a conjecture is clearly untenable. As we have seen, §§36 and 37 prepare the way for §38 as if the question of intersubjective validity were still completely open, even after §21, and §38 itself clearly rejects the putative question of §30 as a possible question for the deduction. And as we shall see in Chapter 10, the metaphysical argument of the Dialectic is a completely illegitimate addendum to the deduction.

Other explanations of the presence of three different attempts at the deduction might be possible, but I shall not try to develop one. Instead, I will simply treat the arguments of §21 and §§38 and 39 as two versions, differing in detail but the same in basic strategy, of the same general argument. Each of these attempts to overcome skepticism about the rationality of aesthetic judgment by showing that the conditions of intersubjective validity in taste are the same as those for cognition generally. Then, I will analyze the argument of the Dialectic as one further attempt to overcome skepticism. This argument may be motivated by Kant's tacit recognition of the limits of his earlier arguments, but it makes no explicit reference to such limits and, moreover, transgresses Kant's own entirely general limits on metaphysics founded in pure reason alone.

8

The Deduction: First Attempt

* *

The Idea of a Common Sense

Kant's first attempt at a deduction of aesthetic judgment is found in the fourth moment of the Analytic of the Beautiful. Here, Kant characterizes the judgment of beauty as the claim to the "necessity of the assent of *all* to a judgment regarded as an example of a universal rule which cannot be given,"[1] or the claim that "everyone should give the object in question his approval."[2] Such a claim, Kant notes, can only be "pronounced conditionally," because, even assuming that one does have "a ground that is common to all, one could count on such agreement only if one were sure that the [given] case [of pleasure] had been correctly subsumed under that ground as a rule for approval." The attribution of a particular feeling of pleasure to its proper source is an empirical judgment, and a judgment of taste dependent on such an attribution must always be less than fully certain. But what is now at issue is the deeper question of the condition under which even a completely certain attribution of one's pleasure to a particular source in oneself could justify the claim to the "necessity of the assent of *all*." The assumption that in attributing a particular feeling of pleasure to the harmony of imagination and understanding one is attributing it to a "ground common to all" is the deepest condition on aesthetic judgment, the condition of its possibility as a form of synthetic *a priori* judgment. The question for its deduction must be, then, the question of whether we have such a ground.

Kant formulates the deep condition on the "necessity advanced by a judgment of taste" as "the idea of a common sense," and thus poses the question of a deduction as whether we have a good reason for presupposing a common sense.[3] Kant's second version of the deduction does not mention a "common sense" until it summarizes its results,[4] and our first question must be whether the use of this term is crucial to Kant's deduction

The answer to this question is complicated by the fact that Kant uses the phrase "common sense" in three different ways.[5] Two of these emerge in §20. Kant begins this section by claiming that unless aesthetic judgment possesses some kind of principle, no one could even consider that it enjoys any kind of necessity. But, of course, it cannot have a determinate objective principle, one which links beauty to other properties of objects by logically universal rules. It can have only a "subjective principle," which allows one to determine what pleases or displeases with universal validity, but through feeling rather than concepts. Kant first introduces the term "common sense" to refer to *this principle;*[6] a common sense would then be a principle which allows one to regard a response as universal and necessary on the basis of one's own feeling. As a principle, the common sense would presumably be a belief or presupposition, such as the belief in the universal similarity of the operations of the higher cognitive faculties, which would allow one to impute a pleasure attributed to these faculties to others. The common sense would be just the kind of principle about what is public in one's mental life which is required by the force of calling something "beautiful." Obviously, a deduction of aesthetic judgment would be provided by a proof that we do have reason for presupposing a common sense, so understood, for this would be a proof that we do have some *a priori* principle to back up the claim on the agreement of others which constitutes the *a priori* element of the judgment of taste.

The situation is confused, however, when Kant uses the term "common sense" as if it referred to a *feeling* rather than a principle. In the second paragraph of §20, Kant asserts that the judgment of taste depends on our presupposing that there is a common sense. This is obvious, if "common sense" is taken in the sense just defined. But Kant glosses this statement by saying that he understands this term to mean not "some external sense, but rather the effect of the free play of our cognitive faculties."[7] However, since the effect of this free play is nothing but the feeling of pleasure which constitutes aesthetic response itself, this suggests that the common sense is a kind of feeling, rather than a principle which may be applied to certain feelings.

Our confusion is compounded by §40, where Kant uses the phrase "common sense" in yet another way. Here, he uses it to mean neither a principle nor a feeling, but rather a faculty or ability; he writes as if the common sense were the faculty of taste itself. He begins this section by arguing that such phrases as a "sense of truth" or a "sense of justice" are misleading in their reference to sense, because ideas such as those of truth or justice "could never enter our thoughts were we not able to elevate ourselves above the senses to higher faculties of cognition." So the common ability to make sound judgments of truth or justice should not be called a common sense. But some judgments may still be ascribed to a common sense, if

> by the *sensus communis* one . . . understands the idea of a *public* sense, that is, a faculty of estimation [*Beurteilungsvermögen*] which in its reflection takes account (*a priori*) of the mode of representation of everyone else, in order, *as it were,* to weigh its judgment against the collective reason of mankind and thereby escape the illusion which arises from subjective private conditions that may easily be taken to be objective, [and] that would have a disadvantageous influence on the judgment.[8]

But in so describing a faculty of estimation by which one's own response can be tested against a conjectural collective voice of mankind, Kant is now identifying the common sense with the *ability* to make judgments of taste.

This becomes clear as §40 continues to characterize this *sensus communis* in ways Kant earlier used to describe taste itself. Thus he asks whether the act of reflection he has just described "is too artificial to be attributed to the faculty which we call *common* sense," and answers that it is not, since "nothing is more natural than to abstract from charm and emotion if one is seeking a judgment that may serve as a universal rule."[9] To abstract from charm or emotion, of course, is precisely what is required to make a judgment of taste. Kant then makes explicit the identity of taste and common sense: "taste can be called a *sensus communis* with more justice than can the sound understanding, and the aesthetic judgment rather than the intellectual can bear the name of a public sense"; as he adds in a footnote, taste may be designated "*a sensus communis aestheticus.*"[10] However, Kant complicates this simple identity by claiming that it depends on what is in fact the second meaning of the term "common sense." He holds that the faculty of aesthetic judgment is appropriately called a "common sense" if one means by "sense" the "effect of mere reflection on the mind . . . for one would then understand by 'sense' the feeling of pleasure." The common sense, it seems, is both a shared feeling of pleasure and the faculty for judging that such a feeling is shared, as well as the principle on which the exercise of this faculty rests.

Fortunately for Kant's deduction of aesthetic judgment, this plethora of senses is more confusing than damaging, for justifying the presupposition of a common sense in any one of its three senses will in fact establish its existence in the other senses as well. If the common sense is the principle on which we can claim necessity and universality for feelings of pleasure, then what is needed to justify its presupposition is a proof that we possess an *a priori* principle grounding claims to intersubjective validity. If the common sense is an effect of simple reflection or of a feeling of pleasure by means of and concerning which[11] universal validity is claimed, then, again, we must be provided with a principle for *a priori* claims to intersubjective validity. Finally, if the common sense is neither a feeling nor a principle, but the faculty of taste itself, proving that we really do enjoy such a faculty still requires proof that we possess a principle licensing imputation of our own pleasures to other persons. In whatever sense we take it, proving that we have a common sense requires proving that we are justified in imputing our own aesthetic responses to others. But that means that Kant's introduction of the phrase "common sense" neither changes the task of the deduction nor advances his argument. It is a needless complexity.

Kant's use of the term "common sense" is connected to another terminological complexity which must be considered before we turn to the argument of §21 itself. Throughout, I have described the task of the deduction as that of establishing the universal validity of pleasures attributed to the harmony of the faculties. But in §40, after having defined taste as itself the *sensus communis,* Kant also characterizes taste as "the faculty of estimating that which makes our feeling in a given representation *universally communicable* without the mediation of a concept"[12] or as "the faculty for estimating *a priori* the communicability of the feelings which are connected with given representation[s] (without the mediation of a concept)."[13]* And in §21 itself, Kant's argument turns on the assumption that a common sense is the necessary condition of the universal communicability of knowledge.[14] Is there a difference between claiming — and justifying a claim of — universal validity and universal communicability? There might well appear to be, for it could be supposed that a feeling is universally *valid* as long as it is really shareable under appropriate conditions, but that it is *communicable* only if the fact of its shareability is supplemented by some means of actually conveying it to other persons, a method for persuading or inducing them to feel it. If this were the case, then a deduction of the universal *communicability* of aesthetic judgment would have to demonstrate that we can communicate as well as impute our pleasures to other persons, and would thus have a more complex task than I have so far assigned it.

However, Kant's substitution of "universal communicability" for "universal validity" does not alter what the deduction of aesthetic judgment must provide, in spite of the pragmatic element which the notion of communicability might seem to add to the more purely epistemological notion of validity. In §9, where Kant first introduces the phrase "universal communicability,"[15*] he clearly means to refer solely to the epistemological status of universal validity, for he opposes universal communicability to private validity,[16] and does not suggest that he means to impose any requirement on aesthetic judgment not already considered in §§7 and 8; but these stated only the requirement of a universal voice.[17] Similarly, the sections preceding the mention of communicability in §21 are concerned only with the justification of taste's claim to the possible assent of all, and not with means for achieving agreement in the face of actual disagreement. And in §40, the common sense is described not as a faculty for conveying one's responses to others, but, quite clearly, as a faculty for simply determining the intersubjective acceptability of one's own responses. By its means, one compares one's own judgment "not so much with the actual as with the possible judgments of others and transposes oneself into the position of everyone else" — an exercise accomplished by the method of the third moment, or by "leaving aside as much as possible what is matter in the state of representation, that is, sensation, and attending merely to the formal characteristics of one's representation or state of representation."[18] In other words, the universal communicability of a feeling or mental state is nothing but its subjective universal validity. The method for determining communicability is identical with that for judging the universal validity of a feeling, and there is no reason to suppose that there must be any difference between a deduction of a principle of communicability and one of a principle of intersubjective validity.

Whether the task of the deduction is described as that of justifying the presupposition of a common sense, that of proving that aesthetic response is universally communicable, or that of providing an *a priori* principle for claims to universal subjective validity, then, the same thing is required: a demonstration that the attribution of a given feeling of pleasure to the harmony of imagination and understanding does indeed license its imputation to any other observer of the object which occasions it. Kant's talk of communicability and common sense does not alter the fact that his deduction must resolve a purely epistemological problem. But Kant's reference to the communicability of feeling is not without significance, for it does point to the key to his deduction. In both of its versions, Kant's deduction of aesthetic judgment turns on claims about the conditions of the communicability of knowledge in general. I shall now turn to the first of Kant's attempts.

Common Sense and the Possibility of Knowledge

Kant's first deduction of taste is found in §21 of the first moment, and proceeds as follows. He first asserts that (1) "cognitions and judgments, together with the conviction that accompanies them, must allow of being universally communicated; for otherwise no correspondence with the object would belong to them: they would collectively be nothing but a merely subjective play of the faculties of representation, just as skepticism claims."[19] This statement presents the fundamental premise of Kant's argument. It maintains, first, that the shareability of a knowledge claim is a necessary condition of its being knowledge and, second, that what must be communicable in any case of knowledge is both a propositional content and a propositional attitude of belief or conviction directed toward this content. These assumptions seem reasonable enough. We do generally take shareability as a necessary condition for knowledge, and this does require not merely that others be able to entertain the propositions we claim to know, but also that they be able to believe them. If no one else could ever convince himself of what I claim to know, that would be as much of an obstacle to my knowledge claim as a general incapacity to understand what I assert. Nevertheless, a serious question does arise about Kant's entitlement to this premise. For the moment, however, we should allow it as plausible and consider the rest of his argument.

Kant's next step is to maintain that (2) "should cognitions allow of communication, then the mental state, that is, the disposition of the cognitive powers for a cognition in general, and indeed that proportion which qualifies a representation (by which an object is given to us) to constitute knowledge, must also admit of being communicated; for without this, as the subjective condition of knowing, knowledge as an effect could not arise."[20] This might appear merely to repeat Kant's first claim that both the content of a knowledge claim and the mental state of conviction (which we might think of as its "subjective condition") must be shareable if there is to be any knowledge at all. But this second step maintains something stronger than the first. It treats the content of a knowledge claim and the conviction it enjoys as together constituting a cognition, and introduces a *third* item as the "subjective condition" of knowledge. This is the particular state of the cognitive faculties which is the psychological basis of *both* entertaining and believing a particular proposition. In fact, step 2 asserts that every instance of knowledge has its subjective basis in a "disposition" (*Stimmung*) or relation between imagination and understanding, and that there is a particular "proportion" between these two faculties, the occurrence of which explains the knowledge of an object.[21]* The existence of this proportion is the condition of there being knowledge of an object on any occasion; and if such knowledge may be shared, it seems that the state of the cognitive faculties being in that proportion must also be shareable.

Kant arrives at this view by treating knowledge (including its conviction) as an effect arising from this disposition or proportion as a cause and by relying on the Humean principle that "the same cause always produces the same effect, and the same effect never arises but from the same cause."[22]* And it does seem plausible that if different persons are to be capable of sharing some cognition, then they must all be capable of being in the state which explains possession of that knowledge. If knowledge has a subjective condition, then it would seem that the subjective condition of knowledge must be as communicable as knowledge itself. But questions may be raised about this assumption of Kant's step 2 as readily as they may be about step 1. Again, however, I will defer these while I continue to expound Kant's argument.

The next stage of this argument is more obscure than those just considered. First, Kant notes that the conditions of communicability outlined in steps 1 and 2 are in fact met in the case "where a given object, by means of the senses, brings the imagination into activity in the synthesis of the manifold, and the imagination brings the understanding into activity, [leading] to the unity of the manifold in concepts."[23] In the ordinary case, where knowledge of an object is constituted by the synthesis of a manifold according to concepts, both the content and conviction of knowledge are communicable, and so the subjective disposition of the faculties involved in such a synthesis must also be taken to be shareable. The relation between imagination and understanding which constitutes the synthesis of a given manifold must be the same in anyone capable of knowing its object. But Kant now introduces some further claims. He maintains that (3) the "disposition of the cognitive powers has a different proportion, according to the difference of the objects that are given." He adds that (4) there must nevertheless be one proportion between imagination and the understanding "in which this inner relationship for the quickening (of one faculty by the other) is the most conducive for both mental faculties of mind with respect to the aim for [*in Absicht auf*] cognition (of given objects) in general." Finally, he asserts that (5) "this disposition cannot be determined except by feeling (and not by concepts)."[24] Kant appears to be arguing the following. Step 3: The proportion between imagination and understanding may differ for different objects, and there are different mental states which may cause knowledge. Step 4: Although any such proportion is ultimately suitable for knowledge, there is a particular proportion between imagination and understanding which in fact is most suitable for "enlivening" them, that is to say, freely disposing them to the relation appropriate to knowledge in general without any determinate concept. Finally, (step 5) the existence of this proportion is revealed only by feeling.

Clearly, the disposition between imagination and understanding characterized by the "proportion" of §21 is nothing other than the harmony of the faculties, the basis of aesthetic response, and the feeling by which this proportion is determined or revealed is none other than the pleasure in beauty which manifests the occurrence of the harmony of the faculties. And from this point, Kant's conclusion quickly follows. He puts it thus: "Now since this disposition itself must allow of being universally communicated, and thus also the feeling of it (in the case of a given representation), but since, however, the universal communicability of a feeling presupposes a common sense, so this [common sense] may be assumed with reason, and indeed without being dependent on psychological observations, but rather as the necessary condition of the universal communicability of our knowledge."[25] That is, (6) the special disposition of the cognitive faculties which is most suitable for knowledge in general must allow of being communicated, and (7) if this disposition is shareable, then the feeling which reveals it to obtain must also be generally communicable. But to maintain this is just to maintain that such a feeling can be rationally imputed to everyone capable of knowledge at all. Or: there is a common sense, whether that be a feeling which is universally communicable, or either a principle or a faculty by which it may be determined that some feeling is communicable. In either case, the assumption on which aesthetic judgment depends is vindicated.

Kant's argument is simple, and rests on plausible assumptions. Its general claim that if knowledge is communicable so is its subjective condition seems licensed by the general principle "same effect, same cause." And its final stages appear to depend on unexceptionable assumptions. Step 6 just asserts that if the subjective condition of knowledge is generally communicable, so, *a fortiori,* is a special instance of this condition, which seems obvious enough; and step 7 only maintains that if this condition is communicable, then so is the feeling which it effects and which manifests it. This appears to depend on nothing but the principle "same cause, same effect."

However, a number of steps in Kant's argument are open to question. We may begin with step 7, on which Kant's crucial transition from knowledge to feeling, or proof of a common *sense,* depends. In inferring that if the harmony of the faculties is communicable, then so must be the feeling of pleasure by which its existence is manifested, Kant assumes that if a given state of mind is one in which all persons may find themselves, then whatever constitutes evidence of being in that state is available to everyone. There are several reasons why this may appear plausible. As mentioned, it may be taken merely to apply the Humean principle "same cause, same effect." If a feeling of pleasure is an effect of the harmony of the faculties, and this cause is a state which may occur in anyone, then, so it seems, may its effect. Or, leaving aside general principles of causation, one might instead invoke the transparency of mental states. With Locke, one could suppose that a mental state just is a state of which one must be able to be conscious, or that "to say a Notion is imprinted on the Mind, and yet at the same time to say, that the mind is ignorant of it, and never yet took notice of it, is to make this Impression nothing."[26] Thus it would be absurd to suppose that someone could be in a particular mental state without knowing it; and if the feeling of pleasure just is the way in which the harmony of the faculties is present to consciousness, it would be absurd to suppose that someone could be in that state without feeling pleasure. If the free play of the faculties itself is universally communicable, pleasure in the beautiful must also be universally valid.

But such arguments are not above criticism. Although the general principle "same cause, same effect" may be a general canon of causal thinking, we must always consider whether what we are calling the cause of something else really constitutes a sufficient condition for the occurrence of the latter. The application of the principle to any given relation of cause and effect requires proof that there is nothing which may interfere with the operation of the cause, and prevent it from bringing about its normal effect. So the general principle of causation itself could not prove that anyone capable of the subjective condition of knowledge must be capable of feeling its effect of pleasure.

Problems also arise if we think of pleasure as the *evidence* for rather than just the *effect* of the harmony of the faculties. Although some mental states, such as knowledge, might be transparent, there are surely other mental states in which one can be — for instance, loving or hating someone — without necessarily knowing it. It is even conceivable that someone might be incapable of knowing himself to be in a particular state because of some deep neurosis or gross insensitivity. And if the harmony of the faculties is not a state of knowledge, and is a cause of pleasure, then to suppose it transparent, or a state the evidence for which must be available, requires the assumption that the principle that the attainment of an objective always occasions a feeling of pleasure precludes any possible interference between cause and effect. But Kant himself has allowed that certain conditions, such as repetition or predictability, may interfere with the operation of this principle.[27] At the least, it is safe to say that Kant's crucial step 7 is not self-evident, but needs a defense that Kant does not give it. Because his justification of the presupposition of a common sense depends on step 7, this is enough to render Kant's first attempt at a deduction inconclusive.

However, problems with its final step are not the deepest difficulties that beset Kant's argument. More troublesome questions may be raised about its opening step, as well as about all those steps depending on the notion of a unique proportion between imagination and understanding in aesthetic response. I turn now to these questions.

Knowledge, Communication, and Proportion

Kant asserts that his deduction of a common sense depends on the "necessary condition of the universal communicability of our knowledge, which must be presupposed in every logic and every principle of knowledge which is not skeptical."[28] But what is the real status of Kant's step 1, the assumption that knowledge must be communicable? Is the communicability of knowledge a genuine condition of its possibility, and is an argument which assumes that it is a truly transcendental deduction of aesthetic judgment from an unimpeachable condition of the very possibility of experience itself? Historically, at least, our answer to these questions must be negative, for Kant himself never really argues that intersubjective validity is a condition of the possibility of experience itself. Neither version of the *Critique of Pure Reason* demonstrates that the possibility of sharing one's beliefs with others is an essential condition for the possibility of one's own experience.

To be sure, both versions of the first *Critique*'s Transcendental Deduction turn on the assumption that knowledge is produced only by following a rule. The requirement that experience be governed by rules is the basis of Kant's deduction of the *a priori* categories, since they are nothing but the general forms for concepts of objects, themselves nothing but rules for synthesis. But what rules are required to establish is not the intersubjective communicability of knowledge, but the unity of one's own consciousness. Thus the first edition of the *Critique of Pure Reason* maintains that

> our thought of the relation of all knowledge to its object carries with it an element of necessity; the object is viewed as that which prevents our cognitions from being haphazard or arbitrary, and which determines them *a priori* in some definite fashion . . . This *unity of rule* determines all the manifold, and limits it to conditions which make unity of apperception possible . . . But a concept is always, as regards its form, something universal which serves as a rule.[29]
>
> The objective unity of all empirical consciousness in one consciousness, that of original apperception, is thus the necessary condition of all possible perception; and the affinity of all appearances, near or remote, is a necessary consequence of a synthesis in imagination which is grounded *a priori* on rules.[30]

From the mere fact of apperception, or the possibility of knowing that different items of empirical consciousness do belong to a single self, Kant argues to the subsumability of such items under rules, or concepts of objects, on the ground that without such rules there could in fact be no certainty of the unity of one's consciousness. But though a concept or rule "is always, as regards its form, something universal," Kant does not actually argue that it must be *intersubjectively* valid. The deduction is written from a standpoint of methodological solipsism, and the particularity to which the universality of a rule contrasts is that of one's manifold at one moment as opposed to another, rather than the uniqueness of one's manifold as opposed to someone else's.

The deduction of the second edition emphasizes perhaps even more clearly than the first version the necessity of rules for knowledge. Here, Kant considers what is required "to distinguish the objective unity of given representations from the subjective,"[31] or what can impose necessity on the otherwise purely contingent subjective sequence of representations. Such necessity is required solely so that I may ascribe different representations "to the identical self as *my* representations," or "comprehend them as synthetically combined in one apperception through the general expression '*I think*,'"[32] and it is because such self-ascription is a necessary condition of experience that knowledge requires rules. As Kant argues, I can assert a "relation to original apperception, and its *necessary unity*" of a given set of representations only if I can establish that "they belong to one another in *virtue of the necessary unity of apperception* in the synthesis of intuitions, that is, according to principles of the objective determination of all representations . . . Only in this way does there arise from this relation a judgment, that is, a relation which is *objectively valid*."[33] Subjecting the items of one's manifold to rules is a necessary condition of being conscious of the unity of that manifold. But again, the universality or objective validity of these rules is conceived of in contrast to the "subjective validity" of the particular sequences presented by the faculty of "reproductive imagination."

A rule does not necessarily distinguish what is valid for oneself from what is valid for others, but rather distinguishes the order in which the representations constituting a manifold must occur from any particular sequence in which they might seem merely to happen to occur. This conception of the function of rules is also evident in Kant's discussion of the law of causation in the Second Analogy of Experience. There, Kant writes that "if we inquire what new character *relation to an object* confers upon our representations, what dignity they thereby acquire, we find that it results only in subjecting the representations to a rule, and so in necessitating us to connect them in some one specific manner; and conversely, that only insofar as our representations are necessitated in a certain order as regards their time relations do they acquire objective meaning."[34] Kant simply does not consider whether the rules that knowledge requires must be shareable, or whether their function in the synthesis of one's own manifold entails their intersubjective validity. He argues that the unity of one's own consciousness requires thinking of the order of one's impressions as dictated from without, by rules valid *of objects,* but not that the unity of one's own consciousness — the Archimedean point of his deduction — requires that one's rules be valid *for others* as well. Thus he does not argue that communicability is a necessary condition of knowledge.

The Transcendental Deduction in the *Critique of Pure Reason* simply does not consider whether knowledge must be intersubjectively valid. There are, however, two places where Kant does touch on the issue of the communicability of knowledge. One of these is a late section of the *Critique of Pure Reason*'s Doctrine of Method called "Opining, Knowing, and Believing." Here, Kant maintains that the "possibility of communicating" a judgment "and of finding it to be valid for all human reason" may serve as a "touchstone" (*Probierstein*) for considering something true. For "truth depends upon agreement with the object, and in respect of it the judgments of each and every understanding must therefore be in agreement with each other"; and where there is a possibility of communication, "there is then at least a presumption that the ground of the agreement of all judgments with one another, notwithstanding the differing characters of individuals, rests upon the common ground, namely, upon the object, and that it is for this reason that they are all in agreement with the object."[35] But even here intersubjective validity is not made a direct condition of the possibility of knowledge. Truth is defined as agreement with an object, or as objective validity. Agreement with others, or intersubjective validity, is a consequence of truth, and a "touchstone" for it, just because objective validity is the best explanation of intersubjective validity. But the requirement of truth may entail a requirement of intersubjective validity only on the assumption — here taken for granted — that there are in fact others with whom one can communicate and who can be expected to make the same judgment as oneself, if one's own judgment is correct.

The possibility of intersubjective validity is not itself a condition for submitting one's own manifold to rules, or for securing the possibility of transcendental apperception. It is not what *constitutes* the correspondence of cognition with its object, as Kant supposes in step 1 of the argument of §21, and it is thus not a condition which must obtain if there is to be any experience at all. Rather, *given* the possibility of intersubjective validity, objective validity may be expected to bring actual intersubjective agreement in its train. But the possibility of using intersubjective validity as an empirical criterion of objective validity does not mean that experience itself requires the communicability of knowledge. A situation in which only one subject existed, or could exist — a situation in which there was no possibility of communication, or even of an estimate of communicability — would not obviously preclude the possibility of a synthesis of that subject's experience according to rules.

In the *Prolegomena to Any Future Metaphysics,* however, Kant does assert that "objective validity and necessary universality (for everybody) are equivalent concepts,"[36] thereby suggesting that step 1's assumption that the communicability of knowledge is a necessary condition of experience is well founded. But an examination of the argument from which this conclusion is supposed to follow shows that Kant does not prove that the possibility of determining what might be communicated to other persons is a prerequisite for the unification of one's own experience. Like the section "Opining, Knowing, and Believing," the *Prolegomena* simply assumes that intersubjective validity will be a consequence of objective validity, taking for granted that others do exist and that one can determine what is communicable to them. In this work, Kant distinguishes between "judgments of perception" and "judgments of experience," the latter being objectively valid judgments asserting necessary connections among the items of one's manifold. He then argues:

> All our judgments are at first merely judgments of perception; they hold good only for us, that is, for one subject, and we do not until afterward give them a new reference, namely, to an object, and intend that they shall always be valid for us at all times and in the same way for everyone else; for when a judgment agrees with an object, all judgments in the same object must also agree among themselves . . . for there would be no ground, why the judgments of others must necessarily agree with my own, unless it were the unity of the object.[37]

I may assume that an objectively valid judgment is intersubjectively valid, and will certainly assume that an intersubjectively valid judgment is objectively valid. Presupposing the existence of others with cognitive capabilities like my own, that is, I will take my knowledge to be universally valid. But there is no argument here to show that I can obtain the unity of consciousness only if I do suppose either that there are others like myself or that if there were I could determine that to be the case. The possibility of rationally imputing any cognitive condition to others has not been shown to be a condition of my own experience.

We must conclude that Kant possesses, or at least offers, no argument which can actually demonstrate that the possibility of intersubjective validity is a necessary condition of experience. If this is what is assumed in its step 1, then the third *Critique*'s first attempt at a deduction of aesthetic judgment cannot prove what it must. It cannot show that the communicability of knowledge, let alone feeling, "is presupposed in every logic and every principle of knowledge that is not skeptical."

This criticism might appear unfair. It may be objected that a rule is just something about which different persons may agree, or something intrinsically communicable, and that if Kant has shown that knowledge must employ rules then he has shown that it must be communicable, whether or not communicability plays any role in his deduction. But several points must be noted. First, if it is to serve for the justification of the imputation of aesthetic response, the communicability of knowledge in general cannot consist in the mere fact that if knowledge uses rules then it is possible that more than one person may enjoy it. Rather, to found the universal imputation of taste, the possibility of knowledge must require that we can determine that other persons are in fact capable of using and compelled to use the rules on which our own knowledge depends. But Kant argues nothing like this. The link he draws between objective and intersubjective validity assumes that we have the general capability to judge the cognitive capacities of others, and that we can therefore infer from objective to intersubjective validity. What the deduction of taste requires, however, is a proof that the possibility of our own experience depends upon the ability to determine the cognitive faculties of others, and Kant simply never argues this.

Second, and perhaps even more important, to the extent that the argument of the first *Critique* does imply that the communicability of experience is a necessary condition of its existence, it does so through the fact that the possibility of experience requires rules. Experience requires necessary connections, and the latter can be supplied only by rules which may be valid for any observer of a given object. But if there is in fact a form of experience which is not subject to rules — the contention of Kant's aesthetics, after all — then it may escape the net of this argument. The possibility of my own experience may directly imply that rules valid for possible others apply to it, but it does not depend on the actuality or possibility of there being others with faculties like my own, or on the assumption that the faculties of others will function just like my own where they are *not* bound by rules. These, however, are the implications which the deduction of aesthetic judgment assumes.

In his second attempt at a deduction, Kant does not suggest that communicability is a necessary condition of the possibility of any experience at all, but does concern himself more exclusively with showing that if any knowledge is communicable, then so is aesthetic response. Perhaps we can take this subtle shift in his assumptions as an implicit acknowledgment that the possibility of taste cannot be founded on a constitutive principle of the very possibility of experience — something which, we shall see, Kant himself intimates in §22. If this is so, then what we should really consider is the force of Kant's argument that the communicability of pleasure in the beautiful really does follow from the universal validity of knowledge in general. Here too problems arise.

The first of these concerns Kant's step 2, the assumption that if a cognition is valid for all, then there is also a single subjective state associated with it and equally valid for all. I have already noted that the conviction associated with a belief must be regarded as a subjective state different from that mental condition which explains a person's possession of a cognition, conviction included. But while there must be a communication of conviction if there is to be a communication of knowledge, this does not generally imply that different persons may share a cognition only if the subjective states explaining their possession of that knowledge are the same. This is clear enough when we equate the subjective conditions of a cognition with the experience in which a person's evidence for it is acquired. Thus two persons might both know that some event occurred, one having seen it with his own eyes and the other having read of it in an authoritative source years later. In such a case, both know of the event, but the causal conditions of their knowledge are hardly identical, the state of seeing something being very different from that of reading about it.[38*] As far as evidence is concerned, at least, cases in which the identity of knowledge are accompanied by the identity of its subjective conditions seem more like exceptions to the general situation than the general rule itself. Now, whether this implies that the identity of knowledge permits variation in the states of the faculties of different observers, as well as in their evidence, is not immediately apparent. But it is far from obvious that different observers must have similar faculties in similar dispositions in order to be capable of shared knowledge. This is certainly not so in the case of machines. Two computers with entirely different circuitry may arrive at the same output by entirely different sequences of operations. At the least, it seems that the premise that the communicability of knowledge entails an identity in the subjective conditions or dispositions on which knowledge is based must be proved rather than just assumed. Kant's premise may be plausible, but his first deduction of aesthetic judgment leaves open whether the particular mental state regarded as the condition of aesthetic response must be communicable just because knowledge in general is universally valid.

Even more pressing questions may be raised about the concept of proportion which Kant employs in steps 2, 3 and 4 of his argument. Two questions are particularly crucial. First, do these steps imply two different theses about a proportion between imagination and understanding as the basis of cognition? And if they do, can Kant's argument succeed?

In step 2, Kant describes "that proportion which qualifies a representation (by which an object is given to us) to constitute knowledge"[39] as that which must be communicable if knowledge is to be communicable at all. This implies that in all cases of representation which are in fact suitable for knowledge, the imagination and understanding are disposed toward each other in the same proportion, and thus that what we attribute to anyone else in supposing knowledge to be communicable is the capacity to experience this proportion. While hardly felicitous, this metaphor of proportion might then be understood to refer to the relationship between the unifiability of any manifold presented by the imagination and the unity required for the application of a concept by the understanding, which is necessary for there to be knowledge of the manifold. The proportion would consist in the fact that the multiplicity of items in the manifold may be seen as a unity from the point of view dictated by some concept or another. If this is so, then all manifolds suitable for representation of an object would display the same proportion—namely, reducibility to unity.

But Kant's step 3 supposes that the proportion between imagination and understanding may differ in different cases of knowledge. As Kant puts it, "the disposition of the cognitive powers has a different proportion, according to the difference of the objects that are given."[40] He then argues that a certain instance of the general proportion required for knowledge is optimal for the special condition of the "enlivening" of both imagination and understanding, and further infers that anyone capable of the proportion of knowledge in general will also be capable of experiencing this optimal case, and will thus be sensitive to the feeling of pleasure produced by the harmony of imagination and understanding. But this argument is in serious difficulty if it derives its concept of proportion from step 2, or assumes that the proportion required for knowledge is the reducibility of a manifold to unity under some concept. For then the proportion is either always the same, regardless of any difference in objects presenting the manifold, and there is no case which is optimal or best adapted for knowledge, or else the concept of proportion alone does not explain optimal adaptability. If Kant is committed to the view of the first *Critique* that any manifold of which one can be conscious as a manifold can in fact be unified in accord with some concept or another, then all manifolds may display the proportion appropriate for knowledge in general. Then either aesthetic response requires more than just this proportion, or else every object may be beautiful.

The view that the proportion between manifold and unity may vary in the case of different objects, only some of which are most suitable for the exercise of both imagination and understanding, could explain why some but not all objects are beautiful. The existence of such a proportion could thus figure in an argument that it is rational to believe not merely that others are capable of aesthetic response in general, but that they should take pleasure in the particular objects which produce it in oneself. But Kant's general theory of knowledge offers no basis for the postulation of such a variable proportion, since it includes only the general claim that every manifold must be reducible to unity under some concept. The variation which Kant's argument requires may be introduced only if we think of it, not as anything like variation in the value of some mathematically expressible function, but rather as a psychological variation in the ease with which the unity of a given multiplicity may be detected. The harmony of the faculties would then obtain when a manifold presented by imagination is so well adapted to the understanding's general need for unity that it can be felt to be unified without reflection on its possible subsumption under any concept at all.

Such an interpretation would not introduce any inconsistency into the argument of §21. However, Kant's notion of proportion would then be not a purely epistemological concept of the general unifiability of all manifolds, but a psychological concept of the ease with which given manifolds may be felt to be unified. But it is hardly clear that the general assumption that any subject capable of cognition at all must be capable of unifying manifolds entails that each subject possesses the same facility in the perception of unity as any other. The ease with which any person may detect unity in his manifolds of intuition, or how well adapted any object is to produce the harmony of the faculties in any particular person, it might be contended, raises questions concerning contingent psychological similarities or differences among people. That everyone is capable of unifying manifolds under empirical concepts does not imply that everyone will automatically strike on the same empirical concepts to do so; therefore, it can hardly imply that the special case of unifying a manifold without any empirical concept at all must occur in precisely the same circumstances for everyone.

Kant's argument could then establish neither that everyone is capable of aesthetic response in general nor that everyone will experience it with regard to the same objects. The communicability of knowledge requires only that everyone be capable of the synthesis of recognition in concepts and the synthesis of imagination on which that depends, but not that everyone be capable of the latter synthesis apart from the former, or capable of it in the very same circumstances.

Kant's use of the concept of proportion, then, suggests that his deduction of aesthetic judgment does not depend solely on transcendental principles of epistemology, but also rests on more particular psychological assumptions. If so, then his argument is threatened by a serious dilemma. On the one hand, if Kant's proportion is interpreted as an entirely general cognitive capability, the universal imputation of sensitivity to this proportion may be permitted, but the particularity of aesthetic response becomes inexplicable. On the other hand, if a unique ease or facility in synthesis is what is really connoted by Kant's concept of proportion, the difference between aesthetic response and cognition in general may be preserved, but the intersubjective validity of aesthetic response is then not entailed by the general communicability of cognitive capacity itself. In this case, Kant's strategy for the deduction of aesthetic judgment may not be fully compatible with his explanation of aesthetic response.

Common Sense — Regulative or Constitutive?

Although this dilemma presents the fundamental problem for Kant's justification of judgments of taste, I will defer its further consideration for the discussion of Kant's second attempt at a deduction, and now turn to the questions about the argument of §21 which Kant suggests in §22. In this section, Kant himself apparently casts doubt on whether §21 has really justified the presupposition of a common sense as a necessary condition of knowledge by asking "whether there is in fact such a common sense in ourselves for higher ends."[41] One would have thought that Kant's derivation of the possibility of aesthetic judgment from the communicability of knowledge in general, and the description of the latter as a condition of the possibility of experience itself, meant that common sense must be a constitutive principle or condition of the possibility of experience itself. But, surprisingly, Kant now asserts that the question of whether it is constitutive or merely regulative is one which he "will not and cannot here yet investigate," having so far sought "only to analyze the faculty of taste into its elements and finally to unify these in the idea of a common sense."[42*] If this question is indeed still open, it would explain why the deduction of aesthetic judgment is yet to be offered by §38. But how could Kant suppose it to be open after having just produced the argument of §21?

Before we can attempt to answer this, we must consider whether the conclusion that the principle of taste is regulative would really represent a retraction of §21. That it would is not entirely obvious, for Kant uses the contrast between regulative and constitutive principles in a number of different ways, and his argument in §22 may be designed to show that the principle of common sense is regulative in a way which is not incompatible with its also being founded on a condition of the possibility of experience itself.

Three different ways in which a principle might be regulative are actually intimated in §22. Two of these parallel possibilities are explored in the first *Critique;* these are the possibilities that the principle of taste is regulative because it is indeterminate, and cannot be mechanically applied to particular objects of taste, and that it is regulative because it is not a necessary condition of the possibility of experience itself, but rests on some lesser necessity. The third contrast between regulative and constitutive suggested in §22 is new to the *Critique of Judgment*. On this contrast, a principle is constitutive if the faculty for its application is an "original and natural faculty," and regulative if this "faculty is artificial and yet to be acquired."[43] The possibility that the principle of taste is regulative in the first or third of these senses would not conflict with the conclusion of §21, for principles might be indeterminate in application or in need of cultivation and yet still be conditions of the possibility of cognitive (or moral) experience. It is only if the question whether the principle of taste is regulative in the second of the ways I have mentioned is still open that §22 might undermine the argument of §21.

The first paragraph of §22 does not establish that the principle of taste is regulative in a way incompatible with the argument of §21. This paragraph covers familiar terrain. Kant starts by reminding us that the judgment of taste claims universal validity, or bases itself on a "public" rather than "private feeling." In so doing, "it says not that everyone *will* agree with our judgment, but rather that everyone *should* agree with it." Because it makes such a claim, it cannot be founded on experience. Therefore, Kant continues,

> the common sense, as an example of the judgment of which I here offer my judgment of taste and on account of which I attribute it *exemplary* validity, is a merely ideal norm, under the presupposition of which one could correctly make a judgment which accords with it, and which correctly makes the expressed delight in an object into a rule for everyone: since the principle, though only subjective, nevertheless, assumed to be subjectively universal (an idea necessary for everyone), could, in what concerns the unanimity of different judges, demand general agreement like an objective principle: if only one were certain that one had correctly subsumed [a given feeling of pleasure] under it.[44]

This dense sentence makes several points. First, it concludes that the common sense — here the principle of taste — is a merely ideal norm, and can support particular judgments with merely exemplary validity, because it cannot be founded on experience. But this really states no special restriction on taste, for if a principle is ideal just because it cannot be confirmed by experience, then the basic *a priori* principles of science and morality must also be ideal. Since some of the latter are surely constitutive rather than regulative, the ideality of the principle of taste would not require it to be regulative rather than constitutive. The second part of Kant's sentence, however, does bear more directly on this issue. Written in the subjunctive, the last five lines of the paragraph suggest that aesthetic judgments must always be uncertain, and this might be a reason for regarding the principle on which they are grounded as merely regulative.

Still, it must be noted that there are two different reasons why particular judgments based on a general principle might always be uncertain. They might be so because the general principle itself is uncertain, or because the general principle, while itself certainly true, does not possess criteria so determinate as to allow an absolutely certain decision that any given case is an instance of that rule. Kant's arguments in the Analytic of the Beautiful suggest that individual judgments of taste are uncertain for the latter reason,[45] and so does Kant's description of common sense, in the opening line of the second paragraph of §22, as an "indeterminate" rather than an "ideal norm."[46] The indeterminacy of the criteria for the application of the principle of common sense, rather than the uncertainty of this principle itself, could be what leads Kant to suspect it of merely regulative status; and if this is all that he has in mind, then his recognition of its possibly regulative force would not imply an acknowledgment of any problem with the argument of §21.

That indeterminacy in application alone may make a principle regulative can be seen by referring to the *Critique of Pure Reason*. There, Kant offers the principles of *manifoldness, affinity,* and *unity,* principles governing the relations of classificatory concepts in science, as paradigmatic examples of principles which have a merely regulative employment,[47] and says this about them: "The remarkable feature of these principles . . . is that they seem to be transcendental, and that although they contain mere ideas for the guidance of the empirical employment of reason—ideas which reason follows only as it were asymptotically, i.e., ever more closely without ever reaching them—they yet possess, as synthetic *a priori* propositions, objective but indeterminate validity, and serve as rules for possible experience."[48] Kant also claims that such principles must be merely regulative because "principles of pure reason can never be constitutive in respect of empirical *concepts;* for since no schema of sensibility corresponding to them can ever be given, they can never have an object *in concreto,*"[49] and because the application of such principles does "not yield knowledge of the object itself (as in the case of the application of the categories to their sensible schema), but [yields] only a rule or higher principle for the systematic unity of all employment of the understanding."[50] Since the criteria of disinterestedness and formal finality by which we judge the universal validity of aesthetic response are also indeterminate and correspond to no definite schemata for objects, the principle of common sense can have no schema. Principles of reason such as manifoldness and affinity have no schemata because they characterize not particular objects, but systems of concepts of objects; the principles of taste which Kant expounded in the first and third moments of the Analytic — and which may be regarded as the criteria by which the general principle of common sense is applied, just as manifoldness, unity, and affinity are the criteria by which the general idea of systematicity is applied — lack schemata because they do not furnish concepts of objects or systems of concepts, but rather constitute general constraints on the relation to subjects by which objects may occasion pleasure. Nevertheless, just as manifoldness and the other principles of reason are indeterminate, in that one can never be certain that they have been maximally instantiated, so the principles of aesthetic judgment are indeterminate. They can exclude certain cases of pleasure but never fully specify the objects which might fall under them; and because they require causal judgments about one's own mental history, it can never be fully certain that they have been complied with. For this reason, then, the principle of taste, like a principle of reason, may be called regulative. But, it must be concluded, this does not imply that it cannot be linked to a necessary condition of the possibility of experience. The principle of taste may be regulative because of its indeterminacy, but this in itself would not entail that the assumption of the communicability of knowledge is not required for determining the objective validity of one's own experience.

If it is on account of its indeterminacy, then, that Kant suggests that the principle of common sense may be merely regulative, this would not necessarily represent a retraction of the claims of §21. In the second paragraph of §22, however, Kant does ask whether the common sense is a constitutive principle of the possibility of experience, or only a regulative principle; and this question, which does put the results of §21 into doubt, appears to be raised by the immediately preceding consideration of the ideality and indeterminacy of the principle of taste. Perhaps Kant's conclusion that the principle of taste resembles the regulative principles of science in its function or mode of application led him to wonder whether it is not similar in its epistemological status as well. His model of regulative principles, that is, may have inclined him at least to leave open the question which, it seems, he had just settled. For the first *Critique*'s conception of a regulative principle does include the view that such a principle is not only indeterminate in application but less than a condition of the very possibility of experience as well. This emerges in the pages of the Appendix on the regulative employment of ideas just quoted. Kant claims that regulative principles must be treated as "maxims," and defines "maxims of reason" as "all subjective principles which are derived, not from the constitution of an object, but from the interest of reason in respect of a certain possible perfection of the knowledge of an object."[51] Of the specific examples of manifoldness and unity, he claims that "since neither of these principles is based on objective grounds but solely in the interest of reason, the title 'principles' is not strictly applicable; they may more fittingly be entitled 'maxims.'"[52]

In the *Critique of Pure Reason,* in other words, the principles which express desirable constraints on the form of systems of scientific concepts are taken to be both indeterminate in function *and* due to a higher or "speculative" interest of reason rather than to the faculty of understanding.[53] By this, Kant means that adoption of the assumptions that nature displays maximal variety in its varieties and maximal unity in its principles of operation is not necessary to make any objectively valid judgments about one's experience, but only necessary to attain higher goals of systematicity among empirical judgments, goals which must be attributed to reason rather than to understanding. The discovery of systematicity among one's empirical concepts and judgments is not a condition of the possibility of making any empirically valid judgments, but an end desirable in itself, representing an interest in the form of knowledge that goes beyond a concern for its mere possibility.[54]*

If the principle of common sense stems from a higher interest of reason in the same way as these regulative maxims of natural science do, that would indeed cast the argument of §21 in a new light. It would suggest that the possibility of the intersubjectivity or communicability of knowledge is not a necessary condition of making objectively valid judgments, but rather the object of a higher-order interest of reason. That knowledge be shared would not be a minimal condition of its possibility—a position for which, as we saw, Kant in any case has no argument — but a further objective, like the objective that it be systematic and satisfy reason as well as the understanding. And if this were the case for knowledge in general, then the communicability of aesthetic response might be part of the goal of the intersubjectivity of knowledge in general, because of the relation between this response and the conditions of cognition in general, and be supported by the same principle of reason which supports the assumption that knowledge in general is not only systematic but shareable as well. But then the assumption that aesthetic response must be universally valid would be not an absolutely unimpeachable *a priori* principle, but rather a goal regulating one's response to objects and, in particular, one's attempts to find ways of actually communicating such response to other persons.

Such a conclusion would have the great merit of confirming the suggestion made in my discussion of the third moment, that the intersubjective validity of aesthetic judgment may be better regarded as a goal or regulative ideal, rather than as a rigorous principle which can exclude from the sphere of taste even responses which would otherwise conform to Kant's explanatory model of aesthetic response. But such a conclusion would also raise questions, perhaps about the very possibility of a transcendental deduction of judgments of taste, and certainly about the form of any such deduction. For the *Critique of Pure Reason,* as a few references will show, takes a very cautious position on the issue of furnishing a deduction of regulative principles.

At one point, Kant apparently goes so far as to deny that regulative principles admit of any transcendental deduction at all. Following the description of regulative principles as possessing "objective but indeterminate validity" which I have already quoted, he continues: "They can also be employed with great advantage in the elaboration of experience, as heuristic principles. A transcendental deduction of them cannot, however, be effected; in the case of ideas . . . such a deduction is never possible."[55] If this were so, then the possibility that the common sense might be a merely regulative idea would certainly undermine the argument of §21 and any other attempt at a transcendental deduction of aesthetic judgment. However, it is not clear that this quotation actually represents Kant's considered opinion. For a few pages later, he writes that "we cannot employ an *a priori* concept with any certainty without having first given a transcendental deduction of it. The ideas of pure reason do not, indeed, admit of the kind of deduction that is possible in the case of the categories. But if they are to have the least objective validity, no matter how indeterminate that validity may be . . . a deduction of them must be possible, however greatly (as we admit) it may differ from that which we have been able to give of the categories."[56] Here Kant suggests that any concept—or, we may suppose, principle—which cannot be justified by an appeal to experience must be justified by some sort of transcendental deduction, although it may not be of the same form as the first *Critique*'s deduction of the pure concepts of the understanding. That is, it may be possible to give a transcendental deduction which does not show that a certain idea or principle is an absolutely necessary condition for the fundamental intellectual task of conceiving of objects of experience and making objectively valid judgments about them. Kant even describes what the form of such a deduction would be like in the case of the regulative ideas with which the *Critique of Pure Reason* is concerned:

> If, then, it can be shown that the three transcendental ideas (the psychological, the cosmological, and the theological), although they do not directly relate to, or determine, any object corresponding to them, nonetheless, as rules of the empirical employment of reason, lead us to systematic unity, under the presupposition of such an *object in the idea,* and that they thus contribute to the extension of empirical knowledge, without ever being in a position to run counter to it, we may conclude that it is a necessary maxim of reason to proceed always in accordance with such ideas. This, indeed, is the transcendental deduction of all ideas of speculative reason, not as constitutive principles for the extension of our knowledge to more objects than experience can give, but as *regulative* principles of the systematic unity of the manifold of empirical knowledge in general.[57]

By being shown to aid in the development of knowledge even without being absolutely necessary for its existence, an idea may receive a transcendental deduction.

If, as Kant may suppose, the indeterminate applicability of the principle of common sense does imply that it must also be limited to the epistemological status of a merely regulative principle, this paragraph might outline the form of a more successful deduction than is furnished by §21. A deduction of the common sense would not show that the assumption of the communicability of knowledge is a necessary condition for the mere possibility of experience, but would show that this assumption does aid in the extension of knowledge in general, and it would then attempt to show that the justifiability of this assumption with regard to cognition in general carries over to the case of aesthetic response as well. Should it turn out that the principle of taste were merely regulative in status—which, we must keep in mind, is not obviously entailed by its indeterminacy in application to particulars—then §22 would suggest some modification of §21. That section's claim to have shown the principle of aesthetic judgment to be implied by the mere possibility of knowledge at all would have to be surrendered, and a deduction more along the lines sketched in the previous paragraph would have to be provided.

I will shortly consider whether Kant's attempt at a deduction in §38 does conform more closely to this proposed pattern for the deduction of regulative ideas than that of §21. Before doing so, however, two more points about §22's intimation that the idea of common sense may be merely regulative should be mentioned. The first of these has already been noted: the fact that in asking whether the principle of common sense may be merely regulative, §22 suggests that it may require cultivation rather than being absolutely "original and natural." This possibility is raised when, immediately after asking whether the common sense is a constitutive or merely a regulative principle produced in us by reason for higher ends, Kant continues:

> whether therefore taste is an original and natural faculty, or only the idea of an artificial and yet to be acquired faculty, so that a judgment of taste with its imputation of universal agreement is in fact only a demand of reason, to bring forth such unanimity in the mode of sense, and whether the ought, that is, the objective necessity of the confluence of the feeling of everyone with the particular feeling of each, only signifies the possibility of becoming united, and whether the judgment of taste merely presents an example of the application of this principle: this we neither will nor can here investigate.[58]

Here, Kant writes as if a principle which is constitutive must be innate, and in need of no cultivation, but a principle which is regulative is a mere ideal in need of cultivation, and not efficacious without some effort and training. Given Kant's insistence throughout the third *Critique* that the judgment of taste claims what the responses of others should be—under ideal circumstances—and that the capability to make judgments of taste requires exercise and education,[59] it may seem obvious that taste must be an ideal and "artificial" faculty, and thus that its basis must be a regulative principle. But it should be noted that Kant never really considers whether principles which are constitutive and *a priori* must be innate, and whether those which are merely regulative must be acquired. There is no place where Kant argues that the principles of geometry or the analogies of experience can be employed without the benefit of any experience or education or that the regulative maxims of science must be acquired rather than innate.[60]* Thus that the principle of taste may be regulative need not imply that it is a mere ideal; or — more important, since the fact that judgments of taste are ideal has been conceded throughout Kant's argument — the ideality of the principle of taste does not itself imply that it has a merely regulative status as far as its epistomological basis is concerned.

It must also be noted that Kant's reason for thinking that the judgments of taste might represent a mere demand of reason may have nothing to do with the *epistemological* aspects of either the function or the status of the principle on which they are based. In considering whether the common sense might not be a higher end of reason rather than a necessary condition of experience, Kant may not even mean to put in doubt the theoretical justifiability of imputing feelings of pleasure to others, but may be questioning only the moral justifiability of demanding a consensus in taste. In this case, the higher principle of reason to which he thinks the principle of taste might be due would be not a *substitute* for a constitutive principle of the understanding, but rather a *supplement,* something to justify adding a practical *demand* of agreement to the merely theoretical *imputation* of that agreement. But if this is why taste must be linked to a higher principle or end of reason, Kant would again have no reason to revise the purely epistemological argument of §21, or to downgrade the principle of taste to a merely regulative status. As I have argued earlier, the theoretical and the practical components of the claim of taste must be distinguished; and the fact that an interest of reason may have to be invoked to ground the latter does not itself imply that it must be a speculative interest of reason rather than a principle of the understanding which grounds the former.

The suggestion that the principle of taste might be regulative rather than constitutive, then, raises at least three different questions. First, it raises the question of the function of criteria for aesthetic judgment, or the problem of applying an indeterminate norm in judgment on particular objects. Second, it raises a question about the real epistemological status of the principle of taste. Finally, it raises the question of whether taste might not need cultivation, and the associated question of whether there might not be an interest of reason — practical reason, that is — behind taste's demand for universal assent. Neither the first nor the third of these questions actually constitutes any threat to the argument of §21. That the principle of taste is not completely determinate in nature or mechanical in application is not a possibility first considered in §22, and the argument of §21 is surely designed to take it into account. And that taste may be the object of morally justified cultivation does not threaten the *validity* of the argument of §21, but only threatens its *completeness* as a justification for all of the demands of taste. Only the possibility that the principle of taste may not be a constitutive principle of experience but rather a principle associated merely with some higher-order objective of theoretical reason could undermine the deduction in §21, and thus open a question to be settled by Kant's next attempt at a deduction.

It must remain an open question, I believe, whether in raising the possibility that the principle of taste is regulative Kant merely meant to remind us of its indeterminate applicability and its ultimate link to morality, or whether he really meant to cast doubt on the adequacy of his justification of the presupposition of a common sense in §21 and to prepare the way for a second attempt at a deduction of aesthetic judgment. I know of no evidence which could settle the issue, and so we must simply next consider the actual force of Kant's second deduction of taste.

A final point about the possibly regulative status of the principle of taste: Kant maintains that in the case of any merely regulative principle, we must reckon with the fact that "I may have sufficient grounds to assume something in a relative sense (*suppositio relativa*), and yet have no right to assume it absolutely (*suppositio absoluta*)."[61] In the case of any principle which is employed in our judgment of an investigation into objects, we must take that principle to characterize not merely our own judgment but also the object of our judgment. As Kant illustrates the point, even in the case of such a regulative idea as that of "systematically complete unity," we are not only "entitled, but shall also be constrained, to realize for it a real object."[62] The reason for this, we must suppose, is simply that it would not be rational to allow a principle to govern our attitude toward an object unless we also supposed that the object itself conforms to that principle. However, in the case of a regulative principle which is not an absolutely necessary condition of experience, this supposition that there is an object conforming to our principle, or an objective ground explaining the conformity of objects to it, does not amount to actual knowledge of an object. It can amount to nothing but the application of an analogy from experience to an unknown thing in itself; in Kant's terms, "I may posit [the object] only as a something which I do not at all know in itself, and to which, as a ground of that systematic unity, I ascribe, in relation to this unity, such properties as are analogous to the concepts employed by the understanding in the empirical sphere."[63] In the case of the systematic unity of nature, the object postulated as its ground is a designer, but its postulation is only "representing all connections as if they were the ordinances of a supreme reason, of which our reason is but a faint copy."[64] In other words, "I make none but a relative use of the transcendental assumption . . . for I do not seek, nor am I justified in seeking, to know this object of my idea according to what it may be in itself. There are no concepts available for this purpose."[65]

The full ramifications of Kant's theory of relative supposition need not concern us here. But it is important to realize that this theory places a restriction on the ways in which the idea of a common sense may be supported. While the nature of a regulative idea may lead to the postulation of a ground in things as they are in themselves rather than as they are experienced, such a supposition is not knowledge; and if such a postulation is justifiable at all, it must depend on *a priori* justification of the regulative idea itself on the basis of its significance *within* the realm of experience. This means that the postulation of a regulative idea cannot first be justified by an appeal to any supersensible object or object beyond the reach of experience. We should certainly suppose this to be the case for any principle which is constitutive of experience, but now Kant is implying that it is also the case for merely regulative principles. Thus, whether the principle of taste is constitutive or regulative, its justification cannot be based on an appeal to objects beyond experience, even if it leads to the supposition that there are such objects or that they have any particular characteristics.

It might be thought that such a point hardly needs to be made. But we shall find that in the final sections of the *Critique of Aesthetic Judgment* Kant attempts to ground the possibility of judgments of taste in just such a supposition of an object beyond the reach of experience.[66] What the theory of relative supposition implies is that even if the question of §22 should be resolved by a decision that taste depends on a regulative idea, such a move cannot be accepted. So if we hope to find a deduction of aesthetic judgment which overcomes the problem of §21 and settles the issue of §22, it will have to be somewhere between the Analytic of the Beautiful and the Dialectic of Aesthetic Judgment. We may now see whether the argument Kant offers in §§38 and 39 does accomplish these objectives.

9

The Deduction:
Second Attempt

****

The Subjective Conditions of
Knowledge

Kant's second attempt at a deduction of the judgment of taste differs from
his first in several ways. The most obvious is that it makes no mention of
the common sense in the course of the argument itself, but introduces the
name *"sensus communis"* in §40 only after the argument is complete.[1]
However, as I argued earlier, nothing crucial to Kant's procedure in §21
really depends on this concept, so its absence from §§38 and 39 does not
itself imply any fundamental change in the strategy of Kant's deduction. If
anything, the omission of the common sense makes Kant's second deduction clearer than his first. In the fourth moment of the Analytic of the
Beautiful, three stages were required to accomplish the deduction: the
statement of the claim to the assent of all, or "exemplary necessity"; the
argument that any such claim must depend on the existence of a common
sense; and, finally, the justification of the presupposition of this common
sense. The outline of Kant's argument in §§38 and 39 is simpler. The two
preceding sections (§§36 and 37) state that the judgment of taste is a claim
on the assent of all, in explaining that its status as a synthetic *a priori* judgment is constituted precisely by the *a priori* imputation of universal validity
to the pleasure perceived in one's own case.[2] The deduction itself then
directly addresses the question of the justifiability of such an *a priori* imputation, ignoring the discussion of the common sense as an unnecessary
detour on the route to its main objective.

A more important difference between Kant's two versions of the deduction is that the first, perhaps just because it follows a lengthy analysis of
aesthetic judgment, leaves unclear much about the relation between the

deduction of aesthetic judgment in general and the justification of particular aesthetic judgments, whereas the second version, coming after the long interruption of the Analytic of the Sublime, reintroduces all of Kant's basic theses about aesthetic judgment and response within a few sections, and manages to make clearer than the first both what general assumption the deduction must justify and what the relation of this general assumption of taste is to the assumptions involved in a particular judgment of taste. In the five sections from §35 to §39, Kant restates the core of the Analytic of the Beautiful with remarkable concision. In §35, he expounds his basic explanation of aesthetic response as due to the harmony of the faculties. In §§36 and 37, his argument that it is in its claim to universal validity that aesthetic judgment becomes synthetic *a priori* rather than synthetic *a posteriori* makes the point that the claim to intersubjective validity constitutes the fundamental presumption of taste as neatly as anything in the Analytic of the Beautiful. Finally, §§38 and 39 show how the attribution of a feeling of pleasure to the mechanism described in §35 can justify the claim required by §§36 and 37, and offer a defense of the assumption on which the claim to compliance with this requirement rests. Since the sections prior to §38 have already received detailed discussion in earlier chapters, I will not devote more space to them here; but I will make a few remarks about §35 before turning to §38 itself.

Section 35 introduces Kant's explanation of aesthetic response into his second attempt at a deduction, but may also confuse us about the content of the principle which must be justified. This section's main contention is that the judgment of taste "can only be grounded on the subjective formal condition of a judgment in general."[3] Kant first makes the unilluminating remark that this condition is the faculty of judgment itself, but he then more informatively explains it as the relationship that exists between the faculties of imagination and understanding in general when knowledge, or the representation of an object, is possible. This relationship of course, is the harmony (*Zusammenstimmung*) of the two powers of representation, "the condition under which the understanding in general can advance from intuition to concepts." Kant does expand on this statement in a way consistent with earlier passages. He interprets the harmony of the faculty as a state in which the imagination "schematizes" — or becomes conscious of unity — without a concept, and maintains that because no concept is involved in aesthetic response, our judgment of taste must rest on a "mere feeling of the mutually enlivening" imagination and understanding, or on a "feeling . . . that the object can be estimated according to the finality of its representation . . . for the furtherance of the cognitive faculties in their free play," that is, the feeling of pleasure itself, which manifests the harmony of the faculties. But Kant also inserts a new twist into his theory. The absence of concepts from aesthetic response leads Kant to characterize this response, naturally enough, in terms of a state of the mental faculties, but he then expounds the principle for judgment on such response as a peculiar principle concerning the relation between these faculties themselves. As he puts it, "taste as a subjective power of judgment contains a principle of subsumption, not of intuitions under *concepts,* but rather of the *faculty* of the intuitions or presentations (that is, the imagination) under the *faculty* of concepts (that is, the understanding), insofar as the former *in its freedom* accords with the latter *in its lawfulness.*" What it is to subsume one faculty under another is unclear,[4] but this sentence could easily be taken to mean that taste requires a principle by means of which the harmonious accord between imagination and understanding can be attained, and to imply, insofar as the possibility of taste depends on such a principle, that the deduction of aesthetic judgment must provide it.[5*] But this is to say that the deduction should explain the possibility of the harmony of the faculties, and concern itself with the relation between the different faculties of cognition in general. This, however, is not the issue of the deduction. The deduction is concerned to explain how the "sensation" or "feeling" described in §35 may be attributed to other persons on the basis of its occurrence in oneself; and the principle for which it searches cannot be one directly governing the relation between the imagination and understanding in themselves, but rather one governing the relation between one's own faculties of cognition and those of other persons. The deduction of aesthetic judgment is meant neither to explain the possibility of a free harmony between the faculties, a possibility presupposed since the Introductions to the third *Critique,* nor to furnish a principle for this harmony, a possibility which Kant has abjured. It is rather intended to demonstrate that pleasures attributed to this harmony may be imputed to other persons, as §37 makes clear.

With this possible confusion averted, we may now turn to Kant's second deduction itself. Kant purports to present the whole of his argument in §38, the section explicitly labeled "Deduction of Judgment of Taste."[6] The main text of this section simply points out that if we accept the analysis of aesthetic response and judgment Kant has already given, we exclude all particular subjective sources of delight from the basis of our judgment, leaving only the "subjective factor" of the "accordance of representation" with the conditions of judgment in general, and then asserts that this general subjective factor may be "assumed valid *a priori* for everyone."[7] In more detail, Kant begins by stating that if we assume that the feeling of delight we take in an object is due to a mere estimation of its form, then that feeling can represent nothing but the subjective finality of the representation of the object for the faculty of judgment, for when pleasure is connected with "mere estimation," or, in the language of the First Introduction, "simple reflection," no objective purposiveness can provide a basis for a claim of intersubjective validity.[8] But if one's judgment does in fact adhere to the "formal rules of estimation," and is in fact made "apart from all matter (whether sensation or concept)," then this judgment "can only be directed to the subjective conditions of the use of the faculty of judgment in general (which is limited neither to the particular mode of sense nor to a particular concept of the understanding.)" Such subjective conditions, however, even though referred to in the plural, are nothing but one state, the harmony of the faculties; and in judging that one's pleasure in an object is due to this source, one is also claiming that one's judgment is directed to "that subjective factor which one can presuppose in all persons (as requisite for a possible experience in general)." Thus the "accordance of a representation with these conditions of the faculty of judgment must admit of being assumed valid *a priori* for everyone." In other words, insofar as a given pleasure is in fact due to nothing but the "subjective finality of the representation for the relation of the cognitive faculties in the estimation of a sensible object in general," or to an object producing the harmony of the faculties without the intervention of a concept and without dependence on any purely sensual response, then that pleasure "can be attributed to everyone with justification."[9]

This is all that Kant offers under the actual title of the deduction of judgments of taste. It is obviously incomplete, for justifying a particular judgment of taste by this argument involves making three assumptions which it does not address. There is the assumption (i) that one's particular response is in fact due to "mere estimation," or that one is correct in attributing one's feeling of pleasure to the harmony of the faculties. There is the assumption (ii) that we can in fact presuppose that this "subjective factor" is "requisite for possible experience in general," or that we may justifiably attribute the general capability for experiencing this state to others. Finally, there is the assumption (iii) that we may make a more particular claim about the mental life of others, and rationally suppose that the very same objects which occasion the harmony of the faculties in ourselves must also occasion it in others.

Kant's consideration of these assumptions is found only in a lengthy footnote and a remark appended to §38, and in the subsequent §39, even though assumptions ii and iii are so far from being mere presuppositions of the deduction of aesthetic judgment that their defense really constitutes the deduction itself. Kant's relegation of this defense to mere addenda to his argument is another, if not the worst, of the expository infelicities of the *Critique of Judgment*. But, the formal inadequacy of his second deduction being thus noted, let us see what the substance of the broader argument of §§38 and 39 amounts to, and whether it improves upon the deduction of §21.

The footnote and remark appended to §38 mention two presuppositions we must make to be "justified in making claim to universal agreement for a judgment of the faculty of aesthetic judgment resting on merely subjective grounds."[10] One underlies the validity of claiming such agreement for a particular feeling of pleasure, or for one's response to a particular object; the other concerns the general possibility of universally valid claims about aesthetic response. Since the first of these (assumption i in my classification, but labeled 2 in Kant's exposition) concerns the application of a general principle itself, it may be considered first. Assumption i is simply the requirement that, for any particular feeling of pleasure for which one claims universal validity on the basis of its assignment to the harmony of the faculties as its source, one must actually be right in so assigning it. The remark appended to §38 misleadingly describes the presupposition "that we have correctly subsumed the given object under these conditions" (the harmony of the faculties, now in the plural) as something asserted by the deduction itself.[11] Assumption i is not part of the deduction, which is a general defense of the rationality of a kind of judgment. It is, rather, presupposed in invoking this deduction in defense of a particular judgment of taste. This is brought out more clearly in Kant's footnote, which describes not two assumptions of the deduction, but rather two conditions required to justify particular aesthetic judgments: the general condition that the deduction of aesthetic judgment itself is correct, and the particular condition that one's assignment of a given feeling of pleasure is correct. Here, assumption i is expressed as the presupposition that (2) the judgment has taken regard of this relation (the harmony of the faculties) alone (thus, of the *formal condition* of the faculty of judgment), and is pure, that is, confused neither with concepts of the object nor with sensations as determining grounds.[12]

In both the footnote and the remark, Kant insists that while the correctness of one's assignment of a particular feeling of pleasure to the harmony of the faculties is a condition of the validity of one's judgment of taste, the possibility of error in this reflective assignment does not undermine the justifiability of aesthetic judgment in general. Thus, to his condition 2, Kant adds, "If any error is made in respect of this, that concerns only the incorrect application to a particular case of the right, which a law gives us, whereby the right itself is not suspended."[13]

Kant can make such a claim for two reasons. In general, he does not suppose that certainty is an absolute requirement for the justifiability of making particular judgments which have any empirical component. Thus in his practical philosophy, Kant insists upon the uncertainty of all particular assignments of motives without impugning the permissibility of moral judgment in general, and in his theoretical philosophy, he maintains that the possibility of "dreams and illusions" in no way affects the general argument that "inner experience is possible only through outer experience in general."[14] That he sees no reason to hold judgments of taste to a stricter standard than those of science or ethics is suggested when he claims that the "difficulty and uncertainty concerning the correctness of the subsumption" of feelings under the principle of aesthetic judgment make "doubtful the legitimacy of the claim to this validity for an aesthetic judgment in general, or of the principle itself, just as little as the (though not so often or easily) mistaken subsumption of the logical judgment under its principle can render the latter principle, which is objective, doubtful."[15]

But Kant also has a specific reason for separating the issues of certainty and justifiability in the case of aesthetic judgment. Certainty in particular instances is no requirement for the justifiability of aesthetic judgment in general because the very nature of this judgment itself explains why it should actually be more uncertain than ordinary cognitive judgments, or why it suffers "unavoidable difficulties not affecting the logical faculty of judgment." As Kant puts it, "in the latter the subsumption is under concepts; but in aesthetic judgment it is under a mere sensible relation of the imagination and understanding mutually harmonizing with one another in the represented form of the object, in which case the subsumption may easily prove fallacious."[16] In the case of ordinary judgments, we have concepts which can serve as rules for the verification of beliefs about sequences of impressions, and we still make mistakes; it is all the less surprising, then, that where we have no concepts to serve as rules, but merely the feeling of pleasure itself, which can be determined to manifest the harmony of the faculties only by indirect methods, we should be open to error. But since this possibility of error can be explained by the nature of aesthetic response as a feeling manifesting a mental state achieved without the application of a concept to a manifold, there is no reason why it should unduly disturb us. We do have rules—of disinterestedness and the finality of form—for judgments of taste, and the fact that their application to our responses of pleasure does not yield complete certainty does not mean that we are being irrational in attempting to discriminate these responses and their sources.

Thus the possibility of error in the assignment of particular pleasures to their sources presents no special difficulty for the justification of making aesthetic judgments in general, though the claim that any given judgment of taste can derive intersubjective validity from the deduction must indeed be subject to the proviso that the feeling of pleasure on which it rests has been assigned to the proper source. Assumption i then presents no real problems, but its discussion does not actually advance the case for the deduction. So we must now see what Kant has to say in defense of assumptions ii and iii.

In the body of §38, Kant simply infers from the connection of a feeling of delight with the subjective conditions of the employment of judgment to its dependence on a factor which may be attributed to everyone as a condition of possible experience in general. He thus attempts to accomplish his deduction in a single step. But as we saw, this inference requires the additional assumptions ii that we can attribute the general capacity for the harmony of the faculties to others and iii that this harmony occurs in everyone in precisely the same circumstances. Assumption ii is addressed in the footnote and remark to §38. Kant's remark acknowledges that the argument offered as the deduction itself "merely asserts . . . that we are justified in universally presupposing the same subjective conditions of the faculty of judgment universally in all persons which we find in ourselves,"[17] but does not explain what justifies us in this presupposition. Most of this remark concerns the correctness of particular aesthetic judgments. But the footnote to §38 does attempt to defend assumption ii. It does this by maintaining (as its own condition 1) that "in all persons, the subjective conditions of this faculty [of aesthetic judgment] are identical, as far as the relation of the cognitive faculties there set into activity to cognition in general is concerned; which must be true, because otherwise men could not communicate their representations or even their knowledge itself."[18] The general strategy of this passage is obviously the same as that of §21. Calling upon his explanation of aesthetic response as the relation of the cognitive faculties in the absence of their ordinary connection by a concept, Kant implies that the capability for aesthetic response is entailed by the capability for knowledge in general, and asserts that the latter must be attributed to everyone as a condition of supposing knowledge itself to be communicable.

The present version of this argument is actually more remarkable for what it omits from the version of §21 than for what it adds. First, it makes no mention of conviction as a subjective condition of knowledge, and thus avoids §21's appearance of a slide from the attitude of belief, which is the subjective component of knowledge, to the state of the mental faculties, which, as its subjective condition, explains the possession of knowledge, propositional attitude and all. But any ambiguity on this issue was just a superficial confusion in §21, which really turned on the admissibility of inferring from the existence of an accomplishment (knowledge) to the capabilities necessary for that accomplishment (the subjective conditions of knowledge). What is really an important change in §38 is its caution with regard to the status of just this basic premise. Like §21, §38 assumes that if knowledge can be shared, then so can the capability for it; but unlike §21, §38 does not suggest that the possibility of communication is a necessary condition for the existence of knowledge. There is no hint that the existence of other persons capable of knowledge in general and aesthetic response in particular can be deduced from the mere fact of one's own experience, and thus can be made the subject of a true transcendental deduction—an argument from the unimpeachable fact of one's own experience to the necessary conditions of the possibility of that experience. The possibility of communication in general is not taken to be deducible from any more deeply entrenched premise. Instead, the communicability of knowledge in general is itself the basic assumption of the deduction of aesthetic judgment, and Kant's actual argument is limited to the claim that in attributing to others the capability for aesthetic response, one attributes to them no more than is required to make them capable of knowledge at all—namely, the "subjective condition" of knowledge. No attempt is made to argue that this attribution, or any consideration of others, is a condition of one's own experience, or *a fortiori*, of one's experience of aesthetic response.

The argument of §38 thus differs from that of §21 in a way paralleling the general difference between Kant's mature aesthetic theory and his earlier theory, according to which the existence of others actually plays a constitutive role in one's own experience of aesthetic response. Section 21 is committed to the thesis that without the possibility of communication, one could have no knowledge oneself; this is reminiscent of the theory that without the possible concurrence of others in sensible response to an object, one can take no pleasure in its beauty. The theory of §21, of course, does make the strong claim that if one does have any knowledge, then one must be in a position to communicate it to others; but attractive as its seems, this theory can draw no support from the theory of knowledge which Kant offers in the *Critique of Pure Reason*. The argument of §38, by contrast, is more consistent with the basic theory of the *Critique of Judgment*. It does not make the possibility of communication a condition of either one's knowledge in general or one's capability for aesthetic response, but instead requires that the existence of others with mental faculties like one's own be independently presupposed. There is thus no suggestion that if one is capable of aesthetic response at all, then it must be possible to make intersubjectively valid judgments about that response. Instead, there is the very different suggestion that if one can communicate any cognitive judgment at all, then one can also attribute to others the general capacity required for the intersubjective validity of aesthetic judgments.

Such an argument is formally weaker than that of §21, for to object to it one need only object to the justifiability of making assumptions about communication with others, and would not have to question the very possibility of experience itself. At the same time, however, such an argument remains within the limits of the first *Critique*'s theory of knowledge; and, just because it pretends to less, it is also more plausible than the argument of §21. Moreover, by treating the possibility of communication as the basic premise for the deduction of aesthetic judgment, rather than implying that this possibility itself can be derived from the more general possibility of experience, §38 does not commit Kant to the view that the principle of taste must be a constitutive principle of experience. Remarkably, §§38 and 39 make no mention of the open question of §22, or even of the distinction between regulative and constitutive principles. We thus cannot adopt the charitable interpretation of Kant's repetition of the deduction, namely, that §38 is actually meant to answer a question explicitly left open by §21. Nevertheless, the fact that §38 simply presupposes the principle of communicability means that its argument is compatible with the possibility that the principle of common sense is merely regulative. If §22 implies, intentionally or not, that the assumption of the possibility of the communication of knowledge in general is only regulative in its epistemological status, then this fact about §38 would represent an important improvement over the argument of §21.

However, before we can further pursue this issue—which really raises the question of the ultimate strength of Kant's deduction of aesthetic judgment—another question must be considered. So far, Kant has spoken only to the attribution of the general capacity for aesthetic response to other persons. But the deduction must also assume that we are justified in attributing particular states of mind to other persons, or that the accord of a particular representation with the harmonious employment of one's own imagination and understanding "must admit of being assumed valid *a priori* for everyone." This, my assumption iii, is not addressed by the first and second conditions Kant places on the deduction in the footnote and remark of §38. However, Kant does turn to it in §39, and once again attempts to have his deduction "come to particulars" by means of a concept of the "proportion" of the cognitive faculties.

According to its title, §39 is concerned with the "communicability of a sensation."[19] As usual, by "communicability" Kant means only universal validity or imputability. Thus he is considering not what techniques might actually be available to offer other persons a certain feeling, or communicate it to them, but only how a feeling not connected to a determinate judgment according to rules may be validly attributed to others. He proceeds by considering the three classes of pleasure distinguished in the first moment of the Analytic of the Beautiful.[20] "Sensory feeling," or the sensation of color, sound, and the like, depends entirely upon our physiological response to objects, and cannot be considered universally communicable, because we have no *a priori* basis for a belief "that everyone has a like sense to our own." *A fortiori,* the pleasures of agreeableness, or the pleasures due merely to the character of the sensation caused by an object of sense, cannot be rationally expected of everyone—"it is absolutely not to be demanded that pleasure in the same objects be incumbent on everyone" when this pleasure is the mere "enjoyment" of sense.[21] This is not so in the case of "delight in an action on the score of its moral character." Such delight can indeed be regarded as universally valid, because of the universal validity of the moral law, action on which produces this pleasure. But just because its universal validity has this base in law, the communicability of moral feeling offers no model for the communicability of aesthetic response. Moral feeling admits of general communication only through reason, and even "should [this] pleasure be the same [*gleichartig*] for everyone," it is so "only be means of very determinate practical concepts of reason."[22] Further,

Kant claims, the universal validity of the pleasure in the sublime also rests on moral concepts. Only in pleasure in the beautiful do we encounter a feeling which, unlike mere sensory enjoyment, is regarded as communicable, but not as a mere consequence of the universal validity of a "lawful activity, nor yet [as a consequence] of a rationalizing contemplation according to ideas."

It is to explain this anomaly that Kant invokes the concept of proportion. First he refers to his explanation of aesthetic response and to the basic strategy of the deduction by saying that "without having any end or principle as a clue, this pleasure accompanies the ordinary apprehension of an object by the imagination, as the faculty of intuition, in relation to the understanding, as the faculty of concepts, by means of a procedure of the faculty of judgment, which it must also exercise for the sake of the commonest experience." But while in ordinary experience judgment accomplishes its procedure — the synthesis of a manifold — with an "empirical objective concept," in "aesthetic estimation" it merely perceives the "suitability of the representation for the harmonious (subjectively final) occupation of both faculties of knowledge in their freedom." Nevertheless, Kant now argues, even the response to a particular beautiful object may be rationally imputed to everyone, for "this pleasure must necessarily depend on the same conditions for everyone, since these are subjective conditions of the possibility of a cognition in general, and the proportion of these cognitive faculties, which is required for taste, is also requisite for the ordinary and sound understanding, which one may presuppose in everyone."[23] As long as one is not mistaken in attributing a particular feeling of pleasure to the harmony of the faculties or to the "subjective conditions of the possibility of cognition in general" — as long as one "does not take the matter for the form, or the charm for the beauty" — one is perfectly justified in regarding reflective pleasure in particular objects as universally communicable.

Kant's argument rests on three suppositions. First, it assumes that one can rationally attribute to others cognitive faculties like one's own as well as the general capability of possessing knowledge by means of those faculties, or bringing imagination and understanding into accord under some circumstances. Then, corresponding to my previous assumption ii, it supposes that one can rationally attribute to others the ability to experience this state without the employment of an "empirical objective concept." Finally, corresponding to assumption iii, it claims a propensity to experience this state with respect to the very same objects that occasion it in oneself. The first of these claims is obviously a condition of the possibility of communication in general, and even if it cannot be derived from the mere possibility of one's own experience, it does seem that attempting to communicate with others is rational only if one supposes them to be equipped with the faculties requisite for knowledge and actually capable of knowledge on at least some occasions. We can now see, however, that not only assumption iii but assumption ii as well are meant to be defended by reference to the concept of proportion. Their defense must go like this: first, since the proportion between imagination and understanding is identical in both ordinary cognition and aesthetic response, anyone capable of ordinary cognition is also capable of aesthetic response; and second, since this proportion is produced in everyone by the same objects in ordinary cases of cognition, it must also be so produced in the case of aesthetic response. And then, as long as one is correct in believing a particular feeling of pleasure to be occasioned by the harmony of the faculties rather than by some sensation or interest, one is justified in believing it to be universally valid or communicable.

Conditions and Proportions

An argument of this form could indeed ground an inference from the shared possession of cognitive faculties in general to the universal validity of particular responses of pleasure — if it were sound. But Kant's concept of proportion cannot bear the weight this argument requires it to carry.

First, although Kant may mean us to think of a proportion as a function which produces a unique result for any particular assignment of values to its variables, and thus to suppose that there is only one way to unify any particular manifold — the premise for assumption iii — he never actually argues for such a claim. The first *Critique,* of course, holds that all manifolds must be unified by the same categories, but never shows that no more than one set of empirical concepts can apply the categories to a given manifold. It is certainly not obvious that only one unification of a given manifold by empirical concepts can conform to the general requirements imposed on synthesis by the pure concepts of the understanding, and thus it is even less obvious that everyone capable of cognition must respond in the same way to a given manifold when his response is not guided by concepts at all.

Second, there is a perhaps even deeper problem about whether the concept of proportion can really be employed to move from the universal imputation of the general capacity of knowledge to the universal imputation of the capacity for aesthetic response. The proportion on which Kant's argument is supposed to turn is the requirement that manifolds satisfy the understanding's demand for unity, whether with or without concepts. But all that must be attributed to others to make them capable of cognition in general is the ability to unify their manifolds by some concept or other, and it is not clear that attributing to them the capacity for the syntheses necessary to accomplish such a unification entails attributing to them the capacity to become conscious of unity in a given manifold without the use of any determinate concept.

The gap between the ordinary case of knowledge and the case of aesthetic response may be revealed by considering either the concept of the "subjective conditions of knowledge" or that of "proportion." We may begin with the first of these. Kant's argument revolves on the claim that the basis of aesthetic response is the subjective condition (or conditions) of knowledge in general, and that in attributing the capacity for knowledge to anyone we then also attribute the capacity for aesthetic response to that person. And we have seen that the harmony of the faculties which grounds pleasure in the beautiful *can* be described as a subjective condition of knowledge — it is a state in which a manifold presented by the imagination is felt to be unified, or in which the ordinary psychological concomitants of knowledge, such as memory and feelings of coherence, are present, without reflection upon any objectively valid concept or judgment. But there are several different things that might be meant by a subjective condition of knowledge, and it is not obvious that attributing to someone such subjective conditions as are required to be capable of knowledge at all really does require the further attribution of the capacity for aesthetic response to that person. First, we might think of the subjective condition of knowledge as a condition on manifolds of intuition, that they be unifiable in some way or another. Second, we might think of the subjective condition — or conditions — of knowledge as the faculties or capacities required to possess knowledge. Third, the subjective condition of knowledge may be the mental state or state of the mental faculties characteristic of someone knowing something. Finally, the subjective condition of knowledge — with the emphasis on "subjective," as it were — might be thought of as the special state in which the last-mentioned mental condition obtains in the absence of actual knowledge, and which is specially pleasurable precisely for that reason, or as the capacity to be in this state. It is far from clear that the existence of the subjective conditions of knowledge in any of these senses must imply the existence of these conditions in all the other senses.

It is certainly a condition of both knowledge and aesthetic response that a person possess the faculties of imagination and understanding, as well as the general capability for judgment, or bringing together universals and particulars. It is also a necessary condition of both knowledge and aesthetic response that a given manifold which is the object of judgment be unifiable from some point of view or another. And it is equally a necessary condition of aesthetic response as well as of knowledge that a person be able to perform the syntheses of apprehension and reproduction on a given manifold. But a person may be capable of knowledge even if he can perceive the unity of given manifolds only through the rules furnished by determinate concepts, and even if he is capable of the syntheses of apprehension and reproduction only when he also continues on to the synthesis of recognition in a concept. In other words, the general requirement that a person be capable of knowledge is a requirement that he be capable of subsuming his manifolds under concepts, and of performing whatever acts of synthesis that requires, but it is not a requirement that he be capable of detecting unity and performing syntheses without the use of concepts. Or, to be more cautious, it is not a requirement that a person be able to be *conscious of* unity in a manifold without subsuming it under a concept. Yet this is just what the capacity for aesthetic response is, for pleasure in the beautiful is itself consciousness by feeling rather than conceptual judgment of the unity of a manifold. The capacity to become conscious that an object presents a unifiable manifold without actually synthesizing it by a concept is different from the capacity to merely perform the syntheses of apprehension and reproduction, the performance of which is ordinarily manifest to consciousness only in the synthesis of recognition in a concept. But if this is so, possession of the subjective conditions of knowledge in general, or what might be regarded as the *minimal* conditions for knowledge, does not entail the capacity to become conscious, through pleasure, of the synthesis of manifolds apart from concepts.

The same point may be made by considering the concept of the proportion of the cognitive faculties which is requisite for both taste and ordinary cognition. Whatever connotations it might have, this concept of proportion only expresses the requirement that, for both knowledge and aesthetic response, a manifold must be seen as a unity. It cannot entail that the detection of unity take place through the use of any particular empirical concept formulated in accord with the categories, or that a given manifold be unifiable by only one empirical concept. Nor can it require that the unity of a manifold be immediately apparent, or detectable with any particular degree of ease or facility. Two different persons will possess knowledge of similar manifolds, or detect the existence of the requisite proportion in the manifolds, even if one can readily synthesize the manifold with some simple empirical concept, while the other can synthesize it only with great difficulty and by means of a highly complicated conceptual scheme. But if this is so, then the general ability to detect the cognitive proportion can hardly imply possession of the ability simply to feel unity, or become aware of the proportion without the use of any empirical concept at all.

In one way, Kant's treatment of proportion in §39 may be preferred to §21's discussion. In the earlier passage, Kant's argument was apparently contradictory. It began by claiming that there is one proportion between imagination and understanding which allows any manifold to be a representation of an object, or serve for knowledge, but then went on to maintain that the proportion between the two faculties was different in the case of diverse objects, with only one of the possible values of this ratio being optimal for the mutual harmony of the two faculties and thus giving rise to aesthetic response.[24] This position could explain why every object is not beautiful, although every manifold is ultimately unifiable; but it introduced an unexplained epistemological thesis into the argument, and explicitly threatened the straightforward connection between aesthetic response and the possibility of knowledge in general on which the deduction of aesthetic judgment must turn. In §39, Kant at least superficially avoids that difficulty by retaining the idea of a single proportion which obtains in both knowledge and aesthetic response. This argument thus ostensibly preserves the connection between the general condition of knowledge and the basis of aesthetic response required for Kant's deduction. At the same time, however, it must raise the problem of why every manifold does not occasion the harmony of the faculties and thus represent a beautiful object.

This problem cannot be answered if the concept of the subjective conditions of knowledge which grounds the harmony of the faculties is interpreted, in purely epistemological terms, simply as the capacity to unify a manifold by the cooperation of imagination and understanding in general, since that does not entail the capacity to unify manifolds without concepts. To drive any wedge between the concept of beautiful objects and that of objects for knowledge in general, some additional capacity must be introduced into the interpretation of the harmony of the faculties. Some psychological notion of an ability to actually feel rather than think unity, or to perceive the unity of a particular manifold with an unusual degree of immediacy or facility, must be added if we are both to preserve Kant's link between the harmony of the faculties and cognition in general and to differentiate between beautiful objects, which are always pleasing, and objects of knowledge in general, which are not.

The addition of such a psychological component to the model of the harmony of the faculties will constitute a difference between the proportion requisite for cognition in general and the particular ratio best adapted for quickening the two faculties of knowledge or producing their free and harmonious accord. But once such a step is taken, the chain of necessary conditions, or of necessary possession of capabilities, which Kant's deduction requires is broken. The general ability to unify a manifold under some empirical concept or other will not imply the ability to feel this unity without concepts or detect it in given manifolds with a unique degree of facility. Once a capacity which is not an absolutely necessary condition of knowledge is introduced into the explanation of aesthetic response, so is an element of contingency, and the possibility of an entirely justifiable *a priori* imputation of aesthetic response to others is precluded. Once our interpretation of aesthetic judgment proceeds beyond the abstract talk of the cooperation and proportion between faculties, we see that Kant's explanation of aesthetic response does not entitle him to the assumptions that everyone capable of knowledge at all must be capable of this response and that they must be capable of it with regard to the very same objects as anyone else.

Formally, the second version of Kant's deduction is more attractive than the first, not only because it avoids explicit confusion on the issue of proportion, but also because it does not adopt the unsubstantiated premise that the communicability of knowledge is a condition of the possibility of any individual's experience. This means that the argument could survive the possibility that the principle of the communicability of knowledge in general may be merely regulative rather than constitutive; and this seems appropriate, for although the possibility of its intersubjective validity is surely compatible with Kant's conception of experience as a rule-governed synthesis of impressions, the latter does not entail the actuality or even the possibility of the existence of other persons with faculties like one's own. But Kant's argument is still in difficulty. For even if we assume that he would be willing to concede that the possibility of the communication of knowledge in general is a merely regulative idea — a concession which, even after §22, Kant never actually makes — he is still obviously committed to the view that the intersubjective validity of knowledge in general entails the intersubjective validity of aesthetic response. That is, Kant clearly supposes that the communicability of cognition in general is enough to insure the validity of assumptions ii and iii for any aesthetic response for which assumption i is met. However, we have now seen that this is not the case. Even if the existence of other persons capable of the communication of knowledge in general could be derived from the mere fact of one's own experience, the general capacity for aesthetic response as well as the communicability of such response in particular cases—both of which are required for the intersubjective validity of aesthetic judgment—could not be so derived. The psychological capacity to experience the free harmony of imagination and understanding goes beyond the minimal capacity for knowledge, and with respect to the latter, its occurrence both in general and in particular cases is contingent. It is, indeed, just for this reason that the occurrence of this harmony occasions a pleasure which is not felt in every case of knowledge.

In the end, we might say, Kant's explanation of aesthetic response and his deduction of aesthetic judgment are in tension. Given the element of contingency required by Kant's explanation of the pleasurability of aesthetic response, even a skeptic who has been persuaded to concede the justifiability of whatever beliefs can be shown to be necessary conditions of knowledge might still refuse to accept Kant's deduction of judgments of taste. The principle of aesthetic judgment, that the harmony of the faculties is communicable just because it is nothing but the subjective condition of knowledge, is not, in the brave words of §21, "presupposed in every logic and every principle of knowledge that is not skeptical," for it cannot be derived from Kant's own theory of knowledge.

A Regulative Principle of Taste

However, this conclusion may suggest an unnecessarily pessimistic assessment of Kant's accomplishment. If we think of taste's imputation of agreement as a qualified prediction of aesthetic response under ideal circumstances, then it must be conceded that Kant's deduction cannot justify the claims of taste. This is because aesthetic response requires a facility in the use of one's faculties and a sensitivity to their operations that cannot be regarded as part of the minimal capability for knowledge. But the fact remains that Kant has offered an explanation of aesthetic response which invokes no faculties beyond those required for knowledge in general—a theory which, unlike some of its predecessors, postulates no special sense of beauty — and which also frees aesthetic response from particularities of use and interest. Given this, it does seem fair to say that he has managed to describe aesthetic response as intrinsically shareable. We may not be able to say that everyone will find a given object beautiful, or, as Kant supposes, that everyone should find it so; but his theory certainly allows us to say that anyone *could* find it beautiful. Perhaps this is enough to justify the enterprise of public discussion of taste, even if it cannot ground *a priori* imputations of taste. As long as aesthetic response requires only faculties requisite for knowledge in general, there can be no reason why anyone should not be able to come to enjoy it, even if it does call for a facility everyone may not have. For while facility in the exercise of any faculty may be what Kant calls in his discussion of genius a "gift of nature,"[25] a facility, unlike a faculty, may also be acquired through education and practice.

If this is the case, then perhaps the intersubjective validity of the capacity for aesthetic response may reasonably be made the object of at least a regulative principle. We have seen that Kant's first attempt at a deduction tries to show but does not succeed in showing that the principle of a common sense is constitutive in force; and his second attempt, while offering no further support for such a conclusion, also tries to show that the principle of taste is constitutive. But §22's suggestion that taste may depend on a regulative principle is still open; indeed, we may now recall, the possibility that taste depends on such a principle is not only raised by §22, but also implied by the theory of reflective judgment and the analogy between the principles of the systematicity of nature and of taste which Kant drew in the two Introductions to the third *Critique*. That analogy, I argued, was misleading insofar as it intimated that the principle of taste, like the principle of teleology, was a principle applicable to objects in nature, and was one of the sources of the restrictive formalism and naturalism in Kant's specific aesthetic opinions; as we saw, the principle of taste must concern the judges of beauty rather than their objects. But perhaps the proper analogy between the principles of teleology and taste concerns not their content but their status. Although the deduction of aesthetic judgment cannot justify certainty in even correctly made judgments of taste, perhaps it can point to the adoption of a regulative principle of intersubjective validity.

However, to suggest that taste may rest on a regulative principle is not the same thing as to argue for it, and such a defense can only be a matter of speculation. For Kant simply does not return to the question of §22 in his second deduction of aesthetic judgment, and, *a fortiori,* gives no hint as to how an argument for a regulative principle of taste might proceed. At the end of §40, Kant does raise the question of whether the "universal communicability of one's feeling in itself must have an interest for us,"[26] and he does argue in §42 that we can take a moral interest in the existence of beautiful objects (actually, beauties of nature only).[27] This argument may well be meant to lay bare the "higher principle of reason" or "higher ends" which, according to §22, may make the development of a common sense a regulative principle, although it does not refer back to the earlier passage. But the discovery of a moral interest in taste can only advance the case for the practical demand of taste; it cannot figure in the epistemological justification for imputing capacities and responses to other persons. On how a regulative principle for the latter might be defended, Kant says nothing. Yet if we are to preserve anything of the arguments offered in §§21 and 38, it would be desirable to find a cognitive rather than a moral interest of reason, or a way in which reason as a faculty of cognition rather than action could lead to a regulative principle of taste.

Our only hope for finding a regulative principle for the intersubjective validity of taste lies in following the first *Critique*'s prescription for the deduction of regulative principles. There, after some initial hesitation, Kant decided that such principles could and must be given a transcendental deduction,[28] and that such a deduction could be furnished if it could be shown that a given principle can "lead us to systematic unity, under the presupposition of such an *object in the idea,*" and "thus contribute to the extension of empirical knowledge, without ever being in a position to run counter to it."[29] Perhaps the contribution it might make to the extension of empirical knowledge could also be used as an argument on behalf of a regulative principle of communicability. First, one might argue that thinking of ordinary empirical knowledge as communicable contributes to its extension, because looking toward the shareability of one's conceptual schemes would incline one to the adoption of schemes both already in use and simple in design, and this would result not only in the sharing of knowledge but in its rapid progression as well. Then, one might continue in either of two ways. A close analogy with the structure of Kant's argument in §§21 and 38 might be preserved. If thinking of knowledge as communicable advanced its acquisition, communicability might be postulated as a "necessary maxim" of reason, without being a constitutive principle of experience itself. Then the conditions of its possibility would likewise be made the subject of a universal imputation, though with only regulative force, and the principle would be extended to the case of taste by the argument that the conditions of the communicability of taste are the same as those of the communicability of knowledge in general. Or, one might attempt to go further than Kant and give an independent argument for the universal validity of the special facility in synthesis which may be involved in aesthetic response. Perhaps one could argue that the progress of knowledge as well as its extension to other persons will be best facilitated if one works toward modes of organization which are highly perspicuous, or apparent without much reflection on concepts at all. If this is so, then the postulation of a general ability to detect unity without much reflection might be a regulative principle in the search for knowledge, and a reasonable goal of education as well; and a general capability for aesthetic response, insofar as it involved a unique facility in aesthetic response, might be thought of as the ultimate form of such a capability, and thus itself be postulated by the same regulative principle.

Since Kant himself does not offer an argument for a regulative principle of taste, it may not be worthwhile to develop one beyond these speculations. Even such a bare sketch as I have presented should allow us to say something about what the ultimate force of Kant's deduction can be against someone who doubts the rationality of claiming general agreement in taste on the basis of one's own response. It seems clear that just insofar as any version of his deduction rests on the general principle that knowledge is communicable, it cannot have the same force against skepticism that the first *Critique*'s transcendental deduction of the categories enjoys. That argument (supposing it to be sound) accomplishes the supreme stroke against skepticism by demonstrating that anyone who presupposes as little as consciousness of the unity of his own manifolds of intuition must also concede the justifiability of judgments about external objects and their causal connections. One would have to be very skeptical indeed to doubt the premise of that argument, but skepticism about the communicability of knowledge might be maintained without undermining any capacity so fundamental as that for apperception.

However, it must be noted, doubt about the rationality of aesthetic judgment based on skepticism about the possibility of shared knowledge in general does not turn on anything unique to aesthetic judgment. For while intersubjective validity may be essential to the content of aesthetic judgment, it is surely presupposed for other kinds of judgment as well, and the skeptic who undermines the rationality of aesthetic judgment by attacking the possibility of communicating knowledge in general will be shouldering a large burden indeed.

A more difficult question arises when we consider Kant's inference from the communicability of knowledge in general to the intersubjective validity of aesthetic response. If the subjective conditions of knowledge were, as Kant maintains, identical with the basis of aesthetic response, then he would have shown that suspicion of the rationality of aesthetic judgment is possible only at the cost of doubting the communicability of our knowledge and experience generally. Showing this would certainly constitute a major step in a dialectical confrontation with skepticism about aesthetic judgment; though not making it impossible, it would obviously make it less than attractive. But if my arguments that the capacity for aesthetic response is not equivalent to the minimal conditions of knowledge, and that identity of response to particular objects cannot be inferred from a more general identity of cognitive faculties, are accepted, then it becomes possible to doubt the rationality of making intersubjective imputations of taste without doubting the intersubjectivity of knowledge in general. And this will be the case whether the postulation of the latter be attributed a constitutive or a merely regulative force.

Nevertheless, Kant's explanation of aesthetic response may still be capable of removing some of the impetus for skepticism about the rationality of aesthetic judgment. Although the theory of the harmony of the faculties may not be enough to fully justify the claim to universal validity which his own analysis imposes on judgments of taste, this theory does explain how we may take a pleasure in objects which is truly independent of individual interests and concerns, and which is rooted in an objective — that of the unification of manifolds in general — which may surely be attributed to everyone. Further, by suggesting how uncertainty in aesthetic judgment arises at least in part as a necessary consequence of its own essential freedom from constraint by concepts, as well as from the fact that aesthetic judgment involves an empirical judgment about one's own mental history, Kant may also have succeeded in averting the thrust of skepticism. For it may be supposed that skepticism relies on our unwitting assumption that certainty is a *sine qua non* for any rational form of judgment, and then advances by arguing from an element of uncertainty in our application of some cognitive procedure to the irrationality of that procedure itself.[30] But if Kant has shown that uncertainty is only to be expected because of the special nature of aesthetic response as well as the nature of self-knowledge in general, then he may have reduced the motivation for obsession with this uncertainty. This may not be enough to make genuine predictions of the aesthetic responses of others rational, but it may be sufficient to allow us to think of aesthetic response as potentially intersubjective and as a fit subject for public discourse; and perhaps this is all that should be expected of an aesthetic theory.

There are, then, obvious problems with Kant's deduction of aesthetic judgment, but his entrenchment of aesthetic response and judgment in the more general framework of our capacity for knowledge as a whole does seem to increase the burden that must be shouldered by the skeptic with regard to taste, without forcing aesthetic response into an inappropriate analogy with either sensory or intellectual cognition. The empiricists, in spite of their attempts to explain away disagreements in our judgments of taste, had left aesthetic judgment open to the attacks of skepticism by assimilating aesthetic response too closely to the model of ordinary sensation. The rationalists, by contrast, set aside the threat of skepticism, but only by introducing a divine guarantee for the existence of intersubjectivity in general. Further, by defining aesthetic response as confused knowledge, they made any strategy for dealing with actual cases of disagreement in aesthetic judgment incompatible with the explanation of aesthetic response itself. Kant's own explanation of aesthetic response, as well as the failure of his deduction of aesthetic judgment, may imply that the possibility of disagreement in taste can never be fully excluded, and that no procedure for handling actual disagreements in aesthetic judgment can guarantee a resolution, but it hardly entails the impossibility of the rational discussion and assessment of the intersubjective validity of aesthetic responses. Whatever its flaws, Kant's aesthetic theory certainly comes closer to explaining both the uniqueness and the rationality of aesthetic judgment than previous attempts.

At this point, it might be most appropriate to turn to the final aspect of Kant's treatment of the intersubjectivity of aesthetic judgment with which I will be concerned, namely, the moral demand for taste. But the last paragraph's reference to the rationalist invocation of a divine guarantee for intersubjectivity raises the question of whether Kant himself avoided a flight into dogmatic metaphysics in his attempt to offer a transcendental justification of aesthetic judgment. There are no hints of such a regress in the two attempts at a deduction considered so far, but Kant returns to the problem addressed by these arguments in the Dialectic of Aesthetic Judgment, and there he does seem to invoke dogmatism to answer skepticism. Before leaving the topic of the epistemological foundations of taste entirely, then, it will be necessary to examine the argument which Kant offers in this part of the third *Critique*.

10

The Metaphysics of Taste

****

A Dialectic of Taste

In the Dialectic of Aesthetic Judgment, Kant reopens the question of the intersubjective validity of aesthetic judgment. This time, he attempts to solve it by the postulation of a supersensible substratum, or noumenal reality, underlying both the subjects and objects of taste. This flight into metaphysics, however, is a misguided addition to the aesthetic theory so far considered.

Our suspicion of the Dialectic is immediately aroused by the confusion encountered in its opening §55, which explains why a critique of taste must include a dialectic. Kant's initial moves seem innocuous enough. He begins by claiming that for a faculty of judgment to be "dialectical," or subject to a dialectic, it must be "rationalizing" (*vernünftelnd*). That is, its judgments must make *a priori* claims to universal validity, for it is only "in the opposition of such judgments that dialectic consists."[1] The disagreement between judgments which represent opposing positions but which are not, on analysis, logically incompatible is not dialectical. Thus, the irreconcilability between different judgments of what is agreeable and disagreeable is not dialectical, because such judgments express only differences in "individual taste" (*eignen Geschmack*). There is no occasion for a dialectic if one person claims, say, that canary-wine is agreeable, and another that it is disagreeable, because these claims do not pretend to be valid for anyone but their individual speakers, and there is no logical difficulty if one person claims to like a wine and another to dislike it—both claims may be true. So, we expect, Kant will next contrast this kind of disagreement with the problematic case which cannot be dismissed with a reference to mere private validity. We look for him to argue that if a judgment makes an *a priori* claim to be valid for everyone, there is a problem in the assertion of both that judgment and its contrary, for both cannot be true. When one person says that a painting is beautiful and another denies it, their conflict cannot be resolved by saying that the two judgments actually have different contents ("A likes painting P" and "B dislikes painting P") and thus do not conflict logically. For a judgment of beauty purports to be valid for everyone, and it cannot be correct both that everyone should respond to a particular object (painting P) with pleasure, and that everyone should not.

But this is not how Kant's exposition of the dialectic of taste proceeds; rather, it takes a turn toward obscurity. Kant simply claims that the fact that no dialectic arises from conflicting judgments of individual taste allows no concept of a dialectic of taste but that of a "dialectic of the *critique* of taste (not of taste itself) in respect of its *principles*."[2] This is confusing for two reasons. First, Kant does not explicitly contrast two forms of judgment, as we should have expected, one of which occasions dialectical conflicts while the other does not, but instead contrasts a form of judgment with the theory of that judgment. However, what force attaches to the assertion that the dialectic is not one of taste but of its critique is far from clear, especially since one would assume that the theory of taste includes a dialectic only because taste itself is dialectical. Second, Kant's claim appears to be connected to what is, given his own definition of it, a misuse of the term "taste." The only reason Kant suggests for the view that the dialectic cannot be one of taste itself but instead concerns the critique of taste is that judgments of taste include judgments of agreeableness, or appeals to individual preference. If this were correct, then there would be a ground for denying that taste in general gives rise to a dialectic. But as Kant's own analysis has made clear, and as his remarks in §40 have made particularly explicit, judgments of taste are always intended to be universal. If there is a dialectical problem in claims to universal validity, then it should arise directly from the nature of taste itself.

The topic of the dialectic of taste becomes somewhat clearer when Kant continues by stating that "concerning the ground of the possibility of judgments of taste in general, mutually conflicting concepts naturally and unavoidably appear."[3] However, this is still not free of confusion. Obviously, Kant means to draw a parallel to the Dialectic of the *Critique of Pure Reason,* and especially to its Antinomies. There, mutually conflicting concepts are indeed his topic, insofar as his arguments concern problems arising from predicating incompatible concepts or determinations of the same objects. Thus, for example, Kant considers whether the concept "infinite in extent" or "finite in extent" applies to a single particular, the world, or whether the concept "governed by the causality of nature" or "governed by the causality of freedom" applies to particular selves. In these cases, mutually conflicting concepts are logically incompatible first-order predicates for objects. In the case of aesthetic judgment, however, one has to stretch to find mutually conflicting concepts. What are really in conflict are just two different positions on "rationalizing" aesthetic judgments, or universally valid judgments about pleasure: the position that they are justifiable, and the position that they are not. The conflict between these two positions does not obviously stem from applying incompatible concepts to one and the same object, but seems more like a simple difference of opinion on whether a certain form of judgment is valid at all. Hence it is not apparent that the problem of taste really leads to a dialectic. And if this is so, then it is also not clear that the theory of taste will call for Kant's typical solution to a dialectical problem: the theory that there are actually two objects, appearance and thing-in-itself, where there appeared to be only one.

If the Dialectic is merely to consider whether aesthetic judgment's claim to universal validity is justifiable, we might wonder why the *Critique of Aesthetic Judgment* should even include it, for Kant certainly appears to have dealt with this issue in his deduction. Before we try to explain the existence of the Dialectic, however, we must note that §56 does advance over §55 in characterizing a dialectical question for taste conforming to the first *Critique*'s model. The latter suggests that a dialectic requires mutually conflicting concepts, and the "Representation of the Antinomy of Taste" which Kant offers in §56 does employ the distinct but related concepts of "contention" and "dispute" (*Streiten* and *Disputiren*).[4]

In this section, Kant employs two "commonplaces" of taste to set up a dialectic of taste reminiscent of Hume's opening gambit in "The Standard of Taste."[5] The first "commonplace . . . with which everyone devoid of taste thinks to protect himself from reproach" is simply the old saw that "*everyone has his own taste.*" The adherent of this view maintains that the determining ground of judgments of taste is entirely constituted by the merely subjective fact of gratification or pain, and need not worry about the validity of a claim to universal agreement because he thinks that such a judgment "has no right to the necessary agreement of others." Opposed to this view are those who may "concede to the judgment of taste the right to pronounce with validity for everyone," but who are in no better position to defend such a claim than are the adherents of the first commonplace. They try to shore up their position by resorting to another antique dictum, the proverb that "*there is no disputing about tastes.*"[6] They suppose that they may affirm that the determining ground of taste is objective, but not to be brought into determinate concepts. But in resorting to this position, they in fact take no more responsibility for their judgments than the adherents of the first commonplace do, for they assume that the impossibility of bringing determinate concepts to bear upon their judgments of taste relieves them of the necessity of adducing any concepts at all to ground their claims.

This position, however, cannot be maintained. For those who hold that there is no disputing about taste, and thus no deciding by proofs, do suppose that we can legitimately *contend* about judgments of taste. Contention and dispute resemble each other in that "through the mutual opposition of judgments they seek to bring forth their unanimity," but differ in that dispute accomplishes this objective with "determinate concepts as grounds of proof," or "assumes *objective* concepts" — that is, concepts of objects — whereas there is no hope of this in the case of contention. Thus, it seems, the possibility of contention cannot depend upon concepts. But, Kant claims, this is where a dialectical problem arises, for those who suppose that "*there may be contention about taste* (although not dispute)" actually support a "proposition" *between* the claim that everyone has his own taste and the belief, which no one wants to defend, that there may be proofs of taste. And if even contention is to be allowed, there must be a hope of coming to terms, and thus "grounds of judgment that do not have merely private validity." Then, Kant concludes, even common sense may be forced into a dialectical conflict, because its proposition that there may be contention about taste is, after all, incompatible with its view that everyone has his own taste. As he puts it,

> In respect of the principle of taste, therefore the following antinomy is exhibited:
>
> 1. *Thesis.* The judgment of taste is not grounded upon concepts; for otherwise it would admit of dispute (decision by means of proofs).
> 2. *Antithesis.* The judgment of taste is grounded on concepts; for otherwise, notwithstanding its diversity, the judgment of taste would not even admit contention (making a claim to the necessary agreement of others with this judgment).[7]

This allows a conjecture about the purpose of the Dialectic of Aesthetic Judgment. What Kant has argued is that when the conditions for disputing and contending are properly understood, ordinary views about the possibility of argument in matters of taste must result in a dialectical conflict.

Perhaps, then, it is not that Kant's *own* justification of the claims of taste requires further elaboration; rather, he may now be implying that *unless* his view is adopted, our views concerning a principle of taste must result in contradiction. If Kant's theory of aesthetic judgment could resolve this contradiction without denying the intuitions from which it results — that there may be contention but not dispute about taste — that would confirm its validity. Thus the function of the dialectic in a critique of taste might be the same as that of a dialectic in the theory of knowledge: to offer indirect confirmation of a position which has already been directly argued for by showing that only by its adoption can contradiction be avoided.

If the fact that the antinomy of taste arises from jointly held "commonplaces" about taste is emphasized, and the possibility raised that Kant is suggesting his own theory of taste as the way out of this antinomy, the inclusion of a Dialectic in the *Critique of Aesthetic Judgment* would be natural enough, and alternate explanations of its occurrence could be rejected. First, the view that the presence of a Dialectic in the third *Critique* is due to nothing but Kant's unbridled affection for the architectonic organization he originally devised for the first *Critique* could be denied. Obviously, the strategy of the present argument is based on that of the earlier one; but if Kant does show that there is a contradiction in our views on taste which can be resolved only by the adoption of his own theory, then this strategy is as appropriate to the third *Critique* as it is to the first. Second, the approach of R. K. Elliott, who has suggested that it is in the Dialectic that Kant first "faces the skeptical problem,"[8] might also be rejected. If it were in the Dialectic that Kant first considered how taste's claim to universal validity might be justified, this view would make sense. But Kant has claimed that his argument in §21 shows that judgments of taste rest on a principle "presupposed in every logic and every principle of knowledge that is not skeptical";[9] and though there is no explicit reference to skepticism in the deduction of §§38 and 39, this argument is clearly directed to the same antiskeptical end as §21. The point of the Dialectic cannot be to broach the issue of skepticism about the rationality of judgments of taste for the first time; rather, it can only be to show that skepticism is a necessary consequence of ordinary views on taste which can be resolved only by the adoption of the theory for which Kant has already argued, thereby confirming the solution to skepticism already offered.

This is at least what we should think if Kant resolved the antinomy of taste by using just the aesthetic theory which he has already expounded. However, what we shall discover when we turn to §57 is that Kant does not dissolve his antinomy by invoking the explanation of aesthetic response and deduction of aesthetic judgment which I have examined. Instead, he argues that the antinomy of taste can be solved only if we postulate a supersensible substratum, or underlying common basis, for the subjects and objects of taste. This must lead us to question whether the sole purpose of the Dialectic is really just to confirm the positive arguments for his theory of taste which Kant has already presented.

Reference to a supersensible ground of appearances has so far played no role at all in Kant's exposition of his theory of taste, which has been cast entirely in terms of ordinary empirical objects and the ordinary and not so ordinary uses of our faculties for dealing with such objects. But in his solution to the antinomy of taste we suddenly find Kant maintaining that a "double sense or point of view in estimation is necessary for our transcendental power of judgment,"[10] and this double point of view is nothing but the distinction between the "object of sense . . . as appearance" and the "pure rational concept of the supersensible," or the object which is the appearance as it is in itself.[11] It is possible that this distinction between phenomenon and noumenon is just inserted into the argument because of Kant's love of architectonic and the fact that his resolution of the problems encountered in the first *Critique*'s Dialectic turned on this distinction. But there may also be a deeper explanation of its occurrence. Although Kant's deduction of aesthetic judgment may increase the burden of proof on the skeptic in aesthetics, I have argued, it is not so powerful or convincing an argument as the first *Critique*'s deduction of the categories. Kant's claims for its conclusiveness are certainly modest in comparison to those he made for his proof of the objective validity of the categories,[12] and it is possible that he did recognize that his argument may still leave room for skeptical suspicion. In this case, Kant may have meant the introduction of a supersensible ground for the subjects and objects of taste to provide a more imposing answer to the skeptic. The Dialectic of Aesthetic Judgment is clearly not Kant's *first* attempt to "face the skeptical problem," but it may have been intended as an *ultimate* answer.

Nor is this all that Kant may have meant the Dialectic to accomplish. It may be recalled that §30 intimated that the deduction of taste should explain the natural existence of beauty.[13] This conception of its task, I argued, was inappropriate, and was rejected by Kant himself in §38.[14] But Kant may have been concerned that the existence of such beauty remained an open issue for ontology, and thought that the introduction of a supersensible ground for the objects of taste would provide some kind of explanation. As we shall see, he quickly qualifies the suggestion that the postulation of such a noumenal object may have any explanatory power; but he suggests it nonetheless, and may have supposed that it would somehow silence a lingering objection to his theory.

If these two conjectures about the function of the Dialectic are correct, our real problem would not be to explain why Kant included it but rather how he could have supposed that it would really be any more convincing than the arguments he had already offered. But this question admits of no obvious answer, and instead of considering it further, I will now turn to the detailed analysis of Kant's solution to the antinomy of taste in §§57 and 58.

A Supersensible Substratum

In §54, Kant states that the antinomy he has expounded can be resolved only if it is "shown that the concept to which one relates the object in [an aesthetic] judgment is not taken in the same sense in both maxims for the faculty of aesthetic judgment," that is, in both the thesis and the antithesis of the antinomy.[15] Acknowledging the "double sense" of the expression "concept" in the opposing theses will show the contradiction to be a "natural illusion," he adds, suggesting that if it is the first *Critique*'s Antinomies which provide the model for the formulation of the dialectical problem of taste, it is the Paralogisms and their exposure of a *sophisma figurae dictionis* which provide the model for its solution.[16] Preserving the parallelism with the first *Critique*, Kant also maintains that this natural illusion is unavoidable, but we may ignore this claim, for which Kant offers no separate argument, and concentrate on his solution of the antinomy.

Kant begins by drawing a by now familiar distinction. He argues that the judgment of taste must be connected to some concept, "for otherwise it absolutely could not make any claim to necessary validity for everyone." But from this the thesis that this judgment is open to dispute decidable by means of proofs does not follow, for the mere fact that a judgment is connected to a concept does not mean that it is thereby provable from that concept. This is because "a concept may be either determinable, or else in itself indeterminate and at the same time also undeterminable." A concept of the first type is "determinable by means of predicates of sensible intuition, which can correspond to it";[17] in other words, the rule for the application of such a concept mentions specific properties which may be presented by an object in intuition, and the presence or absence of those properties in a particular object fully determines whether the determinate concept must be predicated or denied of it. A concept which is indeterminate and undeterminable, however, cannot be applied by means of any such rule, nor can it be made determinate by the invention of a rule. Thus, though it may serve a crucial function of concepts, and ground a valid claim to intersubjective agreement, it cannot allow a proof for an aesthetic judgment, that is, a simple decision on whether or not it is true of a given object by reference to the presence or absence of specific sensible properties.

This distinction is exactly what we would expect to find, given Kant's argument in the Analytic of the Beautiful, and its employment in the Dialectic of Aesthetic Judgment would seem to raise no problem. And it would not, if Kant went on to apply it in the way we would expect—namely, by classifying ordinary empirical concepts of objects, and possibly moral evaluations as well, as "determinable" concepts, and by saying that an object's "subjective finality," or its disposition to produce the free harmony between imagination and understanding, can be characterized only by an indeterminate and undeterminable concept. We should look for Kant to argue that aesthetic judgments do not admit of dispute because they are not based on determinate concepts, but that they do admit of contention and rational claims to intersubjective validity because they are based on the indeterminate concept of the harmony of the higher cognitive faculties, which provides a rational ground for expectation of intersubjective agreement without any proofs. But the concept of the harmony of the faculties is not what Kant now adduces as the indeterminate and undeterminable concept which founds aesthetic judgment. Instead, what he introduces into his argument is "the transcendental rational concept of the supersensible, which lies at the basis of all intuition [and] which, therefore, cannot be further theoretically determined."[18]

Nothing has prepared us for the connection of Kant's aesthetic theory to the metaphysical distinction between appearance and thing in itself, but Kant now argues as if aesthetic judgment's "enlarged relation of the representation of the object (and also of the subject) . . . on which we ground an extension of this kind of judgment as necessary for everyone," can only be founded on the basis of a concept of the noumenal reality which underlies both the object and the subject of taste. He argues thus:

> this [extension] must necessarily be founded upon some concept, but a concept which indeed cannot be determined through intuition, through which nothing can be known, and thus also from which no *proof* of the judgment of taste *can be drawn*. Just such a concept, however, is the mere pure rational concept of the supersensible which

grounds the object (and the judging subject as well) as object of sense, and thus as appearance. For if no regard were taken of such a concept, the judgment of taste's claim to universal validity could not be salvaged.[19]

Kant continues by maintaining that if the concept underlying the judgment of taste is supposed to be a concept of the understanding, then, even if like the rationalists we take the concept to be confused, it would be at least ideally possible to decide matters of taste by proofs. This contradicts the thesis of the antinomy, leaving us locked in a dialectical conflict.

> Now, however, all contradiction is abolished, if I say: the judgment of taste is grounded on a concept (of a ground in general of the subjective finality of nature for the faculty of judgment), from which, however, nothing can be known and proved with respect to the object, because [this concept] is in itself undeterminable and unsuitable for knowledge; however, it is at the same time from this very concept that the judgment derives validity for everyone (for each person, of course, as a singular judgment immediately accompanying intuition): for its determining ground perhaps lies in the concept of that which can be regarded as the supersensible substratum of mankind.[20]

Kant's argument asserts that if we are to retain the antithesis of his antinomy and allow any rational claim to the agreement of others, taste must have some conceptual ground; but if we are to avoid contradicting the thesis, we must recognize that this cannot be any determinate concept directly applicable to objects of sense. It must be a different sort of concept, and that means that it must be an indeterminate concept. Kant then proceeds as if the concept of the supersensible or noumenal ground of the existence of both subjects and objects of knowledge and taste were the *only* indeterminate concept available, and infers that it must be this concept which is the ground of judgments of taste. If taste must rest on an indeterminate concept, then it must rest on this one. This conclusion allows Kant to reveal the conflict in the antinomy of taste to be a mere illusion, for he can now suggest that the term "concept" is used in one sense in the thesis — referring to determinate concepts — and in another in the antithesis — referring to an indeterminate concept. And by revealing this illusion, he can save the theory of taste from the skepticism to which it would surely be suspect if its basic principles led to an inescapable contradiction.

However, Kant's argument is clearly invalid. For even if we do have a concept of the supersensible ground underlying both the object of taste and the phenomenally distinct subjects whose agreement we claim, it is not the only indeterminate concept that we have. The concept of the harmony of the faculties, or the subjective conditions of knowledge, is also an indeterminate concept as the latter has been defined, for by its very nature it cannot be specified by any rule; and, if Kant's deduction is valid, this concept meets the requirements imposed at the outset of the present argument. But the concept of the harmony of the faculties is clearly not identical with the concept of any supersensible object. The indeterminate concept of the harmony of the faculties, as we have seen, either is a purely epistemological concept, of the conditions under which manifolds of intuition can be unified, or is a psychological concept, of the mental state in which unity is felt to obtain. The concept of the supersensible, by contrast, is neither an epistemological nor a psychological concept, not being a concept of a property or state of any phenomenal object at all. Rather, it is an ontological concept, a concept of an object — an object of which, to be sure, we know little, but which we nevertheless think to be that which both empirical objects and empirical subjects are in themselves, or the ground of their existence.

The concepts of the harmony of the faculties and of the supersensible may both be concepts of the "ground" of experience, but they are concepts of very different sorts of grounds. The concept of the harmony of the faculties is meant to be a concept of the subjective condition of experience, a mental state or disposition of the faculties of a subject without which the consciousness of unity in manifolds that constitutes both ordinary experience and aesthetic response cannot obtain. The supersensible is not a condition of experience in this sense at all, but rather a putative explanatory ground of the objects involved in the state just described — the ground or real basis of the objects which provide manifolds of intuition and of the subjects which have and unify those manifolds. The supersensible is a concept not of epistemology but of ontology, and, it must be noted, of an ontology which did not have to be invoked earlier in Kant's argument. It now seems to be invoked either because a transcendental dialectic requires transcendental idealism, or because the suggestion that those who make judgments of taste share a common supersensible ground not only with the objects of their judgments but also with one another may be expected somehow to silence the skeptic.

It appears, then, that there is not only an intended equivocation in Kant's antinomy of taste, but also an unintended equivocation in his solution. But perhaps this is too harsh a conclusion. Several passages do suggest a connection between the two different indeterminate concepts which

Kant's arguments have employed, and Kant may have supposed that the reference to a supersensible ground of experience constitutes no addition in the theory of the Analytic. In the second of the paragraphs just quoted, Kant equated the concept of the "supersensible substratum of humanity" with the concept of a "ground in general of the subjective finality of nature for the faculty of judgment." If we take the ground of subjective finality to be the harmony of the faculties — that is, hold that subjective finality is attributed to an object because it produces this harmony — then it is a confusion to suppose that this ground must be anything supersensible, since the harmony of the faculties is not. But perhaps Kant thought of the subjective finality of nature as a state identical with the free play of the faculties, and thus assumed that the ground of either was some supersensible substratum; in this case, he may have supposed that thinking of the former required a concept of the latter, perhaps because the concept of an appearance always requires a concept of that object which it is in itself.[21]

This connection between the harmony of the faculties and a supersensible substratum is, however, tenuous, both in its substance and in its basis in the text. A more revealing passage is found in Kant's first remark to §57. This passage connects Kant's distinct indeterminate concepts of epistemology and ontology by means of his theory of genius.[22] On this theory, the human production of an object of beauty — that is, the production of an object of fine art — is the production of something which is subjectively final, or for which "rule and precept cannot . . . serve as the subjective standard for that aesthetic but unconditioned finality in fine art which must make a legitimate claim to being bound to please everyone." That is, a product of genius is an object which can neither be judged nor produced by reference to any determinate concept, but which yet pleases universally. But then, Kant argues, in products of genius it must be "nature (in the individual) and not a set purpose of art (of the production of the beautiful) which gives the rule." Actually, since neither the estimation nor the production of beauty can be explained by reference to determinate concepts, or "set purposes," nature — the realm beyond specific human intentions — must be the ultimate source for both. And with this assumption Kant then links the harmony of the faculties to the supersensible. Having denied that a standard for either the estimation or the production of beauty can be found in the realm of determinate concepts and intentions, he concludes that this standard must be found "in what is mere nature in the subject, but which cannot be comprehended under rules or concepts, that is to say, the supersensible substratum of all [the subject's] faculties (which no concept of understanding can attain), and consequently in that in relation to which all of our cognitive faculties are to be made harmonious, this being the ultimate end given by the intelligible [basis] of our nature."[23] In this passage, Kant effects a transition from his epistemological analysis of aesthetic response to the noumenal basis for taste which the Dialectic claims we must postulate by supposing that the objective involved in aesthetic response must have an ultimate ground, and introducing an intelligible or supersensible object to be that ground. Kant confirms our interpretation of his basic model of aesthetic response by describing the harmony of our cognitive faculties as an end set for us by our own nature; but whereas previously the existence of this general end of cognition was itself the ultimate presupposition of his aesthetic theory, he now suggests that the theory of taste cannot be complete until this end is given a metaphysical explanation. Until now, Kant's explanation of the occurrence of aesthetic response was confined to an analysis of its relations to the faculties, states of mind, and objectives involved in ordinary cognition; any puzzle as to why we should take pleasure in beautiful objects was to be resolved by showing how aesthetic response, in spite of its appearance, could be regarded as the satisfaction of an objective. Now, however, Kant seems to suppose that both the existence of that objective itself and the existence of objects which can satisfy it — whether products of nature in its ordinary form or in its guise as human genius — need explanation, which can be supplied only if we transcend the limits of the empirical world and the faculties needed to comprehend it, and instead invoke intimations of noumenal reality.

Supposing that a postulation of supersensible reality is needed to fully explain the existence of aesthetic response is not identical with supposing it necessary to fully justify aesthetic judgment, but the two suppositions surely support each other. Kant's introduction of the supersensible into aesthetic theory may also be facilitated by the ambiguity inherent in the claim that "no concept of the understanding attains" or suffices to represent the ground of aesthetic judgment. Such a concept can fail to comprehend the harmony of the faculties because the latter, though a state of the empirical self, does not occur under any determinate conditions; or a concept of the understanding could fail to comprehend an ultimate ground of aesthetic response because the latter is a noumenal object not given in empirical intuition at all. However, these two reasons for the inapplicability of ordinary determinate empirical concepts are quite distinct, and the fact that aesthetic response cannot be assigned determinate conditions does not in itself imply that its occurrence must be given any noumenal explanation.

Further, we must note, it is not only questionable whether there is any need for and force in a noumenal explanation of the harmony of the faculties; it is also dubious whether reference to a supersensible substratum can alleviate any of the difficulties that stand in the way of Kant's aesthetic theory. If there is one problem about the explanatory power of his model of aesthetic response, it is that it is hard to see how the possibility of the harmony of the faculties consists with the first *Critique*'s thesis that synthesis is always subject to concepts; and if there is one problem for Kant's deduction of aesthetic judgment, it is that a general similarity of human cognitive faculties does not seem to entail that we must all respond in the same way to particular objects. Supposing that there is an underlying ground for both the existence of our own cognitive constitution and the existence of various objects besides ourselves would not appear to resolve either of these issues.

Kant's basic model of the harmony of the faculties introduced an indeterminate concept as the basis of aesthetic judgment, which should have sufficed to resolve the antinomy of taste by permitting contention but not dispute over aesthetic judgments, but which required no reference to the ontology of transcendental idealism. Why should the resolution of this antinomy which Kant actually expounds invoke an idea of noumenal or supersensible reality? Section 57 and its remarks reveal several reasons. Part of Kant's motivation, it must be conceded, is his adherence to the architectonic of the first *Critique,* which dictates not only the inclusion of a dialectic in the third but also the assumption that such a dialectic can be resolved only by exploiting the distinction between appearances and things in themselves. This is revealed by the second remark to §57, where Kant emphasizes the claim that each of the higher faculties of the mind generates an antinomy which can be resolved only if the objects of ordinary experience are recognized to be mere phenomena. Thus:

> That there are three kinds of antinomies has its ground in there being three faculties of cognition: understanding, judgment, and reason, each of which (as a higher faculty of cognition) must have its *a priori* principles; since reason, insofar as it judges concerning these principles themselves and their use, in respect of them all inexorably demands the unconditioned for the given conditioned, which, however, cannot be found unless one regards the sensible as belonging to things in themselves and attributes it, as nothing more than mere appearance, to something supersensible (the intelligible substrate of nature outside and within us) as thing in itself.[24]

There is an antinomy for the understanding, for the faculty of pleasure and displeasure, and for the faculty of desire precisely insofar as all of these faculties, "in accord with an inescapable demand of reason, must be able to judge and determine their object *unconditionally*" by principles *a priori*. And, Kant insists, just as antinomies of understanding and reason are inevitable "if [their] judgments take no regard of a supersensible substratum of the given objects as appearance," but can be solved as soon as such regard is taken, so the same is the case with the antinomy of taste. If the distinction between appearances and things in themselves is not introduced, Kant asserts, we have none but the unsatisfactory alternatives explored by rationalist and empiricist aesthetics. Either judgments of taste have nothing but a groundless, even mad claim to necessary agreement based on mere induction, or else "the judgment of taste is really a disguised judgment of reason on the perfection discovered in a thing and the relation of its manifold to a purpose." In this case, the judgment is only called aesthetic "on account of the confusion that attaches to our reflection."[25]

However, Kant's suggestion that the antinomy of taste can be resolved only by the use of transcendental idealism is unpersuasive. Kant's argument depends on the supposition that aesthetic judgment, like cognitive and moral judgment, makes an unconditioned claim about its object which can be saved only if we suppose it to refer to its object as it is in itself. But it is far from clear that aesthetic judgment attempts to make an unconditional judgment about any object. If we take the object of aesthetic judgment to be the thing which it declares beautiful, then it is certain that it makes no judgment which must be understood to be about that object as a thing in itself. For Kant has insisted throughout that aesthetic judgment is distinguished from other forms of empirical judgment precisely by the fact that we are under no temptation to take it as being about objects even as they are in themselves empirically,[26] and that we instead regard it as concerning the relation of empirical objects to human feelings of pleasure and displeasure.[27] If it is part of the very concept of an aesthetic judgment that it concerns the relation of objects to our own faculties, then it would seem incoherent to suppose that such judgment could concern objects alone; and no use of transcendental idealism is needed to reveal this. And if we take the object of aesthetic judgment to be not the thing declared beautiful but rather the collection of subjects to whom agreement is imputed, it is equally unlikely that such judgment involves any unconditioned claim. Kant himself has insisted that the claim to universal validity is a mere imputation, or ideal claim; it is a claim which is explicitly subject to the conditions that one be correct in assigning one's pleasure to the harmony of the faculties, and that we in fact be capable of sharing knowledge with others,[28] and which is implicitly subject to the condition that the others whose agreement one claims themselves abstract from interest and material concerns. Aesthetic judgment has never pretended to make a claim about the totality of persons except subject to these conditions, let alone a claim about persons as they are in themselves. Its claim is essentially a claim about human faculties of cognition and feeling as they are manifested in experience. Aesthetic judgment, then, has been subject throughout to the condition that human faculties be constituted as they are, as well as — and this seems essential to Kant's entire argument — to the contingent existence of objects which can dispose these faculties to their state of free play.

It might be objected that the point of Kant's present argument is to insist on precisely this fact: that those thinking in commonplaces become confused just because they treat beauty as a property of things as they are in themselves, rather than as a property of our experience of things, and thus that the distinction between appearances and things in themselves is the only one which can resolve the antinomy of taste. But this will not do. Throughout the Analytic of the Beautiful, Kant's argument has been that beauty is not an empirical property of objects, or is not determined by their empirical concepts. To resolve the antinomy, all that is required is the concept of the harmony of the faculties, which itself requires only a distinction between *empirical* objects and the experience of such objects. The Analytic makes no use of Kant's ontological doctrine that the ordinary empirical properties of objects, even their spatial and temporal determinations, are themselves nothing but properties of mere appearance. Kant's reference to the unconditional demands of reason fails to alter this fact, for Kant's own analysis of the judgment of taste makes it an essentially conditional judgment.

Metaphysics and Skepticism

The mere fact that aesthetic judgment requires an indeterminate concept does not seem to be a sufficient ground for introducing any notion of a supersensible reality into Kant's argument, and his claim that reason must postulate an unconditioned reality as the object of this judgment is even less compelling. Kant's deepest reason for the introduction of a noumenal basis for taste, however, is probably neither of these, but the feeling that only the suggestion of a metaphysical ground for harmony both among subjects and between subjects and objects will really silence the skepticism which is engendered by the antinomy of taste. This is revealed when §57 argues that the concept of a general ground for the subjective finality of nature will serve as a determining ground for the judgment of taste, not because it is the concept of a mental state common to all humans insofar as they are capable of knowledge at all, but because it is a concept of "that which may be regarded as the supersensible substratum of mankind."[29] This implies that the ground of aesthetic judgment is not merely an epistemological or psychological condition shared by all persons insofar as they are capable of cognition, but rather an aspect of the ultimate reality of all humans—a property of what they are in themselves quite apart from how they may appear to differ. A supersensible substratum is not something which can be attributed to human beings only conditionally on their possession of certain capabilities. It must be something which everyone possesses just in virtue of being human at all. And if the capability for aesthetic response in general, as well as the existence of harmony between human subjects and particular objects of beauty, is dictated by the nature of this supersensible substratum, then there can hardly be any doubt that we may speak with a universal voice even when we come to particulars in matters of taste.

Should the skeptic accept the postulation of such a supersensible substratum, he would be more effectively silenced than he was by any of Kant's previous arguments. He would be so primarily because the idea of a supersensible substratum of humanity intimates a metaphysical guarantee for the ultimate likeness of all human beings. But Kant's resolution of the antinomy of taste also suggests the possibility of a metaphysical guarantee of a predetermined harmony between human being and nature as well as between human being and human being. Kant does this by substituting the phrase "supersensible substratum of appearances" for the phrase "supersensible substratum of humanity." Thus, after grounding taste on the latter, he goes on to argue that if the antinomy of taste is to be resolved, "in its thesis it should therefore read: the judgment of taste is not grounded on *determinate* concepts, but in its antithesis: the judgment of taste is grounded on a concept, although an *indeterminate* one (that, namely, of the supersensible substratum of appearances); and then there would be no conflict between them."[30] Kant's whole argument in §57 depends on the assumption that there is only one indeterminate concept which can serve as the ground of aesthetic judgment; clearly, then, the concepts of the supersensible substratum of humanity and the supersensible substratum of appearances must in fact be identical, and either may then be invoked in defense of aesthetic judgment. But if this is the case, the intersubjective validity of aesthetic judgment does not rest only on the metaphysical likeness shared by all persons. The experience of beauty, or the harmony between nature's forms and our own responses which constitutes the subjective finality of nature for our power of judgment, would also be guaranteed by the ultimate identity of the supersensible substrata of both humanity and nature. This conclusion would further support the intersubjective validity of aesthetic judgment by cementing the experience of beauty to the metaphysical basis of the relation between human beings and nature.

Kant's intention of anchoring both the existence of beauty and the intersubjective validity of its experience to the same metaphysical foundation, as well as his bald substitution of metaphysics for epistemology, is plainly exposed at the end of §57's second remark. Here Kant maintains:

> But if our deduction is at least conceded as much as being on the right track, even if it has not yet been made sufficiently clear in all its details, then three ideas are revealed: firstly, the supersensible in general, without further determination, as substratum of nature; *secondly,* this very same [supersensible], as principle of the subjective finality of nature for our cognitive faculties; *thirdly,* again the same [supersensible], as principle of the ends of freedom, and principle of the harmony of these [principles] with those in the moral sphere.[31]

On Kant's moral theory, of course, the ends of freedom are the regard for intersubjective validity which constitutes the test of moral maxims. Kant apparently believes, then, not only that there is a single metaphysical ground for both the existence of beauty and agreement about it, but also that there is a single ultimate ground for both taste and morality.

The latter belief I will consider in the next chapter; for the moment, we need only note that in suggesting that it is the idea of the supersensible which provides the right track for his deduction, Kant does imply that this idea of an ultimate metaphysical guarantee can furnish answers for both of the questions to which the deduction of aesthetic judgment might have been addressed: the question of intersubjective validity, which is its real concern, as well as the question of the existence of beauty, a matter, I have argued, which must remain contingent, but which Kant nevertheless apparently feels drawn to explain.

Needless to say, the indeterminate idea of a supersensible substratum can resolve the antinomy of taste and provide the ultimate deduction of aesthetic judgment only if it is accepted. That the skeptic who has been unpersuaded by Kant's earlier arguments will be even more suspicious of this idea, and that no modern reader will find it very attractive, are, I think, too obvious to require any argument; Kant's theory of taste must survive by its epistemological analysis of aesthetic judgment if it is to survive at all. What does call for comment, however, is the fact that Kant himself immediately places some qualification on §57's flight into metaphysics. He does this in §58, and we must now consider how much of §57's remarkable suggestion this section takes back.

Section 58 is meant to establish the "idealism of the finality of nature as well as of art, as the unique principle of the faculty of aesthetic judgment,"[32] and this statement reveals the extent of Kant's qualification of §57: Kant hedges on the suggestion that we may adopt a noumenal explanation for the existence of beauty, but not on his intimation of a supersensible ground for intersubjective validity. Kant begins with some terminology for classifying aesthetic theories. First, officially though belatedly, he distinguishes the "empiricism" of taste from its "rationalism": under the first classification falls any theory which allows taste only empirical grounds of determination, and which thus allows no distinction between the beautiful and the agreeable; under the second classification falls any theory which concedes that taste may "judge on an *a priori* ground." Rationalist theories which assume that aesthetic judgment rests on determinate concepts, however, allow no distinction between the beautiful and the good.[33] But there can also be "grounds of delight which are *a priori* . . . which cannot be grasped by *determinate concepts*," and these make possible a rationalist theory of taste which does not obliterate the distinction between the beautiful and the good. Obviously, Kant's own theory is a rationalist theory of this variety. Next, Kant maintains that we may also distinguish between "realism" and "idealism" in theories of taste. By this time he assumes that the reader is convinced that "beauty is no property of the object, considered in itself," so he does not use the distinction between realism and idealism to make this point. Instead, Kant uses the distinction between realism and idealism to make a distinction between two interpretations of subjective finality. Realism is the view that subjective finality is the result of an "actual (intentional) *purpose* of nature (or art) to harmonize with our faculty of judgment"; idealism is the view that subjective finality is an "independently and contingently originating final harmony with the need of our faculty of judgment in regard to nature."[34]

The beautiful forms so prevalent in the realm of organized nature speak well for the hypothesis of aesthetic realism, or the thesis that their existence can only be explained by the postulation of an actual intention—which could obviously be found not in the empirical objects of nature, but only in its supersensible substratum. But, Kant now maintains, "reason, with its maxims always to avoid as far as possible the unnecessary multiplication of principles, sets itself against this assumption."[35] Further, the mechanical processes of nature are actually sufficient to explain the existence of whatever natural forms we do encounter, as Kant illustrates with a lengthy discussion of the phenomenon of crystallization.[36] He concludes that "without taking anything away from the teleological principle for the estimation of an organization, it can well be thought that, as far as the beauty of the forms and the colors of flowers, the plumage of birds, and shells is concerned, this may be attributed to nature and its capacity, in its freedom without any particular guiding purposes, for originating aesthetically final forms even by, [e.g.,] chemical laws."[37] In other words, the actual existence of beautiful forms in nature does not require us to attribute any actual intentions to nature or its creator. We need not adopt realism with respect to natural beauty, but may adhere to the view that there is a purely contingent correspondence between the appearance of nature and our own faculties. But this is just to say that we do not need to go beyond our understanding of nature as phenomena governed by empirical laws to explain the existence of beautiful objects, insofar as we are called upon to offer any explanation of their existence at all. The existence of beautiful objects in nature requires no supersensible substratum to account for something left unexplained by our empirical sciences. Section 57's intimation that it is only by the assumption of a single supersensible substratum underlying both ourselves and nature that we can explain why the latter presents us with beautiful objects appears to be withdrawn.

But even while he states this strict qualification on one speculation of §57, Kant apparently retains that section's claim that we can explain the possibility of taste only if we acknowledge the supersensible basis of our own faculties. Even in denying that the existence of natural beauty requires us to attribute any ends to it, Kant continues to imply that the universal validity of aesthetic judgment must have a metaphysical explanation. This emerges in Kant's final statement of idealism with regard to natural beauty: "The property of nature, that it contains the opportunity for us to perceive inner finality in the relation of our mental faculties in the estimation of certain of its products, and indeed such a finality as should be declared necessarily and universally valid on the basis of a supersensible ground, cannot be a purpose of nature, or, rather, estimated by us as such."[38] The suggestion stands that taste's claim to intersubjective validity requires the supposition of a noumenal ground for the free harmony of our faculties, which by its very nature will secure the identity of those faculties among us in spite of our phenomenal differences. The qualification of this stance which we might have expected to find in §58's statement of idealism is not forthcoming. Instead, we must conclude that in the end Kant overstepped the limits of his own epistemology in an attempt at least to hint at a kind of guarantee for aesthetic judgment that his original deduction could not provide.

As we have seen, Kant's deduction does indeed fall short of providing an absolute guarantee for the universal validity of aesthetic judgment. But insofar as the Dialectic of Aesthetic Judgment tries to buttress Kant's justification of the rationality of aesthetic judgment with ontological intimations, it provides a far less acceptable guarantee. And insofar as the Dialectic invokes the supersensible to resolve the antinomy of taste, it does so unnecessarily, for Kant's notion of the harmony of the faculties and the deduction based on that concept do a far better job of explaining how taste is not a matter of dispute but of rational contention, or reasonable claims to and discussions of intersubjectively valid aesthetic responses. The metaphysics of the Dialectic make no real contribution to Kant's theory of the universal voice; we must now consider whether Kant's attempt to connect taste and moral judgment does any better.

11

Aesthetics and Morality

****

Completing the Deduction?

For most of this study, my concern with Kant's theory of taste has been essentially epistemological. I have considered Kant's view on how reflection on one's own aesthetic response could entitle one to hold beliefs about the pleasures of other persons, for it is the justifiability of such beliefs that Kant's analysis of aesthetic judgment as a claim to intersubjective validity requires. Kant's deduction of aesthetic judgment obviously attempted to provide an *a priori* basis for such beliefs about the mental states of others, and was thus best approached if we understood the "should" in aesthetic judgment[1] in epistemological terms. What we claim in aesthetic judgment is that, under ideal circumstances, everyone presented with a given object would take pleasure in it; so what we need from a deduction of this judgment is a justification for the assertion of such a claim.

But, as we saw, Kant's deduction falls short of a conclusive justification of aesthetic judgment. Thus it is not unnatural to look for something beyond taste's link to the theory of knowledge from which its claim to intersubjective validity might draw support. The obvious place to look is in the connections which Kant draws between aesthetic judgment and morality. As early as §22, it will be recalled, Kant suggested that the basis of aesthetic judgment might lie not in a necessary condition of the possibility of experience, but in "a still higher principle of reason."[2] Although I considered whether a higher function of *theoretical* reason might support aesthetic judgment, the natural reading of this passage is that aesthetic judgment may somehow have its ultimate foundation in *practical* reason. In concluding his main attempt at the deduction of aesthetic judgment, Kant again—and more explicitly—suggested that the complete justification of taste's claim to intersubjective validity may require reference to practical reason. Thus the last paragraph of §40: "If one could assume that the mere universal communicability of his feeling must of itself carry with it an interest for us (an assumption, however, which one is not entitled to conclude from the character of a merely reflective judgment): one would then be in a position to explain how the feeling in the judgment of taste comes to be exacted from everyone as a sort of duty."[3] This seems to state quite clearly that the way in which aesthetic judgment imputes the feeling of pleasure to others — namely, as a "sort of duty" — cannot be explained in epistemological terms alone, or from its mere character as a reflective judgment. Instead, it appears, we must appeal to some kind of interest to explain this imputation. Such an interest, of course, cannot be a privately valid or personal interest; so the only possibility is that taste's imputation of agreement in pleasure must have some foundation in an interest of morality.

These allusions to duty and the higher interest of reason have led some commentators to the view that Kant's justification of aesthetic judgment's claim to intersubjective validity is completed only with his connection of aesthetics and ethics. Thus Donald Crawford has written that the passage just quoted reveals that "the full import of a judgment of taste is not justified simply by the deduction that the basis of judgment is universally communicable,"[4] and that "Kant explicitly declares that what he is after — what the complete deduction requires — is 'a means of passing from sense enjoyment to moral feeling' . . . This transition constitutes the final stage in the transcendental deduction of judgments of taste."[5] In a similar vein, R. K. Elliott has written that

> taste is grounded not on a pre-existing common sense but on an Idea of Reason which, in conjunction with the moral analogy, sets a universal community of taste before us as a regulative idea, to be realized whether or not common sense exists as a condition of experience . . . The connexion with the moral does not destroy the autonomy of Taste but ensures its possibility. If it were not for the moral analogy there could be no judgments of taste, but only private preferences and judgments of objective perfection.[6]

In the course of his argument for this conclusion, Elliott goes beyond reference to the suggestions of §§22 and 40 and claims that Kant "says explicitly that it is only through the analogical connection between the beautiful and the good that the judgment of taste has any right to claim universality and necessity."[7*] The explicit statement to which Elliott refers appears to be this claim of Kant's: "Now I say: the beautiful is the symbol of the morally good, and only in this respect (that of a relation which is natural to everyone, and which may also be imputed to everyone else as a duty) does it please with a claim to the agreement of everyone else."[8] Just what relation Kant thinks is natural to all and also imputable as a duty is none too clear, but it seems to be either the relation of beauty to the morally good as a symbol of the latter, or the perception of this symbolism. By referring us to this passage, then, Elliott commits himself to the view with which Crawford also concludes his investigation of Kant's link between aesthetics and ethics: the view that perception or sensitivity to beauty may be demanded of everyone because beauty is a symbol of the morally good, and sensitivity to such a symbol may be demanded as part of the demand of morality itself. Thus Crawford's summary of the deduction of aesthetic judgment is that "our judgments marking the pleasure in the beautiful (and the sublime, too) can rightfully demand universal assent, not simply because they can be based on what can be universally communicated, but because they mark an experience of that which symbolizes morality."[9] Only with Kant's argument that the beautiful is a symbol of the morally good can his deduction be completed.

This would be a remarkable conclusion for an argument which began by asserting the total independence of aesthetic judgment from any interest of sense or reason. But before we consider whether the beautiful can serve as a symbol of the good or whether the experience of a symbol of morality can be rightfully demanded of anyone, there are some more fundamental questions which must be confronted. We must ask just what claim has to be supported if the task of the deduction is to be accomplished. This question cannot be ignored, for, as we have seen, Kant makes two different claims about the intersubjective validity of aesthetic judgment. First, Kant's theory includes an analysis of the claim that an object is beautiful according to which such a judgment is justified only if the pleasure occasioned by that object can be regarded as universally and necessarily valid. Second, Kant's theory offers an explanation of aesthetic response, a theory of pleasure according to which we are in fact justified in claiming such intersubjective validity for certain feelings of pleasure. Thus Kant's theory of taste includes both a demand for universal subjective agreement and a basis for the rational expectation of such agreement. The argument for the demand for agreement turned on the evidence of linguistic usage about either the meaning of the word "beautiful" or the requirements of the judgmental form ". . . is beautiful"; the argument for the rational expectation of such agreement—that is, for the possibility of compliance with the demand of the judgment of taste—turned on the explanation of aesthetic pleasure as due to the harmony of the faculties and the deduction of the intersubjective validity of that state itself.

There are thus two distinct elements of Kant's theory of taste which might draw support from a link between aesthetics and morality. A connection between aesthetic and moral judgment might justify us in *demanding* agreement in judgments of taste, or it might justify us in *expecting* such agreement under the appropriate conditions. Rightfully demanding something of others and reasonably expecting it of them are obviously different, so we must raise the question — which neither Crawford nor Elliott does — of whether a link to morality can support one or both of these elements. This is particularly important because the deduction of the judgment of taste, carefully defined, concerns only the justification of the *expectation* of agreement in taste, yet §40 most obviously suggests that morality may play a part in taste's *demand* for agreement. Showing that its link to morality can complete the deduction of aesthetic judgment would require proof that this connection can validate not only the demand of agreement from others but the expectation of it as well; the question of the success of this link is thus, I think it fair to say, already more complex than Kant's commentators have supposed.

We must also note that there are different ways in which we can demand something of someone. We may demand someone's concurrence in a linguistic practice, as a condition of recognizing him as a competent speaker, or in a belief, as a condition of taking his assertions seriously. Or we may demand certain actions or performances of a person, possibly subject to some prior condition, such as his having made a promise, or possibly subject to no conditions at all. There may well be some penalties attached to failure to comply with the first sort of demand, but such failure will hardly be considered breach of duty. In other words, we may make demands on others as speakers or knowers, or as agents, and we may make our demands hypothetically or categorically. Whether the rationality of demanding certain responses from others as speakers or knowers can derive support from the justifiability of demanding certain performances from them as agents must certainly be open to question.[10*]

Whether a link to morality might support aesthetic judgment's demand for concurrence or its expectation of agreement is not the only question which must be made explicit before the validity of this link can be considered. Another question is this: even if an analogy with moral judgment can justify us in either demanding or expecting of others *something* pertaining to aesthetic judgment, just what would this be? If the link to morality is to bear on the task of the deduction, the answer to this question should be the feeling of pleasure in a particular object, since it is always such a particular feeling which the judgment of taste imputes to others and which we must be justified in demanding and expecting of them. The analogy with ethics, in other words, should be expected to justify the demand and imputation of particular feelings to others. But this expectation must be carefully distinguished from two other possibilities: that a connection between taste and morality support us insofar as we demand or impute to others a general capacity for aesthetic response; and that it support us insofar as we demand or impute to others a faculty of taste. The difference between supposing that the general capacity for taking pleasure in beauty is shared and that particular aesthetic responses are intersubjectively valid must be obvious by now. And it should also be clear that Kant's theory of taste requires us to distinguish between the mere occurrence of a pleasure and the recognition of its origin and intersubjective validity; so we must distinguish between demanding or attributing to others the capacity for feeling pleasure in particular circumstances, and the capability for discriminating among pleasures, or actually making aesthetic judgments. Thus we must determine whether taste's analogy with morality can bear on the imputation of pleasures to others, or on the imputation of taste as a faculty for reflecting on pleasures. The thesis of the deduction of aesthetic judgment suggests that its connection with practical reason should bear on the first issue; but the actual content of Kant's analogy may suggest a bearing on the second.

This distinction may be obscured by ambiguity in the concept of taste itself, and even Kant can be confused on just what the possession of taste entails. In §40, Kant carefully describes taste as a capacity for making discriminations about pleasures rather than for feeling pleasure itself; thus taste is defined "as the faculty of estimating what makes our feeling in a given representation *universally communicable* without the mediation of a concept."[11] On this definition, imputing taste to someone might mean imputing to him a discriminatory attitude toward his pleasures, rather than actually imputing particular pleasures to him. But Kant also describes taste not as a faculty for estimating pleasures but as a faculty for having certain kinds of pleasures. Thus the Introduction to the *Metaphysics of Morals* distinguishes pleasure which "may be the cause or effect of desire" from "pleasure, which is not necessarily connected with the desire of an object, which is at basis not a pleasure in the existence of the object of representation, but rather adheres to the representation alone, [and which] can be called merely contemplative pleasure or *passive delight*"; and Kant then claims that "the feeling of the latter kind of pleasure is called *taste*."[12] The imputation of taste to others on this definition would mean the imputation of pleasure itself rather than discriminatory capacity. Given the ease with which Kant himself could confuse the concept of taste, then, we must certainly consider whether any given analogy between aesthetics and ethics bears directly on the imputation of pleasure, or whether it does not instead bear on the imputation of a discriminative faculty of taste to others. In the latter case, the analogy's bearing on the imputation of particular pleasures, and perhaps even on that of the general capacity for aesthetic response, might be at best indirect.

Two more distinctions must be made before Kant's actual exposition of the analogy may be considered. First, we must distinguish between the possibility that a connection between aesthetic judgment and practical reason might provide a further reason to expect or demand agreement in the pure judgment of taste itself, and the possibility that such a connection might provide the basis for some additional and not purely aesthetic pleasure in the objects of taste. Kant's view of pure judgments of taste, of course, is that they concern feelings of pleasure connected to neither antecedent nor consequent interests in the existence of objects — they neither depend upon nor occasion such interests. Though Kant actually offered no reason to accept the second conjunct of this thesis, he was explicitly committed to it, and his own intentions for the analogy between aesthetics and morality must be interpreted accordingly. But that means that if this connection provides a reason for an interest in the existence of beautiful objects and founds a universal demand or expectation of agreement about such objects on this interest, it will not automatically furnish a basis for the imputation of disinterested pleasure required by a pure judgment of taste. Practical reason might provide an intersubjectively valid basis for an interested pleasure in beautiful objects, but that will have to be regarded as additional to purely aesthetic pleasure, and its intersubjective validity will not be direct evidence for the validity of the latter. Perhaps the intersubjective validity of some form of morally grounded pleasure in the beautiful will provide indirect support for the validity of aesthetic response which is at issue in Kant's deduction, but the difference between aesthetic response to an object and an interest in its existence entails that such support must be indirect.

Finally, the question of possible support for the intersubjective validity of pleasure in beautiful objects from the realm of practical reason must be distinguished from the question of whether these objects themselves, especially beautiful works of art, must have some sort of moral content or significance. There are several remarks in later sections of the *Critique of Judgment* which suggest that Kant did affirm such moral content, in spite of his earlier distinction between free and dependent beauty. But since this is a different thesis from either the thesis that there is a sufficient analogy between moral and aesthetic judgment to provide a basis for the intersubjective validity of the latter, or the thesis that there is an intersubjectively valid moral interest in the existence of the beautiful, whether or not it has any sort of content at all, I will not consider this thesis part of the analogy between aesthetic *judgment* and moral *judgment* itself. I will turn to the issue of the moral content of art only briefly at the end of this chapter.[13*]

Beauty and the Disposition to Morality

Now that I have distinguished the different ways in which an analogy with morality might bear on the intersubjective validity of aesthetic judgment, the simplest way to consider Kant's actual development of the link will be by a serial discussion of the various passages in which he expounds it.

Kant's first explicit consideration of a possible analogy actually precedes the Deduction of Pure Aesthetic Judgment, and is found in the "General Remark on the Exposition of Aesthetic Reflective Judgment" which he provides in §29 of the Analytic of the Sublime. Here, Kant makes two different points.

The first point emerges in a discussion of differences between the distinct objects of pleasure, the agreeable, the beautiful and sublime, and the morally good. The agreeable, as usual, is nothing but the cause of "mere enjoyment" dependent on the "mass of the agreeable sensation." The beautiful is the object of "finality in the feeling of pleasure"; the sublime, "the sensible estimated as useful in the representation of nature for a possible supersensible employment." Finally, Kant considers the bearing of the "absolutely good" on the feeling of pleasure or displeasure: it is to be "estimated subjectively according to the feeling it inspires" or as the "object of the moral feeling." In this connection, the significance of moral feeling is that it reveals "the determinability of the powers of the subject by means of the representation of an *absolutely necessitating* law." On the basis of this claim, Kant then remarks on the following analogy. Having stated that the effect on feeling in the case of the absolutely good "is not attributed to nature but to freedom," Kant continues:

But the *determinability of the subject* by this idea [of freedom] — and, indeed, of a subject which in its sensibility can be conscious of *hindrances* but also of its superiority over them by its subjugation of them, through *modifications of its state,* that is, the moral feeling — is so closely related with aesthetic judgment and its formal conditions, that [the moral feeling] can serve to make the conformity to law of action from duty representable as aesthetic, that is, as sublime or even as beautiful, without sacrificing its purity; which could not be the case if one were to place [the moral feeling] in natural connection with the feeling of the agreeable.[14]

The tortured construction of this lengthy sentence makes its translation difficult, but its point is clear enough. Moral feeling is the effect of the formal concepts of morality on the otherwise merely natural feelings of pleasure and pain connected with the existence of objects or actions; its production is thus analogous to the way in which the formal conditions of knowledge produce an effect on the faculty of pleasure and pain in aesthetic response, so we may use the predicates of aesthetic judgment to characterize moral feeling without introducing any inappropriate naturalism into ethical evaluation.

But if this is the content of the present analogy, then it does not entail that the intersubjective validity of aesthetic judgment may be supported by the universal validity of moral judgment. An analogy between the production of feeling in aesthetic and moral judgment allows us to use terms for the former to characterize the latter, but there are no real relations of dependence between the two kinds of feeling themselves. Aesthetic feeling is not a necessary condition of moral feeling, nor is the latter a necessary condition of the former; nor does the analogy imply any connection between the capabilities for experiencing these two different sorts of pleasure. There is thus no obvious way in which the present analogy might employ the intersubjective validity of moral feeling — which, in any case, has not been mentioned — to defend the validity of aesthetic response. It should also be noted that Kant himself insists on an important disanalogy between the two forms of feeling, for he precedes the passage just quoted with the statement that moral feeling is "especially distinguished" from other feelings, that of the beautiful included, "by the *modality* of a necessity resting on *a priori* concepts, which contain not a mere *claim,* but also a *command* of approval from everyone."[15] This suggests that the claim in aesthetic judgment *cannot* be considered anything like a moral command for agreement. Thus the present analogy does not promise to advance the thesis that either the demand or the attribution of agreement in aesthetic judgment may receive support from its analogy with moral judgment. Rather, contrary to the intimation of §40, it suggests that agreement in aesthetic response cannot be regarded as any sort of duty.

The first analogy between aesthetic and moral judgment, then, seems designed to supplement the characterization of moral feeling, but not the theory of taste itself. In the final paragraph of the page from which I have been quoting, however, Kant suggests a second and stronger connection between aesthetic response and moral feeling than that of mere analogy. Here he says that the beautiful and the sublime, "both united in the same subject, are final in relation to the moral feeling. The beautiful prepares us to love something, even nature, apart from any interest; the sublime, to treasure something, even in opposition to our own (sensuous) interest."[16] This passage implies not merely that the nature of aesthetic response makes possible the employment of aesthetic predicates for the description of moral feeling, but that it may actually serve the purpose of moral feeling itself, or aid us in attaining its end — presumably, moral action. Finding that aesthetic response is final with respect to the ends of practical reason, even if not directly based on any such end, would certainly raise the possibility that at least the demand for aesthetic response has a deeper basis than linguistic usage. If the experience of the beautiful is not just analogous to the feeling of being determined by moral law, but actually assists in the development of a disposition suitable for moral action, then aesthetic response may be a means to an end legitimately required by practical reason itself. But it seems that if an end may be legitimately demanded of everyone, so may the means to it be universally required. Thus aesthetic judgment's connection with the disposition to morality would create a new ground for its demand that everyone experience pleasure in beauty.

I will reserve a full assessment of this argument until all of Kant's attempts to expound it have been considered, but will make several general points about it now. The first concerns the question: how does this argument stand with respect to the distinction with which I began this chapter? Most obviously, it supports the justifiability of demanding agreement in aesthetic response, rather than the rationality of expecting such agreement. By describing aesthetic response as final with respect to moral feeling, Kant suggests that it might reasonably be demanded as a means to the latter; but this does not imply that the expectation of agreement in taste has a basis not just in the general conditions for the communication of cognition but in a shared capability for moral feeling as well. This is not to say that such an argument might not be made, but only to point out that Kant gives no hint of one here. Otherwise, however, the present link between aesthetics and morality does seem relevant to the deduction of aesthetic judgment. Thus the fact that aesthetic judgment demands at least a certain capacity for feeling from others is paralleled by the fact that in the case of moral feeling an ability to experience pleasure under certain conditions (apart from or even against any sensuous interest) can apparently be required of other persons. That is, it is aesthetic response itself rather than the discriminatory faculty of taste which is being demanded of other persons. My second point is that the present argument does suggest a reason for demanding aesthetic response itself from others, rather than some further feeling of pleasure. Although the demand for agreement in taste is now being based on its finality or usefulness *for* moral feeling, this finality is founded precisely on the fact that aesthetic response is a pleasure experienced apart from the consciousness of any interest; thus what may be demanded of others on the basis of this finality must be aesthetic response itself rather than some additional but interested response to the existence of beautiful objects. Finally, the argument of §29 does not imply that beauty must have a moral content. It turns on the structure of the experience of aesthetic response, and is obviously meant to be compatible with the conception of free beauty as a purely formal object of disinterested pleasure.

On first glance, then, the only problem for this connection between aesthetics and morality appears to be that it grounds the demand for agreement in aesthetic response rather than the rational imputation of such response to others. In fact, however, two other problems must be considered. The essence of the present suggestion is that the formal similarity between aesthetic response and moral feeling makes the development of the ability to experience the former conducive to the disposition to experience the latter; as an experience conducive to the possibility of moral action, then, aesthetic response may be demanded of other persons. But, first, is moral feeling itself something that may legitimately be demanded of others? Kant's references to moral feeling in §29 and elsewhere in the *Critique of Judgment* may suggest that moral feeling is a necessary component of moral action, but his ethical theory also distinguishes actions' being done out of any particular feeling from their being done simply with a certain intention—that of conforming to duty. On the standard reading, Kant's ethics demands that persons act conformably to duty and with the intention of conforming to duty, but not that they act with any particular feeling. And even if one could demand that they act with a certain feeling, this would be at best the mixed feeling of respect which is a *motive* for moral action, and not this moral feeling, which appears to be an unmixed pleasure *resulting* from moral action. But if this is so, then one cannot directly demand that other persons experience moral feeling itself, and the legitimacy of demanding of them yet *another* form of feeling because it conduces to moral feeling must also be questioned.

Second, even if moral feeling could be rightfully demanded of others, there would still be the problem of demanding of them another feeling just because it might be conducive to the first. Does the finality of aesthetic response with respect to moral feeling mean that the experience of pleasure in the beautiful (or sublime) is a *necessary* condition for the development of the capability for moral feeling, or only that it is a *sufficient* condition, or merely that it is a *conducive* but not a sufficient condition? If the experience of aesthetic response is anything short of a necessary condition for the disposition to moral feeling, then the legitimacy of demanding it of others because of its finality for moral feeling would be compromised; but nothing Kant has so far said is strong enough to imply that the connection between the two cases of feeling is necessary. Of course, if the capacity for aesthetic response were connected with that for moral feeling, and we had a reasonable expectation of the latter capacity in everyone, then we might have an argument for the *expectation* of aesthetic response in others even without a legitimate basis for *demanding* it of them.

Moral Interest in the Beautiful

Leaving aside for the moment these general questions about the real character of Kant's ethical theory and about the possible strength of any link between his analysis of taste and that theory, I turn to Kant's next approach to the connection between aesthetic judgment and morality. This is found in §§41 and 42, immediately following §40's question of whether an interest in communicability might explain how we come to exact taste from everyone as a sort of duty. Before we consider the two possibilities of "empirical" and "intellectual" interest in the beautiful, however, Kant's topics in §§41 and 42, we may note that the mere formulation of §40's question itself suggests that any support that they might lend to the thesis of the deduction must be complex. The hypothesis of §40 is that some interest in the communicability of our feeling in general may explain the demand for the "feeling in the judgment of taste" from others. A complex argument will be needed to convince us that the deduction may be supplemented by this hypothesis because the obvious consequence of an interest in the communicability of our feeling will be a demand that everyone have a regard for the communicability of his feelings, rather than that everyone have a particular feeling; and even if we leave this aside, an interest in communicability appears more likely to ground a demand for the experience of a feeling which might be the topic of communication rather than a rational expectation of that feeling in others. Whether Kant's argument in §§41 and 42 can buttress the *deduction* of aesthetic judgment rather than the *analysis* of that judgment's demand for universal subjective validity is far from obvious.

The opening of §41's discussion of the "empirical interest in the beautiful" does not bode well for the further deduction of aesthetic judgment. Kant starts by asserting that it has been sufficiently proven that the judgment that something is beautiful "must have no interest as its *determining ground,*" but that this does not entail that an interest of some kind cannot enter into combination with pure aesthetic judgment. Such a combination, Kant maintains, "can never be anything but indirect," which implies that "taste must . . . first of all be represented in conjunction with something else, in order to connect with the delight in mere reflection upon an object a further *pleasure in the existence* of the object (as that wherein all interest consists)."[17] This suggests two points: first, that what an empirical interest in the beautiful concerns and may ground is not a reason for attributing aesthetic response itself to others, but some additional pleasure in the existence of beautiful objects; second, that the way in which such an interest will work is by means of a basis for interest in the possession of taste, the ability to make discriminations about pleasures, rather than by any direct bearing on the feeling of pleasure itself. In that case, any support for the demand or imputation of particular aesthetic responses that might be drawn from an empirical interest in the beautiful must be indirect. Such an interest will first bear on the possession of taste, and then require some further argument to take us from the demand and imputation of taste in general to a demand and imputation of pleasure in response to any specific object.

But to continue Kant's argument: if we are to go beyond the mere judgment of taste to an interest in the existence of its object, taste must be combined with something else, and a candidate for the latter role is required. There are, according to Kant, two possibilities. "This other can be something empirical, namely, an inclination proper to human nature"; that is, taste may enter into combination with some psychological component of human nature, as part of the realm of nature in general, which can be known only empirically. Or taste may be combined with "something intellectual, as a property of the will through which it is capable of rational determination *a priori*"; taste may be connected with the laws of freedom rather than the laws of nature, and the connection may be open to *a priori* rather than merely empirical knowledge. In either case, Kant himself points out, the new factor will explain "a delight in the existence of the object, and so furnish the ground for an interest in that which has already pleased of itself and without regard to any interest."[18] Even if an interest in the existence of the beautiful is the subject of an intersubjectively valid demand or imputation, Kant implies, some argument will still be needed to extend that validity to the disinterested response and judgment of taste itself.

An interest founded on an element of human nature which is known only empirically — an empirical interest — is the candidate for connection with taste which is considered in the rest of §41. Kant argues that there is an empirical interest in the beautiful which exists only in society. It is founded on an "impulse to society natural to mankind," a "natural inclination" to existence in society which produces an interest in both the state of social existence and the property of "sociability," or the "suitability for and the propensity to" social existence. Whatever might conduce to the satisfaction of this inclination becomes the object of an interest by the natural laws of inclination and pleasure. A faculty through which "one can communicate even his *feeling* to everyone else" falls under this description, since the communication of feeling can promote the existence of sociability. Thus such a faculty will become the object of an interest founded on the natural inclination to society, "as a means of promoting that which the natural inclination of everyone requires."[19]

Though Kant had long believed in the existence of such an inclination,[20] the later paragraphs of §9 placed strict limitations on the significance for the deduction of aesthetic judgment of any interest it might found.[21] Thus we already know what Kant shortly asserts, namely, that an interest founded on such an empirically known inclination can be the subject only of empirical claims, and cannot advance the case for any genuinely *a priori* claim of taste. But, even if there were not this problem about its epistemological status, could a natural inclination to society furnish a link between aesthetic and moral judgment that could supplement the deduction of the former? Kant's exposition does not make it obvious that it could, for he goes on to explain only an interest in the possession of the faculty of taste itself rather than an additional basis for belief in even the ideal unanimity of particular aesthetic responses. The basic conclusions which Kant draws from the existence of the natural inclination to society are that one "is not quite satisfied with an object if his delight in it cannot be felt in communion with others," and that "one expects and requires of everyone a regard to universal communication . . . just as if it were required by an original contract dictated by humanity itself."[22] In other words, the inclination to society creates an interest in the means to society, among which is a regard to universal communicability; so such a regard is demanded of others, though on the basis of a mere inclination rather than a purely rational ground. This is to say that the existence of this inclination provides at least a psychological explanation of why we demand taste from others, but no new basis for expecting actual agreement in aesthetic response. Furthermore, the nature of this inclination seems to be such that its frustration — in the absence of an opportunity for communication — actually stands in the way of a purely aesthetic response to an object, or at least prevents complete satisfaction with it. Perhaps this frustration does not actually detract from the pleasure of pure aesthetic response, but it does detract from the greater satisfaction to be obtained from the combination of aesthetic pleasure with satisfaction of the inclination to society.

Kant's exposition of this last point suffers from a badly chosen example. Kant maintains that "for himself alone a man abandoned on a desert island would not adorn either himself or his hut, nor would he look for flowers . . . in order to decorate himself with them." "Only in society," Kant concludes, "does it occur to one to be not merely a man, but man [refined] after the manner of his kind." This may be so, but it hardly bears on the issue of aesthetic response. These remarks are obviously reminiscent of Kant's earlier view that there is no pleasure in beautiful forms in solitude, but are not quite equivalent to it, for the denial that a solitary person will use beauty for self-adornment or make any special attempt to have the beauty of nature appear to his own advantage does not entail that aesthetic response itself is affected one way or the other by the absence of society. Kant asserts that society can lend a value to charms or sensations which they otherwise would not have, just because they permit of universal communication. But this is not to say that truly beautiful objects would not furnish the pleasure of aesthetic response outside society; it is to say only that when we are in society our interest in communication can cause us to take pleasure in objects which otherwise would have no particular tendency to please.

Although Kant is somewhat confused here, these last remarks do reveal what is at issue in the discussion of the empirical interest in the beautiful. If one *assumes* that we do have similar responses to beautiful objects—that is, that the claim of intersubjective validity implicit in calling something beautiful is in fact satisfied—beautiful objects do furnish an occasion for communication. Thus, given our interest in communication itself, they provide the basis for an additional element of pleasure in society. Further, given that our inclination to society leads us to demand a regard to communicability from others, the fact of the communicability of the pleasure in the beautiful provides a reason other than the linguistic force of aesthetic judgment itself for demanding a concern for this pleasure, and perhaps even agreement in it, from others. Finally, the existence of beautiful objects is of interest to us in society—quite apart from questions of personal pleasure or self-adornment—because these objects do provide occasion for communication, and may advance the level of communication in general. But these implications all rest on the validity of the deduction of aesthetic judgment, rather than providing any additional ground for accepting that argument. Pleasure in the beautiful is an occasion for communication and a ground for interest only if we do in fact have a reasonable basis for expecting agreement in this response. By itself, the possibility that an intersubjectively valid pleasure could satisfy our inclination to sociable communication may provide a reason for demanding agreement in aesthetic response, but it is not a reason for expecting such agreement.

If we could base a duty in an empirical inclination, our natural inclination to society could explain how we come to exact aesthetic response as a sort of duty, but it could not advance the deduction's argument for the rationality of *imputing* agreement about this feeling to others. This is the real problem with the empirical interest in the beautiful, and the structure of this problem suggests that it may arise even if our interest in demanding regard to and agreement in response to the beautiful has an "intellectual" rather than a merely empirical base. But Kant himself does not suggest the real problem in using an interest in the beautiful as a buttress for the deduction of aesthetic judgment. In preparing us for §42's discussion of an intellectual rather than an empirical interest in the existence of the beautiful, he claims that if an *a priori* basis for such an interest can be found, then taste would indeed "reveal a transition on the part of the faculty of estimation from the enjoyment of sense to the moral feeling." That is, if such an *a priori* connection can be found, taste not merely will be in the service of an empirical inclination to society, but will figure in a truly moral relation to others. It will thus, presumably, derive an increased security from its instrumental connection with morality. And, Kant continues, in the case of the discovery of an *a priori* rather than an empirical ground for interest in the beautiful, not only would we "be better guided to make final employment of taste, but taste would further be represented as a link in the chain of human *a priori* faculties, on which all legislation must depend."[23] This suggests not only that the faculty of taste may have an instrumental value for morality, but also that its connection with morality provides taste with some new guidance for its own employment — that is to say, with a new basis or even new criteria for its claims of intersubjective validity for specific feelings of pleasure. But, as we have seen, it is not clear that any new basis for the demand for agreement in aesthetic response, whether pure or empirical, can lend any support to the epistemological thesis that such agreement may be rationally expected under certain circumstances. Only if a demand for agreement also entails the expectation of its fulfillment — as Kant supposes the obligatory demand of the moral law to entail human freedom — might the discovery of a new basis for the demand of taste provide support for the deduction's assertion that such agreement may really obtain. Let us now see whether Kant's discussion of the intellectual interest does bear more directly on the issue of the deduction than did his discussion of the empirical interest.

An intellectual interest in the beautiful is one connected with the *a priori* determination of the will by reason. More simply, it is one connected with our capacity for acting on moral concepts or ideas of practical reason rather than with our natural inclinations, whatever their object. To argue that we do have such an interest in the existence of beautiful objects, Kant argues that there is a sufficient analogy between the pure judgment of taste and the moral judgment from concepts of practical reason for the kind of interest we have in the natural existence of objects conformable to the latter to be extended to the existence of objects conformable to the former as well.[24] He then suggests that we may use this interest in beautiful objects to demand a like interest from others, and that we are justified in holding in contempt "as coarse and low the habits of thought of those who have no *feeling* for beautiful nature . . . and who devote themselves to the mere enjoyment of sense."[25]

Even before considering its details, we can see the difficulties which such an argument will encounter if taken as an attempt to supplement the deduction of aesthetic judgment. First, as in the cases already considered, it will more obviously serve to base a demand for response to the beautiful, as a sign of moral character, than it will to base a rational expectation of agreement in such response. Second, it is also obvious that the response at issue in such a demand will actually be not aesthetic response itself, since that must be disinterested, but rather some additional component of interested pleasure in the totality of our response to beautiful objects. Again, in other words, the bearing of agreement in an interest in the beautiful on agreement in aesthetic response can be at best indirect. Even if the analogy between aesthetic and moral judgment showed that one is justified in demanding and even expecting a certain interest in the beautiful, it would still remain to be argued that a pure aesthetic pleasure is a condition for the existence of this further interest in an object, and thus is legitimately imputed to anyone to whom the intellectual interest is imputed. We will see, however, that Kant does not carry his argument through these final steps.

With these considerations in mind, let us turn to Kant's exposition in §42. Kant begins by drawing a contrast between the moral significance of interest in the beauty of art and in the beauty of nature. It is with the best of intentions, he says, that many "hold it to be a sign of a good moral character to take an interest in the beautiful generally." But the adherents of such a view may be readily contradicted by those who assert that "virtuosi of taste" or connoisseurs of art are "usually vain, capricious, and given to injurious passions." In fact, "interest in the *beautiful of art* gives no proof at all of a habit of mind attached or even inclined to the morally good"; it is only "an *immediate interest* in the beauty of *nature*" which characterizes a good soul. A habitual interest in the contemplation of nature or its beautiful forms, Kant maintains, is indicative of a "disposition of mind favorable to the moral feeling," and is thus a disposition which might be affected by a demand for moral feeling.[26]

It is natural to ask why an interest in the beautiful forms of nature should be indicative of anything about a person's moral character, as well as why there should be a difference in this regard between beautiful objects of nature and of art. I will not pursue the latter question here — though it may be argued that this distinction between interest in nature and interest in art is inconsistent with the implications of Kant's most basic views on both the response to and the creation of art[27] — and will confine my attention to the first of these questions. After some further praise of the man who "turns to the beautiful in nature," praise which comes at the expense of the "connoisseur or art fancier," Kant explains the moral significance of interest in natural beauty. He begins his answer with one of his most fundamental statements of the analogy between aesthetic and moral judgments. Both of these are judgments directed to peculiarly formal features of their objects; both determine an *a priori* connection of delight to their object, and make this delight into a rule for all; and neither is founded on a prior interest in its object. It is worth quoting Kant's analogy in full:

> We have a faculty of merely aesthetic judgment, for judging forms without concepts, and finding, in the mere estimate of them, a delight that we at the same time make into a rule for everyone, without this judgment being founded on an interest, nor yet producing one. On the other hand, we also have a faculty of intellectual judgment, for determining an *a priori* delight for the mere forms of practical maxims (so far as they are of themselves qualified for universal legislation), which delight we make into a law for everyone, without our judgment being founded on any interest, *though here it produces one.* The pleasure or displeasure in the former judgment is called that of taste; the latter is called that of moral feeling.[28]

Aesthetic and moral judgments are structurally analogous, for on the basis of formal properties of their objects but no prior interest in their existence, they connect pleasure with these objects and assert that connection to be valid for everyone. They differ in two respects, however: aesthetic judgments employ no concepts of objects (and for that reason, perhaps, can set up no interests), whereas moral judgments, obviously, must employ the concept of universal legislation in order to estimate the forms of maxims; and only moral judgments can, without presupposing an interest, produce one.

Kant next uses this analogy between the two forms of judgment to explain the moral significance of interest in the beautiful, but two questions about the application of the analogy may be raised even before we consider this explanation. First, if there is to be a strict analogy between the two judgments concerning the universality of delight, we must interpret moral judgment as requiring moral feeling and not just moral action of everyone; and it is certainly a question whether this is actually entailed by Kant's moral theory. Second, this passage suggests that Kant's view of the moral significance of interest in natural beauty rests on his thesis that aesthetic response itself can produce no interest in the existence of beautiful objects. Only if that is the case does it seem necessary to invoke an analogy with

moral judgment to explain such interest, and to attribute moral significance to it. But, as we have seen, Kant's thesis that aesthetic response not
only is based on no prior interest in an object but also produces no subsequent interest in its existence has no real ground. If the thesis of the moral
significance of interest in the beautiful depends on this view of the disinterestedness of taste, it too will be questionable. Should it presuppose this
view, any attempt to support the intersubjectivity of aesthetic response by
that of an interest which may be added to it will also be problematic.

I now return to Kant's argument. After having expounded the analogy
between the two faculties of judgment, Kant proceeds by pointing out a
further fact about moral judgment, and arguing that this further fact obtains in the case of aesthetic judgment as well. What Kant observes is that
the ideas involved in the maxims which are the subject of moral judgment
are, after all, ideas of "objective reality" — concepts of objects or actions to
be realized in the actual world of nature — and that the interest which is
produced in us by the moral feeling is an interest in the existence of such
objects. Moral judgment produces not merely a universally valid delight in
our own intentions but also an interest in the existence of certain realities.
And insofar as such existence depends on the cooperation of nature with
the interests stemming from our reason, moral judgment also produces an
interest in nature's manifestation of accord with the conditions of our own
moral feeling. Kant then generalizes this interest in nature's cooperation
with the conditions of our delight to the nonmoral but analogous case of
the delight of aesthetic response:

> But now, since it also interests reason that the ideas (for which it ef-
> fects an immediate interest in the moral feeling) have objective reality,
> that is, that nature at least show a trace or give a hint that it contains
> in itself a ground for assuming a lawlike harmony of its products with
> our wholly disinterested delight (which we acknowledge *a priori* as a
> law for everyone, without being able to ground it on proofs): so reason
> must take an interest in every manifestation on the part of nature of a
> harmony similar to this; consequently, the mind cannot reflect on the
> beauty of *nature* without finding itself at the same time interested.
> But this interest is by its relationship moral; and one who takes such
> an interest in the beautiful of nature can do so only insofar as he has
> already founded his interest in the morally good.[29]

This interest in the existence of the beautiful in nature is an interest in the
harmony of nature with the conditions of our own disinterested delight,
which is to say, with the conditions of our response to beauty. Such an

interest in objective reality can be explained only on the basis of a moral interest in the reality of our ideas. Thus an interest in the existence of beautiful objects can be due only to a moral interest in the accordance of nature with human objectives. This is why an interest in natural beauty reveals a good moral character. It is because of our interest in the development of a good moral character "that the analogy between the pure judgment of taste, which, without depending on any interest, allows us to feel delight and at the same time to represent it *a priori* as proper to all mankind, and the moral judgment, which does the same thing from concepts . . . leads to the same sort of immediate interest in the objects of the former as in those of the latter."[30] And because interest in beauty is a product of a good moral character, it may be demanded of others, and they may be criticized for insensitivity to such beauty.[31]

What are we to make of such an argument? As Kant expounds it, it depends on the thesis that aesthetic response itself does not produce an interest in the existence of beautiful objects, or even on the more general thesis that an interest in the objective reality of our ideas is always a moral interest. The first thesis is questionable enough. Kant never really offered a reason why the pleasure occasioned by a beautiful object should not itself be enough to produce an interest in its existence, and it was only by substituting a definition of interest drawn from Kant's moral philosophy for that of the third *Critique* that we could produce an argument even for the weaker thesis that the pleasure of aesthetic response could not produce interest in determinate classes of beautiful objects. The second thesis seems even more problematic, and indicative of some confusion on Kant's part. An interest in the reality of an idea is not intrinsically moral, but is moral only if the idea is itself moral. But if that is so, then an interest in nature's conformity to our disinterested delight in beauty is not a moral interest, if the idea of that delight is not itself a moral idea—no matter how analogous to one it might be.

Kant's argument thus involves at least one questionable premise, and does not appear to be sound. But even if it were sound, would it supplement the deduction of aesthetic judgment? The real problem with §42 is that it is addressed to the justification of what was already assumed by that deduction, that is, the demand for agreement in response to the beautiful, and that it does not bear on the legitimacy of the actual imputation of such agreement at all. Kant does not ask whether our demand for an interest in beautiful objects of nature from others should actually be expected to be fulfilled; even less does he argue that the purely disinterested pleasure in the beautiful which produces such an interest may be expected to be found in all. Had Kant offered an argument that the intellectual interest in the existence of the beautiful, because of its foundation in the moral interest in the objective reality of our ideas, may be imputed to all, he might then have argued further that disinterested pleasure in the beautiful is a presupposition of this interest, and must be imputed to others if the latter is. But there is no hint of such arguments in §42. This section's link between response to the beautiful and moral interest might have been meant to distract our attention from the problem about the intersubjectivity of taste that arises as long as that attention is confined to the epistemological considerations of its earlier deduction, but the section offers no direct arguments on the issue of intersubjectivity, and no direct supplement to the deduction of aesthetic judgment.[32*]

What about the demand for an intellectual interest in the beautiful itself? Does Kant's present argument at least succeed in going beyond the purely linguistic considerations which initially anchor taste's demand for agreement in aesthetic response? Here too there are problems. First, it is obvious that if anything may be directly demanded of others because of taste's analogy with moral feeling, it is interest in the existence of the beautiful, and such an interest is by definition distinct from the disinterested pleasure in beauty which is the true subject of a judgment of taste. This would not present a problem if a demand for agreement in the possession of such an interest entailed at least a demand for agreement in aesthetic response itself — that is, identity of response to particular objects. But it is far from clear that the latter demand is entailed by the former. It might be argued that the demand for the intellectual interest in the beautiful entails demanding the capacity for aesthetic judgment itself, as an ability to discriminate between disinterested and interested pleasures. One could argue this by claiming that we can take a morally significant interest in nature only insofar as we are interested in nature's being in accord with our disinterested delight, and by maintaining that such accord can be considered only if we are indeed conscious of some delight as disinterested. But unless disinterestedness itself entails intersubjective validity — which, apart from the success of the deduction, it does not — this would not imply that different persons must take disinterested delight in the *same* objects in order to take a morally grounded delight in the existence of beautiful objects in general. It would certainly be compatible with the general idea of intellectual interest in the beautiful that different objects produce the feeling of beauty in different persons, and that each person then takes a morally significant interest in the existence of whichever objects produced that response in him. At best, the demand that all persons reveal good moral character by their interest in beautiful objects can license a demand that they all take an interest in the existence of whatever they conceive of as natural beauty, not a demand that they actually find the same objects beautiful.

A second question for the present basis for the demand for agreement in aesthetic response is whether its analogy with interest in the objective reality of the ideas of morality in fact justifies the demand that everyone demonstrate an immediate interest in the existence of the beautiful. Kant has argued that the fact that an interest in the beautiful can be explained only by a fundamental interest in the morally good furnishes "cause to suspect at least a tendency to a good moral disposition in one to whom the beauty of nature is of immediate interest."[33] But this does not actually establish a connection between moral interest and interest in the beautiful appropriate to justify any exaction of duty in the case of the latter. In his first consideration of the link between aesthetic and moral judgment in §29, Kant argued that the development of taste conduces to the development of moral feeling, and though there a problem arose about demanding what is at best a mere instrument rather than an actual necessary condition for the development of morality, one could at least see why we should take an interest in other persons' possession of taste if it can lead to moral feeling. But here it appears that a good moral disposition is required to develop an intellectual interest in the beautiful, rather than *vice versa*. If that is the case, it is hard to see how any demand of moral interest from others could legitimate a demand for interest in the beautiful. If the capacity for aesthetic response and its attendant interest were a condition for moral action, it might be demanded as part of the capacity for morality that we surely do demand of others. But if it is a consequence rather than a prior condition of moral capacity, the demand for it cannot be legitimated in the same way. If it is a basis in the requirements of morality that could give a demand on others a more than purely linguistic foundation, then the present explanation of interest in the beautiful does not succeed in so supplementing the Analytic of the Beautiful's justification of the demand for agreement in aesthetic response. The intellectual interest in the beautiful might have a basis in a good moral disposition, and even be a sign of the latter, but it is no requirement of morality.

The argument of §42 does not advance the deduction of aesthetic judgment. Kant's account of the moral foundation of interest in the beautiful might explain why we actually take great interest in the taste and aesthetic responses of other persons. We certainly do take such interest, and the fact that we do does require explanation. But Kant's argument can justify neither a demand for nor an expectation of agreement in aesthetic response. To see whether Kant can improve on this argument, I will now turn to his final consideration of the connection between taste and morality, the discussion of "beauty as the symbol of morality" in §59.[34] (There is one reference to a connection between taste and morality in the sections between §42 and §59 but since it bears on the question of whether art must have a moral content rather than on the question of whether taste itself has some moral significance which can secure the assumption of its intersubjective validity,[35] its discussion can be deferred.)

Beauty as the Symbol of Morality

For those interested in the *Critique of Judgment*'s claim to effect a "union of the legislation of the understanding and of reason by means of judgment,"[36] or to offer "a mediating link for the union of the realm of the concept of nature with that of the concept of freedom,"[37] the thesis that beauty is the symbol of morality has been of great interest. It appears to be the thesis by which Kant's promissory note of systematic significance for his aesthetics can be cashed in.[38*] My own interest, however, has been confined throughout this study to the intersubjective validity of the judgment of taste, and I have limited consideration of the larger systematic pretensions of the third *Critique* to their bearing on this issue. I will maintain this policy in the discussion of §59, and restrict my discussion of this rich and suggestive section to its implications for the thesis that judgments of taste rationally demand intersubjective agreement in pleasurable response to given objects from others and impute it to them.

One interpretation of this part of the *Critique* which has had a similarly limited objective is that of Crawford, who maintains that the argument that beauty is the symbol of morality completes Kant's deduction of aesthetic judgment. Crawford's view is that the connection of aesthetic judgment to morality can supplement the results of the deduction from more purely epistemological grounds only if the requirement of aesthetic judgment can actually be deduced from the requirements of morality, or if "there is a basis for implying that others ought to agree with our judgments of taste, because they ought to be morally sensitive." Given this, he holds that "to complete the deduction, Kant must argue or assume that moral sensitivity implies a sensitivity to that which symbolizes the basis of morality"; he then argues that §59 accomplishes such a completion, for what this section demonstrates, he says, is that "our judgments marking the pleasure in the beautiful (and the sublime, too) can rightfully demand universal assent, not simply because they can be based on what can be universally communicated, but because they mark an experience of that which symbolizes morality."[39] In Crawford's opinion, the fact that the beautiful symbolizes morality allows aesthetic sensitivity to be demanded of others in a way that the fact that the development of taste may be conducive to the development of a morally good disposition does not.[40] The argument of §59 is thus supposed to be an improvement over the earlier thesis that the harmonious accord in the play of the cognitive faculties merely "promotes the sensibility of the mind for moral feeling."[41] Since Crawford thinks that §42's theory of interest in natural beauty also constructs only a "tenuous link between the aesthetic and the moral, simply because this contemplation [of natural beauty] does not itself seem to be any firm indication of a morally good disposition,"[42*] he believes that the argument of §59 must improve on the argument of that section too. I have also argued that the theories of §§29 and 42 cannot accomplish what appears to be required of the link between aesthetics and morality. The question that now arises, then, is whether the thesis that beauty is the symbol of morality is in fact significantly different from the thesis that taste may be conducive to morality and thus demanded on the grounds of morality. Does the argument of §59 in fact improve over those of §§29 and 42?

The obvious place to begin is with Kant's conception of the nature of symbolism itself. Symbolism is one of three species of what Kant calls "hypotyposis," or the rendering of concepts in terms of sense. Just as there are three types of concepts, namely, empirical concepts, pure concepts of the understanding, and rational concepts or ideas—for instance, the concept "dog," the concept "causation," and the concept "freedom"—so there are three ways in which concepts may be rendered in sense, or in which their reality may be verified. For empirical concepts, *examples* may be furnished—for the concept "dog," we may provide an actual example of a dog. For pure concepts of the understanding, *schemata* may be furnished —for the pure concept of causation, we may supply the appropriately defined schema of temporal succession. Finally, for a concept of reason or an idea, we may furnish a *symbol*—an intuition which is an indirect representation of a concept "which only reason can think, and to which no sensible intuition can be adequate," and which therefore cannot really be said to "verify" the concept. Examples of the symbolic representation of ideas are the use of a living organism to symbolize a constitutional monarchy and of a handmill to symbolize an absolute monarchy. Neither an organism nor a handmill is an example — an instance — of a kind of government, obviously, nor is either a schema, a form of intuition corresponding to a logical relation, as temporal succession corresponds to the relation of ground and consequent. Instead, these objects serve as symbols of analogies between themselves and what they symbolize.[43]

All of these forms of hypotyposis differ from "characterisms" for concepts, that is, arbitrary sensible signs which invoke the thought of a concept merely "according to the imagination's law of association."[44*] Although symbols are not direct presentations of concepts — sensible intuitions which actually contain the properties picked out by the concept — there must nevertheless be an intuitive or more than merely arbitrary connection between a symbol and what it symbolizes. Kant explains this connection in terms of analogy, but analogy in a particular regard. What he claims is that in symbolism the concept is supplied with an intuition such that the "procedure of judgment in dealing with it is merely analogous to that which it observes in schematism." In schematism, the components of a complex intuition are subsumed under a concept because a rule which the latter involves can determine the order of thought in reflection on the intuition; in symbolism, what agrees with the concept "is merely the rule of [judgment's] procedure, not the intuition itself; thus it accords merely in the form of reflection, and not according to the content."[45] This interpretation of symbolism is illustrated by the example of the handmill as a symbol of despotism; Kant claims that "there is certainly no similarity between a despotic state and a handmill, but there surely is between the rules of reflection upon both and their causality."[46] In both these cases, presumably, one thinks in a similar chain: of objects (grain, persons) being subjected to operations entirely outside of their control (being ground, being dictated to) and being converted into whatever the mechanism (the mill, the despot) is designed or designs to produce (flour, slaves). The actual content of the symbol — a mechanical device — is not an instance or schema of what it symbolizes — a human institution — but there is a similarity in the way in which ideas are connected in thinking of either the symbol or what is symbolized. The structure of reflection in considering the operation of a handmill is analogous to the structure of reflection in thinking of the workings of a despotism, and thus the former may serve as a symbol of the latter. But there is no connection in content—a handmill is certainly neither a part of nor a kind of despotism.

This fact suggests that the connection between a symbol and its referent will be looser than that between examples or schemata and their respective referents. Nothing but a dog can serve as an example of the concept "dog," and, given the nature of our sensible intuition, nothing but an objectively valid temporal succession can serve as a schema for the pure concept of ground and consequent. But anything which allows one to relate ideas in the same way as does the handmill—some other mechanical device, perhaps, or some other form of human relation—could serve equally well as a symbol of despotism.

On Kant's theory of symbolism, then, there is no intrinsic connection between a symbol and what it stands for, or no way in which the content of one representation is essentially connected to that of another. One thing may serve as the symbol of another only because the structure of reflection is similar in the two cases. But if this is the nature of symbolism, then the thesis that the beautiful is the symbol of morality cannot be expected to differ radically from the analogy between aesthetic and moral judgment which Kant has already drawn in §42. The thesis will not mean that the representation of a beautiful object itself contains any moral content, or is itself a schema for moral action. The beautiful need not have any content or make any reference to a concept of morality. Instead, what the thesis suggests is that there is an analogy between the "rules of reflection" upon both the beautiful and the morally good, or between the "procedure of judgment" in dealing with the beautiful and that for dealing with the moral. But this seems to mean just that there are structural similarities between aesthetic and moral judgment, for it is these which are our procedures of judgment with respect to the beautiful and the morally good. Beauty is a symbol of the morally good only because there is an analogy between aesthetic and moral judgment.

For the most part, this is precisely what Kant's exposition of the symbolism of beauty maintains. The argument is presented in two paragraphs. The first describes the general significance of the analogy between aesthetic and moral judgment, or what it is about morality that beauty symbolizes on the basis of the analogy between the procedures of judgment in reflection on these two objects; the second describes the specific similarities between judgments on beauty and judgments of morality in virtue of which beauty may in fact be taken to symbolize the morally good. Since the second paragraph thus states the evidence for the more general claim of the first, we may consider it first.

The specific similarities between aesthetic and moral judgment are described by Kant as follows:

> (1) The beautiful pleases *immediately* (but only in reflective intuition, not like morality, in a concept). (2) It pleases *apart from all interest* (the morally good is, to be sure, necessarily connected with an interest, but not with one of a sort that precedes the judgment on the delight, rather [with] one that is thereby first effected). (3) The *freedom* of the imagination (and thus of the sensibility of our [cognitive] faculty) is in the estimation of the beautiful represented as in harmony with the understanding's conformity to law (in moral judgment the freedom of the will is thought of as the accord of the will with itself according to universal laws of reason). (4) The subjective principle of the estimation of the beautiful is represented as *universal,* that is, valid for everyone, but not as recognizable through any universal concept (the objective principle of morality is also declared to be universal, that is, [valid] for all subjects and also for all acts of the same subject, [but] also [to be] recognizable through a general concept).[47]

Basically, this is just an elaborated statement of the similarities between aesthetic and moral judgment already employed in Kant's argument for the intellectual interest in the beautiful. The first point asserts that both forms of judgment are immediate: this is not a phenomenological point about the speed or any other characteristic of the experience of pleasure in a beautiful or moral object, but rather a reference to the fact that neither the beautiful nor the moral pleases as a means to some further end, be that sensuous gratification or some other form of happiness. Each pleases in itself, or is itself the satisfaction of an ultimate end — the harmony of the faculties, or the possession of a good will. Thus, neither is merely contingently pleasurable owing to its instrumentality in the achievement of some other pleasure. Second, both the beautiful and the morally good please without consideration of any prior interest, although, as Kant once again insists, they differ in that only the moral is capable of creating an interest. This is just another way of saying that each of these objects pleases apart from any consideration of its potential as a means to the satisfaction of some specific practical objective. Third, Kant draws an analogy between, on the one hand, the way in which the harmony of the faculties in response to beauty may be interpreted as an accord between the imagination's unruled movement through a manifold of intuition and the understanding's need for unity, ordinarily satisfied with a rule, and, on the other hand, the fact that in the moral determination of the will the natural faculty of choice (*Willkür*) is in accord with the faculty for the representation of the moral law (*Wille*).[48]* Both aesthetic response and the determination of action by moral judgment represent remarkable instances of cooperation between the sensuous and intellectual aspects of human nature. Finally, and obviously enough, aesthetic and moral judgment resemble each other in claiming universal validity.

As the basis of beauty's symbolism of morality, these four points do indeed express analogous structures of reflection, each involving a harmonious accord between different faculties of mind. Each form of reflection is similar in excluding the ordinary relationship of means to end as a source of value for its object, and is thus immediate and free of all interest. Each form of reflection claims the same status, namely, universal validity. To the extent that Kant's general analysis of symbolism does dictate what he means in calling one thing a symbol of another, these analogies should exhaust the content of the assertion that beauty is a symbol of morality. A beautiful object is a sensible particular which can be taken to symbolize something like morality to which no sensible intuition is adequate just because there are these analogies between judgments upon the two objects.

As I said, beauty's symbolism of the morally good is characterized in more general terms in the paragraph preceding the one just discussed. In fact, this paragraph makes two claims about the significance of the symbolism, one of which is clearly just a more general statement of the four points which follow it, but one of which seems to go beyond these analogies. Beauty's symbolization of the "basis of morality" might be interpreted by reference to either of these two claims; and since, as we have seen, it is its representation of this basis that some commentators suppose crucial to the completion of the deduction of aesthetic judgment, it will be important to distinguish these two claims carefully.

Kant begins the paragraph with the assertion that it is only as a symbol of the morally good that beauty pleases with a claim to the agreement of everyone, and then suggests that in being pleased by such a symbol, one becomes "conscious of a certain ennoblement and elevation over the mere receptivity to pleasure from sense impressions." He then adds, with considerable obscurity, that in connection with this pleasure one also "values the worth of others according to a similar maxim for their judgment." His view appears to be that in aesthetic judgment we become conscious of the fact that our feelings and desires may be determined by grounds higher than mere sensory stimuli, and that we thus also become capable of recognizing this ability in others and demanding it of them. In a sentence even more opaque than what has just preceded, Kant then says that "this is that *intelligible* to which taste, as has been indicated in the previous paragraph, extends its view."[49] What the antecedent of the opening "this" is meant to be cannot be univocally determined, but something like the following seems to be what Kant has in mind. As the previous paragraph has stated, symbolism consists in the representation of a rational concept or purely "intelligible" object by a sensible intuition or directly perceivable object. Thus we use such phenomena as handmills or the flowing of fluids to represent such purely intelligible objects as a form of government or a logical relationship like entailment. If that is the case, then to the extent that the experience of beauty and, by extension, a beautiful object itself symbolize something, they must symbolize an "intelligible," a concept to which no sensible intuition is directly adequate. The concept which beauty symbolizes is then suggested to be that of our capacity for morality itself, the capacity for a moral rather than sensuous determination of the will. The pleasure we take in the beautiful, because it involves elevation above the merely sensuous, represents the elevation above determination by the pleasures of the senses that is a condition of the possibility of morality. Presumably, our elevation above the rule of sense impressions is sensible in the case of aesthetic response, but not in the case of the moral determination of the will; so the sensible intuition of beauty must be used to symbolize the purely intelligible basis of morality.

If this is what Kant is saying, then his reference to taste's extension of its view to an intelligible is basically another statement of the third point of analogy in the subsequent paragraph—the analogy between the harmony of the imagination and the understanding in aesthetic response and that of choice and reason in moral action. The next few lines of the paragraph under consideration are compatible with this conclusion. Thus Kant suggests that there is an analogy between the way in which the beautiful brings our cognitive faculties into accord and the way in which the intelligible — our capacity for morality — "brings even our higher cognitive faculties into accord, and is that apart from which sheer contradiction would result between their nature and the claims put forward by taste."[50] That is, without the ultimate capacity for an elevation above sense and a free harmony between the sensuous and cognitive aspects of our nature, neither the claims of taste nor those of morality could be met. Similarly, taste resembles morality in that in it "the faculty of judgment does not find itself subjected to a heteronomy of laws of experience, as is otherwise the case in empirical esti-mation; rather, in respect of the objects of such a pure delight [as that of taste], judgment gives itself the law, as reason does with respect to the fac-ulty of desire." Thus, as products of free accord between two faculties, aesthetic response and moral judgment are both autonomous, judgments in which the mind is not determined by merely natural and contingent causal connections. In both, the mind's own nature — whether that be understanding's aim for unity or reason's respect for law — determines the nature of our response to empirical objects.

There is one obvious way, then, in which beauty may symbolize the basis of morality. If we understand the basis of morality to be our capacity to determine the choices that we make as beings in the world of nature by our rational representation of the moral law, then the beautiful, through the nature of aesthetic judgment, symbolizes the basis of morality precisely by symbolizing this capacity. The basis of aesthetic judgment, one capacity for harmony among our faculties, symbolizes the basis of moral judgment, another capacity for harmony among our faculties.

As Kant continues, however, he makes another claim for his analogy, a claim which implies that the beautiful symbolizes the basis of morality in another sense. Kant now introduces as the basis of morality not our capa-city for morality, but instead the purported metaphysical basis of that capacity — the supersensible or noumenal basis of our phenomenal nature. Thus, Kant argues that judgment "sees itself, on account of both this inner possibility [for ennoblement and elevation] in the subject and this external possibility of a nature in harmony with it, as related to something in the subject and outside of it, which is not nature, and not freedom, but which is connected with the ground of the latter, namely, the supersensible, in which the theoretical faculty is united with the practical in a common but yet unknown manner."[51] Our response to beauty is not interpreted as manifesting solely the capacity for harmony between imagination and understanding, or as symbolizing just our capacity for harmony between choice and reason in moral action. Rather, the experience of the beautiful is taken to represent the supposed supersensible basis of the harmony of the cognitive faculties, and thus to symbolize the supposed supersensible basis of our capacity for moral action. It is in virtue of its own connection with a supersensible basis that the experience of the beautiful may symbolize the basis of morality, as the supersensible ground of the latter.

It is no surprise, then, that the theory of beauty's symbolism of morality finds a home in the Dialectic of Aesthetic Judgment, the only part of the

Critique where Kant attempts to connect the analysis of aesthetic judgment with the ontology of transcendental idealism. The four specific points of analogy expounded in the penultimate paragraph of §59, as well as Kant's first claim for the significance of these analogies in the preceding paragraph, may be interpreted in the epistemological and psychological terms of Kant's theory of mental activity, and do not transcend the theory of aesthetic judgment expounded in the Analytic of the Beautiful and the corresponding analysis of moral judgment. Only with this final reference to the supersensible do we find a theory of the symbolism which breaks these bounds and attempts to explicate the link between aesthetic and moral judgment in a way radically different from those encountered earlier in Kant's text.

What is the force of Kant's final exposition of the link between aesthetics and morality? It must be kept in mind that if §59 were to constitute a successful completion of the deduction of aesthetic judgment, beauty's status as a symbol of morality would have to justify both the demand for *and* the imputation of intersubjective agreement in taste. Crawford has argued only that beauty's symbolism of the basis of morality justifies the *demand* for agreement in aesthetic response, so our first question may be whether the thesis of symbolism can accomplish even this much. It is by no means clear that it can; and it should be noted that, even though Kant claims that it is only insofar as it is regarded as a symbol of the morally good that beauty has a claim to the agreement of all, the thesis that he actually proposes after detailing the analogies underlying beauty's symbolic status really amounts to a restatement of the instrumental value of aesthetic judgment in the development of a moral disposition. What Kant actually concludes is simply that "taste, as it were, makes possible the transition from sensuous charm to a habitual moral interest without too violent a leap, insofar as it represents the imagination even in its freedom as purposively determinable for the understanding and teaches us to find a free delight in the objects of the senses even without sensuous charm."[52] In other words, the development of taste requires us to develop the capacity to abstract from and go beyond the pleasures of mere sensuous agreeableness—in the case of aesthetic judgment itself, to pleasures due to other sources. This ability to go beyond exclusive attention to the pleasures of the senses is also required for the development of a good moral disposition, although in this case we must go beyond consideration of any kind of pleasures whatsoever. Thus the skill acquired in the development of taste conduces to the development of the ability to act morally. This thesis we have seen stated as early as §29, and I have already noted the major problem with it: the propriety of actually demanding of other persons, as a sort of duty, a skill or response which may be conducive to something we can legitimately demand of them, but which is by no means a necessary condition of the latter.

Why should Kant have been so cautious in going beyond his original interpretation of the link between aesthetic and moral judgment after first suggesting an apparently much stronger result for the thesis of symbolism? A good reason for his caution is the fact that sensitivity to a *symbol* of morality is not itself a state requisite for moral performance, and thus not something which can be *demanded* as part of a demand for moral action.[53]* Another reason for caution is the fact that in *neither* of its possible senses is the basis of morality which the beautiful may symbolize identical with the moral law, consciousness of which is requisite to a moral performance and knowledge of which could be legitimately demanded of others as part of the demand for morality itself. A final reason for caution in trying to cash in the promise of beauty's symbolism of the morally good is the fact that one of the ways in which beauty may represent the basis of morality—namely, by its representation of a supersensible ground for the harmony of the faculties—depends on the thesis that aesthetic judgment does indeed involve such a representation; this, as we have seen, is a highly questionable thesis.

I will expand on these points somewhat. The last of the three may be most briefly explained. The problem with using its purported reference to a supersensible as the basis for beauty's symbolism of morality is really twofold. First, it is only by a tenuous argument that the experience of aesthetic response itself may be interpreted as any sort of experience of a supersensible, for it was only by exploiting the ambiguity of the notion of an indeterminate concept that the Dialectic of Aesthetic Judgment was able to link aesthetic judgment to a supersensible.[54] And even if the argument to the postulation of a supersensible substratum of subject and object were permissible, this would hardly entail that aesthetic response is an *experience* of the supersensible by means of which the intuition of beauty could become a symbol for the rational concept of morality, as a strict adherence to Kant's analysis of symbolism would require. The actual experience in aesthetic judgment, even on the argument of the Dialectic, remains one of the "harmonious accord of all our faculties of cognition"; the Dialectic's addition is not a new characterization of aesthetic experience, but, rather, the putative explanation that the objective in this experience, the satisfaction of which produces aesthetic pleasure, is set by our intelligible nature or is due to a supersensible ground. Even if we were to allow the argument from aesthetic response to a supersensible substratum, then, there would still be a problem about taking experience of the beautiful as a symbol of any kind of supersensible, and it would no more be a direct representation of this ground than is moral feeling itself.

The second problem with this interpretation of beauty's symbolism of the basis of morality arises from Kant's ethics. If we demand that others respond to beauty because it is a symbol of the basis of morality, then we are demanding of them a form of knowledge of the basis of morality.[55*] For this demand to be justified, knowledge of this basis must be required as part of morality itself. But it is questionable whether any knowledge of the existence of a supersensible ground of ourselves and our actions, or of the accord between our sensuous and our rational natures, is actually required for morality on Kant's ethical theory. What is required of a moral agent is consciousness of the moral law and of his obligation to comply with this law; without such consciousness, a person may perform morally acceptable actions, but he cannot perform morally praiseworthy ones, because he cannot act out of the incentive of duty—consciousness of his obligation under the moral law. Knowledge of the moral law, then, may be demanded of other persons on purely moral grounds; and if we take the categorical imperative itself to be the basis of morality—as the basic incentive of moral action—then at least discursive if not symbolic knowledge of the basis of morality may be demanded of everybody. But this may not imply the further thesis that knowledge of the *noumenal* basis of morality may be demanded of everyone, which would certainly be necessary to justify a universal demand for sensitivity to a symbol of this basis. For we cannot demand that everyone make the inference from his obligation under the moral law to the existence of a supersensible basis for his action.

Kant does argue that consciousness of moral obligation entails consciousness of freedom, for one can be conscious of an obligation only if one is conscious of being able to carry it out. Thus, as he puts it in the *Foundations of the Metaphysics of Morals*, "a free will and a will under moral laws are identical,"[56] and from this, he supposes it to follow that "in respect to their will, all men think of themselves as free."[57] But Kant then argues only that the *philosopher* who undertakes a critique of practical reason must recognize the difference between our phenomenal and noumenal selves in order to explain how we can be free. Knowledge of the possible supersensible basis of our freedom is neither required for knowledge of the fact of our freedom and our obligation under the moral law itself, nor entailed by it. Every person has a knowledge of his freedom from his mere consciousness of his moral obligation, and needs nothing more to act morally; in particular, he does not need to know about transcendental idealism, and it is even part of Kant's argument that everyone *is* aware of freedom without knowing about any such philosophical theory.[58]

But what all of this means is that although the philosopher might have to introduce the idea of a supersensible substratum of humanity as the ultimate explanation of the possibility of morality, knowledge of the basis of morality in this sense is not required for the performance of moral action itself. Thus knowledge of a supersensible substratum cannot be demanded of anyone as part of the requirement of morality; *a fortiori,* neither can sensitivity to a symbolic representation of such a basis be demanded. The possibility of employing the beautiful as a symbol of morality because reflection on it may involve a reference to a supersensible ground of our nature does not justify the demand of a response to beauty from everyone, so long as the basis of such a demand must be confined to what is strictly required for acting with a good will.

This argument should be sufficient to substantiate the last of my three reasons for caution with respect to the thesis of beauty's symbolism of morality. A similar argument may be offered concerning the second of them, or that part of it which remains unargued. I argued earlier that §59 suggests two different ways in which beauty symbolizes the basis of morality: the beautiful symbolizes both the possibility of harmony among our faculties which is requisite for moral judgment and action and the supersensible basis of this harmony. I have just considered the problem with the second version of this symbolism, and can now develop the argument concerning the first. Again, one may maintain that what morality requires of everyone is consciousness of obligation under the moral law. Just to the extent that consciousness of such obligation is equivalent to consciousness of freedom, morality may require consciousness of freedom. But one could then argue that the latter requires only that a person think of himself as capable of complying with the moral law; conceiving of freedom as the possibility of harmony between the will as a natural faculty of choice (*Willkür*) and the will as the source of the moral law (*Wille*) is required for the philosophical explanation of the possibility of freedom, but not for consciousness of the fact of freedom itself. But since it is not the *fact* of freedom which the beautiful symbolizes, but the *nature* of freedom as a harmony among different faculties, consciousness of what the beautiful actually symbolizes is not required for conformity to the basic demand of morality. *A fortiori,* sensitivity to the symbol of the nature of freedom cannot be required as part of the simple demand that everyone be moral.

Both of these arguments lead to what is really the underlying problem with the supposition that beauty's symbolism of morality can be used to justify demanding aesthetic response from others, namely, the justifiability of demanding of anyone sensitivity to what is *merely* a symbol of morality, regardless of what aspect of morality or its basis it symbolizes. A symbol is not identical with the object or thesis that it symbolizes, and the justifiability of demanding knowledge of the latter from everyone thus does not entail the justifiability of demanding sensitivity to the former. If a symbolic representation of something were the only representation possible, and knowledge of that matter were justifiably demanded of everyone, then perhaps sensitivity to its symbol could also be universally demanded. But supposing that this is so in the case of beauty's symbolization of morality would conflict with one of the most fundamental tenets of Kant's moral philosophy, the thesis that everyone is immediately aware of his obligation under the moral law. Insofar as Kant maintains that this consciousness is equivalent to a consciousness of one's freedom, he is then committed to the view that every human being is immediately aware of the fact of his freedom; at the very least, Kant is certainly committed to the view that anyone may become conscious of his freedom simply by reflection on his obligation under the moral law.[59*] But then no merely indirect or symbolic representation of either the categorical imperative or the fact of freedom can actually be required for compliance with the demands of morality. To argue the contrary would be to undermine a basic part of Kant's moral philosophy.

It is small wonder, then, that Kant actually refrains from expounding the argument for the significance of beauty that Crawford attributes to him, and instead confines himself, in the actual conclusion of §59, to the claim that taste may assist in the smooth development of a habitual moral interest. The attribution of such an instrumental value to taste is sufficient to explain why we do take an interest in other persons' possession of taste, and the fact that taste may be conducive to a good moral disposition as well as to mere sociability is sufficient to explain why our interest in taste may be dignified with the title of an "intellectual" rather than a merely "empirical" interest. But the fact that taste may be helpful in the development of that ability to override the claim of purely sensuous pleasure which is requisite for compliance with the moral law does not make it a necessary condition of such compliance, and, as we have just seen, Kant could only have undermined a basic aspect of his moral philosophy if he had claimed that either aesthetic response or aesthetic judgment is such a condition.

Finally, two further points should be noted. First, it may be observed that Kant is extremely cautious in the claims he makes for taste as even a mere instrument for the development of morality. In fact, the concluding section of the *Critique of Aesthetic Judgment,* the Appendix called the "Methodology of Taste," which is Kant's only explicit discussion of aesthetic education, actually maintains that it is the development of morality which is conducive to the development of taste, and not that taste is conducive to morality. Here, Kant asserts that "taste is basically a faculty for the estimation of the sensible rendering of moral ideas," from which he concludes "that the true propaedeutic for the foundation of taste is the development of moral ideas and the culture of moral feeling; for only when the sensibility is brought into harmony with the latter can taste assume a determinate, unchangeable form."[60] This passage does not actually preclude an instrumental role for the development of taste in the development of morality, for there might be a reciprocal relation between the two dispositions which allows the development of each to advance that of the other at different stages in the total development of a person or culture. But the passage does suggest that Kant is cautious in his claim for the moral significance of taste. It seems that the most he is really willing to commit himself to, in spite of the grand claims of §59, is something like the thesis of §42: the possible value of taste for the development of morality may explain why we not only take pleasure in the appearance of the beautiful, but also have an intellectual interest in its existence.

My last point about §59 is obvious. It is just the observation that, even if the various arguments based on the symbolic status of beauty could be accepted, they would still be arguments justifying only the demand for agreement in response to the beautiful, and not the expectation of such agreement. That is to say, the arguments of §59 could at best offer support for the analysis of the claims of aesthetic judgment which precede its deduction, and not for the deduction itself. To complete the task of this deduction, §59 would have to argue that a response's symbolic significance with respect to the demand of morality provides a good reason for imputing a capacity for this response to every person as a moral agent. But there is simply no intimation of such an argument in §59 or, for that matter, in any of the other sections of the *Critique of Judgment* which explore the link between aesthetic and moral judgment. Perhaps, in analogy with the deduction he does offer, Kant could have argued that imputing moral responsibility to everyone presupposes the universal imputation of the capacity for moral judgment, and then the imputation of the capacity for aesthetic response as well because of its connection with the first capacity. But Kant does not construct such an argument.

This essentially concludes my consideration of whether the analogies which Kant draws between taste and morality can supplement the deduction of aesthetic judgment. I have argued that these analogies do not do so. The fact that the development of taste may be conducive to the development of a critical attitude toward one's own pleasures and a regard for the intersubjective validity of both maxims and one's feelings can explain the great interest we take in the taste of others, given our deep and legitimate interest in the possibility of communication in general and morality in particular. It is certainly an accomplishment on Kant's part to point this out, or to reveal that our fascination with the very issue of taste represents more than a purely epistemological interest — an accomplishment which my arguments in this chapter are hardly meant to demean. But the connection which his analogies discover cannot actually justify a *demand* for agreement in aesthetic response, let alone an *expectation* of such agreement, so long as such a justification must derive solely from consideration of the requirements of morality. Perhaps the most general problem with attempting such a justification is that, whereas the judgment of taste requires us to attribute a specific feeling of pleasure to other persons, an occurrence in the realm of nature, it is in fact questionable whether morality can require us either to demand specific feelings of other persons or to attribute such to them.

Kant's references to moral feeling in the *Critique of Judgment* might be taken to suggest both that this feeling is a pleasure and that experience of it is a requirement of morality. But both these points are far from clear in Kant's moral philosophy. Kant's theory of the association between feeling and morality is too complex a subject to be fully discussed here, but at least some of his statements must be acknowledged to suggest that we should be hesitant about interpreting any demand for feelings of pleasure in connection with moral action as part of the demand for morality, and thus even more cautious about demanding any capacity for other instances of pleasure on the basis of a demand for a feeling of pleasure linked to morality. At one point in the *Critique of Practical Reason,* Kant warns against any attempt to "pass off" even the most refined sort of pleasure "as a mode of determining the will different from that of the senses," because "the possibility of these pleasures . . . presupposes, as the first condition of our delight, the existence in us of a corresponding feeling."[61] Kant's view is that anyone's capacity for the experience of a kind of pleasure is an empirical and contingent matter, and not properly involved in a demand of morality. Now, one might argue that the composition of this passage preceded Kant's decision that the pleasure in the beautiful has an *a priori* basis, a decision reached only after the completion of the *Critique of Practical Reason,* and that it could be revised in view of Kant's aesthetic theory itself. But one would still have to face two further questions: First, is the moral feeling of pleasure which Kant invokes in the third *Critique* in fact identical with the feeling of respect? And second, even if it is, is what allows it to be demanded of other persons valid for any other case of pleasure, even one with an *a priori* basis? It is not obvious that either of these questions can be answered affirmatively.

First, it is by no means clear that the moral feeling of respect is actually a feeling of pleasure. Kant characterizes this feeling as consciousness of the constraint of the moral law, and holds that "as submission to a law, i.e., as a command, it contains therefore no pleasure but rather displeasure proportionate to this constraint." He also says that "since this constraint is exercised only through the legislation of one's own reason, it also contains something elevating, and the subjective effect on feeling . . . can also be called self-approbation with respect to pure practical reason."[62] But a feeling of self-approbation may not be identical with a feeling of pleasure, and what Kant defines here is in any case the effect of the moral law on one's natural feelings for the production of a motive, or *for* the determination of the will; it is *not* in fact identical with the feeling of pleasure which the third *Critique* treats as the *result* of the determination of the will to moral action — the pleasure which is, one might say, not so much the *motive* as the *reward* for moral action.

Second, Kant does assert that the practical law not only "produces" this feeling of respect, but also "absolutely commands it." However, the basis for its command seems to be just that reason may demand "subjective respect for the law as the sole mode of determining the will through itself."[63] In other words, as creatures with one foot in the realm of nature and one in that of reason, we require a feeling which can compete with our other, pathological inclinations if we are to be moral; it is as such a necessary condition of moral action that the feeling of respect might be demanded of everyone. But this argument legitimates a demand for feeling *only* as a necessary condition of morality. Other cases of feeling, no matter how analogous or even conducive to the feeling of respect they may be, could not actually be commanded as part of the requirement of morality. Indeed, Kant even suggests, making too much of our susceptibility to anything like a feeling of our free conformity to the law—which is what the feeling in aesthetic response is, according to §59—may be "tantamount to believing that we could finally bring it about that . . . we, like the independent deity, might come into possession of holiness of will."[64] This would be incompatible with our recognition of the imperative nature of morality. For several reasons, then, we must be wary of using Kant's analogies between moral and aesthetic feeling as a justification for demanding that anyone feel delight in the beautiful.

Art and Morality

There now remains to be considered only one aspect of Kant's connection of the aesthetic with the ethical. This is the thesis, asserted several times in later sections of the *Critique of Judgment,* that works of art must have a moral content, or represent moral ideas. As I argued at the opening of this chapter, this thesis is not identical with the view that there is a moral significance to the experience or judgment of the beautiful which justifies the demand or imputation of aesthetic response to others. The latter opinion is, first of all, asserted of beautiful objects in general, or, in the case of §42, of beautiful objects of nature only; but it is certainly not a thesis specifically about objects of art. It is also a view based on the nature of aesthetic reflection and analogies between the latter and the structure of morality, rather than a thesis which turns on any particular characterization of beautiful objects themselves. Indeed, given the emphasis which Kant places on the freedom of the imagination in aesthetic response in the passages which expound the connection between aesthetic and moral judgment, one might even expect Kant to use the link to morality as another reason for the view that the proper object of pure aesthetic judgment is a free beauty, an object which has no content or representational significance at all but pleases on account of its form alone. According to the Analytic, it is only in response to pure forms—whether natural or artificial —that the imagination is truly free; and thus, one would think, the response to objects of this sort should ground the analogy with the free determination of the will by reason in moral judgment. Why should Kant instead suggest that art must represent some moral content?

In one of the passages where this thesis is asserted, it does seem to emerge from a simple confusion between the idea that aesthetic judgment has moral significance and the idea that its objects must have moral significance. Such a confusion underlies the final paragraph of the *Critique of Aesthetic Judgment;* to quote again a sentence previously quoted in part, "taste is basically a faculty for the estimation of the sensible rendering of moral ideas (by means of a certain analogy in the reflection on both), from which fact, and from the greater susceptibility for the feeling for the latter (that is, the moral feeling) which depends on it, derives that pleasure which taste declares to be valid for mankind in general, and not just for the private feeling of an individual."[65] The first part of this sentence appeals to the analogy just expounded in §59, but appears to misstate its significance. In §59, Kant did not establish that the faculty of taste judged the rendering or symbolization of moral ideas; rather, what he showed was that because of similarities in the "procedure of judgment" in aesthetic and moral judgment, the faculty of taste itself could be taken as a symbol of the capacity for morality, or, less directly, of the object of morality, the morally good. The symbolic status of the faculty of taste was quickly transferred to its object, the beautiful, but this was permissible just insofar as the beautiful was the object of a reflection with a structure analogous to that of moral judgment. Kant did not demonstrate that beautiful objects have or must have any connection to morality *apart* from the structure of our reflection upon them. Thus he did not argue that beautiful objects must have moral content, or signify morality by what they represent. Yet when Kant states that the analogy in our reflection on both moral and aesthetic judgment implies that taste judges of the sensible rendering of moral concepts, he seems to assume that the objects of taste themselves render moral concepts. This is not a consequence of his theory.

As the sentence continues, however, it suggests a deeper ground than mere confusion for the unexpected twist in Kant's argument. Its second half implies that it is an object's representation of moral ideas which makes it an object of pleasure "valid for mankind in general, and not just for the private feeling of an individual." In other words, not relying on §59's theory of symbolism, but instead appealing directly to taste's requirement of a universally valid basis for pleasure, Kant now hints that the rendition of moral concepts may be the ultimate foundation for intersubjectivity in aesthetic response. If the content of an object is something to which we all respond with equal pleasure, Kant may be supposing, then so will be the object itself; and if this is true, Kant can find a final guarantee for the intersubjective validity of aesthetic response to particular objects, as long as he just assumes that moral ideas themselves occasion such a response. Kant certainly does assume that art typically represents ideas, and moral ideas at that — poets, for instance, essay "to render sensible rational ideas of invisible beings, such as the realm of the blessed, the kingdom of the damned, eternity, creation . . . death, envy, and all the vices, as well as love and fame"[66] — and he may well take this purported fact about art[67*] to be a real basis for its intersubjective appeal.

In other words, perhaps Kant himself recognized that neither the connections between aesthetic and ordinary cognitive judgment nor those between aesthetic and practical judgment could really justify the absolute and *a priori* claim to intersubjective validity which he required of the judgment of taste, and thus appealed to the intersubjective acceptability of moral ideas in desperation. Indeed, it is interesting to note that although the conclusion of §60 may be in conflict with Kant's doctrine of free beauty, there is actually a basic similarity in the arguments which must underlie both §60 and Kant's formalism. In deriving the formalist strictures of his theory of free beauty, Kant did not restrict himself to what was entailed by the explanation of aesthetic response as the harmony of the faculties, but excluded from the grounds of pure judgments of taste any aspects of objects, such as their colors or tones, which could not be assumed to produce the same pleasure in everyone and, thus, compliance with the requirement of universal validity. Similarly, the Analytic can also be regarded as having excluded the representational significance of objects from consideration in the pure judgment of taste because that too could occasion unwanted disagreement. Thus, having argued that the distinction between free and dependent beauty is in part a distinction between objects regarded as beautiful apart from any content they may have and those regarded as beautiful because of such content, Kant asserted that "through this distinction one can settle many quarrels on beauty between critics, insofar as one shows them that one [critic] is dealing with free beauty, and the other with dependent beauty, the former making a pure judgment of taste, and the latter one that is applied."[68] Kant may be making a similar move in §60, but instead of *excluding* certain properties from those considered by the pure judgment of taste because of their tendency to produce *disagreement,* he now *includes* certain factors, even making them essential, because they instead promise *agreement.*

But such an argument would indeed be a product of desperation. Although the nature of aesthetic response as a harmony of the faculties did

not actually preclude the inclusion of symbols of morality or other ideas in
the manifold of imagination, as Kant initially supposed, to make the representation of such ideas the basis of aesthetic response and its intersubjective
validity would be to pay too high a price for the deduction of that validity.
It would undermine the basis of Kant's aesthetic theory, making the representation of a certain content and the fulfillment of the determinate ends
of morality the basis of aesthetic response and the judgment of taste, and
thus removing the free harmony of the faculties from its fundamental role
in both the explanation and the justification of taste.

Section 60 is not, however, the only place where Kant suggests that art
must have a moral content. Before entirely rejecting this thesis as nothing
but a desperate attempt to link the intersubjective validity of taste to that
of moral judgment by any means available, we must consider one other
argument. This is found in §52, in the midst of those sections of the *Critique of Judgment* explicitly devoted to the theory of art rather than of aesthetic judgment in general. Kant begins this section by considering the
possibility of combining different media of art in a single object, as rhe-
toric is combined with pictorial representation and music in the case of an
opera. This leads him to the consideration of the relative merits of different artistic media which occupies §53, but before embarking on that discussion he asserts that no matter what media are combined in a given object, what remains essential in all fine art is the "form which is final for
observation and for estimation," and not the "matter of sensation (charm
or emotion)."[69] In regard to the latter, he goes on, our aim is merely enjoyment, "which leaves nothing behind it in the idea, and renders the soul
dull, the object by and by distasteful, and the mind dissatisfied with itself
and ill-humored because of its consciousness of a disposition contrary to
reason in its judgments." Kant then claims: "If the fine arts are not, either
proximately or remotely, brought into combination with moral ideas,
which alone bring with them a self-sufficient delight, this is their ultimate
fate. They then only serve for diversion, of which one will be all the more
needful as one has already used it to drive away the mind's dissatisfaction
with itself, so that one makes oneself ever more useless and dissatisfied with
oneself. In general the beauties of nature are most useful for the first objective [of combination with moral ideas]."[70] This is a remarkable passage,
which could not be fully explained without a detailed consideration of
Kant's peculiar contrasts between the beauties of nature and art, which is
beyond the scope of this book. But I will suggest a similarity between this
attempt to require moral significance in the objects of aesthetic judgment

and the attempt found in §60. There, I suggested, Kant may have tried to compensate for the ultimate insufficiency of his deduction by appealing to the intersubjective validity of moral ideas; and the insufficiency of the deduction which motivates this appeal, one could argue, is due to the fact that the harmony of the faculties must ultimately be acknowledged to be a psychological rather than a purely epistemological concept. The present passage may also be motivated by a recognition of the ultimately psychological nature of the harmony of the faculties. Kant may now be conceding a problem that can arise from his explanation of aesthetic pleasure. That explanation turned on the fact that the harmony of the faculties is a mental state in which the general cognitive objective of the unification of manifolds is fulfilled apart from its ordinary condition, subsumption under a concept, and thus a state in which this fulfillment is, in a sense, unexpected. The pleasure we take in an object which disposes the mind to this state is due to just this unexpectedness of the unifiability of its manifold. But if that is the case, then it would seem to follow that familiarity with an object should diminish the pleasure one takes in it, as Kant suggests is the case with cognitive success generally. This would be the case because even if repeated experience of a beautiful object produced no empirical concept to guarantee the harmony of the faculties, such repetition might nevertheless produce an expectation of unifiability, and thus undermine one's pleasure in it. Aesthetic pleasure itself, then, would require some ground other than the mere harmony of the faculties if it is to retain its interest in spite of familiarity. The representation of moral ideas could provide this deeper basis.

However, there are many problems with this argument. First, it may be maintained that in the case of a truly great work of art each experience of it reveals new features, or creates new possibilities for the harmony of the faculties. No amount of exposure to such a work can ever make one's response fully predictable. Or one might maintain that even if the pleasures of aesthetic response are less enduring than those of moral consciousness, that is no reason for Kant to modify his aesthetic theory. It might just be a fact about aesthetic pleasure that, although it is more truly free than any other pleasures, it is less enduring than some. If so, the theory of the harmony of the faculties would explain this peculiarity, and need no revision. But I cannot expand these remarks here; I can only suggest that Kant's attempt to link aesthetic response with morality may well be connected with his at least implicit recognition of the limitations placed on aesthetic judgment by its ultimately psychological basis. The unexpected claim of

§52 may confirm what I have already argued: the psychological element which must be attributed to Kant's concept of the harmony of the faculties, though it is crucial to much of the explanatory power and interest of his aesthetic theory, must also be recognized as placing limits on the success of the deduction of aesthetic judgment.

This chapter has had to be long and complex to cope with the diversity, suggestiveness, and, as it has turned out, inconclusiveness of Kant's attempts to link aesthetic and moral judgments, but its results may now be briefly summarized. Kant's attempt to construct such a link may well have been motivated by his concern to buttress his deduction of aesthetic judgment. This objective, however, could have been accomplished only if the connection between taste and morality justified not just the demand for agreement in aesthetic response but the imputation of it as well. But the arguments which Kant actually offered hardly touch on the latter requirement, and though they seem better suited to proving the justifiability of the demand for agreement in taste, even here they run into difficulty. Kant's attempts to justify the demand of taste by its significance for morality are either not strong enough—they do not make taste a necessary condition of morality—or else too strong—they undermine basic tenets of Kant's aesthetics or ethics. Ultimately, Kant's attempt to secure the intersubjectivity of taste in the conditions of cognition, whatever its deficiencies, is more successful than his attempt to secure it in the nature of morality.

It is Kant's analysis of the epistemology and psychology of taste which is his most impressive contribution to aesthetics. Though his deduction of aesthetic judgment falls short of his own objectives, his analysis of aesthetic judgment and explanation of aesthetic response must be recognized as great accomplishments. Kant's explorations of the claims of taste, the psychology of taste, and the kinds of assumptions we make about both ourselves and others in venturing judgments of taste are often problematic, but clearly do make real strides in integrating the phenomenon of taste into a general model of human thought and feeling. And even though Kant's analysis of the moral significance of taste fails to complete his own deduction of aesthetic judgment, it does reveal some of the grounds of our deep interest in the very question of taste itself. Thus it too sheds light on the role of taste in establishing the intersubjective validity of our thought and feeling—the true subject of Kant's concern in a work which is both brilliant and confused by turn, but surely the most profound investigation of its subject which philosophy has yet to offer us.

Translations Consulted

All quotations from Kant's writings on aesthetics are my own translations, though I sometimes follow the versions of earlier translators with little change. Quotations from Kant's other writings are generally drawn from standard translations, but are occasionally modified. The translations I have consulted or followed are:

Anthropology from a Pragmatic Point of View. Trans., with Introduction and Notes, by Mary J. Gregor. The Hague, Martinus Nijhoff, 1974.

Critique of Judgment. Trans., with an Introduction, by J. H. Bernard. New York, Hafner Publishing Co., 1951 (originally published in 1892).

Critique of Judgment. Trans., with Analytical Indexes, by James Creed Meredith. Oxford, Oxford University Press, 1952 (originally published in 1911).

Critique of Practical Reason. Trans., with an Introduction, by Lewis White Beck. Indianapolis and New York, Bobbs-Merrill Publishing Co., 1956.

Critique of Pure Reason. Trans. Norman Kemp Smith. London and New York, Macmillan and Co. and St. Martin's Press, 1964 (originally published in 1929). Quoted with permission of the publishers.

First Introduction to the Critique of Judgment. Trans. James Haden. Indianapolis and New York, Bobbs-Merrill Publishing Co., 1965.

Foundations of the Metaphysics of Morals. Trans., with an Introduction, by Lewis White Beck. Indianapolis and New York, Bobbs-Merrill Publishing Co., 1959.

Kant: Philosophical Correspondence, 1759-1799. Ed. and trans. Arnulf Zweig. Chicago, University of Chicago Press, 1967.

Logic. Trans., with an Introduction, by Robert S. Hartman and Wolfgang Schwartz. Indianapolis and New York, Bobbs-Merrill Publishing Co., 1974.

Metaphysical Elements of Justice. Trans., with an Introduction, by John Ladd. Indianapolis and New York, Bobbs-Merrill Publishing Co., 1965.

Metaphysical Foundations of Natural Science. Trans., with an Introduction and Essay, by James Ellington. Indianapolis and New York, Bobbs-Merrill Publishing Co., 1970.

Prolegomena to Any Future Metaphysics. With an Introduction by Lewis White Beck. Indianapolis and New York, Bobbs-Merrill Publishing Co., 1950.

Selected Pre-Critical Writings and Correspondence with Beck. Ed. G. B. Kerferd and D. E. Walford. New York, Barnes and Noble, 1968.

Abbreviations Used
in the Notes

Ak.   *Kant's gesammelte Schriften, herausgegeben von der Königlichen Preussischen Akademie der Wissenschaften* (now the Deutschen Akademie der Wissenschaften zu Berlin). Berlin, Walter de Gruyter & Co., 1902 — . (This is generally known as the *Akademie* edition.)

APPV   *Anthropology from a Practical Point of View*
CJ   *Critique of Judgment*
CPR   *Critique of Pure Reason*
CPrR   *Critique of Practical Reason*
FI   *First Introduction to the Critique of Judgment*
FMM   *Foundations of the Metaphysics of Morals*
GR   General Remark
L   *Logic*
MFNS   *Metaphysical Foundations of Natural Science*
MM   *Metaphysics of Morals*, I (*Metaphysical Elements of Justice*)
PFM   *Prolegomena to Any Future Metaphysics*
R   *Reflexion*

Notes

Citations of Kant's writings are given according to the following method. For Kant's published works, the abbreviated title of the work is followed by an Arabic (preceded by "§") or Roman section number, if Kant provided one, and then by the volume and page number of the passage as it is found in the *Akademie* edition of Kant's writings, abbreviated *Ak*. Exceptions to this rule are: the volume numbers are omitted from the many references to the *Critique of Judgment*, which appears in volume 5 of the *Akademie* edition, and its *First Introduction*, which appears in volume 20; and citations to the *Critique of Pure Reason* use the standard pagination of its first (A) and second (B) editions instead of the location in the *Akademie* edition. For Kant's *Reflexionen*, the unpublished fragments collected in those volumes of the *Akademie* edition constituting *Kant's handschriftliche Nachlass*, the letter *R* is followed by the number of the fragment and then by the volume and page of its location in the *Akademie* edition.

Introduction

1. *CJ*, §36, p. 289.

2. *CJ*, §8, pp. 215-216. The reader will immediately note that I have characterized Kant's theory of taste by reference to his analysis of judgments of beauty alone, and have made no mention of judgments on the sublime. In what follows, the latter will be mentioned only in passing. There are at least three reasons sufficient for excluding any extended discussion of the sublime from a study which, like this one, is intended to examine only Kant's solution to the problem of taste rather than the whole of his aesthetics. First, Kant himself makes no reference to the sublime in his introductory account of his project (see *CJ*, VII, p. 190; VIII, p. 193), nor does his fundamental explanation of aesthetic response as a harmony between imagination and understanding leave any room for the feeling of the sublime, which involves the faculty of reason instead of understanding (contrast *CJ*, VII, and *FI*, VIII, passim, with *CJ*, §23, p. 245, and §27, p. 257). Although Kant's explanation of our response to sublimity might be taken to supplement and enrich his basic model of aesthetic response, it does seem something of an afterthought, or a concession to the standard topics of eighteenth-century aesthetics (or taste!). Second, Kant actually denies that any deduction of intersubjective validity is needed in the case of the judgment of the sublime (*CJ*, §30, pp. 279-280); and though I shall argue in Chapter 7 that Kant's reason for this rejection is inadequate, his dis-

cussion of the sublime does minimize the question of intersubjectivity, which is my main concern. It thus adds nothing to the subtle analysis of the relations between subjective aesthetic response and intersubjectively valid aesthetic judgment which is the heart of Kant's discussion of the beautiful and the main source of its continuing interest. Finally, even if there is historical interest in Kant's discussion of the sublime, I think it safe to assume that his analysis of this particular aesthetic merit will not be of much interest to modern sensibilities, and thus that most of what we can or will learn from Kant must come from his discussion of judgments of beauty.

3. *CJ*, §36, p. 288.

4. For the sake of brevity, I shall refer to the *Critique of Judgment* even when I in fact mean only its first half, the *Critique of Aesthetic Judgment,* and the two versions of the Introduction to the work as a whole (on which see note 1 to Chapter 2, below). The second half of Kant's book, the *Critique of Teleological Judgment,* will not be discussed in this study.

5. *CJ*, §58, p. 346.

6. I shall present a more detailed study of the historical background of Kant's aesthetics in Ted Cohen and Paul Guyer, eds., *Essays in Kant's Aesthetics* (University of Chicago Press, forthcoming).

7. *CJ*, §58, p. 346.

8. *CJ*, §29, GR, p. 278.

9. *CJ*, §29, GR, p. 278.

10. *CJ*, §57, Remark II, pp. 345-346.

11. *CJ*, §29, GR, p. 278.

12. *CJ*, §19, p. 237.

13. *CJ*, §29, GR, p. 278.

14. *CJ*, §57, Remark II, p. 346.

15. *CJ*, §15, p. 228.

16. *CJ*, §5, p. 210.

17. Hutcheson, *An Inquiry into the Original of Our Ideas of Beauty and Virtue: In Two Treatises,* 4th ed., corrected (London, D. Midwinter et al., 1728), I, xii, xiii, p. 11.

18. Hume, *A Treatise of Human Nature,* ed. L. A. Selby-Bigge (Oxford, Clarendon Press, 1888), II, I, viii, p. 299.

19. Burke, *A Philosophical Enquiry into the Origin of Our Ideas of the Sublime and the Beautiful,* ed. James T. Boulton (London, Routledge and Kegan Paul, 1958), pp. 149-150. See *CJ*, §29, GR, p. 277, where Kant calls such "psychological observations . . . extremely fine," but thinks them suited only for "empirical anthropology."

20. Hutcheson, *Inquiry,* VI, iv, p. 73.

21. Hutcheson, *Inquiry,* VI, xi, p. 80.

22. Hume, *Enquiries concerning the Human Understanding and the Principles of Morals,* 2nd ed., ed. L. A. Selby-Bigge (Oxford, Clarendon Press, 1902), pp. 170-173.

23. Hume, "The Standard of Taste," in *Essays Moral, Political, and Literary* (Oxford, Oxford University Press, 1963), pp. 238-239.

24. Burke, *Philosophical Enquiry,* p. 11; see also p. 20.

25. Kames, *Elements of Criticism,* new ed. (New York, F. J. Huntington and Mason and Law, 1852), ch. XXV, p. 467. Henry Home, Lord Kames, is properly referred to by "Kames," the title he adopted on his ascendency to the Scottish high bench. The reader should note, however, that Kant, no adept in the rules of Scottish etiquette, referred to him as "Home," and this usage will be followed in several quotations in Chapter 1.

26. Kames, *Elements of Criticism,* ch. XXV, p. 468.

27. Kames, *Elements of Criticism,* ch. XXV, p. 469.

28. Baumgarten, *Aesthetica* (Bari, Jos. Laterza et Filios, 1936), §1.

29. Leibniz, "Remarks on Shaftsbury," in Gottfried Wilhelm Leibniz, *Philosophical Papers and Letters: A Selection,* 2nd ed., ed. Leroy E. Loemker (Dordrecht, D. Reidel Publishing Co., 1969), p. 634.

30. Wolff, *Vernünfftige Gedancken von Gott, der Welt, und der Seele des Menschen,* new ed. (Halle im Magdeburgischen, Rengerischen Buchhandlung, 1751), §§316, 319, 321.

31. Wolff, *Vernünfftige Gedancken,* §§404, 417.

32. Baumgarten, *Metaphysik,* trans. G. F. Meier (Halle im Magdeburgischen, Carl Hermann Hemmerde, 1767), §452.

33. Meier, *Anfangsgründe aller schönen Künste und Wissenschaften* (various editions) (Halle im Magdeburgischen: Carl Hermann Hemmerde, 1754-1769), §23.

34. Baumgarten, *Metaphysik,* §73.

35. Meier, *Anfangsgründe,* §24.

36. See Baumgarten, *Aesthetica,* §§177, 182, 183, 189.

37. Baumgarten, *Aesthetica,* §72; cf. *Metaphysik,* §§394, 395.

38. Leibniz, *Monadology,* §60, in Loemker, p. 649; Baumgarten, *Metaphysik,* §553.

39. Leibniz, *Discourse on Metaphysics,* §14, in Loemker, p. 312.

40. Baumgarten, *Metaphysik,* §291.

41. *CPR,* A 339/B 397.

42. *CPR,* A 298/B 355.

43. *R* 647, *Ak.* 15, I, p. 284; see also *R* 627, p. 273; *R* 710, p. 314; *R* 1850 and 1854, *Ak.* 16, p. 137.

44. *R* 640, *Ak.* 15, I, p. 280; see also *R* 712, p. 316.

45. *R* 1850, *Ak.* 16, p. 137.

46. *CJ,* §9, p. 219.

47. *CJ,* §40, p. 295.

48. Eva Schaper, "Kant on Aesthetic Appraisals," *Kant-Studien,* 65, no. 4 (1973), 443.

49. *CPR,* A 51/B 75.

50. Some of the difficulties in the structure of the *Critique of Judgment* are discussed by Wolfhart Henckmann in "Das Problem der ästhetischen Wahrnehmung in Kants Ästhetik," *Philosophisches Jahrbuch der Görres-Gesellschaft,* 78, no. 2 (1971), e.g., pp. 324 and 327, where he quotes Luigi Pareyson's description of the third *Critique* as a "ricchezza tumultuosa e un po' disordinata."

1. Kant's Early Views

1. Letter 313, to K. L. Reinhold, December 28 and 31, 1787, in *Ak.* 10, pp. 513-515; Zweig, *Kant: Philosophical Correspondence,* pp. 127-128.

2. Letter 70, to Marcus Herz, February 21, 1772, in *Ak.* 10, pp. 129-135; Zweig, pp. 70-76 (the quotation is from p. 71).

3. See "The Approach to an *a priori* Principle," in Chapter 1, above.

4. *R* 623, *Ak.* 15, I, p. 270.

5. *R* 1787, *Ak.* 16, p. 114.

6. See Baumgarten, *Metaphysik,* §395.

7. *R* 1588, *Ak.* 16, p. 27. This *Reflexion,* as well as those referred to in notes 8 and 16 of this chapter, were first brought to my attention by Paul Menzer, *Kants Ästhetik in ihrer Entwicklung, Abhandlungen der Deutschen Akademie der Wissenschaften zu Berlin, Klasse für Gesellschaftswissenschaften,* 1950, no. 2 (Berlin, Akademie Verlag, 1952), pp. 30-31.

8. *R* 1585, *Ak.* 16, p. 26.

9. *R* 1856, *Ak.* 16, p. 138.

10. *R* 1587, *Ak.* 16, p. 26.
11. *R* 1787, *Ak.* 16, p. 114.
12. *R* 1848, *Ak.* 16, p. 136.
13. See Menzer, *Kants Ästhetik,* pp. 30-31.
14. *L, Ak.* 9, p. 15.
15. See Meier, *Anfangsgründe,* §470 ff.
16. *R* 1579, *Ak.* 16, p. 19.
17. *R* 1579, *Ak.* 16, p. 17.
18. *R* 1579, *Ak.* 16, p. 18.
19. *R* 1579, *Ak.* 16, p. 19.
20. *R* 1579, *Ak.* 16, p. 19.
21. *FI, Ak.* 20, p. 239; *CJ,* §19, p. 237.
22. *L, Ak.* 9, p. 15.
23. Baumgarten, *Aesthetica,* §1.
24. *R* 1895, *Ak.* 16, p. 151.
25. *R* 1794, *Ak.* 16, p. 118.
26. *R* 625, *Ak.* 15, I, p. 271; see also *R* 630, *Ak.* 15, I, p. 274.
27. *R* 625, *Ak.* 15, I, p. 272; see also *R* 1799, *Ak.* 16, p. 119.
28. *R* 1798, *Ak.* 16, p. 119.
29. *R* 1794, *Ak.* 16, p. 118.
30. *R* 715, *Ak.* 15, I, p. 317.
31. *R* 875, *Ak.* 15, I, p. 384.
32. *R* 878, *Ak.* 15, I, p. 385.
33. *R* 1845, *Ak.* 16, p. 135.
34. See "The Key to the Critique of Taste" in Chapter 4, above.
35. *R* 851, *Ak.* 15, I, p. 376.
36. *R* 648, *Ak.* 15, I, p. 284.
37. *R* 851, *Ak.* 15, I, p. 386.
38. *R* 653, *Ak.* 15, I, p. 289.
39. *R* 701, *Ak.* 15, I, p. 311.
40. *R* 686, *Ak.* 15, I, p. 306.
41. *R* 1791, *Ak.* 16, p. 116.
42. *Logik Blomberg, Ak.* 24, I, pp. 45-46.
43. *Logik Phillipi, Ak.* 24, I, p. 354.
44. *Logik Phillipi, Ak.* 24, I, p. 355.
45. *CJ,* §9, p. 218. Kant fails to notice, however, that a trace of the rejected view has surfaced only a few paragraphs before.
46. *R* 878, *Ak.* 15, I, p. 385.
47. *R* 630, *Ak.* 15, I, p. 274.
48. See Herman-J. de Vleeschauwer, *The Development of Kantian Thought,* trans. A. R. C. Duncan (Edinburgh, Thos. Nelson and Sons, 1962), pp. 124-127.
49. *CPR,* A 21.
50. *CPR,* B 35-36 (my emphasis).
51. See *FI,* p. 237, and *MFNS, Ak.* 4, pp. 468-471.
52. See the letter to Reinhold, *Ak.* 10, pp. 513-515; Zweig, pp. 127-128.

2. The Theory of Reflective Judgment

1. My interpretation will draw from both the first Introduction to the *Critique of Judgment* and the published Introduction. The first Introduction, which was rejected by Kant

"simply because it was disproportionately extensive for the text" (Letter 549, to J. S. Beck, December 4, 1792, in *Ak.* 11, p. 381; Kerferd and Walford, *Selected Pre-Critical Writings,* p. 149), and was not published in its entirety until 1922, has been the subject of many grand claims following its nineteenth-century denomination as *Über Philosophie Überhaupt.* A number of interpretations of Kant's aesthetics have been based upon it in the belief that it offers more insight into the systematic significance of aesthetics than does the published Intro- duction (for instance, K. Kuypers, *Kants Kunsttheorie und die Einheit der Kritik der Urteils- kraft,* Amsterdam and London, North-Holland Publishing Co., 1972). My own view is that both of these Introductions make equally important contributions to our understanding of the internal structure of Kant's theory of aesthetic judgment and to the systematic signifi- cance of that theory, although they do not always make precisely the same contribution. Kant is less clear in the third *Critique* about matters of methodology than he was in either of the first two *Critiques*—as if the haste with which he tried to finish his work in what he saw as his few remaining years of life left him little time for such niceties—and the disparities of the two Introductions reflect that fact. The interpretation of the *Critique of Judgment,* however, can- not affort to reject any clues to the true structure of its theory. Consequently, in what follows I shall draw upon both Introductions, noting differences between them where these seem inter- esting or important.

2. In arguing that Kant's subsumption of aesthetic judgment under reflective judgment confuses his treatment of the former as much as it illuminates it, I am departing from the tra- dition of those who use the connection with reflective judgment to argue that the major con- cern of Kant's aesthetics is the problem of "individuality," or our grasp of particular objects. The major work in this tradition is Alfred Baeumler, *Das Irrationalitätsproblem in der Ästhetik und Logik des 18. Jahrhunderts bis zur Kirtik der Urteilskraft* (Halle, 1923; re- printed by the Wissenschaftliche Buchgesellschaft, Darmstadt, 1967).

3. The problems in Kant's treatment of the relations between nature and art cannot be fully explored in this study. Some of these issues are further discussed in my article "Interest, Nature, and Art: A Problem in Kant's Aesthetics," *The Review of Metaphysics,* 31, no. 4 (June 1978), 580-603.

4. See *CJ,* IX, pp. 195-197. Commentators on the third *Critique* have often made this role the focus of their interpretation; in my view, to the detriment of the analysis of Kant's theory of taste itself. One work in this vein is A. C. Genova, "Kant's Complex Problem of Re- flective Judgment," *The Review of Metaphysics,* 23, no. 3 (March 1970), 452-480.

5. Such a view is maintained by Victor Basch, *Essai critique sur l'esthetique de Kant,* 2nd ed. (Paris, J. Vrin, 1927), pp. 153-154.

6. *FI,* II, p. 201; cf. *CJ,* Preface, p. 167.

7. The third *Critique,* it may here be noted, generally identifies the faculty of "reason" with pure practical reason, the source of moral reasoning, and omits reference to the faculty of pure theoretical reason cautiously admitted to the *Critique of Pure Reason's* model of mind. This could well be because the faculty of reflective judgment actually takes over the main constructive function earlier assigned to theoretical reason (see note 41, below).

8. *FI,* II, p. 202; *CJ,* Preface, p. 168.

9. *CJ,* Preface, p. 169.

10. *FI,* II, p. 202.

11. *CJ,* Preface, p. 169.

12. *CJ,* II, p. 177.

13. *CJ,* Preface, p. 169.

14. *CJ,* II, p. 174.

15. *CJ,* III, p. 177.

16. *CJ,* Preface, p. 169.

17. *FI,* III, pp. 205-206; cf. *CJ,* III, pp. 177-178. Kant notes that earlier philosophers

(the rationalists) had attempted to reduce all of these capacities to cognition, but that "it has now been obvious for some time that such an attempt to bring unity into the plurality of faculties . . . is futile" (*FI*, III, p. 206). One of the philosophers who made this obvious was Moses Mendelssohn, who insisted (though *not* in his early writings on aesthetics) that "between knowing and desiring there is approval, approbation, satisfaction of mind" (*Morgenstunden*, 2nd ed., Berlin, 1785, p. 118; quoted and discussed by Lewis White Beck in *Early German Philosophy*, Cambridge, Mass.: Harvard University Press, 1969, pp. 328-329).

18. *CJ*, III, p. 178.
19. *FI*, III, pp. 207-208.
20. *CJ*, III, p. 177.
21. *FI*, III, p. 207.
22. *FI*, III, p. 206.
23. *FI*, III, p. 207.
24. *FI*, III, p. 208.
25. *CJ*, IV, p. 179.
26. *FI*, V, p. 211.
27. *FI*, V, p. 212.
28. *CJ*, IV, p. 179.
29. *CJ*, IV, p. 179.
30. *FI*, V, p. 211.
31. *FI*, VII, p. 220. See above, Chapter 3.
32. *CPR*, A 126.
33. *CPR*, A 122.
34. *CPR*, A 123.
35. *CPR*, B 142.
36. *CPR*, B 164-165.
37. *CPR*, A 642-668/B 670-696.
38. *CPR*, A 647/B 675.
39. *CPR*, A 651/B 679.
40. *CPR*, A 648/B 676.
41. A fuller discussion of the theory of reflective judgment would have to include an examination of the first *Critique*'s theory of the regulative principles of reason more detailed than what can be included here (some discussion of this theory may be found in Gerd Buchdahl, *Metaphysics and the Philosophy of Science*, Oxford, Basil Blackwell, 1969, pp. 495-509). It must suffice here to say that the first *Critique* is never as insistent as the third that science requires principles additional to the categories for its very possibility. In his University of Pittsburgh doctoral dissertation "Reason and Truth in Kant's Theory of Experience" (1977), Thomas E. Wartenberg has argued that the Dialectic's introduction of systematicity provides a necessary component of Kant's theory of the justification of empirical judgments. This may be so, but Kant's return to the issue in the third *Critique* suggests that, at the least, he may not have been aware of what he had really established about systematicity in the first.
42. *FI*, II, p. 203.
43. *FI*, II, p. 203 (Kant's emphasis omitted).
44. *FI*, V, 213-214; cf. *CJ*, V, p. 185, and *CPR* A 655-658/B 683-686.
45. *FI*, IV, p. 209.
46. *FI*, IV, p. 210.
47. *CJ*, V, p. 185.
48. *FI*, V, p. 210.
49. *FI*, IV, p. 209.
50. *FI*, V, p. 212 (my emphasis); see also *FI*, V, p. 215.
51. *FI*, IV, pp. 208-209.

52. *FI*, II, p. 202.
53. *CJ*, IV, p. 180.
54. *CJ*, IV, p. 180.
55. *CJ*, V, p. 183.
56. *CJ*, V, pp. 183-184.
57. *FI*, II, p. 202.
58. *FI*, IV, p. 210.
59. *FI*, IV, p. 209.
60. *FI*, V, pp. 211-212.
61. *FI*, II, p. 204.
62. *FI*, V, pp. 213-214.
63. *CJ*, V, p. 184.
64. *FI*, IV, p. 209, V, p. 215; *CJ*, V, p. 185.
65. *CJ*, V, pp. 185-186.
66. *CPR*, A 122; see also A 100-101.
67. *FI*, V, p. 214.
68. *FI*, V, p. 214.
69. *FI*, IV, p. 210.
70. *FI*, V, p. 212.
71. *FI*, V, p. 213.
72. *FI*, V, p. 214.
73. *FI*, V, p. 216 (Kant's emphasis omitted).
74. A similar point is made by Francis X. J. Coleman in *The Harmony of Reason: A Study in Kant's Aesthetics* (Pittsburgh, University of Pittsburgh Press, 1974), p. 9.
75. This aspect of the theory of reflective judgment will be considered at length in Chapter 3.
76. *FI*, IV, p. 210; cf. *CJ*, V, p. 182.
77. See *CPR*, A 662/B 690.
78. *CPR*, A 644/B 672.
79. *CPR*, A 662/B 690.
80. *CPR*, A 663/B 691.
81. *FI*, V, p. 216. The choice of a translation for *Zweckmässigkeit* is difficult. Neither Bernard's "purposiveness" nor Meredith's "finality" is completely satisfactory. "Purposiveness" reproduces the structure of the original and preserves its connection to the concept of purpose (*Zweck*), but may also connote more of a connection to purpose than, in the end, Kant actually intends. "Finality" has an artificiality to it which allows it to function as a technical term, deriving its meaning solely from Kant's definitions rather than from any preestablished connotation; but at the same time it may lose all reference to "end" or "purpose." Occasionally, words such as "appropriateness" or "suitability" have been suggested as translations of *Zweckmässigkeit*, but these translations, while possibly capturing all the sense which *ultimately* attaches to Kant's concept, are unsatisfactory precisely because they obscure the problem *about* Kant's concept, namely, that of determining what connection between beauty and purpose it really allows. In the face of these difficulties, I will generally use "finality" in virtue of its artificiality, but will sometimes uses "purposiveness" and its cognates where emphasis on the original connection to purpose seems appropriate.
82. See *CJ*, V, p. 183, and *FI*, V, p. 212. Both of these passages introduce reference to the first *Critique*'s schematism — that is, its provision of rules concerning spatiotemporal relations as empirical criteria for various purely logical notions — as the means by which determinant judgment works, and thus create the impression that there will be some analogue of schematism for the case of reflective judgment.
83. See *CJ*, IV, p. 180.

84. *CJ,* IV, p. 180.
85. *CJ,* IV, pp. 180-181.
86. *CJ,* IV, p. 180.
87. E.g., Aristotle, *Physics,* bk. II, ch. 8.
88. *CJ,* IV, p. 180.
89. *CJ,* V, p. 185.
90. *CJ,* IV, p. 181.
91. *FI,* V, p. 215 (my emphasis).
92. *FI,* V, p. 216.
93. *CJ,* IV, p. 181.
94. *FI,* V, p. 216.
95. *FI,* VI, p. 217.
96. *FI,* V, p. 216.
97. *FI,* IX, p. 234.
98. *FI,* V, p. 211.
99. *FI,* VI, p. 217.
100. *FI,* VI, pp. 217-218.
101. *FI,* VII, p. 219.
102. *FI,* VII, p. 220.
103. *FI,* VII, p. 220.
104. *FI,* VII, pp. 220-221.
105. *FI,* VII, p. 219 (my emphasis).
106. *FI,* VII, p. 221.
107. *FI,* VII, p. 219.
108. *FI,* IX, p. 232.
109. *CJ,* VIII, p. 192.
110. *CJ,* VIII, p. 192.
111. *FI,* IX, p. 212.
112. *CJ,* VIII, p. 192.
113. *FI,* IX, p. 236.
114. *FI,* IX, p. 236.
115. *FI,* IX, pp. 232-233.
116. *CJ,* §30, pp. 279-280; see Chapter 7, above.
117. *FI,* IX, p. 235.
118. *CJ,* VIII, p. 193.
119. *CJ,* §57, pp. 340-341; see Chapter 10, above.
120. *FI,* X, pp. 238-239.
121. *CJ,* VIII, p. 193.
122. *FI,* IV, p. 210.
123. See *CJ,* §5, p. 211; §9, p. 219; §17, p. 236; and §22, p. 240.
124. *CJ,* §22, p. 240.

3. The Harmony of the Faculties

1. This is essentially the approach of Eva Schaper in "Kant on Aesthetic Appraisals." It is also, in a sense, the strategy of more traditional readings of Kant's theory as resting on the concept of disinterestedness. Such an interpretation is criticized in Michael Neville, "Kant's Characterization of Aesthetic Experience," *Journal of Aesthetics and Art Criticism,* 33, no. 2

(Winter 1974), 193-202. Neville adduces Monroe Beardsley, Marshall Cohen, and Jerome Stolnitz as adherents of such an interpretation (pp. 194, 201).

2. Such a view is implicit in Mary Warnock's belief that there is really no difference between Kant's theory of what is involved in making a judgment of taste and his theory of what is "involved in creating or expressing something upon which an aesthetic judgment is to be passed by another" (*Imagination,* Berkeley and Los Angeles, University of California Press, 1976, p. 41). But this leaves out Kant's whole interest in the *justification* of judgments of taste, and completely obscures the subtle relationship between justification and explanation which is crucial to Kant's theory. Although Warnock's view is motivated by her interest in Kant as a precursor of the Romanticists, it fails to see just how Kant forms the link between eighteenth- and nineteenth-century aesthetics by his discovery that the solution to the problem of taste, the predominant concern of eighteenth-century theorists, entails a theory of artistic creation, soon to become the predominant concern of the nineteenth-century thinkers.

3. *CJ*, VII, p. 188 (emphasis added).

4. This characterization of the theory of the first *Critique* actually comes from the third: *CJ*, VII, p. 189.

5. *CJ*, VII, p. 189.

6. *CJ*, §3, p. 206. The *Critique of Pure Reason* denies that space and time on the one hand and phenomena such as colors on the other are subjective in the same sense, because only the former possess genuine "ideality," that is, are both subjective *and* necessary components in any knowledge (*CPR*, A 28/B 44). The third *Critique* does not actually involve any change in this position, but only acknowledges that, in spite of their contingency, sensations of color and the like are incorporated into *empirical* concepts, differing in this regard from sensations of pleasure and pain.

7. Kant's definition of objective validity; see, e.g., *CPR* A 104-105, B 137.

8. "Logical" is a term which Kant often uses where we would use "epistemological"; see, for instance, *CJ*, VII, pp. 188-189.

9. *CPR*, B 45.

10. *CPR*, A 820-821/B 848-849.

11. *PFM*, §19, *Ak.* 4, p. 198.

12. *CJ*, VII, p. 189.

13. *CJ*, VII, p. 188.

14. *FI*, VIII, p. 221.

15. *CPR*, B 35-36; see Chapter 1, above.

16. *FI*, VIII, p. 222.

17. *FI*, VIII, p. 222.

18. *FI*, VIII, p. 223.

19. *CJ*, §35, p. 287.

20. *FI*, VIII, p. 223.

21. *FI*, VIII, pp. 223-224.

22. *FI*, VIII, p. 224.

23. *FI*, VIII, p. 224.

24. *FI*, VIII, pp. 224-225.

25. Locke, *An Essay concerning Human Understanding,* bk. II, ch. 8, §18; in the edition by Peter H. Nidditch (Oxford, Clarendon Press, 1975), pp. 138-139.

26. Berkeley, *Three Dialogues between Hylas and Philonous,* First Dialogue; in *The Works of George Berkeley, Bishop of Cloyne,* ed. A. A. Luce and T. E. Jessop (London, Thos. Nelson and Sons, 1949), II, 175-180.

27. *CJ*, VII, p. 188.

28. *CJ*, VII, p. 189.
29. See *FMM, Ak.* 4, p. 422.
30. *CJ*, VII, p. 189.
31. *CJ*, VII, pp. 189-190.
32. *FI*, VIII, pp. 230-231. It is a serious question whether it is actually true that all pleasures must incline us to their continuation, as Kant supposes, or whether at least some pleasures may not be such as to require their own cessation. In this study, however, I will have to confine myself to an examination of Kant's theory of aesthetic response in terms of his general theory of pleasure, and cannot pursue all the questions which might be raised about this general theory itself.
33. *CJ*, VI, p. 187.
34. *CJ*, §22, GR, p. 242.
35. E.g., *CJ*, §2, p. 204.
36. So argues Ralf Meerbote in "Reflections on Beauty," forthcoming in Cohen and Guyer, *Essays in Kant's Aesthetics.*
37. *CPrR, Ak.* 5, p. 119.
38. He also makes no use of the second *Critique*'s theory of the primacy of practical reason, or of the subordination of the objectives of other faculties to the interest of practical reason.
39. *CJ*, VI, p. 187.
40. Evidence for this claim will be presented in Chapter 3.
41. *FI*, VIII, p. 230.
42. Conceivably, one could argue that the connection of pleasure to the fulfillment of objectives is a condition of the possibility of human action. But Kant includes no hint of such an argument, certainly not in the present context.
43. *CJ*, VI, p. 187.
44. *CJ*, VI, p. 188.
45. *CJ*, §22, GR, p. 242.
46. *FI*, VIII, pp. 223-224.
47. See *FI*, VIII, p. 223: "imagination (which merely apprehends the object)"; *CJ*, §35, p. 287: "the *faculty* of intuitions or presentations, i.e., the imagination."
48. *CPR*, A 98.
49. *CPR*, A 100.
50. *CPR*, A 99.
51. *CPR*, A 100, 102.
52. This repairs my elision in the last quotation, in which a synthesis of reproduction was actually defined as what obtains when one representation "can, in accordance with a fixed rule, bring about a transition of the mind" to another (*CPR*, A 100).
53. *FI*, VII, p. 220.
54. *FI*, VII, pp. 220-221.
55. *FI*, VIII, p. 223.
56. *FI*, VIII, p. 224.
57. *FI*, VII, p. 220.
58. Berkeley, *A Treatise concerning the Principles of Human Knowledge,* Introduction, §13, in Luce and Jessop, II, 33.
59. *FI*, VIII, p. 224; see Chapter 2.
60. Mary Warnock attempts to interpret Kant's theory by supposing that the imagination brings its object under an "indeterminate concept" of the understanding, and by supposing that such a concept is "simply" any concept which "is not a scientific concept" (*Imagination*, pp. 55-56). But Kant does not actually use the phrase "indeterminate concept," and the only

candidates for such a term which come to mind are the indeterminate *scientific* concepts of affinity, etc. If one does not wish to saddle Kant with the view that aesthetic response involves the sort of concepts to which Berkeley objected, one must suppose that the imagination supplies the general *condition* for the use of concepts without supplying any concepts at all.

61. *CJ*, VII, pp. 189-190.

62. *CJ*, §9, pp. 217-218.

63. *CJ*, §9, p. 219.

64. All quotations in this paragraph are from *CJ*, §35, p. 287.

65. See *CPR*, A 137-138/B 176-177.

66. *CJ*, §35, p. 287.

67. *CPR*, A 140/B 179.

68. *CJ*, VII, p. 190.

69. The General Remark which follows §22 is clearly not just a continuation of the argument of that section, but a concluding remark on the whole of the Analytic of the Beautiful, which may consequently be used in its interpretation without consideration of location.

70. *CJ*, §22, GR, p. 240.

71. *CJ*, §22, GR, pp. 240-241.

72. *CJ*, §22, GR, p. 241.

73. *CJ*, §22, GR, p. 242.

74. *CJ*, §22, GR, pp. 243-244. See also the discussion of Kant's deduction of aesthetic judgment in Chapters 8 and 9 above.

75. There will be some discussion of these problems in my treatment of Kant's formalism in Chapter 6. The reader may also see my "Formalism and the Theory of Expression in Kant's Aesthetics," *Kant-Studien*, 68, no. 1 (1977), 46-70.

76. *CJ*, §53, p. 329.

77. *CJ*, VI, p. 187.

78. *CJ*, VII, p. 190.

79. *CJ*, §9, p. 219.

80. *CJ*, §53, p. 329.

81. *CPR*, A 99.

82. The fact that what is apparently a proper aesthetic pleasure may dim with familiarity seems to be something of a counter-example to Kant's general thesis that pleasure is a state of mind which tends toward its own preservation (*FI*, VIII, p. 230), at least if that is interpreted as a tendency of indefinite duration.

83. *CPR*, B 161.

84. *CPR*, B 141.

85. *CPR*, B 134.

86. See, for instance, *CPR* A 105-106, A 108, B 132-133, B 139.

87. A somewhat more detailed sketch of this kind of interpretation may be found in my review of W. H. Walsh's *Kant's Criticism of Metaphysics*, in *The Philosophical Review*, 86, no. 2 (April 1977), 274-282. A more detailed argument for what I think is a similar view is presented in Dieter Henrich, *Identität und Objektivität: Eine Untersuchung über Kants transzendentale Deduktion* (Heidelberg, Carl Winter, 1976). A criticism of verificationist interpretations of the transcendental deduction is offered by Richard Rorty, "Verificationism and Transcendental Arguments," *Nous*, 5, no. 1 (February 1971), 3-14.

88. In the *Manifold in Perception: Theories of Art from Kant to Hildebrand* (Oxford, Clarendon Press, 1972), Michael Podro attempts to solve the problem of the possibility of the harmony of the faculties by distinguishing between interpretations of the Transcendental Deduction on which the mind *imposes* unity on its contents, and on which it must merely *seek* for unity (pp. 14-15). But this distinction alone will not suffice, for it would still have to be ex-

plained how, seeking for unity, the *understanding* should ever fail to find it, or how unity could ever be *found* without a concept. Only my distinction between a (psychological) sense of unity and the actual possession of verifiable knowledge, I believe, can explain this.

89. This element may also be explained as due to Kant's general thesis about the uncertainty of our beliefs about our own motivations, and about the connection of interest and pleasure; see Chapter 5.

90. This problem will be explored in Chapters 8 and 9.

91. See the quotation and discussion of *CJ*, §53, p. 329, in the preceding section of this chapter.

92. *FI*, VIII, pp. 224-225.

93. *FI*, VIII, p. 229.

94. *CJ*, §9, p. 218.

95. *CJ*, §9, p. 219.

96. *CJ*, §12, p. 222.

97. Cf. *CJ*, VII, p. 189.

98. *CJ*, V, p. 187.

99. *FI*, VIII, p. 224.

100. *FI*, VIII, p. 226.

101. *CPR*, A 103.

102. *FI*, VIII, p. 223.

103. *FI*, VIII, p. 224.

104. *CJ*, VII, pp. 189-190.

105. *FI*, VII, pp. 224-225.

106. *CJ*, §12, pp. 221-222.

107. *CJ*, §12, p. 221.

108. They are argued to constitute such evidence by Richard E. Aquila, in "A New Look at Kant's Theory of Aesthetic Judgments," *Kant-Studien*, in press.

109. Cf. Mary Mothersill, *"Apprehensio Ipsa Placet:* A Starting Point for Aesthetics," *Journal of Philosophy*, 74, no. 11 (November 1977), 734.

110. *CJ*, §37, p. 289.

111. I will consider this problem later in this chapter and also in Chapter 7; see also Lewis White Beck, "Kritische Bemerkungen zur vermeintlichen Apriorität der Geschmacksurteile," in A. J. Bücher, H. Drue, and T. M. Seebohm, eds., *Bewusst sein: Gerhard Funke zu eigen* (Bonn, H. Bouvier Verlag, 1975), pp. 369-372.

112. As far as I can tell, Kant uses the term *Gemüth* to refer to the mind and all of its activities, whether conscious or not, but I cannot find evidence adequate to preclude the possibility that he means a *conscious* state of mind by *Gemüthszustand* in the present context, for he does not use this word as a technical term with a determinate meaning. Several paragraphs in the *Anthropology* do use the terms *Gemüth* and *Zustand* in close proximity; but while one of these suggests that states of mind need not be conscious states (*APPV*, §3, *Ak.* 7, p. 131), at least one other is most naturally read as treating such states as states of consciousness (*APPV*, §4, *Ak.* 7, p. 134n.). Thus, the meaning of the passage from *CJ*, §12, must be decided on the basis of its context and larger considerations of coherence, and I think that my suggestion is completely coherent with the rest of Kant's argument.

113. See Hume, *A Treatise of Human Nature*, bk. I, pt. III, sec. xiv (Selby-Bigge, p. 155).

114. *FI*, VIII, pp. 224-225.

115. *CJ*, §9, pp. 216-218.

116. *CJ*, VII, p. 190.

117. In his discussion of "Stage I" of Kant's transcendental deduction of aesthetic judgment, Donald Crawford also argues that we must distinguish between the "estimation of the object" and the "judgment of taste" if we are to make Kant's theory intelligible, and in some

points my own argument is quite similar to his. But Crawford makes no mention of the fact that Kant himself uses the terms for this distinction neither regularly nor consistently; thus he does not mention the passages in the second Introduction where "estimated" is used in connection with the judgment of taste rather than with the initial, pleasure-producing response to the object. He also attributes only the "estimation of the object" to reflective judgment, whereas what I am arguing is that if we are to conform to Kant's division of faculties at all, and to his frequent use of "aesthetic judgment" and "reflective judgment" as equivalents, we must regard reflective judgment's involvement in producing a judgment of taste as the complex one of both producing pleasure and assigning a given pleasure's production to reflective judgment rather than to any other source. Cf. Crawford, *Kant's Aesthetic Theory* (Madison, University of Wisconsin Press, 1974), pp. 69-74.

118. *FI*, VIII, p. 224.

119. *FI*, VII, p. 220.

120. Although Kant's argument in the opening paragraphs of §9 (pp. 216-217) in fact seems to express such a view; this problem will be considered in Chapter 4.

121. Crawford argues in a similar way in *Kant's Aesthetic Theory*, pp. 70-71.

122. *FI*, VIII, p. 229.

123. *CJ*, VII, p. 190.

124. *CJ*, VII, p. 191.

125. *CJ*, §8, p. 216.

126. *CJ*, VII, p. 191.

127. *FI*, VIII, pp. 224-225.

128. *FI*, VIII, p. 225.

129. Cf. *CJ*, §3, pp. 205-206.

130. *FI*, VIII, p. 224.

131. *CJ*, §5, p. 210.

132. According to H. W. Cassirer, for instance, in the latter section "Kant compares what he calls the three specifically distinct kinds of delight" (*A Commentary on Kant's Critique of Judgment*, London, Methuen, 1938, p. 182); more recently, John Fisher and Jeffrey Maitland have held that "Kant is committed to the existence of types of pleasure which can be introspected and compared independently of their objects," on which account, they believe, Kant's "theory of appreciation does not make sense" ("The Subjectivist Turn in Aesthetics: A Critical Analysis of Kant's Theory of Appreciation," *The Review of Metaphysics*, 27, no. 4, June 1974, 747). See also Warnock, *Imagination*, p. 47.

133. *CJ*, §5, pp. 209-210.

134. Lewis White Beck, *A Commentary to Kant's Critique of Practical Reason* (Chicago, University of Chicago Press, 1960), pp. 93-94.

135. *FI*, VIII, p. 232.

136. *CPrR*, Ak. 5, p. 23.

137. Letter to Reinhold, *Ak*. 10, pp. 513-515; Zweig, pp. 127-128.

138. *CPrR*, *Ak*. 5, p. 9n.

139. *FI*, VIII, pp. 230-231.

140. *CJ*, §10, p. 220.

141. *APPV*, "Division" of bk. II and §60, *Ak*. 7, p. 230.

142. *APPV*, §67, *Ak*. 7, p. 240.

4. A Universal Voice

1. *CJ*, VII, p. 191.

2. *FI*, VIII, p. 225.

3. *CJ,* VII, p. 190.

4. By which Kant means something as restrictive as, in the case of painting, linear design rather than color (see *CJ,* §14, p. 225, and §16, p. 229). The details of this view are discussed in Chapter 6.

5. *CJ,* §9, p. 216.

6. *CJ,* §§5, 9, 17, and 22.

7. *CPR,* A 70/B 95, A 80/B 106.

8. *CJ,* §1, p. 204.

9. *CJ,* §1, p. 203n.

10. *CJ,* §2, p. 205.

11. *CJ,* §3, pp. 205-207.

12. *CJ,* §3, p. 207; §4, pp. 207-209.

13. *CJ,* §5, p. 211.

14. *CJ,* §2, p. 204; §4, p. 207.

15. Perhaps the most recent expositor of such a view is Robert L. Zimmerman, who claims that, according to Kant, "in aesthetic experience the mind is presented with contents from the noumenal world" ("Kant: The Aesthetic Judgment," in Robert Paul Wolff, ed., *Kant: A Collection of Critical Essays,* Garden City, N.Y., Doubleday, 1967, p. 386). I will criticize such an interpretation in Chapter 5; the reader may also find sound criticism of this view in Podro, *The Manifold in Perception,* pp. 16-17.

16. *CJ,* §6, p. 211.

17. *CJ,* §7, p. 212.

18. *CJ,* §8, pp. 214-215.

19. *CJ,* §8, pp. 215-216.

20. *CJ,* §9, p. 217.

21. *CJ,* §9, p. 219.

22. *CJ,* §9, p. 219.

23. *CJ,* §10, p. 219.

24. *CJ,* §11, p. 221.

25. *CJ,* §13, p. 223.

26. *CJ,* §14, p. 225.

27. *CJ,* §15, p. 227.

28. *CJ,* §16, p. 229.

29. *CJ,* §16, p. 229.

30. *CJ,* §16, p. 230; §17, pp. 231-236.

31. *CJ,* §18, pp. 236-237.

32. *CJ,* §18, p. 237.

33. *CJ,* §20, p. 238; §21, p. 238.

34. *CJ,* §22, p. 239-240.

35. Donald Crawford remarks that "the detailed correspondence to the table in the *Critique of Pure Reason* is inexact" in the case of each moment of aesthetic judgment (*Kant's Aesthetic Theory,* p. 17), but does not mention that such inexactitude undermines Kant's sole methodological support for the outward structure of the Analytic of the Beautiful and calls for a serious reconstruction. I have made this point in my review of Crawford's book in *The Journal of Philosophy,* 22, no. 3 (February 1975), 78-79.

36. *CPR,* A 70/B 95.

37. The categories drawn from the division of modality into problematic, assertoric, and apodeictic; cf. *CPR,* A 80/B 106.

38. *CPR,* A 219/B 266.

39. *CJ,* §8, p. 215; cf. §37, p. 289.

40. Kant's thesis is that "This rose is beautiful" or "This statue is beautiful" is the exem-

plary form of aesthetic judgment (§8), but this does not conflict with the view that empirical concepts do not determine the judgment of taste. Terms such as "rose" or "statue" may be used to identify the objects of judgment, but cannot ground inferences to their beauty. (Obviously some roses and many statues, for example, are not beautiful.)

41. The *Critique of Practical Reason* does use the table of categories for a classification of "the concepts of good and evil," but this comes late in Kant's argument and plays no role in his basic analysis of the requirement(s) of the categorical imperative as the *a priori* principle of morality. See *CPrR, Ak.* 5, pp. 66-67.

42. *R* 1918, *Ak.* 16, pp. 156-157.

43. *CJ,* §2, p. 205.

44. Cf. *CJ,* §5, p. 209.

45. *CJ,* §6, p. 211.

46. For the use of the term "normative" in connection with Kant's aesthetics, see Beck, *A Commentary to Kant's Critique of Practical Reason,* p. 114, and Roger Scruton, *Art and Imagination* (London, Methuen, 1974), pp. 138-139.

47. A similar account of the invalidity of Kant's "deduction" of the second moment from the first is suggested, but not quite stated, by Maitland and Fisher, "The Subjectivist Turn in Aesthetics," pp. 734, 741.

48. *CJ,* §6, p. 211.

49. *CJ,* §8, p. 214.

50. *CJ,* §1, p. 203n.

51. *CJ,* §2, p. 205.

52. *CJ,* §6, p. 211.

53. *CJ,* §7, p. 213.

54. *CJ,* §6, p. 211.

55. *CJ,* §8, p. 214; cf. *FI,* VIII, p. 223.

56. *CJ,* §7, p. 212.

57. As Stanley Cavell has put it, in this case we may *"retreat* to personal taste" ("Aesthetic Problems of Modern Philosophy," in Cavell, *Must We Mean What We Say?,* New York, Scribner's, 1969, p. 91).

58. *CJ,* §7, p. 212.

59. *CJ,* §8, pp. 213-214.

60. *CJ,* §7, p. 213.

61. As did Burke, for instance, who only added an essay on taste as an Introduction to the second edition of his *Philosophical Enquiry into the Origin of our Ideas of the Sublime and Beautiful* (see the edition by James T. Boulton, London, 1958, p. 3). For Burke, the problem of taste did not seem to be the essential question of aesthetics, but "a matter curious in itself" which merely "leads naturally enough to the principal enquiry," the explanation of aesthetic response. Kant's realization of the interdependence of the analysis of aesthetic judgment and the explanation of aesthetic response was not anticipated by Burke.

62. Cf. the *Enquiry concerning the Clarity of the Principles of Natural Theology and Ethics,* First Reflection, §3 and Second Reflection (*Ak.* 2, pp. 282, 289); *CPR,* A 727-732/B 756-760.

63. *CPR,* A 9/B 13.

64. *CPR,* §19, B 141-142.

65. *PFM,* §19, *Ak.* 4, p. 300. We shall see later that this statement is problematic.

66. *CJ,* §6, p. 212.

67. *CJ,* §7, p. 213.

68. *CJ,* §8, p. 214.

69. *CJ,* §8, p. 216.

70. *CJ,* §7, pp. 212-213.

71. *CJ*, VII, p. 191.
72. *CJ*, §6, p. 211.
73. *CJ*, §7, p. 212.
74. *CJ*, §8, p. 214.
75. *CJ*, §8, p. 214.
76. *CJ*, §40, p. 296.
77. *CJ*, §19, p. 237.
78. For instance, Crawford, in *Kant's Aesthetic Theory*, and R. K. Elliott, in "The Unity of Kant's 'Critique of Aesthetic Judgment,'" *British Journal of Aesthetics*, 8, no. 3 (July 1968), 244-259. (I will give more detailed reference to their views in Chapter 11.)
79. *CJ*, §6, p. 211.
80. *CJ*, §38, p. 289.
81. *CJ*, §7, pp. 212-213.
82. *CJ*, §8, p. 214.
83. *CJ*, §8, p. 216.
84. *CJ*, §8, pp. 215-216.
85. *CJ*, §8, p. 216.
86. Or than there has appeared to be to some commentators. Crawford thinks that Kant's concept of postulation is clear enough to be pressed into service here without further comment (*Kant's Aesthetic Theory*, pp. 130-131), but we shall see that this is not the case.
87. *CJ*, §8, p. 216.
88. *CPR*, A 218-219/B 265-266.
89. *CPR*, A 234-235/B 287.
90. *CPR*, A 234/B 287.
91. *L*, §38, *Ak*. 9, p. 112.
92. *CPrR*, *Ak*. 5, p. 122.
93. Beck, *A Commentary to Kant's Critique of Practical Reason*, pp. 251-252.
94. For a discussion of the obscurity of Kant's concept of postulation, see Beck's discussion of the Postulates of Pure Practical Reason in his commentary, ch. XIII, §6 (pp. 251-255).
95. *CJ*, §8, p. 216.
96. Cf. *CPR*, A 663/B 691.
97. I use this term as an adjective derived from "idea," and not in the substantival sense in which Kant uses "ideal" in the first *Critique* to refer to the postulation of an unconditioned entity (*CPR*, A 340/B 398).
98. *CJ*, §8, pp. 213-214.
99. *CJ*, §1, p. 203.
100. *CJ*, §1, p. 204.
101. *CJ*, §6, p. 211. Kant admits an exception to this rule in the case of "pure practical laws," which do produce a feeling of pleasure. In §6, he denies that this is relevant because of the disinterestedness of aesthetic judgment, a denial which he cannot make yet on my reconstruction of his argument. But in the first Introduction, as we saw, this case could actually be excluded following the definition of aesthetic judgment as a judgment actually *based* on the feeling of pleasure; for it is Kant's general position that no moral judgment of any kind is based on a feeling of pleasure. Any judgment based on a feeling, even in an ethical context, would be an aesthetic judgment (though a sensory rather than a reflective one, and therefore not a judgment of taste).
102. *CJ*, §8, p. 214.
103. *CJ*, §8, pp. 214-215.
104. *CJ*, §8, p. 215.
105. Podro comes close to stating this view, but does not get it quite right. He says that

Kant eliminates "not only the *interest* of concepts from the interest of the pure judgment of taste," but also "the *use* of concepts in the pure judgment of taste"; but, he continues, since in any judgment "the mind must employ some concepts," Kant must mean "by not employing concepts . . . not employing concepts which in some sense 'go beyond' the pure sensory determinations of things and lead us to classify the things of the world as objects of a certain kind" (*The Manifold in Perception*, p. 22). However, Kant has no place for anything like purely sensory concepts; concepts always represent the work of the understanding on the material furnished by sensibility (see, e.g., *CPR* A 20/B 34). Kant must instead be interpreted to mean that aesthetic judgment, though it may have to use concepts to refer to its object, does not base its connection of pleasure to the object on the subsumption of the object under any concepts.

106. *CPR*, A 104.

107. *CJ*, §6, p. 211.

108. *CJ*, §8, p. 216.

109. *FI*, VIII, pp. 223-224. The reader may be reminded that I do not attribute to Kant the view that aesthetic judgments must result from two phenomenologically distinct acts of reflection.

110. This point is well argued by Crawford (*Kant's Aesthetic Theory*, pp. 70-71). Crawford does not observe, however, that some of the remarks in §9 in fact conflict with this view.

111. *CJ*, §9, p. 216.

112. *CJ*, §9, pp. 216-217. I have followed Crawford in amending the first clause of this quote (see p. 71 of his book); Kant's use of the words *vorhergehe* in the opening question and *Ginge . . . vorher* in the answer make it clear that the latter is still dealing with the two terms, pleasure and estimation, the relative priority of which (to use Meredith's expression) is at issue.

113. Kant uses the term "communicability" (*Mitteilbarkeit*) instead of "validity" (*Gültigkeit*) in §9, and thus considers the conditions of universal communicability rather than of universal validity. But there is nothing in §9 to indicate that he means anything more by universal communicability than he does by universal validity, and the fact that the opening paragraph of §9 contrasts universal communicability with private validity is evidence that "communicability" and "validity" are in fact synonymous.

114. The last three quotes are from *CJ*, §9, p. 217.

115. *CJ*, §9, p. 218. The fact that Kant concludes his argument with an explanation of "universal subjective validity" rather than of "universal communicability" is further evidence for the synonymy of the two expressions.

116. *CJ*, §9, p. 218. Both Bernard and Meredith translate the key phrase in this sentence which I have given in German as "must be fundamental," which is vague. Crawford offers two slightly different translations of this sentence (one supposed to be "slightly less cumbersome" than the other), both of which come close to mine (*Kant's Aesthetic Theory*, pp. 72-73). I have tried for a literal rendition, taking only the liberty of translating *zur Folge* as "as its consequence."

117. Crawford interprets the claim that the universal communicability of the mental state in the given representation must have the pleasure in the beautiful as its consequent as meaning that "the pleasure in the beautiful, in order to be distinguished from mere sensuous pleasure, must itself be based on a universally communicable mental state brought about by the reflection and contemplation . . . of [*sic*] the beautiful object" (*Kant's Aesthetic Theory*, p. 72). But these two statements are not equivalent; the latter requires a certain property of whatever explains pleasure in the beautiful, but the former makes that property itself (communicability) the explanation of this pleasure.

118. *CJ*, §9, pp. 217-218.

119. This has been noted by several authors. See, for instance, Anna Tumarkin, "Zur transscendentalen Methode der Kantischen Ästhetik," in *Kant-Studien,* 11 (1906), 375, and Schaper, "Kant on Aesthetic Appraisals," p. 444.

120. *CJ,* §9, p. 218.

121. Cf. *CJ,* §6, p. 211.

122. The *Critique of Judgment,* like the first *Critique,* shows every sign of having been written in considerable haste, and of having been subjected to no great amount of revision. There is no statement about its composition as revealing as Kant's famous admission to Mendelssohn that the first *Critique* was completed "hastily, in perhaps four or five months" (letter 206, August 16, 1783, in *Ak.* 10, pp. 344-346; Zweig, p. 105); but on May 26, 1789, Kant did write to Marcus Herz that he was still "burdened with the extensive work of completing [his] plan (partly in preparing the last part of the critique, that of *judgment,* which should appear soon)" (letter 362, *Ak.* 11, pp. 48-55; Zweig, p. 151). This letter, written just the year before the third *Critique* actually appeared, suggests that Kant did not spend too long writing it.

123. *CJ,* §41, p. 296.

124. For the references and discussion of this point, see above, Chapter 3, and notes 110 through 113.

125. Such a paradox was attributed to Kant by Edward Bullough, who interpreted him as saying "that aesthetic judgment *precedes* appreciation, that we *judge* a flower to be beautiful and *therefore* like it (the famous judgment *a priori*)," in *Aesthetics: Lectures and Essays,* ed. E. M. Wilkinson (Stanford, Stanford University Press, 1957), p. 52. Kant, of course, precludes any such interpretation of the apriority of aesthetic judgment in §37 (p. 289). Walter Cerf also claims that "Kant should be understood to assert that the judgment of taste is the cause of the pleasure felt" (in his translation of the *Analytic of the Beautiful,* Indianapolis, Bobbs-Merrill Publishing Co., 1963, p. 95). He thinks paradox may be avoided if one realizes that "judgment" is ambiguous, between "tasting" and "passing a verdict," and disambiguates Kant's confused concept by distinguishing between a "causal relation between psychic events" and "a logical relation . . . of a norm of justification to what is to be justified." He gives no indication, however, that Kant himself makes this distinction quite clear in many places, including §9's opening distinction between the *Beurteilung des Gegenstandes* and the *Geschmacksurteil,* and only fails to observe this distinction in the present passage.

126. That the key to the critique of taste must be so interpreted was argued by Tumarkin in 1906, when she wrote that Kant's key must separate "three steps, the aesthetic estimation, which we know as the play of the cognitive faculties, the feeling of pleasure called forth from this estimation, from the harmonious play of the faculties of representation, and finally the judgment resting on this feeling" ("Zur transscendentalen Methode," p. 373). (She held Kant to be inconsistent in his development of this view, however, though not because of the passages I have considered, but rather because he confused the universality of "estimation" with the universality of "judgment." This does not seem to me to be a real problem.) Crawford also argues for the resolution of the paradox which I have suggested (*Kant's Aesthetic Theory,* pp. 70-74), but does not concede that any of Kant's own statements are actually paradoxical; thus he asserts that "a careful consideration of the text shows that Kant does not claim that the pleasure must be consequent to the judgment of taste" (p. 73). This may be, but Kant does assert that pleasure is a consequent of the communicability of a mental state, and this is a paradox, since the mental state involved is a state of pleasure.

127. *CJ,* §9, p. 218.

128. *CJ,* §9, 219.

129. *FI,* VIII, p. 225.

130. *CPR,* B 4.

131. *CJ,* §18, p. 236.

132. *CJ*, §18, p. 237.
133. *CJ*, §8, p. 214.
134. *CJ*, §9, p. 218.
135. *FI*, VII, p. 221.
136. *CJ*, §19, p. 237.
137. In the article earlier mentioned, Beck has argued that Kant's characterization of aesthetic judgments as *a priori* leads to the false conclusion that there is no room for error in such judgments ("Kritische Bemerkungen," p. 370). Though such a denomination of the judgment may suggest this conclusion, the present passage from §19 (as well as §8, p. 214, which Beck quotes, and §38, p. 290n.) make it clear that Kant himself did not draw it, and did not think the transcendental deduction of aesthetic judgment obliged to demonstrate its certainty. In other words, that aesthetic judgments claim a kind of necessity does not mean that they must all be true; only *if* they are true are they, in the appropriate sense, necessary, just as mathematical assertions (for some) are necessarily true *if* true, but not all true.
138. The last three sections of this moment are, of course, very significant, for they represent Kant's first attempt at a transcendental deduction of aesthetic judgment; but for that reason I shall consider these sections in the discussion of Kant's deduction rather than of his analysis of taste.
139. Cf. *CJ*, §8, pp. 214-216.
140. *CJ*, §9, p. 219.
141. *CJ*, §20, p. 238.
142. *CJ*, §8, p. 216.
143. *CJ*, §37, p. 289.
144. *CJ*, §36, p. 288.
145. *CJ*, §37, p. 289.
146. *CJ*, §37, p. 289.
147. In his article, Beck interprets the concluding lines of §37 to imply that "the *a priori* judgment here in question is not an aesthetic judgment on an object, which actually pleases me, but a theoretical judgment in the meta-language of aesthetics" ("Kritische Bemerkungen," p. 370). This interpretation is inspired by a proper concern with the question of how aesthetic judgments can ever be erroneous if they are *a priori,* but fails to consider the possibility that a particular aesthetic judgment on a given object might be both empirical, and thus potentially wrong, and also *a priori.* Further, the judgment which Kant actually calls *a priori* in the sentences quoted by both Beck and myself is the judgment that a *given* object is beautiful, that is, that the delight *it occasions* may be imputed to everyone as necessary. This is certainly an "aesthetic judgment on an object, which actually pleases me," and not a meta-aesthetic proposition.

5. The Disinterestedness of Aesthetic Judgment

1. *CJ*, §1, p. 203; see my earlier discussion in Chapter 4.
2. *CJ*, §2, p. 204.
3. *CJ*, §5, p. 211.
4. *CJ*, §5, p. 210.
5. *CJ*, §2, p. 205n.
6. *CJ*, §2, p. 204.
7. *CJ*, §6, p. 211.
8. *CJ*, §1, p. 203n.
9. *CJ*, §29, GR, p. 267.
10. *CJ*, §5, p. 210.

11. *CJ*, §5, pp. 209-210.

12. *CJ*, §5, p. 210.

13. *CJ*, §5, p. 210.

14. See Chapter 3.

15. *CJ*, §3, p. 205.

16. *CJ*, §3, p. 206.

17. *CJ*, §3, p. 206.

18. See Chapter 3.

19. *CJ*, §2, p. 204.

20. *CJ*, §4, p. 207; an action, of course, may be an "object" of the will.

21. *CJ*, §41, p. 296.

22. Crawford discusses the significance of the inclusion of "representation" in §4's definition in *Kant's Aesthetic Theory*, pp. 38-41. He argues that one can take its inclusion as insignificant, or as a mere expression of Kant's general view that we are in fact acquainted with all objects by means of representations; but since we can have an interest in a nonexistent object — especially an object which may not yet exist — it may in fact be necessary to say that such an interest is connected with the representation of the object rather than with its actual existence. However, Crawford does not attempt to resolve the difficulty so presented, concluding that "the ultimate plausibility of either account of interest need not concern us here" (p. 41). In fact, I suggest, this difficulty is crucial, for Kant's argument in the first moment actually requires treating interest not as a kind of pleasure at all, but rather as a kind of representation — a concept of an object which provides a reason for its real existence, either by promising pleasure in that existence or in some other way. This will be argued in the section of this chapter entitled "Interests and Existence."

23. This seems the natural reading, but Kant's words *Ein solches* could be taken to refer to the interest as well as to the delight which defines it.

24. *CJ*, §2, p. 204.

25. *CPR*, A 598/B 626.

26. *CJ*, §2, p. 204.

27. Similar examples may be found in Hume, *A Treatise of Human Nature*, bk. II, pt. I, sec. viii (Selby-Bigge, p. 299), and in Kames, *Elements of Criticism*, pt. I, ch. 1 (in the New York edition of 1852, pp. 27-29).

28. *CJ*, §2, p. 204.

29. *CJ*, §2, p. 205.

30. *CJ*, §2, p. 205.

31. *CJ*, §2, p. 205.

32. *CJ*, §3, p. 207.

33. It should be noted that Kant does not actually *say* that the delight in the beautiful *is* disinterested in this paragraph.

34. *CJ*, §2, 205n.

35. Most of §4 actually concerns the difference between the agreeable and the good rather than that between the good and the beautiful.

36. *CJ*, §4, p. 207.

37. *CJ*, §4, p. 207.

38. The application of the term or concept "beautiful" to an object is not a counterexample to this claim, because it depends on the experience of pleasure and reflection on that experience, and is not a condition of that experience.

39. *CJ*, §4, p. 207.

40. *CJ*, §4, p. 209.

41. Whether the promised pleasure is produced by the existence of the object or related to it in some other way may be left undetermined for the moment.

42. *CJ*, §10, pp. 219-220.

43. See note 141 to Chapter 3.

44. *CJ*, §12, p. 222.

45. It is undoubtedly wrong to believe that *all* pleasures must produce a drive toward their own preservation; many pleasures are surely such that they can be enjoyed only for limited periods. But Kant, apparently, does not recognize this fact, and in any case makes no direct attempt to argue that the pleasures of aesthetic response do not conform to the general rule about pleasures which he enunciates.

46. Crawford spends several pages arguing that "beautiful objects tend to maintain and hold our interest" (*Kant's Aesthetic Theory*, p. 51). It seems to me that this needs no proof; what is required instead is further inquiry into Kant's concept of interest, to see whether it in fact commits him to the counter-intuitive claim that aesthetic judgment produces no interest in its object, as well as inquiry into the question of whether Kant actually offers arguments in support of the view against which Crawford argues.

47. *CPrR, Ak.* 5, p. 79.

48. *FMM, Ak.* 4, p. 459n.

49. *FMM, Ak.* 4, p. 413n.

50. *CPrR, Ak.* 5, p. 21.

51. *CPrR, Ak.* 5, p. 79.

52. *CPrR, Ak.* 5, p. 21.

53. *CPrR, Ak.* 5, p. 33.

54. *CPrR, Ak.* 5, p. 78.

55. *FMM, Ak.* 4, p. 413n.

56. *FMM, Ak.* 4, p. 459n.

57. This is a convenient place to note one problem with Kant's use of disinterestedness in the third *Critique*. Kant writes as if any judgment based on an interest is partial, or based on merely private or personal conditions (cf., e.g., *CJ*, §2, p. 205, and §6, p. 211), and, conversely, as if "disinterested" and "universally valid" are extensionally equivalent. This view conflicts with his theory that interest may arise either from pathological conditions of gratification or from an objective law of morality. The latter creates an interest, but one with intersubjective validity. Thus not all interested delights are partial and only privately valid, and aesthetic judgment cannot be inferred to be disinterested just because it must be universally valid. Rather, the judgment of beauty must be disinterested because it is both intersubjectively valid and free of determination by concepts.

58. *CPrR, Ak.* 5, p. 60.

59. E.g., *CPrR, Ak.* 5, p. 38. The connection between this satisfaction in moral action and the feeling of respect is both complex and obscure. It is clear that the latter is hardly an unmixed feeling of pleasure (cf. *CPrR, Ak.* 5, p. 80), a fact which will turn out to be of significance later on (see Chapter 11); but it is also clear that a feeling of satisfaction, and thus apparently of pleasure, whether or not related to the feeling of respect which *motivates* moral action, is a *consequence* of such action. As we will see, the Introduction to the *Metaphysics of Morals* says that practical pleasure may be the cause *or* effect of desire (*Ak.* 6, p. 212), and the first Introduction to the *Critique of Judgment* treats the feeling which results from the "objective determination of the will" quite unequivocally as a feeling of pleasure (*FI*, III, pp. 206-207).

60. *MM, Ak.* 6, p. 212. I have omitted Kant's claim that the connection is valid for the subject only; this relates to his tendency (also evident in *CJ*, §2, p. 205n.) to describe moral

judgment as arising from no interest, but producing one. The *Foundations* and the *Critique of Practical Reason* may be read more simply as contrasting pathological interest in an object and moral interest in an action (cf., e.g., *FMM, Ak.* 4, p. 459n.) as two sources of action, and suggesting that moral interest is not valid just for a given subject. That seems to be the relevant view with which to compare the argument in the *Critique of Judgment.*

61. *MM, Ak.* 6, pp. 212.

62. Kant's insistence in *CJ,* §3, that no kind of pleasure, whether of sense or reflection, can furnish knowledge of an object, is at odds with his physiological interpretation of the pleasures of sense, and must be tempered by that theory. A proper statement of his thesis would be that an object's disposition to produce such pleasure may not be included in the public empirical concept of that object, because physiology may differ from one person to the next, but that it might be included in a possible private empirical concept.

63. The force with which Kant expresses this claim suggests that there are reasons for his adoption of it in addition to an overly broad interpretation of the implications of his argument. In fact, as we shall see in Chapter 11, it is Kant's belief that there are moral grounds for interest in the beautiful (of nature) (§42) and empirical grounds for interest in the beautiful (of art) (§41). His concern to distinguish pleasure based on the fulfillment of these interests from aesthetic appreciation may have led him to overstate his point, and to deny that aesthetic response creates any interest at all, rather than just distinguishing an interest founded on aesthetic appreciation from other interests in beautiful objects.

64. Cf. Kant's discussions of the effects of repetition on aesthetic response in *CJ,* §22, GR, pp. 242-244, and §53, p. 326.

65. *CJ,* §2, p. 205.

66. *CJ,* §5, p. 209.

67. E.g., *FI,* VIII, p. 225, and *CJ,* §1, pp. 203-204.

68. Cf. *CPR,* A 225/B 272.

69. *CPR,* A 219/B 266-267.

70. *CPR,* A 599/B 627.

71. *CPR,* A 218/B 265-266.

72. *CPR,* A 225/B 273.

73. Cf. *CJ,* §14, pp. 224-225.

74. *CJ,* §4, p. 207; §16, p. 229.

75. This simple fact is enough to refute any interpretation of Kant's distinction between mere representation and real existence as meaning that he thinks that the objects of taste are something other than ordinary empirical objects, and to require us to find some other interpretation of the distinction.

76. *R* 557, *Ak.* 15, I, pp. 241-242. This note has not been dated with much precision, and is said to stem either from 1776-1779 or 1780-1789. A crossed-out passage connects delight in the enlivening of sensibility with that "through feeling, judgment of taste."

77. *R* 697, *Ak.* 15, I, p. 310.

78. *R* 678, *Ak.* 15, I, p. 300.

79. *CJ,* §2, p. 205.

80. *R* 827, *Ak.* 15, I, p. 369.

81. *R* 868, *Ak.* 15, I, p. 382.

82. Kant's example, of course, uses an object of taste that is an actual physical object or token, rather than an object which is a type—such as a poem or musical composition. In the case of the latter, it may indeed be true that the object of aesthetic judgment is not an ordinary physical object. But this is certainly not the case *because* of the disinterestedness of aesthetic response, as idealist interpretations of Kant would have us believe, and the abstractness of such objects as poems certainly does not place them in the noumenal realm.

83. *CJ*, §12, p. 222.
84. See note 72, above.
85. *R* 697, *Ak.* 15, I, p. 310.
86. *R* 696, *Ak.* 15, I, p. 309.
87. *CJ*, §5, p. 209.
88. *CJ*, §14, p. 225.
89. Cf. *CJ*, §43, p. 303.
90. *CJ*, §11, p. 221.
91. Cf. *CJ*, §44, p. 305.
92. See Scruton, *Art and Imagination*, p. 15.
93. *CJ*, §6, p. 211.
94. *CJ*, §3, p. 206.
95. *CJ*, §22, GR, p. 241.
96. *CJ*, §5, p. 210.
97. *FMM, Ak.* 4, p. 419.
98. *FMM, Ak.* 4, p. 407.
99. *CJ*, §8, p. 216.
100. *CJ*, §19, p. 237.
101. *CJ*, §38, p. 290n.

6. The Form of Finality

1. *CJ*, §10, p. 219.
2. *CJ*, §14, p. 225.
3. *CJ*, §17, p. 236.
4. To allow attention to be focused on Kant's arguments in the third moment, without being distracted by the connotations of terminology, I shall now translate *Zweckmässigkeit* exclusively as "finality." I shall continue to use "purpose" as well as "end" to translate *Zweck*.
5. The major thesis of the third moment is that already intimated by the Introductions to the *Critique of Judgment:* the claim that aesthetic response is a response to the form of objects, and thus to an aspect of them. This suggests that any object may be beautiful, regardless of what kind of object it is. But some paragraphs in §§16 and 17, following upon the original location of aesthetic judgment as part of the reflective judgment of nature, suggest that certain kinds of natural objects are intrinsically fit to be objects of pure aesthetic judgment, and that certain kinds of manmade objects are intrinsically unfit for such a role. I will discuss this question later in this chapter.
6. *CJ*, §17, p. 231.
7. *CJ*, §34, pp. 285-286.
8. In a recent article, Robert Burch has taken the passage from §34 to mean that Kant never attempts to provide *any* sort of rules which would directly govern the application of "beautiful" to objects ("Kant's Theory of Beauty as Ideal Art," in George Dickie and Richard Sclafani, eds., *Aesthetics,* New York, St. Martin's Press, 1977), pp. 688-703. Such an interpretation fails to recognize the difference between determinate and indeterminate concepts or rules, and is therefore incapable of explaining Kant's intentions in §§13 through 17.
9. *CJ*, §14, p. 225.
10. *CJ*, §16, pp. 229-230.
11. *CJ*, §16, p. 230; §17, p. 236n.
12. Section 17 contains a peculiar argument in which Kant connects beauty to a concept, rather than dissociating it from concepts, apparently in an attempt to supplement the previ-

ous sections with a doctrine on which certain objects of taste would be models or archetypes for everyone.

13. *CJ*, VII, pp. 189-190.
14. *FI*, VIII, pp. 232-233.
15. *CJ*, §10, p. 220.
16. *CJ*, §10, pp. 219-220.
17. *CJ*, §10, p. 220.
18. *CJ*, §10, p. 220.
19. *CJ*, §11, p. 221.
20. Cf. *CJ*, §3, p. 207.
21. In a trivial sense, of course, where the intention is to create something beautiful, a beautiful object pleases in virtue of the same "property" whereby it fulfills this intention — namely, its beauty. However, since the harmony of the faculties involves no determinate empirical concept and no determinate empirical judgment, it cannot be a response to the perception of an object as having been created in the fulfillment of some specific intention, let alone to the perception of it as being a successful fulfillment of intention. I have explored this point more fully in "Interest, Nature, and Art."
22. The view which is ordinarily criticized as the intentionalist fallacy is the view that an author's intentions determine the *meaning* or *interpretation* of a work of art, and not its aesthetic *merit*. One well-known discussion of this subject, however, does begin by attacking the view that an author's intentions may be a standard for the "success of a work of literary art" (William Wimsatt and Monroe Beardsley, "The Intentionalist Fallacy," in Wimsatt, *The Verbal Icon*, Louisville, University of Kentucky Press, 1954, p. 3), though its arguments are more appropriately directed against the intentionalist theory of interpretation than of evaluation. But in any case the view that an artist's success in accomplishing his intentions is an intrinsic ground for the attribution of merit to his product does seem to be a common view, and can be attacked as a fallacy concerning intentions.
23. Kant's confusion about the role of the artist's intentions in the evaluation of his work emerges in §45; I have discussed this in "Interest, Nature, and Art."
24. *CJ*, §11, p. 221.
25. *FI*, VII, p. 220.
26. *FI*, VII, p. 221.
27. *CJ*, VII, pp. 189-190.
28. *CJ*, §12, p. 222.
29. *CJ*, §12, pp. 221-222.
30. *CJ*, §12, p. 222.
31. *CJ*, §12, p. 222.
32. See Chapter 3, above.
33. *CJ*, §11, p. 221, and §13, p. 223.
34. *FI*, IX, pp. 232-233; *CJ*, VIII, pp. 192-193.
35. *CJ*, VII, p. 189.
36. *CJ*, §10, p. 220.
37. Crawford, *Kant's Aesthetic Theory*, p. 93.
38. *CJ*, §15, pp. 227-228.
39. *CJ*, §64, p. 371.
40. Crawford, *Kant's Aesthetic Theory*, p. 94.
41. In §43, Kant supposes that we must think of bees as having a "representation" of their remarkably regular cells in order to produce them, but not a conscious "thought" (p. 303), but we need not follow him in this supposition. If this example is contentious, however, one might consider instead a hexagonal pattern in a crystal.

42. See, for instance, Plato's *Timaeus*, 27d-36d.

43. *CJ*, §14, p. 223.

44. That is, the division of the objects of pleasure into the agreeable, the beautiful, and the good (*CJ*, §5, pp. 209-210).

45. *CJ*, §13, p. 223.

46. *CJ*, §14, p. 225.

47. *CJ*, §14, p. 224.

48. *CPR*, A 20/B 34. All of the quotations in this paragraph and the next are from *CPR*, A 20-22/B 34-36, and will not be individually noted.

49. *CPR*, A 20-21/B 35.

50. Locke, *Essay*, bk. II, ch. viii, secs. 9-10 (in Nidditch, pp. 134-135). The subject of Kant's attitude toward the distinction between primary and secondary qualities is pursued in Crawford, *Kant's Aesthetic Theory*, pp. 102-110.

51. *CJ*, §16, p. 230.

52. Barrows Dunham, "Kant's Theory of Aesthetic Form," in George T. Whitney and David F. Bowers, *The Heritage of Kant* (Princeton, Princeton University Press, 1939), pp. 372-373.

53. Crawford uses the example of a Pietà in which the "total effect of the work is partially the result of an intense contrast between the deathly pale white body of Christ and the warm browns of the earth below him" (*Kant's Aesthetic Theory*, p. 110) to undermine Kant's limitation of beauty to spatial and temporal form; however, as Crawford's own vocabulary suggests, this contrast could easily be assigned to the realm of charm or emotion. The example of the Albers paintings, I think, can make this point more clearly.

54. Hilton Kramer, "Albers," in *The Age of the Avant-Garde* (New York, Farrar Straus and Giroux, 1973), p. 364.

55. Kramer, "Albers," p. 364.

56. Dunham, "Kant's Theory of Aesthetic Form," p. 374.

57. Crawford suggests a position essentially similar to mine when he writes that "Kant's exclusion of the so-called secondary qualities from the realm of the aesthetic is based partly on a hasty application of the form-content distinction, but mostly on an independent view concerning the inferior epistemological status of secondary qualities" (*Kant's Aesthetic Theory*, p. 110), but the point that the concept of the harmony of the faculties does not itself entail Kant's interpretation of the distinction between form and matter still deserves emphasis. In particular, since Kant's theory of knowledge might be loosely taken to comprehend both his theory of judgment and his theory of space and time, it is important to emphasize that these need not stand or fall together, and that the theory of taste may be regarded as linked with the former without being connected to the latter.

58. *CJ*, §14, p. 224.

59. In *The Notion of Form in Kant's Critique of Aesthetic Judgment* (The Hague, Mouton, 1971), Theodore E. Uehling, Jr., discusses the question of whether Kant actually agreed with Euler's theory. The problem is raised by the fact that in the first two editions of the third *Critique*, the text has Kant doubting the theory (*gar sehr zweifle*), but in the third, Kant does not doubt it (*gar nicht zweifle*) (Uehling, pp. 22-26). There seems to me little doubt that Kant did affirm Euler's theory, but, as we shall see, that affirmation is hardly sufficient to make his view on the aesthetic potential of qualities like color satisfactory.

60. *CJ*, §51, p. 325.

61. *CJ*, §14, p. 224.

62. *CJ*, §53, p. 329.

63. Uehling supposes that the merit of Kant's adoption of the theory that pure colors or tones are beautiful lies in the fact that it allows manifolds of colors or tones to be considered

beautiful insofar as their individual parts can be so considered; he supposes that "if we are to call [e.g.] a painting beautiful, we would do so on the same grounds that we could call any constitutive part of the painting beautiful" (*The Notion of Form*, p. 34). This is a bizarre supposition, and totally misses Kant's point that pleasure in beauty is a response to the non-rule-governed unity *of a manifold*. Although his whole work is devoted to Kant's theory of form, Uehling fails to notice that there is nothing in Kant's theory of the harmony of the faculties which can require that it be occasioned only by what the first *Critique* identified as the form of appearance.

    64. *CJ*, §49, p. 316.
    65. *CJ*, §49, p. 315.
    66. *CJ*, §49, p. 317.
    67. *CJ*, §51, p. 320.
    68. *CJ*, §49, p. 315.
    69. *CPR*, A 29/B 44.
    70. *CPR*, A 29-39/B 45.
    71. In *CJ*, §3, p. 206, Kant apparently is willing to allow that colors, for instance, may be incorporated into the empirical concepts of objects.
    72. *CJ*, §14, p. 224.
    73. Cf. *CJ*, §9, p. 218, and §29, GR, pp. 277-278: "if the judgment of taste . . . cannot be *egoistic*, but must necessarily, from its inner nature, be allowed a *pluralistic* validity . . . then it must rest upon some *a priori* principle (be it subjective or objective), and no amount of prying into the empirical laws of the changes that go on within the mind can succeed in establishing such a principle." This is said in the context of Kant's criticism of Burke's theory of taste.
    74. *CJ*, §15, p. 226.
    75. *CJ*, §15, p. 226. Kant refers the rejection of utility to the previous two *Hauptstücken*, or main parts; he obviously refers here to the first and second moments of the Analytic rather than to the immediately preceding §§13 and 14.
    76. *CJ*, §15, p. 227.
    77. *CJ*, §11, p. 221.
    78. These and the following quotations are from *CJ*, §15, p. 227. Why Kant should distinguish these two sorts of judgment as "qualitative" and "quantitative" is less than clear. The words do not seem to be used in senses already established in the first or third *Critiques*. Kant gives a reason for the denomination of quantitative perfection—that it involves a determination of the extent to which a particular object conforms to the general requirements of its type —and perhaps this is all he really has in mind in invoking the contrast between "qualitative" and "quantitative." It should be noted, however, that these two species of perfection are not actually mutually exclusive. If someone's intention is to produce an object of a given type, then the qualitative perfection of his effort will in fact consist in its quantitative perfection. Still, there is a difference between the case in which the concept for the evaluation of an object is taken from an intention connected with it, and the case in which it is not.
    79. *CJ*, §15, p. 227.
    80. *CJ*, §43, p. 303. Cf. §45, p. 306: "art always has a determinate intention to produce something."
    81. *CJ*, §45, p. 307.
    82. *CJ*, §48, p. 311.
    83. *CJ*, §16, p. 229.
    84. *CJ*, §16, p. 231.
    85. *CJ*, §16, p. 229.
    86. *CJ*, §16, pp. 229-230.
    87. *CJ*, §16, p. 230.

88. Cf. Hume, *A Treatise of Human Nature*, bk. II, pt. I, sec. viii (Selby-Bigge, pp. 298-299), or *An Enquiry concerning the Principles of Morals*, sec. VI, pt. II (Selby-Bigge, pp. 244-245).

89. *CJ*, §53, p. 323n.

90. In her article "Free and Dependent Beauty," in *Kant-Studien*, 65 special no. (1974), 247-262, Eva Schaper has made this point, and carefully considered the possible ways in which the concepts of depicting and serving a purpose might be related.

91. Cf. Schaper, "Free and Dependent Beauty," p. 255.

92. *CJ*, §48, p. 311.

93. *CJ*, §48, p. 312. Since one of Kant's examples of such an object of representation is "the devastations of war," it is obvious that he is not really contrasting the natural with the manmade, but rather the actual existence of objects with their representation or depiction.

94. *CJ*, §49, p. 314.

95. Cf. *CJ*, §49, pp. 316-317.

96. *CJ*, §51, p. 320. In "Formalism and the Theory of Expression in Kant's Aesthetics," I have criticized what Kant claims in the phrase I have omitted from this quote, namely that this thesis is true of natural as well as artistic beauty.

97. H. W. Cassirer, for instance, did not even discuss §16 in his *Commentary to Kant's Critique of Judgment*, and Crawford paraphrases Kant's distinction without questioning its appropriateness. Schaper has drawn attention to the present problem ("Free and Dependent Beauty," p. 249), but suggests no explanation of what she calls Kant's "apparent inconsistency."

98. *CPR*, A 90/B 122.

99. Peter Heintel has suggested that Kant's distinction between free and dependent beauty opposes his own conception of beauty to the "alltägliche Vorstellung der Schönheit" ("Die Bedeutung der Kritik der Ästhetischen Urteilskraft für die transzendentale Systematik," *Kant-Studien Ergänzungsheft*, no. 99, Bonn, H. Bouvier & Co., Verlag, 1970, p. 70), thus intimating such an explanation. Two further points might be noted. First, Kant's description of dependent beauty is not far from the explanation of beauty typical of rationalist aesthetics and of at least some empiricist aesthetics (see note 81, above). Second, the fact that Kant does appeal to the common view of beauty to buttress his own view of the matter of universality (and, less successfully, disinterestedness) does not mean that he cannot depart from it on other issues; obviously, he does.

100. *CJ*, §16, p. 230 (ll. 2-3 and 27-29).

101. Cf., e.g., Crawford, *Kant's Aesthetic Theory*, p. 115: "Kant seems to hold that the free-dependent beauty distinction is one between kinds of judgment and not between kinds of objects of judgment."

102. *CJ*, §16, p. 230.

103. *CJ*, §16, p. 231.

104. *CJ*, §16, p. 230.

105. *CJ*, §17, p. 236n.

106. Schaper analyzes the conflict between the two views on the nature of the distinction between free and dependent beauty which underlies Kant's examples ("Free and Dependent Beauty," p. 256), although she does not relate it to the claim about the judgment of art made in §48. Nor does she consider any explanation for the apparent conflict in Kant's views.

107. *CJ*, §22, GR, p. 241.

108. *CJ*, §15, p. 227.

109. *CJ*, §16, p. 231.

110. Crawford argues that the distinction between free and dependent beauty "depends upon Kant's notion of *abstraction*," and supposes that Kant's position is that "we can abstract

from any concept of a purpose determining the form of what we are considering" (*Kant's Aesthetic Theory*, pp. 115-116). It is far from clear that Kant's position is as unambivalent as this suggests.

111. *CJ*, §29, GR, p. 277.

112. In the language of the first *Critique*, he might have thought this a question of "applied" rather then "transcendental logic" (*CPR*, A 53-56/B 77-80).

113. *CJ*, §29, GR, p. 278.

114. *CJ*, §17, p. 231.

115. *CJ*, §17, p. 232.

116. *CJ*, §17, p. 232.

117. *CJ*, §17, pp. 233-234.

118. *CJ*, §17, p. 235.

119. *CJ*, §17, p. 236.

120. Such an interpretation was argued for by David White, in a paper called "The Relation between Beauty and Moral Goodness: Plato and Kant," presented at the Ohio University Kant Conference, March 1977.

7. The Task of the Deduction

1. *CJ*, §19, p. 237.

2. *CJ*, §6, p. 211.

3. This and the following quotations are from *CJ*, §31, p. 280.

4. *CJ*, §31, pp. 280-281.

5. *CJ*, §31, p. 281.

6. The quotation is the title of *CJ*, §36, p. 287.

7. *CJ*, §36, p. 288.

8. *CJ*, §36, p. 289.

9. *CJ*, §36, pp. 288-289.

10. *CJ*, §37, p. 289.

11. *CJ*, §36, p. 288.

12. See *CPR*, B 19; *PFM*, Ak. 4, p. 216; *FMM*, Ak. 4, p. 440.

13. See Chapter 4, above.

14. *CJ*, §19, p. 237.

15. *CJ*, §40, p. 296.

16. *CJ*, §41, p. 297.

17. Crawford, *Kant's Aesthetic Theory*, p. 69.

18. *CJ*, §38, pp. 289-291.

19. Thus, Elliot devotes only a single paragraph to the problem of the epistemological deduction before proceeding to the link with morality, which he views as Kant's attempt to make up for the inadequacy of his first argument ("The Unity of Kant's 'Critique of Aesthetic Judgment,' " p. 245). Crawford's discussion of the epistemological deduction occupies only six and a half pages of *Kant's Aesthetic Theory* (pp. 125-131), and his discussion of the actual force of Kant's argument essentially consists in a reference to an analogy which he supposes to obtain between the "postulation" of a common sense in the case of aesthetic judgment and the postulates of practical reason (pp. 130-131). Francis Coleman has also confined his discussion to "some parallels between [Kant's] conceptions of ethical and aesthetic autonomy" (*The Harmony of Reason*, p. 146). Those few writers who have addressed Kant's deduction of aesthetic judgment without preoccupations with the link to morality have also had little to say about its real structure or force. Berel Lang supposes that "the Deduction in the *Critique of Aesthetic*

Judgment depends directly on the Transcendental Deduction in the *Critique of Pure Reason*" ("Kant and the Subjective Objects of Taste," *Journal of Aesthetics and Art Criticism,* 25, no. 3, Spring 1967, 253), and A. C. Genova claims that "Kant's deduction of how judgments of taste are possible is an analogon of logical deduction" ("Kant's Transcendental Deduction of Aesthetic Judgments," *Journal of Aesthetics and Art Criticism,* 30, no. 4, Summer 1972, 470). The latter of these claims is too vague to mean very much, and the former, we shall see, is actually quite mistaken. Basically, little of any worth has been written about the deduction of pure aesthetic judgments; consequently, the present and succeeding chapters will, unlike previous ones, proceed essentially without reference to commentators.

20. See the beginning of Chapter 4, above.

21. Like the first *Critique,* the third also includes a Doctrine of Method to parallel its Doctrine of Elements. This section (§60) is included partly for the sake of architectonic completeness, and Kant himself begins it by asserting that the division between the Doctrines of Elements and Method is inapplicable to the critique of taste (pp. 354-355), because both the appreciation and production of fine art can be taught only by example and illustration, and not by precept (pp. 355-356). Obviously, there are many earlier sections into which §60's observations on this matter could have been inserted.

22. I shall argue in Chapter 11 that, whether or not they are so intended, they do not in fact advance the deduction of aesthetic judgment.

23. *CJ,* §30, p. 279.

24. *CJ,* §23, p. 244, through §29, p. 266. The GR appended to §29 contains material applicable to judgments on both the beautiful and the sublime.

25. *CJ,* §23, p. 244.

26. *CJ,* §23, p. 246.

27. See, e.g., *CJ,* §24, p. 247.

28. *CJ,* §26, p. 253.

29. *CJ,* §30, p. 280.

30. *CJ,* §22, p. 266.

31. *CJ,* §30, p. 279. The remaining quotations in this and the next paragraph are also from this passage.

32. This and the following quotations are from *CJ,* §30, p. 279.

33. *CJ,* §38, p. 291.

34. Of course, if this conclusion is accepted, the hope of an explanation for there being more than one deduction of aesthetic judgment which was offered by §30 must come to naught.

35. Donald Crawford has considered the possibility of criticism on Kant's aesthetic theory in ch. 8 of *Kant's Aesthetic Theory* (pp. 164-171), and in an earlier article, "Reason-Giving in Kant's Aesthetics," *Journal of Aesthetics and Art Criticism,* 28, no. 4 (Summer 1970), 505-510. Space does not permit me to pursue this topic, but I would note that while, for reasons made clear in Chapter 6, I am less sanguine than Crawford is about the potential of purposiveness of form as an informative critical notion (*Kant's Aesthetic Theory,* p. 169), I do think that the possibilities for understanding criticism as a form of discourse both for removing obstacles to understanding and appreciation and for directing attention to sources of merit, following the notions of disinterestedness and the form of finality, are greater than Crawford allows.

36. *CJ,* §31, p. 281.

37. See "The Necessity of Aesthetic Judgment" in Chapter 4, above.

38. *CJ,* §33, p. 285.

39. This and the following quotations are from *CJ,* §32, p. 282.

40. *CJ,* §32, pp. 281-282.

41. Hume, "The Standard of Taste," p. 232.

42. *CJ*, §33, p. 284.

43. *CJ*, §33, pp. 284-285.

44. *CJ*, §34, p. 285.

45. *CJ*, §33, p. 285.

46. That is, made not in advance of any particular empirical instance of a concept, but independently of any empirical evidence at all, or on the basis of a purely *a priori* inference about the application of concepts. Cf. *CPR*, B 2.

47. *CJ*, §33, p. 284.

48. *CJ*, §33, p. 284.

49. Unless one supposes, as does W. H. Walsh, that Kant's transcendental deduction in the first *Critique* works by showing certain concepts to be means for securing intersubjective agreement (*Kant's Criticism of Metaphysics*, Edinburgh, University of Edinburgh Press, 1975, p. 42). I have criticized this interpretation in the review earlier mentioned.

50. Such an interpretation is employed by Graham Bird, in *Kant's Theory of Knowledge* (London, Routledge and Kegan Paul, 1962). See, e.g., pp. 138-139.

51. *CPR*, A 94/B 126.

52. I have briefly sketched such an interpretation in my review of Walsh.

53. *CJ*, §38, p. 290.

54. Cf. *CPR*, §§16 and 17 (B 132, 138).

55. See earlier discussion in this chapter.

56. *CJ*, §20, p. 238.

57. *CJ*, §21, p. 239.

58. *CJ*, §22, pp. 239-240.

59. *CJ*, §57, pp. 339-341.

60. I have not been able to consult the work of Giorgio Tonelli on this subject ("La formazione del testo della *Kritik der Urteilskraft*," *Revue Internationale de Philosophie*, 8, 1954, pp. 423-448). However, reports of his results elsewhere imply that while the *Critique* as a whole was not written in the order in which it appears, the Analytic of the Beautiful, §§30 to 40, and the Dialectic were written in the order in which they appear in the published text, and within a reasonably short period of time. This suggests that a history of the text will not explain why Kant treats the same problem several times.

8. The Deduction: First Attempt

1. *CJ*, §18, p. 237.

2. *CJ*, §19, p. 237.

3. *CJ*, §21, p. 238.

4. *CJ*, §40, p. 293.

5. In his discussion of "common sense," Crawford distinguishes only two of these ways (*Kant's Aesthetic Theory*, pp. 128-129). He does not raise the question of whether the term "common sense" is crucial to Kant's argument at all.

6. *CJ*, §20, p. 238.

7. *CJ*, §20, p. 238.

8. *CJ*, §40, p. 293.

9. *CJ*, §40, p. 294.

10. *CJ*, §40, p. 295.

11. See *FI*, VIII, p. 229.

12. *CJ*, §40, p. 295.

13. *CJ*, §40, p. 296. Both of these quotations, by the way, reveal Kant's failure to make a clear terminological distinction between the simple reflection on an object which leads to aesthetic response and the act of reflection on that response which leads to aesthetic judgment, for both use the term *Beurteilung*, linked in §9 to the first of these forms of reflection, to mean the second of them.

14. *CJ*, §21, p. 239.

15. He uses two different phrases, actually: at §9, p. 217 (l. 1), *allgemeine Mitteilbarkeit;* and at l. 8, *allgemeine Mitteilungsfähigkeit.* I cannot detect any difference of significance between these.

16. *CJ*, §9, p. 217.

17. *CJ*, §8, p. 216.

18. *CJ*, §40, p. 294.

19. *CJ*, §21, p. 238.

20. *CJ*, §21, p. 238.

21. Meredith obscures Kant's commitment to the view that there is one proportion between imagination and understanding which grounds knowledge by translating Kant's words *diejenige Proportion* as "the relative proportion" (Meredith, p. 83); Bernard's translation "that proportion" (Bernard, p. 75) allows the implication of Kant's assertion to appear more clearly.

22. Hume, *A Treatise of Human Nature*, bk. I, pt. III, sec. xv (Selby-Bigge, p. 173). I do not mean to suggest that Kant states anything like this principle.

23. *CJ*, §21, p. 238.

24. *CJ*, §21, pp. 238-239.

25. *CJ*, §21, p. 239.

26. Locke, *Essay*, bk. I, ch. II, sec. 5 (in Nidditch, p. 49).

27. See *CJ*, VI, pp. 187-188, and §22, GR, pp. 242-243.

28. *CJ*, §21, p. 239.

29. *CPR*, A 104-106.

30. *CPR*, A 123.

31. *CPR*, B 142.

32. *CPR*, B 138.

33. *CPR*, B 142.

34. *CPR*, A 197/B 242-243.

35. *CPR*, A 820-821/B 848-849.

36. *PFM*, §19, *Ak.* 4, p. 299.

37. *PFM*, §18, *Ak.* 4, p. 299.

38. The fact that the ultimate cause of both cases of knowledge—the event itself—must be identical does not affect this argument, since the event itself is not a *subjective* condition of knowledge, or a mental state explaining a given person's cognition.

39. *CJ*, §21, p. 238.

40. *CJ*, §21, p. 238.

41. *CJ*, §22, p. 240.

42. *CJ*, §22, p. 240. This last remark suggests that the basic meaning of common sense for Kant is neither the universally valid feeling of aesthetic response nor the principle of its universal validity, but the faculty for determining the universal validity of feeling, that is, the faculty of taste itself.

43. *CJ*, §22, p. 240.

44. *CJ*, §22, p. 239.

45. See especially *CJ*, §8, p. 216, and §19, p. 237.

46. *CJ*, §22, p. 239.

47. *CPR*, A 662/B 690.
48. *CPR*, A 663/B 691.
49. *CPR*, A 664/B 692.
50. *CPR*, A 665/B 693.
51. *CPR*, A 666/B 694.
52. *CPR*, A 667/B 695.
53. Cf. *CPR*, A 666/B 694.
54. Kant's remark that "without reason [there can be] no coherent employment of the understanding, and in the absence of this no sufficient criterion of empirical truth" (*CPR*, A 651/B 679) may represent a more accurate assessment of the actual role of higher-order constraints on relations among concepts than the one presented in my text, but this remark seems to be an isolated insight in Kant's discussion of regulative principles; the view I have expounded in my text is the predominant one.
55. *CPR*, A 663-664/B 691-692.
56. *CPR*, A 669/B 697.
57. *CPR*, A 671/B 699.
58. *CJ*, §22, p. 240.
59. E.g., *CJ*, §32, p. 283; §47, pp. 309-310; and §60, pp. 355-356.
60. Kant claims, of course, that "though all our knowledge begins with experience, it does not follow that it all arises out of experience" (*CPR*, B 1). But the force of this is precisely to separate the issue of epistemological status from the psychological issue of whether a given principle is innate or acquired during the temporal course of experience.
61. *CPR*, A 676/B 704.
62. *CPR*, A 677/B 705.
63. *CPR*, A 677-678/B 705-706.
64. *CPR*, A 678/B 706.
65. *CPR*, A 678-679/B 706-707.
66. *CJ*, §57, pp. 339-341.

9. The Deduction: Second Attempt

1. *CJ*, §40, p. 293.
2. *CJ*, §37, p. 289.
3. *CJ*, §35, p. 287.
4. See "Pleasure and the Goal of Cognition" in Chapter 3, above.
5. I believe that Wolfgang Bartuschat succumbs to such an interpretation when he takes the purpose of the deduction to be to prove the possibility of a mental state of *Selbstbezüglichkeit*, or the possibility of a harmony between imagination and understanding in which they are "self-related," or related without the benefit of a conceptual intervention (*Zum systematischen Ort von Kants Kritik der Urteilskraft*, Frankfurt am Main, Vittorio Klostermann, 1972, p. 134). Clearly, the general success of Kant's aesthetic theory depends on the possibility of this state, but the deduction itself surely presupposes its possibility and attempts to demonstrate its intersubjective validity, a status which Bartuschat seems to suppose automatically characterizes the harmony of the faculties (p. 135).
6. *CJ*, §38, p. 289.
7. *CJ*, §38, pp. 289-290.
8. *CJ*, §38, pp. 289-290.
9. *CJ*, §38, p. 290.
10. *CJ*, §38, p. 290n.

11. *CJ*, §38, *Anmerkung*, p. 290.
12. *CJ*, §38, p. 290n.
13. *CJ*, §38, p. 290n.
14. *CPR*, B 278.
15. *CJ*, §38, p. 291.
16. *CJ*, §38, *Anmerkung*, pp. 290-291.
17. *CJ*, §38, p. 290.
18. *CJ*, §38, p. 290n.
19. *CJ*, §39, p. 291.
20. Cf. *CJ*, §5, pp. 209-210.
21. *CJ*, §39, pp. 291-292.
22. *CJ*, §39, p. 292.
23. *CJ*, §39, pp. 292-293.
24. See *CJ*, §21, p. 238, and Chapter 8, above.
25. *CJ*, §46, p. 307.
26. *CJ*, §40, p. 296.
27. *CJ*, §42, pp. 298-301. See my article "Interest, Nature, and Art."
28. *CPR*, A 669/B 697. See the final section of Chapter 8, above.
29. *CPR*, A 671/B 699.
30. See, for instance, Hume's argument "Of Skepticism with regard to reason," *A Treatise of Human Nature*, bk. I, pt. IV, sec. i (Selby-Bigge, pp. 180 ff.).

10. The Metaphysics of Taste

1. *CJ*, §55, p. 337.
2. *CJ*, §55, p. 337.
3. *CJ*, §55, p. 337.
4. *CJ*, §56, p. 338.
5. Hume, "The Standard of Taste," pp. 234-235.
6. Both quotations are from *CJ*, §56, p. 338. Hume refers to the latter saying as an "axiom" which, "by passing into a proverb, seems to have attained the sanction of common sense" ("The Standard of Taste," p. 235).
7. *CJ*, §56, pp. 338-339.
8. Elliott, "The Unity of Kant's 'Critique of Aesthetic Judgment,' " p. 254.
9. *CJ*, §21, p. 239.
10. *CJ*, §57, p. 339.
11. *CJ*, §57, p. 340.
12. Cf., e.g., *CPR*, A 130.
13. *CJ*, §30, p. 279.
14. *CJ*, §38, *Anmerkung*, p. 291.
15. *CJ*, §57, p. 339.
16. *CPR*, A 402.
17. *CJ*, §57, p. 339.
18. *CJ*, §57, p. 339.
19. *CJ*, §57, pp. 339-340.
20. *CJ*, §57, p. 340.
21. Cf. *CPR*, Preface to 2nd ed., B xxvi-xxvii.
22. This theory is expounded in §§56 through 60. I have not considered it here, but have discussed some aspects of it in "Interest, Nature, and Art."

23. *CJ*, §57, *Anmerkung*, I, p. 344.
24. *CJ*, §57, *Anmerkung* II, p. 345.
25. *CJ*, §57, *Anmerkung* II, pp. 345-346.
26. Cf. *CPR*, A 29-30/B 44-45.
27. *CJ*, §1, pp. 203-204.
28. *CJ*, §38, pp. 290-291.
29. *CJ*, §57, p. 340.
30. *CJ*, §57, pp. 340-341.
31. *CJ*, §57, *Anmerkung* II, p. 346.
32. *CJ*, §58, p. 346.
33. *CJ*, §58, p. 346.
34. *CJ*, §58, p. 347.
35. *CJ*, §58, p. 348.
36. *CJ*, §58, pp. 348-349.
37. *CJ*, §58, pp. 349-350.
38. *CJ*, §58, p. 350.

11. Aesthetics and Morality

1. Cf. *CJ*, §19, p. 237.
2. *CJ*, §22, p. 240.
3. *CJ*, §40, p. 296.
4. Crawford, *Kant's Aesthetic Theory*, p. 143.
5. Crawford, *Kant's Aesthetic Theory*, p. 145. Crawford refers to the deduction of universal communicability as stages I through IV of the deduction, and to the transition to the realm of morality as stage V, thus clearly committing himself to the view that these different considerations constitute a single connected argument. (The quotation within Crawford's last passage is from *CJ*, §41, p. 297.)
6. Elliott, "The Unity of Kant's 'Critique of Aesthetic Judgment,' " p. 259.
7. Elliott, "The Unity of Kant's 'Critique of Aesthetic Judgment,' " p. 255. He refers here to §59 and pp. 224-225 of Meredith; the passage he must have in mind actually begins on p. 223 in Meredith.
8. *CJ*, §59, p. 353.
9. Crawford, *Kant's Aesthetic Theory*, p. 156.
10. Jeffrey Maitland, in "Two Senses of Necessity in Kant's Aesthetic Theory," *British Journal of Aesthetics*, 16, no. 4 (Autumn 1976), 347-353, criticizes Crawford and Elliott for confusing "the problem of justifying the *possibility* of aesthetic *judgments* and the problem of justifying the *significance* of aesthetic *experience*" (p. 347), and for failing "to recognize the two kinds of demands aesthetic experience can make: (1) one ought to agree with aesthetic judgments . . . (2) one ought to cultivate an appreciation for beauty" (p. 351). These criticisms are in a vein similar to mine, though I believe it is more important to distinguish between demanding and expecting agreement in the cognitive sphere before considering whether cognitive demands are like practical demands. Maitland does not raise the question of whether a link to morality could be expected to lend any support to taste's *demand* for or *expectation* of agreement.
11. *CJ*, §40, p. 295.
12. *MM, Ak*. 6, p. 212.
13. A fuller discussion of the problem of Kant's views on the content of art than will be offered here may be found in "Interest, Intention and Art."

14. All quotations in this paragraph are from *CJ*, §29, GR, pp. 266-267.

15. *CJ*, §29, GR, pp. 266-267.

16. *CJ*, §29, GR, p. 267.

17. *CJ*, §41, p. 296.

18. *CJ*, §41, p. 296.

19. *CJ*, §41, p. 297.

20. As was evidenced by the passage quoted from the *Logik Blomberg, Ak.* 24, I, pp. 45-46; cf. Chapter 1, above.

21. Cf. *CJ*, §9, p. 218.

22. *CJ*, §41, p. 297.

23. *CJ*, §41, pp. 297-298.

24. *CJ*, §42, p. 301.

25. *CJ*, §42, p. 303.

26. *CJ*, §42, pp. 298-299.

27. I have argued this in "Interest, Nature, and Art."

28. *CJ*, §42, p. 300.

29. *CJ*, §42, p. 300.

30. *CJ*, §42, p. 301.

31. *CJ*, §42, pp. 302-303.

32. One possibility for constructing such an argument might exist: if one were to interpret the idea in the objective reality of which moral feeling creates an immediate interest (p. 300) as itself the idea of intersubjective agreement in general (a conceivable extension of the interpretation of the categorical imperative as dictating laws for a realm of nature), then nature's hint of accordance with our own subjective conditions might be a hint of its provision of such a community. But such an argument would have to be considered a speculative supplement to Kant rather than anything derivable from the text itself, and would in any case have the dubious status of Kant's own teleological arguments.

33. *CJ*, §42, pp. 300-301.

34. *CJ*, §59, p. 351.

35. *CJ*, §52, p. 326.

36. *CJ*, IX, p. 195.

37. *CJ*, IX, p. 197.

38. An example of this kind of interpretation may be found in the book by Peter Heintel, who interprets Kant's theory of symbolism as meant to resolve the problem of the typic of practical reason, or making moral ideas intuitable; according to him, in §59 "so geht es jetzt um die fundamentale Reflexion jeder möglichen Bestimmbarkeit von Vernunftbegriff, Idee und Sittlichkeit . . . Also kann . . . nur das Schöne, als die Aufhebung sowohl des theoretischen als auch des praktischen Moments, zur Darstellung der Vernunftbegriffe herangezogen werden" (*Die Bedeutung der Kritik*, pp. 13-135).

39. Crawford, *Kant's Aesthetic Theory:* the first two quotations are from p. 149, the last from p. 146.

40. Crawford, *Kant's Aesthetic Theory*, p. 146.

41. *CJ*, IX, p. 197; cf. §29, GR, pp. 266-267.

42. Crawford, *Kant's Aesthetic Theory*, p. 148. This sentence, however, does not state the problem with §42 correctly. If Kant's argument there were valid, interest in the beautiful would be a clear indication of a good moral disposition; the flaw is that it would not be a necessary condition of such a disposition, and thus could not be legitimately demanded or imputed on the basis of the requirements of morality alone.

43. *CJ*, §59, pp. 351-352.

44. *CJ*, §59, p. 352. According to Kant, the current (Leibnizo-Wolffian) usage incor-

rectly contrasts symbolic knowledge with intuitive, thus taking symbols to be mere signs, when the symbolic is in fact a species of the intuitive. The interpretation of a symbol as an arbitrary sign does seem to prevail in Leibniz's "Meditations on Knowledge, Truth, and Ideas" (Loemker, pp. 291-292), though it is not so obviously correct for Leibniz's usage in the later *Monadology* (cf. §61; in Loemker, p. 649). Baumgarten classifies "intuitive" and "symbolic knowledge" as two forms of knowledge of objects involving signs, and distinguishes them only according to whether the representation of the sign is "greater" than that of the thing signified (this is the case with symbolic knowledge), or whether the representation of the thing is "greater" than that of the sign (intuitive knowledge)" (Baumgarten, *Metaphysik*, §460).

45. *CJ*, §59, p. 351.
46. *CJ*, §59, p. 352.
47. *CJ*, §59, pp. 353-354.
48. The two partners in harmony on the moral side of Kant's analogy are, I think, aptly brought out by the use of the terms *Wille* and *Willkür*, which Kant used in his later discussions of the freedom of the will to distinguish its two aspects. This distinction is especially prominent in *Religion within the Limits of Reason Alone;* see the discussion in J. R. Silber's introduction to the revised translation by T. M. Greene and H. H. Hudson (New York, Harper & Row, 1960), pp. xcv-xcvi and ciii-cvi.
49. *CJ*, §59, p. 353.
50. *CJ*, §59, p. 353.
51. *CJ*, §59, p. 353.
52. *CJ*, §59, p. 354.
53. Jeffrey Maitland, in "Two Senses of Necessity in Kant's Aesthetic Theory," claims that the problem with Crawford's interpretation of the necessity of aesthetic judgment as resting on beauty's symbolism of morality is that Crawford does not show that beauty is a *unique* symbol of morality, and thus leaves the demand for sensitivity to the symbol underdetermined (p. 349). The real problem with the view, however, is with the legitimacy of demanding attention to anything that *merely* symbolizes morality, even if it does so uniquely.
54. *CJ*, §57, pp. 340-341.
55. A symbol is, after all, a form of "intuitive" representation or knowledge (*CJ*, §59, p. 351).
56. *FMM, Ak.* 4, p. 447.
57. *FMM, Ak.* 4, p. 455.
58. Cf. *FMM, Ak.* 4, p. 404.
59. See, e.g., *CPrR, Ak.* 5, p. 42. Kant's commitment to the view that any person has all the knowledge necessary for moral action, whether or not he is aware of beauty's symbolism of morality, seems to preclude any attempt to ground the necessity of aesthetic response or judgment in morality. This applies not only to Crawford's argument, but also to the view developed by Ted Cohen in "The Formal Basis of Kant's Claim That Beauty Is the Symbol of Morality" (forthcoming in Cohen and Guyer, *Essays in Kant's Aesthetics*), where he argues that the beautiful plays a crucial role in symbolizing the morally good because, as purposive without a purpose, it represents what otherwise could not be represented, an end in itself which is not quite any end at all. Even if this argument rested on a viable interpretation of the categorical imperative, which I do not think it does, it would still fall victim to Kant's insistence on the universal accessibility of that imperative. But while Cohen cannot do better than Crawford in establishing the moral *necessity* of a regard for either taste or the beautiful itself, which is the only point I am considering in this chapter, he certainly goes a long way toward an interpretation of Kant's discovery of the moral foundation of our *fascination* with the phenomena of beauty and taste.
59. See, e.g., *CPrR, Ak.* 5, p. 42.

60. *CJ*, §60, p. 356.
61. *CPrR, Ak.* 5, p. 24.
62. *CPrR, Ak.* 5, pp. 80-81.
63. *CPrR, Ak.* 5, p. 81.
64. *CPrR, Ak.* 5, pp. 81-82.
65. *CJ*, §60, p. 346.
66. *CJ*, §49, p. 314.
67. Of course, if §16 is read to allow that any works of art may be free beauties, this "fact" would only be contingently true of such works of art of which it was true at all.
68. *CJ*, §16, p. 231.
69. *CJ*, §52, pp. 325-326.
70. *CJ*, §52, p. 326.

Index of Passages

This index locates all quotations from the sections of the *Critique of Judgment* and its *First Introduction* in the present work.

General Index

A *posteriori* principles of taste, 17-18, 30

A *priori* principle of taste: Kant's first claim of, 14-15; not admitted in Kant's early theories, 16-17, 19, 29-30; not determinate, 17-18, 31, 36, 301, 304; possible without particular a *priori* judgments, 19; precluded by communicability theory of pleasure, 26-28; concerns ourselves rather than nature, 34, 50, 53, 61, 63-64; analogical arguments for, 35-39; deduction of, 50-51, 258-259; regulative status of, 52-53, 304-306, 325-327; and common sense, 280, 282. *See also* Common sense; Deduction of aesthetic judgment

Abstraction, 146, 228-229, 239, 241, 247-248, 250-253

Aesthetic, meaning of term, 71-72

Aesthetics, Kant's views on discipline of, 16-19, 30-31

Aesthetic ideas, 92, 233-234, 245, 391

Aesthetic judgment: as synthetic a *priori*, 1, 9, 164-166, 258-259, 308, 309, 417; as universally valid, 4, 7, 8-9, 10, 15, 18, 112, 113, 120, 133-147, 157; as outcome of complex reflection, 8, 12, 110-113, 151, 158-159; as empirical, 22; distinguished from aesthetic response, 22, 28-29; and reflective judgment, 31, 33, 41, 58-67; and nature, 34, 60-61; and art, 34, 201-202, 241-242; and finality, 57, 59-63; and systematicity, 62-64; and indeterminacy, 66; and pleasure, 72, 75, 100-101, 112; and estimation, 110-111, 158-159; as logically singular, 126-129, 147-151, 271, 273; justification of particular judgments, 147, 309, 311-314; and necessity, 160-166; as pure or empirical, 224-225; supersensible ground of, 277; and skepticism, 278, 327-330; and dialectic, 331-337; not un-

conditional, 344-345; and moral judgment, 357-361, 368-370, 376-378, 380-381. *See also* Aesthetic response; Deduction of aesthetic judgment; Pleasure; Reflection; Reflective judgment

Aesthetic response: distinguished from gratification and evaluation, 3, 9, 198-200; explanation of, 4, 8, 9, 69-70, 79-99, 236, 309-310, 324, 353-354; as confused perception, 6-7; and intersubjectivity, 15, 324-325; distinguished from aesthetic judgment, 22, 28-29; and solitude, 26-27, 158; two theories of, 27; as single event, 28-29; and reflective judgment, 51; and synthesis, 85-99, 104; consciousness of, 99-110; and communicability, 153-154, 197; and interest, 168; and conceptual judgment, 195-196, 237; and finality, 216-218; and abstraction, 248; and criteria, 254; and proportion, 295-297, 317-324; capacity for, 315-319, 320, 324, 255-356; distinguished from faculty of taste, 355-356, 360; and moral feeling, 359-361. *See also* Harmony of imagination and understanding; Pleasure

Agreeable, the: distinguished from the beautiful and the good, 2, 115, 116, 170-171, 173, 182, 188-189, 194-195, 198-200, 357; analysis of judgments on, 135-137, 139; and classification of aesthetic judgments, 224; and interest, 177-178, 185; and will, 180-181; and communicability, 317

Albers, Josef, 231, 233

Anthropology, Kant's view of, 21

Anthropology from a Pragmatic Point of View: on pleasure, 118, 182; on states of mind, 410

Antinomies: in *CPR*, 332; three kinds of, 343

Antinomy of taste, the: analysis of, 333-345; and skepticism, 346

Apperception, 42, 45, 98, 289-290

Aquila, Richard E., 410

Architectonic, in *CJ*, 128-131, 262-263, 335-336, 343, 427

Art: and reflective judgment, 31, 33; and taste, 34; and disinterestedness, 200-202; and aesthetic judgment, 201; and nature, 208, 209, 220, 237, 367-368, 420; and representation, 237, 243-246; and intentions, 240-241; and free and dependent beauty, 242-246; and perfection, 249-252; and deduction of aesthetic judgment, 263-264, 267-268; and genius, 341; and moral content, 356-357, 360, 389-394; media of, 392

Autonomy, of aesthetic judgment, 258, 269-271

Baeumler, Alfred, 403

Bartuschat, Wolfgang, 430

Basch, Victor, 403

Batteaux, Abbé Charles, 272-273

Baumgarten, Alexander Gottlieb, 2, 6, 7, 16, 17, 19, 30, 72, 434

Beardsley, Monroe, 407, 422

Beauty: as paradigmatic aesthetic predicate, 1; intersubjectivity and meaning of, 1, 7, 8, 21, 113, 126, 128, 133-137, 139, 147, 150, 151, 353; distinguished from the agreeable and the good, 3, 116, 170-171, 173, 179-180, 182, 188-189, 194-195, 198-200, 357; Meier's definition of, 6; and reflective judgment, 33-34; and interest, 175, 181-183, 362-373; and will, 181-183; and concepts, 188-189; and perception, 193-197; and finality, 214; two concepts of, 246-250; and proportion, 295-297; as symbol of morality, 352-353, 373-389; and supersensible substratum, 346-349. *See also* Free and dependent beauty

Beck, Lewis White, 116-117, 145, 404, 410, 411, 413, 414, 417

Berkeley, George, 76, 88, 409

Bernard, J. H., 405, 415, 429

Bird, Graham, 428

Buchdahl, Gerd, 404

Bullough, Edward, 416

Burch, Robert, 421

Burke, Edmund, 2, 4-5, 19, 253, 413, 423

Cassirer, H. W. 411, 425

Categorical imperative, the. *See* Moral law

Categories: and systematicity, 42-43, 46; and pleasure in nature, 82; as necessary conditions of experience, 97-98

Causal connections: between harmony of faculties and feeling of pleasure, 106-110, 118; and existence, 193-196; and beauty, 200; and subjective finality, 217-219

Causal judgments: uncertainty of, 205-206; and ends, 213-214

Causal terminology, 106, 109

Causality: Kant's schema for, 108-109; and pleasure, 182, 198, 217-218

Cavell, Stanley, 413

Cerf, Walter, 416

Charm and emotion, 225-226, 231, 281. *See also* Agreeable

Cognition, faculties of, 35, 58, 61, 63-64

Cognition, intuitive, 6, 434

Cognition, objectives of, 20, 22, 47, 49, 50-51, 65, 77, 79-99, 102, 107, 157

Cognition, subjective conditions of: and harmony of imagination and understanding, 73-76, 84-86, 148, 153, 154; and formal finality, 216-219; and appearance of design, 221-223; and deduction of aesthetic judgment, 284-287, 288, 290, 292-294, 308, 311, 314-316, 318-321, 322-324

Cohen, Marshall, 407

Cohen, Ted, 434

Coleman, Francis X. J., 405, 426

Color, 70-71, 199, 209, 219, 225-226, 230-235, 252-253, 317, 423

Common sense: and empirical rules, 18; and exemplary necessity, 128; and deduction of aesthetic judgment, 277, 279-288, 308; whether regulative or constitutive, 297-306, 316; and dialectic of taste, 321; meaning of, 429

Communicability: claimed by taste, 8, 111, 254; and pleasure, 22-29, 152-159; relation to intersubjectivity, 282-283; conditions of, 284-287, 288, 290, 292-294, 314-316, 319, 323, 359; as condition of knowledge, 297, 301-303; of sensation, 317-318; and regulative principle of taste, 326-327; interest in, 361-365; meaning of, 415, 429. *See also* Intersubjectivity

Composition, 209, 219, 225-226, 252

151, 152-155, 157, 159-160, 235-237, 256-257; never fully clarified, 11, 248-255; early theories of, 19-22, 25-26; and reflective judgment, 33-34, 59-60, 67; and subjective conditions of cognition or synthesis, 41, 73-75, 82, 84-87, 88-89, 91, 92, 93, 96, 311; relation to feeling of pleasure, 78-79, 87, 99-110, 114, 204; and subsumption, 90, 309-310; and schematism, 90-91; as state or event, 93-96; compatibility with *CPR*, 96-99; psychological interpretation of, 98, 296-297, 322-324, 393-394; and uncertainty, 99; and common sense, 128, 279-282; and disinterestedness, 131, 179; and imputation, 146-147; and apriority of aesthetic judgment, 163-166; and formalism, 209-210, 237; and form of finality, 216-220; and form, 230-233; and aesthetic ideas, 233-234; and freedom of imagination, 251-252; and proportion, 286-287, 295-297, 322-324; and particular judgments, 312-314; and deduction of aesthetic judgment, 314-315, 318-324; and antinomy of taste, 338, 340, 344, 350; and the supersensible, 340-343, 380-381, 382-383; analogy to willing, 377-380; and content in art, 391-392. *See also* Facility, in cognition; Imagination
Hedonism, 172-173
Heintel, Peter, 425, 433
Henckmann, Wolfhart, 401
Henrich, Dieter, 409
Herz, Marcus, 14, 416
Human figure, the, 254-255
Hume, David, 2, 4, 198, 208, 272, 285, 287, 333, 418, 424, 431
Hutcheson, Francis, 2, 4

Idea, universal voice as, 145-146, 150
Ideal of beauty, the, 237, 254-255
Idealism in taste, 348, 350
Imagination: as defined in *CJ*, 85; and objects, 91; and concepts, 98; and aesthetic ideas, 233-234; freedom of, 247, 248, 250-253. *See also* Harmony of imagination and understanding
Immediacy, 377
Imputation: meaning of, 139-142; interpretation of, 142-147, 271-272; and

uncertainty, 151
Inaugural Dissertation, 16
Inclination: to society, 156, 363-364; and agreeableness, 170-171; and beauty, 182; and interest, 184. *See also* Agreeable
Indeterminacy, 146-147, 298-300. *See also* Regulative principles; Uncertainty
Indeterminate concepts, and dialectic of taste, 337-340, 346
Induction, and aesthetic judgment, 142-143, 146, 272-274
Innateness, 304-305
Intention: and finality, 215; and qualitative perfection, 239-240; and art, 240-241; and beauty, 422. *See also* Ends
Intentionalist fallacy, the, 215, 422
Interest: definition of, 125, 174-175, 183-184, 187, 190; role in Kant's argument, 167-170; and aesthetic judgment, 167-168, 356-357, 419; and kinds of pleasure, 171-172, 190; and beauty, 187-191; and existence, 191-198, 369-372; consciousness of, 204-205; and uncertainty, 205-206; and classification of aesthetic judgments, 224-225; in communicability, 352; empirical, 362-366; intellectual, 363, 366-373, 385; and analogy of aesthetic and moral judgment, 377-378. *See also* Disinterestedness; Existence
Intersubjectivity, 133-147, 160-166; as criterion of aesthetic judgment, 1, 2, 9, 11, 15, 34, 63-64, 65-66, 68, 108, 110-111, 115, 121-122, 129, 132-137; and reflection, 8, 69; criterial *versus* explanatory theories of, 10-11, 15, 22-25, 27-28, 151-152, 154-160; and empirical principles, 16; uncertainty of, 66; as regulative or constitutive principle, 66-67, 236, 302, 324-327; place in Kant's argument, 125-127; distinguished from objective and logical validity, 71, 148-150; and disinterestedness, 132-133; and predication, 138-139; relation to necessity, 160-166; and exclusion of matter, 234-236; and deduction of aesthetic judgment, 256-259, 261-262, 268, 276-278; and the sublime, 265-266; and states of mind, 271-272; and universal communicability, 282-283; and *CPR*, 288-291; and *PFM*, 291-292;

as condition of cognition, 301-302; presupposition of, 312, 314-316, 317-324; and skepticism, 328-329; and the supersensible, 349-350; demanding *versus* expecting, 353-355, 359, 362, 365-366, 367, 370-371, 381, 386-387; and interest in the beautiful, 356-357; and moral feeling, 357-361; and analogy of aesthetic and moral judgment, 378; and moral content in art, 390-392. *See also* Communicability

Judgment, faculty of: two exercises of, 8, 112, 114, 151-160; not in Kant's early theories, 19; definition of, 35; and universals and particulars, 36, 39-41; and the subjective, 38-39; and systematicity, 45-46, 49. *See also* Aesthetic judgment; Reflection; Reflective Judgment
Judgments of experience and perception, 292

Kames, Henry Home, Lord, 2, 5, 16, 17, 19, 418
Knowledge. *See* Cognition, faculties of; Cognition, intuitive; Cognition, objectives of; Cognition, subjective conditions of
Kramer, Hilton, 231
Kuypers, K., 403

Lang, Berel, 426
Lawfulness, 90-91
Laws: of sensibility, 16, 20-22; of understanding, 20-21. *See also* Empirical laws; Moral law
Leibniz, Gottfried Wilhelm, 2, 6, 7, 434
Lessing, Gotthold Ephraim, 272-273
Linguistic usage, and aesthetic judgment, 135-139
Locke, John, 76, 228, 287
Logic (Kant's): on aesthetics, 19; on postulation, 145
Logical functions of judgment, 123-124, 128-131, 133
Logik Blomberg, 24-25
Logik Philippi, 26-27

Maitland, Jeffrey, 411, 413, 432, 434
Mathematics: and music, 92; and postulation, 145
Matter, of appearance, 224-229, 234-235.

See also Form
Maxims, of natural science, 51-52, 57, 65-66, 301, 305
Meerbote, Ralf, 408
Meier, Georg Friedrich, 2, 6, 18
Mendelssohn, Moses, 404, 416
Menzer, Paul, 401, 402
Meredith, J. C., 405, 415, 429
Metaphysical guarantee for taste: in empiricism, 4-5; in rationalism, 6-7; in Kant, 7, 11, 64, 277-278, 307, 329-330, 331-350
Metaphysics of Morals: on interest, 186-187; on taste, 355-356
Methodology, in *CJ*, 124, 138-139, 403
Mind, faculties of, 37
Modality, of aesthetic judgment, 128-129, 130-131, 144-145, 160-166, 192, 358. *See also* Necessity
Moments, of aesthetic judgment: and maxims of natural science, 65-66; official exposition, 122-128; actual status, 128-131. *See also* Disinterestedness; Finality, formal; Interest; Intersubjectivity; Necessity
Monadology, 7
Moral feeling: and interest, 186-187, 367-369, 372; communicability of, 317-318; and claims of taste, 357-361, 387-389
Moral judgment: and pleasure, 170, 414; analogy to aesthetic judgment, 357, 368-370, 376-378, 380-381
Moral law: and postulation, 145; and interest, 185-186; and symbolism of beauty, 382-383, 388-389; and pleasure, 414
Morality, 351-394; and imputation, 141-142; and deduction of aesthetic judgment, 254, 260-262, 305-306, 313, 326, 347; requirements of, 360-361, 372, 382-385, 387, 388-389; and symbolism of beauty, 373-389. *See also* Moral feeling; Moral judgment; Moral law
Mothersill, Mary, 410
Music, 92-93, 100, 232, 242, 244
Mutual assistance, 75, 87. *See also* Harmony of imagination and understanding

Natural science, 41-43. *See also* Maxims of natural science
Nature: and reflective judgment, 33-67; as